Praise For *The Sec* *Thirty-Four* by Terence W. Barrett, PhD

"Terry Barrett has provided us a valuable gift. He has written, with clarity and passion, the most detailed description of Medal of Honor recipients I've ever read, and brought them to life. These were real men! He also recounts the times in which they lived, giving us an historical context of true proportions. We are grateful for his significant achievement!"

—Brigadier General Thomas V. Draude, USMC (Ret.)
President & Chief Executive Officer
Marine Corps University Foundation
Quantico, VA

"Dr. Terry Barrett has delivered an important and interesting treatise on the nature of physical courage. We've been a nation at war for a decade, yet fewer and fewer Americans understand the sacrifice our servicemen and women make on our behalf routinely. The examples given to us by Dr. Barrett are anything but routine. They illustrate the best of our nation's warrior spirit and the limitless reaches of human endurance and ability."

—Dr. Joseph J. Thomas, LtCol, USMC (Ret.), PhD
Lakefield Distinguished Military Professor of Leadership
United States Naval Academy

"The research for this book into the backgrounds and heroic actions of U.S. Marine Corps Medal of Honor recipients is very impressive. The result is a series of stories about truly great heroes who seemed to have been forgotten by their hometowns and who should be remembered. This is remarkable reading for anyone interested in a better understanding of what makes a person act in heroic ways to protect and preserve the freedoms we hold so dear. God bless them, the United States Marine Corps, and our great country."

—Jack Lengyel
Director of Atheltics (Ret.)
United States Naval Academy

"My life has been changed by reading this book—not only in the way I look at my father and his USMC service, but because this whole project really highlights some of the work out there that still needs to be done."

—Dr. Kim Crowley, PhD
Bismarck State College
author of *How to Write About Sylvia Plath*

"When I was a kid, I delivered newspapers during the Viet Nam war. Every day the front cover of the *Columbus Dispatch* would list the number of war dead. To a kid, these were just numbers, but Terry Barrett makes them human and not just statistics from a war many Americans would just as soon forget. Each Marine and soldier has a story, and Dr. Barrett tells them brilliantly. *The Forgotten Thirty-Four* guarantees that these brave men will not ever be forgotten again."

—Tom Becka
Radio Talk Show Host/ author of
There's No Business Without The Show!

THE SEARCH FOR THE FORGOTTEN THIRTY-FOUR

Also by Terence W. Barrett, PhD,
Life After Suicide: The Survivor's Grief Experience

THE SEARCH FOR THE FORGOTTEN THIRTY-FOUR

HONORED BY THE U.S. MARINES, UNHERALDED IN THEIR HOMETOWNS?

TERENCE W. BARRETT, PhD

Printed by CreateSpace. Publication funded by Aftermath Research, Fargo, ND.

The accounts in this book are factual. All efforts were made to validate details, in most cases from two or more sources. Some unverified details have been excluded from the text. Suppositions are noted with such words as "likely" and "probably" or explained in the Notes. Any errors of fact discovered in this rendering are solely the author's responsibility.

Barrett, Terence W., 1949-

Library of Congress Catalog Number: 2011909052

Includes bibliographical references.
ISBN-10: 1461104246
ISBN-13: 978-1461104247

1. Military History. 2. United States Marine Corps. 3. Medal of Honor Recipients. 4. Bravery. 5. World War II, Korea, Vietnam War.

Cover photo provided by Bruce Salisbury.
Back Cover photo provided by Patty Becka.

Interior photo credits are provided in the Notes.

To find out more about our books, join us online at www.createspace.com.

Printed in the United States of America

To four men who died in service to our country:

Sergeant James Patrick Byrne, U.S. Marine Corps (22-years-old)
Date of Loss, March 8, 1967
In Quang Tri, South Vietnam

Corporal Terrence Patrick Kilbane, U.S. Army (20-years-old)
Date of Loss, February 6, 1969
In Pleiku, South Vietnam

Corporal Timothy Richard Ptacek, U.S. Army (19-years-old)
Date of Loss, May 21, 1969
In Quang Ngai, South Vietnam

Major Jeffrey P. Nye, U.S. Air Force (29-years-old)
Date of Loss, February 6, 1976
At Terrejon Air Base, Madrid, Spain

To all those Killed In Action and Missing In Action in Vietnam.

CONTENTS

ACKNOWLEDGMENTS

Those I wish to thank for their help, support, and interest in the research regarding United States Marine Corps Medal of Honor recipients are those who knew about this project and who provided much in its completion.

I am grateful to my parents, William and Mary Barrett, who lived through the Great Depression, survived World War II honorably, valued education and service, and ensured their five children had opportunities they had not experienced themselves. My mother for years mailed newspaper articles about WWII servicemen and enriched this research.

My heartfelt thank you goes to my wife, Rachel Dittmer Barrett, for listening to endless stories of Medal of Honor Marines, for her thoughtful suggestions, and for encouraging this writing. My brothers, sisters, aunt, and nieces often asked about the research: Timothy and Jan Barrett, Mary Anne Cody, Susanne Barrett Kazmer, Dennis Barrett, Barbara Lasso, Leslie Barrett Hall, Katie Barrett Nowak, Heather Kazmer, Jillian Kazmer, and Shanna Kazmer. I am fortunate to be a part of their lives.

Many family members of the recipients provided information about the lives of their Marines, in correspondence, phone conversations, and in personal meetings. Their contributions are noted in the text and Notes. Special thanks go to Pamela Carter, Marmont "Monty" Edson, Lauren Edson Lewan, Sharon Houston, Donel L. (Feyerherm) Swisher and Quonieta (Feyerherm) Murphy, Justice Marion "Mike" Chambers Jr., Benjamin Chambers, Rolland J. Julian, Ralph Julian, Lorraine Hansen, Owen Smith, Ryerson Mausert, Jr., John and Patricia Barnes, Janet (Coker) Artz, Robyn Nicodemus, and Jay Morgan.

I am especially grateful to the USMC Medal of Honor recipients who took of their time to review material, in whole or in part, to ensure its accuracy: Colonel Harvey C. Barnum, Jr. (Ret.), Colonel Wesley L. Fox (Ret.), Major General James E. Livingston (Ret.), Master Sergeant Richard A. Pittman (Ret.), Everett P. Pope (now deceased), and Private First Class Robert E. Simanek (Ret.). Theirs are inspiring lives of service and bravery, deserving of our nation's admiration.

The contributions of Jack Closson, USMC (Ret.), Bruce Salisbury, USAF (Ret.), Ann (Salisbury) Phelps, David Noyes, Thomas A. Chamberland, Karen (Ball) Greenly, Joan Earnshaw, and Lois Monson are included in the text and Notes. They each provided considerable assistance in researching information about individual recipients.

Tim Barrett, Paul Becka, Michael Feighan, and Tim Cleary, proud son of a WWII Marine who fought on Saipan and Okinawa, walked with me among gravestones in National Cemeteries to remember the Medal of Honor Marines. Paul and Patty Becka visited the gravesites of two of the Marines in private cemeteries separated by more than five hundred miles, left Memorial Day tributes, and often inquired about the discoveries derived from this research.

I am indebted to my friends, Eric and Pati Walz, for their help in finding threads to the lives of two Marines, for traveling to a Memorial Dedication for one of them, for planning a weekend friends' outing to his monument, and to their daughter, Amanda, for her interest in one Marine's mysterious background.

Long-time friends were unwavering in their humor and believed writing a book meant something: Joe Arnold, James Barry, grandson of a WWI Belleua Wood Marine, Tom and Susan Boardman, Kevin Byrne, Richard Clark, Tom Coughlin, Gerald Fallon, Tim Harkness, Kevin Keegan, Ron and Kitty Maltarich, Regis McGann, Tim McManamon, Kevin O'Malley, Daniel and Cheri Reed, John Richilano, Dennis and Maureen Salettel, and Don and Pam Sandborg.

Jack Lengyel provided his enthusiasm and encouragement, took time to read the manuscript, and connected me with others who believed in the value of this book. Kevin Keegan and Lou Sahadi took initiatives to locate an agent and editor.

My gratitude and respect go out to retired Marines who saw value in researching bravery: Lieutenant General Ron Christmas, USMC (Ret.), Marine Corps Heritage Foundation, Major General Donald Gardner, (Ret.), Marine Corps University, and Colonel Walter G. Ford, (Ret.), Leatherneck Magazine. Lieutenant Colonel Joseph J. Thomas, (Ret.), PhD, United States Naval Academy, was constant in his interest and support over the last five years. Brigadier General Thomas V. Draude, (Ret.), Marine Corps University Foundation, expressed immediate and consistent enthusiasm for this project and carefully read the material for its factual accuracy. Major General Thomas L. Wilkerson, (Ret.), United States Naval Institute, provided literary suggestions and extended his encouragement for the publication of this work.

Carol Cepregi, Congressional Medal of Honor Society, Mt. Pleasant, South Carolina, readily assisted me in contacting Medal of Honor recipients.

My thanks to James Tougas, Nancy G. Waller, Timothy Teig, and Dave Seifert, Fargo Vet Center staff members whose interest in bravery and recommendations of current books furthered this research.

Special thanks go to Christy Bright for the technical help she provided in formatting this work before it went to print, and to Kim Crowley for her skilled editing of the final draft of this book.

Terence W. Barrett
Fargo, North Dakota
2011

FOREWORD

The Search For The Forgotten Thirty-Four is a study of bravery. Within these pages are the accounts of brave men, Marines, the history surrounding them, and the events that defined their legacies. More than telling stories, this book focuses on the greatness of America and those who chose to wear the uniform—men willing to put themselves into difficult situations and finding within the capacity to deal with dire circumstances as they unfold. They are inspiring examples, impressing upon the reader that "average" or "ordinary" individuals possess the potential to act bravely. In this, as stated in the text, our culture can be less anxious, fearful, or cowered by the intimidations of terror.

One thing *The Forgotten Thirty-Four* makes clear is that the demonstration of bravery is a reflection of personal character. Another is that bravery does not just spring forth when an individual finds himself in a particular circumstance. The roots of bravery are traced back into childhood. Personal background is searched out to better understand later actions.

The men described here did not join up to become Medal of Honor recipients. No one who earns this award intended to do so. They wanted to be Marines, first and foremost. Those who have earned the Medal did so because they were in events that drew forth the character honed in early experience. The hope is that communities will not let any brave hometown son or daughter be forgotten. Bravery is passed from one generation to the next. *The Search For The Forgotten Thirty-Four* gets to the heart of the matter. We must remember them.

Semper Fi.

Major General James E. Livingston, USMC (Ret.)
Medal of Honor recipient

CHAPTER 1
A Name Forgotten

"The legacy of heroes is the memory of a great name and the inheritance of a great example."

British Prime Minister Benjamin Disraeli [1]

The floor of the Bo Ban hut was not the most comfortable place to recline. Despite the wrenching pain in his leg, he took sleep when it came. Five comrades stretched out nearby. Another friend had taken the watch. Outside in the dark, the enemy had detected the ambush site and quietly advanced to the hut.

"Grenades!"

The warning and the sound of a grenade landing near him startled the Marine lance corporal from sleep. He had been in enough combat to know the danger. In that instant he made a decision.

After the grenades detonated in Bo Ban, there was no question how his life ended. Witnesses to his death provided the details in an investigation conducted afterwards. His Medal Citation, available since 1970, described the bare events.

Tracking down this Marine in public sources thirty-two years later provided little information about him. One photograph appeared on various Web sites, along with his Medal Citation. Archives provided a few newspaper articles, circa 1970. Marine records held a bit of biography. Beyond his award Citation, background was limited to his birth date and place, foster parents' names, date and place of enlistment, and his gravesite. Facts regarding his family, childhood activities, education, and extracurricular activities were scarce.

The First Search for Kenneth Lee Worley

The service records most easily accessible to those looking for Ken indicate that he was born April 27, 1948, and apparently spent his childhood in Farmington, in rugged northwestern New Mexico, on the eastern edge of the Navajo Indian Reservation. During WWII, the Marines had recruited Natives from the Reservation who would eventually be revered as the Navajo Code Talkers.

Farmington was an "Oil Field Town" in 1948, home to about 3,290 people. The population had exploded to nearly 24,000 by the time he left. As years passed, the number of residents who might remember him later would shrink to a small number, and confusion about who he had been would grow.

The town sits in the San Juan Mountains at the confluence of the San Juan, La Plata, and Animas rivers. Colorado's San Juan Mountains and the desert highlands of Arizona and Utah are within sight. The Animas River, believed to mean "River of Lost Souls," comes out of the high mountains, where its ferocious currents and rapids churn up boulders and rocks. Local Farmington residents are proud of the deposits of unique *river rocks* along the banks of the river.

Fly-fishing for Rainbows on the San Juan River is a favorite pastime for the locals, even in the winter. Older Farmington residents remember Ken fishing in the Las Animas River when he was a boy and sometimes tell stories of him playing with his little friends in the neighborhood, finding happiness where he could. To those who looked for him later, it would be clear that he had not been born into a "well-to-do" or leading family in the community.

After graduating from elementary school in 1962, Ken ended up 270 miles south as the crow flies. The records suggest he attended Hot Springs High School for two years in arid Truth Or Consequences, New Mexico, on the muddy Rio Grande River. The small town of under 8,000 residents is in the eastern foothills of the wrinkled Black Range Mountains, between Elephant Butte Lake and Caballo Lake State Parks. His classmates would have been as much Hispanic and Native American as Anglo.

Ken's arrival in Truth Or Consequences would be one of the many mysteries of his young life, as the high school has no record that Ken Worley was ever a student there. He left New Mexico around 1964, when he was 16-years-old, relocating to Modesto, California, which he gave as his Home of Record when he enlisted in the Marines.

Just before Christmas, 1966, Donald and Rosemary Feyerherm, who already had eight children in their care, took Ken in and provided a foster family for him. Having been an "only child" for years, Ken was now called "brother" by Quonieta, Donel, Austin, Carla, Lura, Conni, Russell and Vella Feyerherm. [2]

The Feyerherms had little information about his past, except that he was from Farmington, had run away from home, and had been on his own since age eleven. They knew he had lied about his age and had been driving a truck since he was fourteen. At the time they met him, he had been driving truck in San Jose and had been living in a trailer with no amenities. [3]

Thus began the belief that Ken was an orphan. In later newspaper reports, he would sometimes be referred to as "the orphan Marine."

Presents from the Feyerherms that first Christmas brought Ken to tears. Later, both Orange County, California and Snohomish County, Washington would claim the young Marine as one of their own. Another mystery.

"A wild, impetuous, wonderful kid"; it became clear to his foster parents that Ken wanted to be part of the family, and he intended to give back. [4] Rosemary remembered him insisting that he was part of the family, too, and telling her "I'm going to pay my way." [5]

Ken enlisted in June 1967. His training went well at the San Diego Recruit Depot, and he was promoted at the expected times. Following recruit training, he had twenty-one days of leave accumulated before he was to report to Camp Pendleton in August. As his foster father would tell it, Private Worley spent most of those days with the Feyerherms, working eighteen of the days to earn more money. He spent most of his paycheck to treat the family to a day at Knotts' Berry Farm.

Private First Class Worley completed individual combat training and basic infantry training in October. His orders to Vietnam came that November, five months after he had enlisted. He arrived in Vietnam on Friday, November 24, 1967. The north monsoon season was underway.

He slogged about in the mud on combat base hills, his poncho pelted by the rain. Besides being under rocket and mortar attacks for the first time in his life, he heard warnings about malaria and dysentery and trench foot. Snakes abounded in the jungles, but hookworm and ringworm accounted for more casualties than did snake bites. And no matter how deep the fighting holes were dug or how reinforced the defensive bunkers were built, he saw the bloody death of comrades.

Lance Corporal Worley served as a rifleman and machine gunner with Company L, 3d Battalion, 7th Marines, occupying a series of low hills southwest of Da Nang, Quang Nam Province, Republic of Vietnam.

On a Sunday night, elements of his Company went out on a patrol to set up an ambush site in Bo Ban Hamlet. In the dark of early Monday morning, at 5:55 on August 12, 1968, the Marines with Lance Corporal Worley were awakened by warnings their platoon leader, Second Lieutenant John J. Hewitt, shouted out:

"Grenades!"

The enemy had detected the site of the ambush, crawling and crouching past security, and had thrown grenades into the house in which the Marines were sleeping. One of the grenades rolled near Lance Corporal Worley and five of his companions. He immediately dived onto the grenade.

The news reached California as it usually did: *For Immediate Release.* The Department of Defense announced on August 14, 1968, its Vietnam Weekly Casualties Statistical Summary. LCPL Kenneth L.

Worley, listed as Killed as a Result of Hostile Action, was identified as "friend of Mr. Donald FEYERHERM, 5348 Harvey Way, Longbeach." [6]

Lance Corporal Worley's body was brought home. There was no parade to celebrate his return to home soil. He was buried with military honors in Westminster Memorial Park in Orange County on Saturday, August 24, at 10:30 AM, in a grave donated by the owners of the cemetery. The Feyerherm family attended.

By then the Feyerherms, the only family he had on record, lived nearby in Anaheim. They were notified that Ken had been awarded the Medal of Honor, but the original paperwork submitted by First Lieutenant Joel S. Brummer and signed by First Lieutenant W. F. Sawyer was lost and the process was initiated a second time.

The Feyerherms moved to Edmonds, on the Puget Sound, in the northern sprawl of Seattle. Don opened D&K Woodworking Company, the D for himself and the K for his silent partner, Kenneth. [7]

When the time for the awarding of Ken's Medal came, the Marines made sure the entire Feyerherm family traveled to Washington, D.C., making all the arrangements and covering the expenses. At that time the children were between the ages of six and twenty-one. The ever-vigilant and supportive Marine escort provided "sitting" service for the younger children, one evening traveling out of D.C. with them to find a McDonald's restaurant to accommodate their preferences. Vice President Spiro Agnew presented the family Ken's award on April 20, 1970, in a ceremony at the White House. [8]

By the following year Don was working as a heavy equipment operator at Naval Air Station Moffett Field, near the south end of San Francisco Bay, and Rosemary was nearby working as a clerk-typist at the California State Department passport office. She had become disenchanted with the government and protested the war policies, announcing her candidacy for the Democratic nomination for president. [9]

Afterwards, the public notice given to Ken Worley's life and heroism did not seem to reach back to New Mexico.

Ken's name was inscribed on the California Vietnam Memorial in Sacramento. On the wall of the Sacramento Military Entrance Processing Station (MEPS), [10] passed by those entering the service, a framed, color-enhanced photograph of Ken is fixed above a framed copy of his Medal Citation.

A newspaper article in the *Everett Herald* did list Ken as having graduated from an Edmonds high school in 1967, [11] and UPI articles across the country noted he was from Edmonds. [12] There was a plaque at the old Carnegie Library in Edmonds that said he attended Edmonds School District 15. At the same location at 118 5th Avenue North, now the Edmonds Historical Museum, beside the flagpole to the left of the front entrance, stands a seven-foot granite monument dedicated in honor of local men who were killed in action in all wars. [13] Ken's name is engraved on the memorial with seventy-eight others. His name is also included on a memorial for local Medal of Honor recipients at the Snohomish County Courthouse in Everett, Washington, but he is not listed on the Medal of Honor plaque in Olympia.

While the Feyerherms moved to 7016 196th Street, Edmonds, after Ken's death, it does not appear that he ever lived there, and certainly did not graduate from the high school there.

Later in the search for Ken's family ties, some Farmington residents thought there might have been an article about him in the local newspaper at the time he was killed, but they could not be certain.

Remembered Among Others by the Nation in 1982

Searching for Ken Worley inevitably leads to the Vietnam Veterans Memorial Wall in Washington, D.C. His name can be located on Panel 48W-Line 1 of The Wall.

Correspondences with several Marines who served in Vietnam revealed confusion associated to whether or not the Worley they remembered was the same Marine who had been killed in action and earned a Medal of Honor. Walking along the Memorial Wall provides an explanation for their uncertainty.

Thirteen Worleys from across the states in all branches of the military are honored on the Memorial Wall panels. Four were Marines. The thirteen ranged in age from 18-years to 48-years at the time of their casualty. Nine were 21-years-old or younger. All but two were enlisted men. Their ranks stretched from private first class (E2) to major general (O8). Five left wives behind at home.

Not the first Worley to go to war in Vietnam, Ken was the eleventh Worley to give his life in Vietnam. Three Worleys died before Ken received his orders to Vietnam. Army Sergeant Robert Keith Worley, a married man from Saltville, Virginia, died early in the war on February 13, 1966. Army SP6 Rom Worley, married and from Walnut, North Carolina, died on April 27, 1967. Marine Corps Private First Class Stephen Ray Worley of West Monroe, Louisiana, was killed in action on October 14, 1967.

Following the North Vietnamese New Year's Tet Offensive, 1968 proved to be a fatal year for eight Worleys who went to Vietnam. Their dying began in March and continued into August. The first was Army Corporal Stephen Michael Worley of South Charleston, West Virginia, who died on Sunday, March 10, 1968. Air Force Staff Sergeant Don Franklin Worley, married, from Bald Knob, Arkansas, died in Laos the next day on March 11. [14] Two days later, March 13, Army SP4 William Paul Worley from Altoona, Pennsylvania, died at Pleiku nine days after his arrival in country. On April 21, Marine Lance Corporal Thomas James Worley, from Detroit, Michigan, died in Quang Tri Province. Marine Sergeant James Ronald Worley of Hartsville, Tennessee, died in Quang Tri nine days later, on April 30. The next week, Army SP4 Robert Lee Worley, from Las Vegas, Nevada, died May 6. The oldest and highest ranking Worley to die in Vietnam was Air Force fixed wing pilot, Major General Robert Franklin Worley of Riverside, California. He died on July 23 in Thua Thien Province, near Hue. Three weeks would pass before Ken earned his Medal of Honor in August.

Two more Worleys died in the war after 1968. Army First Lieutenant Michael Gregg Worley of Leicester, North Carolina, was killed in action June 11, 1969. Army Corporal Garry Lee Worley, 18-years-old, of Bristol, Tennessee, was the last Worley to give his life in South Vietnam. He died on April 23, 1970.

Records indicate that none of the other twelve Worleys were directly related to Ken.

The nationwide media attention given the Vietnam Veterans Memorial Wall in 1982 provided an opportunity for New Mexico, the *Land of Enchantment*, to recognize Ken Worley. Among the 58,195 names on The Wall, 399 of the war dead had listed New Mexico as their home state when they entered the military. Ken, however, does not show up on this list.

Thirteen Medal of Honor recipients across three wars are associated to New Mexico. Only six are actually "accredited" to the state. Ten of the recipients were born in New Mexico. Nine served in the Army, born in Albuquerque (3), Cerrillos, Loving, Gallup, Governador, Silver City, and Taos. Seven of these earned their Medals in Vietnam. Ken Worley is the only Marine from New Mexico to earn the Award, and the only recipient born in Farmington. With him, five others have their names etched into the shiny black face of the Vietnam Veterans Memorial Wall.

The Marine Corps does not capriciously recommend one of its own to be awarded a Medal of Honor. For any community to be able to claim itself as the birthplace of one of these men should be a source of immense pride.

When the Four Corners Vietnam Memorial Wall was dedicated July 4, 1993, at the local Farmington Veterans Park, Ken's name was not among the eighty-three servicemen listed as Missing In Action or Killed In Action.

Phone calls, letters, and e-mails to individuals in his hometown initially yielded no further information about him. The Veterans of Foreign Wars (VFW) officer who answered a call knew nothing of the Marine. There was no tribute to him at the local service organization. The reason given: if he were killed in action, he would not have been a member.

The Farmington schools would release no information about their former student, unless a request was made by an immediate family member or by court order. The local museum director was able to find nothing about the former resident in archived school annuals. As it turned out later, searching for Ken Worley in any school records would have yielded nothing anyway.

Ken's life prior to the Marines was mysterious and the discovery of it was circuitous. He had moved from his hometown when he was 14-years-old. He moved several times in the years that followed, to different towns, different schools, and finally to a different state. His life was to be brief. He earned his Medal of Honor and died when he was only 20-years-old.

When Ken left his home and family, he took with him the kind of character that ultimately results in heroic bravery. The life experiences in Farmington that had helped shape the man he had become were unknown. The people he had encountered, family, friends, teachers, classmates, clergy, and neighbors, who could tell stories about his boyhood had never come forward.

Certainly, he was remembered by his family, by friends he had made across his short life, and by the Marines who had served with him in combat. Yet, his was the name first noted among thirty-four Marine Medal of Honor recipients to be without tribute in their hometowns. Without memorial or tribute, had the news of his heroism in Bo Ban Hamlet, Vietnam, not reached to Farmington, New Mexico?

This initially was all that could be known from accessible public records about this young Marine. His life experience in New Mexico remained an enigma. The search for facts about his childhood intensified. Questions about Ken would eventually have answers, but not easily.

Farmington was a class-conscious small town when Ken lived there. Residents tended to stay out of the personal business of neighbors and other families. Gossip, viewed to be socially rude, was carefully restricted to backrooms. The population might have expanded since 1968, when Ken died, but some old attitudes have survived. The Medal of Honor recipient was known by some still living in Farmington. They were not talking.

CHAPTER 2
The Passing of Forty Years

"They shall not grow old, As we who are left grow old. Age shall not weary them, nor the years condemn. At the going down of the sun, and in the morning, We will remember them."

For The Fallen, *The Times*, September 21, 1914
By Robert Laurence Binyon
British poet, dramatist and art scholar

Bravery and heroism are serious things—not to be taken lightly or for granted or set aside on a shelf to collect dust.

Learning about bravery requires recognizing and remembering heroic individuals. The stories of the heroic, brave men in this book were drawn from histories of one hundred eighty-one Marines in WWII, Korean, and Vietnam battles. All had demonstrated extraordinary bravery in combat circumstances and earned Congressional Medals of Honor.

The Forgotten Thirty-Four were unquestionably brave. The Marine Corps at one time acknowledged their bravery. For the most part, however, autobiographies, memoirs, and biographies have not been written about them. Their names are mentioned in lists, sometimes in passing.

Some seem no more than footnotes in books about other heroes. The backgrounds from which they had come, the personal characteristics they possessed, and the men they had been are little known to the wider public.

The extent to which the Thirty-Four had been largely disregarded was a concern calling out for correction. Their forgotten stories are moving as well as inspiring.

Starting with twenty-two U.S. Marines who fought in World War II on an island called Iwo Jima, *Semper Fidelis, A Psychological Study of Heroic Bravery,* set out to discover the roots of heroic bravery. [1]

Bravery reaching the range of heroic requires that a person's behavior demonstrates unordinary courage or strength, appears to be characteristic of the person across time and circumstances, involves personal risk, perhaps the sacrifice of one's life, and results in uncommon outcomes and accomplishment. Afterwards, the person's heroically brave actions are celebrated and honored, remembered to the point of becoming almost legendary.

Hometowns, communities, and schools find pride in heralding one of their own heroes.

In most cases, that is. There are heroes whose brave deeds have been forgotten—fallen dormant in the memories of their own hometowns. The Forgotten Thirty-Four are counted among these.

Encountering such inspiring lives, the *Semper Fidelis* study went back to the Civil War and began again—at the beginning. As it progressed, the investigation became as much about learning why these thirty-four Marines had been forgotten as it had been about discovering what could be learned from their lives.

In Search of Bravery

Go in search of bravery and a good place to look is among the Marines. The U.S. Marine Corps began as an idea raised by a group of men planning sedition on a Friday in November. As Marine traditions tell it, members of the fledgling Continental Congress were gathered together talking strategy in Tun Tavern in Philadelphia. They wanted to establish an American Corps of Marines, organized in just two battalions similar to those in the regiments of the Continental Army.

The men drafted a brief resolution that would become a Congressional Act and transmitted it to "The General." The war was on with Great Britain and it was 1775, November 10.

The Resolution Establishing the Continental Marines was recorded in the Journal of the Continental Congress. The Marines had been envisioned as a select corps of elite fighting men who would enter the war to fight for freedom. No person could be appointed as an officer and no man enlisted into the ranks within the Battalions unless they were able seamen, acquainted with maritime affairs. These selected men were to be skilled marksmen and intrepid fighters. Not just anyone could *sign up*. Each had to be a known and proven combatant.

Congressional Act of the United States Senate and House of Representatives passed the Resolution into law on July 11, 1798. The Marines were to "provide for the naval armament," meaning they were to serve as the security force "on board the frigates, and other armed vessels and galleys employed in the service of the United States." Meant to be deployed as a force serving on the seas, the Act also granted the president the discretional power to direct the Marines at any time to fulfill duties "in the forts and garrisons of the United States, on the sea-coast, or any other duty on shore." [2]

At the time, and for the most part, ever since, the Marines have constituted the smallest fighting force organized by the United States, maintaining the smallest number of officers and enlisted men of all the fighting branches of the military.

When the Continental ship *Providence* was being readied for "a short cruise" out of Boston, Captain William Jones, USMC, decided to recruit more Marines to fill the ship's security complement. On March 20, 1779, he advertised in the *Providence Gazette* for "a few good men." Captain Jones' choice of words has echoed across generations of Marines for more than 200 years. [3] Those who once sailed aboard the *Providence* would recognize the current recruiting slogan displayed on posters, billboards, Web sites, and youtube.com. "The Few. The Proud. The Marines."

These few men and women *are* proud of that legacy. Marines have always "done more with less." They, at times not so humbly, proclaim the honor of being "first to fight, first to die." History proves they have done a lot of both since their inception in Tun Tavern.

Ever since Congress passed the Act for Establishing and Organizing a Marine Corps, the president has frequently ordered the deployment of Marines to troubled spots around the world. The Marines have campaign flags memorializing armed engagements in the Revolutionary War, Quasi-War with France, Barbary Wars, War of 1812, Creek-Seminole Indian War, Mexican War, American Civil War, Indian War Campaigns, Interim 1866-70, 1871 Korean Campaign, Interim 1871-98, Spanish-American War, Philippine Insurrection/Samoa, 1899, China Relief Expedition (Boxer Rebellion), Interim conflicts 1901-11, Nicaragua, 1912, Action against Philippine Outlaws, 1911, Mexican Campaign (Vera Cruz), 1914, Haiti 1915, Interim 1915-16, Dominican Campaign 1916-20, World War I, Haiti Campaign 1919-20, Second Nicaraguan Campaign 1926-33, Interim 1920-40, World War II, Korean War, Dominican Republic, 1965, Vietnam War 1963-74, Lebanon, 1982-84, Grenada, 1983, Persian Gulf, 1988, Panama, 1989, Persian Gulf War 1990-91, Somalia 1992-94, Iraq and Afghanistan 2003-present.

The Marines who have fought in wars serve as examples of individuals in circumstances that draw upon bravery. Among these thousands of men and women are a group of 294 men recognized for their bravery, who earned the nation's highest award for valor in combat. These men were in extraordinary combat circumstances, such that their highest character emerged and prevailed, and they demonstrated extraordinary bravery. Their stories provide the material for us to better understand the quality of bravery, the personal characteristics associated to it, and the actions that spring from it.

The Medal of Honor [4]

In 1782, George Washington initiated the awarding of a *Purple Heart* to honor brave soldiers, sailors, and Marines wounded in combat. Additionally, Certificates of Merit and "brevet" promotions were awarded to those who acted gallantly in battle. The idea for the Medal of Honor emerged during the Civil War as a way to acknowledge *exceptional* heroism among brave men. This *badge of valor* was the first military decoration for enlisted men of the Navy and Marine Corps formally authorized by the American Congress and approved by President Abraham

Lincoln on December 21, 1861. Seven months later, the Medal of Honor for the Army and Voluntary Forces was authorized on July 12, 1862.

The Medal of Honor is the highest award for bravery given to individuals in the United States, earned primarily for valor in action against an enemy force. Its awarding is recommended by senior military officers, investigated for justification, and authorized finally by the President of the United States. President Theodore Roosevelt signed an Executive Order into law on September 20, 1905, directing that the Medal should be presented at ceremonies of award always "with formal and impressive ceremonial." Recipients of the award should "when practicable, be ordered to Washington, D.C.," so the president, as Commander in Chief, or a representative of the president, can present the Medal.

This award is commonly called the *Congressional Medal of Honor* because it is awarded "in the name of the Congress of the United States," but Congress actually seldom awards special Medals of Honor. In reality, the award is a matter to be decided among military men and their Commander in Chief.

In judging men for receipt of the medal, each military service has established standards by which the award is recommended. The USMC requires that the individual's valor must be exemplary enough to clearly exceed the obligations of duty and to distinguish it from other common acts of bravery in combat. The individual's actions must be uncontested by those present, beyond any justified criticism, and attested to by at least two eyewitnesses. Medal of Honor bravery must involve actions that unquestionably place the individual's life at risk.

The president, in the name of Congress, has awarded 3,466 Medals of Honor to the nation's bravest Marines, Sailors, Soldiers, Airmen, and Coast Guardsmen since the decoration's creation in 1861. Nineteen men have been awarded two Medals. [5] The first Marine recipient was Corporal John F. Mackie in 1862.

Sixteen Marines were awarded the Medal of Honor during the Civil War. Sixty-three Marines earned the award in the 1871 Korean Campaign, the Spanish-American War, the Philippine Insurrection and the Boxer Rebellion. Nine Medals were awarded to Marine officers for the landing at Vera Cruz, Mexico in 1914, and thirteen more were conferred on enlisted Marines and officers during the Caribbean "Banana Wars," 1912-35. Only two Marines, Major General Smedley D. Butler and Sergeant Major Daniel Daly were awarded Medals of Honor for two separate actions: Vera Cruz (1914) and Haiti (1915) for Butler, and Peking (1900) and Haiti (1915) for Daly. Seven Marines received the Medal for actions during World War I, eighty-two during World War II, and another forty-two for the Korean War. A total of fifty-seven Marines were awarded the Medal during the Vietnam War. One Medal of Honor has been awarded to a Marine who died in action in Iraq in 2004.

The Citations describing the heroism and brave acts of these men are public record. Initially, once awarded, the official records of each individual's actions were maintained in government archives and sporadically printed. The U.S. Senate finally, in 1973, ordered that the Citations be compiled together and printed in a book. The first volume published was *Committee on Veterans' Affairs, U.S. Senate, Medal of Honor Recipients: 1863–1973.* The book was updated and reprinted in 1979. [6]

Remembering Heroes

Since the attack on Pearl Harbor on December 7, 1941, 182 Marines have earned Medals of Honor: Eighty-two during World War II, forty-two in the Korean War, and fifty-seven Marines from the Vietnam War. Corporal Jason Dunham was awarded the Medal for his actions in Iraq in 2004. Of these Marines, 124 (68%) did not return home after their wars. Photographs of young men in Marine uniforms would present an unchanging image of each of them as the years passed and as those who remembered them aged. Such photographs and memories exemplify the images British poet Robert Laurence Binyon had in mind when he wrote the verse at the start of this chapter. [7]

Their lives might have ended, but their impact has not. Marines treat their Medal of Honor recipients with regard, admiration, and special courtesy. Travel to MCB Quantico and see that the golf course is dedicated to them and streets, buildings and dining halls are named in their honor.

Immediate family members of the recipients met presidents or official representatives of the White House to receive posthumous Medal awards. Fathers, mothers, sisters, brothers, wives and children traveled to Washington to participate in ceremonies. They involved themselves in societies and organizations dedicated to remembering fallen heroes. Fellow Marines of the Medal recipient contacted families. And family members were invited to attend veteran's groups and unit reunions as guests of honor.

The men who had been saved or rescued by the recipients continued their lives, daily remembering the actions of these heroes, committing themselves to make a difference in life. They often lobbied for recognition and memorialization of the Marines who had sacrificed themselves on their behalf.

The generations that were raised in the shadows of this bravery were affected. The recipients' children, nephews, nieces, and cousins heard the stories and carried the pride of the family with them. No matter how distant, the heroism resonated with them. The sentiments seem consistent: "Merritt Edson is a great great great uncle of mine and it makes me proud to have the Marine Corps blood in me. My father and brother were both in the Marine Corps..." [8] and "I never had the opportunity to know my great uncle because I was very young when he died. He left a proud legacy that will never be forgotten." [9]

"Jimmy Phipps was my cousin and we spent a lot of happy years together. He came from a very loving happy family. His death brought much grief to our family. We were all very proud of Jimmy's sacrifice. I will always remember him and be proud of him for what he did." [10]

"Jack Kelso was not only my Uncle but is also my Hero. He gave his life for his country. He gave his life to save the lives of others. We did not get the chance to know him but our Grandparents and our Mom, his sister, told us about him and how he lost his life.... Now we tell our Kids about him and they share with their classmates about a great hero." [11]

To William David Morgan: "Always my Hero, always in my thoughts, forever in my heart, forever my Uncle. Rest in Peace. Love always...your niece." [12]

Children were named after their heroic father, grandfather, great uncle, or distant cousin. Generation after generation entered the Marines to pay tribute to a family member they perhaps did not personally know, but whom they wished they had.

What can be said with certainty is that the majority of the men achieved a level of respect that remains to impress and inspire family, friends, former companions in battle, and present Marines who are introduced to their stories in recruit training courses. The legacy of these Marines will not die nor pass away.

This is as it should be.

Medal of Honor recipients are remembered on a national level, sometimes on a state level. Their names are found on various Medal of Honor Memorials across the United States. The Congressional Medal of Honor Museum is on board the historic aircraft carrier USS *Yorktown*, docked at Patriots Point, Charleston Harbor, South Carolina. Other museums, monuments and memorials are located in places like Chattanooga, Tennessee; Valley Forge, Pennsylvania; Indianapolis, Indiana; Pueblo, Colorado; Riverside, California; San Antonio, Texas; and Bell Chasse, Louisiana.

Whether inscribed on glass panels or engraved in bronze, steel, granite, or on marble walls, or fiberglass obelisks, all the names of Medal of Honor recipients, from the Civil War to the present, are there. "Home of the brave," America tends to remember its heroes. Yet, remembering goes beyond inscribing a name on a panel.

One of the First

When the Medal of Honor was first established, Andrew J. Tomlin, born in Goshen, New Jersey, was 17-years-old. Four years later, he was Corporal of the Guard, detached aboard the USS *Wabash*, a warship, headed for a confrontation with the Confederates in a bid to capture Wilmington, North Carolina, the only remaining major port open for southern ship traffic. The Union blockade had been unable to cut Wilmington off from sea trade, due largely to the presence of Fort Fisher at the mouth of the Cape Fear River.

Under the command of Colonel William Lamb, the fort had been enlarged and fortified into an intimidating bastion during the war. It encompassed one mile of defense facing the sea and a third of a mile facing land. Its artillery batteries of forty-seven guns sat upon a multitude of earthen mounds thirty-two, forty-five, and sixty-feet high and were connected by underground tunnels. A nine-foot-high palisade fence protected Fort Fisher on its land side from ground assaults.

The Union forces attacked at Cape Fear on December 24, 1864, and failed to take the fort, withdrawing and regrouping. On January 12, 1865, Union ships began a bombardment to open up a second assault.

Over 8,000 Union troops assaulted the palisade fence on the land side. The palisades were breached and Federal forces were able to advance towards the fort, but the outcome was in doubt after two days of fighting.

During the assault on Fort Fisher, 200 Marines were dispatched ashore. During a particularly bitter engagement, more than two-thirds of the attacking Union forces retreated from the fort "in panic." The Confederates threatened to counterattack in force, and the Marines were ordered to hold a line of entrenchments to the rear of the fort.

Corporal Tomlin held a position in the line of 200 Marines on the night of January 14, remaining there until relief troops arrived in the morning. During the withdrawal, one of his comrades was wounded by enemy fire on an open plain near the palisades. Corporal Tomlin "unhesitatingly advanced under a withering fire of musketry...and assisted the wounded man to a place of safety," for which he would receive the nation's highest military honor. After six more hours of ferocious battle on January 15, Fort Fisher fell to the Union forces.

Sergeant Richard Binder, Sergeant Isaac N. Fry, Corporal John Rannahan, Private John Shivers, Private Henry A. Thompson, and Corporal Andrew J. Tomlin, six Marines, were each awarded Medals of Honor for intrepid actions taken under fire during the assault on Fort Fisher. Corporal Tomlin, the last Marine in the Civil War to earn the Medal, was also the first to receive the Medal of Honor for putting his life in danger to save another Marine. His was the kind of conspicuous gallantry that would be repeated by many Marines in campaigns and engagements right into the twenty-first century.

Andrew returned home to Goshen after the war. He lived honorably in his community, serving terms as commissioner and as Cape May County sheriff. He died November 1, 1906, at the age of 61. Sarah, his wife, lived until 1940, dying at the age of 92. They are buried together beside a white country church in Goshen Methodist Cemetery.

A dark gray granite stone, the polished face engraved with a description of Andrew's heroism at Fort Fisher, stands above the Tomlin grave. A small, white marble block, engraved with the Medal of Honor insignia was more recently placed at the base of the Tomlin monument. Beyond the U.S. Marines and the U.S. Navy, who remembers this young man who earned a Medal for exceptional valor over 140 years ago?

Consider that Americans reside in more than 33,000 cities, towns, villages and communities in the United States. This averages out to only one town in ten potentially being able to claim a recipient as a native son. The possibility of a recipient having lived down the street is actually smaller, as several cities can claim more than one recipient as their own: Leeds, Alabama, Pueblo, Colorado, and Six Mile, South Carolina, are examples.

Goshen, New Jersey, an unincorporated community, was home to 15,490 residents in 2009. Since a less than 9.6 percent chance of claiming a Medal of Honor recipient exists for any town, it is reasonable that Andrew J. Tomlin be honored in Goshen. That the birthplace or home of record of a Medal of Honor recipient takes pride in claiming one of these valiant men as a native son makes good sense. So do tributes in hometown halls, in local school halls of fame, and in neighborhood parks: these honors go beyond a monument in a cemetery and a name on a wall.

"Sacrifice was their duty, remembrance is our mandate." [13]

The actions of brave individuals deserve to be remembered beyond photographs shared among family members. Their sacrifices earn them the grateful acknowledgment of communities, states, and the nation. It is as retired Air Force officer Greg Boyington Jr. said at a September 22, 2007, ceremony to pay tribute to his father: "Pappy belonged to the nation." [13]

Some in a position to remember take action to ensure tributes are established to Medal of Honor recipients. Maine's Secretary of State is an example, taking to heart his responsibilities to maintain the historical record and to oversee the Maine State Archives. Fifty-three Medal of Honor recipients born in the State of Maine have their awards accredited to Maine. Fourteen more recipients born in other states or countries, either having moved to or enlisted in military service there, are accredited to Maine, totaling sixty-seven awards. Additionally, twenty-nine recipients were born in Maine but were residing in another state when they entered the service. Their awards are accredited to other states. A total of ninety-six Medals of Honor are, therefore, associated to Maine.

Few Maine recipients have had memorials dedicated to them. The Pine Tree State's Secretary of State decided to change that. In October 2006, he initiated a project to promote historical and civic awareness in the communities related to the recipients. The Secretary emphasized the importance of paying tribute to the recipients, encouraging their hometowns and the communities in which they are buried to recognize them with memorials. [15] One of the ninety-six Maine warriors was a Marine, David Bernard Champagne of Waterville. His story is told in a later chapter.

Texans have accepted the mandate to remember in a big way. The Woodlands sits on 25,000 Texas acres twenty-seven miles north of downtown Houston. The community commissioned its Town Green Park and positioned it along Lake Robbins Drive. On the east side of the park, along a perennial garden near the waterway, a monument was dedicated on Friday, May 25, 2007, Memorial Day Weekend. The Texas Marine Medal of Honor Monument pays tribute to "seventeen brave Marines from the great State of Texas who selflessly went above and beyond the call of duty defending freedom wherever it was threatened."

Across the United States, memorials and tributes abound for at least one hundred-eleven Marine Medal of Honor recipients from World War II, Korea, and Vietnam. While family and friends and fellow Marines might recognize the tributes to these men, for most Americans the names of the recipients and their memorials might be just that, names and monuments. In cities, towns, parks and plazas across the States, thousands of people encounter their memories daily without recognizing their significance.

Statues or monuments have been dedicated to twenty-three Marine recipients in their hometowns and war memorials or plaques to nine others. The Navy has commissioned fifty-five ships in the name of Marine Medal of Honor recipients. [16] Fourteen public schools, seven VA Hospitals/Medical Centers or clinics, six Veterans Nursing Homes, at least one Federal Building, six U.S. Post Offices, fourteen Marine camps and bases, forty-one Legion Posts/VFWs/AMVETs/Marine Corps Detachments, Reserve Centers, and Associations, one Disabled American Veterans Chapter, thirty-five buildings/halls/rooms, one

National Guard Armory, one museum, and five airports have been named after them.

Nationwide, names of Marine recipients have been dedicated to twenty-two streets/avenues/drives/roads, eight highways, thirteen highway bridges and exchanges, three memorial pavilions and highway rest areas, fourteen parks and playgrounds, ten athletic fields, and one college campus. Fifteen awards, trophies, or scholarships granted annually, one competitive team, and two commemorative stamps or envelopes issued by the Post Office bear the name of a Marine recipient. From time to time, a July Fourth or a Memorial Day Parade is dedicated to one or the other in their home state, and an annual golf tournament is named for one of them.

Long-Remembered Bravery

That a hero is forgotten at home is put into greater contrast in the example of how one community pays tribute to its hometown son.

All United States Marines remember "Manila John" Basilone. Sergeant Basilone landed on Guadalcanal Island with 4,200 of Lieutenant Colonel "Chesty" Puller's 1st Battalion, 7th Marines on September 18, 1942.

Over a month into the fighting, Sergeant Basilone was positioned with his squad of fifteen men on Lunga Ridge, also called *Bloody Ridge*, along the south defensive perimeter protecting Henderson Airfield. A little more than a week from his 26th birthday, Sergeant Basilone, was a platoon sergeant in charge of two sections of heavy, water-cooled .30-caliber machine guns. Tasked to keep the Japanese from exploiting a narrow pass to Henderson, his outpost was positioned well forward in the jungle at the Tenaru River.

The enemy had not yet relinquished the idea of pushing the Marines off Guadalcanal and they came in earnest in late October. As the Zodiac signs on horoscope astrology charts drifted out of Libra into Scorpio, 3,000 frenzied warriors charged out of the steamy night jungle, through the rain, determined to crest the ridge and recapture the airfield.

The waves of Japanese attacked Sergeant Basilone's position head on. Mortars, grenades, and gunfire relentlessly pounded the machine-gunner's foxhole. Severely outnumbered, the machine gunners went into action, as much to hold the line as to repel the determined enemy assault.

Comrades would remember later that Sergeant Basilone kept the two sections of machine guns firing through three days and nights of unrelenting *Banzai* assaults. He went without food, sleep, rest of any sort, and relief. His heroic actions culminated on the night of October 24, and into the next morning. On that final night, the *Banzai* assault began around 10:00 PM and advanced in seven waves throughout the night. Sergeant Basilone's outpost was soon flanked and nearly surrounded by an enemy force intent on overrunning them.

In the onslaught, one of Sergeant Basilone's positions was bombarded, the weapons destroyed, and the gun crew killed. He raced 200 yards to the position, exposed to enemy fire, carrying a ninety-pound machine gun. Immediately engaging the enemy advance from the machine-gun position, he repaired one of the other machine guns and manned both himself, keeping a constant fire of 400 to 600 rounds of bullets a minute against the Japanese. When hostiles attacked from the rear of his emplacement, he kept the machine gun firing forward and killed those behind him with his Colt .45 pistol.

Replacements made their way to the beleaguered outpost, and Sergeant Basilone resumed his role as platoon leader. He raced between gun pits, encouraging his gunners, directing their fire, clearing jammed guns, and relieving them when they grew fatigued. His hands blistered from the heat of the machine guns as his crews kept firing throughout the assault.

To prevent the supply of ammunition from growing desperately low when the supply lines were cut off from the outpost, Sergeant Basilone repeatedly ran alone 200 yards through the jungle and enemy positions, back to the perimeter and an ammunition dump. Then he dashed back to distribute an armload of machine-gun shells between the two gun pits.

Reinforcements pushed ahead to the outpost on the morning of the 25th and the enemy assault was repulsed. Sergeant Basilone was in his gun pit, resting his head on the rim of the emplacement, his first pause in three days. Only two others in his squad survived with him.

Over 1,300 Japanese soldiers died in front of the line held by the 7th Marines. Sergeant Basilone's outpost accounted for over 100 of these enemy dead. Around his gun pit were 38 dead, many of them within arm's length of his machine gun.

The Marines held Guadalcanal secure by February 9, 1943, and Sergeant Basilone was one of the first American heroes of the war. He was awarded a Congressional Medal of Honor that May 1943. He was returned to the States in July to promote a war-bond campaign. 30,000 people gathered in his hometown of Raritan, New Jersey, for a Sunday, September 19, parade in his honor. The October 11, 1943, *Life* Magazine issue featured a four-page story about the parade: *Life goes to a hero's homecoming.*

"Manila John" was promoted to Gunnery Sergeant, crossed the United States on a promotional tour, had his photograph taken with Hollywood screen stars, served safely at Camp Pendleton, was offered the opportunity to be commissioned an officer, and married Sergeant Lena Mae Riggi, Marine Corps Women's Reserve, on July 10, 1944.

Gunnery Sergeant Basilone did not want acclaim, notoriety, or an officer's commission. He longed for life among his Marine comrades, and he requested to be returned to action in the South Pacific islands. Preparation for another island campaign was underway. He shipped out for Hawaii on August 11, 1944. He would live through another hour and forty-five minutes of combat.

"Manila John" landed on Iwo Jima at Red Beach 2 with the 5th Marines on D-Day, February 19, 1945. He refused to bunch up or hesitate in the black volcanic sands on the beach as the landing forces stalled under the withering Japanese fire. He encouraged and cajoled his unit forward and pushed them off the beach. Alone, he charged an enemy blockhouse and destroyed it and its occupants. As he pressed the assault with his platoon, an artillery shell exploded at his feet at 10:45 AM, killing him and four other Marines.

Gunnery Sergeant John Basilone, 28-years-old, was remembered by General Douglas MacArthur to be "a one-man army." Marines have remembered him ever since as a legend.

The memory of John Basilone's bravery has remained beyond the Marine Corps. *Time* Magazine, March 19, 1945, featured HEROES:

The Life & Death of Manila John. The U.S. Navy paid tribute to him, twice commissioning the USS *Basilone* (DD/DDE-824). His name appears on roads, memorial highways, overpasses, plaques, and plazas from east to west coast. Sgt. John Basilone Lodge 2442, Order Sons of Italy in America is located on Long Island, New York. An apartment development in Pacoima, California was named Basilone Homes.

"Raritan's Hero"

As the years passed in his hometown, the Marine Corps League Detachment 190, Legion Post 280, and the Knights of Columbus Council #1326, a freeway bridge, a memorial room in the Public Library, a park, and a football field were dedicated in his name. An oil portrait was hung in the Town Hall. A life-sized statue of John holding a heavy machine gun stands in Basilone Park at Canal Street and Old York Road, just north of Raritan River.

Then in September 1981, Raritan held another parade in John's honor. A highlight of the annual community calendar, The John Basilone Memorial Parade enjoyed its twenty-ninth year in 2010.

Raritan, New Jersey, knows to preserve the memory of a hero.

Communities would do well to remember what President Calvin Coolidge said: *"The nation which forgets its defenders will itself be forgotten."* [17]

Another generation is being introduced to John Basilone's bravery, and anyone interested in learning about him can discover much about his life. A book was published about John in 2004. On November 10, 2005, the U.S. Postal Service issued the "Distinguished Marines" stamps. John was one of only four Marines to appear on a commemorative stamp. Another book about him was published in early 2010. [18]

Now, sixty-five years after John died, Steven Spielberg and Tom Hanks have participated in producing a 10-part miniseries for HBO. *The Pacific* premiered March 14, 2010. John Basilone is one of three Marines featured in the series. The two others are authors Robert Leckie and Eugene Sledge.

Like John Basilone, many Marine Medal of Honor recipients have been memorialized with more than one tribute. The names and stories of recipients have appeared in books, magazines, movies, and television shows. The lives of men like Greg Boyington, Merritt Edson, John Basilone, Mitchell Paige, Joe Foss, and Wesley Fox are described in books. Besides some appearing on the covers of magazines like *Life*, *Time*, and the *Marine Corps Gazette*, magazine and newspaper articles record the exploits of many recipients. For a good number of recipients, like Harold Bauer, Internet Web sites provide extensive background details and histories of their lives.

Surviving recipients are routinely asked to appear at civic functions, to preside over July 4th and Memorial Day ceremonies, to serve as Grand Marshall at parades, to dedicate monuments and memorials, and to give public speeches.

More than fifty-five years after Mitchell Paige had earned his Medal on Guadalcanal, a G.I. Joe action figure was modeled after him in 1998. Private First Class Jack Lucas earned his Medal on Iwo Jima in 1945 for cradling two grenades under his body, was the youngest Marine to ever be awarded the Medal of Honor, and sat beside the First Lady during President Bill Clinton's January 1995, State of the Union Address.

While most communities do remember their valiant Marines, thirty-four Medal recipients seemed to have been unrecognized at home. Why had their hometowns let dust settle upon their bravery? Do a person's heroically brave actions have to become legendary to be celebrated and honored? Must a hero be idealized or his image perfected in order to be remembered?

Forgetting and the passing of time

His name is Kenneth Lee Worley. Farmington, New Mexico, was his home for the first fourteen years of his life. There was little to find of him there in 2000.

In an alphabetical roster of the 181 Marine recipients from the three wars, Ken's is the last name. On Medal of Honor monuments including all 3,466 recipients, his name is thirty-seventh from the last.

Ken's name is etched into Panel 48W-Line 1 of the Vietnam Veterans Memorial Wall, the eleventh of thirteen Worleys to give his life in Vietnam. It is also inscribed on the California Vietnam Memorial in Sacramento. A framed, color-enhanced photograph of Ken is fixed above a framed copy of his Medal Citation on the wall of the Sacramento Military Entrance Processing Station (MEPS), [19] passed by those entering the service.

His name was included on a list of honorary names sent aboard NASA's *Stardust* comet-sample return mission that was launched on February 7, 1999, visited Comet Wild 2 on December 31, 2003, saw 2004 begin, and then steered for its scheduled return to earth in January 2006.

Ken Worley's name also topped a list begun in 2000.

Data about the 181 Marine Medal of Honor recipients of WWII, Korea, and Vietnam gathered during *Semper Fidelis*, a study of heroic bravery, was first organized into a chart. Columns included various background features, like family members, education, marital status, early interests and activities, and place of action. The chart's last column indicated memorials and tributes to each Marine following the Medal's awarding. That column was obviously empty for Ken Worley. His name began a list.

Medal of Honor Citations provided the initial and most readily accessible information. The Citations are available at a variety of Web sites. The recipients' personal backgrounds were then considered, accessed from the public records available to any researcher, including archival records, biographies, and newspaper articles. Looking for similarities in the early experience among the 181 men might identify important developmental factors that influence an individual to act heroically brave. Did these men have experiences that set them apart from ordinary people and which would have made their later actions predictable?

Google searches were conducted for all recipients. Five Web site sources were initially heavily relied upon: the United States Marine Corps Headquarter's History and Museum Division, *Who's Who in Marine Corps History*; medalofhonor.com; Americans.net; C. Douglas Sterner's HomeofHeroes.com, and arlingtoncemetery.org.

At the conclusion of the *Semper Fidelis* study, in addition to Ken Worley, thirty-three more names had been added to the list: no significant public memorials or lasting tributes had been dedicated to twelve recipients from WWII, ten from Korea, and twelve from Vietnam. These thirty-four men were a distinct group of Medal recipients deserving further research and recognition.

Since the majority of Marine recipients have had fitting tributes, that thirty-four seemed all but forgotten came as a surprise. Their bravery had certainly reached into the range of heroic. Their actions had demonstrated extraordinary courage or strength, appeared to be characteristic of them across time and circumstances, involved personal risk, perhaps the sacrifice of their lives, and resulted in uncommon outcomes and accomplishment.

The roster of the Thirty-Four Forgotten developed because the original search methods resulted in minimal background information. For these Marines, the search was extended. Phone calls to the Chamber of Commerce in hometowns, to local museums, to VFWs, to school librarians, as well as letters to newspaper features editors, often provided no additional information. The thirty-four recipients truly seemed forgotten.

The memories about men like Joe Julian of WWII, Jack Kelso of Korea, and Ken Worley and Ron Coker of Vietnam seemed to have faded, certainly from the greater public's awareness. Perhaps extended family remembered them. Perhaps old friends in their hometowns carried their memories. Perhaps their graves were tended to by respectful civic organizations, and maybe their high schools had dedicated a plaque to their memories.

Trying to understand how one man's brave actions seem to be unheralded in a hometown leads to conjecture. Is there no one to speak up and advocate for a tribute to the native son? Does the community for some reason believe the Medal of Honor recipient does not deserve to be remembered? Is it because his family moved from his birthplace when he was a child and no one remains in the town to recall his having lived there once? Did the news of his heroism not reach the town?

For some unheralded Medal of Honor Marines sixty years have passed since demonstrating their valor, for others fifty, and for the more recent war, it has been forty years since the Medals were awarded. These brave men might have been forgotten, but their bravery was still a force to inspire. Time does not lessen bravery's impact.

Whether bravery has been remembered cannot always be determined by time's passage. Ten months after John Basilone died on Iwo Jima, the Navy first launched DD 824, the USS *Basilone*, on December 21, 1945. Charles Joseph Berry also died on Iwo Jima, diving on top of a grenade to protect others. Nearly fifteen years passed before DE-1035, the USS *Charles Berry*, was launched.

Darrell Samuel Cole, wounded twice as he sustained a one-man assault against three enemy pillboxes on Iwo, died on the first day of the island assault, the same morning as John Basilone. Someone remembered Darrell Cole, a 24-year-old Marine from a small town in Missouri, long after his heroic actions and petitioned for a ship to be commissioned in his name.

Henry Lawrence Garrett III, the 20th Secretary of the Navy, approved the naming of a ship in his honor, ordered on January 16, 1991. The guided missile destroyer DDG-67, the USS *Cole*, was christened on a Saturday morning, April 8, 1995, fifty years after Darrell died in the black volcanic ash. Lee Perry, wife of then Secretary of Defense William J. Perry, sponsored the *Cole* by breaking a bottle of champagne across the bow and formally naming the ship. The world would be reminded of this Medal of Honor Marine four years later when the ship named in his honor was attacked by terrorists at Aden Harbor, Yemen, on October 12, 2000.

The petition to honor a Medal recipient after decades have passed might come from a family member, a friend, a Marine companion, a local politician, or a veteran's organization. Someone who personally knew the recipient or who somehow came to know of his heroics might submit the petition. For the thirty-four Marines for whom no memorials or tributes were listed in that chart's last column, had so much time passed that no one remembered or recognized their bravery?

As the nation dealt with the suicide attack on the USS *Cole*, strangers who knew nothing about Ken Worley's life and death were going to resolve to honor him. A groundskeeper asked about three letters on a faded, bronze military grave marker. The 20-year-old Marine was not buried in the cemetery's Veterans section. One or two veterans had passed by his marker to pay him homage from time to time. More than thirty years after he had been brought home from war, the bravery of this one of *The Forgotten Thirty-Four* was going to again inspire others to take action.

Communities are made better by honoring their heroes.

More than forty to sixty years have passed without much public notice of the lives and heroism of *The Forgotten Thirty-Four*. These men rose above natural fear in moments of extreme peril and acted honorably. It is time for them to be remembered in their birthplaces.

The following chapters provide what information can be known about them from archival investigation and chronicles the efforts of some hometown historians to bring proper recognition to their local heroes.

The purpose in telling the stories ahead is four-fold. First and foremost is to bring recognition to thirty-four Marines who appeared to have been forgotten at home. The second is to provide examples of bravery to the public in order that "ordinary" people can find inspiration. The third reason is to highlight the personal characteristics of Medal of Honor recipients so that the men they had been can teach us what kind of person has the potential to be heroically brave in difficult situations. Finally, it is hoped *The Forgotten Thirty-Four* will also provide encouragement to Marines on active duty who put themselves in harm's way on behalf of their fellows, their Corps, and their nation.

CHAPTER 3
Discovering a Forgotten Hero

"Cover them over with beautiful flowers;
"Deck them with garlands, those brothers of ours;
Lying so silent by night and by day..." [1]

William "Will" McKendree Carleton, American poet, (1845–1912)

Thirty-four years passed after Ken Worley's death before any community claiming him to be one of their own remembered him. It was not his hometown, where he had lived for nearly the first three-quarters of his life that remembered him. In Farmington, civic-minded individuals were unsure if Ken was someone who should be heralded in their community. Because he had moved?

Another six years of searching passed before some of the mysteries were resolved. Addresses were not the only things that had changed in Ken's life before he enlisted in the Marines.

Finding Witnesses

When bravery is recognized, its influence is deep and it is wide. Bravery touches the heart and spirit of those who bear witness to it.

Bravery stirs and kindles an impulse to take meaningful action. Like the beat of a drum, bravery compels one to draw together with others and march ahead.

Some, like the Feyerherm siblings, remembered Ken as they went on with their lives. The Marines of Lima Company, 3d Battalion, 7th Marines who were with him when he died protecting five companions from a grenade, certainly remembered him. Some Marines of other platoons would not forget him either. Forty years after the ambush at Bo Ban, Daniel D. Poland, a sergeant in another platoon, recalled learning of Ken's heroism and death the next day, affirming, "I still remember the day. Just as I remember the day Kennedy was killed." [2]

For the most part, however, Ken's actions faded into obscurity for thirty-two years. Having operated more as platoons in Vietnam than as companies, even Marines who had served in Lima, 3/7 at the time did not know the circumstances of his death or that he had been recommended for a Medal of Honor. Some veterans attending a L/3/7 reunion in August 2009, did not remember when Lance Corporal Worley was killed. [3]

"You may be lost...
but you are not forgotten." [4]

Ken's grave is in the central part of Westminster Memorial Park, not far from the front entrance off Beach Boulevard. Across from the mausoleum, his flat bronze marker sits between trees ten markers in from the road. In 1994, someone began leaving flowers from time to time.

An Army veteran had come across Ken's grave when visiting his own grandparents' graves. That a fellow veteran, a few months apart in age from himself, with MOH on his marker, was lying there apparently forgotten and his legacy neglected was upsetting to Peter C. Gianarakos, who stopped by the grave whenever at the cemetery.

Wanting to get Ken into a national cemetery or where he really might have belonged, in Arlington, the only things Peter was able to do until someone with more authority took an active interest, was leave flowers and write to the *Orange County Register* newspaper. He talked to a Brigadier General about the forgotten Marine in the grave at Westminster. He seemed to encounter "lack of true interest." A Veterans Administration worker, Peter did not give up on the idea. Fifteen years passed before he read about events in Ken's birthplace. [5]

On Memorial Day, 2002, George Grupe, a WWII bomber pilot and amateur military historian, went to Westminster Memorial Park to say a few words at a veteran's grave. A cemetery worker asked him about a weathered, flat bronze grave marker, in another section of the park with an MOH inscription, wondering what the letters meant.

George understood that MOH probably meant the 20-year-old Marine buried there had earned a Medal of Honor, the highest award the Nation gives to its brave servicemen. He set about learning what he could about this Marine. Newspaper articles followed.

That December, Ken's Medal Citation and photograph were added to the Find-A-Grave Web site and Westminster Memorial Park added his name to its list of ten famous people buried in the cemetery. Between December 23, 2002 and August 12, 2009, 104 messages were left for him on the Find-A-Grave Web site. Inquiries about Ken began appearing in the Worley Family Genealogy Forum, presented by Genealogy. com, around January 29, 2002, but there was no response from family in New Mexico, or anywhere else for that matter.

The local newspapers announced a wreath and garland ceremony scheduled for Friday, May 30, 2003 at Westminster. Ken's story caught the attention of Sonny Martinez, a Marine who had served in Vietnam with Company C, 1st Battalion, 4th Marines and was then living in Anaheim. Planning on attending the ceremony, Sonny posted his thoughts online.

"This ceremony was long over due." [6]

The following year, George Adams, a Lima 3/7 Marine and former platoon commander wrote that he "would like to honor Lance Corporal Worley at a future Lima reunion." [7] Lance Corporal Scott Reynolds, a former Lima 3/7 machine-gunner, had been near Bo Ban with another platoon the morning Ken jumped on that grenade. His thoughts about honoring Ken appeared in a newspaper article. He summed up the thoughts of many Marines when he said, "It's the right thing to do. People should never forget."

As a result of the renewed recognition, George Grupe, Jack Closson, a retired Marine first sergeant, Anaheim's American Veterans (AMVETS) Post 18, and other local veterans began searching for Ken's history and advocating that the young Medal recipient be honored by the community. They accomplished much in two years. In time, West Coast newspapers proclaimed the results of their efforts.

The May 23, 2004, front page *Sunday Spotlight* announced the news in bold and capital letters: HERO'S SACRIFICE NOW RECOGNIZED. "He lay buried in Westminster Memorial Park for 35 years, a hero unknown to Orange County." [8] This was a story that would become instrumental in ensuring Ken's heroism would enter our nation's consciousness.

Dennis Foley, a columnist and dedicated reporter at the *Orange County Register*, was able to locate Quonieta (Feyerherm) Murphy and her son, Robert. A fellow Lima Company Marine, Charles Black, contacted Dennis and told him about Ken's Seiko watch. Dennis suggested that Charles send it to the local veterans.

The reporter did all he could to learn about the Medal of Honor Marine. He searched for information about the Marine's birth parents and childhood in Farmington. He contacted the longtime school librarian at Truth of Consequences High School who checked all the records and yearbooks and found no record of a Kenneth Worley. He interviewed local veterans who were discovering bits and pieces of Ken's life prior to his enlistment, some of which could not be confirmed elsewhere. Just "disjointed fragments" sounding more like rumors and gossip than facts.

Dennis made a point of crossing the States to stand in front of the D.C. Vietnam Memorial and found the name etched on the Wall. He even posted a request on Classmates.com asking anyone who might have known Ken to contact him. No one did. Ken's life prior to his arrival in California remained a mystery to the reporter and to the readers of the *OC Register*. [9]

The California discoveries did not involve Farmington. As far as those on the West Coast believed, Ken had no family. Any ties to New Mexico had been severed long ago. Westminster was going to adopt him as its own son.

A Search by a Local Historian

With the resurgence of interest about Ken in California, a local historian closer to Ken's birthplace began searching out information about the Marine in 2003. His efforts and frustrations demonstrate what can be done when someone remembers, advocates for, and persists on behalf of one of our fallen warriors. Proof again that the passage of time does not diminish valor.

A retired U.S. Army and Air Force master sergeant by the name of Bruce Salisbury had once lived a few blocks from where Ken had grown up in Farmington, although he had not known Ken personally. In fact, he was already in the service himself when Ken was born.

The Salisbury family had moved to Farmington in the summer of 1945, when Bruce was 14-years-old. He was drafted into the service less than a year later, before he had finished a single semester of high school. [10] After retiring from the service in 1966, the Korean War veteran settled in Aztec, a small community north and east of Farmington.

Bruce understood the significance of the Medal of Honor award. Learning that someone born in his town had earned the Medal buoyed him with pride. He revered Ken Worley as a hero and was determined to see that a tribute be paid to the young Marine. Bruce was also resolute: any and all obstacles he encountered to honor Ken Worley would neither stop nor slow him down. If nothing more, the Farmington Marine at least deserved to have his name added to the Four Corners Vietnam Memorial Wall.

For five years, the face of Farmington's lone Marine Medal of Honor recipient remained on Bruce's mind as he searched for Ken's history. He petitioned the local newspaper to write a story, having periodic conversations with Debra Mayeux, a features editor at the *Farmington Daily-Times*. He spoke with the mayor, who had been a Marine, county commissioners, and members of other Veteran organizations, wondering if a tribute could be paid to this hometown hero. It seemed to Bruce that he "kept stumbling into a wall of reluctant resistance." [11] Dead ends were frequent. Ken Worley just was not much remembered by most Farmington residents. The grade school that official records would indicate he had attended no longer exists.

Bruce took every opportunity to spark the local memory. Hoping to draw attention and interest, and perhaps meet someone who knew the Worley family, Bruce made sure the VFW 614 booth featured a display of Ken's picture and Citation at the fall, 2007, San Juan County Fair.

The photo from Ken's HQMC records found on Internet Web sites was the only known existing image of the young man. Wearing the drab green utility uniform and a combat helmet, it was likely taken when he was nearing his graduation from boot camp: a serious image of a young Marine, who seemed to have little to smile about.

Although no one in Farmington would have known Ken as he appeared in the photo, several people stopped at the VFW booth and commented that they had known the young Marine's family, saying little more about him. Theirs had been a community that had long ago adopted the "mind your own business" anthem. [12] Family matters were to be kept private and probing into personal affairs could be taken as an affront. Bruce asked few questions and the locals volunteered little information.

What he did learn was simply that Ken Worley had been a "young kid" to those who remembered him, a "nice little guy."

Researching history is furthered by having connections with others who feel passion for both the subject and for digging around in the past. Setting up Ken's display at the San Juan County Fair VFW booth was going to bring Bruce unexpected collaboration.

Ann (Salisbury) Phelps stopped by the VFW booth to say hello to her older brother. She stared at Ken's photo. In a moment of recognition, memories of events more than fifty-years past were stirred. The face under the combat helmet in that photo was familiar. So was the name. Ann remembered going to school with a Worley girl who had a little brother, eight years younger, named Kenny.

Having not been close friends to the Worley children, Ann first remembered the sister's name to be Sue, then Beverly. The Salisbury and Worley families had lived many blocks apart, but attended the same schools. The two girls had sometimes met at the corner of North Orchard Avenue and Apache Street on their way to school. Having been classmates throughout, both graduated from grade school in 1954.

Ann, herself impassioned to have looked into the eyes of a young boy who would later earn a Medal of Honor and to have walked the same sidewalks as he had, joined Bruce in his quest to honor the forgotten son of Farmington. She began talking to local officials and writing letters. Bruce and Ann searched for obituaries in newspaper archives at the San Juan College Library and walked among rows of gravestones in the Farmington cemeteries, hoping to discover the roots to Ken's life.

They located Worleys buried in the town's cemeteries. J.D. Worley, born August 17, 1906, died November 28, 1982, is buried in Greenlawn Cemetery. Two other Worleys are buried nearby; one who preceded J.D. in death by seven years and one who followed him ten years later.

Lettie Mae Worley came to Farmington in 1955 from Eastland County, Texas, when she was 46-years-old. By then, Ken Worley was eight-years-old and in school. Lettie Mae had two daughters and a son, who was then twenty-two. One of her daughters married and eventually moved to Westminster, California. Lettie Mae died in 1992, leaving behind her two daughters. A nephew and grandchildren remained in Farmington. Lettie Mae's son had died in 1975 and was buried in Greenlawn. His name was Kenneth Rae Worley.

Cemetery records and obituaries provided no links between these Worleys and the Medal of Honor Marine.

Ken's name was added to the Four Corners Vietnam Memorial Wall's granite surface at Farmington's Vietnam Veterans Memorial Park. No indication of his service branch, rank, or MOH was attached to his name. When *fourcornerstour.com SW US* modified its Web site May 21, 2008, Ken was recognized as Farmington's Medal of Honor Recipient, providing links to *homeofheroes.com* and *wikipedia.org*.

Ken appeared in a book written by a history professor at the University of New Mexico-Valencia County Branch in 2007. He is mentioned briefly on page 324 of *Buried Treasures: Famous and Unusual Gravesites in New Mexico History.* The book is advertised to be about "noteworthy men, women, and children, usually deserving of high praise and admiration," although few have been honored with monuments to memorialize their achievements. [13]

The Search From North Dakota Continued

In today's world of Internet technology, research into a variety of archives has been made relatively simple. Yet, the challenge for those interested in finding out more about Kenneth Lee Worley was in finding witnesses to his early life. The common end in the search for his history became familiar. Dead ends. Eventually, more newspaper articles turned a search light onto the mysteries of his childhood.

Any possible connection to Ken and the Worley name was explored. If the name was Worley and was associated to New Mexico, that it might also be related to the mysteries in Ken's life was worth considering. For example, there is a baseball field in Farmington with an intriguing history.

East of the Four Corners Regional Airport, on the flight path of Runway 5/23, at East 30th Street and North Butler Avenue, is a baseball diamond commuters can look down on. The Farmington High School plays its games there. The diamond is called Worley Field. That the field might have been named in tribute to Ken Worley's heroism was encouraging. By 2006, current Park Board members did not know why the ball field was so named. There is no plaque at the field. The museum curator and the mayor looked into the matter and found no answers; just more dead ends.

Later in the search, Jim Clay, a Farmington baseball historian, dated the naming of Worley Field to have been in the early 1960s, when Babe Ruth baseball first came to town. Those who remember that era believe the field was named for a man who worked at El Paso Natural Gas and had been instrumental in getting the company to donate equipment for the construction of the park. Other locals remembered that Thomas Worley had been a well-liked Farmington baseball coach and thought that "Worley Field" was named as a tribute to him.

No one was certain of any family relationship that either Mr. Worley might have had to Ken.

California family members knew a little. Ken had told someone in his foster family about the ball field's name. They knew the field was not named in honor of Ken, since Worley Field already existed when Ken left Farmington. Perhaps the field had been named for a relative of his, but the Feyerherms were uncertain. Ken was not one to tell much about his New Mexico family or his childhood in Farmington. That he told people in Modesto about a ball field suggests that being a "Worley" meant something to Ken. [14]

Of the Worleys currently living in New Mexico, and among the dozen or so who corresponded with this author, none seemed to have any knowledge of Ken's biological lineage. It was as if, before the Modesto Feyerherms took him in, Ken had no family.

In trying to establish Ken Worley's genealogy, the search for a sister, Beverly Worley, was equally without reward. On the off chance that her name remained the same, e-mails and letters were sent to seven Beverly Worleys in the current national database. Those who responded denied knowing anything about a Kenneth Worley.

Sometimes dead ends mean going back to the beginning and starting over. Perhaps the way to find Ken's childhood was to trace his ancestors. The earliest Worleys to immigrate to America had names like Joshua, Jacob, Isaac, Elijah, Hiram, Abraham, and Achor. Jacob Worley, believed to be a man in his late thirties, decided to leave his home in Germany. He boarded the ship *Phoenix* and arrived in Philadelphia in August 1750, according to the ship's passenger manifest. Jacob was not the first Worley in Pennsylvania, as Achor Worley is reputed to have purchased Indian Orchard from the local Natives, operated a sawmill on Big Sweet Root, and been one of the original settlers of Town Creek Valley in 1728. [15]

Further south, John Worley was recorded buying acres of land in North Carolina in 1717. By 1720, another John Worley Sr, born before 1699, was buying up acres of land near Swift Creek, south of the James River and just outside of Richmond, Virginia. He later deeded property to William Worley in Franklin County, Virginia and wrote his Will in March 1757, in Cumberland County.

The Worley settlers had a great number of children, who migrated quickly across state lines. Families appear on early tax rolls and censuses in Maryland, Virginia, North and South Carolina, Georgia, and Alabama. The Worleys went west into Ohio, Kentucky, Tennessee, Indiana, Illinois, Wisconsin, Iowa, and South Dakota. By the 1860 Census, Worleys were in Kansas, Missouri, Oklahoma, Texas, and Colorado. The 1920 United States Federal Census listed 174 Worley families in the United States, the greatest number living in Ohio.

Wagons loaded with families and belongings began the trek out of Independence, Missouri in 1821, and rolled along the Santa Fe Trail. The first Worleys arrived after the pioneering had been accomplished in New Mexico, not too much before the Cactus State became the 47th State in 1912. The 1920 and 1930 United States Federal Census listed only about 49 Worleys living between the north-to-south New Mexico borders, all in the eastern counties of Colfax, Curry, Union, and Eddy. The first Kenneth Worley in New Mexico was born in Eddy County in 1917. Back in the east, on September 22, 1932, the First Chapter of the Purple Heart Association of United States was formed at a gathering of veterans in Connecticut at the state armory. T. W. Worley of Ansonia was elected as an executive committee officer. Some Worleys would remain where they settled, one generation after another. Others would move on, leaving New Mexico for different places. Whether they moved or stayed, some Worleys would leave a legacy behind them. One was Nelson Worley.

The City of Clovis, New Mexico, Police Department had nine patrolmen in 1941, when Nelson was 23-years-old. Nelson became the tenth patrolman, the youngest hired by Clovis. In November 1945, he became Clovis police chief and later served several elected terms as the Curry County Sheriff. Nelson retired from law enforcement in 1983. Due to the high esteem in which the citizens held him, Clovis dedicated the Nelson Worley Law Enforcement Complex in June 2000, four years before the dedicated public servant passed away. [16]

Worleys were spread throughout the country. The family appears to have arrived in Idaho around the 1880s. One of the arrivals was assigned duties as the superintendent of the Coeur d'Alene Indian Reservation, in the rugged northwest of the territory. A small town within the Reservation was named for him.

East of the town is the Worley Cemetery, where the earliest recorded burial date is 1917. There are many burial sites with no stones, or illegible markers, but it appears that no Worleys are interred there. Today, about fifty-four families reside in Worley. The eighty-six Worleys mentioned in the 2000 Idaho census live in cities and towns other than Worley.

Likely all but forgotten, except by historians searching town archives and descendants researching their genealogies, the migration of the Worleys left a mark on communities across the States. Avenues are named after Worleys in Sunnyvale, California, Holyoke, Colorado, Arcadia, Merritt Island, and Orlando, Florida, Columbia, Missouri, Canton, Cleveland, Dayton, and Trotwood, Ohio, and in Clarksburg, West Virginia. In Bouse and Yuma, AZ, Sutter Creek, California, Starkville, Mississippi, Columbia, Missouri, Fayetteville and Monroe, North Carolina, Washington Court House, Ohio, Sumter, South Carolina, and Amarillo, Texas, the Worley name is inscribed on street signs. Worley Roads can be traveled in Suisun City, California, Graceville, Florida, Ball Ground and Pitts, Georgia, Banner Elk, Marion, and Princeton, North Carolina, Greenville, South Carolina, Hampton, Virginia, and Beckley, West Virginia. Lanes in Montgomery, Alabama, Brandenburg and Thornton, Kentucky, Pink Hill, North Carolina, Brandon, Mississippi, Wallhalla, South Carolina, Whitwell, Tennessee, Bolt, West Virginia, and Gretna, Virginia are named after a Worley.

If migration and transportation bring to mind the Worley ancestors, the reminders will be more than roadways. A small airport near Henry Fork, Franklin County, Virginia is named Worley Field. Near Temple, Texas, where Milam County Road 428 crosses a deep chasm cut by the flow of the legendary San Gabriel River, an old iron and steel truss bridge challenges vehicles to rumble across its metal deck.

Built around 1910, the historic Worley Bridge, narrow at 12-feet wide, can convey one vehicle at a time. [17] For some locales, recreation will be the reminder. Worley Lakes can be found in Charlton County, Georgia, near Pekin, Tazewell County, Illinois, and in Cottle County, Texas.

Obviously, Kenneth Lee was one of the Worleys who did not settle down in his birthplace. How the Worley ancestry applied to Ken was unknown. Tracing forward from Achor and Jacob Worley did not uncover a link to Ken's birth in Farmington.

Of the more than 25,000 descendants accounted for in the 1990 U.S. Census, twenty years after he had been awarded the Medal of Honor, no Worley ever publicly claimed to be related to him.

The Roots of Bravery

Journalists and reporters have to consider their readership. They ask themselves, why is this story of interest? Who would be interested in this? Newspaper reporters decided Ken Worley's story deserved telling. Their articles served to finally bring researchers together with one of Ken's foster sisters, his girlfriend, his son, and a cousin. Why searching for Kenneth Worley's childhood had provided such mystery and had led to so many dead ends would become clear: Ken's battles and heroism had begun long before he was a Marine. [18] The one certainty as the search for his roots continued: nothing can change what he made of himself, the valor he demonstrated in the last fourteen months of his life, or the honor the Marines have extended toward him.

In certain sources, Ken is described as "orphaned," although little was written or known about his parents. His Family of Record was Mr. and Mrs. Donald Feyerherm of Edmonds, Washington. Tracking a foster family, last cited in a newspaper article in 1970, proved equally challenging as the search for the Worleys. Fortunately, when Jack

Closson's Young Marines appeared in newspaper articles and formed an Honor Guard at Ken's gravesite for Memorial Day ceremonies, Ken's foster sisters, Quonieta Murphy of Salem, Oregon, and Nell Swisher of Escondido, California, attended. They began to fill in details of Ken's life, at least from the time he was 16-years-old until the award of his Medal of Honor at the White House.

The Feyerherm girls knew that Ken had come from Truth Or Consequences around 1964, when he was 16-years-old. Family disruptions of some sort had sent Ken to live with various aunts and uncles. They believed he had relocated to Modesto, California, possibly to live with an aunt. Ken made friends easily and found work. He seems not to have ever enrolled in high school again after leaving New Mexico.

Searching newspaper archives for articles from the 1960s turned up some tantalizing "tidbits" that seemed promising, but tended to lead nowhere in the search for Ken's history. For example, a Legal Notice appeared in a newspaper across the bay from San Francisco on April 30, 1963, a year before Ken left New Mexico. Dated April 27, 1963, it read "NON RESPONSIBLE I will not be responsible for any debts or commitments made by anyone other than myself on or after this date," and was signed by KENNETH WORLEY of 5673 D Street, Hayward, California, just seventy miles west of Modesto. From whom Kenneth was severing financial responsibility is not indicated. Any relevance to Ken from Farmington cannot be known at this point in time. [19]

In early July 2008, Debra Mayeux, the Features Editor at the *Farmington Daily Times* began her own investigation into Ken's life. She consulted local historians about Ken, his family, and Worley Field. Debra's headline news story, *Mystery surrounds Farmington's lone Medal of Honor recipient* went into print on July 13, 2008. [20] The *Daily Times* story did not seem to reach any of Ken's relatives, nor unearth any new information about him.

On the 40th anniversary of Ken Worley's death, Jim Belshaw of the *Albuquerque Journal* wrote a story headlined *A Brave Marine Who Left*

No Trace, published August 12, 2008. This article, with its familiar photograph of Lance Corporal Worley, immediately caught the attention of John and Sharon Houston, living near Albuquerque. Sharon called a cousin living in Farmington, and they shared their similar memories of the Marine in the newspaper story. Certain of Ken Worley's identity, Sharon contacted Jim Belshaw and identified herself as Ken's first cousin. The dead ends had ended—most of them, anyway.

In mid-November 2008, the search for Ken Worley's roots experienced a boost. Joan Earnshaw, Bruce Salisbury's cousin, learned of his efforts to have a tribute dedicated to Ken in Farmington. A retired IRS Agent, Joan is now a private investigator (PI) who is a member of a network of female investigators who sometimes help each other work cases. Touched by the story of Ken's bravery, Joan took an active interest and volunteered her investigative resources. The search into a Marine's background was somewhat personal to her. Her husband's uncle was retired USMC Brigadier General Joseph W. Earnshaw, a Kansas native who had been in command of the African-American 52d Defense Battalion between 1944 and 1945. [21]

In August 2009, Joan discovered a 60-year-old document that added more mystery to Ken's early life. The search into his background had reached the meeting place of a cousin's childhood memories, family secrets, misinformation grownups give their children, the passing of 50 years, and archived documents.

CHAPTER 4
The Making of an Orphan

"When there is not love for a child to remember…"

Roger Dean Kiser, short story author

Kenneth Lee Worley kept his life experiences to himself no matter where he traveled. He told bits and pieces to those who knew him for a few years in Modesto, California. He confided even less to his Marine comrades about his early experience. Later, when reporters asked questions, it was as if his life had centered around Modesto. Not much about Ken can be discovered in public records.

Ken's bravery can be better understood and appreciated when listening to the stories of those who saw him at play, who looked upon his bruises, and who wept for him. Unfortunately, few people could be located to provide first-hand accounts of his early life. The reader will find, as researchers discovered, tracking Ken's family line is complicated and confusing.

For those wanting to bear witness to his childhood, his history began in Texas when a Horlacher girl decided to change her name to Smithee.

Reuben Pickett Smithee was born September 29, 1878, in Lawrence County, Arkansas, son of John A. Smithee, a blacksmith. [1] When the 1900 United States Census was completed, Reuben, age 21-years, was living near Hale Center, Texas, in the Panhandle on the northwest side of the state.

The area is flat land with distant vistas. Agriculture, cotton and corn, sheep and beef production were the economic main stays when Reuben lived there. Oil would not be discovered there until 1946. Comprising about 1,225 square miles of the Lone Star State, Hale County might have included fourteen small towns, scattered among 259 farms and ranches. The 1900 Hale County Census recorded a population of 1,680. All this could make it challenging for a man to find a wife. Reuben was still a single man at the time of the Census, but would be married with children by the next Census. Were it not for the realities of a frontier settler's life, Ken Worley would have later known him as Grandpa Rueben.

Mary Eliza Horlacher was born in Plainview, Hale County seat, on September 13, 1886, the second of four children. Her father, Samuel, had come from Pennsylvania; her mother, Sarah, had come from Corinth, Mississippi. [2] Her parents married in Wise County, Texas, on December 10, 1882, and moved to Hale County. [3] Among the first settlers in the county, the Horlachers began ranching.

Reuben and Mary had travel in their blood and travel they did.

Reuben, nearly 23-years-old, went up to Plainview on August 13, 1901, and entered into holy matrimony with Mary, who was one month from her fifteenth birthday. The newlyweds began their family in Hale Center, the second largest town in Hale County, on Route 27. And they would discover that the lifespan of children, adults, and marriages could be short on the frontier.

Marriages ended by death or divorce. Some spouses just walked away from a marriage without bothering about the legal papers. Some frontiersmen had wives and children in more than one location as they ventured about. Rueben and Mary were actually successful in keeping their marriage together. Rueben would spend twenty-four of his years married. Mary would spend more than fifty-three of her seventy-nine years as a married woman.

The Smithees had eight children: Carrie Meneavia (sometimes written Minerva) was their first, born about 1903. Family travel was still by horse and wagon, even after the Santa Fe Railway reached Plainview in 1907. When their first boy, Robert Littleton Ardell, was born the next year, the Smithees were living in the New Mexico Territory.

Reservations, Expansions, and Border Towns

The borders of Indian Reservations were excellent locations for military camps, supply depots, and trading posts. Commerce with the Natives fostered enterprises and industries. Roads made travel along well-trodden trails more comfortable and efficient. Surveyors, engineers, contractors, and laborers began migrating to the frontier areas. Mail had to be delivered. The railroad magnates saw the opportunities for shipping and transportation. Mills provided building materials. In seemingly short time to the Native Americans, the white farming and trading communities grew to be small towns, often referred to as "border towns." All of this meant a great influx of men and families hoping to find steady work.

The 3.5 million-acre Navajo Reservation had been established in 1868. At the turn of the century the Navajo population was about 2,500. On the Reservation's edge, the town of Farmington was incorporated in 1901. Livestock and agriculture were the principal occupations, corn, pumpkin, peaches, and various fruits being plentiful. The town became the county trade center.

When Robert Littleton Smithee was born, fewer than 550 residents lived in Farmington. Although the local sawmills and brick factories were busy and a commercial district was expanding along Main Street, Reuben decided not to stay in New Mexico.

Somewhat nomadic in the years when the "wild" western frontier days were coming to their end, the Smithees returned to Hale Center. More children followed. J.C. was born in 1910 and Virgin Marie in 1912, only six months after New Mexico and Arizona became the 47th and 48th States. The fifth Smithee child died at birth July 31, 1913, and was buried in an unmarked Lot 2W grave in Hale Center Cemetery. This unnamed Smithee "infant child" provides the little evidence that the family came out of Texas. [4] Luella Ravenia was born next about 1915.

Some Smithee family members, perhaps related to Rueben, lived, married, and died in Hale Center. For example, Reverend James Taylor Smithee was born there February 26, 1898, married Eulah May Monroe on August 24, 1916, stayed there and died there May 16, 1984.

Rueben and Mary did not stay—in any place for that matter. Moving about, they looked for work to sustain their poor and expanding family. Rueben's work is not remembered, but he was likely a laborer. Mary had skills as a midwife and nurse. After leaving Texas, at various times they lived in New Mexico, Arizona, and Colorado.

At the time of the 1920 United States Census, Rueben and Mary were in Farmington again. Littleton was twelve, J.C. was nine, Marie was seven, and Luella was five-years-old. Living in Farmington, the Smithee family had grown by two more children. Nannie Opal, born in Placitas, Sandoval County, January 22, 1918, was eleven-months-old when Rueben filled out the Census forms. Vera Derall, born in 1919, was three-months-old. The two youngest girls were in Farmington when the town had grown to nearly 800 locals.

Carrie Meneavia was 16-years-old when Harold March caught sight of her. There is no record of how many locals turned out for their wedding in 1919. Nannie and Vera were too young to remember that family event. The extended Smithee family could not say what happened to Carrie afterwards. According to various Horlacher genealogy message boards today, she died in the small community of Rochester, California, east of Los Angeles, in 1993.

The 1920 United States Census proved to be the last for Reuben.

As in many eras, raising a large family was a hardship for the Smithees. The family's travels, travails, and life circumstances hardened the Smithees. They might have appeared cold, unloving, unbending, unemotional, bitter, and even hating to outsiders, but they tended to be closed and protective of each other to the same outsiders. Understanding the hardships of Ken Worley's childhood depends upon learning the experiences of the Smithee children.

It is good to remember that the Smithees were not in "just any era." Reuben's boyhood had been during the time when there were only thirty-eight United States. New Mexico and Arizona were their own Territories. The Army was building forts on the frontier, streets and roads were not paved, gunfights in western towns were the grist of popular tabloids, and the Native Americans were fighting off the incursions of white people onto their ancestral lands.

The valley between the southeastern Arizona Gila and Pinaleño Mountains, surrounded by desert, had been drawing peoples from far away for centuries. Apache tribes and bands were roaming the valley when the Spanish Conquistadores passed through from the south in the mid-1500s. Some Conquistadores remained near Mount Graham, with its tree-covered summit reaching an elevation of 10,720 feet. Kit Carson guided the Army of the West out of the New Mexico Territory and along the Gila River in 1845 on its way to California.

The Indian Wars between the eastern Arizona Chiricahua Apache and the Americans broke out in 1860. Chief Cochise led the Apache warriors. The arid San Carlos Apache Indian Reservation was established in 1871, as a means of forcibly consolidating and containing the Apache bands. The Apache stayed in the fight for twelve years before Cochise accepted a peace treaty in 1872 and settled the Chiricahua on reservation land. The Apache chief died in the Dragoon Mountains in 1874, four years before Reuben was born.

Camp Thomas broke ground in 1876, intent upon keeping the Apaches on the farmlands along the Gila River. That same year, 15-year-old William Oliver Tuttle drove a team of horses into Arizona, having taken six months to do so. [5] Born in Pepin, Wisconsin, August 1, 1860, William was eight-months-old when the American Civil War erupted at Fort Sumter in South Carolina. His father had been killed in a Civil War battle, and William was looking to make it on his own. Remembered as a man short in stature, Bill was a scrapper, not afraid of a fight. He was also hardworking and enterprising, and people found him to be of an engaging and pleasant nature. He hired on as a message carrier, growing into manhood as history was made around him.

Reservation life and politics would play a part in Bill's life, but he was not necessarily looking for a fight. More than that, he was looking for a place to put down roots and start a family of his own.

Geronimo and other Chiricahua Apache chiefs had had enough of reservation life. In April 1877, they broke out and began raiding forts and settlements. Geronimo was recaptured, returned to the reservation, and then fled again with his warriors. His final surrender came in September 1886. Some Apaches refused to return to San Carlos and were never captured. They conducted the last Indian raids from the mountains up through November 1900.

Soldiers had been dying as much from typhoid fever and malaria as from deadly encounters with hostiles, and Camp Thomas was moved further south in 1878 where it became Fort Thomas. Eventually, the fort included twenty-seven log and adobe buildings. As happened in most places where soldiers built a fort, a town grew around the Army encampment. At times, the houses of prostitution and saloons outnumbered the resident houses.

The Clanton family operated a cattle ranch near Fort Thomas. One of the Clanton boys was involved in a gunfight at the O.K. Corral one hundred miles south in Tombstone in October 1881. Wyatt Earp, Doc Holiday, and Frederick Remington all frequented Fort Thomas at various times while William Tuttle earned his keep there.

William was busy with agency affairs on the San Carlos Indian reservation. He worked for the federal government as an Indian agency farmer in 1891, all the while conducting the affairs of a merchant. He was installed as the reservation police chief and served as such until 1905. In that capacity, Marshall William is noted to have rounded up intoxicated carousers and saved hunters stranded in mountain blizzards.

He tried his hand at ranching for a while in 1900, but eventually established himself in a prosperous business. William began his own trading post on the reservation, dealing in general merchandise. Tuttle's Station, a stage stop and inn on the military supply road from San Carlos to Fort Apache, was a busy place. Big game bear and deer in the surrounding mountains made Tuttle's a convenient stop for hunters. On September 15, 1910, two deserters from the U.S. Army murdered two hunters there. The incident was sparked when a dog owned by one of the deserters bit one of the hunters.

William sold Tuttle's Station in 1913, and opened another general merchandise store in Fort Thomas, which developed into a prosperous business over the years. His customers spoke well of the manner in which he conducted business. He might have been a short man; nonetheless, William was prominent in the town, respected by most who encountered him. He began serving long terms as a Republican member of the county central committee in 1912, and into the 1920s. He was also an active member in the Globe Lodge No. 489, (B.P.O.E.), on the western edge of the reservation. William left an impression admirable enough that his biography appeared in a 1930 book, *History Of Arizona*. [6]

Work and sustenance on the western frontier proved to be a challenge for the Smithees in Farmington. Rueben moved the family to Fort Thomas, Graham County, due west of Truth or Consequences, sometime between the two World Wars, not for history, debauchery, or degradations, but for employment.

There was work around Graham County in mining camps, vineyards, and on farms. Lumber was coming down from the mountains in the Gila Valley to the sawmills. The government was funding improved road projects. Later in the 1930's, the Civilian Conservation Corps (CCC) would provide employment opportunities for young men in the county during the Depression, setting up work camps on and around Mount Graham.

Fort Thomas also provided work. In 1924, William Tuttle's General Store was destroyed by fire, but because of his fine reputation and available laborers, he was able to rebuild and in time was back in business. He became well acquainted with the Smithees, perhaps because Rueben helped in the rebuilding or because Mary did her grocery shopping at his store.

At some point Mary Smithees's mother, Sarah Minerva Harrison Horlacher, moved to Fort Thomas, perhaps to live with her daughter. She had been living in Farewell, on the Texas-New Mexico border when her husband, Samuel, had died around 1912. Mary was going to share the experience of widowhood with her mother, perhaps not a complete surprise since they had all been born in the 1800s when the average life expectancy at birth was about forty-five to fifty years.

As the families prepared for the year-end holidays, Rueben, 47-years of age, died in Fort Thomas just before Christmas, 1925.

With children and teens to provide for, Mary, 42-years-old, married again in Fort Thomas in April 1929, to William Oliver Tuttle. Twenty-six years his junior, Mary Horlacher Smithee was William's third wife. [7] The Smithee children settled down for a few years and began finding their own suitable partners for marriage.

The grocery store owner had had his own children, twelve with his second wife. Four of his daughters had died in childhood. All his children had been born between 1885 and 1909. This meant that his two youngest children were born at the same time that Reuben and Mary were starting their own family. William's surviving children were all adults when he married Mary.

The Great Depression and the Dust Bowl years were ahead. So were deaths, marriages and divorces and remarriages, inter-family affairs, family secrets, and questions about paternity. Birth certificates and last names would not always accurately identify the father of a particular child. The turmoil Ken Worley was to experience early in life was in motion.

Around 1930, J.C., Mary's third child, married Pauline Francis Kerby, from Pima, eleven miles down Route 70 from Fort Thomas.

The couple had seven children, four of whom were boys. These would be the next generation of Smithees and Ken's first cousins.

Virgin Marie was next in the Smithee family line. Some called her "Virgie" when she was a girl. Two years apart in age, she and J.C. had a close relationship all her life. Her big brother did not hesitate to "stand up" for her. Marie was 16-years-old when her mother married Mr. Tuttle. Her own marital status and whereabouts during the next years were initially unknown.

That Marie might have met her husband in either Graham or Pinal County and married in the early 1930s seemed likely. The Smithee women tended to marry young and begin their families and marry more than once. Marie might have been advised by her mother to marry a younger man. Establishing that Marie married in Arizona was a challenge and was learned late in the search for Ken's roots. Since Arizona is a "closed record" state, vital records like Birth, Death, and Marriage & Divorce Records are not considered public records. Only the individual registrants or immediate family members have access to such records. Texas Registry records, however, provided some hints to Marie's whereabouts.

A man by the name of James Edward Worley married in 1932 in Safford, Arizona. [8] The town is twenty miles south of Fort Thomas, and nine miles from J.C. and Pauline's wedding chapel. James' bride was 19-year-old Virgie Marie Smithee. Genealogy sites suggest that the couple moved to the Dallas, Texas area and had children. The Texas Birth Index for Dallas County lists Beverly Lorraine Worley, born January 15, 1940, and Betty Sue Worley, born February 13, 1942, as their daughters.

What became of James Edward Worley has not been determined. His marriage to Virgie Marie likely ended. Whether or not he ever lived in Farmington is unknown. Virgie's life between 1932 and 1947 is now without witnesses. Efforts to later track and validate the identities and relationships of Betty Sue Worley and Beverly Worley added further mystery to the search for Ken Worley's background. Marie's nieces knew nothing of this marriage or of her life outside of Farmington.

Luella Smithee, born into the family after Marie, was 18-years-old when she married Pat Cassidy in 1933 in Globe, Arizona, where her stepfather, William, belonged to Globe Lodge No. 489. That same June 7, William Tuttle died of pneumonia and was buried in the Fort Thomas Cemetery.

Mary Eliza Horlacher Smithee Tuttle still had children at home in 1933. Her second-born, Robert Littleton, had polio. Unlike his siblings, he did not marry and needed special caring and treatment. Mary's two youngest daughters, Nannie Opal, 15-years-old, and Vera, 14-years-old, had not yet found husbands. Mary and Nannie Opal would continue ties with the Tuttle family.

Frank J. Tuttle was William's fourth-born child, and one of three sons. He had a tenth grade education, having attended Roswell Military Academy in Roswell, New Mexico. When he was 22-years-old, working as a hotel keeper in Fort Thomas, he had married a 15-year-old Texas girl in Solomonville, Graham County, Arizona, on June 29, 1914. Twins were born to them before a year had passed, and two more children were born before their fourth anniversary. Two of the children survived into adult life, but their marriage did not. Frank, 36-years-old, married a second time on August 13, 1929, to a 21-year-old young woman from Utah. They lived in Lordsburg, Hidalgo County, New Mexico, where he worked as a laborer. They had a son ten months later, and then their short marriage ended.

Mary Tuttle and her companion, John Thomas Deal, left Fort Thomas with Nannie Opal, crossed over the border into New Mexico, and went to Lordsburg. According to the State of New Mexico, County of Hidalgo Marriage Book No. 8, page 4922, Mary and John stood before Pastor M.C. Moore of the Baptist Church and witnessed a marriage. [9]

On July 6, 1935, Nannie Opal Smithee, 17-years-old, married Frank Tuttle, who had been her older stepbrother for six years. Frank was also twenty-six years older than Nannie, now his third wife. In addition to Frank's five-year-old son, Nannie was stepmother to his son and daughter who were older than her. Nannie and Frank had one child, who later had the surname Brooks. [10]

Mary's mother, Sarah, died on April 18, 1939, and was buried in Fort Thomas. Afterwards, Mary decided a younger husband might make more sense in terms of longevity. She married John T. Deal in

1939. Born August 29, 1888, in Indian Territory, Oklahoma, John was two years junior to Mary. While the Tuttle surname was renowned in Fort Thomas, the Deal surname was also of particular note in eastern Arizona. A young man by the name of Pony Deal had earlier been a friend of John Ringo and a member of the Clanton cowboy gang.

John T. Deal was the man Ken and all his cousins would know as Grandpa Deal.

As for Nannie Opal Tuttle, her husband had trouble with alcohol and liked to roam from home. Predictably, the marriage ended. Frank married a fourth time in Lordsburg, on February 13, 1953, and died three years later at the age of 63. He was buried in Section 14, Lot 122 of Globe Cemetery, Globe, Gila County, Arizona.

Chain stores like J. C. Penney's and Piggly Wiggly Grocery had been arriving in Farmington for ten years when Mary and John married, and it seemed like maybe the town was not so affected by the Depression. The Deals decided to relocate there from Fort Thomas and stayed until 1962. They settled onto a property on North Allen Street, a few blocks east of the Four Corners Regional Airport. The property was a bit like a farm, with scattered fruit trees and a big, deep irrigation ditch on the west side. Struggling with poverty, various extended family members would set up trailers in back of the North Allen Deal property for years at a time. Cousins slept in tents.

Some Smithee family secrets were hoped to have been left behind in Arizona.

The growing and extended Smithee family struggled to provide for themselves. U.S. Highway 550 had been completed between Farmington and Durango in 1933. For a time, the families migrated up the road near Bayfield, Colorado, northeast of Farmington, as the men worked on the Pine River Dam at the intersection of Highways 160 and 501.

Nannie Opal Smithee Tuttle moved to Farmington at some point. She lived on North Allen, next door to the Deal property, with her second husband, Bernard "Red" Brooks.

Vera Derall was the youngest and last of the Smithee daughters to marry. Having watched the disruptions in her sisters' lives, she had pledged to have a more stable life for herself. Vera married Roy Z. Scribner. Roy had come from California and had extended family in Modesto. He worked in construction and sometimes went back and forth between New Mexico and California on visits. Vera and Roy and their four children, Ken's first cousins, lived near the Deals in Farmington. Their daughter, Sharon, was the woman who contacted *Albuquerque Journal* reporter Jim Belshaw in 2008, forty years after Ken had died in Vietnam, and identified herself as his first cousin.

While the Deals, Smithees, and Tutttles toiled and persevered, World War II broke out, and some men in the family went off to fight. "Red" Brooks, went into the Army and was held as a POW in the Philippines for many years. Roy Scribner went into the Navy. With the surrender of the Japanese, and with husbands returned home, the couples tried to make the post-war adjustments. More hard times were ahead, and battles within the families were going to erupt that would last longer than the war had.

"Virgie" Marie was also back in Farmington, living on the Deal settlement. Available records contradict how the next generation of cousins remembered the family genealogy in regard to their aunt.

As far as Ken's cousins knew, their Aunt Marie had only one husband, Charles Peace, a man believed to have come from Texas, but whose background is largely unknown. There were Peace families residing in Plainview at the same time Marie's mother was growing up there and others living in Hale City. An investigator discovered one document indicating that Charles was born August 13, 1918, in Winkleman, Arizona. Winkleman, a small mining town of under 400 residents at the confluence of the Gila and San Pedro rivers, is thirty-five miles west from Fort Thomas, and on the southwest edge of the San Carlos Apache Indian Reservation.

If accurate, Charles was five years younger than Marie. He was a docile man, often overwhelmed by the Smithee personality. He was a handyman and a bit of a vagrant when it came to working, picking fruit and doing odd jobs for people. Charles disappeared from time to time, ostensibly to find work. One of his brothers-in-law, Roy Scribner, helped him get work in construction from time to time. Cousins remember Betty Sue as Marie and Charles' first child, their only daughter, born around 1940.

Charles Peace moved his small family into a school bus, parked in front of the Deal's house. In the class-conscious town, this would have raised eyebrows. Living in any kind of trailer suggested the family was transient and belonged at the bottom of the social ladder. A school bus put the Peace family on the lowest rung.

Unknown to some cousins until much later in their adult lives, Marie, between marriages, had an affair of unknown length with a brother-in-law in 1947. Her pregnancy triggered suspicions among the families living on or near the Deal property.

Kenneth Lee was born April 27, 1948. Because he was so much like the brother-in-law in appearance, the family did not doubt his lineage. Ken's paternity was a matter of rancor among his aunts, the Smithee girls. Nannie Opal found the affair especially egregious, and Ken's birth set off interfamily hostilities and hatred that would be directed at him. Whether or not the families talked or argued about the affairs of Virgie Marie in front of the children, Ken had cousins who were also his half-sisters. And some of the cousins knew it.

Charles and Marie must have migrated up to Nyssa, Malheur County, on the southeast border of Oregon. Perhaps they moved to get away from the family wrangling or to find work. The region along the Snake River provided work for potato and sugar laborers. Maybe Marie wanted to be closer to the Smithee she cherished most. Her brother, J.C., was living 50 miles down the road near Boise, Idaho.

According to the Oregon Death Index, Marie Peace died in Nyssa, February 26, 1950, of cancer and kidney failure. [11] Marie was buried in Farmington's old Greenlawn Cemetery, a few blocks northeast of Allen Street. The cemetery owner reports her age as having been 36-years. If there was ever a stone marking her grave, as of 2008 it was no longer on the lot where cemetery records indicate she is buried. Over the years a daughter would infrequently contact the cemetery to inquire about the care of her mother's grave. [12]

A Walk into the San Juan County Court House

Later inquiries challenged the childhood memories of Kenny's cousins. Private Investigator Joan Earnshaw persisting in the search for his sister, Betty Sue, found a curious document at the San Juan County Court House.

On August 9, 1949, six months before Virgin Marie Smithee Peace died of cancer, a couple walked into the San Juan County Court House in Aztec, New Mexico, the small town fourteen miles northeast of Farmington. They filled out an Application for Marriage License. The County Clerk, Liska Diel, issued them a Marriage License at 1:50 PM. The next day the couple stood before D. Clarence Burd, Minister of the Gospel, [13] in Farmington and joined "in the Holy Bonds of Matrimony in accordance with the Laws of the State of New Mexico," recorded in Marriage Record Book No. 13. [14]

Charles F. Peace, 30-years-old, of Winkleman, Arizona, [15] then a resident of Farmington, had married Marie Worley, 36-years-old, of Hale Center, Texas, then a resident of Farmington. The last name now shared by the couple was Peace. At the point of this marriage, Ken was 16-months-old and Betty Sue, his half-sister, would have been close to 10-years.

The 1949 marriage document raised more questions and doubts. At the point Joan Earnshaw discovered it, researchers had not yet found evidence of Marie's earlier marriage. Was this the same Charles Peace who, according to cousins, had been married to Marie Smithee, Ken's mother, all along? Did another Charles Peace live in Farmington at the time? The similarities of names, ages, and hometowns seemed too much a coincidence.

Did Charles, anticipating the death, marry another Marie before Virgin Marie died the following February? From what is remembered of him, it is difficult to believe Charles could have done well in life without a wife taking care of him, but marrying another woman even before his wife died? Could Charles have led a secret life that no one else knew about? Did his absences to find work beyond Farmington really entail being with his other family?

If Charles married a Marie Worley in 1949 and he already had two children, did this Marie Worley also have children, Beverly being one of them? Perhaps Beverly Worley, who later changed her name to Peace, became a stepsister to Ken by this marriage? As small as the town was then, it is hard to believe Charles could have married a Marie Worley with no one else knowing. Liska Diel could answer such questions, but she has been dead for years. [16]

Ken's cousins, Sharon Scribner, Joyce Smithee, and Valerie Brooks were all nearly three-years-old when this marriage took place. The girls spent a good amount of time around Ken when he was a boy. They witnessed some of the things that happened to him, but were unaware of the adult family dynamics for a good portion of their lives.

Sharon Scribner Houston today was initially certain that Charles did not marry a Marie Worley before her aunt died in 1950. Also, there was never a Beverly Worley in their family. The cousins had believed that Marie and Charles Peace had long been married and that Betty Sue was their first child. Sharon had always known her cousins as Betty Sue Peace and Kenny Peace.

Sharon was emphatic about these details. Charles had been close to the Deals and Smithees. There was no other woman in Charles' life after her aunt Marie died, until twelve years later when Charles married her other aunt. The cousins had close ties to him and would have known about it. [17]

That it was Virgin Marie Smithee's husband who walked into the Aztec Court House that August in 1949 to obtain a license to join "in the Holy Bonds of Matrimony" with Marie Worley is made more likely by the witnesses to the marriage the next day. Standing with Charles and Marie were J.C. Smithee and Mrs. R. M. Goodding. J.C. was Marie Smithee's older brother, Joyce's father, and Ken's uncle.

The questions for researchers became, who was Marie Worley and why would J.C. Smithee condone this union while his sister was ill? J.C. might have answered these questions as the search for Ken Worley's roots began, except that he had late-onset Alzheimer's. Six months after the wreath and garland ceremony at Ken's Westminster grave, his Uncle J.C. died on December 11, 2003, at the age of 93-years. With him, the firsthand memories of the Smithee family experiences in Hale Center, Texas, and Fort Thomas, Arizona, went to the grave.

Lacking definitive answers to the questions raised by the 1949 Worley-Peace marriage record, researchers are left to speculate. Some possible answers would include more "perhaps" qualifiers than others. Some family history is apparently not well known by extended Smithee family members. In a family with as many secrets as the Smithees held, unlikely explanations can be equally plausible. However, the simplest explanation can also be the accurate one.

Charles Peace might not have been a Smithee in-law as long as it seemed to Ken's cousins. The presence of J.C. Smithee, Virgie Marie's older brother, as a witness to the 1949 marriage is a strong indication that the Marie Worley marrying Charles was J.C.'s younger sister. One week after Marie celebrated her 36th birthday she married Charles Peace and would not live to see her 37th birthday.

It makes sense that Virgin Marie Smithee, the next in the family line after J.C., did not wait until she was 36-years-old to marry. The Smithee family had moved from Hale Center, Texas to Farmington and to Fort Thomas, on the south side of the San Carlos Indian Reservation, where Rueben died. The Smithee children closest to Marie in age, J.C. and Luella, had met their spouses and married while the family lived in Arizona. Marie was six years older than Nannie Opal. That Mary Horlacher Smithee Tuttle was witness to Nannie's marriage before moving from Fort Thomas back to Farmington, suggests that Marie had already married.

Marie likely met a husband in Fort Thomas by the name of Worley, marrying in the time frame of 1930-35, either in Graham or Pinal County. Charles was not her first husband and neither Betty Sue nor Ken was his biological child. If this were the case, and if they were available to researchers, birth certificates would indicate that Marie Smithee Worley brought both into this world. Charles had changed their names to Peace when he became their legal guardian by marriage.

Kenny Lee was just 22-months-old when Marie died. Held in the protective embrace of his Aunt Vera, the only Smithee adult to provide him solace, he would have no memories of having had a mother. Charles, in reality a stepfather, raised Kenny as his own son, doing the best he could with the two children, staying in the school bus on their grandparents' property. Since Charles was often on the move for work, taking the school bus, Betty Sue and Kenny stayed with the various extended families in town. This sometimes meant trips to Truth or Consequences, Las Cruces, and Sorocco.

Charles loved Kenny in his own way, but several aunts did not treat either child well. Not understanding why, the cousins, in particular Sharon, Joyce, and Valerie, remembered Kenny as having been "treated horribly," "treated like a dog" by their aunts. The scars on his body gave testimony to how the aunts felt about him.

Sharon's mother, Vera, stayed out of the family hostilities and provided her children with as peaceful an upbringing as possible. Vera and Roy had a special place in their hearts for their niece and nephew, doing what they could to help them. Having had a difficult childhood himself, Roy was protective of them when they were in his care. Vera stored away letters from Betty Sue and photographs of the two children playing with various cousins. One of those photos shows Kenny Lee, five-years-old, standing beside an older cousin, Sharon's brother, and aiming down the long barrel of a toy rifle.

Fifteen years later, he would be doing the same thing in Vietnam, only for real and with an air-cooled weapon that had an attached bipod and was capable of 100 rounds-per-minute rapid-fire bursts.

Kenny and Betty Sue, separated by eight years, faced childhood challenges. Rather than being overwhelmed, they each tapped into the resilience within themselves and found ways to overcome their hardships.

Betty Sue was the envy of many of the younger cousins and girls in the Farmington neighborhood. As she got into her teen years, she was meticulous about how she did her hair, wore make-up, and customized with jewelry. She kept herself clean and preferred wearing dress up clothes. Poor maybe, but she was attractive and sophisticated-looking all the same. Social and engaging, Betty began dating and became all the more the envy when she had a boyfriend.

Once finished with eighth grade, Betty Sue ran away to California with her boyfriend, Alec, in 1954, when she was about fifteen. Betty Sue wrote Vera and Roy sometimes, and came for visits. On one photograph, the smiling teenager wrote, "To my favorite Grandparents and Uncle, With love, Betty Sue." She signed her letters and photographs as Betty Sue Worley, no longer using Peace as her surname. Whether Betty Sue had married Alec or not, the cousins, having no knowledge of Marie having had a husband before Charles Peace, believed that Betty Sue must have married someone named Worley while she was in California.

And, if Betty Sue's husband's name was Worley, whether he was in any way related to the Farmington Worleys, Lettie Mae or Thomas, the baseball coach, or the Modesto or Hayward Worleys was uncertain. Whatever the case, her cousins are sure her marriage did not last.

Once away from Farmington, Betty Sue Worley had a son by the name of Ricky. Kenny was an uncle with a nephew believed to be living in California. Betty Sue's letters to family stopped around 1963, and her contacts ended altogether in the 1970s after her brother was awarded the Medal of Honor.

Private Investigator Joan Earnshaw joined in the search for Betty Worley.

Joan posted a message on the Worley Family Genealogy Forum, April 16, 2009, "looking for the family of Kenneth Worley... Any info as to the location of Betty or other family members would be appreciated." As of this printing, the site administrator reported *"No followups yet."*

Joan located a 1962 newspaper wedding announcement that offered some clues. Betty Louann Worley, who had lived in Hayward, California, married Hans Werner Schneider on November 11, 1962. Betty's brother, Kenneth attended as an "Usher." A niece, Debbie Worley, served as a "Flower Girl." [18]

This wedding occurred after Kenny Peace had graduated form eighth grade and moved from Farmington. The wedding announcement raised the question of whether Kenny had been the usher at a Hayward wedding when he was 14-years-old.

As the earlier search for Ken had shown, there were other Kenneth Worleys living in various places east and west of New Mexico. There might have been a Worley family living in Hayward, but of unknown connection to the family in Farmington. The Hayward *Daily Review*, Thursday, June 29, 1961, page 12, had announced a wedding of Lester Lee Worley, son of Ree Worley. Betty Worley was a bridesmaid in a green satin frock and yellow carnations and Kenneth Worley was an usher. Were these sister and brother of Lester? [19]

This Betty Worley was active in high school, was often in the news, and had made headlines on Saturday, December 27, 1958, when she was installed as president of the Future Business Leaders of America Club of Tennyson High School. [20] She was in charge of tickets for the all-day "Lancers" Friday Carnival and evening dance, May 8, 1959. [21] This Betty Worley was likely the one who married Hans Werner Schneider three years later. The later article mentions Betty's brothers: Lester, Kenneth, Norman, and Robert. Joan was able to find Hans Schneider in June 2009, and talked with him by phone. His wife, Betty, had died in 2002. Hans believed that her brother Ken had been too young to be the Marine who had earned a Medal of Honor in Vietnam. Another dead end. [22]

Checking the 1960-85 California Marriage Index, Joan discovered a marriage between Betty Sue Worley and Larry L. Loucado in Orange County, September 27, 1965. [23] Larry, about 71-years-old at the time of the search, was listed as living with his wife, Betty Sue, in Ventura. The couple did not respond to inquiry letters about Ken's family background. Some hints surfaced from different sources that Betty Sue Peace Worley, aka unknown, was deceased. Ken's sister, Betty Sue, and his nephew, Ricky, have not been located.

What Peace in Farmington?

For Ann Phelps, childhood memories involving the Worley, Peace, and Smithee families continued to bubble up to the surface of her awareness. Ann remained certain that Ken had at least one sister, possibly two. Maybe one was a half-sister. [24] Ann never really knew Betty Sue, just who she was. She knew Beverly Worley better. Beverly looked up to Betty and told Ann that she wore Betty's handed down clothes. Betty did seem a little older. Both girls were really slender and had cheerful smiles and sparkling eyes. Betty Sue had dark hair and dark eyes. Beverly Worley was blonde and fair skinned. She had light eyes like Kenneth, more gray than blue, and similar skin coloring.

Ann recalled the time in grade school when Beverly "bailed out' from a school yard swing. The skirt of her dress caught on the swing's wire and ripped completely off, left dangling back and forth on the swing. Beverly was a shy and modest girl, and there she stood in her slip and the top of her dress. Ann walked Beverly home to change clothes, shivering and crying, with what was left of her skirt wrapped over her slip. More Betty Sue handed down clothes.

Beverly's mother had a heart condition and her health declined when Beverly was in the final years of grade school. She is remembered to have died about the time Beverly started her 1954-55 freshman year at Farmington High School. Members of the Class of 1958, Ann and Beverly shared a freshman locker. But, Beverly did not enroll in high school as a Worley. Her last name had changed. Her picture was in the 1955 "Naniskad" Annual. She was then Beverly Peace. And when the yearbook was distributed to the freshmen, Beverly was not at school to receive her copy.

The reason for her absence was a stark memory for Ann. Beverly was at her locker one morning, attended classes, and by evening had been checked out of school. Beverly left school that day without saying good-bye, and Ann never saw her again. Her name appeared again without a photograph in the 1956 Annual as a freshman.

One of Beverly's books had been left in the locker. Forest green hardcover, the title in gold letters on a faded and somewhat frayed spine, *The Hoosier Schoolmaster* was not a library book. [25] Ann was unsure if the novel had been left on purpose or if someone other than Beverly had cleared out the locker, not realizing to whom it belonged. Ann had a strong sense that Beverly had left the book for her to find, perhaps as a gift since she had not had a chance to say good-bye. She took the book home with her.

Wanting to know that her locker mate was okay, Ann called the Smithee children who Beverly had said were her cousins, and asked if they might tell her where she could return Beverly's book. The cousins, perhaps brusquely, said they had never heard of Beverly Worley Peace.

No matter where she inquired, Ann encountered what she believed was "serious stonewalling." At school, the teachers and the librarian, at home, her mother, everywhere and anywhere she asked, others refused to give information about Beverly, to the degree of denying the girl had existed. No one claimed the book. Thus, *The Hoosier Schoolmaster* became a reminder of the Worley-Peace children in the years that followed. Ann kept the book after she graduated and married. Somewhere, the book was lost, possibly damaged and discarded from a Colorado storage shed.

Betty Sue Peace Worley is remembered by her cousins to have run away from Farmington at nearly the same point in time that Ann remembers Beverly Worley Peace in one day disappearing from Farmington High School. There is little to explain the presence of Beverly Worley Peace in Ken's history. When his sister, Betty Sue, left Farmington, Kenny Peace was left alone to deal with his extended family for the next nine years.

Class-conscious Farmington was a small town, in which people were to know their places and children were taught whom to invite to their birthday parties. Mothers dictated the relationships among their children, especially when dating began in their adolescence. The well-to-do northsiders were to keep away from the southside toughs, unless they wanted trouble with their own mothers. Those with wealth found their friends among the wealthy. Mormons congregated with other Mormon, Catholics with Catholics, Baptist with Baptists, Native Americans with tribes people. Mandatory attendance at church groups was a common way to keep children from street activities. [26] If at all, Kenny would have felt welcomed in only a small, closed circle of relatives.

Before Kenny started off to school, one of his Smithee cousins was earning celebrity in Farmington. J.C.'s son, Arthur J. Smithee, was often in the local newspaper sports column and was well known in the town. [27] Art was born in Pima, Arizona, December 2, 1934. He knew neither his Grandpa Rueben nor Grandpa Tuttle. As he grew up, Grandma Mary married Grandpa Deal and the families moved north to Farmington. Art was into his teens when Marie and an uncle joined in an affair and Ken's life began.

Playing high school team athletics, Art helped the distance medley relay team capture titles. He also played end on the football team, lettering three consecutive years. In his senior year, some sports reporters referred to Art as "a 180-pound workhorse," "the backbone of the offensive line," and "a rangy pass grabber." Passes he caught from quarterback Max Webb helped lead the Scorpions to an 11-1 season in 1951, and an undefeated season and Class A Conference Football Championship in 1952.

Art was a cousin Kenny could have admired and looked up to, except that he was only four-years-old when Art graduated from high school. During the years of searching for background information, Art might have been able to provide details of extended family life while Kenny was growing up, except that he had died in Nampa, Idaho, June 7, 1987, nearly nineteen years after his cousin had died in Vietnam and fifteen years before Ken's grave was rediscovered in Westminster.

The four elementary schools Kenny attended were within walking or running distance of the school bus on the Deal property where he had lived. The schools sat in one long city block between North Wall and North Court Avenues and East Apache and East Main Streets. Kenny would have walked up a small hill to have his lunch at the school lunchroom at the top of the block on East Apache. From there he might have looked across the street to the High School, wondering, maybe, why Betty Sue was not there.

Ken walked to Farmington Elementary School, across from La Plata Street for first through third grades. [28] This was also called the North Wall School. For fourth grade, he went to Wall Street School; an old, two-story brick building that had been used as an elementary as early as the 1920s. It was on the little hill just north of the parking lot between the two grade school buildings.

The smell of chalk, dirt, old brick, people, wax, and lunch food cooking permeated the entire Wall Street School. Fourth graders, the closest to the lunchroom, found the smells to be appetite suppressants. While standing in line along the brick hallway leading to the lunchroom, some boys whiled away the time scratching graffiti on the wall, an activity for which teachers were constantly on the look out. Once students were in the lunchroom, teachers had to stand over them and compel them to eat every bite of the food placed in front of them. Many a student had to gag down the much-despised raisin salad.

Grades five and six were located across the block from the earlier grades, in a building facing Court Avenue (Swinburne Elementary?). The seventh and eighth grades were in another two-story brick school.

Ken's grade school records might be archived somewhere, but they are inaccessible to all but his immediate family. Ann Phelps had some ideas about what his classroom and school yard experiences might have been like.

Teachers at the time Ken was sitting in their classrooms seemed to understand the town's class lines. Students from prominent, "well-to-do" families did not face much discipline. A hands off attitude also prevailed for the children of business owners, professionals, school board members, and for those who had teachers in the family. The harsh, and sometimes severe, corporal punishment seemed to be reserved for the kids whose school and church clothes were also their play clothes. When poor students were naughty, they were actually relieved to be "put in Coventry," meaning they were to be ignored and shunned by teacher and classmates. Coventry could be good for laughs and left no bruising.

In the care of his family, Kenny was not allowed to play much, and sports and extracurricular school activities were out of the question. His playmates were essentially his cousins living on North Allen. Since he was among Farmington's "poorest of the poor" families, companions outside of the family would have been the street kids and maybe some of the "rowdies." Play was improvised and without expense. Some of it was adrenaline-fueled, and much of it was against the rules.

Some degree of gymnastic skills was in order. The grade schoolers liked to turn themselves inside out on the horizontal metal handrail at the top of the Wall Street School cellar steps. Suspended by the arms from the rail, they swung their legs and feet between their arms, completing a revolution called "skin the cat." The danger, of course, was that a fall down the steps could result in broken bones. Sliding down the metal cellar door also garnered thrills.

The playground swing sets also provided ample exhilaration. A favorite game was to swing as high as one dared and then "bail out" of the swing at its apex. Soaring through the air to land on one's feet was the objective. Ripped clothes, scraped and bleeding knees and palms, and the occasional broken arm were not deterrents to aiming for greater heights. Taking a swing to go higher than the top bar, as if it was possible to do a complete circle in the seat, and managing the jostling oscillations as the swing's chains gave way to gravity, inducing a rapid downward arc, heralded many a boy's bravery. Those up to the greater risks would climb the side A-frames and cross the top pipe, as if walking along a round balance beam. Teachers held their breath, saving it for the lectures that would follow.

Like other kids of his time raised on war movies, Kenny likely played war by the wooden structure housing the school's old fire escape slide and looked for ways to sneak into the Farmington Lumberyard on East Main Street and Wall Avenue to climb on the stacks of lumber. Walking from home in the school bus on North Allen to the Animas River for some fishing, and then back, Kenny would have at times passed by Farmington Drug at 101 Main Street, where the older kids liked to hang out. Ensign Glen Howard Rickelton was the son and nephew of the drug store's owners. "Rick" graduated from Farmington High School in 1949, a little more than a month after Kenny turned one-year-old, and attended New Mexico State University. He went on to be a Navy pilot, flying a VF-51 Grumman F9F2 *Panther* off the carrier deck of the USS *Essex* during the Korean War. Ensign Rickelton was shot down and killed in combat January 6, 1952. [29] Might this have been a hero's story familiar to Ken?

Kenny probably looked into The Malt Shoppe beside the Junior High School building, wistfully hoping for a treat. He would have walked past the local grocery store, just to the north of the ice cream place, at the corner of Apache Street. The owners once had a float in the Fair Parade, calling themselves the *Beatum & Cheatum Market.* That name stuck. Kenny likely ran errands to the market for his grandparents, aunts, and uncles. [30]

One Move Among Many

Mary and John Deal wanted to be closer to the New Mexico hot springs in order to attend to Littleton Smithee's health. They thought about it for years, as the North Allen area of Farmington was rapidly filling with residential housing developments, closing in on the Deal farm. Ken's grandparents made their decision. They moved to Truth or Consequences in 1962, after Ken had finished elementary school. Their house was eventually torn down.

The Deals lived for a time on Platinum, and then moved again to another street. Charles moved with Kenny to Truth or Consequences and the 14-year-old registered to attend Hot Springs Junior High in the fall. The Hot Springs High School has records that Kenneth Peace attended there for only the 1962, fall semester. His photo was not in that year's school yearbook, possibly excluded because he was a student there for so short a time, or more likely, because he had not been present when photos were taken.

Another chapter was about to be written in Ken's story. Charles Peace remarried after moving from Farmington. His bride happened to be Marie's younger sister, Kenny's Aunt Luella. Having a stepmother who had already shown her lack of fondness for him did not bode well for the teenager. Kenny had already been storing up years of anger towards his family. He likely had never done well in school because of the trouble in the family, and now he began getting into trouble with the law.

Roy Scribner got Charles some construction work in Socorro, where he stayed for a year or so. The schools have no record of Ken attending there. Around this time, he was away from family, living in the northeast corner of New Mexico, on HW25, on the old Santa Fe Trail. He had been sent to the Youth Correction Center in Springer, New Mexico, for about eighteen months. As bad as that experience was for him, he did not believe returning to his family would improve his circumstances any.

Kenneth Lee Peace was near his sixteenth birthday when he was released from the Springer Youth Facility. How much Ken and his sister were in contact during his adolescence is unknown, but when he returned to Truth or Consequences, he planned that it would be a short stay.

Sharon Scribner had married John Houston in 1963. While they were visiting the family in Truth or Consequences, Ken told his cousin that he was "sick of it all" and was going to run away and change his name. Another cousin was visiting from Farmington. On a walk to the drug store, Ken told her he was going to run away and take the name Worley. Later, when the search for Kenneth Worley's past was underway, even his cousins had no idea why he might have chosen that name. They thought perhaps Worley was his sister's married name, since they remembered the photos of her sent from Betty Sue Worley.

Both Peace children, Betty Sue and Kenny, were teenagers when they ran away from New Mexico, and both changed their names as soon as they separated from the family circle. The Worley name obviously held some significance for both of them. Their cousins might be correct, that Worley was Betty Sue's married name. Betty Sue might have been writing to Kenny when he was held in Springer, and he had decided to change his name to hers and meet up with her in California.

The 1949 Worley-Peace marriage license suggests another reason. As soon as they freed themselves from the overbearing influence of family, the two teenagers each returned to their legal surname, Worley, the name on their birth certificates.

Whatever the reason Ken changed his name from Peace to Worley when he left New Mexico, the name change explained why finding traces of Ken Worley in Farmington had been difficult. Anyone who had known him as a boy would have remembered him as Kenny Peace.

Ken's running away from home can be viewed in many ways. Experiencing early personal challenges was one background factor

Semper Fidelis identified that resulted in strong personal character and later heroically brave actions among Marine Medal recipients. Humans instinctively attempt to escape from adverse situations. Staying in the situation can result in defending or fighting for change, but the possibility of adapting a helpless attitude or a hopeless outlook is real when events are ongoing and out of a child's control. However, running away from hardships is not answer enough. Some people who are able to escape their realities do so without necessarily improving their situations or themselves. Escaping might be a solution. How that solution works out depends on the character of the person.

Seeking to better themselves and their situations was a trait shared among the Medal of Honor recipients. They tended to not give in or capitulate to unwelcome circumstances. Instead, they looked for ways to get beyond the status quo when finding themselves in situations not to their liking.

It is a common sentiment among siblings, friends, and classmates remembering a Medal of Honor recipient; those people remember that, as boys, the recipients had been somehow special or different than the rest. They persistently demonstrated a strong drive to make things better for themselves.

"He was the strong one."
"He was the good one."
"He could do anything he put his mind to."
"We knew he would make something of himself."

When family income was lacking, they found jobs. When jobs were not available in their own community, and they were old enough to do so, they moved to cities where work was more plentiful. When they lacked an education, they earned GEDs. When they grew up in troubled neighborhoods or disturbed families, they joined the Marines, rather than immersing themselves in troubling or disturbing situations. Even those who were raised in stable, strong, and exemplary families sought to build on what they had been provided and looked for ways to improve things.

The desire to better oneself or one's circumstances might be viewed by some as a kind of restlessness. Men such as these definitely bring a sense of movement to their lives, no matter how "good" things might be for them. "Settling" just is not in their nature.

Ken shared many of the personal characteristics demonstrated by these warriors. This became more apparent when he ran from New Mexico. Ken's departure is an indication that he was finished with being treated badly and that "settling" was not in his nature either. There would be some hardships ahead, but leaving would also bring better things his way.

Kenneth Peace left New Mexico around 1964. He arrived in Modesto as Kenneth Lee Worley. No one knows for sure where or with whom he stayed for the next two years. As far as anyone can tell, he never looked back. Nor did he ever attempt to reengage with family in New Mexico. This was apparent more in his absence than in his lack of effort to explain to anyone why he had run from family. Ken's Grandma Mary Eliza outlived her third, and younger husband. Grandpa Deal died September 11, 1964, two days before Mary's birthday. Grandma Mary, 79-years-old, died November 1, 1965, in Sierra, New Mexico. Neither Ken nor Betty Sue returned to New Mexico for the funerals.

When their nephew ran away, Vera and Roy Scribner tried to find him, putting ads in the newspapers for him to come home, reassuring him that they would take care of him. None of the cousins knew at the time that Ken had moved to Modesto, or made any connection to the whereabouts of Betty Sue or the West Coast Scribner family. Roy's adult children believe that it would have been just like him to arrange for Betty Sue and Kenny to run to Modesto and not tell anyone of his involvement on their behalf.

Later, someone in California knew enough about Ken's life to know that the Lance Corporal Worley named in 1968 "Immediate Press Release" reports had once been Kenny Peace and had family in New Mexico. That someone called Charles and Luella to report Ken's death in Vietnam. When the stepparents made inquiries about Ken's death benefits, they learned from the Marines that Lance Corporal Worley had made no official mention of the Peace family. The Feyerherms were

Ken's only family on record. In 1970, Charles and Luella were also informed by someone in California that Lance Corporal Worley had been awarded the Medal of Honor. What that tribute meant to Charles is unknown: he was not invited to the White House.

Sharon Houston had long been married and raising her four children when she heard from family in the early 1970s that her cousin had died in Vietnam in 1968. The last time she had seen Charles Peace was in 1973. Her aunt Luella had by then divorced him, and he was remarried to another woman. He seemed bitter and unhappy. [31] Charles died either in Truth or Consequences or Williamsburg, Sierra County, New Mexico, June 27, 1997. He was nearly 79-years-old.

Sharon's mother, Vera, gradually provided her details of Kenny's early life and the family events that surrounded him. Sharon learned much later that a family had taken him in before he enlisted in the Marines. She believed that the California family had given Kenny the only love he had likely ever known, that they had played a beautiful part in his life, had helped turn his life around, and were the redeeming factor in his life. For that, she was grateful.

Whatever his reason, Kenneth Lee wanted to be a Worley. That was the teenager who arrived in California.

Life in Modesto

Around the fall of 1966, as the holiday season was approaching, Ken had been driving big diesel trucks, hauling Christmas trees out of the mountains. He had injured his foot, requiring a cast, and was unable to drive until the injury healed. [32] At the time, he was living alone in a little camper trailer with no running water, electricity, or heat. Things might have looked bleak for Ken, but things were about to turn, much for the better.

Quonieta Feyerherm was 16-years-old, a sophomore at Grace M. Davis High School, on Modesto's north side. [33] A girlfriend wanted her to meet a friend of her boyfriend and introduced her to Ken, "a handsome truck driver passing through town." Quonieta and Ken liked each other instantly. As they spent time together, talking and getting to know one another, Quonieta learned that Ken, two years older than she, had been "bounced from pillar to post" among his extended family. He did not say much about his parents, but it seemed that they had come out of Texas. Quonieta sensed that Ken believed "he had never belonged anywhere," and in a way, seemed like a "lost soul." [34]

Quonieta took him along for a hot, home-cooked meal. Her father, Don Feyerherm, immediately took a strong liking to Kenny. The whole family seemed to agree that the their father and this 18-year-old truck driver with a cast on his leg were like "kindred spirits." Don told the teenager to go collect his belongings and move in with the family until he could get himself back to work. Never mind that Don and Rosemary had eight children at home with them, the oldest of whom was Quonieta. Kenny did just that and became one of the family overnight. Although he now had six foster sisters and two foster brothers, no one thought of Kenny as a "foster brother." He blended in easily, becoming like one of their own, and stayed until he joined the Marines.

Kenny seemed to jump in wherever he was needed and to do whatever a brother might do without thinking twice about it. He was the kind of person who did more than he was asked to do. He helped the younger brother Butch with chores and watched over Nell, who remembers being a pre-teen and wild. She was attending Stanislaus Elementary, a school on the outskirts of town surrounded by agricultural fields on Kiernan Avenue, much closer to home than Davis High.

Despite the cast on his foot when he joined the foster family, Ken was not one to let an injury keep him down, a characteristic that would be evident in Vietnam. Don was the manager of a full-service Modesto Regal Gas Station. Ken went to work at the station, cast and all. He ran the pumps, filled tires with air, and helped with the mechanical services in the garage.

Ken enjoyed things mechanical. Anything with an engine was something he liked getting his hands on. He had a cherished old pink Desoto and could frequently be found under the hood, tinkering with the engine, fixing here and there. Well liked by his coworkers, Ken was smart and savvy and hard working. He had an uninhibited sense of humor and could bring the best out in those around him. He might have been a teenager, but Ken was respected as a man, demonstrating a sense of ethics and morals, wanting to do the right thing.

All who knew him well would say he was a "loving and caring person." When Quonieta wondered if she might be pregnant, Ken drove her to the Orange County Hospital. The test came back positive. Ken proposed marriage, unconcerned about paternity. Quonieta would not have hesitated to marry him, but Rose Feyerherm would not hear of such a union. She insisted that her daughter marry her high school boyfriend, who was by then in the Navy.

Don Feyerherm had been a fireman in the Navy for sixteen years, working on boilers in the engine room of ships. Raising such a large family had presented a hardship, and he left the service. He talked favorably about his experiences. Kenny loved the way his foster dad talked about the Navy, and considered joining that branch of the service. The Selective Service Board, however, settled the issue. Somewhere around early June 1967, when he was 19-years-old, a letter arrived. Ken was going to be drafted into the Army, not the service branch of his choice. His lack of high school records, though, was an obstacle that could not be overcome for the Navy recruiters.

Ken, tall, slender and muscular, with wavy, sandy blond hair, got in his Desoto, drove the forty-five miles down to Fresno, and enlisted in the Marines. He gave his home of record, as noted in documents, as Modesto. Later, both Orange County, California, and Snohomish County, Washington, would claim the young Marine as one of their own.

Prior to his departure to the San Diego Recruit Depot, the Feyerherms, neighbors, friends, and gas station coworkers gathered for a goodbye party. They knew enough not to have him make chili for the guests. He had once brewed what came to be known as "five-alarm chili," so hot that his eyes watered, his nose ran, and his forehead and body poured sweat. The physical discomfort had not stopped him from eating the combustible concoction. The neighbors had come to adore the young man and would miss Ken greatly. That was not an experience he had ever known in New Mexico when he was Kenny Peace. [35]

CHAPTER 5
First Time on a Team

"There was always talk of espirit de corps, of being gung ho,
and that must have been a part of it. Better, tougher training,
more marksmanship on the firing range, the instant obedience
to orders seared into men in boot camp."

James W. Brady, author and columnist [1]

A heroically brave man does not necessarily stand out in a crowd, at
least not in the ways one might think.

Once he arrived at the San Diego Recruit Depot, and for the rest
of his life, Ken would have been known simply as "Worley" to his
drill instructors, comrades, and commanders. By tradition, Marines call
those below the non-commissioned officer (NCO) ranks, the privates,
privates first class, and lance corporals, by their last names.

One of his fellow "Boots" can still see "Worley" standing on the
yellow feet painted on the pavement. Although he would now be told
where to plant his feet, how to stand and march, and how to address
those who gave him orders, Ken stood on those yellow feet looking
"happy and proud." [2] He was now a member of Platoon 396, living
with others in a Quonset hut, which had to have seemed better than

living alone in a trailer without running water, electricity, or heat. Certainly it was an improvement over living in a school bus. By the end of summer, 1967 Boot Camp, Platoon 396 would be the Honor Platoon at MCRD San Diego.

Private Worley, quiet and introspective, was a loner who did not talk much. Other Boots did not pay much attention to him, nor think much of him. Some of the privates liked to make jokes and poke fun at him. They mistook his easy, quiet, far away-in-thought attitude to mean he was "slow" and a dummy.

Private Rey Mejia learned otherwise. About three-quarters through boot camp, he was paired with Worley to stand guard over the rest of the platoon's gear. They began talking, a little at a time. Private Mejia asked him why he put up with the hazing some of the others gave him. Worley just shrugged his shoulders, as if he did not care, and smiled a bit, as if to say the teasing did not bother him much.

"He's been through this before," Private Mejia thought to himself, noting that his companion on guard duty had strong, rough features and looked older than his 19-years. Private Worley's hands had the toughened appearance of someone who had had to work hard. His smile and his hands told a story; Private Mejia saw in them a rough life. What Private Worley did not tell him was that he once had a stepmother who had burned his fingers when she caught him biting his nails, or that he was once made to stand up outside for hours in the sun, holding on to a pole.

Private Mejia was a deep thinker himself. He recognized that Ken was not a dummy, nor stupid. As he got to know him, he began to see Worley as he really was. Above all the meanness of this world, Private Worley saw the world different than most. He knew that people could be mean, but seemed able to see beyond cruelties. Sure of himself, Worley always tried to make the best of what came his way.

Of course, two privates in boot camp do not tend to talk to each other about such things. When Private Mejia found out Ken was from Modesto, he told him he was from just down the road a little, in Fresno. The privates understood where their training was going to take them, and Rey said he would visit Ken when they got back from Vietnam. Rey had sisters, one of whom lived in Modesto.

"Okay," Ken simply said to the idea.

As the two talked a while longer, Private Mejia told him about his family.

As others would remember later, Private Worley did not say much about his family. He just listened. To Private Mejia it seemed like Ken did not have a family. Ken talked a bit about a little sister and his mom and dad in Modesto and that was it.

After their day on guard duty, the two did not talk much again until they arrived in Vietnam. But from that day on, Private Mejia thought of Ken in a different way. Without understanding why, he recognized that Private Worley was a special person, one with "a real kind spirit."

There it is, "spirit." While author James Brady mentioned *espirit de corps* as being part of the Marine boot camp experience, there is more to this. The *spirit* within Medal of Honor recipients was consistently obvious to others before they entered combat. Childhood friends, school companions, and teammates recalled it, and fellow recruits recognized it early in training.

Today, Rey understands that the memories of friends left behind in Vietnam will follow him all his life. The emotions are deeply felt and when he tries to write about them, he puts his pen down after a time. He has been blessed in life, married since 1981 and with five children, now adults beginning their own families. Rey believes it is because of men like Ken Worley that he came home. His gratitude towards and admiration of his fellow Marine is evident in his writing.

Private Worley's training went well, and he was promoted at the expected times. While he was at boot camp, Quonieta traveled to Hawaii and married her high school boyfriend. Her marriage did not change the affection Ken felt for her. Following recruit training, he was transferred to Camp Pendleton in August 1967, for individual combat training and basic infantry training, which he completed in October.

He visited the Feyerherms when he could, a trip made easy by Don's penchant for moving. Don had moved the family to Anaheim after Ken had left for recruit training. Ken took leave and visited the family for the last time after his orders to Vietnam came that November, five months after he had enlisted.

Lima Company, 3d Battalion in Vietnam

Private First Class Worley arrived in Vietnam on Friday, November 24, 1967. His boot camp friend, Private First Class Mejia, was transferred to the 5th Marines in mid-December.

Monsoon rains and cold weather did not stop the Marines from patrolling, but they did reduce the number of enemy encounters. Private First Class Worley was introduced to listening posts, small-scale patrols, nighttime ambushes, wary sleep, overhead illumination flares, the echoes of mortar rounds dropping down tubes and arching into the sky, convoy security details, radio watch, booby traps, swollen rivers, and flooded rice paddies. The rain began to subside in late December and the temperatures warmed. Enemy sniper and sapper attacks escalated.

Private First Class Worley served as a rifleman and machine gunner with the 3d Battalion, 7th Marines in the Da Nang area of Quang Nam Province. The 3/7, seeming to be consistently among the "first to fight," had a proud history dating all the way back to Guadalcanal in WWII. Ten of its Marines had already earned Medals of Honor across the three wars, the last of whom was Roy Mitchell Wheat of K Company. On August 11, 1967, Lance Corporal Wheat dived onto an antipersonnel mine to protect two other Marines from the detonation. Five more 3/7 Marines would go on to earn the Medal after Ken, the most recent being in Iraq on April 22, 2004.

Company L, 3d Battalion, had been in Vietnam from the beginning. General William Westmoreland, the head of Military Assistance Command-Vietnam, had requested a Marine battalion to be dispatched to Qhi Nhon, a major American logistics base with little protection, 175 miles south of Da Nang. The 3rd Battalion came ashore on July 1, 1965, to guard the base. The battalion also participated the next month, August 18, in the first major Marine offensive action in Vietnam: *Operation Starlight*. The Battalion engaged 1500 veteran fighters of the Viet Cong's Main Force Regiment on the Van Tuong Peninsula, 15 miles southeast of Chu Lai airfield.

The 7th Marines were moved onto a series of low hills southwest of Da Nang, Quang Nam Province, where they remained for most of the war, part of the defensive perimeter protecting the airfield from attack. In an agricultural district, the hills sat amidst rivers and rice fields. Depending on assignments, moving on and off one, moving from one to another, Private First Class Worley lived out the remainder of his life on these hills.

The Regimental Command Post was established on Hill 55, (Nui Dat Son on some tactical maps) located between the Yen and Vu Gia rivers in Dien Ban District, on grid maps at coordinates AT970620. The Marines needed to move men and material quickly across the Song Thu Bon south to An Hoa or to a jump off point for various operations particularly on Go Noi Island. Down river to the southwest of Hill 55, the Marines constructed Liberty Bridge at coordinates AT923532, in Dai Loc District. The bridge was a point of contention with the Viet Cong, was under attack constantly, and destroyed and rebuilt more than once.

Between Hill 55 and the Liberty Bridge sat Hill 37 at coordinates AT916582. An old French Colonial Fort dominated the hill. A solid stone structure, with good walls, overlooking the plains at an elevation of over 130 feet, the old fort was ideal as a command bunker. During the monsoon rains, when the Song Vu Ghia and nearby rivers flooded, Hill 37 became an Island. A landing pad allowed dry helo transport onto and off the hill.

First Lieutenant David Noyes graduated from The Officers' Basic School at Quantico in August 1967. He arrived in Vietnam that October, reporting to the 3d Battalion Command Post on Hill 37. He was in command of a Mike Company platoon, when Private First Class Worley arrived in country in November. The following February, First Lieutenant Noyes became the Battalion Intelligence Officer at the Hill 37 CP, until he requested to go back into the field. He was given command of First Platoon, Lima Company in May and served as their Executive Officer. [3]

As he had done wherever he was remembered, Private First Class Worley made an impression on others. Marines who had survived boot camp with him, trained with him, and gone to Vietnam with him experienced him as a good, quiet person. At one point, he was assigned temporary duty in the mess hall on Hill 37. He made friends with Marines from other 3/7 companies while there. He did not talk about having any family. Later, the Marines of Lima Company and Mike Company who came home would recall him as having been a fine person and would think of him often. [4]

In country for a month, on a hill in Vietnam, Private First Class Worley might have been remembering Christmas with the Feyerherm family the previous year; the best he had ever known. But, Modesto would have seemed a world away. Christmas 1967 was quiet for the Divisions of Marines in Vietnam, but not necessarily peaceful and relaxing. A cease-fire had been established with the North Vietnamese, in part to respect their traditional new year, *Tet*. The year of the Monkey, according to the Chinese/Vietnamese calendar, was about to commence. Private First Class Worley was among the more than 5,025 Marines fighting in Vietnam that year who would not live to celebrate Christmas 1968.

In a calculated, strategic move the NVA used the quiet time to prepare for a major offensive. They began staging tens of thousands of soldiers and tons of materiel to the north of the 17th Parallel and along the border in Laos. The Marines, wary of the lull in combat, dug in for an expected assault in places like Khe Sanh and Vandegrift Combat Base. Cease-fire or not, the Marines in the Da Nang area were on 100 percent alert.

Private First Class Worley and Quonieta Feyerherm wrote often to each other. He talked about being lonely, of going out on patrols, and of the men with whom he was serving. Being a Marine had become like being in a real family, and he had a sense of belonging. He wrote about things he would like to do with his life once he was back home. When Quonieta's son, Robert, was born January 21, 1968, she wrote to let Ken know. He wrote back expressing how happy he was for her, letting her know that he loved her and the baby. Quonieta did not learn until years later that Rob was Ken's son, but she believes Ken might have believed he was the father right from the start. [5] The birth of a son might have been on Private First Class Worley's mind, but matters closer at hand also had his attention.

For days prior to Tet, the enemy forces were massing and probing. Da Nang was under attack. In the early hours of January 31, Tet, the full NVA offensive began. Nearly 100,000 North Vietnamese soldiers swept into the south and, in a surprise move, simultaneously attacked the capital city in every province. Six major cities, thirty-six provincial capitals, twenty-three airfields and military bases all came under siege. Da Nang was one of the major cities attacked.

Whatever hill Private First Class Worley might have been on, he experienced a thunderous mortar bombardment. At 11:45 AM he was involved in an intense fight in a rice paddy about 2,000 meters west of Hill 55, on the other side of a bend in the Yen River, as both Lima and Mike Companies blocked the advance of a large-sized enemy unit. [6] Engagements with enemy forces continued on and around the 7th Marine's sector until February 14.

Private First Class Ken Worley wrote regularly to the Feyerherms while he was a Marine. His letters arrived for his siblings, for Don and Rose, and for the entire family. His growing maturity was evident in his writing. Initially, he was uncertain of the American involvement in the conflict. His letters from Vietnam took a more serious, somber tone as his nine months in-country passed. In one of his last letters to Rose, he expressed a sense of understanding his purpose in being in Vietnam.

The Feyerherms would long cherish those letters.

Promoted in May 1968, four days after his birthday and at the end of the north monsoon season, Lance Corporal Worley saw a good share of combat in Vietnam. He had demonstrated his bravery countless times in five major combat campaigns, as reflected in the four bronze campaign stars attached to his Vietnam Service Medal. He was remembered to have pulled an injured platoon commander to safety during one firefight.

Although his level of valor and heroism was evident to his companions, it would become unquestionable to the Nation before autumn reached America. Lance Corporal Worley must have participated in the March *Operation Nutcracker* when the 7th Marines struck back at the enemy after Tet. *Operation Worth* followed in April. Then in the spring when the 36th and 38th North Vietnamese Regiments positioned themselves for an attack on Da Nang, the Marines launched *Operation Allen Brook* to stop them. The May through August operation would be the longest for Lance Corporal Worley.

Looking northwest, the Regimental Commander on Hill 55 could see another hill across the Yen River. Largely cleared of any vegetation, at grid AT934664 and an elevation of 135 feet, the Combat Base on Hill 41, sitting above Phuoc Nhan village, was occupied by companies of the 7th Marines. Engineers had carved out roads. Hill 41 could seem a barren place, covered with rock and rusty colored soil. It was a terribly muddy place from May to September when the south monsoon set in. Having lived in arid places in New Mexico and the dry places of southern California, Lance Corporal Worley must have experienced more rain during his nine months in Vietnam than he had ever seen before.

To the west and northwest of the command post were lush, green-covered mountains. The hill faced the entrance to Happy Valley and the climb up Charlie Ridge was to the west. The Marines had so named these places because the area was a primary infiltration route for the Viet Cong intent on having Da Nang for themselves. Happy Valley, with its streams and six to eight-feet-tall elephant grass, was also an enemy staging area favored by NVA 122-mm rocket units. Charlie Ridge, enveloped in choking vegetation, was a ten-mile-long mountain range rising to above 3,600 feet. Triple canopy trees added another 125 feet to the ridge elevations. The crest was often shrouded in fog or clouds. Besides the enemy enclaves, caves and camps, and unfriendly hamlets, tangles of vines, low scrub brush, deep gorges, and steep cliffs made passage along Charlie Ridge most inhospitable for the Marines.

Firefights were a constant on Hill 41, as if the Viet Cong had the command post surrounded. Rocket, RPG, and mortar attacks were so frequent that Lance Corporal Worley, like his Lima Company companions, likely learned to go about his duties, ignoring the attacks. First Lieutenant Noyes recalled that the mortar attacks would zero in on the Hill's mess hall and Officer and NCO clubs. The RPG and rocket attacks were more likely to gain the attention of the Marines, since the Viet Cong had to be close to launch those projectiles.

The August humidity brought heaviness to the air and the temperatures were beyond 100 degrees. In the days ahead, in addition to battle casualties, nearly half of Lima fell exhausted by the heat. Lacking reinforcements, platoon strength was down to 20-25 men, depleted by the casualties. Short of men, a mess sergeant was assigned as the platoon sergeant. Determining that the sergeant was inexperienced in combat and could not read a grid map, First Lieutenant Noyes replaced him with a corporal.

Personnel changes were frequent and common among Marine units in Vietnam. Marines went where they were needed. Moving from hill to hill, sometimes patrolling through waist-deep water, and transitioning from one platoon to another might have been familiar to Lance Corporal Worley and reminiscent of his childhood displacements.

First Lieutenant Noyes, having led the platoon and Lance Corporal Worley through three months of combat engagements, stayed on as Lima Company Executive Officer when Second Lieutenant Hewitt, fresh from Quantico, was placed in command of First Platoon in August. First Lieutenant Noyes remained in the XO position until November when he rotated back to the States.

In addition to the rising August temperatures, combat engagements were also going to heat up more for the Marines. The Viet Cong were planning to begin another offensive on Monday, August 12, by attacking more than 150 targets in South Vietnam.

Heroism at Bo Ban Hamlet

On a Sunday night in August, at 7:45, Lance Corporal Worley left Hill 41 with eleven other Marines and elements of Lima Company patrolling for enemy forces in western Hieu Duc District. The evening temperature was about 95 degrees Fahrenheit and the humidity was up over 80 percent. The temperature might drop into the mid-80s by dawn. Like most Marines after months in the bush, Lance Corporal Worley had likely dropped twenty percent of his body weight since arriving in Vietnam.

A 45-cal pistol on his web belt, a plastic bottle of lubricant strapped to his helmet, he carried his 7.62mm, M-60 machine gun loaded with a belt of ammo ready to fire. Additional ammo belts were slung across his shoulders. The weight of his M-60, an additional nineteen pounds, would have been of no concern to Lance Corporal Worley. He had quickly mastered the use of the weapon in training in Da Nang, later remembered by his trainer as "the most focused guy I'd ever met." Gung ho to a degree, Lance Corporal Worley was "solemn and serious" at the same time. [7] His assistant gunner trailed behind him, carrying more machine-gun ammunition.

Reaching Bo Ban Hamlet, about ten miles southwest of Da Nang and fifteen miles northwest of Hoi An, the patrol intended to set up a night ambush along a trail into the hamlet. Setting up an ambush site would not have been the only thing on their minds, however. Besides relentless mosquitoes and parasitic leeches, those who served in the bush, rice fields, and jungles of Vietnam were watchful of booby traps set by the enemy. Trails might have made for easier movement, but they made for dangerous passage. Night had closed in, overcast. Moisture was in the air.

Lance Corporal Worley fell into a hole as they approached Bo Ban and wrenched his right thigh. Their corpsman, Doc Kevin Reade, provided first aid. Rather than return to Base, and despite his injured leg, the young combat veteran hobbled forward. They stopped 50 meters from the original ambush site. In a flat, wooded area stood a hut, surrounded by the cover of dense shrubbery. The squad took positions in the hut. When security was positioned, the main body of the ambush set up for some sleep. Doc Reade was right beside Lance Corporal Worley.

Once they were hunkered down, Lance Corporal Worley gave his Seiko wristwatch to his companion, Lance Corporal Charles G. Black, to keep track of time during sentry duty. The two had become friends, talking late into the nights about getting home and what they wanted to do once back in the States.

Why the Marines took shelter in the hut in Bo Ban caused some consternation later. Experienced combat Marines knew better. Doing so gave the enemy an advantage. Hooches required a protective perimeter outside: more men. Tossing grenades through a door or window provided the Viet Cong immediate protection and the ease of slipping back into the darkness from which they had come.

Bo Ban has no place on most maps. It was hardly a village or hamlet. Comprised of fewer than twenty buildings, surrounded by woods and rice paddies, it was a place to traverse quickly and with caution. While the scenery provided by green caribe-pine forest covered hills, small villages, countryside, and quiet rivers might give the area a peaceful appearance, Bo Ban has a history that suggests otherwise. The area had an important strategic location because of its proximity to Da Nang City.

In the early 19th century, the locals built a Communal House to worship the village gods and bygone sages and to celebrate annual festivals. In August 1945, the people gathered at the house to demonstrate against French Colonialism. Bo Ban was the first local polling booth in January 1946, for the national congress election of the Democratic Republic of Viet Nam. [8] Earlier, in 1939, the French had established a military defense base nearby for protecting Da Nang, bringing extended bitter fighting between the French army and local troops, until the French capitulated power in 1954.

When the American military began building up its forces in 1964, the local Bo Ban people again gathered at the Communal House and decided to wipe out the enemy "mercenaries." They began confiscating the arms and storehouses in the District. The Viet Cong intended to saturate the area with their presence and launch rocket attacks against the Da Nang airbase. Their activity would always be strong around Bo Ban; Marines knew to expect landmines, booby-traps, ambushes, and local hostility when maneuvering and patrolling there.

Most places in Vietnam provided hostile environments to the Marines and required bravery to pass through, pause in, or "set up" on them. Some places took on greater significance due to the battles that were fought there. Khe Sanh, the Rockpile, Cam Lo, the A Shau Valley, Chu Lai, the Arizona Territory, Liberty Road, Con Thien, Hue City, and Charlie Ridge are among the places where more than one Marine went "above and beyond" and earned a Medal of Honor. Bo Ban hamlet was also such a place.

Lester William Weber of Aurora, Illinois, west of Chicago, three months younger than Ken, was assigned duties as a Second Platoon machinegun squad leader for Company M, 3d Battalion, 7th Marines. Six months after Lance Corporal Worley went to the Bo Ban ambush site, Lance Corporal Weber, near the end of his tour, earned a Medal of Honor when he launched a one-man assault to help extract a squad of Marines who had been on patrol around Bo Ban and had come under assault by an entrenched battalion-size force of Communist guerrillas.

The Marines in some locales had an understanding that, in significant ways, "the night belonged to the VC." Dawn tended to bring a sense of relief when those on the ground could again call upon air, artillery and Naval gunfire for support. In the dark of early Monday morning, at 5:55 on August 12, 1968, there would be no chance to call for support of any kind. The Marines with Lance Corporal Worley were awakened by warnings their platoon leader, Second Lieutenant Hewitt, shouted out.

"Grenades!"

The enemy had detected the site of the ambush, likely with the aid of Bo Ban residents, slipped past security, and had thrown four grenades into the hooch in which the Marines were sleeping. One of the grenades rolled near Lance Corporal Worley and five of his companions. Immediately alert and recognizing the danger, he dived onto the grenade, ensuring the protection of the others as the grenades detonated.

Lance Corporal Kenneth Worley, 20-years-old, his body shattered and severed, died instantly in Bo Ban Hamlet.

The Marines who had known him and gone to battle with him would not forget him. The news of his death and his valor circulated through Lima Company the next day. A sergeant in another platoon wrote, "I still remember the day. Just as I remember the day Kennedy was killed." [9] Thirty-six years after his death, one of the Marines saved by his actions expressed it clearly: "Even to this day I feel the loss of his friendship and camaraderie." [10]

And the memories held are consistent, no matter the passage of time. Ken was engaging and kind. He was quiet, talking little about his life prior to Modesto.

"He was a straight-shooter and an overall good guy." [11]

The grenade blasts at the Bo Ban ambush site shattered the crystal of Ken's Seiko, held by Lance Corporal Black, the young Marine who had stood watch before the attack. Injured in the grenade blasts, Lance Corporal Black spent six months in the hospital recovering. Although the Seiko had never worked again, he kept the damaged timepiece in memory of his slain companion. Some thirty-six years later, the former Marine returned the watch to Quonieta and her son.

After the Bo Ban fatality, the Marines attempted to notify the Feyerherms, Ken's family of record in Modesto. Rose, a government computer keypunch operator, was working at Seal Beach Naval Weapons Station, which sits on the Pacific Coast between Long Beach and Huntington Beach. The family's whereabouts was determined when one of her friends provided the Marines a telephone number. Rose was informed of the death over the phone, before the Marine contingent pulled up in the green sedan and walked to the family's door. During the funeral services, Don kept vigil over his foster son, who was dressed in his Marine Dress Blues and laying in an open casket with a glass cover.

Forty years had passed since family and friends said their goodbyes to Ken in his casket and watched him be lowered into the donated grave. Had it not been for the MOH inscription on his weathered grave marker, Ken's story might have ended there. His kind of bravery is an example of what happens when someone remembers it.

No matter the passing of time, bravery inspires action. Tributes to Ken were under consideration in two different locations; in one place because someone walked past his grave, and in another place because someone was proud to have lived in a community in which a Medal of Honor recipient had been born.

CHAPTER 6
Farmington Remembers Its Hero

Give them the meed they have won in the past;
Give them the honors their merits forecast;
Give them the chaplets they won in the strife:
Give them the laurels they lost with their life. [1]

William "Will" McKendree Carleton, American poet, (1845–1912)

After George Grupe stood at Ken Worley's grave on Memorial Day 2002, the initiatives to pay fitting tribute to the fallen Medal of Honor Marine gained momentum. The California AMVETS Service Foundation was asked to pledge a $10,000 contribution.

In the City of Westminster, California, April 21, 2004, City Council meeting, Mayor Margie L. Rice said she would like to see the City do something to acknowledge Lance Corporal Worley. In their May 19 meeting, the City Council, acknowledging that Ken had no family, unanimously approved a motion to grant honorary Westminster citizenship to him so that the city could honor his service.

Leaving Ken's gravesite in Westminster Memorial Park, driving east on Bolsa Avenue for five miles, a visitor can find the community of Santa Ana's Civic Center. Just off North Broadway, near the Hall of Administration, forty large American flags fly over the Medal of Honor Memorial. Then, a semicircle of eight three-foot-high concrete pedestals looked upon a central four-sided monument that honors servicemen who served in WWI, WWII, Korea, and Vietnam.

Bronze plaques are fixed to the pedestals, each telling the story of an Orange County servicemen who has earned a Medal of Honor, one in WWI, five in WWII, and one each in Korea and Vietnam. Two Marines, Kenneth Ambrose Walsh, the fourth ranking USMC World War II fighter "Ace" pilot, and William Earl Barber, of the Korea breakout at the Chosin Reservoir have pedestals. Dedicated in 1998, the tribute is called the *Walk of Honor* Memorial.

On Thursday, May 27, 2004, more than 200 visitors made sure they were at the Orange County Circle of Honor along Santa Ana's Walk of Honor before 1:00 PM. Quonieta Murphy and Ken's son, Robert, were present, their travel from Oregon paid for by local veterans. High school history students were among the crowd. George Grupe, Jack Closson, Jeff Sharp, AMVETS Post 18 commander, Veteran Don Zweifel, and Larry Muhlenforth, who had trained Lance Corporal Worley in the use of an M-60 machinegun in Vietnam, were pleased with the turnout.

The sounds of a bugler, a bagpiper, and twenty-one rifle shots echoed across the Civic Center. U.S. District Judge David Carter, a former Marine and decorated Vietnam veteran, gave the keynote address. They had gathered that day to dedicate a ninth pedestal to the Walk of Honor, paid for by the California AMVETS Service Foundation. The new plaque that had been added was dedicated to Lance Corporal Kenneth Worley.

The Seiko wristwatch Ken had worn into Bo Ban hamlet was presented to Quonieta and Robert at the Santa Ana ceremony. [2]

The next month, June 2004, up Route 605 eleven miles northwest of Ken's resting place, a youth education and service program was named in his honor in Bellflower. The Lance Corporal Kenneth L. Worley Young Marine unit, "a living memorial" to the Medal recipient, is under retired Marine First Sergeant Jack Closson's dedicated guidance. [3, 4] Ken's bravery became an inspiration for boys and girls, ages eight to eighteen years, who have served in the youth education and service program.

Westminster is fittingly proud of Ken Worley, though the young Marine likely never even passed through the city. Four years after Ken's plaque was dedicated at Santa Ana's Walk of Honor, B. J. Savage, former Marine and retired Westminster Deputy Chief of Police, presented a request at the June 11, 2008, Westminster City Council/Agency Board Regular Meeting. He had discovered in 2006 that a Medal of Honor recipient was buried at Westminster Memorial Park. Without knowing much about Ken's life, a commitment emerged to see a permanent memorial erected to honor the young man's service and heroism. [5]

The City Council considered honoring the 40th anniversary of Ken's death by placing a memorial plaque at the Vietnam Memorial in Sid Goldstein Freedom Park, next to the Westminster Civic Center, a few blocks northeast of Ken's final resting place. [6] A motion was made in favor of the request; it was seconded, and then passed by a 5-0 vote. [7]

People began arriving at the Westminster Civic Center flagpoles well before 1:00 PM on Saturday, August 29, 2009. For the third straight day, the temperature had surpassed 100 degrees in parched Orange County. Blue awnings, matching the color of the overhead sky, provided shade from the bright sunshine for rows of chairs as the temperature rose to 105 degrees.

A Marine Color Guard from Camp Pendleton arrived in their Summer Dress uniforms. The Commanding General of the 1st Marine Division, the 1st Marine Division Band, Vietnam veterans groups, and members of the 1st Marine Division Association gathered. At 12:30 PM, Jack Closson and Nelson and Terry Rodriguez del Rey formed up the Kenneth Lee Worley Young Marines, no fewer than 36 strong, in their red unit t-shirts, camouflaged utilities, and ribbons. The NCOs wore their Class "C" uniforms. The Young Marines were there to provide an Honor Guard. The Nicholson Pipes and Drums performed in honor of the Medal of Honor Marine, then dead for forty-one years.

Rey Mejia, the Boot Camp comrade who had deployed to Vietnam with Lance Corporal Worley, was there. Westminster's mayor, a Federal Judge, a District Congressman, and B. J. Savage were pleased to greet the crowd of citizens sitting under the awnings. A Vietnam Veterans motorcycle club formed a line in the rear, standing watch over the proceedings.

Nell Swisher, Ken's foster sister, had traveled from Escondido and sat among the guests of honor. Of all who attended, only she and Rey Mejia had known Ken personally. In the crowd of over one hundred were private citizens like Eric and Pati Walz, who had for years been learning about Ken and had driven up from Temecula to witness this tribute. [8] The local TV station sent out a cameraman to record the ceremony. They had all gathered for a formal groundbreaking ceremony. A memorial plaque was to be dedicated by the City to Lance Corporal Kenneth L. Worley.

The formal dedication of Lance Corporal Worley's plaque took place at the Westminster Civic Center, 11:00 AM, on Veterans Day, November 11, 2009, the day after the Marine Corps 234th Birthday. The plaque sits beneath three flagpoles, topped by the photograph of Ken under helmet, and flanked by the Medal of Honor emblem and the Marine Corps emblem. Over his name are the proud words upon which Corps training is built: Honor-Courage-Commitment. His Medal Citation is inscribed under his name.

In Farmington, Ken's birthplace, where he lived until graduating from elementary school, local residents began to awaken to his heroic legacy. Debra Mayeux's *Farmington Daily Times* July 13, 2008, headline story had an impact. Readers expressed their support for a Memorial to the forgotten Marine. These included Donel L. Swisher who was moved by the idea that Kenny was "find[ing] his way home to Farmington" after forty years and hoped the community would recognize this hero and "Farmington son." [9]

During their Work Session the following Tuesday, the Farmington City Council discussed Debra's article and whether the city should be involved in creating a memorial for their Medal of Honor recipient. The mayor was hesitant. What were Ken's ties to the community? One councilman expressed support for the city to provide a location for a memorial, but believed such a project should be privately funded.

The Council's hesitance is understandable. It makes sense that a community would want to know as much as possible about a hometown hero before it went about erecting a monument to his memory. The Marines had witnesses to Ken's heroism who left no doubts about the kind of man he had become. But, what of his childhood in Farmington? Who had he been and what had he contributed?

A handful of Farmington residents continued to advocate that the Medal of Honor Marine be recognized. The City Council, Chamber of Commerce, the Marine Corps League 736, and the New Mexico Secretary of Veterans Services became more invested in a memorial around October 2008. Through all of this, a controversy was ignited: what fitting Memorial should be dedicated to this native son? Some proposed a plaque on a stone in the local park, others advocated for a bronze sculpture of the young Marine. Some were opposed to a monument for Ken alone, proposing inclusion of other veterans.

"Few dispute he was a hero." [10]

Newspaper headlines followed in *The Daily Times*. *Memorial for fallen soldier stalls: No money raised for Marine's remembrance*, by Steve Lynn, January 3, 2009. *City, veterans should resolve memorial issue*, January 7, 2009. *Donations sought for Marine's memorial*, January 8, 2009. Readers began posting Internet comments. One Albuquerque reader wrote on Saturday, January 3: "Oh and it's not too much to ask for someone who has made the ultimate sacrifice for their Country. In fact a little City funding for the memorial to be placed somewhere in Orchard Park would be an excellent place. I think a full size statue, similar to the Minuteman in Lexington, MA would be great, listing the citation of LCpl. Worley's receiving the CMOH is very fitting." On January 18, Jack Lengyel wrote from Surprise, Arizona: "I believe a statue of Medal of Honor recipient Kenneth Lee Worley is the appropriate way to recognize his valor to his fellowmen and country. We should do no less to honor this brave American." [11]

The newspaper printed a simple poll, asking readers to vote a preference. When the polling closed on January 19, the results seemed conclusive. 602 votes had been cast. 287 votes (47.67%) favored a bronze statue. 168 votes were for a stone with a plaque (27.90%), 112 votes

(18.60%) were for anything that did not involve public money. 35 votes (5.813%) preferred some other idea.

The matter of a Farmington memorial had reached a compromise of sorts, but had not been concluded. As a *Daily Times* staff writer reported, "Farmington's once forgotten soldier finally will get his mark on the community." [12]

A little bit of a walk south and east from the old Deal property where Ken grew up on North Allen, off San Juan Boulevard and at the end of South Tucker Avenue is what some call "Cobble Center." On the river walk, at a bend along the north banks of the Animas River in Berg Park, is Farmington's All Veterans Memorial Park. A tribute to men and women who served to preserve the freedoms of our nation, the park recognizes and honors the contributions of America's veterans from the Revolutionary War through the present and into the future. [13]

By April 2009, a memorial for Ken was in the planning stages, to be erected in the All Veterans Memorial Park. At a total cost of $58,000, funded primarily by private donations, the memorial was to be comprised of four, five-foot columns of Animas river rock, each displaying a copper plaque. One column would have a bronze eagle at its top with a plaque explaining the Congressional Medal of Honor. The other three columns would be dedicated to Farmington's Medal of Honor recipients, each with a plaque of their Citation, under a proclamation, "Above And Beyond The Call Of Duty."

The city established a reserve fund of $10,000, if the project needed to be supplemented. [14, 15] Referred to as the *Three Heroes Memorial*, the pillar-pyramid to Ken, locally known as the "once forgotten soldier," was initially expected to be built and dedicated by Veterans Day, November 11, 2009. [16]

Memorial Day weekend, May 23, 2009, came, a thunderous and rainy Saturday. The red, white, and blue balloons bunched up around All Veterans Memorial Park withstood the weather, as did those who gathered for the groundbreaking of the Medal of Honor recipients' monument. The mayor was there with city officials, family, servicemen, veterans, U.S. Senator Tom Udall (D-NM), and House Representative Ben Ray Luján, Jr. (D-NM).

Bruce Salisbury, the local historian and veteran who had worked so tirelessly for Ken to be recognized in his hometown had not been invited to the ceremony. The speakers who gave credit to themselves for their year of work did not mention him. His name did not appear in the two newspaper articles written about the long-awaited memorial. [17] Bruce attended the event anyway, leaving early from his 60th Farmington High School reunion and 52 fellow graduates, to be there. The first chance he had, he approached Senator Udall and Representative Luján with an idea. The Farmington Post Office building had no name. Perhaps a Joint Resolution to name the Post Office in honor of Ken Worley could be entered at the next Legislature session. The lawmakers seemed to like the idea. [18]

Bruce had not given up on the idea of a statue commemorating the local hero. If Farmington did not want the bronze statue, maybe the Marines would agree to have the tribute erected at Camp Lejuene, North Carolina, or any other Marine base. Reaching out to active and former Marine Corps personnel, Marine Corps Reservists and all families and friends of Marines, he continued to advocate for "a bronze figure of this Medal Of Honor Hero, standing easy, along with a Young Marine." [19]

The Mount KIA/MIA Memorial, a nonprofit organization, voted the Kenneth Worley Bronze as their first major fundraiser. Tom White, a well-known Maine sculptor, began donating his time to sketch drawings of the Kenneth Worley and Young Marine Bronze statue in an effort to help with fund raising. [20]

Another idea had begun to fester with Bruce in January 2009. It seemed fitting that the Navy should commission a ship in honor of his hometown hero. He consulted with a friend, retired Navy Rear Admiral Bruce Black, about this possibility. By July he was ready to send the request to the Secretary of the Navy, the Honorable Raymond E. Mabus, Jr., asking him to consider naming a ship in tribute of Ken. Bruce took his proposal to Congressman Ben Ray Lujan on August 26. The Congressman committed to personally contacting the Secretary of the Navy concerning the request when he returned to D.C.

The research for this effort brought to mind another Marine. Corporal Jason L. Dunham was from the small town of Scio, on the

Genesee River in the Allegheny Mountains of western New York. He was assigned as a squad leader for Company Kilo, 3rd Battalion (Ken Worley's Battalion), 7th Marines in September 2003. A little after noon on April 14, 2004, Corporal Dunham rushed with his 14-man team to the town of Husaybah, Iraq, to reinforce a convoy that had been taken under attack. During a skirmish, he yelled a warning, covered a charged grenade with his Kevlar helmet and fell on it. Corporal Jason Dunham, 22-years-old, died of his wounds at 4:43 PM on April 22, 2004.

President George W. Bush authorized on March 14, 2006 that the U.S. Post Office building in Scio be named after him. The president announced on November 10, 2006 that Corporal Dunham would be awarded a Medal of Honor, the first Marine in the Iraqi War to be so honored and the first since Vietnam.

The Navy named a 520-foot guided missile destroyer, DDG-109, in his honor, as well as a barracks at the King's Bay Naval Submarine Base, Georgia, where he had served in the security force company for two years. USS *Jason Dunham*, the 59th destroyer in her class, is the 56th ship named to honor a Medal of Honor Marine. Bath Iron Works in Bath, Maine, built the ship. Jason's mother was selected by the Navy to be the ship's sponsor. The USS *Jason Dunham* was christened August 1, 2009, five years after Corporal Dunham's death, and officially commissioned November 13, 2010. The ship's homeport is Norfolk, Virginia.

Jason's story has been told in *The Gift of Valor*, a book by Wall Street journalist Michael M. Phillips, who was embedded with his battalion at the time of the Husaybah ambush, and in a chapter within *Uncommon Valor: The Medal of Honor and the Six Warriors Who Earned It in Afghanistan and Iraq.* [21] His life is chronicled on several Web sites, including jasonsmemorial.org.

Bruce Salisbury spent hours looking at the sites honoring Jason Dunham, especially the memorial page featuring a slide show of Jason's life. That tribute to Jason put in contrast the two known photos Bruce had of Ken Worley and made the Farmington hero's "lonely life stand out in more stark terms." The tributes to Jason strengthened Bruce's resolve to see a memorial to Ken in his hometown and to pursue the

naming of a ship. [22] Should the Secretary of the Navy endorse this tribute, the USS *Kenneth Lee Worley* would be the 57th ship named in honor
of a Marine Medal of Honor recipient.

Bruce set up his VFW booth for the August 10-16, 2009 San Juan
County Fair, touted as the largest county fair in New Mexico. He had
a quality, white on green street sign made reading WORLEY WAY.
Under the sign he positioned a large photo of Kenneth, his Citation,
and other available data. Several people came by the booth more than
once to talk about Ken. Folks who just wanted to honor the young man
in the photo shed tears.

As had been true in the past, some long-time locals had knowledge of the Worley and Deal families, but were reticent to talk more
about the past in such a public setting as a county fair. One was a
woman whose brother is a VFW Post member. The same age as Ken,
her brother would have gone to the same schools for eight years. Bruce
hoped to one day have a chat with him.

On the second day of the fair, a Farmington businessman who
had set up a commercial booth just aisles away from the VFW booth
stopped by to visit a little. Clyde Chappell, a retired USMC lieutenant colonel and Vietnam Veteran, expressed surprise that the young
man in the photo under WORLEY WAY had served in the 3/7 during *Tet*. The name did not register with Clyde, who had been a 3/7
Company Commanding Officer during and after Tet. He recalled that
"the Battalion was so screwed up and replacing men so fast during Tet,"
that it did not surprise him that he did not remember the Marine by
name. Clyde was assigned as the 3/7 Battalion Commander three weeks
after the ambush at Bo Ban. [23]

The connections to Ken in Farmington seemed to be multiplying,
some private, some ironic, and some miraculous. He might have been
born into circumstances of little renown and a family lacking prestige,
but he would eventually hold a position of esteem in the New Mexico
community.

On Friday, October 23, 2009, Michael Doyle, reporter for the
McClatchy Newspapers in Washington, D.C. wrote "California

lawmakers seek to have ship named for Vietnam War hero." California Democratic Senators Dianne Feinstein and Barbara Boxer, Representative Dana Rohrabacher, R-Huntington Beach, Representative George P. Radanovich, R-Mariposa, Representative Dennis Cardoza, D-Merced, and New Mexico Representatives Ben Ray Lujan, D-Santa Fe, and Harry Teague, D-Hobbs, were all signatories to a letter sent to Navy Secretary Raymond E. Mabus Jr. dated October 26, 2009, requesting that this tribute be extended to Ken. [24]

In five brief paragraphs, the letter to Secretary Mabus went beyond the details of Ken's Medal of Honor Citation, noting his background; "To fully understand the sacrifice made by LCpl Worley, we believe it is necessary to look not only at his service as a Marine, but the hardship he overcame to become one...orphaned at a young age...evident to us that the sacrifices he made while growing up helped him develop into the selfless hero he became as a Marine...can think of no finer tribute to LCpl Worley, his family, and his fellow Marines than to name a Navy vessel in his honor."

Meanwhile, construction of the *Three Heroes Monument* progressed in Farmington's All Veterans Memorial Park. The city and San Juan County each provided $10,000, and another $3,500 was contributed through private donations. On Tuesday, October 27, the mayor invited Bruce Salisbury to attend the Dedication ceremony, to be held November 7, 2009. [25] Bruce began notifying others, including Quonieta Murphy, Ken's son Robert, Donel Swisher, Sharon Houston, Jack Closson, and retired Admiral Bruce Black, sending them "Invitations to The Dedication at All Veterans Plaza."

The Farmington *Daily Times* also posted the announcement with photos of the four memorial pillars, on Monday, November 2. According to the article, the city chose to have the unveiling ceremony on Saturday instead of November 11, Veterans Day, to avoid any conflict with the Aztec veterans parade. The article cited Bruce's efforts to have Ken recognized in his hometown and the mayor's crediting him with bringing Ken's story to his attention the previous year. [26]

Ann Phelps read *The Daily Times*. She and her husband, Perry, went down to the Animas River site, touching the bronze on Ken Worley's monument. Bruce had already left a stemmed red rose atop Ken's plaque. While there, Ann remembered her friend, Beverly Worley Peace. The next evening, she and Perry made an unplanned visit to the Farmington Goodwill store, "cruising" among the shelves. Being an avid reader and writer, she wandered over to the book section. Among all the books on the shelves, one captured her attention and she recognized it immediately. She bought the book and took it home with her.

The Hoosier Schoolmaster, an 1899 edition, was an exact copy, if not the same book, Beverly had left for her in their freshman school locker. Ann wrote *Angels?* [27] in the e-mail Subject block to her older brother. She planned to take a photo of Beverly to the Memorial Dedication, hoping to see a familiar face in the crowd.

That Saturday, over 100 people gathered for the Medal of Honor Memorial unveiling and dedication. Among them were family and friends of fallen servicemen. Members of the American Legion, state and local Marine Corps Leagues, Disabled American Veterans, Veterans of Foreign Wars Posts 614 and 2182, Military Officers Association, the Farmington National Guard, Blue Star Mothers, and the County Commissioner Chairman attended. [28]

The mayor officiated, introducing the various speakers. An unscheduled speaker was called to the rostrum to make an important announcement. The New Mexico Marine Corps League Department Commandant and former Commandant of the Jerry Murphy Detachment 381 in Albuquerque stepped forward and made a statement that surprised Bruce Salisbury; reading a copy of the Request Letter to Secretary Mabus, which Bruce had provided him before the ceremony, the MCL Commandant told the public that a U.S. Navy vessel would be commissioned in Ken Worley's name.

As the cottonwood trees rustled and the Animas River flowed nearby, Francis Mitchell, Navajo medicine man, stood before the four pillars, under the eagle and the dedication to Valor, and blessed the Memorial. Following the red ribbon cutting, as a bugler sounded

Taps, a 21-gun salute echoed among the Heroes' columns. "God Bless America" was sung and all present released red, white and blue balloons, watching them float above the trees into a sun-filled blue sky.

The mayor had said that the columns would "stand the test of time and the test of nature."

Ken Worley had been tested throughout his brief life. His memory had come home, and future Farmington sons and daughters who walk along the Las Animas will long remember his life and actions.

On Saturday, November 7, 2009, Journalist Michael Doyle, resolved to keep Ken's story in the public mind, posted a lengthy synopsis, *Mystery in life; renowned in death: Those who knew him 'awed' by efforts to pay tribute to Marine.*

Neither Quonieta Murphy nor Donel Swisher were able to attend the Farmington dedication. Among the few people alive today who knew Ken in life, the Feyerherm sisters sometimes have different and contrasting views of the days when Ken was with them. About who he was as a person, they agree, using similar descriptions. Ken was a sweet, nice young man, spectacular in some ways, giving and considerate of others, and quiet.

The sisters remain "awed" and "amazed" at the public recognition extended to the hero who was to one a "brother" and to the other a boyfriend. Nearing her sixties, Quonieta looks back on those days and remembers that Ken was "just a kid." Both sisters are sure that Ken would be "just blown away" by the efforts to pay fitting tribute to him.

He was "a lost soul" who has found a place for himself.

Bruce Salisbury continues to write letters and magazine articles to promote tributes to his hometown Marine hero. He is persistent in this matter. Bruce received a welcome correspondence in July 2010. Ayse Weiting, Fox News Channel Producer, wrote to him. Ken's story was under consideration by retired USMC Lieutenant Colonel Oliver North for a future "War Stories" episode. [29] One positive conclusion in the search for him is certain. Lance Corporal Kenneth Lee Worley's heroics have reentered public awareness.

CHAPTER 7
The Lessons of Heroic Bravery

"I was scared all the time. ...But you dealt with it."

Captain Joseph Jeremiah McCarthy, USMC
Medal of Honor recipient
About events on Iwo Jima [1]

Brave acts occur every day. Great numbers of humans possess qualities of moral strength, purpose of mind, and courage. Finding themselves in the right difficult circumstances they demonstrate bravery. Most brave individuals go unheralded because their lives seem unremarkable or because they perform unwitnessed acts of bravery. Sometimes the witnesses to their bravery do not survive the circumstances.

Bravery is a personal quality, usually understood to be an inner core of strength and courage. Bravery is demonstrated by a deliberate and conscious choice to quickly, perhaps immediately, initiate an action in a difficult and challenging situation. That action will be in a manner uncommon (perhaps) to most people and performed in a socially accepted and respected way. Put simply, bravery is the demonstration of courage.

Reading local, regional, national and international newspapers and listening to news broadcasts can identify brave individuals. Exceptional acts of bravery are often referred to as *heroic* in the media. These can be recognized because they remain a story of interest longer in the media and often result in community acknowledgments. People think and talk about the brave.

Specific situations occur in which individuals are recognized to possess some degree of bravery: for example, firefighters responding to three-alarm urban fires or raging forest fires, police officers in a shoot-out, Coast Guard lifesavers rescuing shipwrecked boaters from stormy seas, and juries of twelve people deciding a capital murder court case. Among individuals in such circumstances will be those who possess bravery and act heroically.

Obviously, brave actions can be observed and reported to others. Personal qualities and motivations cannot be seen, however. Qualities and motivations are inferred to be present by the demonstrated actions. To say that a man charged ahead *bravely*, that he possessed *valor*, or that he was *courageous* involves observation of action and *inference* about things unseen.

For example, to say that Lance Corporal Ken Worley jumped on a grenade before it exploded and deliberately sacrificed his own life so that others might live infers internal motivation for his observed actions.

Most people would say that Ken Worley was brave. But, while bravery tends to be commonly viewed as a single quality of person, as is courageous, it is more likely a blending of traits that merged within him during his childhood development.

Many who have written about Medal of Honor recipients have noted that they were "ordinary" men, suggesting that their extraordinary actions resulted from their being in extraordinary circumstances. In other words, were it not for their acts of heroic bravery in combat, the men might have seemed like so many other everyday people. When some of the recipients were boys, family or friends would not have thought of them as likely to someday be brave or heroic. Childhood friends remembered more than one recipient as not just an unlikely hero but as an unlikely Marine. These recipients had not yet demonstrated actions that would have suggested bravery.

Looking more closely, identifying characteristics true of Medal of Honor recipients sheds a different light on these men and on bravery. The actions they demonstrated later in combat are a reflection of their personal makeup, not of the circumstances that surrounded them. They each possessed certain traits evident in childhood that were predictive of their later actions. The combination of personal qualities Medal of Honor recipients possess made their heroically brave actions likely. While common, ordinary, and average in a variety of aspects, they were certainly also special in others.

That heroic bravery is a reflection of ingrained personal characteristics becomes clearer when considering the backgrounds of the Medal of Honor recipients. A variety of personal qualities associated to events and behaviors across the lifetime of these men, starting in childhood, were identified during the *Semper Fidelis* study. These qualities, or some combination of them, are closely associated to their heroically brave actions in combat.

Individuals who demonstrate such characteristics early in life are more likely to demonstrate heroic bravery at some point in their lives than are people who might lack such qualities. Many of the characteristics are described in the chapters ahead.

For emphasis sake, studying the lives of the Medal of Honor recipients makes one fact certain. Among heroically brave individuals, bravery demonstrates a pattern of behavior rather than a single, isolated act. If enough background information regarding each recipient could be explored, a pattern of behavior and the characteristics resulting in heroic bravery when in combat circumstances would be discovered to have already been evident earlier in their lives. The foundation for bravery is laid down in childhood. Once in combat situations, the bravery becomes evident.

Ralph Waldo Emerson said so long ago:

"The characteristic of genuine heroism is its persistency." [2]

Persistency means continuing tenaciously, persevering, enduring.

As some Medal recipients had already been honored in their communities for various contributions and achievements before going to war, investigating their early personal backgrounds can yield further information about heroism.

Aquilla James Dyess is one example.

In the summer of 1928 after his freshman year of college, Jimmie, as he was called, was vacationing in Charleston, South Carolina. A young woman nearly drowned in the ocean surf. Jimmie struggled for thirty minutes to help her to shore, resuscitating her when once back on the beach. At the age of nineteen, he was awarded the Carnegie Medal for Heroism. While being interviewed, Jimmie characteristically gave credit for the rescue to another young woman who had first responded to the woman in trouble. [3]

Lieutenant Colonel Dyess was in command when the 2d Battalion, 24th Marines went ashore on Namur Island, Kwajalein Atoll in the Marshall Islands on February 1, 1944. The Marshalls are comprised of thirty-four scattered, low coral atolls with sandy beaches and impressive lagoons 600 nautical miles south of Wake Island and 2,200 nautical miles east of Samar. The islands provided cover and concealment for the Japanese and devastating interlocking fields of fire.

Sixteen years after his Charleston vacation, Lieutenant Colonel Dyess personally led the advance on the second day of the assault, directing his companies against key positions, driving the Japanese backwards out of their fortified positions, inspiring his men by his lack of concern for his own personal safety. Often exposed to intense automatic weapons fire, he remained at the forefront of the attack. When the enemy forces were reduced to a constrained area of resistance, he directed a flanking movement to complete the assault and secure the island. As he stood exposed in an antitank trench, Lieutenant Colonel A. James Dyess, two weeks beyond his 35th birthday, was killed by an enemy machine gun.

Jimmie Dyess was remembered afterwards. His leadership, his dedication to assigned missions, and his care for men under his command were honored long after the events on Kwajalein Atoll, where today a

U.S. missile base remains. The airfield on Roi was named in his memory, and the U.S. Navy launched a destroyer, DD-880, in tribute to him in January 1945. Based on a pattern established early in his life, Jimmie Dyess would predictably have achieved further accomplishment, and probably acclaim, had he survived the war.

Persistency of bravery across time might not be obvious in the lives of all the Medal recipients. Medal of Honor Citations describe some Marines who died early in their combat careers. In the case of these recipients, it could appear that their heroic bravery occurred in a single moment of time and is a solitary event in which they distinguished themselves. For example, John Vincent Power died within hours of landing on Namur Island during his first combat experience. William Adelbert Foster died after a month of combat on Okinawa having had no other combat experience. Richard Kraus had been out of the United States for only three months when he jumped onto a grenade to save companions on Peleliu.

Dying early in their combat careers tells little of what these men were like prior to going to war. Thinking that their Citations describe their first and only act of bravery would likely be an erroneous conclusion. Each of them had already been brave before stepping onto the beaches of hostile enemy islands.

The Citations of the majority of Medal of Honor Marines state that they had demonstrated "extraordinary heroism through repeated acts of valor," rather than a single act. Additionally, many of them had previously earned medals for bravery in other combat engagements and other wars.

In the three wars considered, there were among these men those who had experienced extended months in combat, participated in numerous campaigns, and volunteered for extended or return tours. At least thirty-six recipients had received citations for valor in previous wars, campaigns, or battles. Nine were WWII "Ace" aviators who had been involved in numerous air combat events extending over months of time. Additionally, other recipients continued demonstrating brave deeds following their Medal of Honor actions, when they could have remained removed in safe circumstances.

Lewis Bausell was killed in combat on Peleliu three days after he had earned his Medal. He had earlier spent four months fighting on Guadalcanal. John Basilone died on Iwo Jima two years after he had earned his Medal on Guadalcanal and celebrity at home. Ross Gray was killed on Iwo six days after he earned his Medal of Honor; Tony Stein two weeks after earning his on Iwo. Dale Hansen was killed four days after the battle for Hill 60 on Okinawa. Lee Phillips earned his Medal for actions on Hill 698 in Korea after already fighting in Seoul and at the Chosin Reservoir. Missing in action three weeks after the fight on Hill 698, he was declared killed-in-action.

Persistency.

The Demonstration of Courage

There is no argument that people in the same situation respond differently to unfolding events. Put twelve people together in a jury room, and they will not react to the decision-making process in the same way. Put one hundred-fifty people into a darkened theater, and they will not react the same when an earthquake sends tremors across the floor. All men and women who leave their homes and go to war are brave. Yet, put four thousand brave men on a beach and order them to assault concrete fortifications with hostile machine guns and cannons pointed at them, and they will act bravely in different ways.

We look to the brave and naturally ask questions. Perhaps we wonder if only special individuals are capable of heroic bravery. In the presence of another's bravery, do all people have the potential to act bravely? Curious about what compels heroes to do the things they do, we wonder about the backgrounds from which they have come and what traits comprise their personalities. What do heroes think of themselves? Are they ever afraid—of dying, at least?

We do learn from brave men and women.

While perhaps humbling, knowing and learning about brave individuals can inspire a person to higher achievements and put day-to-day trials and tribulations into proper perspective. Having others to look up to, perhaps to emulate, to have as guides or role models promotes character building. Wanting to be like them, we practice what heroes have done. Understanding one man's bravery can move others beyond fear and inspire more brave acts. Bravery is contagious. That is why a community must keep the memory of its heroes alive.

Lessons to learn about bravery from Medal of Honor recipients.

The *Semper Fidelis* study of *heroic bravery* began with the Medal of Honor Citations. To better understand this extreme form of courage, the backgrounds and personal qualities of Marines who earned the Medal were investigated, in addition to their brave actions. This involved searching for information about them before their service in the Marines. Studying the lives and heroic actions of Medal of Honor recipients provides insight into human reactions to danger. Before telling more stories of the thirty-four forgotten Marines, a few things learned from them are described below.

Heroically brave actions

The context of combat engagements in which Marines find themselves has changed in the over two hundred years of their history. Tactics have evolved in close association to advances in technology. Yet, certain things about combat have remained consistent. It is noisy, disorienting, fatiguing, and frightening. Threat and danger are posed to self and comrades. Injury and death are constant realities.

Across time, individual ways in which Marines might demonstrate heroism and bravery have sometimes been specific to the situation and, therefore, unique to the combat circumstances. In other important ways, the actions that reflect conspicuous gallantry and dauntless courage have remained generally unchanged since the Marine Corps was first organized.

Examination of Medal of Honor Citations suggests that Marines repeatedly perform in certain ways in their demonstration of heroic bravery. Nine general actions were identified to be ways in which Marines earned the nation's highest award for bravery in battle:

1) Do what is asked for or required and more.
2) Fend off an enemy assault, especially one of unequal odds.

3) Volunteer for a challenging task potentially dangerous to one-self.

4) Turn the outcome of an engagement with the enemy by initiating an assault.

5) Demonstrate leadership that inspires others to take action despite imminent danger.

6) Sustain deliberateness of purpose despite extended duress.

7) Carry on one's duty in spite of grievous, debilitating, and life-threatening wounds.

8) Put self in harm's way, disregarding danger, to rescue others.

9) Act in defense of fellow combatants, even to the risk of one's self.

A hero's age at the time of action does not determine bravery.

Age does not determine heroic bravery. The age range of all the recipients studied, spanning 17-years to 55-years-old, indicates that heroic bravery cuts across age groups. Jack Lucas was 17-years-old when he pulled two grenades beneath his body to protect his comrades on Iwo Jima. Alexander Archer Vandergrift was 55-years-old when he was in command of the initial 1st Marine Division 1942 landings in the Solomon Islands.

In general, the Marines who went to war from WWII to Vietnam were progressively younger, and the percentage of recipients in the 21-years and younger age range increased in each war. Prior to Vietnam, recipients were most likely to be in their mid-twenties. This changed dramatically in Vietnam.

The histories of these men and their Medal of Honor Citations also make it clear that men who are heroically brave risk their lives, do not live forever, and more often than not, do not live long, natural lives. Sixty-nine percent (124) of these heroically brave men were killed in action. More than half of the men whose actions were explored during the *Semper Fidelis* study died before their twenty-fifth birthday.

Of the 181 recipients, seventy-four men (41%), were 21-years and younger. Thirty (17%) of them were teenagers when they earned their Medals. These men demonstrate that young men are capable of brave actions. Men in these age groups were also more likely to die than were the older recipients. Sixty-one (82%) of the 21-years and younger men died in combat. Twenty-five (83%) of the teenagers died being heroically brave. Among the 107 men who were 22-years or older, sixty-four (60%) died in the wars.

In each of the two later wars the younger recipients were more likely to die in combat. Thirty-two percent of the WWII recipients who received posthumous awards were 21-years and younger. Forty-six percent of the recipients who died in combat in Korea were 21-years and younger. In Vietnam seventy-one percent of the recipients who received posthumous awards were 21-years and younger.

The age range of the 181 Medal of Honor Marines across the three wars; their average ages; the number, age ranges, and average ages of recipients who died in combat; the number of recipients who were 21-years and younger and who died in combat; and the number who were teenagers and received posthumous awards are detailed in the columns below.

	WWII	Korea	Vietnam
Number of USMC Medals of Honor	82	42	57
Age Range	17 to 55	18 to 35	18 to 37
Average Age	25-years	24.4-years	22.9-years
Killed-In-Action	52 (63%)	28 (67%)	44 (77%)
Posthumous Age Range	18 to 36	18 to 33	18 to 33
Average Posthumous Age	23.25-yrs	23.2-yrs	22-yrs
Recipients 21-years and younger	27 (33%)	15 (36%)	32 (56%)
21-years or younger Killed-In-Action	17 (21%)	13 (31%)	31 (54%)
17 to 19-years-old	11 (13%)	6 (14%)	13 (23%)
Posthumous Awards 17 to 19-years-old	6 (7%)	6 (14%)	13 (23%)

The youthfulness of so many of the recipients is balanced by the fact that 59% were 22-years and older and that their age range stretched out to 55-years. Bravery is not a reflection of youthful inexperience or a sort of naiveté regarding the realities of war, combat, and the proximity of death. All the recipients understood the realities of the dangerous situations they were in.

"I'm not much of a brave person."

Those who are acknowledged for their bravery resist recognizing and admitting their own personal bravery.

"Brave? I don't know that I was brave. I had to do what I did at that time. I did what anybody would have done."

"I'm not much of a brave person."

"I'm no more brave than the next guy."

"I just thought I was being *stupid*!"

We tend to idealize our heroes, sometimes putting them into a light they might find uncomfortable. The men described throughout this book were in extraordinary circumstances, such that their highest character emerged and prevailed. While public attention might celebrate them as heroes, they recognize their own flaws, human frailties, and weaknesses. Among those who have raised themselves by their actions to the level of hero, most would admit that there is no perfect man wearing a Medal of Honor.

This being reality, we must avoid diminishing our view of these men and their accomplishments when we discover questionable elements in their backgrounds or conclude that they were in many ways ordinary. That a recipient seemed ordinary at one time in life or came from a troubled background are not justifications for allowing brave actions to be forgotten. Nor is recognition of personal imperfections an excuse for allowing the memory of a native son's heroic bravery to slip from community awareness.

As General Walter E. Boomer wrote of one of the Medal recipients, "...less than perfect in his personal life...his human frailty allows us to better appreciate him as a person, not a mythological hero." [5]

Bravery does not mean fearlessness.

American author Mark Twain had traveled, worked on the Mississippi steamboats, and watched the Civil War nearly tear the nation apart. When he wrote the following comment, he was 59-years-old. He was not trying to be funny; he was serious when he said; "Courage is resistance to fear, mastery of fear—not absence of fear." [6]

Mark Twain and others have long understood that fear and bravery go hand-in-hand.

Acting with bravery means that a person must perceive a danger or threat, real or imagined. Bravery is then demonstrated by an admirable human action, an indifference to fear, and a disregard for the personal danger. Note, however, that indifference to fear does not mean the absence of it. A person recognized to possess bravery consciously rises to meet a challenge that triggers fear, draws upon this personal quality, and takes an initiative few might endeavor.

The award Citations for the recipients repeatedly describe their heroic actions with specific words: included among these are admirable, bold, courageous, daring, dauntless, fearless, gallant, honorable, indomitable, intrepid, resolute, stout hearted, tenacious, unfaltering, unwavering, valiant, and valorous. The words impart a certain sense to the actions of these men.

Can we accept the implied meaning as accurate? Is *dauntless* a measurable and quantifiable personal quality? How might *courage* best be defined? A person described to be *dauntless* is believed to be *without fear*, unintimidated by danger. The words dauntless and courageous are often used interchangeably. Both are considered synonymous with *brave*. Yet, dauntless and courageous do not mean the same thing.

There can be no question that the Marines described in this book acted courageously. That they acted without fear at the same time is not accurate. A person does not have to be dauntless to be brave.

The Medal recipients, who demonstrated heroic bravery in obviously dangerous and life-threatening situations, *did* experience natural fear. They say so in their own words:

Joseph Jeremiah McCarthy said: "I was scared all the time. Any man tells you he wasn't scared was an imbecile. But you dealt with it." [7]

John Lucian Smith willingly admitted to being afraid during the early days on Guadalcanal, the first American offensive of WWII: "... they were just as scared of us as we were of them." [8]

James Elms Swett, who also flew at Guadalcanal said: "I was, number one, scared— number two, frightened—number three, ready to bail out of that darned thing...you couldn't believe how nervous I was." [9]

Everett Parker Pope said of his actions on Hill 100, Peleliu Island: "We were all scared but able to overcome our fears and do what was expected of us." [10]

Even famed Merritt Austin Edson, reputed to have willingly and coldly looked death in the eye, wrote of his extensive combat experiences: "I have been scared half to death more than once, more often than anyone realizes..." [11]

Another reason heroes hesitate to consider themselves as *brave* is that they realize they have been at times in situations in which they had been afraid and did not *feel* brave. Fear is the body's physiological and emotional reaction associated to the presence of a threat or danger. Fear puts us in a heightened state of agitation in which attention is concentrated and focused upon a target perceived as a threat. Fear is about the nervous system and the instinct to survive an impending danger.

Bravery is about managing fear, not about being without it. *Bravery is all about personal character.*

Bravery is not a denial of danger.

That many of the 181 recipients were teenagers and so many of them had just entered their adult years when they earned their Medals, the conclusion that their actions reflect youthful inexperience or an adolescent sense of invulnerability is understandable, but must be avoided.

The majority of these men were in their first period of military service, some lacking any previous combat experience before they earned a Medal of Honor. Yet, a good number of them were seasoned combat veterans. Seventeen recipients had served in previous wars. At least an additional forty-one had been involved in previous significant combat campaigns. This means at least 32% of the recipients had survived earlier combat events and had a rational concept of the dangers they faced. The percentage of those with previous combat experience is likely higher than this.

The Marines in Vietnam were often out on patrols and engaged in fire fights with an enemy force that appeared suddenly, fought fanatically, and then receded back into jungle tangles, tunnels, and caves. These engagements were not recorded in history books like the major battles on Guadalcanal, Iwo Jima, and at Chosin. Therefore, it is difficult to accurately determine how much combat the Vietnam recipients experienced prior to earning their commendations. From available records, it is reasonable to conclude that young men like Jimmy Wayne Phipps, who died in Vietnam when he was 18-years-old, were veterans of enough combat to understand the realities of the situations in which they found themselves. No one can say a young recipient "did not know any better."

Volunteering to go into harm's way

"Then I heard the voice of the Lord saying, 'Whom shall I send? And who will go for us?'
Then I said, 'Here I am, send me!'" [12]

Something spiritual pervades the willingness to put one's self in danger on behalf of others. The author of the Book of Isaiah, 6:8, touched upon this characteristic.

Taking on an unwelcome or intimidating job or responsibility that others avoid or abandon presents a special challenge. A person who does so risks frustration, fatigue, and failure, sometimes even ridicule and criticism. Along with the willingness to face such risks, when a task involves possible injury and pain, as well as threats to life and limb, it is certain that volunteering demonstrates bravery. The Medal recipients showed a readiness to encounter fear, danger, and death.

An obvious example of this tendency is that 107 of the recipients enlisted in the Marines during a time of war or national emergency, even if it meant lying about their age to do so. Vietnam illustrates this well. It was uncertain who might be called for military service in the years prior to the televised draft lottery (December 1, 1969). Once enacted, the draft seemed to be on the minds of most 18-year-old men who were required to present at a local draft board to *register*, indicating that they were now eligible to be called for service, or inducted.

The numbers of men being drafted for service increased appreciably each year during the years of the Vietnam War. Eventually it was such that adolescents in high school, from sophomore year on, had Vietnam on their minds. In every high school across America, there was a good chance that students knew someone from their school, neighborhood, or town who had been "called up" to go to war. Knowing the prospects of being drafted put a different spin on dropping out of school. And knowing the prospects of being sent to Vietnam put a different spin on volunteering for military service.

Of the 57 Vietnam recipients, all but two of the men enlisted for service and forty of these did so while the conflict was underway in Southeast Asia. Fourteen of these men enlisted at age 17-years, fourteen quit high school or college to enlist, and thirteen enlisted immediately or within six months following graduation from high school or college. The descriptions of these men suggest an eagerness to put themselves into challenging and extraordinary circumstances.

Brave individuals do not "just happen" to be in circumstances in which bravery emerges. They tend to knowingly and willingly put themselves in such circumstances.

The Character of Heroic Bravery

The character of the recipients clearly had an impact upon those around them. As boys, teens, teammates, team captains, friends, and fellows in arms they were able to motivate others to action. On fields of play or on fields of battle, their efforts elevated companions to greater efforts. Their drive and ambition and single-mindedness could be contagious.

As boys, the recipients might have been the first to try something, but because they sought affiliation, they tended also to include others in their endeavors. They encouraged friends to not give up on objectives, to try harder, or to do more. Some were viewed as *instigators* during their school years, including others in their pranks and mischief.

Once they were men, the Marine Medal of Honor recipients were able to draw the best out of others. Men who associated with them evidently admired and looked up to them. Among their Marine companions, some were viewed as having been like big brothers. The older recipients were father figures to many of their men. They are remembered to have been exemplary, to have demonstrated inspiring initiative, or to have given a heroic example to others.

A significant number of Medal Citations describe recipients' efforts to encourage, embolden, and quicken the courage of their comrades in dire circumstances. Their own actions served to inspire others to "heroic efforts" or to "such aggression" that the enemy was overcome.

No fewer than ninety-two Citations include the word *inspire* or *inspiring* in the details of heroically brave actions. While we might take this one quality for granted, it is a difficult characteristic to define. That someone is inspirational, by definition means the person must possess some quality that draws higher levels of aspiration, effort, and achievement from others. The word itself is derived from the Latin word meaning *to breathe into*. What is it these men were able to breathe into others?

This aspect of heroic bravery is called *spirit*. These Marines possessed innate and vigorous spirit. Its presence among these men is incontestable. Heroically brave action is unlikely among those who do not possess *spirit*. Medal of Honor citations often mention the *spirit* demonstrated by recipients. They are described as having an exceptional *spirit of loyalty*. They possessed a courageous, dauntless, indomitable, intrepid, invincible, relentless, tenacious, or valiant *fighting spirit*. They demonstrated a heroic, loyal, resolute, unfaltering, or valiant *spirit of self-sacrifice* in the service of others and in the face of certain death.

The United States Marine Corps deliberately and proudly fosters *esprit d'corps* within the ranks of enlisted men and officers. This *spirit* of loyalty and devotion to fellow Marines, to the greater Marines Corps, and to the mission of the Corps is taught and drilled into the fabric of thought of young Marines.

Most Marines will feel some attachment to former Marines like Corporal John Mackie, Gunnery Sergeant Dan Dailey, Sergeant John Basilone, Private First Class Wesley Phelps, Major Smedley Butler, Major Gregory "Pappy" Boyington, and Captain Joe Foss. Steeped in legend and tradition, their historically factual stories are told over and over in boot camps and officer training schools.

And most Marines will feel some attachment to present and future Marines. *Esprit* becomes natural. It is *spirit* that the Corps attempts to imbue in its members, believing that this quality is what brings a man or woman through the carnage wrought by battle and perhaps raises the individual to heroically brave efforts. Perhaps the Corps is only drawing upon a characteristic already present within those drawn to be a Marine.

Without question the Medal of Honor recipients had a full measure of *spirit*, evident in their actions long before they entered combat. Childhood friends, school companions, and teammates recalled it. Fellow recruits recognized it early in training. And commanders counted upon it when they sent these men into harm's way. This is the quality that the recipients breathed into the comrades who witnessed their heroic bravery. Only from *spirit* can come inspiration.

The men described in the following chapters lived and died in circumstances in which few people in the general population will ever find themselves. The majority of people will never know if they possess this brand of bravery, because heroic bravery is seldom called for in everyday events.

Realistically, not all people are capable of heroic bravery. Yet, many more than are aware, "average" and "ordinary" individuals, do have the potential to experience bravery. Reading about bravery and learning about heroes might help us discover this quality within ourselves and practice it deliberately. We might find ourselves less troubled by fear.

Medal of Honor recipients provide us examples. By encouraging children and adults to take the nine actions described of these men and fostering the development of the traits they exemplify, people would accomplish much in life with greater confidence and more certain esteem for themselves.

Our culture would also discover itself to be less anxious, fearful, or cowered by the intimidations of terror.

CHAPTER 8
Some Would Choose Not
To Remember The Brave

"And I won't forget the men who died
Who gave that right to me"

Lee Greenwood [1]

Singer Lee Greenwood sees bravery in one way. Others see it in a different way.

"We should protest this man's evil actions." [2]

"He's not an example of the sort of person we want to represent us."

For one recipient, it was never about a community forgetting him. He had earned a Medal of Honor and returned home after the war. The public took to him immediately and celebrity followed the awarding of his Medal at the White House. Parades and accolades were common. Then the years passed.

He and Ken Worley shared one evident similarity. His friends and classmates had known him by one name, and he joined the Marine Corps with a different name. Neither of his names was fictitious.

After he died, petitions to establish a permanent memorial or monument in tribute to this brave warrior began. So did the protests. Community members proposed to change the name of the airport in his birthplace, an issue upon which the city council was split for years. In a neighboring state, a university student government rejected a resolution to build a memorial in honor of him, its most legendary graduate. The ensuing debates serve as examples of the cherished freedom of speech right extended to American citizens in our two-party system. While we might respect the varied opinions possible about a single issue, in matters of the Medal of Honor the final say regarding tributes should go to those who understand the kind of heroic bravery required to earn this recognition.

People who would rather not acknowledge another's bravery have to learn to look above their own opinions. Peering into the vastness of the sky might expand their views.

It Started at Kitty Hawk

The twelve-second first flight of Wilbur and Orville Wright's *Flyer* at Kitty Hawk, North Carolina, on December 17, 1903, was like a catapult into a new era. Eleven years later British and German pilots in their biplanes began taking shots at each other over Belgian battlefields in the opening days of World War I. Within the next four years, pilots went from forward observer duties to fighter responsibilities. Air battles became an integral part of waging war.

As they had done aboard ships at sea, the Marines began providing security to others in the skies.

Second Lieutenant Ralph Talbot and Gunnery Sergeant Robert G. Robinson were assigned flight duties in the 1st Marine Aviation Force in France and Belgium. They were crewed together on October 14, 1918, flying a De Havilland-4 airplane. Their assignment was to protect the rear of an attack squadron during a high-bombing raid over Pittham, Belgium. By day's end their airmanship, gallantry, and performance above and beyond what was asked of them distinguished both as the first Marine aviators in history to earn Medals of Honor, and as the last two Marines to earn the distinction in the First World War.

Second Lieutenant Talbot was awarded his Medal posthumously, and his body was buried in the military cemetery of Les Barracques, near Calais, France. Gunnery Sergeant Robinson survived the war and returned to Michigan to live out his life.

For many in America, aviators became a new breed of swashbuckling adventurers.

Following WWI, pilots came home with heightened enthusiasm for flight. Many found jobs as "Barnstormers" during the first half of the 1920s. Natural daredevils, men like Clyde Edward "Upside-Down" Pangborn thrilled crowds at county fairs pulling breathtaking stunts and demonstrating the acrobatic possibilities of airborne contraptions. Boys and girls stood in the fields, mouths agape, wide-eyed, gazing into the skies, wishing one day to be able to fly into clouds. The Barnstormers were happy to give them rides. At least two of those boys would later be Marine "Aces" with their handsome images on *Life* Magazine covers.

Aviation was thriving in North America. And it was wild enough at times that Air Traffic Control was established in 1926. Some aviators bridled with irritation that they should fall under the control of an agency. They had taken to the air to escape ground-bound rules and regulations. Even greater government oversight was inevitable as aviation became an industry that rivaled rail and road transportation. Eventually, on August 23, 1958, pilots, the airways, and civil aviation safety became the responsibilities of the Federal Aviation Administration.

Aircraft engineers and designers remained busy in the years between the two World Wars. Beyond civil transportation, leaders also envisioned military advantages in procuring aircraft. Nations built forces intent on having control of the skies above their lands. Marine aviation continued to grow into its own fighting force, and the 1918 air battle over Belgium would not be the last time a Marine aviator distinguished himself.

Before the United States entered WWII, a pilot serving in the Royal Canadian Air Force described the experience men had been discovering since Kitty Hawk. John Gillespie Magee, Jr. put pen to paper on August 18, 1941, and mailed his thoughts home to his father. He had "slipped the surly bonds of Earth...danced the skies on laughter-silvered wings...put out [his] hand and touched the face of God."

Ever since, his *High Flight* poem has adorned the walls of aviators. [3]

Within just months of John Gillespie Magee, Jr.'s writing a poem, Marine aviators were soaring with their own "eager craft through footless halls of air" fighting off Japanese invasion forces. Eleven of them would earn a Medal of Honor in WWII, providing air support for Marines on Pacific islands. Henry Talmage Elrod was the first.

During one low-level strafing and bombing run on December 11, 1941, in the defense of Wake Island, Captain Elrod closed in on the Destroyer *Kisaragi*, released his bombs, and scored a direct hit. The Japanese destroyer exploded into flames and quickly sank. Captain Elrod thus earned the distinction of being the first fighter pilot to sink a major warship with small caliber bombs. Later, when no planes remained on the island, Captain Elrod, 36-years-old, was shot and fell mortally wounded as he was throwing a grenade. The first Marine in WWII to earn a Medal of Honor, he was buried on Wake Island.

The ten aviators who followed with their own acts of heroic flying were Richard Eugene Fleming, John Lucian Smith, Robert Edward Galer, Joseph Jacob Foss, Harold William Bauer, Jefferson Joseph DeBlanc, James Elms Swett, Kenneth Ambrose Walsh, Gregory Boyington, and Robert Murray Hanson. All their Medals were earned between 1942-44.

First Lieutenant Bob Hanson, 23-years-old, "slipped the surly bonds of Earth" for three months in an F4U Corsair and ascended into the South Pacific skies over Bougainville and New Britain islands. He was an "Ace" after having been a Marine aviator for fewer than nine months. Flight after flight, he demonstrated legendary airmanship, claiming twenty-five enemy aircraft. First Lieutenant Hanson's plane was seen crashing into the sea on February 3, 1944, and he was declared killed in action. His posthumous Medal of Honor was the last to be earned by a Marine aviator in WWII.

Another war and twenty-three years passed. Another war had begun. The next Marine pilot to earn a Medal of Honor was Captain Stephen Wesley Pless flying a UH-1 "Huey" helicopter medical evacuation mission in Vietnam, August 19, 1967. Captain Pless was the only Marine aviator in Vietnam to earn this distinction, and the first and last Marine pilot to do so after Robert Hanson.

In tribute to the Medal of Honor Marine aviators, four Navy ships, three airports, one road, a Marine Corps League Detachment, a university room, dining hall, a monument, statue, university student detachment, an elementary school, and a commemorative U.S. stamp envelope have been dedicated in their names. Three of their stories have been featured in the History Channel's *Dogfights* series.

From Coeur d'Alene to a Medal of Honor

Gregory Boyington had a life before he had fame and celebrity, as well as a life after he distinguished himself in battle.

As was true of each Medal of Honor recipient, Greg faced early challenges in his life. These challenges resulted from life situations in which he had no direct control, beginning with family disruptions so early in his life that he would know nothing about them until he was an adult. Other challenges arose from deliberate choices he made. All his life, Greg found ways to challenge himself. He put himself into situations in which he would be challenged and tested and in which he had an opportunity to excel. His response to most challenges was to face them directly and to find a way to triumph. Some of his responses to challenges were immediate and spontaneous, at times appearing impulsive.

Greg was born in the rugged, upper northern region of Idaho, at Coeur d'Alene, on December 4, 1912, twenty-two years after the state had been declared. His birthplace is part of the sixty-five mile wide buffer between the Montana and Washington borders, narrowing further as it stretches up to Canada. The area is completely mountainous, heavily forested, and mostly wilderness. Stream and river gorges render much of the territory impassible. Except for Highway 90 connecting the three states, the region north of Coeur d'Alene still has few paved roads. The surrounding lands are home to indigenous Native American tribes including the Kutenai, Kalispel, Nez Perce, and Shoshone. [4]

Greg's biological father was Dr. Charles Barker Boyington, a successful dentist. The doctor and his wife, Grace Barnhardt Gregory, an accomplished pianist and music teacher, had married on New Year's Day, 1912. The union was marred by alcohol abuse and violence, and his parents divorced March 4, 1915, when Greg was just two-years-old. By the time the divorce was finalized in court, Grace and Gregory had moved twenty-five miles due west to Spokane, Washington, to live in an apartment with another man and his extended family. Grace and Ellsworth J. Hallenbeck, a bookkeeper, were living as if they were a married couple.

Two years after her divorce from Charles, when Greg was nearing kindergarten age, Grace and Ellsworth moved from the Spokane apartment. Although no documents substantiate a marriage and adoption, Grace and Gregory returned to Idaho with the last name Hallenbeck. Well into his early adult life, Greg believed E.J. Hallenbeck was his natural father. He had no hints of a Charles Boyington living in Coeur d'Alene twenty miles to the north or of a half-brother, Keith, born in 1922. Greg was in *Life* articles, and Keith was an architect in Spokane before they knew anything about their shared lineage.

Greg's earliest memories would be of the years living in the small logging town of St. Maries on the edge of the Coeur d'Alene Indian Reservation, eighteen miles east of the small town of Worley. His half-brother, William Dewitt Hallenbeck, was born there on February 2, 1918. Family life was like an arena for bitter quarreling. Mr. Hallenbeck was a hard-drinking man who was tough on the family, and his alcoholism would have a lasting influence on his stepson. Grace had her own problems with drinking; Greg vowed early he would stay away from drinking alcohol.

One particular event in St. Maries left an indelible mark on young Greg. In autumn 1919, Clyde Pangborn flew a Jenny biplane into Idaho. A famous pilot, Clyde *barnstormed* about the country entertaining crowds with aerial stunts and acrobatics. Twelve years later in 1931, he made the first trans-Pacific Ocean flight. When Clyde landed his plane in a St. Maries meadow near the grade school, six-year-old Greg, having run from the playground after morning recess, was waiting as the biplane taxied to a stop.

Greg was able to talk people into seeing things his way, a trait he seemed to have possessed naturally. He convinced "Pang" to agree to take him flying. Greg was then able to talk E.J. Hallenbeck into giving him the five dollars ($63 in the 2010 economy) necessary for the flight and then persuaded his mother to give him permission to go barnstorming. When Clyde took the young boy flying over St. Maries on Constitution Day, a seed was planted that in the 1970s would grow into a popular nighttime television series. That first flight was also to be a connection to a group of other boys who would go off to war when they were young men.

Greg was not the only boy affected by barnstorming pilots. Aerial demonstrations inspired many boys like him to want to fly. One was Joseph Jacob Foss. Joe was 12-years-old when some history-making men visited near his father's farm. Charles Lindbergh flew into Renner Field on August 27, 1927, three months after his historic trans-Atlantic flight. Joe and his father drove to the haypatch airfield five miles north of Sioux Falls, South Dakota, to watch and his lifelong enthusiasm for flying was sparked. Joe Foss and Greg Boyington would later make their own history over islands in the Pacific.

The Hallenbeck family moved to Tacoma, Washington, in 1926, when Greg was fourteen. Greg graduated from Tacoma's Lincoln High School in 1930 when the Depression was only six months along and had not yet earned its "Great" title. Money and mounting debt were ever an issue in the Hallenbeck family as well as in Greg's life. Despite the economic hardships, he went on to the University of Washington. Mrs. Hallenbeck worked as a switchboard operator to help pay Greg's educational expenses, and he worked parking cars at a garage.

Maneuvering moving vehicles into tight spaces became an avocation for him.

Intensely competitive

Greg shared a characteristic demonstrated by most Marine Medal of Honor recipients. When not challenged by events, he set up his own challenges. And a good number of them were competitions with others.

Competition is obviously not unique to Medal recipients. It is not an American innovation or phenomenon; competition is a fact within nature, especially in situations in which scarcity is perceived. The theory of evolution is, in part, based on the concept of *survival of the fittest*. When there is not enough to go around, all involved must compete in some form for what is available, whether it be food, shelter, warm clothes, a parent's attention, a part in a play, a position on a team, a romantic partner, a seat in the theater, a first-place trophy, a gold medal, a championship, a job opening, an acceptance to a college, a promotion in rank, or a pilot with the most "downed" enemy aircraft.

Americans accept competitiveness: even expect it. Economic principles of capitalism are based upon the competition among suppliers as well as the competing influences of supply and demand. The rule of Democracy and the markets of exchange are built upon the premise that the best will win out or make it to the top.

For Greg to succeed in life, he would necessarily be faced with challenges, he would have to enter conflicts, and he would have to compete with others. Social psychologists have determined that competition is a social reality closely associated to conflict. [5] In fact, competition and conflict cannot exist apart from each other. Once engaged, competition fuels itself; there are various rewards in winning, internal and external, and strong reactions to losing. Individuals strive to gain, achieve, and win as well as endeavoring to avoid depletion, diminishment, and loss. Additionally, individuals demonstrate diverse strategies for competing. The more confident individuals compete openly; those who feel less certain of their chances to succeed compete behind the scenes. In other words, some competitors are obvious in their methods; others are more subtle and manipulative.

To compete means to strive against or to contend or vie with another or others. Any competition implies rivalry, a contest between opponents. Greg found great enthusiasm for facing off with an opponent. It was as apparent in childhood fistfights in St. Maries as it was in his choice of school extracurricular activities. Short of stature, but solidly built, Greg was an athlete throughout his school days, wrestling at Lincoln High School, and competing as a member of the wrestling and swimming teams at the University of Washington. He held the Pacific Northwest Intercollegiate middle-weight (160-pound) wrestling title for a year. Remaining physically fit would be important to him across his lifetime.

Greg's photographs appear in the 1931-34 University of Washington *Tyree* yearbooks as Greg Hollenbeck. [6] His only photograph in the 1931 *Tyree* is on page 185 where he is among the intramural wrestling champions, an independent in the 145-pound class. Greg is on page 236 of the 1932 yearbook, shown as a Lambda Chi Alpha Pledge. He evidently was more active in his junior and senior university years. The 1933 *Tyree* lists him as a member of the Junior Prom Tickets crew (page 78), a Minor Sports Wrestler (page 116), a Lambda Chi Alpha intramural Wrestler, 159-pound class (page 118), and a Lambda Chi Alpha Pledge (page 187 with a photograph). Greg's photograph is on page 97 of the 1934 *Tyree* having participated in the Minor Sports Wrestling at 155 pounds. He is listed among the Lambda Chi Alpha Pledges again, but without a photograph (page 224).

Greg Hallenbeck was obviously a competitor. He had been in the presence of conflict throughout his childhood. He redirected the will to survive and come out on top from his home life to wrestling mats. No matter where he directed his efforts, he strove to go well beyond minimal requirements. Greg earned awards and the admiration of his schoolmates, coaches, and professors. Those who wrote references for him described him as industrious, dependable, exceptional, talented, and of fine character. [7]

Greg's competitive drive, like that of other Medal of Honor recipients, would have been obvious to others in two ways. First of all, he had a drive to excel at the things to which he turned his interests. His immediate competition was with himself: trying to improve upon his last performance, constantly wanting to do better than the last time. For example, if he had taken down and pinned an opponent to the mat in the second period of a wrestling match, he would have strived to pin his next opponent in the first period.

Being impelled to not be "bested"—in anything, whether the matters were minor or major—was the second ingredient of competitiveness Greg exemplified. Not only did he want to constantly get better at what he did, he also did not want anyone else to be better than he was. Greg demonstrated this intense drive not to be bested by the enemy, the hostile opponent, the armed rivals, later in aerial combat, as well as on the ground during twenty months in prisoner of war camps. Giving up when things seemed to be going badly for himself was not characteristic of Greg Hallenbeck. This characteristic would have been quite evident among any of the Medal recipients who competed in events like boxing, wrestling, track, swimming, tennis, golf, and marksmanship.

In the summers during his school years, Greg returned to Coeur d'Alene to do the kind of work that kept him in athletic shape. He took jobs in mining and logging camps, on road construction crews, and in fire watch prevention crews. One summer he worked in gold mine tunnels in Golden, Idaho, where the Clearwater Mountains exceed 3,500-foot elevations.

In addition to competitive sports and working energetically to off-set mounting debts, Greg also enjoyed camaraderie. Besides joining the Lambda Chi Alpha fraternity, spending time at the frat house on 4509 Nineteenth Avenue Northeast on the north edge of campus, he was also a member of the Minor "W" Club in 1934 (*Tyree* page 101). As a letter winner in a minor sport, he had to first apply to join the club and then be accepted by members. Greg was in the Scabbard and Blade fraternity in 1933 (as a pledge, page 261) and 1934 (page 155), an honorary military club for advanced students. He was also active in the Reserve Officers Training Corps (ROTC) and eventually rose to the rank of Cadet Captain.

Greg's involvement in athletics and summers away from home somewhat reduced his availability for dating girls. However, he was charismatic, and girls were easily drawn to him, as he was to them. He finally made room for a serious romance in his senior year at the university.

Roosevelt High School is about a mile north of the Lambda Chi Alpha fraternity house in Seattle. Helene (or Helen) Clark was a senior there when Greg met her in 1933 at a semiformal ROTC dance. The attractive teenager had been orphaned and then given refuge by an "adoptive" family. Helene was Greg's steady girlfriend during his last year at the university. Shortly after her graduation from Roosevelt High, they married on July 29, 1934.

Greg graduated in December 1934, [8] with a Bachelor of Science degree in aeronautical engineering when that kind of degree was still considered akin to pioneering. The 1935 University of Washington Commencement Program lists him as Gregory Hallenbeck. He went to work at Boeing Aircraft Company in Seattle as a drafts-man and an engineer. He also served some part-time active duty in the Coastal Artillery and enlisted in the Volunteer Marine Corps Reserve.

Greg and Helene started their family. Gregory, Jr., was born May 24, 1935, ten months after their wedding.

Striving for individual accomplishment, working diligently, pro-moting team effort, enjoying camaraderie, encouraging others to greater heights, driving towards a personal objective, and leading oth-ers were all aspects of his personality. Where might he find a career that would allow satisfactory expression of who he was?

"Pang's" influence

Of all the ambitions Greg might have had, flying is what most cap-tured his attention. At 23-years-old, fifteen years after he had crewed up with Clyde Pangborn for a fifteen-minute flight, Greg applied for an appointment as an aviation cadet. Admission into the training program required that he provide a copy of his birth certificate. Greg was going to make some new discoveries and make the most out of them. With his birth certificate in hand, Greg learned his natural father's name for the first time. Since the aviation program was admitting only single men, his birth name presented him an opportunity. Greg's cadet appli-cation is one of the first official documents identifying him as Gregory

Boyington. He was no longer a Hallenbeck, and on the record he was no longer married with a newborn son.

Cadet Boyington, having arrived in Pensacola, Florida, as a member of Class 88-C in February 1936, encountered some problems in completing the Navy's flight training. Wrestling an airplane into the skies was different than wrestling an opponent to the mat. It was not barnstorming either. Greg did not naturally take to some of the flight techniques and regulations and had to repeat several flights. He would have to get better to remain in the flight program.

Other problems began to emerge. Greg seemed to have some aversion to taking orders from authority figures. He got into altercations in the Officer's Club and on the flight line, resulting in charges against him. Were it not for the Marine's need for trained pilots, he might have been "bounced" from the program, or worse, discharged from the service altogether. And, although Helene and Gregory, Jr. lived with him in the Pensacola Bachelor Officers Quarters, Greg appeared to earnestly live the life of a single man. He began paying attention to other women.

By most accounts, it would seem that dramatic character changes were witnessed in Greg during his training in Pensacola. Those changes likely hinged on a variety of factors, but many of his problems can certainly be attributed to one significant habit. According to his own version of his life, Greg had abstained from alcohol use through all his years of school and early years of marriage. Not until he was among other pilots at a cadet cocktail party in Pensacola did he start drinking. Consuming too much hard liquor quickly became a habit that would be problematic for the rest of his life. Cadet Boyington was drunk frequently, and functioning in an "alcoholic haze" or in a complete "blackout" became normal.

Greg Boyington was commissioned a Marine second lieutenant on July 2, 1937. On record he was a bachelor, a requirement to receive a "regular" officer commission in the Marines at that time. He and Helene then had two daughters; Janet Sue Boyington was born January 28, 1938 and Gloria Boyington April 24, 1940. When Second Lieutenant Boyington moved his family to Quantico, Philadelphia, and San Diego in the following years, they lived secretly in his Bachelor

Officer Quarters. Many of his squadron mates knew that he was married.

Second Lieutenant Boyington continued to improve his flying skills. He returned to Pensacola as a first lieutenant and as a flight instructor in 1940. His drinking and debt problems continued. His view of regulations and policies was also evident in that he kept his large dog, Fella, a collie-shepherd mix, in the Bachelor Officer Quarters against NAS Pensacola regulations.

After only nine months back in Florida, another flying opportunity promising something peacetime military flying lacked was presented to First Lieutenant Boyington. Chiang Kai-shek, the Chinese leader, was at war with Japan and the Central Aircraft Manufacturing Company (CAMCO), also known as *The Company*, had civilian trade interests in China. Imperial Japan had designs on the resources in China and had endeavored to cut off China's trade with the rest of the world. They had invaded in 1931, working their way along China's eastern coastline, intent on capturing all critical seaports. By 1937, Chiang Kai-shek understood the peril and ordered the construction of a supply route starting in Kunming, Capital of Yunnan Province in southwest China, over the mountains, into Burma, and linking to the Bay of Bengal.

The Burma Road was completed by the end of 1938 and promised to keep China supplied with necessary goods. CAMCO, under contract by China, had been organized to provide protection of the Burma Road from the air. The Chinese referred to these pilots as the *Fei Hu*. The world knew them and their fighter planes as the *Flying Tigers* of China. The hundreds of young men protecting the Burma Road earned the image of being hard-drinking brawlers, "tosspots": swashbuckling, mercenary hired guns serving as air commandos.

Greg Boyington was going to be one of the American volunteers who went to war against Japan before the December 7, 1941, attack at Pearl Harbor. He resigned his commission in the Marines in August 1941, and accepted a flying position with CAMCO. Helene went back to Seattle with their three children, ages one to six-years-old. Greg left on a ship from San Francisco on September 24, 1941: destination Kunming, China.

One week before Greg and the CAMCO fliers docked at Rangoon and one month before the United States plunged into the war, combat of another sort flared. On November 7, 1941, a Seattle judge granted Helene a divorce and custody of the children. The divorce was not amicable. Allegations of abuse and parental absence and incompetence went into the court records. Greg later admitted that he was "emotionally immature" well into his adult years. The same might be said as well for Helene, who had developed her own drinking habits.

While in Kunming later, Greg received a letter from his mother. The Seattle juvenile court had taken Greg Jr., Janet, and Gloria from Helene. The children were in Grace and Ellsworth Hallenbeck's care on an apple ranch near Okanogan in north central Washington on the western border of the Coleville Indian Reservation.

By November 13, Greg was flying combat missions over the Burma Road from an airbase at Toungoo in south-central Burma. After Burma fell to the Japanese, the *Flying Tigers* went back to Kunming. There, Greg served as a CAMCO squadron commander and flew over 300 hours of combat time by March 1942. He had individually accounted for six Japanese planes shot down before the Flying Tigers were disbanded, although that number would be contested in official records.

America was at war with Japan. The Marine's "Cactus Air Force" had been in newsreels for months, finally securing Henderson Airfield and Guadalcanal in early February 1942. When the Flying Tigers were disbanded, most of the surviving pilots were assimilated back into military commissions in the U.S. Air Force. Greg left the Flying Tigers under questionable circumstances in April 1942.

Out of a flying job and no longer holding an officer's commission, he returned to Washington State and reconsidered his options. Work was scarce and he again parked cars in a Seattle garage. Greg was granted custody of the children by the judge in August 1942. However, his wages were not enough to provide for a family. In October, his two older children went to live with Grace again, and Gloria was given into the care of Helene's sister. Through connections in the Marines, Greg was able to talk his way back into the Corps, finagle a major's commission, and get back into the kind of conflict he preferred.

Renowned American Ace pilot Captain Eddie Rickenbacker had established a record in WWI by shooting down 26 German aircraft. He had set the bar high. Only seven American fighter pilots broke the Rickenbacker record before WWII ended, with 27-40 "kills" by a single pilot. At the start of the war, the competition was among the Marines.

Being an Ace was an honor, but a Marine had to be more than an Ace to earn a Medal of Honor. One hundred eighteen Marine aviators shot down five or more enemy airplanes during WWII. [9] Nine of the Aces earned Medals of Honor. These pilots exemplify recipients who demonstrated repeated acts of valor extending over months of time, rather than a single heroic act. At least seven of the Aces were assigned to the "Cactus Air Force" during the air battles over Guadalcanal. Among these were four Medal of Honor recipients: Joe Jacob Foss, John Lucian Smith, Harold William "Indian Joe" Bauer (posthumously), and Robert Edward Galer. By the time Captain Joe Foss of VMF-121 took his last flight on January 25, 1943, he had downed 20 Japanese Zeros, four bombers, and two biplanes, tying the Rickenbacker record of 26. Joe was on the June 7, 1943, *Life* cover.

Upon his arrival in the Solomon Islands, Major Boyington's competitive nature—his drive to excel, his efforts to improve upon his last performance, and his determination to not be "bested"—focused upon knocking enemy aircraft out of the skies, as well as Eddie Rickenbacker's record. By early April 1943, Major Boyington was second-in-command of the Marine Fighter Squadron 121, the same position Captain Joe Foss had filled at Henderson Field during the battle for Guadalcanal. As Executive Officer, Major Boyington flew several combat missions over Guadalcanal that April.

The Marines then made a decision to make use of the best of his talents. While serving at the Espiritu Santo airfield in the New Hebrides, Major Boyington requested and was given the mission to mold a group of twenty-seven young, inexperienced, sometimes undisciplined, replacement pilots into a cohesive fighting team and take them into combat in the South Pacific Solomon Islands. Major Boyington was assigned duties as the Commanding Officer of the newly formed unit, VMF Squadron 214 in August. He and his fledgling fighters would earn themselves the nickname, *The Blacksheep Squadron*. His pilots dubbed him "Gramps," then "Pappy" because, being 31-years-old, he was a senior citizen to them.

In combat, Major "Pappy" Boyington remained a leader. Between September and December 1943, he took the *Black Sheep* on missions over the Russell Islands, New Georgia, Bougainville, New Britain, and New Ireland. During a thirty-two-day period of their first tour, he shot down 14 Japanese planes himself. In the October preparations for the Marines' landing on the Island of Bougainville, he took 24 fighters and persistently circled overhead the Kahili Airfield with its 60 Japanese planes, enticing the enemy to send up a numerically superior force into a dogfight.

Twenty of the Japanese fighters did not return to Kahili; all twenty-four of Major Boyington's planes returned to base. In twelve weeks of combat VMF-214 shot down 94 enemy planes, destroyed or damaged another 103 planes, sank supply and troop ships, and destroyed unnumbered ground installations. Nine pilots in Major Boyington's *Black Sheep* squadron had achieved the rank of Ace.

Once Major Boyington was an established Marine Ace he caught the attention of war correspondents and the newspapers back home. The wartime media began to seek photo opportunities with him. At Turtle Bay, Espiritu Santu on November 26, 1943, a Vought F4U-1A Corsair, Bureau Number 18086, was configured especially for him. Under the cockpit, twenty Rising Sun flag decals were fixed to the fuselage forward of the number 86. "Gregory Boyington, Major, USMC" was stenciled under the cockpit canopy. Uncharacteristically for Marines, a name was also painted in cursive forward of the red and white "kill" flags. The name would become another controversy for Greg when the war ended.

In the existing photograph, Major Boyington sits in the cockpit with helmet and goggles, talking with a crew chief who stands on the port wing above the big flaps. The crew chief's arm stretches out toward the cockpit, obscuring two letters of the angled name, the second of which appears to be the letter "y". The later contention would be whether that name was *Lucybelle* or *Lulubelle*.

Although WWII Marine pilots did not have claim to any single airplane, this plane has come down in history as Pappy Boyington's Corsair. Scale model adaptations of Corsair Number 86 remain popular today.

Presumed Killed in Action

Bougainville Airfield was secured for Marine use in November 1943, and in December, American forces were directing their attention at the Japanese fortress of Rabaul on New Britain Island, Papua New Guinea. By December, Major Boyington was nearing a record number of individual air victories and was closing in on Marine Corps history.

During the first Allied fighter sweep over Rabaul on December 17, 1943, Major Boyington was one airplane short of the Marine Ace record of 26 "kills." Three days into the new year, he established a new record of 28 enemy planes shot down before he was shot down himself. [10] As had been true among his opponents on the wrestling mats, few enemy pilots could claim to have bested "Pappy" Boyington in the air. In fact, there was only one.

On January 3, 1944, Major Boyington led 48 airplanes on a sweep over Rabaul. The fight began at 8:00 in the morning. This time when the squadrons returned to Bougainville, their "skipper" was not with them. A Japanese Zero fighter had shot up Major Boyington's Corsair, and he was last seen crashing into the sea. Declared missing-in-action and presumed killed-in-action, most of the world believed the Marine Ace had died in the air battle.

Words he had said to them earlier in 1943 echoed in the memories of his squadron mates.

"If you ever see me go down...I promise I'll meet you in a San Diego bar six months after the war." [11]

Competitive. Not to be bested.

Major Boyington had survived the downing of his plane and was picked up by an enemy submarine off Rabaul. Taken into captivity, during the following twenty months in prisoner of war camps he endured beatings with canes and baseball bats, torture, and starvation. Along with the other prisoners, he subsisted on a meager rice diet.

Lieutenant Raymond F. "Hap" Halloran, United States Army Air Corps, met Major Boyington on April 1, 1945, at Omori Prison Camp on mainland Japan, located southwest of Tokyo on the way to Yokohama. The Lieutenant, 23-years-old, had already been impressed with the Marine Ace's reputation for aerial combativeness. Over the next four months Major Boyington's natural leadership would impress him all the more.

In spite of his thin appearance, the sparkle in "Pappy's" eyes was evident. He was quietly defiant of his captors and looked out for the other POWs, taking special care of the younger men. In the evenings he tended to them in their Omori barracks, uplifting and encouraging them to stand up to the hardships. Major Boyington took the prison camp situation in stride, never despairing or complaining. His confidence buoyed the POWs. Lieutenant "Hap" Halloran knew he "would be okay as long as Pappy was there." [12]

On August 29, 1945, the world learned of the Marine Ace's survival when he was liberated from Omori Prison Camp. The "thrilling" and "electrifying" news was flashed from the USS *Ancon,* a cruiser in Tokyo Bay. His youngest daughter, five-year-old Gloria, staying at Grandma Grace's farm near Brewster, Washington, told reporters that she had known all along that her daddy was still alive because she had prayed for him. [13]

Lieutenant Colonel Boyington returned to the United States a celebrated war hero and was presented a Medal of Honor at a White House ceremony. On September 12, he joined with *Black Sheep* companions at a bar in San Francisco. The reunion was featured in a three page *Life* Magazine article on October 1, 1945.

For a year or so Greg Boyington remained in the public's consciousness.

CHAPTER 9
The Glamour Was Gone

"To be brave you have to be afraid or it means nothing."

Gregory "Pappy" Boyington [1]

As the public could read in newspaper and magazine columns, Greg
flew through marriages and divorces and battled against alcoholism. As
he moved from place to place, he could not hold on to his money. His
wives frequently received calls from police sergeants to come pick him
up from the "drunk tank." He spent many a night in a jail cell.

Lieutenant Colonel Boyington went to Marine Major Frank E.
Walton's Los Angeles home early in November 1945. Major Walton
was a public information officer at Camp Miramar and had been VMF-
214's intelligence officer. Frances (Relmah) Baker, a "honey-haired"
32-year-old former movie actress, was another guest at dinner. She had
been divorced from a San Francisco restaurant chain owner since 1942
and was working as an X-ray technician. As seemed to happen wherever he went, there was an immediate "hypnotic" magnetism between
Greg and the woman.

They went to Reno, Nevada on New Year's Eve, in part for Greg to break off with a woman by the name of Lucy. Having gotten to know each other for two months, Greg and Frances traveled together to Las Vegas, Nevada, and were married by a justice of the peace on Tuesday, January 9, 1946. Only four months had passed since his liberation from Omori Prison Camp. [2] Ahead were years of exhilaration and depression in Burbank, California.

The marriage triggered legal battles with another woman, an "old flame" who had been engaged to Greg while he had been at war in the Pacific and held in POW camps. At issue were such things as his Navy Cross medal, a three-carat engagement ring, and $20,000 Greg had sent Mrs. Lucy Malcolmson over the years to keep in trust for his three children. [3]

Other "engagements" became problematic for Greg. He was often intoxicated during interviews and public relations engagements, his speaking sometimes garbled and incomprehensible. The Marine Corps retired him from active service for medical reasons in 1947. Psychiatrists and psychologists tried to help him stop his drinking. In the ten years following his release from the POW camps, his name appeared in newspaper, tabloid, and magazine blurbs about arrests for public intoxication. Greg found it "next to impossible" to find and keep employment, going from one job to another. He was hired as a salesman in various venues. His six years as a draught-beer salesman was the longest job he held after leaving the Marines. Greg refereed professional wrestling matches when he was otherwise unemployed or out of money. A fight of one kind or another seemed to await him around every corner.

Having reached the age of forty-two, Greg had to admit to himself that he had never found peace of mind in whatever he had been seeking. He wrote in his memoir, "Shortly after the war the glamour was gone and there was nothing in my life but turbulence for nearly ten years." [4]

With Fran's help, Greg stepped into an Alcoholics Anonymous meeting in 1956 and began to climb out of the stupor he had fallen into after his release from the POW camps. After not flying for thirteen years he was able to pass his aviation medical physical, regain his flight ratings, and was hired as a charter pilot flying out of the San Fernando Valley in California.

Now sober, Greg appeared as one of the guest challengers on the 27th episode of CBS's weekly game show *To Tell The Truth*, airing on July 2, 1957. With Bud Collyer hosting, four celebrities, Polly Bergen, Ralph Bellamy, Kitty Carlisle, and Hy Gardner, attempted to correctly identify Greg, while two other impostors tried to fool the panel into thinking they were Pappy Boyington, the WWII Marine Ace. An indication that Greg's WWII fame had dimmed, none of the four panelists recognized him and only two correctly guessed his identity from questions they had asked.

The panel might have had an easier time identifying Greg the next year. In 1958, the success of his memoir, *Baa Baa Black Sheep*, put him on the *New York Times Best Sellers* book list. More notoriety followed.

In January 1959, Greg went to Colorado Springs to visit his son, Gregory, Jr., and enjoyed one of the proud moments in his life. The United States Air Force Academy (USAFA) was first established in 1954 and graduated its first class in 1959. Greg Jr., had been one of the first USAFA classmen cadets. A photograph of "Pappy" and Fran visiting with Greg Jr. at the Academy appeared on Page 67 of the January 26, 1959, *Life* Magazine.

In the *Life* article entitled *Bright Days for a "Bum,"* Fran was interviewed by Peter Bunzel. She described Greg's iron nerves, his drinking bouts and binges, his three years of sobriety, and the difficulties of their marriage. In the "post-rejuvenation days," a joyful Fran believed they were finally through the worst of it and that their marriage was "wonderful."

Greg was consulting for an upcoming Columbia Pictures movie based on his autobiography. He was traveling to Hollywood and other places distant from home and Fran. That summer he was often seen in the company of an about-to-be-divorced for the second time television actress and cover girl model by the name of Dolores "Dee" Tatum Shade. Dee, at the time married to a plane service operator in Riverside, California, had achieved some of her own *Life* notoriety in those years after "Pappy" had returned to the States from Omori Prison Camp.

In 1947, the Senate War Investigating Committee was looking into playboy millionaire Howard Hughes' failure to meet his wartime aircraft contracts. Mr. Hughes had had business dealings during the war with Julius Albert Krug, then Acting Chairman of War Production Board. Afterwards, President Truman had selected Mr. Krug as his Secretary of the Interior. Another person involved in the Senate investigation was John W. Meyer, a business adviser and public relations man for Mr. Hughes. One of his responsibilities was to arrange entertainment for potential investors and buyers. Dolores Tatum, 20-years-old, was on his roster of entertainers for government officials.

The Investigating Committee was intrigued by the fact that Mr. Meyer had arranged for Secretary of the Interior Krug to be entertained at Windham Hotel in New York City on Sunday October 13, 1946.

A *Life* August 4 issue might have been the first introduction to Dolores for most Americans. In an article titled *Summer Problems: Krug's Woe is a Tabloid Wow*, she is mentioned on Page 27 in a caption under a photo of an evening's expense account. The invoice indicates that John Meyer had paid Dolores $100 for entertaining Secretary Krug at the Windham Hotel the year before.

Dolores had her friend and attorney, Heinz A. L. Hellmold, file a sworn affidavit on her behalf to the Senate War Investigating Committee denying that she had ever met the Secretary and had never been paid by Mr. Meyer. Heinz also wrote a letter to *Life's* Editor. The letter appeared on Page 9 of the September 1, 1947 issue. Repeating Dolores' denials, Heinz also included a portfolio photo of the attractive 21-year-old actress and promoted her upcoming movie.

Dolores' first starring feature was in a romance movie, *Sarumba*, 1950, when she was cast as Maria. Roles in two suspense movies followed. "Dee" was cast as Terry Newell in *Mask of the Dragon*, 1951, and as Connie Duval in *Fingerprints Don't Lie*, 1951. None of these movies were exceptional box office hits.

In July 1959, after he had met Dolores, Greg's second marriage reached its end. He and Frances separated after nearly fourteen years together and were soon divorced on October 13. The reasons cited were his return to alcohol, temper outbursts, and absences from home. Two weeks later, October 27, Greg and Dolores met Chaplain F. W. Carlock of the Air Force Academy for a quiet ceremony in Denver. *Time* Magazine reported the visit in its Monday, November 9, 1959, Milestones section. Gregory ("Pappy") Boyington, 46, married Dolores

("Dee") Tatum, 33-years-old. Greg said his third marriage was the "first time I've been married sober." The couple married again December 21, 1960 to make it official.

The years that followed were difficult ones, as turmoil continued in his life. Columbia Pictures shelved the movie about Greg's wartime experiences. He described his marriage to Dee as one of "mayhem" committed against him and first sued for divorce in March 1964. [5] He and Dee made up and stayed together another eight years.

Greg went through periods of estrangement from his children. For the most part, Gloria, the youngest, had had no relationship with her father in the years that followed his return from the POW camps. Legal conflicts with his elder daughter and son-in-law, former prize-fighter Rocco "Rocky" Slater, emerged. Janet had begun a divorce action against Rocco at the same time her father and Fran were ending their marriage. Greg testified against Janet at divorce and child custody hearings in April and May 1960, when his granddaughter was two-years-old. [6] He and Dolores took over guardianship of Janet's daughter, Candice, and adopted the grandchild before 1965. Alcohol and drugs led to Janet's mysterious death around 1971, when she apparently died by suicide. [7]

A 2002 Internet message posted by Greg's granddaughter provides an example of the alienations and estrangements that were part of his life. Candice Gregg Boyington wrote:

"I was adopted by Gregory Pappy Boyington and Dolores Boyington. I am looking for my real mother, I believe to be Janet Boyington, sister of Gregory Boyington Jr. (nickname Bobby). Do you have any information on how to contact Gregory or Janet Boyington? I am very anxious to receive any information regarding this matter." [8]

Although physical fitness was always important to Greg, he had also been a heavy cigarette smoker. Diagnosed with lung cancer, he and Dee moved to Fresno in 1971 so he could be close to the local Veterans Administration hospital. Cancer surgeries removed a part of his lung and stayed the spread of the illness for a time. His health began a slow, progressive deterioration. He returned for further cancer treatments over the next twenty years.

Greg separated from Dee on October 8, 1971, moving out on his own. The divorce action became newsworthy in March 1972. Unlike his two earlier brides, Dolores did not go away readily. The divorce was not completed until 1973. Greg was single again at age 61. For the most part, the mayhem in his life was coming to a close.

Pappy met Josephine "Jo" Wilson Moseman through friends of a friend. Jo, divorced from a wealthy highway contractor, lived on Fresno's Columbia Drive East in an expensive house near the Sunnyside golf course. She was a strong and assertive woman. A recovering alcoholic herself, Jo took abstinence and sobriety seriously. She insisted that Greg not have a drink in his hand if he intended to be in her life. She also convinced him to play a lot of golf, a game he approached with characteristic vigor. Greg played on the courses with the same competitive intensity that had earned him a wrestling championship at the University of Washington forty years earlier. He and Jo, then 45, married August 4, 1975 at her home. [9] Her address was where friends and former squad mates would find Pappy for most of the rest of his life.

His WWII exploits as VMF-214 squadron commander soon entered American homes via the television set. Columbia Pictures took his autobiography off its shelves and turned it into a made-for-television movie with actor Robert Conrad starring as Pappy Boyington. The two-hour pilot film first aired on NBC, September 21, 1976, and became the popular *Baa Baa Black Sheep* series. Greg was a technical consultant to the show that ran for 36 episodes through the 1976-77 TV seasons. Predominantly off-camera, he had a short walk-on role as a visiting general during the show's second season.

The television series was only loosely based on Greg's memoir. Written for the viewers' entertainment, it created a version of Pappy Boyington for the public. *Baa Baa Blacksheep* depicted the Marine pilots as casual, charming, dauntless, risk-taking, and somewhat non-compliant, oppositional aviators. The storyline typically described the Black Sheep pilots as "a bunch of misfits and drunks." While Greg "Pappy" Boyington had returned briefly to American awareness and enjoyed increased celebrity, the show cost him the long-time friendship of many of his VMF-214 squadron mates.

Pappy and Josephine had happy days together. He believed them to be the most fulfilling years of his life. Into the 1980s, they traveled to air shows around the States where he was pleased to autograph books and color prints for his admirers. The days when he wondered if he had been a "bum" in his life were less frequent.

Greg had developed a love of fighting as a child, often coming home with a bloody nose after having been on the streets of St. Maries with his playmates and neighbors. [10] Pappy's final fight was with cancer, an illness he was not able to "best." The Marine Ace died on Monday, January 11, 1988, in a Fresno hospice for cancer patients. He was 75-years-old. Obituaries noted that survivors included Josephine, retired Air Force Colonel Gregory Boyington Jr. of Alameda, California, Gloria Boyington Schneider of Everett, Washington, his brother, Keith Boyington of Spokane, and eight grandchildren.

Gregory Boyington was buried in Arlington National Cemetery with more than 300,000 other heroes. Near his upright white marble headstone at Section 7-A Site 150 stands the privately-purchased marker for U.S. Army Technical Sergeant Joe Louis (Barrow), the long-running heavyweight boxing champion of the world from 1938-1940.

CHAPTER 10
The Fight To Remember One Man's Bravery

"The first duty is to remember. We have an
obligation to the Captain Waskows of World War II,
and all our wars, to remember." [1]

Rick Atkinson
Military historian

The Marines never forgot "Pappy" Boyington's valor in service to the country. VMA-214 is one of four AV-8B Harrier squadrons assigned to Marine Aircraft Group-13, 3rd Marine Aircraft Wing. The squadron relocated from MCAS El Toro, California to MCAS Yuma, Arizona in 1987. In June 1989, it formed the first night attack squadron with the AV-8B Night Attack Harrier.

VMA-214's mission "is to provide close-air support, conduct armed reconnaissance and limited air-defense for Marine Expeditionary Forces." [2] The sign in front of the squadron's headquarters proclaims VMA-214 to be the Home of the *Blacksheep Squadron*. Theirs is a proud history.

Jan Portugal, a California artist, was commissioned in 1988 to sculpt a life-sized bronze bust of Greg. The 29-inch tall by 12-in diameter bust was presented by Hap Halloran and Consolidated Freightways to VMA-214 in a ceremony on June 22,1989. Josephine Boyington and Greg Jr. were both present among the dignitaries and *Blacksheep Squadron* personnel. [3]

Apart from his lasting legacy within the Marine Corps, Greg Boyington had some celebrity after the war, but it was not sustained in the public mind. For years he seemed to be forgotten, including in his birthplace. In some communities, Americans even protested efforts to remember him. [4]

How Greg might have been remembered in Coeur d'Alene and St. Maries were it not for Veterans determined to honor him is uncertain. Friends and neighbors had known him as Greg Hallenbeck for most of the fourteen years he had lived in Idaho and when he had returned there in later summers to work. He had graduated from Tacoma's Lincoln High School and the University of Washington, Class of 1934, as Greg Hollenbeck.

Eight years after Greg died, the Coeur d'Alene Marine Corps League Pappy Boyington Detachment 966 was first chartered in December 1996, with permission from MCL national headquarters and the Boyington family. Pappy's photograph, Medal of Honor, citation, other medals of valor, a newspaper clipping, a squadron photo, and a model of his F4U Corsair are on public display in the hallway of the Coeur d'Alene Marine Memorial Club.

Around 2004, the 161 Detachment members began a movement to rename the local airport in honor of Greg Boyington. The proposal had the support of the Disabled American Veterans, the Distinguished Flying Cross Society, and every veterans' organization in Kootenai County, where Coeur d'Alene is the County seat. The County commissioners, Airport Advisory Board, and the airport manager were not enthusiastic and rejected the plan to honor the Marine Ace in 2005 by refusing to vote on the proposal. The controversy between the veterans and the commissioners did not go away for the next two years.

There was yet more controversy about honoring Greg Boyington 500 miles west of Coeur d'Alene. In the December, 1998 UW alumni magazine, *Columns*, A Look Back at UW History, Tom Griffin had written a tribute to *Gregory Boyington–Our 'Black Sheep' Hero*. [5] Eight years later, how much of the student body shared his respectful view of the Marine aviator was in question.

The University of Washington student government, in a split vote during its February 2006 deliberations, rejected a resolution to build a memorial in honor of five Medal of Honor recipients who had graduated from UW, in particular its most legendary alumnus. [6] Despite the established standards by which the Medal of Honor is awarded, that the individual's valor include risk to life, that it be exemplary enough to clearly exceed the obligations of duty and to distinguish it from other common acts of bravery, that the actions must be uncontested by those present and beyond any justified criticism, some of the student senators did not believe a Marine set the example of a UW graduate. They thought it inappropriate to honor someone who had killed other people. Some unfounded, derogatory remarks were made about Greg. [7]

Events at the University of Washington to not remember a hero sparked news coverage, newspaper articles, Internet traffic, and e-mail forwards. At the time this controversy appeared in the media, the UW alumni and friends decided to honor Greg Boyington by establishing the Lieutenant Colonel "Pappy" Boyington Memorial Scholarship Fund. The fund provides scholarships to undergraduate students who are either a United States Marine Corps veteran or are the child of a United States Marine Corps veteran.

Opposing a statue honoring Greg Boyington on the UW campus might serve as an example of freedom of speech and having one's own opinion. Veterans on the campus voiced their own strong opinions about remembering the heroics of a brave man and the student government's decision. Not one of the student senators who protested the tribute to Greg had experienced years of brutal treatment in an enemy POW compound during a war that threatened the freedoms of people around the world.

Had the student government done more thorough research, they might have been swayed by the fact that their university had more graduates who had earned Medals of Honor than any other public university—eight. Only the service academies could claim more.

The UW student council did reverse its decision and withdrew their opposition to honor the Medal of Honor alumni. In April, the Student Senate of the Associated Students at the University of Washington (AS) passed a resolution to commemorate the Medal of Honor recipients and called for a memorial on the Seattle campus.

In October 2006, the students formed a task force to fulfill the Medal of Honor Memorial Project through the University of Washington Foundation. [8] In its pledge drive, the Project acknowledged the Medal recipients as "heroes—ordinary men who find themselves in extraordinary circumstances and act with unfathomable courage." By December 2007, the Task Force volunteers had presented a plan for the memorial to the administration, received approval, raised over $100,000 from private sources and were working with an artist on the final design. Initial hope was that the memorial would be a reality by fall, 2008. [9] Private contributions rose to $152,000.

The monument was built on a five-point star laid down in a traffic circle on Memorial Way, in the center of campus. The university president stated, "The memorial will be a permanent, powerful reminder of the extraordinary things that can happen when ordinary people take action." [10] His comment might just as well describe those who persisted in making the Memorial a reality as it does the Medal recipients. One of the Seattle sculptors who worked on the monument hoped students would be inspired to their own "extraordinary feats" by walking through the inner circle of the Monument, enclosed in the words Courage, Sacrifice, Resolve, Valor, and Humility.

The Dedication Ceremony took place on Veterans Day, November 11, 2009, when a color guard, bands, sixteen Medal of Honor recipients, Veterans organizations, ROTC and JROTC units, and Washington's governor began a march at 10:00 AM.

In Coeur d'Alene, the North Idaho Marines reacted to the 2006 UW incidents by reinvigorating their efforts to honor Greg. The Kootenai County commissioners continued their opposition. The stalemate was resolved by the election of two new commissioners who favored the idea. Once they took office in 2007, Detachment 966 again proposed dedicating the local airport in "Pappy's" honor.

Greg "Pappy" Boyington was paid tribute in his birthplace 64 years after he earned the Medal of Honor. On August 8, the commission voted the name change into effect. At a Saturday ceremony on September 22, 2007, active Marine Harrier pilots, former Marines from around the state as well as the nation, Kootenai County commissioners, a state representative, and Greg Boyington, Jr. gathered at the airport.

In 1991, just years after Greg Boyington had died, State Representative Margie Chadderdon and her husband had bought a legacy print, a photograph of "Pappy" framed inside a star. Mrs. Chadderdon gifted the print to the county commissioners at the September 2007 dedication. The print will hang in a memorial at the Kootenai County Courthouse, possibly to be moved to the airport later.

Since September 22, 2007, flights land at Coeur d'Alene Airport/ Pappy Boyington Field.

For MCL Detachment 966 the memorial effort did not end with the naming of Pappy Boyington Field. The Detachment gathered contributions for the cost of the airport's new signage. The former Marines also resolved to raise funds for a memorial at the airport, including a proposed statue sculpted by Bryan Ross, to honor the Marine Ace from Coeur d'Alene.

Kevin Gonzales, having served in the Marines, 1984-88, is a member of Detachment 966. He was inspired by the efforts of the many veterans he watched fight to pay tribute to a Medal of Honor recipient. Remembering Greg Boyington's bravery, the veterans seemed to have grown more determined in the face of resistance from others. Kevin featured these veterans in a 90-minute documentary that chronicles the community events surrounding the efforts to change the name of Coeur d'Alene Airport. [11]

The tenacity, determination, and bravery of one man have an impact on those around him and upon future generations. Greg Boyington showed others the will and spirit to improve upon his last performance.

Competitive.

CHAPTER 11
What Tribute Is Paid to The Living?

"For without belittling the courage with which men have died, we should not forget the acts of courage with which men have lived."

President John F. Kennedy [1]

"Stand, Marines. He served on Samar!"

The Island of Samar in the Central Philippine Islands was an inhospitable place for Marines at the end of the nineteenth century. A revolution had broken out in the islands in 1896 when Filipino insurgents decided to establish self-rule. The commanding U.S. Army general called for the Marines in the autumn of 1901. Assigned to secure the southern part of Samar, a battalion of Marines comprised of thirteen officers, two surgeons, and 300 enlisted Marines landed on 24 October and got down to business immediately.

Initially small expeditions were sent out from Basey and Balangiga, small towns on Leyte Gulf, to counter the roving bands of insurgent guerrillas. The *insurrectos* established themselves in trenchworks along the Sohoton and Cadacan Rivers, but could not withstand the Marine operations. Within days, their numbers had been reduced and they withdrew to a cave fortress in the cliffs above the Sohoton River.

In mid-November, the battalion split into three columns with a mission to penetrate the region that no white soldiers had ever entered and take a cliff stronghold believed to be impregnable. The march would require the Marines to overcome guerrilla defenses, jungle terrain, swollen rivers, and serrating volcanic rock. On November 17, 1901, the Marine columns launched a surprise attack across the Sohoton River, along trails booby-trapped with poison spears, bamboo guns, pits, and suspended boulders. They climbed bamboo ladders and skirted narrow ledges to reach enemy positions in the sheer cliffs 200 feet above the river. By the time they reached their objective, many of the men were without shoes, having had them cut from their feet by the volcanic stone.

Bleeding feet or not, by the time the fighting was over, the insurgents had been driven from the cliffs and their camps.

The Marines were then tasked to cross Samar, east to west coast, to lay down a route for a telegraph line. On December 8, they left Basey in two columns abreast to determine their starting point on the east coast. After thirty-five excruciating miles, the Marines reached the port of Lanang. With this as the "jump off" point, a detachment of fifty men departed inland on the morning of December 28 to reconnoiter a possible trail for the telegraph cable.

The march encountered wild tropical jungle, swollen rivers, treacherous rapids, heavy rains, continually wet and shredded clothing, fevers, serious illness, exhaustion, swollen and bloody feet, reduced rations, near starvation, lost trails, disrupted communication, flooded camps, men physically incapacitated or losing rational thought, and many dying along the trails. The situation became desperate and the column split into segments, one pushing ahead eventually arriving at Basey, another staying in place in the midst of the jungle, and a third finding the way back to Lanang. A relief effort to retrieve the stranded contingent of men left in the jungle finally brought the starved Marines to the coast in mid-January 1902.

The mission had covered about 190 miles. Some in the patrol had marched nearly 250 miles, having participated in the relief expedition.

When it was over, the battalion commander reported that his Marines had "marched without murmur for twenty-nine days." Ten Marines died in the march across Samar.

The battalion was withdrawn March 2, 1902, after 129 grueling days on Samar.

For years after the Philippine Insurrection, the officers and men who survived Samar were recognized in a traditional tribute paid by their fellow Marines. When one of them walked into a room, the others would rise to the command: "Stand, Marines. He served on Samar!"

Those who returned home

As introduced earlier in this book, 181 Marine Medal of Honor recipients were researched during the *Semper Fidelis* study. Fifty-seven (or 31%), having demonstrated heroic bravery, survived their wars and came home. Thirty earned their Medals in WWII, fourteen in Korea, and thirteen in Vietnam. Like Gregory Boyington, their stories did not end with their Citations.

By the start of *Semper Fidelis*, twenty-five of the recipients who had survived the wars were deceased. Thirty-two recipients remained alive: thirteen from WWII, eight from Korea, and eleven from Vietnam.

During the research, Douglas Thomas Jacobson, WWII, died September 10, 2000, at the age of 74-years. William Earl Barber, Korea, died November 30, 2002, at the age of 83-years. Joseph Jacob Foss, WWII, died January 1, 2003, at the age of 87-years. Mitchell Paige, WWII, died November 15, 2003, at the age of 85-years. Raymond Gilbert Davis, Korea, died September 3, 2003, at the age of 88-years. Raymond Michael Clausen, Jr., Vietnam, died May 30, 2004, at the age of 56-years. Richard Earl Bush, WWII, died June 7, 2004, at the age of 79-years. Richard Keith Sorenson, WWII, died October 9, 2004, at the age of 80-years. Louis Hugh Wilson, Jr., WWII, died June 21, 2005, at the age of 85-years. Robert Edward Galer, WWII, died June 27, 2005, at the age of 91-years. George Herman O'Brien, Jr., Korea, died March 11, 2005, at the age of 78-years. Reginald Rodney Myers, Korea, died October 23, 2005, at the age of 85-years.

Raymond G. Murphy, Korea, died April 6, 2007, at the age of 77-years. Jefferson J. DeBlanc, WWII, died November 22, 2007, at 86-years. Jack H. Lucas, WWII, the youngest Marine to earn the Medal, died June 5, 2008, at 80-years. James E. Swett, WWII, died January 18, 2009, at 88-years. Everett P. Pope, WWII, died July 16, 2009, the morning of his 90th birthday.

Among these men, only Richard Earl Bush appeared to have been forgotten in his hometown.

As of December 2010, fifteen Marine recipients remained alive: two from WWII, three from Korea, and ten from Vietnam. The two living WWII recipients were in their mid-eighties. The average age reached by the thirty WWII veterans following their return from war had reached 76-years at that time. Two living recipients from Korea were in their early eighties and one was seventy-nine. The average age reached by the Korea recipients following their return from war was then 74-years. The average age of the three Vietnam recipients who had died is fifty-one years. The ten living recipients from Vietnam are all in their mid-sixties and well into their seventies. The average age reached by the thirteen veterans who survived the Vietnam War had reached 67-years.

Of the fifty-seven men who came home, afterwards twenty-nine continued their military careers in the Corps: ten from WWII, eight from Korea, and eleven from Vietnam. The other twenty-eight recipients returned to civilian life after their wartime service: twenty following WWII, six following Korea, and two following the Vietnam War.

Lasting tributes dedicated to those who returned home

Remembering heroism, paying tribute to the brave, does not have to be a posthumous memorial or monument. Recognition of those who survived the battles, returned from distant wars in places most citizens would never see first hand, has been extended. Honors to living native sons have been important to many communities.

In addition to being on the cover of *Life*, *Time*, and *NRA* magazines, being interviewed or highlighted on TV programs, marshaling parades, and giving presentations, many permanent public tributes have been paid to the Medal recipients who survived. An airport, American Legion Post, two schools, five statues, a street, memorial display, commemorative issue stamp envelope, combat base, highway bridge, National Guard Armory, athletic field, a sign outside childhood home, town historical marker, a city park, playground, and a high school auditorium were dedicated to honor various living recipients.

Dedications have also followed for those who returned from the wars and have since died. Four Navy ships, two airports, U.S. Post Office, two highway bridges, a highway, two streets, a building, USMC Base, V.A. Hospital, two commemorative halls, an AMVETS Post, four Marine Corps League Detachments, a Purple Heart Chapter, school, wing of a school, scholarship, college dormitory, three memorial displays, a Veterans Nursing Home, three Veterans parks, a baseball field, two monuments, and an inscription on a monument have been named in tribute to these men.

Stand, America. He fought on Iwo Jima.

Wilson Douglas Watson was an "Arkie" from Earle, Arkansas, born on February 16, 1921. Whether he was actually born in Earle is not clear. Some records give his birthplace as Tuscumbia, Arkansas, or Alabama. [2] Identifying his birthplace is only one of many difficulties encountered in searching for the facts of his life. There remains little to be discovered about him on Internet sites.

Wilson, or Will, preferred his middle name and was known as "Doug" to those who were familiar with him. Most who knew him would have lived on nearby farms or attended seven grades of school with him in Earle.

Earle, home to about 1,900 residents, was a town of less than three square miles on the eastern edge of Arkansas, twenty-two miles west of West Memphis on State Route 64. The surrounding land is flat, covered in arable soil deposited long ago by Mississippi River flooding and irrigated by numerous rivers, tributaries, and streams. Small remnants of swampland remain, like the Gibson Bayou north of town. The Earle area is beset by annual tornadoes at one of the highest rates in the United States.

Doug was eight-years-old when immense dust storms darkened the skies west of the 100th Meridian and drought scorched the land. His family was among those two-thirds of farmers who were able to hold on to their land during the Dust Bowl years of 1929-33, when 375,000 people migrated out of the affected states to start over in California.

Instead of spending hours sitting at a school desk, Doug worked on the family farm, helping in the fight for subsistence. Hunting game and shooting varmints with rifles and shotguns were a natural part of his boyhood. He is one of the sixty-two recipients who did not finish high school, having stopped going to school in the seventh grade when the drought years were reaching their climax.

Earl High School, home of the "Bulldogs," sits on Route 64 on the edge of town. Getting to the school building would not have been a hardship for Doug. As was true for all of the Medal recipients, the opportunity for education was available to him. Doug's choice to quit his formal schooling provides insight into what part education and book learning play in later Medal of Honor actions.

Bravery does not rely on school education

Among those for whom school records could be determined, the majority of Marine Medal recipients, 134, attended public schools. At least eighteen attended parochial or private schools. Nine attended rural or county schools, five attended military academies for their high school education, and four attended technical high schools. Two earned GEDs.

Book learning was not necessarily the challenge these men sought and academics generally did not hold their early interest. If they could not associate schoolwork with the occupations they envisioned for themselves, academic learning took an obvious secondary importance. These men likely had low tolerance for boredom and generated their own excitements to avoid being bored. Focusing attention on anything found not exciting presented them difficulties.

Many of the Medal recipients were said to have skipped classes or been truant from school. John Basilone and Jack Lucas are two of many examples. John was often truant, took ten years to finally graduate from grade school, and chose at the age of fifteen not to go on to high school. Jack left school at the age of fourteen to go to war. Five others besides Doug Watson (3%) did not attend any high school. An additional 56 (31%) quit junior high or high school before graduating.

Doug Watson did not drop out of school to go into Earle to hangout at the pool hall or on a street corner. He was like the other Medal recipients who stopped going to school to get busy at life or went to work to earn income and provide support for their families: like William Robert Caddy, who worked as a helper on a milk truck and turned his paychecks over to his mother. After dropping out of school early, six, like Doug, went to work on the farm, four drove trucks, several joined the Civilian Conservation Corps, three operated machines or equipment, three were store clerks, two worked in foundries, another two in factories, two were mechanics, and two others were laborers.

Work available to those who did not have high school diplomas also included welding, carpentry, painting, construction labor, textile work, bartending, draftsman work, and taxi driving. Thirty of these men quit high school specifically to enlist in the Marines, for most because a war was ongoing and they did not want to wait until graduation to get involved.

Fifty-six (31%) of the men had some college after high school. Of these, 37 (20%) graduated with college degrees before the actions that earned them Medals. Some of the recipients did excel at their studies, earning A's throughout their school years. At least seven of them earned either academic or athletic scholarships to college. Everett Pope graduated magna cum laude from Bowdoin College in Maine and was designated a Phi Beta Kappa. Two recipients graduated with Law degrees and one earned a Master's level graduate degree.

The college graduates attended a variety of colleges and universities, large and small, state and private. Among them are graduates of Auburn University, Baylor University, Clemson, Duke, Harvard, Holy

Cross University, Loyola, the Naval Academy, Princeton, Texas A & M, and Yale. Twelve men interrupted their higher education, quitting college or junior college specifically to enlist in the Marines.

Lack of education by those who dropped out of school is often evident in letters they sent home. Had a school English teacher graded their correspondences, the letters would have been marked with red pen for poor spelling, grammar, and punctuation. These men seemed at times to have limited vocabularies, punctuating their conversations with the vulgarities and slang often common among enlisted Marines. However, their sentiments and perspective on events surrounding them could be evocative and insightful.

Lance Corporal Thomas Elbert Creek, for example, was still 17-years-old when he enlisted in the Marines and saw extensive combat in Quang Tri Province, Vietnam. The scars on his face were testimony to the realities of six months in a war. He had completely lost the hearing in his right ear to the noise of battle and had developed a three-packs-of-cigarettes-daily habit to keep his nerves in check. Marines Lance Corporal Creek called friends were killed in large numbers during the 1969 *Operation Dewey Canyon*. In letters home to family in Amarillo, Texas, he discouraged his 17-year-old brother from enlisting in the Marines, hoping that neither he nor his older brother would come to Vietnam and experience the hardships he had endured. He was far from being the teenager hanging out at Palo Duro High School whom Amarillo teachers and fellow students might have remembered. [3]

Education did not end for the Medal recipients when they joined the Marines. They were accomplished students and learners in areas of interest. When once in the Marines, they did well in training, giving full attention to the lessons and often requesting or being assigned to advanced or specialized courses of training. They tended to score within *expert* ranges for Marine skills. Promotions came at an accelerated rate for many, especially during times of war. Those who had started out as enlisted men and accepted commissions as officers (called "Mustangs") were just as competitive for positions and promotions as the men who had gone directly from college into the officer ranks.

Academic performance, grades in school, and level of education reached are not determining factors in heroically brave actions. Nor is level of accomplishment in school a reflection of the intelligence of these men.

Pick up skills and learn lessons easily.

While their teachers might have been frustrated by some of the recipients not working up to their full scholarly potential, the acumen of those with less than a high school education was apparent in other areas of endeavors like mechanics, athletics, outdoorsmanship, and skilled trades. They seem consistently to be remembered as being skilled in the things they chose to do. Their employers, trainers, and drill instructors likely appreciated the ease with which they learned skills, duties, and responsibilities.

Men like Doug Watson were happy to learn when they could turn their attention to things that interested them. The majority of the recipients were promoted to successive ranks in either expected or accelerated intervals. Many were assigned duties as instructors in military schools and classes. Several were assigned to recruit duties as representatives of the Marine Corps.

Doug worked on the farm near Earle until he was twenty-one. When America entered WWII, he faced a decision. Having learned that a person had to fight and work hard to hold on to something important to him, and characteristic of the recipients seeking to better themselves and their situations, Doug decided to go over to Little Rock. He enlisted in the Marines on August 6, 1942.

Four months later, after his recruit training in San Diego, Private Watson went overseas as an automatic rifleman with the 2d Battalion, 9th Marines, 3rd Division. He spent more than nine months training for amphibious assaults ahead on island shores. Private Watson landed with the Marines on the bloodied beaches of Bougainville on November 1, 1943, and fought in the nearby jungles for 57 days. Leaving that island two days after Christmas, he went to Guadalcanal for more training and preparation. His next destination was a volcanic island shaped like a peanut, thirty-miles long and four to eight-miles wide. The 2d Battalion left their departure line at 7:40 AM on July 21, 1944, and landed on Guam's Blue Beach.

On this island, Private Watson participated in some of the fiercest fighting the 9th Marines had yet encountered. He helped capture Mount Tenjo Road, fought over ridges, into caves, and through rugged terrain. For five days he battled along with Captain Louis Wilson to seize and hold the Fonte Plateau. And once Guam was declared secured on August 9, he stayed on the island to help sweep it of stragglers and to prepare for the next island.

After the battle for Guam, just over a year had passed since Private Watson had enlisted. He had experienced eighty-two days of combat on two islands and more was ahead. The Marines were anticipating that they would be hopping Pacific islands until they reached mainland Japan. Another three months passed before Private Watson trudged through the surf carrying his automatic rifle to fight for more land. The terrain of the next island was not like the tropical jungles of Bougainville and Guam, and certainly nothing like the agricultural lands around Earle, Arkansas.

Private Watson celebrated his 24th birthday just before Navy battleships began pounding Iwo Jima in preparation for the Marines' invasion. When the first assault waves motored towards Iwo, he remained behind as part of a floating reserve, ready to be called into the fight at any time.

On February 24, five days after the D-Day landings, the companies of 2d Battalion landed on the island. They moved into position on the southern end of the Motoyama Plateau in the central portion of the island, taking 3rd Division's left flank. Although relatively flat, the terrain was rough and jagged, and well defended. The 9th Marines were going to have to hammer against the backbone of the enemy's defenses for three days of grueling combat.

On February 25 at 7:00 AM, the 9th Marines pushed the attack across Airfield No. 2. The going was slow, fought an inch at a time, pillbox by pillbox, under a barrage of artillery, mortars, and machine-gun fire. The 2d Battalion found the going the slowest, encountering intense enemy resistance. By evening their advance had progressed only a couple hundred yards to the southwestern edge of the airfield.

Private Watson was given the word: get what sleep he could. The next day the attack through the center was to kick off at 8:00 AM.

The Japanese were well established in the high ground past the airfield, especially on Hill 199-Oboe. Positioned in the volcanic sandstone of high ridges, in the draws, and in the crags and rocky outcroppings, the northern high ground gave the enemy excellent crossing fields of fire to lay down upon advancing forces. Minefields and tank ditches obstructed the approaches to the hill. As Private Watson's squad used fire and movement to advance, intense machine-gun fire pinned them in place.

Private Watson charged a pillbox, firing his automatic weapon into the pillbox opening. Assaulting alone, he kept the position silenced with his constant fire until he was able to close the distance and lob a grenade inside. He then rushed to the rear of the pillbox and killed the soldiers attempting to escape. His platoon was able to move again toward Hill 199-O. The day ended with the 2d Battalion digging into defensive positions as dark descended.

On the morning of February 27, while the attack toward Hill 199-O gained momentum, Private Watson's platoon was halted again by enemy fire from the high ground. With his assistant gunner, he rushed up a small rise, scaled a jagged ridge, and charged for the crest of a hill. The Japanese counterattacked from their positions on the reverse slope with knee-mortars, grenades, and machine-gun fire.

Standing erect and exposed on the top of the hill, firing his automatic rifle from his hip, Private Watson fought back the Japanese for fifteen minutes, allowing his platoon to advance to his position. Only when his weapon was emptied of ammunition did he stand down long enough for re-supply. By then, he had been wounded seven times and had killed an estimated sixty enemy combatants. By day's end, the uphill battling had gained the Marines Airfield No. 2, the commanding terrain north of the field, and Hill 199-O.

Private Watson fought for three more days during the advance toward Hill 331 in Iwo's northeast sector. Ninety of his days in the Marines had been in combat. During the March 2 assault, a gunshot to his neck wounded him. He was evacuated from Iwo Jima and treated aboard a hospital ship. He recovered from his physical and medical wounds. Seven months after he left the island, President Harry S. Truman presented Doug Watson his Medal of Honor at the White House on October 5, 1945. He was back on home soil.

Doug was one of seven men from Arkansas who earned Medals of Honor in WWII. The six others were born in the small towns of Lonoke, Morrilton, Lepanto, and Harrison and from the larger cities of Blytheville and Little Rock. Four served in the Army and two were in the Navy. Doug was the only WWII recipient from Arkansas in the Marine Corps. Three of the recipients were killed in action. The bodies of two of these were returned to Arkansas for burial. One, a Navy Medic killed on Iwo Jima assisting wounded Marines the day after Doug was evacuated from the island, was buried in Missouri.

Of the four recipients who returned home after the war, one later served ten terms as the sixth Lieutenant Governor of Arkansas. Another played professional football with the Detroit Lions and later served as the seventh Lieutenant Governor, narrowly defeating the other in a close general election. One recipient remained in the Army, reaching the rank of master sergeant and retiring in 1965, living out his life in Florida.

The folks in Arkansas were proud of Doug. A few days after he met President Truman at the White House, *Doug Watson Day* was celebrated in Marion, Arkansas. On Thursday, October 25, 1945, Doug Watson was officially welcomed home in Earle by the state governor, a state representative, and the state commander of the American Legion. The streets and the high school auditorium thundered with the shouts of the Earle locals welcoming their native hero home. [4] On Armistice Day,

November 12, he led the parade down the main streets of Memphis, Tennessee.

After his discharge from the Marines in 1946, Doug decided not to return to the farm or to try to settle into civilian life. He joined the Army in September and would again fight later in Korea, alongside the Marines. He reached the rank of Army Staff Sergeant as a mess hall cook.

There is little information about Doug Watson's life following the Korean War. Counted among the *Forgotten*, he is one of the recipients for whom the tributes to his actions appeared to have culminated in a Citation for valor, a meeting with the president at the White House, and in post-war parades. Newspaper archives provide some hints of turmoil in his life. For a while in early 1963, photographs and articles about him appeared in the national AP news outlets.

Doug married a woman by the name of Vida, and the couple had a son in 1954. Over the passing years, he was in and out of hospitals for treatments for his battle wounds. Then while serving as a mess sergeant at Fort Rucker, Alabama, he eventually "got tired of messing" with the Army. He had been "passed around" enough, had been promised a discharge, and wanted out after more than twenty-one years of service. Frustrated that the service had gotten "his records all messed up," and reminiscent of his initiating a charge up Hill 199-O on Iwo Jima, Sergeant Watson left of his own accord. He drove from Fort Rucker in his car on Saturday, October 27, 1962, headed up Route 167, kept traveling for 390 miles, and went home to Earle.

Perhaps events unfolding in the world news had been having an impact on him. Sergeant Watson's departure from the Army was not initially newsworthy. For the previous two weeks, most journalists had their attention fixed toward the Caribbean and the possibility that another World War was about to erupt.

The Cuban Missiles Crisis began on October 14, 1962, after a U.S. reconnaissance plane had photographed several nuclear missiles sites on the island, supplied by order of Soviet Premier Nikita Khrushchev.

In a TV address to the nation, President Kennedy declared a naval blockade on Cuba. He also threatened to attack the USSR if a Cuban missile was ever launched against the United States. The president dispatched a U.S. fleet, including eight aircraft carriers, to patrol an arc 500 miles east of Cuba, and prepare to fire on the approaching Soviet vessels. The world was pensive, wondering if a nuclear World War III was about to break out. Khrushchev backed down on October 28, 1962, ordering the Soviet ships to turn back to the USSR.

Doug was back in Arkansas by the time the ships reversed course.

A bulletin did go out that Sergeant Watson was AWOL. After thirty days, on November 26, he was declared to have deserted. Sergeant Watson was in Marked Tree, Arkansas, a town due north of Earle, staying at his mother-in-law's with his wife and son. He was arrested there on February 11, 1963. On Thursday, February 14, he was held at the Crittenden County Jail in Marion, the town east of Earle that had dedicated a day to him eighteen years earlier. [5]

What the residents living in the 144-square-mile area of these three towns thought of Doug's arrest would be interesting to know. One, a jailer in Marion and a longtime friend, fondly remembered attending the Earle grade school with him. [6] On Friday, Doug said goodbye to his friend and was transported to the Little Rock Air Force Base to be transferred to Fort Sill, Oklahoma to face desertion charges. Sergeant Watson met with an officer from the Judge Advocate General's Staff who would represent him if he faced a court martial and needed legal assistance.

That Saturday, an Army spokesman reported that no charges had been filed, that Sergeant Watson was not under arrest or detention, and that he had been hospitalized for rest and evaluation. [7] The next Saturday afternoon, February 24, his Army dress uniform showing the rank of private, he was flown to Walter Reed Army Hospital in Washington, D.C. for further medical evaluation. [8] The date of his discharge is not in public records. A question mark stands in the space that would indicate the end of his U.S. Army Years of Service. The discharge likely came in 1963, following his hospitalization at Walter Reed. His rank at discharge was Army Specialist 5, equivalent to a Marine corporal.

What happened in Doug's life between 1963 and 1994 was not discovered during the searches for him. He appears to have finished out his life across the state from his hometown, in a secluded region of mountains, valleys, rivers, picturesque waterfalls, and springs in northwest Arkansas. Records indicate that he lived in Russellville. But for the forests, the terrain in the Arkansas River Valley might have served as a reminder of Iwo Jima and Korea.

It might have been interesting to ask Doug about his reactions to an event in the Russellville news during the 1987 Christmas season. A 47-year-old retired United States Air Force sergeant massacred fourteen of his family members gathered for a reunion in nearby Dover between December 22 and 26. Two days later, he drove into downtown Russellville and shot two more people dead and wounded four others. What impact did this news have on the Medal of Honor recipient who nearly forty-three years earlier had charged up a rugged slope, stood exposed on the crest of a hill, and fended off an enemy counterattack?

Doug lived to the age of 72-years. He died on December 19, 1994, and is buried at Russell Cemetery, a small country cemetery outside of Ozone, Johnson County. The Ozark Highlands Scenic Highway is a mile or so south of his gravesite. Four other WWII Medal of Honor native sons are buried in Arkansas cemeteries. They have impressive monuments and head stones with the appropriate Medal of Honor insignia for their service branch.

The uncertainties about Wilson Douglas Watson's life and background must have continued up to the time of his burial. Visitors to his grave might notice that his simple, bronze military marker does not mention his USMC service; instead, the inscription states US Army. While the marker does acknowledge his Medal of Honor award, the

Medal image above his name is the Army Medal, not the Navy/Marine Corps Medal presented to him by President Truman in 1945.

Some people remember Doug from time to time. Ten years after his death, a letter about his Army service appeared in the *World War II Magazine*, "A Hero Among Us." [9]

CHAPTER 12
After the awarding of a Medal of Honor

"I can't forget one single name. Those men are with me still.
If I don't remember them, I ask you then who will?"

Robert A. Gannon [1]

Ken Worley received a posthumous Medal of Honor and was forgotten in his hometown for nearly forty years. What his life might have been like had he survived the war in Vietnam and returned home would now only be supposition. Greg Boyington came home from a prisoner of war camp, was awarded a Medal, and experienced periodic celebrity and notoriety until his death forty-two years later. Resistance in his hometown had to be overcome in order for a public tribute to be extended to him. Doug Watson returned to his home state eighteen years after earning a Medal on Iwo Jima and after more than twenty years of military service. There appears to be no tributes to him in the town on record as his birthplace.

This chapter is not so much about forgotten Medal of Honor recipients. It is meant to give perspective to what might have been in the lives of recipients had their awards not been posthumous and as a testimonial to why all Medal of Honor recipients should be remembered. The names of the fifty-seven recipients who survived their battles and wounds are listed below, some mentioned with brief details. The majority of these recipients have been honored at home in fitting ways. Events involving James Everett Livingston and Joseph Jacob Foss are described in greater detail. The chapters that follow return to the stories of forgotten recipients.

Heroic bravery, distinguished actions, and the earning of a medal for valor tend to have an enduring impact. Acknowledgment and acclaim for one's actions changes things. This reality is tangible. As Richard Sorenson, a WWII recipient, said, "You become conscious of what you do and how you do it because you're living in a glass bowl. You have to be careful that what you do won't tarnish your name or the Medal of Honor Society." [2]

They returned from the wars. As in childhood, as in combat, and now in adulthood, the Medal of Honor recipients continued to be determined to overcome challenges and pursue life. However their war experiences, as well as their Medals, had altered their attitudes toward their own lives. They lived as if they could hear the final words of Private First Class William Adelbert Foster, of Cleveland, Ohio.

Private First Class Foster was a rifleman with Company K, 3rd Battalion, 1st Marines, when they landed on Okinawa. A month of fighting followed. On May 2, 1945, Private First Class Foster joined others in a ferocious assault against a strong enemy fortification. The 3rd Battalion was ordered to hold its present position, and Private First Class Foster dug in, sharing a foxhole with another Marine at the point of the perimeter defense line.

Japanese soldiers did not give up ground easily and typically counterattacked "fanatically." Some were able to penetrate within the defensive perimeter and engaged the Marines in close proximity. Private First Class Foster and his companion fought to maintain their position, exchanging hand grenades with the closing enemy soldiers. A grenade landed in their foxhole, just beyond their reach, and Private First Class Foster dived upon it, smothering the explosion with his body.

Stunned and terribly wounded, his life seeping into the Okinawa ground, he had time enough to consider himself, his injuries, his fate, to think of his homeland, his family back in Cleveland, Ohio, who would receive a telegram about him, or to recite a prayer. Instead, Private First Class Foster's thoughts were of his mission and his duty. He concentrated his remaining strength for one last heroically brave action. He had two grenades left with him in the foxhole. Without the strength to throw them himself in the ongoing fight, he handed them to his fellow Marine.

Before dying from his wounds, Private First Class William Foster, 30-years-old, spoke his last words to his comrade. "Make them count."

Making life count

War experiences affected Medal recipients in a variety of ways long after their return. Most had battle injuries to continue to remind them of enemy engagements. Some had bouts with illnesses contracted in theaters of war. The memories of fallen comrades were frequently on their minds. Marines, as much in lore as by tradition, do not leave fallen comrades behind on battlefields. The recipients brought dead companions home with them and seldom let them be far away in thought. Some experienced tinges of *survivor's guilt*, wondering why they had come home and others had not. For most of these men, however, it was not a guilt they felt, it was more a sense of responsibility for those who had died in the battles in which they had survived. They lived not just for themselves, but for their comrades as well. Listen carefully to how they explain the motives for all they have achieved in life, and you will hear them say in so many ways, "We represent *them*."

Surprisingly perhaps to civilians, the recipients' lives were not made easier by the awarding of a Medal of Honor. Perhaps naturally restless, these men found it difficult to sit still after returning from war. Active, productive, and involved, doing as much as they could do, they might have appeared to some who knew them to be "workaholics."

Among those who made the Marines a career

Marines treat their Medal of Honor recipients with regard, admiration, and special courtesy. Of the fifty-seven recipients who survived their wars and came home, twenty-nine remained in the Corps. They had earned the respect of fellows and that respect went with them wherever they served. And unlike their civilian counterparts whose bravery and medals might have been set aside in closets and on shelves, those who remained in uniform had many opportunities to wear their medals in ceremonies, parades, and official functions. Their valor would be frequently remembered.

Researchers accept that social support provided to warriors after battle ameliorates posttraumatic stress reactions. Those who remained in the Marines were likely to experience a good amount of such support. They would also have had opportunities to talk about their war experiences within groups of men who could appreciate such conversation. Environments in which conversations about battle experiences can occur in safety are known to decrease the nervous system agitation triggered by battle.

The twenty-nine recipients who remained in the Marines after their awards were: William Earl Barber, Harvey Curtiss Barnum, Jr., Henry Alfred Commiskey, Sr., Raymond Gilbert Davis, James Lewis Day, Merritt Austin Edson, Wesley Lee Fox, Robert Edward Galer, Jimmie Earl Howard, Arthur J. Jackson, Alan Jay Kellogg, Jr., Howard Vincent Lee, James Everett Livingston, John James McGinty III, Alford Lee McLaughlin, Reginald Rodney Myers, Robert Joseph Modrzejewski, Mitchell Paige, Richard Allen Pittman, Stephen Wesley Pless, David Monroe Shoup, Carl Leonard Sitter, John L. Smith, Jay R. Vargas, Jr., Alexander A. Vandegrift, Kenneth Ambrose Walsh, Archie Van Winkle, Harold Edward Wilson, and Louis Hugh Wilson, Jr.

These men continued to distinguish themselves in their military careers, in part because of who they were, and in part because of what they had done. Several served in later wars. They rose in rank over time, serving long terms stretching from twenty to forty-three continuous years. They also continued going to military schools and were typically promoted into the highest enlisted and officer ranks. Two earned college degrees. Jim Day had dropped out of high school in East St. Louis and joined the Marines when he was seventeen so he could fight in WWII. He began as a private, fought on the Marshall Islands, Guam, and Okinawa, earned his GED, went on to earn a college degree, then a master's degree, and retired at the rank of major general.

Three of the recipients who returned from wars reached the rank of four-star General and served tours as the Commandant of Marines, the highest level of command in the Marines. Alexander Vandegrift, who had completed two years of college before joining the Marines, steadily rose in rank and was the first four-star general in Marine Corps history, becoming the 18th Commandant. Before he died in 1973, seven universities, including Harvard, had awarded him honorary Doctorate degrees.

Four recipients were eventually promoted to Major General, and three were Brigadier Generals. Another served as Assistant Commandant. One served as Deputy Assistant Secretary of the Navy. Eight attained the rank of Colonel, two Lieutenant Colonel, four Major, and one Captain. The enlisted recipients who did not seek or accept officer commissions rose in rank also. One reached the Chief Warrant Officer rank, one reached Sergeant Major, two Master Sergeant, one Gunnery Sergeant, and one Specialist 5 in the Army.

After 30 years of service in the Marines, retiring at the rank of colonel when he was 58-years-old, then working in social services, Carl Leonard Sitter, veteran of Hagaru-ri and the Chosin Reservoir breakout during the war in Korea, entered the Union Theological Seminary in Richmond, Virginia, at the age of 75-years to earn a Masters of Divinity. He wanted to be a Presbyterian minister. [3]

Among the recipients who remained in the Marines, James Everett Livingston had demonstrated such characteristics as leadership that inspired others to take action despite imminent danger in Vietnam battles, sustained deliberateness of purpose despite extended duress, and carrying on his duty in spite of grievous, debilitating, and life-threatening wounds.

Born January 12, 1940, in Towns, a community of eighty-two residents on the Little Ocmulgee River in south central Georgia, he graduated from Auburn University in 1962 with an engineering degree. James accepted a commission as a second lieutenant that same June.

He would later earn a Master's Degree in management from Webster University in Parris Island, South Carolina.

Second Lieutenant Livingston demonstrated comfort with command and was assigned a variety of leadership positions. He had been promoted to captain by the time he landed in Vietnam in August 1967, for his second tour of duty. He assumed command of E Company, 2d Battalion, 4th Marines, with half a year ahead before the Communists unleashed their 1968 *Tet* offensives.

In April 1968, the Marines began launching operations in the eastern fortified villages and hamlets below the Demilitarized Zone (DMZ) in response to Tet. Dai Do was one: a hamlet circled by bunkers, spider holes, hedgerows, snipers in trees and huts, and 12.7-mm machine-gun emplacements. Resistance from NVA regulars was fierce, as Marines fought hand-to-hand, penetrating through dense jungle. At Dai Do the Marine advance stalled at the edge of the hamlet. Casualties were high, and a remnant of the battalion was cut off from the rest.

On the morning of May 2, 1968, Captain Livingston maneuvered Echo Company into position to advance across 550 yards of open rice paddies to reach isolated Golf Company. Under intense mortar and machine-gun fire, which decimated the company, disregarding the blast of rounds near him, he charged his men into the fortified bunkers, overwhelming one after another as they breached the enemy defensive ring and gained Dai Do.

Wounded twice by grenade fragments, Captain Livingston refused medical aid and remained in command, encouraging his men, rallying them each time it seemed that their advance had run out of steam. He kept up the assault on the complex of mutually supporting bunkers until more than one hundred of them had been silenced and the combined companies forced the NVA out of Dai Do.

The NVA counterattacked with a battalion-size force at the adjacent village of Dinh To. Captain Livingston swiftly maneuvered his men into Dinh To, accompanied by Hotel Company, and blocked the NVA counterattack, incurring a third wound. This time he was crippled and unable to stand or charge ahead. Undaunted, he remained in the open, giving orders, deploying men into advantageous fighting positions, and directing the evacuation of casualties. Later in the day, a relief force reached the embattled Marines, providing covering fire as the companies disengaged from the larger enemy force.

Captain Livingston, 28-years-old, refused to be evacuated from the battle until he was certain that the withdrawal and safety of his surviving men had been ensured. After hours in the field with his legs mangled, he was medevaced to the USS *Iwo Jima,* where the surgeries began. Within days, he was flown to Honolulu, Hawaii, to undergo weeks of surgery and months of therapy. Finishing out his tour in Asia at Camp Hanson, Okinawa, recovered from his wounds, Captain Livingston returned to the States and continued in his Marine career. [4] He instructed at the Army's Infantry School, and then served as Director of the 1st Marine's Division Schools. In March 1975, he returned to Vietnam for a third brief tour, participating in the evacuation of Saigon. Retired as a major general in 1995, after more than 33 years of continuous military service, he served as an executive vice president of a company and a member of various business and volunteer boards.

Lumbar City, Georgia, made sure that James Livingston would be remembered. An historical marker citing his valor in Vietnam was erected at the entrance to the city in 1993.

Like Major General Livingston, many of the career Marines continued to excel after reaching retirement. They earned honorary degrees and sat on business and volunteer boards of directors. One served as a vice president of a major corporation, another as Commandant of Cadets at a military academy. Three worked within the Veterans Administration services. Merritt Edson, a WWII recipient, later served as the Director of the National Rifle Association as well as the first Commissioner of the Vermont State Police, which he helped organize. Eleven years after retiring from the Marines in 1992, having served as the Regional V.A. Liaison Officer, Jay R. Vargas received a Civil Servant of the Year Award. On the night of May 1, 1968, Captain Vargas, in command of Company G, cut off from the rest of 2d Battalion, had found refuge in a deep drainage ditch on the edge of Dai Do.

Those who returned to civilian life

Those who left the Marines following the wars did so for various reasons: several had been medically discharged from service because of their disabling wounds, some were released because of a reduction in force size following the war, some wanted to return to careers interrupted by the war, and others preferred to return to home and family because they had seen enough of combat.

Service in the Marines for many men and women becomes a defining point in life, a reference point for future experience. Later events are measured by and contrasted to their military experience. "In the Corps, we..." becomes a familiar reprise. A tour in the Marines, especially combat experience, unquestionably changes people and can shape who they will be for the rest of their lives. There is a good degree of truth in the adage, "Once a Marine, always a Marine."

The twenty-eight recipients who survived their heroically brave actions and returned to civilian life include: Gregory Boyington, Richard Bush, Hector Albert Cafferata, Jr., Anthony Casamento, Justice M. Chambers, Mike Clausen, Jr., Jefferson Joseph DeBlanc, Duane Edgar Dewey, Robert H. Dunlap, Joseph Foss, William G. Harrell, Douglas Jacobson, Robert Sidney Kennemore, John H. Leims, Jacklyn H. Lucas, Joseph Jeremiah McCarthy, Raymond Gerald Murphy, George Herman O'Brien, Jr., Robert Emmett O'Malley, Everett Parker Pope, Carlton Rouh, Luther Skaggs, Jr., Franklin E. Sigler, Robert Ernest Simanek, Richard Keith Sorenson, James Elms Swett, Douglas Watson, and Hershel W. Williams.

As civilians, at least three completed college programs or earned advanced degrees once back home. Jack Lucas is an example. After cradling two hand grenades to protect his companions on Iwo Jima, he went back to high school once he was discharged from the hospitals and the service. He is likely the only high school freshman in history who had earned a Medal of Honor in combat before attending classes. Jack also went on to earn a college degree.

The men involved themselves in work, community affairs and organizations, and volunteered their services in a number of ways. Some earned civic awards for their community endeavors. Six wrote books and three hosted television programs. One was a state governor, another a hometown mayor. Five furthered their higher education; Jeff DeBlanc, for example, went on to earn two Masters degrees and a Doctoral degree.

However it appeared to others, the recipients were doing more than cramming as much living into life as they could. As Marines are trained to do, they were going above and beyond. They more likely lived as if they had to live more than one life.

While the recipients had been able to suppress natural fear, override nervous system reactions to danger, or turn the agitation generated by the nervous system into an aggressive reaction against the threat, their nervous systems had registered the events. Memories, perhaps pushed away, were stored somewhere in brain cells. And for many, the agitation would not subside. The majority channeled it into action of some kind, typically work. Some tried to still the unease with alcohol or nicotine. Some drank large amounts of caffeine to forestall going to sleep and falling into nightmares. Hershel "Woody" Williams experienced visual memories of events on Guam and Iwo Jima into his eighties and lost nights of sleep if he watched a war movie. [5]

Twenty-four of the fifty-seven recipients were already married when they returned from the wars, and at least another seventeen married afterwards. The majority of them had children and raised families. Two of the men outlived their first wives and remarried. Their relationships with spouses could be more challenging than expected in marriage. The emotional vulnerability natural to intimacy had to be guarded against because it brought with it the memories of emotional connections to men who had not returned from battle and to horrendous sights of carnage wrought by combat. For decades these men avoided the triggers for tears. The emotions and tears periodically found them in their later years when they talked openly about the companions who did not come home.

Additionally, their activity, productivity and the pursuit of accomplishment kept them absent, perhaps distant, from home for periods of time. At least five of the men divorced after returning from the wars, two of them more than once.

The Opening of Doors

Heroic bravery and the earning of a Medal of Honor definitely opened doors. Their names and stories have appeared in numerous books, magazines, movies, and television shows. The recipients are routinely asked to appear at civic functions, to preside over July 4th and Memorial Day ceremonies, to serve as Grand Marshall at parades, to dedicate monuments and memorials, and to give public speeches. They have encountered unsolicited job offers, been awarded honorary degrees, been asked to sit on corporate boards of directors, to advise government committees and testify at Senate hearings, and to sit on the podium at a President's inauguration and attend a State of the Union Address. They are honored guests at the funeral services of comrades.

Joseph Jacob Foss was born April 17, 1915, near Sioux Falls, South Dakota. He and his brother grew up working on their father's farm, where electricity had yet to be installed. He enjoyed the out-of-doors, finding whatever time he could for hunting and fishing. One month before he turned 18-years-old, his father, Frank, was killed in an accident. After high school graduation, Joe worked in a gas station to pay for college and flying lessons. He was remembered as a person who overcame hardship with an abundance of optimism and self-confidence.

Joe attended Augustana College, then Sioux Falls College, before transferring to the University of South Dakota. His education was gradual, sometimes interrupted to help his mother out on the farm. Besides boxing in college, he played on the football and track teams. He was a member of the Sigma Alpha Epsilon fraternity. And he took a Civil Aeronautics flying course. In his senior year at USD, he joined the South Dakota National Guard, then enlisted in the Marines before he graduated at the age of twenty-five.

Captain Foss landed at Henderson Field on October 9, 1942, during the battle for Guadalcanal. He was assigned to duties as Executive Officer, second-in-command of VMF-121, leading flights of F4F Wildcats into air fights. Variously described as "outspoken," "gregarious," "blunt," "brash," or "bold," he was a straight-talking, no-non-sense kind of man with a Marine's vocabulary. Within nine days he was a Marine "Ace." By the time he took his last flight on January 25, 1943, he topped the list for numbers of enemy aircraft shot from the sky by a Marine aviator.

Captain Joe Foss, 28-years-old was on the June 7, 1943, *Life* cover. His celebrity could have taken him a lot of places after the war; instead he chose to return to South Dakota and went into business for himself, opening a charter flying business and a car dealership. He and his wife, June, had four children to raise.

Joe was instrumental in organizing the SD Air National Guard and rose to the rank of Brigadier General in the Guard. He was called back to the active Marine Corps during the Korean War.

In civilian life, Joe helped establish a children's hospital in Sioux Falls and served as the President of the National Society of Crippled Children and Adults. He got involved in state politics, eventually being elected governor for two terms. Joe was also selected to be the first Commissioner of the American Football League and was the President of the National Rifle Association. He appeared on TV shows and had his own TV series for a while. The Sioux Falls Airport was named in his honor in 1955. He authored two books. When Tom Brokow wrote his book, *The Greatest Generation*, a chapter was dedicated to the farmer's son from South Dakota. [6]

Following his war experience, Joe Foss' life was filled with accomplishment, but was not without its hardships. He was restless and could not settle into a serene life style. Two of his four children had serious illnesses and disabilities. His professional activities resulted in his being an absentee father a good part of the time. His marriage suffered, a separation ensued in 1957, and then a divorce. June died a few years later of complications from diabetes. Two of his four children died. Joe had his own near-death experience with an illness related to arsenic poisoning. Life was not always a trial. He remarried in 1967 to Donna "DiDi" Wild Hall.

Joe had carried a small Bible in the pocket of his flight suit when he flew with the Cactus Air Force over Guadalcanal. In the last quarter of his life, he turned his attention to his Christianity. Like everything else to which he had attended in his life, he was ardent about his faith and happy to talk honestly about his strong religious convictions.

He became active in the Campus Crusade for Christ and the Fellowship of Christian Athletes. No matter the tragedies Joe encountered, he was a man who turned things around. [7]

He will not be forgotten in Sioux Falls.

Most recipients who returned to civilian life did well, although not all experienced the fame attained by Joe Foss. They lived lives of responsibility, raising families and earning livings. Some did experience failed business enterprises and economic hardships at times, but success and accomplishment were more frequent among them and giving up was not in their nature.

Six recipients worked for the Veterans Administration: three as counselors, two as Division Chiefs, and one as a VA officer. One was a high school teacher, another a geologist, one a salesman then a bar owner. Another was a bank president. One rose to the rank of Fire Chief in Chicago. Justice Chambers returned to the practice of law and served as a staff advisor to the Senate Armed Services Committee. Carlton Rouh, who had protected comrades from a grenade blast, eventually served a term as the mayor of his hometown, Lindenwold, New Jersey. Clearly, the men continued to seek affiliation. Some were members of Community Affairs organizations, corporate boards, and veteran organizations. Douglas Jacobson organized a Marine Corps League chapter in Port Charlotte County, Florida.

Few appear to have left the Marines entirely behind. At least five continued part-time careers in the Marine Reserves. Two eventually retired from the Reserves as Colonels, one as a Lieutenant Colonel. Joe Foss retired from the South Dakota National Guard. Most of the men attended unit reunions and Medal of Honor Association functions.

And then there were accidents.

Captain Hiram Bearss earned a Medal of Honor on Samar Island, and then served bravely in France during World War I as part of the 4th Marine Brigade. He was given command of the 102nd Infantry and the 51st Brigade, reaching the rank of Brigadier General before he retired. Some believed that his abrasive personality had prevented him from being promoted to the rank his accomplishments deserved. He died in an automobile accident in 1938, at the age of 63-years.

Two recipients who had returned from Vietnam had significant traffic accidents. Stephen Pless died in a motorcycle accident in Florida six months after receiving his Medal of Honor. Mike Clausen was critically injured in a car accident, lost an eye, and was in a coma for months before fighting his way back into life.

The agitation these heroically brave men experienced after returning from war might have originated in childhood experiences. Available public records suggest that at least thirty-two of the 181 Medal of Honor recipients experienced significant, emotion-laden events in childhood. Even before combat, some might have been predisposed to act beyond the dictates of life-threatening events, fueled by the past.

The agitation, at times, later emerged as depression for some recipients. Such episodes were managed effectively—as long as the recipient could turn his attention to other challenges. Loss and failures in life become intense experiences for such men because of their competitive natures. For a few, a belief there was nothing more to accomplish, that their individual best had already been attained, or that only decline or despondency lay ahead, appears to have triggered taking action even against depression. John Lucian Smith's heroic bravery is described in a later chapter.

CHAPTER 13
A choice to live in relative obscurity?

"None of them looked like boys anymore.
None of them ever would again." [1]

Seargeant Clint Van Winkle, USMC
Iraq, 2003

Available information regarding Luther Skaggs, Jr. and Richard Earl Bush, both of who earned Medals in WWII and returned to civilian life, is scarce.

Henderson, Kentucky, lies on a bluff overlooking the Ohio River, in the northwest corner of the state, across from the southwest corner of Indiana. River traffic had to look up high banks of red clay soil to see the town.

At the turn of the twentieth century, Henderson was the major dark tobacco producer in the world, exporting much of it to Great Britain. Downtown then had great tobacco factories, stemmeries, and warehouses. By the 1920s, however, the economic high tide had come to an end for Henderson's tobacco trade. Corn, soybean, and coal production became the leading sources of employment.

John James Audubon State Park, a range of hills and ridgelines reaching up to nearly 600 feet in elevation, is northeast of Henderson. Trails in the park provided opportunities to make long climbs with steep inclines and descents and hikes along ridgelines. The park's namesake, naturalist and painter John James Audubon, lived in Henderson for several years, as did W.C. Handy, a famous blues performer. Husband E. Kimmel, commander of the U.S. Pacific Fleet during the Japanese attack on Pearl Harbor is a Henderson native son. The community is also proud to proclaim that Abraham Lincoln's first love, Ann Rutledge, was born just outside of the city.

Henderson's list of notable natives seems to be incomplete. Its only Medal of Honor recipient is not included on the list. [1a]

Luther Skaggs, Jr. was born in Henderson, on March 3, 1923. Very little is known regarding his family life and childhood, but he likely was a descendant of the Kentucky pioneers. Frontiersmen came into Kentucky through the Cumberland Gap. Before Daniel Boone, Irishmen like Henry, Charles, and Richard Skaggs came in the late 1760s. Skaggs Trace, an old hunters' trail in Lincoln County, is named after Henry, a "long hunter." Henry ranged further west and helped establish the site for what is now Bowling Green. Nearby Skaggs Creek runs out of the hills heading toward the Barren River. Skaggs men continued west and north into Kentucky, many settling along the Ohio.

Luther was remembered by friends to have been a "mighty nice, quiet kid," with a soft, musical Kentuckian voice. He would grow to be five-feet-eight-and-one half-inches tall and about 140 pounds. He had brown hair, and there was something about his eyes. Luther had pale, soft blue eyes that lit up like a flash fire when there was a fight at hand; then, he was "unflinching." In his heart, Luther was "a tough little guy." [2]

Although little information is available about Luther's life on the Ohio River, history provides some sense of it. He must have known a good amount about living through catastrophes. The Great Depression began when he was six, and the Dust Bowl years when he was seven.

When Luther was nearly 14-years, the winter water levels on the Ohio began to rise. In early January 1937, a severe winter storm swept southern Indiana. For two weeks snow, sleet and heavy, record-making rains covered the states. Flood warnings were sounded as the river began to swell and overflow its banks.

Major cities, from Pittsburgh, Pennsylvania to Cairo, Illinois, were inundated as floodwalls were breached. Water supplies were cut off in towns and streetcar services lost. For some cities the water levels reached anywhere from 54 to 80 feet: Pittsburgh, Cincinnati, Evansville, Indiana, Louisville, and Paducah, Kentucky were all under water. Martial law was declared across the river from Henderson in Evansville. By January 27, seventy percent of Louisville was flooded.

By the time the Ohio was falling below flood stage in the affected regions on February 5, a million people were homeless, and 385 were dead. Businesses were devastated, materially and financially. Property losses were estimated to be $500 million. [3] According to a Consumer Price Index conversion, that would be more than 7.2 billion dollars in 2007. Although the rising river waters would have had Henderson residents on alert, due to its elevated position on the bluff, the city was spared much of the devastation of the Ohio River flood of 1937.

Luther had some experience with personal disasters. His parents, Luther and Ida, divorced at some point, and he does not appear to have finished high school. His father relocated to Brownsville, northeast of Bowling Green and near Mammoth Cave. Ida remarried a Mr. Stoermer in Henderson. Prior to the outbreak of war, Luther was employed as an apprentice power lineman for the Rural Electrification Administration in Henderson.

Ten months after the attack at Pearl Harbor, Luther joined the Marines on October 6, 1942. After recruit training at Parris Island and infantry and mortar training at Camp Lejeune, North Carolina, he embarked for overseas duty on March 1, 1943, two days before his twentieth birthday.

Private First Class Skaggs was a mortarman and served as a section squad leader with King Company, 3d Battalion, 3d Marines, landing with them at 8:08 AM on Red Beach 1, the Island of Guam on July 21, 1944. The Battalion was on the far left flank of the Division's 2,500-yard-wide beachhead. The beach looked ahead at the heights of Adelup Point, the Chonito Cliff, and Bundschu Ridge.

The heights overlooking Red Beach were intensely defended by a battalion-sized force with the advantage of looking down on the Marines intent on ascending to the high ground. Enemy snipers had concealed themselves in snares across the heights. The Marines encountered artillery and mortar barrages as well as interlocking machine-gun fire as they crossed the beach and attempted to climb the rises. Enemy grenades easily rolled into the Marine positions.

His section leader and seven of his buddies were taken out of action by mortar fire shortly after landing under the sandstone Chonito Cliffs. Private First Class Skaggs took command of the 81-mm mortar section. He led them across 200 yards of beach scathed by machine-gun fire. His actions throughout the day and night and into the next morning would demonstrate why his companions seemed always to conclude that he was a tough little guy.

The irregular terrain would have provided little challenge to a young man who might have spent time in eastern Kentucky's Cumberland Mountains, except that a reinforced battalion-size Japanese force waited in their fortifications in this irregular terrain. The defenders held the high ground and were well concealed within the folds, ridges, and caves provided by the cliffs.

The mortar team made its way off the beach and up the cliff. By late morning Private First Class Skaggs had set the mortars up in an advantageous position on Chonito. They got down to business, providing covering fire for the landing force. From their own heights, the enemy forces registered the mortar section's position and directed fire upon them throughout the afternoon and evening.

There was going to be no sleep or rest for Private First Class Skaggs that Friday night.

The Marines' 81-mm mortar rounds were having their effects, and the Japanese continued in their efforts to silence the mortars pounding them. They attacked Private First Class Skaggs' position into the night and early morning. Under his determined direction, the section was able to repel each counterattack that came out of the dark and keep their mortar tube hot.

During the first engagement, the enemy charged within throwing range of the mortar position. A hand grenade was hurled into Private First Class Skaggs' foxhole and exploded, shattering the lower part of his left leg. He quickly fashioned a tourniquet and fastened it to the injury. Despite his serious wound, the fighting was not over for him. He propped himself up in his foxhole and for the next eight hours fought off the enemy incursions with his rifle and hand grenades.

Private First Class Skaggs did not call out for a corpsman or for assistance. He remained calm, reassuring his comrades that he was still in the fight, not wanting to put others at risk or hamper the defense of the beachhead by taking Marines away from their positions to care for him. Instead, he waited for morning's light on July 22. Private First Class Skaggs crawled from the cliff himself, made his way to the rear, and continued in the fight from there until the Asan-Adelup beachhead was secure. Thirteen of the fourteen Marines defending that sector of the beachhead died.

When his lieutenant wrote a report of Private First Class Skaggs' actions, he described the little Marine's "courageous conduct the greatest inspiration possible."

Evacuated from Guam with other Marine casualties, Private First Class Luther Skaggs, 21-years-old, was hospitalized. His leg was amputated and the healing process began. Newspaper reports began circulating news in February 1945, that an unnamed medal for valor had been approved by Secretary of the Navy James Forrestal.

Eleven months after the battle for the Chonito Cliffs, Luther went to the White House on June 15, 1945. President Truman presented him a Medal of Honor at noon, placing the ribbon around Luther's neck as he supported himself on his crutches, standing erect with his shoulders square. From records of the President's calendar, it does not appear that any Skaggs family members attended the ceremony.

Luther participated in war bond drives and appeared on national radio programs. On June 26, 1945, he returned to Henderson for a parade through flag-draped streets and the town's Central Park to the cheers of thousands of Henderson County residents. Luther was promoted to corporal on April 4, 1946, and discharged from the Marines.

Driven to overcome personal or perceived shortcomings.

Some Medal recipients had experienced serious illnesses, infirmities, and health problems in childhood. Some had physical disabilities that could not be corrected; one had a leg shortened by polio, one was colorblind, one had impaired depth perception, and another had dyslexia. Others bore the scars and physical remnants of early accidents. A good number of them were shorter in stature than their average playmates and classmates.

Before they enlisted in the Marines, the recipients had already demonstrated intense efforts throughout their childhoods to let nothing stand in the way of their objectives and ambitions. As other recipients did, Luther would demonstrate this characteristic after the awarding of his Medal.

Newspaper articles stored in archives provide some sense of his life after his discharge. For most of the next thirty years, Luther lived on the East Coast. He initially worked as a Veterans Administration contact man in Philadelphia. Out of the Marine Corps for just a week, on April 12, 1946, he fell on a wet floor in his Philadelphia apartment building, re-injuring his leg. A dispute with the landlords followed over who was responsible for his fall. He filed a $50,000 lawsuit against the landlords on August 22, 1946.

Luther met Rose, the woman he would marry, while he was in the Philadelphia hospital. Rose involved herself in the affairs of the Marine Corps League Detachment Ladies' Auxiliary. After two and a half years working for the Veterans Administration, Luther and Rose moved to Henderson around 1949. They lived with his mother and stepfather for a while, and Luther unsuccessfully tried his hand in politics. [4] He and Rose eventually moved back east, living in Churchton, Maryland, near Washington D.C., where he worked as a budget analyst with the Defense Supply Agency. [5]

Short AP articles about Luther appeared between the mid-1950s into the late-1960s. On Saturday night February 11, 1956, he helped judge the contestants and picked the Beta Sigma Phi *Sweetheart Ball* Queen in Beckley, West Virginia. He was elected President of the Third Marine Division Association's Washington DC Area Chapter when it was newly formed in 1958. The following year, five years after the Marine Corps War Memorial had first been dedicated outside Arlington National Cemetery, Luther was one of the guests of honor at the Association's annual reunion. Part of the ceremonies was a tribute to him and four other surviving recipients at the Iwo Jima Memorial.

The Congressional Medal of Honor Society evolved from its predecessor, the Medal of Honor Legion, in 1946, three years after Luther had earned his Medal on the Island of Guam. The Society's mission was to perpetuate the ideals embodied in the Medal: promoting patriotism and fostering a love of country in the aftermath of World War II. [6] Luther served as President of the Medal of Honor Society for two terms, beginning in January 1961, and stepping down in October 1964.

Luther's various involvements sometimes returned him to the White House. Seventeen years after President Truman had met him there, President John F. Kennedy sent him an invitation. When the president spoke with Descendants of Civil War Medal of Honor Winners on the White House South Lawn, April 28, 1962, at 9:45 AM, Luther Skaggs, Jr. was present as a guest. President Kennedy thought well of Luther. He ensured Luther was selected to place a wreath at the Tomb of the Unknown Soldiers in Arlington on July 12, 1962, the one hundred year anniversary of President Lincoln signing the legislation that authorized the Medal of Honor. [7]

When Wayne State University students in Detroit protested against President Kennedy in October 1962, Luther had an opinion. While he granted that free protests were part of the American way of life, he also found the student protests disgraceful. Later, on a cold Saturday, October 23, 1965, he led a march of 3,500 through Philadelphia streets to a rally at Independence Hall in support of the Administration's policy in Vietnam.

Always active, in 1967, Luther served as a special assistant to Harold Russell chairman of the President's Committee on Employment of the Handicapped.

The newly formed Annapolis Detachment of the Marine Corps League (MCL) honored Luther by presenting him with a life-time Gold Membership card on Monday, May 15, 1967. The MCL cites its mission as: "Members of the Marine Corps League join together in camaraderie and fellowship for the purpose of preserving the traditions and promoting the interests of the United States Marine Corps, banding together those who are now serving in the United States Marine Corps and those who have been honorably discharged from that service, that they may effectively promote the ideals of American freedom and democracy, voluntarily aiding and rendering assistance to all Marines, FMF Corpsmen and former Marines and FMF Corpsmen and to their widows and orphans; and to perpetuate the history of the United States Marine Corps and by fitting acts to observe the anniversaries of historical occasions of particular interest to Marines." [8] The Gold card indicates the highest rank of membership, acknowledging that Luther had performed service "above and beyond" the principles advocated by the MCL.

Luther seems consistently to have accepted leadership roles: of his own initiative, as he did under the Chonito Cliffs, and by invitation or election. Only nine-years-old when the Purple Heart Association of United States was first organized at the Connecticut State Armory on September 21, 1932, [9] Luther served as the National Commandant of the Purple Heart Association in 1967-68. [10]

No further information was discovered in available public records during this research regarding Luther Skaggs, Jr. He died April 4, 1976, 53-years-old, and is buried in Section 46, Arlington National Cemetery.

Luther Skaggs obviously was a dedicated man who led a life of service and distinction. His courageous actions in battle and his "unflinching" attitudes toward any challenges he faced make him a man worthy of recognition. There are places in Kentucky where he is remembered.

The Marine Corps Coordinating Council of Louisville Kentucky was founded January 1, 1991. Among its roster of thirteen Kentucky Legends are seven Medal recipients. Luther's short biography is provided on their Web site. [11] Luther's name is also included with fifty-five other veterans on a plaque at the Kentucky Medal of Honor Memorial, erected on the old Jefferson County Courthouse grounds, the corner of Fifth and Jefferson Streets in downtown Louisville on Veteran's Day 2001. The Henderson County Public Library Genealogy and Local History does include a reference to him in its Kentucky Information Files.

Luther, however, is not included among Henderson's Notable natives listed on the Wikipedia community profile. [12]

As described above, President Kennedy thought well of Luther. All the towns and cities where a Medal of Honor recipient was born would profit from reflecting on the president's remarks at Amherst College on October 26, 1963: "A nation reveals itself not only by the men it produces but by the men it honors, the men it remembers." Beyond the June 26, 1945, parade through Henderson streets and Central Park a week after he received his Medal at the White House, it is not known if his hometown ever paid him further tribute.

One hundred forty miles southeast of Luther's birthplace is the town of Glasgow, sitting on one of the early trails through south central Kentucky. Just north of Skaggs Creek, Glasgow is now the seat of Barren County.

Barren County is a watershed area. The plentiful rivers and streams make the region perfect for agriculture. Primarily rural, with rolling farmlands and meadowlands, growing of burley tobacco and hay, as well as dairy and cattle, remain predominant. When work is finished, the many streams provide favorite respite for those who enjoy fishing for smallmouth bass.

While Saint Patrick's Day is celebrated in Glasgow with gusto, the Scottish heritage of some of its pioneers is most evident. The Glasgow

Highland Games have been celebrated there annually since 1986 on the weekend after Memorial Day.

Richard Earl Bush was born in Glasgow on December 23, 1924; twenty-one months after Luther Skaggs came into the world. His ancestors had been in Barren County for more than 100 years. The County Court House has marriage records of males with the Bush surname dating as far back as 1803.

Not much is written about his early life, but one thing is sure: Richard, as quiet and humble as he was by nature, showed a propensity for volunteering. After finishing one year of high school, he decided helping out on the family tobacco farm was more important than returning for a second year. He worked for the next several years driving a tractor for his father.

In September 1942, when he was 17-years-old, he and his brother went the thirty-seven miles over to Bowling Green to enlist in the service. Although the war was underway, they tried to reassure their father that they had no intentions of volunteering for anything hazardous or of earning medals.

Edson's First Marine Raider Battalion was formed within months of the Pearl Harbor attack. The mission was to operate as amphibious light infantry, landing on enemy-held islands in rubber boats, and penetrating behind enemy lines. Envisioned to be "commandos" who would make quick strikes from the sea and then disappear, the Raiders took on the aura of an "elite" force. Marine Corps historians cite the Raiders as the first special operations force in the United States.

Marines had to volunteer to join the Raiders and be individually accepted by the commanders. Since higher risks of combat and casualties were anticipated, higher standards for entry were implemented. These included to be exceptionally physically fit, to be able to make long marches at a fast pace, and to be a strong swimmer. The inflatable boats might not always make it to and from the beaches, and the Raiders might have to be their own means of transportation on and off islands.

The reassurances Private First Class Bush gave his father when he enlisted apparently had slipped his mind. He joined the 1st Raiders in mid-1943 and served with the Battalion in the Pacific Solomon Islands. He rose to the rank of corporal. The Raiders were disbanded the following January, and Corporal Bush was reassigned with the rest of the 1st Raiders to the 1st Battalion, 4th Regiment, 6th Marine Division in February 1944. The regiment did its training on Guadalcanal. Some of the bloodiest fighting for the Marines in the Pacific was ahead.

Corporal Bush survived the eighteen-day battle for Guam, July 21—August 8, 1944, the battle in which his fellow Kentuckian, Private First Class Luther Skaggs, earned a Medal of Honor. The 1st Battalion began preparations for its next amphibious landing. They were going to enter a battle that would be the longest and most costly engagement in the Marine Corps' history, entailing eighty-two days of combat. In those days, eleven Marines would be awarded Medals of Honor. When it was over, 19,500 casualties would be recorded.

Okinawa Shima

The Marine's Island Campaign secured Iwo Jima in March 1945. One more island awaited their beach landing. The place was Okinawa Shima, a heavily fortified outpost island of mainland Japan sitting between the East China and the Philippine Seas.

Corporal Bush, a rifle squad leader, would have been awake and briefing his men before dawn. There were probably some prayers—not just because of the day's plans, but because it was Easter Sunday, April 1, 1945. There might also have been some jokes or pranks, because it was April Fool's Day. Standing along the ship's railings the previous day, the Marines would have seen their objective.

The steep cliffs of Okinawa's northern coastline, green with vegetation, presented a formidable sight from the sea. Mount Yonaha-dake on the island's northeast reached to 1,643 feet above the sea. Mount YaeTake on the northwest Motobu Peninsula rose to almost 1,500 feet. The midsection of the island, south of the Ishikawa Isthmus, was most inviting for an amphibious assault. The land there around Hagushi, mostly cultivated by local farmers and sparse of vegetation but for green conifers, sloped gently from the beaches toward inland hills.

Two strategic airfields, Kadena and Yontan, had been installed about a mile inland. The Marines had been tasked to seize the airfields.

Pre-invasion intelligence gathering had provided some sense of what awaited the assault forces, and casualties were expected to be high. Japanese forces numbering about 115,000 men had been deployed to defend the island. Japanese commanders had selected the most advantageous pieces of terrain from which to fight and committed carefully designated units to defend their positions. They had doubled the amount of artillery common in defense networks, even incorporating naval guns. Impressive howitzers, mortars, and antitank guns were readied, with ample munitions stockpiled. The enemy had positioned themselves to be protected by mutually supporting ridgelines and steep defiles. Snipers had had more than enough time to pick advantageous hiding places.

Corporal Bush and his squad waited for the order to board the landing *tractors* for what was to be the largest amphibious assault of the island campaigns. The command came over the loud speakers at 4:06 AM.

Twenty minutes before dawn, American ships in the East China Sea began a naval bombardment of the landing areas on the western side of Okinawa. The coast was soon obscured by smoke and dust. At 8:00 AM, from two miles out, a line of landing craft nearly eight miles long began the approach to the beaches. By then, the sky was bright with sunshine, and the air was a cool 75 degrees. Visibility was good and the sea was calm, disturbed only slightly by a mild breeze. The surf along the shoreline amounted to only ripples. There was no significant enemy response to the bombardment or to the amphibious assault. The first landing craft arrived at their designated landing sites at 8:30 AM.

The Marines landed north of the line formed by the Bishi River. The 4th Regiment was in the middle of the line as the Marines swept northeastward across the island. They had secured Yonton Airfield without much resistance by 11:30 AM. By nightfall, the forces had advanced nearly three miles inland.

By April 4, the Marines had crossed the entire island and established their lines north of Ishikawa. The orders came down from the top: sweep to the north, up the Ishikawa Isthmus. What might have been considered "hospitable" terrain for maneuvering ground forces was going to be behind them. Once inland, the Okinawa terrain to the north turned from hills into mountainous rises. The roads were primitive, unsurfaced and narrow. Steep ravines hampered traffic. Partially concealed trails traversed wooded hills and ridges. The coral walls, crags, and cliffs of the mountains were pitted with caves.

As Corporal Bush pushed the squad forward, they encountered small units of Japanese and stragglers who had been forced north. The afternoon of April 4, a major rainstorm that lasted into the next day also slowed them down, turning the roads and trails into muddy quagmires.

The enemy seemed to be making their way towards Motobu Peninsula, blowing road bridges as they moved. During the thrust northward, Corporal Bush would maneuver his squad over eighty-four miles, as the 6th Marine Division captured 436 square miles of hostile terrain. Working their way up the northern portion of the island, by day's end on April 8, the Marines had stretched their line across Motobu and had reached the sprawling, steep slopes of Yae Take. There, in six-square miles of heavily wooded ravines and twisting rocky ridges, the Japanese had established defensive outposts and the commander's fortress.

The Marines faced an enemy skilled in mountain combat; Yae Take was heavily defended by field artillery, light mortars, 25-mm naval guns fixed into hill emplacements, and plentiful machine guns. Caves hidden by vegetation and short trees provided sites from which the Marines could be ambushed. To make matters more challenging, another tropical storm had drenched the island with rain all day Tuesday, continuing into April 11 and shrouding the peninsula in gray storm clouds.

The Marines had the mountain surrounded by Wednesday, April 11. For two days they reconsolidated their positions, reconnoitered and probed the enemy defenses, and planned the assault on Mount Yae Take.

Two weeks into the battle for Okinawa, the Marines pushed off from their positions from the west and east of the peninsula on the morning of the 14th. By evening they held half the lower ridgeline around the mountain, forcing the enemy forces further up the slopes. The battalions were tasked to destroy a fortified enemy stronghold on Yae Take, an uphill assault from the lower ridge. On April 15, the enemy emplacements within the mountain fortress were directing their own barrage of artillery, mortars, and rifle fire at the advancing force. The Marines reached the stronghold's forward position and halted.

The next day, Monday, April 16, Corporal Bush was in the vanguard of the final assault on the Mount Yae Take fortress. As the enemy artillery concentrated its fire upon the advance, he directed his squad up the precipice, over the ridge, and into the enemy trenches. Their assault drove the Japanese out of their fiercely-defended positions. He pressed his men forward.

Corporal Bush's squad was the first to penetrate Mount Yae Take's inner defensive perimeter, and they took casualties. He was among the casualties, initially ignoring his own serious wounds. Ordered to a makeshift field medical station, Corporal Bush was evacuated to a "protected" place with a rocky outcrop above. Lying prone among other injured Marines being provided treatment, he saw an enemy grenade land near him. Medical staff and other wounded Marines were in danger. Later cited to have been as "alert and courageous in extremity as in battle," Corporal Bush, 20-years-old, instantly grabbed the grenade and pulled it into his own body, smothering the shattering explosion and containing its violent impact to himself.

He lost several fingers from one hand and sight from one eye. And he survived.

The Marines finally swept over Yae Take on April 17 and cleared Motobu peninsula of any significant resistance the next day. The 6th Marine Division lost 207 Marines killed in the battle. Corporal Bush was counted among the 757 wounded. Over 2,500 enemy soldiers were killed. Only 46 were captured and taken prisoners.

At war's end, Corporal Richard Bush was discharged from active service. He married Stella Ramsden, and they raised a daughter, Judith, and a son, Richard Jr.

Richard worked his way to a rank of Master Gunnery Sergeant in the USMC reserves. Working as a counselor at the Chicago Veterans Administration, he continued his life of coming to the aid of other veterans. Richard was awarded a variety of civilian honors in recognition of his efforts.

As had been true during the war, Richard outlived others he cared about. Stella died in 1989. Judith, his daughter died in 1995.

Richard died on June 7, 2004, in Waukegan, Illinois, fifty-nine years after he had pulled a grenade to himself. He is buried at Ascension Cemetery in Libertyville, Illinois. His obituary and biography appeared on page 4 of the Wednesday, June 9, 2004, *Glasgow Daily Times*. The *New York Times* reported his story on Sunday, June 13. [13] What one newspaper reported after he died might reflect how Richard was remembered in other towns and cities across the United States. Hendersonville, North Carolina, is separated from Glasgow, Kentucky, Richard's birthplace, by two state lines, the Great Smoky Mountains and Blue Ridge Divide, and a straight-line distance of only 220 miles. The *Hendersonville Times-News* printed a brief, four-line announcement of Richard's death in its June 17, 2004 publication. Four lines.

Richard Bush does continue to be remembered in various places. In 2008, on the anniversary of his April 16 Medal of Honor actions on Okinawa, the *Leasing News* Web site of Saratoga, California, printed his Citation in its *This Day in American History*. [14] He is included among the thirteen Marine Corps Coordinating Council of Louisville Kentucky's *Kentucky Legends*, and his name is on the plaque at the Kentucky Medal of Honor Memorial.

How much Richard Bush is remembered in his hometown is in question. A 1998 obituary gave evidence that the Glasgow Marines have never forgotten him.

James (Jimmy) Simmons was a WW II Veteran and a retired Glasgow High School history teacher. His obituary was posted online, on April 6, 1998. Listed among his awards was the Richard Bush Award, presented to him by the Glasgow Marine Corps League (Detachment 584). [15] The award was made in recognition for Jimmy's service to the community and to the country. Beyond Jimmy's obituary, searches provided no other references to validate this award. A telephone call to Glasgow cleared things up. It turned out that Jimmy was the second recipient of the annual award.

Jerry V. Stahl, a veteran of the Korean War, former and acting Commandant of the Glasgow Marine Corps League Detachment, was the first to be honored with the Richard Bush Award, in 1996. Having known Richard personally, the award meant a lot to Jerry. He was the one who had presented the award to Jimmy in 1997. A total of nine veterans received the honor until the award was renamed the *Patriot Award* in 2004, after Richard's death. [16]

The population of Glasgow, Kentucky, was 14,200 at the 2000 census. There is an Honor Roll in the town square that includes Richard E. Bush as a Medal of Honor recipient. The town also has had its own Web site since 1995. Glasgow's eleven Notable natives are listed on the Wikipedia community profile. [17] Diane Sawyer, journalist and TV News Host, is one of the Notables. Richard is not included among them.

CHAPTER 14
Iwo Jima

"Victory was never in doubt. Its cost was...What was in doubt, in all our minds, was whether there would be any of us left to dedicate our cemetery at the end, or whether the last Marine would die knocking out the last Japanese gun and gunner."

Major General Graves B. Erskine, USMC
Dedication of Iwo Jima 3rd MarDiv Cemetery
March 1945

The machine-gun bullet had done its damage. Frothy blood gushed from his mouth, making his efforts to speak more gurgling than mumbling. The sucking, hissing sound as he struggled to breathe made it plain to the corpsman. The Marine's chest cavity was no longer sealed. His lung had collapsed, air was escaping into the pleural cavity between the lung and the chest wall, and the wounded officer was in immediate danger of dying. The field dressing would slow his expiring, but he needed more than first aid. The field hospital station on the beach would also likely be inadequate to save him. The cold and rainy afternoon, with all the noise, mud, and stench, did not hamper transfer of the wounded as much as did the artillery, mortar, machine-gun, and sniper fire.

The Marines were pinned down in a crisscrossing blaze of firearms. Explosions of grenades, tank and artillery and oversized mortar shells sent shrapnel, rock, and dirt into the air. Eardrums were shattered. The smell of death and rot made a man want to cover his nose. The cries of men for a corpsman or "doc" intensified the need to do something.

To stand up in this, already wounded, and lead men out of craters and ditches, that is what he wanted to do. It is the kind of action, the kind of bravery that defies description.

He had been in the fight on four other islands; this had been his fifth amphibious landing. A mortar blast had felled him on the first island. The multiple fragmentation wounds and two fractured wrists had been healed for about two years. Just a year earlier, concussion wounds had taken him out of action when an ammunition dump exploded near him. After each wounding, the option of returning to the United States would have been approved by his superiors.

More than 4,500 white crosses and stars would fill the rows of the 3rd, 4th, and 5th Marine Division cemeteries on the island under the ancient volcano; 1,462 of the dead would be from his Division. In hopes of keeping Marines out of these Division cemeteries, hospital ships, like the USS *Samaritan* and USNS *Comfort*, were anchored off shore to receive the casualties needing surgery and life-saving care. Before the fighting was over, more than 13,737 wounded Marines and corpsmen would be evacuated to a hospital ship. Many Marines died of their wounds on the ships.

Some say that as life seeps from a body, from memory the person's life "passes in review." As he was moved for evacuation with a shattered collarbone and sucking chest wound, the Marine had thirty-seven years to review.

YEAR 1945

Iwo Jima is a small island, eight square miles: two miles wide and five and a half miles long, in the shape of a pork chop. Its most prominent feature is the 550-foot volcanic crater called Mount Suribachi, sitting the length of four football fields away from the first landing site, black volcanic ash beaches. Over 70,000 Marines of the 3rd, 4th, and 5th Divisions fought on the island for thirty-six days and nights.

Amphibious tractors transporting the Marines from the ships dropped the first wave of Marines on the island at 9:05 AM on Monday morning, February 19, 1945. The Japanese allowed the arriving waves of American forces to assemble and bunch up on the two-mile stretch of soft black volcanic sand, rock really. Men, tanks, trucks, and artillery pieces sank into the terraced beaches, enmired.

Two thousand men of the 28th Regiment were ordered to cut Mount Suribachi off from the larger portion of the island and seize the fortified mountain from the elite 2,000 Japanese soldiers dug into caves and ravines to hold control of it. The main Marine force had been ordered to take the rest of the island and its three airfields.

The upper half of the pork chop shaped island, with its hills, ridges and crevasses, tunnels and caves, and fortress-like emplacements provided concealment for thousands of determined enemy fighters. What the Marines were actually going to have to take were 21,000 Japanese soldiers in steel-reinforced concrete fortifications, pillboxes and blockhouses, and in caves and caverns, underground bunkers, and tunnels.

Around 10:15 AM, Lieutenant General Tadamichi Kuribayashi ordered carnage to be unleashed upon the Marines. He had given clear orders to his men: each was to kill no less than ten Marines before sacrificing his own life for the Emperor. "Annihilation" was a consistent directive in Japanese mission orders. The Marines were immediately busy charging machine-gun emplacements, blasting enemy fortifications, destroying pillboxes, exchanging hand grenades, probing for mines, and clearing routes through the volcanic rock for their tanks.

Once the battle was engaged, the 28th Marines took five days to progress the four hundred yards to capture Suribachi. The 5th Marines slowly progressed up the western third of the island. The American flag was raised over Iwo Jima on Friday, February 23.

Perhaps the most remembered of the Marines who fought, and either died, or came home from this island are the six Iwo Jima Flag Raisers. Corporal Ira Hayes of Gila River Indian Reservation, Arizona, Corporal

Harlon Block of Texas, Sergeant Michael Strank of Pennsylvania, Private Franklin Sousley of Kentucky, Private Rene Gagnon of New Hampshire, and Navy Corpsman John Bradley of Wisconsin are remembered in millions of copies of the famous Joe Rosenthal/AP photograph, as well as in books and movies. Three of the Flag Raisers died during the fight for the island. Only Corporal Hayes, Private Gagnon, and Corpsman Bradley returned home after the war.

Although climbing the ridges of Suribachi and raising the second flag over Iwo was an act of bravery, lifting that makeshift pole did not go "above and beyond" the call of their duties. None of the six Flag Raisers were awarded a Medal of Honor. They are each, however, rightfully memorialized, stretching upward symbolically for all Marines, in the Iwo Jima Monument at Arlington National Cemetery.

There would be no weekend off before returning to work for the six, or any other Marines, after Mount Suribachi was taken. Another thirty-one days of fighting were ahead before Japanese resistance gave way and the fighting stopped on the island. Marines died every day.

By official casualty reports following the battle, 4,554 Marine officers and enlisted men were killed during the hostile action. 1,331 more died of wounds received in the battle. Forty-six were never found or identified afterwards and were presumed dead. An additional 17,272 Marines were wounded in the action; 2,648 were reported to have been the casualties of combat stress and fatigue.

Navy officers and sailors were also among the casualties at Iwo Jima—363 were killed in action, 70 more died of their wounds, 448 were reported missing and presumed killed, and 1,917 were wounded in action. The island defenders died in greater numbers. The Japanese recorded 20,703 on their death rolls. Only 216 survived the battle, having been captured and taken prisoners during the month-long assault.

Brave actions occurred in countless numbers on Iwo Jima. Men sacrificed their lives in the accomplishment of their orders and the mission. Thousands died. While many more might have deserved the honor, twenty-two Marines were awarded the Medal of Honor for their actions on the volcanic island. The nature of their gallantry must have been truly conspicuous to stand out from the thousands of courageous acts occurring daily on the island.

Captain James G. Headley understood this. A lawyer from Cincinnati and USMC reserve officer, he was a company commander who took command of a battalion when his commander was wounded in action and evacuated from the island. Five months after the war ended, he summed up his impressions of the battle. Jim Headley saw "so many acts of courage and bravery that it's almost impossible to remember them all. They died so fast that the whole business of heroes and death is a little mixed up in my mind. You'd see a man do something almost unbelievable and a minute later you'd see him die. It's pretty hard to pick out any outstanding man or men." [1]

All Marines remember Iwo Jima as the island that forever ensured the Corps' existence. More Medals of Honor were earned there than in any other single engagement or campaign in which Marines have served. In fact, more Medals were awarded in five months in 1945 than in any other full year in the Corps' history.

Iwo Jima Medals of Honor [2]

Charles J. Berry *	Jacklyn H. Lucas
William R. Caddy *	Jack Lummus *
Justice M. Chambers	Harry L. Martin *
Darrell Samuel Cole *	Joseph Jeremiah McCarthy
Robert H. Dunlap	George Phillips *
Ross F. Gray *	Donald J. Ruhl *
William G. Harrell	Franklin E. Sigler
Douglas T. Jacobson	Tony Stein *
Joseph R. Julian *	William G. Walsh *
James D. LaBelle *	Wilson D. Watson
John H. Leims	Hershel W. Williams

Twenty-two names make up the list of Marine Iwo Jima Medal of Honor recipients. Twelve of the names are followed by an asterisk. The glyph indicates Posthumous Awards. Therefore, ten Iwo recipients survived their actions and returned home after the war. Six ships, four bridges, five streets, a memorial highway, an American Legion Post, four Marine Corps League Detachments, a National Guard Armory, Veterans' nursing home, university dorm, university memorial display, two scholarships, a town monument, city park, and an athletic field have been named in tribute to one or the other of these twenty-two men.

Jack Lucas died June 5, 2008, at the age of 80. Only Hershel "Woody" Williams, 87-years-old, continued to attend Medal of Honor reunions as of this printing. At the start of this research, the *Thirty-Four Forgotten* initially included Justice M. Chambers, Franklin E. Sigler, and Wilson D. Watson.

Some recipients preferred to have no tribute or memorial extended to them at all.

Justice Marion Chambers grew up in Huntington, West Virginia, between where the Big Sandy and Guyandotte Rivers drop out of the Appalachian ridges and spill into the Ohio River. The area is rich in silica deposits, and glass manufacturing provided work for a large segment of the town's people. Children across America played with colorful glass marbles made in the region.

Huntington shares a corner with Ohio and Kentucky. The city is the Cabell County seat, spreading across a county line, divided by the Four Pole Creek, into Wayne County. Most of the city is in Cabell. The smaller Wayne County portion of Huntington is mainly comprised of the Westmoreland neighborhood.

Arthur Chambers, Justice's father, was the family patriarch. He grew up in the years prior to the turn of the twentieth century and did not find employment in glass manufacturing or marbles. He was a persuasive talker, however, and was able to talk people into buying things. After marrying Dixie Maryland Justice, he went on the road.

His younger brother, Boyd, stayed in school and played athletics. [3]

Arthur was a furniture salesman, traveling into eastern Kentucky and points south. Interestingly, he did not like to drive himself. Arthur preferred to hire drivers to take him to his distant customers. Much later, when his younger son, Arthur Jr., was experiencing the joys of automobiles, he gave his father a driving lesson. The pull of horsepower was unsettling for Arthur Sr., and he continued in his habit of hiring drivers.

The Chambers bought a small, bungalow style house in Westmoreland to raise a family. Located at 3137 Brandon Road, where it bends into Auburn Road, the home was just a short walk from the Auburn Road Bridge that carried traffic over the Four Pole into Cabell County.

Gladys was their first child, born in 1905. Justice was born February 2, 1908. All three years apart, Arthur, Jr. was born in 1911 and Martha, their youngest child, in 1914.

Since Arthur Sr. was out of town five nights a week, home only on the weekends, Dixie showed her children how to manage a household with only one parent present to keep things in order. And education was the first order of business for the Chambers children. They all first went to Westmoreland Grade School, then crossed the bridge into Cabell County to attend the old Huntington "Pony Express" High School, a relatively new school at the time. Established in 1889, it was then the only high school in the city.

Justice's was a modest background, but he was energetic and enthusiastic about many things. He might have played with marbles, but education was what drove him. His athleticism, but not his determination, was hampered by an episode of polio when he was a child, which shortened one of his legs. [4] Not to be "bested" by an illness, his unwillingness to let polio handicap him also gave evidence of his mental toughness. The men he led into battle later would call him "Jumping Joe" because of the way he ran to compensate for the shortened leg.

Family remembers the two eldest Chambers children as strongminded and intent on finding their own way. Gladys and Justice liked having the initiative and neither were individuals others could tell what to do, although they tried with each other. And early in their lives, Gladys did have an influence on her younger brother.

Marshall College

Less than four miles east from their house on Brandon Road, on the Cabell County side of town, was the home of the *Thundering Herd*, Marshall College.

As Justice entered Huntington High, Gladys went off to college. Marshall was an obvious choice for higher education, not only because of its close proximity, but because of family ties. The Chambers children were familiar with the Marshall campus, especially the football stadium, where the first Marshall football game was played on a Wednesday afternoon, November 9, 1898. Their Uncle Boyd Chambers [5] played football for the *Thundering Herd* in 1900 and baseball from 1900 to 1901. He graduated from Marshall College with the Class of '01, and stayed on. Boyd was an innovator and tactician and knew the game. His alma mater hired him. He was head coach for baseball, basketball and football, and served as director of athletics until 1917. [6]

The year after Justice Chambers was born, 1909, Boyd became head football coach. He held the position until 1916, compiling a 31-26-3 record. As Justice was making his way through the early grades at Westmoreland, his uncle became famous. On April 28, 1915, "Big Green" first appeared in print as the nickname for the baseball team— Boyd's idea. There was more.

Among coaching colleagues, Boyd earned the nickname "Fox," and for good reason. The 1915 football season had not gone well for the team and their coach, finishing with one win and eight losses. The 92-6 loss to rival West Virginia University on Saturday, November 6, 1915, might have seemed particularly forgettable, maybe even humiliating, but was in fact memorable, history-making actually.

To ensure at least one score that day, Coach Chambers had designed and practiced a play for which the quarterback threw a pass to a receiver standing on the shoulders of another player at the end zone. Boyd had the chance to introduce the play in the *Thundering Herd*'s fourth possession of the game, already behind 21-0, when Marshall recovered a *Mountaineers'* fumble. The play worked, the *Herd* scored, and the *Mountaineers'* coach protested.

Despite the controversy, the play was ruled fair and the final score stayed in the record books at both schools. The play, featured in the 1916 Marshall yearbook as the "skyrocket pass," was outlawed in college football for the 1916 season. More commonly remembered as the "Tower Pass" or "Tower Play," some Marshall football historians might say it is remembered more than any other play in Marshall gridiron history. The extended Chambers family never forgot it. Not long after this history-making game, Boyd B. "Fox" Chambers ventured down the Ohio River and was the head football coach for the Cincinnati Bearcats, 1918-21.

Persuasive talking, being on the move, innovation, and designing tactics were in the blood of the Chambers.

Looking for Justice and his siblings in Huntington High's *The Annual Tatler* yearbooks took some extra effort. Gladys was probably at Huntington High between 1918-22. Justice was next in 1921-25, Arthur, Jr. in 1927-31 and Martha, the youngest child, in 1930-34. Based on this information, Jennifer J. Day, current Library Media Specialist at the high school was able to find Justice in the 1925 yearbook. [7]

Under his picture are listed his extracurricular activities: he was a Cheer Leader in 1923 and 1924, participated in the Glee Club, Crucible Club, and Dramatic Club, and in the Senior Play. The yearbook staff summed up their impression of Justice. "This busy boy just can't sit still, he's the life of the class." This view of Justice as the life of the class would echo all the way to the island of Iwo Jima.

After high school, Justice stayed in Huntington and attended Marshall College for three years, working his way through school. His elder sister had already finished her formal education. The first four-year baccalaureate degrees at Marshall were conferred on June 11, 1921. Gladys graduated with hers and began teaching in Huntington, briefly having Athur Jr. and Martha as students. She married, had one son, divorced, and moved to New York City where she found a career in modeling.

Then, with the encouragement of his parents and his elder sister, Gladys, Justice transferred from Marshall to George Washington

University in Washington, D.C. From there he went on to National University to earn a law degree.

A Natural Leader

While in college, by then having reached a height of six-foot three-inches, Justice enlisted in the peacetime Naval Reserves for two years in 1929. When the country later plunged into the Depression, he plunged into the Marine Corps as a private and then was commissioned an officer in 1932.

Besides the oath to "support and defend the Constitution of the United States against all enemies, foreign and domestic," Justice also vowed to love and cherish Johanna Maria Schmutzer when they married on Christmas Day, 1932. By the time Washington's 5th Marine Regiment was activated for service in summer, 1940, he and Johanna, called "Hansi," had started a family, raising a daughter, Patty, and a son, John. [8]

Justice's acumen for leadership had been recognized while he was serving in the Reserves. When the Marines started organizing two Raider Battalions following the attack on Pearl Harbor, he was recruited into "Red Mike" Edson's 1st Raider Battalion at the rank of Captain. He embarked by train to the West Coast on Washington's Birthday, February 22, 1942, to join the Raiders. "Red Mike" was pleased to have him.

Captain Chambers was vigorous in training his company as the Marines prepared for their island hopping campaign in the South Pacific. The Raiders concentrated on physical fitness, marksmanship, weapons use, small-unit tactics, individual skills, hand-to-hand fighting, and night operations, all of which Captain Chambers ardently pursued.

When *Operation Watchtower*, the first American ground offensive of WWII, simultaneously landed the Marines on Guadalcanal, Tulagi, and Gavutu-Tanambogo on August 7, 1942, Captain Chambers was in command of the Battalion's D Company. Aboard ship on their way to the Solomon Islands, he gave detailed assault plans to his platoon commanders. He also gave vigorous pep talks to his Marines, readying them for what was ahead. Engaging the enemy for real was not going to be like the amphibious assault rehearsals in the Fiji Islands in the previous weeks.

Tulagi is a small coral island, stretching southeast to northwest, about four thousand yards long and only a thousand yards wide. A thickly forested ridge reaching to 350 feet in elevation comprised most of the island. Tulagi's low ground was to the southeast, a saddle between the ridges: a smaller hill of 208 feet and a 281-foot hill on the southeastern tip of the island. The Japanese had been in possession of the island since May and had established defensive positions in trenches, tangled ravines, and caves in the high ground as they built a seaplane base in the harbor.

Edson's 1st Raiders approached Tulagi to the sounds of American planes and naval guns pounding the island, as well as the machine guns of their landing craft providing them covering fire. Captain Chambers was in the first assault wave that climbed out of Higgins boats at 8:00 AM and waded one hundred yards to the coral beaches of Tulagi. Dog Company was at the point of the assault.

Before evening had fallen on D-Day, Captain Chambers had fallen to a mortar blast. That night during enemy incursions, despite his serious wounds, he directed the evacuation of other wounded men and the defense of the battalion aid station. His actions earned him a Silver Star for valor and a Purple Heart for his wounds. While Captain Chambers recovered from his wounds in New Zealand, his recuperation was brightened by the news that Johanna had given birth to their second son, Justice Marion "Mike" Jr., September 3, 1942.

Captain Chambers was one of the fifty-five Raiders wounded during the capture of Tulagi, but not among the thirty-eight killed. He would lead men into battle again. [9]

Promoted, Lieutenant Colonel Chambers was given command of the 3d Battalion, 25th Marines, 4th Marine Division. The impact he had on the men under his command was later described in 1945 magazine articles. "[A]s much a marine as any man who ever lived, handsome, good-natured and rather young for his rank," he trained them first at Camp Lejeune, then at Camp Pendleton, California, keeping them in the field five days and nights a week. He was home from battalion training only on the weekends.

As a commanding officer, Lieutenant Colonel Chambers was going to be remembered as making things rough for his troops in training so they would perform gallantly when tested in battle. Before the war ended, he was "known throughout the Marine Corps as one of the finest guys and one of the toughest commanding officers in any man's army." He said it to his officers as soon as he assumed command of the 3d Battalion: "[G]entlemen, we are going to war. And when we get there, we are going to be ready." [10]

Lieutenant Colonel Chambers left San Diego on January 13,1944, and led his battalion into the Marshall Islands. Their objective was the capture of the airfield on Roi Island, connected by a spit of land and a causeway to Namur Island. Lieutenant Colonel Chambers took his men into a lagoon on mid-afternoon, January 31, and by evening had secured Ennugarret and Ennumennet, the two small islets nearest Namur. From there the battalion provided cover and support of the main assault the next day, and then spent six days securing fifty more small islets adjoining Roi-Namur.

Lieutenant Colonel Chambers, "a strapping big fellow," led his battalion across Yellow Beach in the second assault wave on Saipan Island on Thursday morning, June 15, and established his men 700 yards inland from the beach. Five days into the battle, when the Marine sweep had turned north, he led a well-planned and well-organized assault that captured Hill 500. At dawn on June 22, Lieutenant Colonel Chambers' men led the assault north toward Death Valley and Mount Tapotchau in central Saipan. To the west of Tapotchau was Garapan City, where some later researchers believed Amelia Earhart died in a Japanese prison in 1937. [11]

At 3:15 that afternoon an enemy ammunition dump exploded and Lieutenant Colonel Chambers was taken out of action with concussion wounds. He returned to the 3d Battalion command post the next day. Stalking about like a pirate, with a pistol on his hip, another under an armpit, and a "wicked looking knife" dangling from his belt, he eventually led the battalion up the eastern side of Saipan, through Karaberra Pass to the airfield under Mount Marpi on the north tip of the island.

Banzai and Suicide Cliffs

Marpi Point, overlooking the Pacific, with knife-like coral and bone-crushing surf hundreds of feet below, earned different names in the final days of the battle for Saipan.

Twenty-two days after Lieutenant Colonel Chambers had crossed Yellow Beach with his men, 3:00 AM on July 7, a Friday morning, the Japanese commander ordered an all-out massive banzai charge into the Marine lines on the western side of the island. The yelling, shooting, artillery explosions, bayonet lunges, rock throwing, and hand-to-hand fighting was not stopped until 6:00 PM. Over 4,200 Japanese soldiers died.

Although Saipan was declared secured by the Marines at 4:15 PM, July 9, the dying did not end. And as horrible as the carnage had been between the combatants battling for the island, more scenes of horror awaited the Marines. Between July 8 and 12, Japanese civilians began killing themselves, in part, in tribute to their Emperor and, in part, to avoid capture.

The Marines watched the Japanese shoot, grenade, and decapitate each other. Groups of civilians blew themselves up with grenades. Mothers threw babies and fathers pushed children off the cliffs at Marpi Point, and then jumped to their own deaths. Lines of civilians sacrificed families to avoid the shame of a military defeat and the harrowing capture by Americans their homeland propaganda had warned them to expect. The bodies piled up on the coral under the cliffs, the surf red with blood. The stench in the air from bloated bodies would be a haunting memory for many veterans in the years ahead.

Reports from the island estimated that more than 10,000 civilians committed *gyokusai,* translated as "shattered jade," in the final days. Today's maps mark the Marpi Point sites as "Banzai Cliff" and "Suicide Cliff."

Lieutenant Colonel Chambers was proud of his Marines: how they fought, how they endured and rallied, and in particular how respectfully and compassionately they had treated the frightened civilians. In those last days, he had witnessed enemy "fanaticism" that tempered his thoughts about what the 3d Battalion would face as the island hopping to Japan continued. And he was certain it would be "terrible."

The 3d Battalion immediately entered into the planning for the assault upon nearby Tinian. On July 24, Lieutenant Colonel Chambers led his men into the face of coral cliffs and across the left side of White Beach 2. He and his battalion remained fighting on the island until it was declared secured at 6:55 PM on August 1. Ahead for Lieutenant Colonel "Jumping Joe" Chambers was one of the fiercest battles in Marine Corps history.

On February 19, 1945, participating in his fifth major amphibious assault of the war, Lieutenant Colonel Chambers took the battle-hardened 3d Battalion across the right flank of Blue Beach 1, Iwo Jima. Their objectives were to capture the Rock Quarry cliffs and to anchor the front line to East Boat Basin. He was 37-years-old and had had enough combat experience to understand what was ahead when he charged out of that landing craft. He knew that any assaulting unit covering a flank, as was his mission, would be exposed to the most intense enemy resistance.

Iwo Jima provided no cover and protection for the assault troops. The high ground of Hill 382 and the cliffs near the quarry to the right and Mount Suribachi to the left provided the enemy ample advantage to lay withering fire down on the Marines at the landing site. Heavy mortar, machine gun, and rifle fire spewed from the quarry. Artillery rounds pounded the volcanic stone terraces leading up from the beaches. The enemy barrage, smoke and noise, and the mangled bodies of dead and wounded comrades trapped the Marines on the terraces.

Once ashore, his combat mettle having first been forged on Tulagi with Edson's Raiders, Lieutenant Colonel Chambers moved into the front line and began encouraging his men to pivot to the northeast and inch toward their objective, the ridge top facing the quarry. He remained in the open, exposed to enemy fire, as he reconnoitered the 25th Regiment's line of responsibility and organized his battalion for the assault on the high ground. By D-Day's end, after an eight-hour battle, Lieutenant Colonel Chambers had pushed the battalion to its first objective and anchored the regiment's protecting flank.

Historians have drawn conclusions about the battle for Iwo's Rock Quarry on the right flank. Gaining the cliff tops on D-Day has been recognized as a reflection of the *strength of character* of Lieutenant Colonel "Jumping Joe" Chambers and his executive officer, Captain James G. Headley. [12]

As on other islands, the battalion had been at the point of attack and experienced the realities of combat. More than half of the battalion's key officers, twenty-two, and nearly half of its troops, five hundred, had been lost to casualties. The battalion was placed in reserve for the next day's assault.

At 2:30 PM, February 21, "Jumping Joe" Chambers pushed the remnant of his reorganized battalion back into the front line. Exposed to extremely rugged terrain, under intense enemy fire, the companies moved forward from their reserve position a yard at a time, painstakingly closing a gap that had opened in the Marine line. For the third night, harassing artillery, mortar, machine-gun, and sniper fire as well as enemy incursions, kept the battalion alert.

The flag over Mount Suribachi

On D-Day plus four, February 23, at 10:20 AM, the first American flag was raised over Mount Suribachi.

Lieutenant Colonel Chambers was not on the island to witness the event.

On the previous cold and rainy day, having positioned his forces in a tactically sound manner, he had moved among his men, "zealous" in his efforts to bolster their morale as they held the center of the regimental line. Observing formidable enemy emplacements on a hill in front of them, Lieutenant Colonel Chambers coordinated a rocket and machine-gun attack that killed over two hundred enemy fighters.

Near 3:30 that afternoon, ignoring the intense enemy fire along the line, Lieutenant Colonel Chambers, twenty days past his thirty-seventh birthday, left his forward observation post and was hit by machine-gun fire. A bullet hit him in the left collarbone, passed through his chest and his lung, and exited his back. He was removed to an aid station, then from Iwo Jima to a ship for surgery. [13]

The recommendation that he be awarded the Medal of Honor began its way up the chain of command on April 7, 1945. The war ended and five years passed.

After seventeen years of military service, Justice Marion Chambers was promoted to colonel and medically retired from the Marines.

"Jumping Joe" went on to serve in various official offices, including staff advisor to the Senate Armed Services Committee. He settled with his growing family in Rockville, Maryland and later was president of his own consulting firm. His career of "professional lobbyist" focused upon international social concerns. [14] "Almost a legend," stories of Colonel Chambers' wartime heroic actions appeared in newspapers, magazines and books from time to time. [15]

Johanna gave birth to twin sons, Pete and Paul, on March 17, 1950, St. Patrick's Day. The family traveled to the White House that November so that President Harry S. Truman could present Justice a Medal of Honor for his endurance and courageous leadership on Iwo Jima.

November 1, an unseasonably hot, Indian Summer day in Washington D.C., was also an interesting and historic day for both the Chambers family and President Truman. The White House had been undergoing extensive reconstruction and renovation since 1948, and the president's residence had been temporarily moved across Pennsylvania Avenue to the Blair House. President Truman had his first meeting at the White House that Wednesday at 10:00 AM. He had the pleasure of meeting with the extended Chambers family and presenting the Medal to Colonel Chambers at noon. At least four Marine dignitaries in their dress uniforms attended the fifteen-minute ceremony. Thoughts of Iwo Jima, the Marines, and heroes might have been much on President Truman's mind after he had retired to the Blair House for lunch and a nap. At 2:15 PM, twenty-nine pistol shots rang out under his bedroom window during a shootout between the White House policemen and two Puerto Rican nationalists who stormed Blair House in an obviously unsuccessful attempt to assassinate the president. [16]

The attack on the president did not entirely overshadow media portrayals of the White House Medal ceremony. Newspaper columns described the two twins, Peter and Paul, seven-months-old, one held in each of their father's arms, eagerly trying to snatch the Medal from the president with their "chubby little hands." [17] Paul, reaching from the left, tried to pull President Truman's handkerchief from his suit pocket.

A Medal of Honor and photos of the family with President Truman at the White House would not be centerpieces of the Chambers' household. Like many Medal recipients who returned home, Justice was quiet and humble about his war experiences, preferring that attention not be paid to his service. Iwo Jima left indelible marks on the spirits of the men who fought on that island. Pushing memories of combat just to the edge of awareness, most chose afterwards not to talk about the war. They often insisted that their children and grandchildren not ask or talk about the medals, badges, and ribbons that once adorned their uniforms.

Always a modest man, Justice restricted his children and grandchildren from talking to others about his Medal, admonishing them "You are never to talk about my accomplishments or bring them to the attention of others." [18] In fact, Justice never talked to his children about the War or what he did in it. He did attend the February weekend 1st Raider Reunions when Battalion survivors gathered to reacquaint themselves with old comrades. As his third-born child grew, Justice took Mike Chambers along with him to the reunions.

His family was a priority for Justice. Like his father before him, on the road and away from home, working and providing was the focus. While Johanna remained home to raise the children, he was out of the house before 7:30 AM and back for dinner at 6:30 PM, five days a week. [19] Being home only on the weekends had become a Chambers family tradition. A grandson, who would know him for only twelve years, experienced Justice as a "loving and doting Grandfather" who was happy and proud that he had raised a wonderful, loving and close family. [20]

As many returning from war discover, Justice's marital relationship with Johanna was fraught with tensions that could not be resolved. They separated during Christmas vacation, 1962, and a divorce followed. While working in his own business as a professional lobbyist, Justice married Barbara Fornes, with whom he remained for the duration of his days.

There seemed little time for rest. In the same way the Marines and "Red Mike" Edson had, presidents appreciated Justice and his ability to organize and lead. And he did have a law degree. He served as Deputy Director of Civil Defense for President Truman. After President Eisenhower was elected, he left government service and turned to lobbying. President John F. Kennedy appointed him to the post of Deputy Director of the Office of Emergency Planning in 1962, a position in which he served with distinction until his retirement. Among other positions, he served as National President of the Fourth Marine Division Association.

Justice typed a brief note to his children in November 1972. True to his humble nature, he expressed the belief that he had too few virtues to extol. Recognizing that his family was going to face problems in the days ahead, he wanted them to know that they had "a strain" in them that would help them prevail. With the note were included copies from the Senate's December 21, 1950, Congressional Record of his Medal of Honor Award and magazine articles about his actions in command of Marines on the Pacific Islands. [21]

Justice died July 29, 1982, at the age of 74-years. He was buried in Section 6, Site 5813-A-9, in Arlington National Cemetery, with full military honors and in the presence of several hundreds of mourners, including family, friends, Marines, generals, various Association members, and seven Medal of Honor recipients. As he had requested, six Marines in camouflage combat utility uniforms and helmets were pallbearers. Six colonels in full-dress white uniforms served as honorary pallbearers. [22]

The honor guards meticulously folded the flag of the United States that had been draped over his coffin. A Marine officer presented the flag to Barbara, repeating the words heard by thousands of wives and mothers across the years: "As a representative of the United States Marine Corps, it is my high privilege to present you this flag. Let it be a symbol of the grateful appreciation this nation feels for the distinguished service rendered to our country and our flag by Colonel Justice Marion Chambers."

After his father's death when Mike Chambers was stationed at Quantico, he would serve each year as the Base sponsor for the Raider Reunion. He recalls meeting "some truly remarkable and great men and women there." Like his father, the Tulagi veterans said little about the War. Occasionally, a Raider would pull him aside, point to a man, and quietly tell a story of what the old Marine had once done. The tales were poignant, full of love and respect. And the ending seemed always to come with an admonition: "Don't ever tell him I told you."

Mike recognized this characteristic time after time as "the nature of all the veterans I have known."

"They don't talk—they just remember." [23]

That his five children and grandchildren, his nephews and cousins, and their children into the next generation were proud of Justice is evident. A son and grandson, both named after him, served as career Marine officers.

And as the years passed after Justice was interred at Arlington, many of his Marine comrades would remember him. The Marine Corps League Colonel Justice M. Chamber Detachment #555 in Mentor, Ohio, is named in his honor. On October 15, 1993, General Carl E. Mundy, Jr., 30th Commandant of the Marine Corps, directed the signing of Marine Corps Order (MCO)1650R.35B, the Chambers Award for Outstanding Leadership. The Marines continue annually to present this award to a Reserve Junior Officer.

But was he honored in West Virginia?

There was a time when Justice's heroism was overlooked in his home state. In 1963, he was a successful attorney living in Baltimore. At that time, the West Virginia State Board of Public Works had authorized that a bronze plaque bearing the names of all the state's Medal of Honor recipients be mounted in the State Capitol Rotunda in Charleston, thirty-eight miles east of Huntington. The plaque included names of sixty-two recipients, ten of who earned their awards in WWII. Of these ten, two had been born in Huntington. The list was based upon an article that had been presented by historian Boyd B. Stutler at the Annual Meeting of the West Virginia Historical Society on October 1, 1955. [24] Boyd noted a discrepancy when the time came for the West Virginia's Medal of Honor Recipients plaque at the State Capitol. There should have been eleven from WWII and three from Huntington—one of the awards had been made belatedly and the recipient's name had not been added to the state's list. The name, Justice Chambers, marked the 63rd name inscribed on the plaque. [25]

A four-hour drive northwest of Huntington, 227 miles into the rises and valleys of the Appalachians, travelers on I-68 near the upper northeast border with Maryland might stop for a rest. In Hazelton, Preston County, before leaving West Virginia, is another tribute. The rest area at Mile Marker 30, the Medal of Honor Recipients Statewide Memorial Plaza, is replete with flags, memorial stones, and bronze plaques. Justice Chambers is listed on the ornate plaque among the names of the WWII recipients. [26]

No other information about Justice Chambers was available in the West Virginia Archives and History or the database at the time of this printing. [27]

"An oversight that should be corrected" in his birthplace.

Huntington residents had been proud of their native son when Justice visited the White House in 1950. His parents had lived to take pride in his heroism and the acclaim in his hometown. His mother, Dixie, died in 1953. Arthur Chambers Sr. died in 1957. His three siblings all outlived Justice and had longer lives. Arthur, Jr. died in 1988 at the age of 78-years. Gladys died in 1989 at the age of 84-years. Martha, the youngest, lived the longest, dying at 87-years in 2001. None of his siblings lived to see their hometown dedicate a tribute to him.

Beginning in 1986, the City of Huntington Foundation began to recognize individuals who had made "significant contributions to the greater Huntington area through civic or political achievements, artistic endeavors, athletic accomplishments and/or acting as an outstanding ambassador for Huntington." The "Greater Huntington Wall of Fame" became a reality. The wall is located in the lobby of the downtown Civic Center, now called the Big Sandy Superstore Arena. A brass plaque for each honoree featuring their name, picture, and a brief description of their accomplishments is displayed on the wall. [28]

Annually, the Foundation asks for nominations in the spring and selects up to five individuals to add to the wall. Then in the autumn, the Foundation hosts an awards dinner to announce the new inductees. H. Woodrow "Woody" Williams, Charles E "Chuck" Yeager, former Marshall football coach Bobby Pruett, and Soupy Sales are among the citizens who have been recognized over the years. All of the Huntington inductees, some of whom were known to Justice Chambers, certainly deserved the recognition.

Virginia Ruth Egnor was among the 1998 inductees, the second plaque dedicated to her by a Huntington mayor over a period spanning nearly fifty years. She had grown up there and gone to Huntington High in 1934-38, nine years after Justice had graduated from there. Then she had been known as Ruthie.

When Colonel Chambers was photographed with the president at the White House, Ruthie was also in the public's view; only her name had been changed. America knew her as Dagmar; pronounced "dow-mahr." She was the first major female star of television on NBC's first late-night show, Broadway Open House, 1950-52. Her beaming image shone from the July 16, 1951, cover of *Life.* [29]

Prior to that issue hitting newsstands, Dagmar went home to Huntington. She bought a former mayor's house in Westmoreland for her family, down from the Chambers' on Brandon Road. She was referred to as "Huntington's first citizen" by local media. On June 25,

1951, the Chamber of Commerce and Mayor Walter Payne presented her with a plaque "from the grateful citizenry to Dagmar for distinguished service in publicizing her hometown."

The town had also invited its two best-known celebrities home for a July 4th celebration. Dagmar and Justice Chambers rode in the parade together in a Buick convertible.

Stars and starlets have a certain allure in hometowns, and Huntington remained reasonably enamored with Dagmar over the years. She was featured on the cover of the *Huntington Quarterly*, Issue 35, Spring 1999, two years before she died. First published in Autumn 1989, seven years after Justice's funeral in Arlington, the magazine is "devoted to showcasing the positive stories of the Huntington community." Soupy Sales, H. Woodrow "Woody" Williams, Chuck Yeager, and Bobby Pruett have each had a cover story or feature dedicated to them in the *Quarterly*. As of Issue 72, Winter 2010, it appears that Justice Chambers has had no mention in the Huntington magazine, nor is he included among the magazine's *Famous Folks*.

Following the 2010 awards, 100 plaques have been mounted on the Greater Huntington Wall of Fame. There is no plaque for Justice Chambers.

Public records searches, phone calls to the chamber of commerce, and correspondence inquiries suggested that Justice Chambers might not have been much remembered in his hometown after riding with Dagmar in a parade. What at first exploration might have appeared to be forgetting was not at all the absence of memory. Sometimes remembering just takes time—or someone deciding the wait has been long enough. According to a November 13, 2001, *Herald-Dispatch* news article, a local effort in Huntington had begun to have Justice Marion Chambers memorialized in some manner. [30] It had, two years earlier, because one Iwo Jima veteran and Medal of Honor recipient would not rest until a tribute at home was paid to his friend.

H. Woodrow "Woody" Williams

"Woody" Williams spent his childhood and young adulthood in the northern reaches of West Virginia in the foothills of the Appalachians, an area abundant in forests and state parks. He was born in Quiet Dell on October 2, 1923, a small town sitting at an elevation of 1,046 feet off the main north-south highway through the state. When he was eight years old, his hometown was in the headlines of national newspapers when West Virginia's most notorious multiple murderer, Harry Powers, the *Bluebeard of Quiet Dell* was arrested in 1931.

"Woody" moved north to Fairmont at some point, where he worked for a time as a taxi driver, as a laborer, and as a truck driver for a construction company. He married Ruby Dale Meredith of Fairmont and they had two daughters. Woody went down to Charleston in 1943 and enlisted in the Marines on May 26, when he was 19-years-old, weighing in at 145 pounds. Corporal Williams earned a Medal of Honor on Iwo Jima by single-handedly destroying a Japanese strong point on February 23, 1945. Woody and Justice became fast friends after the war, meeting at annual reunions.

An athletic field in Huntington and a bridge at Barboursville are named in Woody's honor. He was inducted into the Greater Huntington Wall of Fame in 1999, West Virginia's only surviving Medal of Honor recipient.

Around the time Woody Williams' plaque was added to the Wall of Fame, he and D. J. Turley Jr., Huntington's Marine Corps League Detachment 340 Commander, began planning. Woody believed the lack of recognition for Wayne County's only Medal recipient since the Civil War "was an oversight that should be corrected." County Commissioner Rich Wellman agreed. Having a native Medal of Honor recipient was "quite a distinction" according to Commissioner Wellman. He thought "it should be part of our history." [31] Justice's two nephews, Ben and Carter, both Huntington residents, assisted.

On May 11, 2002, Wayne County remembered their native son, unveiling the Chambers Memorial Plaque to honor the patriotism of the Iwo hero. Honored guests included the Colonel's daughter, Patricia, two sons, Justice M. "Mike," Jr. and Peter, and his two nephews. Woody Williams was a guest speaker. Various members of the West Virginia Fifth Senatorial District and House of Delegates attended. At Woody Williams' and the Marine Corps League's invitation, U.S. Senator John D. Rockefeller IV was also a guest speaker. [32] The plaque is on display at the Wayne County Court House, fifteen miles south of the Chambers' Brandon Road home.

Huntington City Council members on the Wayne County side of town, Woody Williams, and the West Virginia Marine Corps League saw this dedication as only a beginning. They wanted a tribute to the Huntington Medal of Honor recipient closer to home. As Justice had lobbied for others in his lifetime, now citizens lobbied for him.

At their Thursday, February 19, 2004, meeting, the West Virginia House of Delegates considered a message from the Senate. The Clerk of the Senate announced the adoption by the Senate, without amendment, of a concurrent resolution of the House of Delegates. Senate Concurrent Resolution No. 29, submitted by Senators Jenkins, Plymale and Dempsey, stated: "Requesting the Division of Highways name the bridge on U. S. Route 60 crossing Four Pole Creek from Cabell County to Wayne County, the 'Colonel Justice M. Chambers Memorial Bridge'." As resolved by the Legislature, the Division of Highways was requested to name the bridge the "Colonel Justice M. Chambers Memorial Bridge" with signs so indicating on either approach to the bridge. [33]

Route 60 runs through the center of the Marshall University campus. The "Colonel Justice M. Chambers Memorial Bridge" is 3.6 miles west of the university, where Adams Avenue crosses into Waverly Road. The green highway signs are on both sides of the bridge, the one on the west sitting beneath the shade of trees is in Wayne County. Underneath, flanked by acres of trees, shrubbery and vegetation running for miles, the Four Pole Creek empties into the Ohio River a tenth of a mile north. Justice's boyhood home is a short walk from the green sign on the Wayne County side of the bridge now bearing his name.

Justice is now listed among the Notable People from Huntington on the Wikipedia.org site. At the time of this writing, a plaque for him has not been added to the Greater Huntington Wall of Fame. It appears that Marshall University has not dedicated a tribute to Colonel Chambers. [34]

CHAPTER 15
"Unable to adjust himself to the public"

"…worldwide praise can never substitute for loyalties learned
and tested under the tribulations of the battlefield."

James Webb [1]

Thirty miles north of Raritan, New Jersey, where the annual John Basilone Memorial Parade takes place, there is another community that could have its own annual parade to honor a hometown Medal of Honor recipient. Actually, more than one community could have parades for this Marine.

Those who migrated to America seem to have passed down an acquired habit for moving on. Mobility, going from one place to another, changing residences or communities, has always been an important feature of American life, primarily to pursue economic opportunities and to provide more space "for the children." In the era when the WWII veterans were born, between the start of the 1900s and the war, approximately twenty-three percent of Americans moved from the states in which they were born. [2]

At least fifty-seven Medal of Honor recipients moved in childhood, either to a different state or to a town distant enough from their place of birth to mean new friends, new school, and possible changes in contacts with extended family members. The ages at which they moved varied from toddler to teenage years. At least seven of the men moved several times while in childhood. One of these men, Harold William "Indian Joe" Bauer, a Guadalcanal "Cactus Air Force" Ace, kept track of where he lived at certain points in his life based on which Nebraska or Kansas town his family was residing in when he, his two brothers, and his two sisters were born.

Franklin Earl Sigler did not cross a state line, but did move from his birthplace to a new town. Born November 6, 1924, Frank was a city kid who spent his youth on the west side of the Hudson River. His parents, George and Elsie Sigler, lived in Glen Ridge/ Montclair, New Jersey, when they started their family. Their first child, William C. was born November 12, 1921. Frank followed three years later. By the time Frank was five-years-old, the Siglers had moved five miles north to Little Falls with their two sons. More sons and a daughter were born in Little Falls. Frank went to Passaic Valley High School in Little Falls. That is where he was when the war began.

Death of an older brother

Patriotism was strong in the Sigler family. William was the first to join the Marines at the start of the war and to go to the Pacific Islands. When he had time, he would send a letter home with news from the islands. Frank waited in New Jersey for his chance. Following the Marine's victory on Guadalcanal, 18-year-old Frank enlisted on March 23, 1943. He reported for boot camp at Marine Corps Recruit Depot Parris Island, South Carolina. For seven weeks, most of his hours were spent in weapons training, physical fitness, field training, extensive marching, and close order drills as the drill instructors prepared him to go to war as an infantryman. Like many of his fellow recruits, Private Sigler had stories to tell about his older brother, the Marine at war, in their down time in the barracks.

Just as another muggy summer was arriving at Parris Island, and Private Sigler was nearing recruit graduation, the telegrams reached Little Falls.

USMC Private First Class William C. Sigler, 22-years-old, was killed June 11, 1943, in the South Pacific. At that time, the Marines were preparing for their landing assaults on the New Georgia group of islands in the central Solomons that began June 20, 1943. William's body was returned to the States and buried in Arlington National Cemetery at Section 12 Site 2815. [3]

There is no way to measure the impact of a brother's death in war. Stationed in South Carolina, Frank would have had a chance to get home to be with family in Little Falls after the news arrived. He was now the eldest son and brother. But grief would have to wait. Having finished recruit training, he spent ten more months, a damp 1943 winter and then spring, in South Carolina. Assigned to the Guard Company at the Charleston Navy Yard, Private Sigler waited to go to war.

He finally left the States in July 1944, training with Company F, 2d Battalion, 26th Marines in Hawaii as they prepared themselves for the capture of another Japanese island.

Private Sigler had his first taste of battle February 19, 1945, spending the day waiting to go ashore. Having boarded its landing crafts just before 8:00 AM, Fox Company was not ordered across their line of departure until after 3:00 PM. They crossed Red Beach on Iwo Jima around 5:30 PM.

Private Sigler sank ankle deep into the black volcanic sand and found he could not run up the terrace to the high ground. Nor could he dig a foxhole for cover from the withering enemy machine-gun and mortar fire. As 30,000 other Marines had discovered that day, the only alternative was to literally plow forward. He did for the next twenty-three days, a time in which his leadership and heroic bravery emerged.

Having fought past Hill 362-B, Company F began the painstaking and costly advance toward the last Japanese holdings on Kitano Point and Hill 165, the northernmost enemy outpost on Iwo. In the center of the Marine line, the advance had been slowed for several days by strongly-fortified and well-placed enemy gun positions.

Impervious to gunfire, many of the positions could be silenced only by grenades or flamethrowers.

On March 14, Private Sigler took the kind of actions demonstrated by the heroically brave. When the encounters with the enemy positions seemed bleak, he initiated a one-man assault. He also carried on his duty in spite of grievous, debilitating, and life-threatening wounds, as well as putting himself in harm's way and disregarding danger to rescue fellow Marines.

During the advance, his squad leader became a casualty under fire of a gun position. Private Sigler took command and led the squad on a charge toward the enemy emplacement. Reaching it first, he destroyed the position with hand grenades. The squad attempted again to advance. Other Japanese in supporting tunnels and caves opened fire. Private Sigler immediately climbed up the ridge to the enemy positions and assaulted them alone. Seriously wounded in his assault, he crawled back to his squad as the Japanese continued to fire upon them.

He refused evacuation or first aid. Having determined the enemy locations, he directed machine-gun and rocket fire into the cave openings. Three of his companions were wounded during the fight. Private Sigler carried each, one at a time, through the enemy fire to safety in the rear. Despite his own wounds, he returned to his squad and remained with them, directing their fire. Through his determined efforts, the enemy gun positions were destroyed. Fox Company moved forward and within two days the line of advance reached Hill 165.

Private Franklin Sigler, 20-years-old, was ordered to withdraw. He was evacuated from Iwo Jima, hospitalized for a time in Bethesda, awarded the Medal of Honor by President Truman at the White House on October 5, promoted to private first class in June 1946, and medically discharged from service. He walked with a slight limp afterwards.

Months after the war in the Pacific ended, the Newspaper Enterprise Association (NEA) News Service called together an unofficial committee representing various veterans' organizations and newspapers to review the combat records across the services to identify a Medal of Honor recipient who most closely resembled the legacy of U.S. Army Sergeant Alvin York of WWI. Private Sigler was among those whose valorous actions were considered for this honor. Luther Skaggs and Wilson "Doug" Watson were also considered. [4]

Following his return from the war Frank married, had a daughter, and lived with his parents in Little Falls, New Jersey, until he was able to own his own home. He did not talk to family about the events on Iwo Jima or call attention to his Medal of Honor.

Frank tried various civilian jobs after his return: a game warden, county court attendant, and a county detective. The jobs were short-lived. He was treated for "recurring nervous disorders" at the Lyons, New Jersey, Veterans Administration Hospital. According to his mother, Elsie Sigler, proud of all her children, her son was "unable to adjust himself to the public." He also gradually isolated himself from his friends. [5] The dark wood interior of his house seemed to reflect the moods that overtook him. Extended family sometimes experienced him as a bit gruff. The barber in Sparta considered him a life-long friend and "a great guy."

Not much was written about Frank in the public record after 1949. He served as Commandant of the Semper Fidelis Detachment of the Marine Corps League in Passaic, retiring in 1950. In April that year, he presented Senator Joe R. McCarthy (R-WI), himself a WWII Marine veteran, the League's National Americanism award.

Frank's photograph appeared in newspapers again in October 1977, holding his personalized FES CMH (Franklin Earl Sigler, Congressional Medal of Honor) auto license plates issued to him by New Jersey. [6] These were the first license plates ever designed to specifically honor men who had earned the military's highest decoration.

Franklin died January 20, 1995, at the age of 70-years. He was buried on a cold, clear day on a hill in Arlington National Cemetery. His funeral included caissons and full military honors. His daughter and brothers and sister were in attendance as well as nieces and in-laws. His grandson, a Marine recruit, was there with other young Marines. Robin S. Gardner, his grandniece, attended with her husband. Eleven years after the funeral, she would be elected to her first term as Falls Church

City, Virginia, mayor, and was nearing the end of her second term at this writing. [7]

Franklin's white headstone is in Section 12 Site 2799, just yards away from his brother's.

Sigler family members continued to attend annual Iwo Jima commemorations and stayed involved with the Medal of Honor Society. A perpetual Memorial Scholarship has been established in Franklin's name through The Marine Corps Scholarship Foundation in an effort to "enrich the lives of deserving young men and women with the gift of education."

Cradling grenades

There has never been a drill in basic Marine training that teaches young men to fall upon and cradle explosive devices to their bodies to shield others. Few would ever think about doing such a thing. The indomitable resolve to jump on a grenade comes from within the individual. Doing so is heroically brave in the extreme.

William Gary Walsh, born on April 7, 1922, in Roxbury, Massachusetts, came from a long line of Irishmen who were proud to do public service and respond to people in dire need. Arlington National Cemetery records indicate that his father was a Boston fireman, who died during the rescue of people from a burning building. After Bill's service in WWII, his brother, a Franciscan priest, serving as an Army Chaplain with the 180th Regiment, 45th Infantry Division in Korea would earn a series of medals for valor, coming to the aid of wounded soldiers while under enemy fire. A bridge joining Boston and Quincy was later named in the Father's memory. [8]

Bill attended public schools in Boston. He walked into a Marine recruiting station in April 1942, when he was 20-years-old, and enlisted. After boot training, he was assigned duties as a Marine Scout, and then saw duty with Carlson's Second Raider Battalion. He quickly gained combat experience and rank, participating in the campaigns on Guadalcanal, Bougainville, Tarawa, and the Russell Islands.

After two years of fighting, he briefly retuned to the States in 1944 and married Mary Louise Ponrod, who had been a member of the USMC Women's Reserve. Gunnery Sergeant Walsh then joined the 5th Marine Division as they prepared for their entry into the Pacific Theater. He returned to the Pacific, assigned duties as an infantry platoon leader with Company G, 3rd Battalion, 27th Marines.

Spending most of the morning of February 19, 1945 in an LVT with his platoon, he watched the smoke and fires rise from the beaches of Iwo Jima, as the waves of his sister battalions were bunched up and pinned down on Red Beaches 1 and 2. As the Marine line progressed across the narrow portion of the island, George Company came ashore at 11:30 AM and joined the fighting, staying 200 yards behind the lead battalions. Gunnery Sergeant Walsh led his platoon in mopping up enemy positions that had withstood the lead assault. By 3:00 PM the Marines had reached the west coast and Company G dug in only 200 yards from the cliffs.

Each day George Company took casualties as they advanced north past the western edge of Airfield No. 1, through the hostile bluffs, over jagged ridges, and beyond Airfield No. 2 to the east. Having moved forward about 300 yards on the eighth day of fighting, the company dug into night positions about 800 yards south of Hill 362-A. George Company waited for the inevitable enemy incursions and counterattacks. Sleep was fitfull on Iwo if it came at all.

At 8:00 AM on the morning of February 27, Gunnery Sergeant Walsh and his platoon went forward on the right flank towards the base of the barren hill rising sharply from the rocky island floor. They encountered fortified pillboxes, machine-gun bunkers, and static medium tank positions dug into hollows on the hill.

The enemy was as much in the hill as on it. Caves and a tunnel complex provided the Japanese significant advantage for fighting, protection, and re-supply. Artillery and mortar shells from both forces pounded the terrain around the Marines as they pushed forward. By noon, intense enemy machine-gun fire from interlocking positions and mortar fire from adjacent high ground had stalled George Company. The platoons were being pummeled.

Pinned down at the base of a steep ridge, Gunnery Sergeant Walsh defied the Japanese mission orders to annihilate the Marines. He charged ahead with his platoon against a machine-gun position dug into the ridge and a trench full of Japanese soldiers. The enemy responded with increased fire and grenades and repelled the attack. Gunnery Sergeant Walsh reorganized his depleted platoon and attacked again, ignoring the steady flow of automatic weapons fire directed at him.

This time, the platoon reached the ridge crest and, before the remnant of his men could consolidate, a barrage of enemy hand grenades thrown from reverse-slope defensive positions confronted them. His men took shelter in whatever depressions and trenches they could reach.

When a grenade landed among some of his men sheltered in a low trench, Gunnery Sergeant Walsh did not hesitate.

Among the 294 Marines awarded the Medal of Honor, no fewer than seventy-one received the Medal for acting against natural survival instincts to save others from explosive projectiles. The first mention of a life-threatening encounter with a grenade in a Marine Medal of Honor Citation occurred between the two World Wars.

Corporal Donald Leroy Truesdell was the first, during the Nicaraguan expedition, a civil disturbance between 1926 and 1933. Bandits were attempting to overthrow the government. A Marine expeditionary force was sent to help quell the insurrection. 25-year-old Corporal Truesdell was part of a patrol in the Sierra Madres Mountains in the north, near the Honduran border. It was rugged terrain, covered in jungle.

On April 24, 1932, the patrol was following a path near the Rio Coco. Corporal Truesdell moved along in the formation, alert and ready for a hostile encounter. During the patrol's advance, a rifle grenade slipped from its carrier and fell upon a rock, igniting the detonator. An explosion was imminent within seconds, putting several members of the patrol in danger. Corporal Truesdell saw what happened, was yards away from the grenade, and had time to protect himself by taking cover. Instead, he hastened to the explosive, picked it up, and tried to throw it away from the patrol. The grenade detonated before he could dispose of it, blowing off his right hand and causing multiple serious fragmentation wounds to his body. His firm grasp of the grenade restricted the explosion to himself, thereby protecting the lives of others close by.

Corporal Truesdell survived this encounter with a grenade. He took an action inconsistent with instinctive reactions. Although he could have sheltered himself away from the blast, wholly consistent with survival instincts, he instead tried to get the hurtful object away from himself and others. Many more Marines would follow this example of heroic bravery. Unlike Corporal Truesdell, few would survive.

Of the 82 Marines awarded the Medal of Honor in the Second World War, twenty-seven hurled themselves onto grenades to save fellow Marines. Eight of the twenty-two Marines (36%) who earned Medals of Honor on Iwo Jima made quick decisions about the danger grenades posed to comrades. Gunnery Sergeant Walsh was one of them.

Not a reflexive or impulsive act

Some might conclude that Gunnery Sergeant Walsh reacted to a reflexive impulse rather than acting on his own conscious decision. Perhaps, if he was the only man to have ever jumped on a grenade to protect others, investigators might reasonably say he acted on reflex. However, when a group of sixty-seven Marines in various situations, and across time, risk catastrophic injuries in order to save companions, the action of jumping on a grenade must be considered much more than a reflexive impulse. [9]

Psychology recognizes that most human behavior, if not all, must occur in the sequence of sensation, perception, conclusion, decision, and action. From a behavioral standpoint, Gunnery Sergeant Walsh had to first see or hear the projectile, recognize it, understand its explosive capacity, and consider that the average grenade explodes within four seconds after it is charged, therefore demanding action.

Obviously Marines do not jump on grenades when alone. When a grenade lands in a lone Marine's fighting hole, natural instincts take over. He will either vacate the position by diving out of the hole or he will try to throw the grenade back in the direction from which it came. Unable to do either, he might just as likely keep fighting until the explosion.

The decision to jump on a grenade is made in that instant in time when all other alternatives seem without merit or without the necessary time to accomplish. Rather than cradle a grenade to their bodies, some of the Medal recipients did attempt another alternative. The actions of Private First Class Luther Skaggs, Jr., fighting off counterattacks to secure Guam's Asan-Adelup beachhead; of Private Hector Albert Cafferata, Jr. keeping the Toktong Pass open as the Marines fought their way out from Yudam-ni at the Chosin Reservoir; of Corporal David Champagne during the assault on the North Koreans' fortified positions on Hill 104 and Tumae-ri Ridge; of Private First Class Jack William Kelso saving a bunker at Combat Outpost Warsaw, near Sokchon; of Staff Sergeant Lewis Watkins counterattacking the crest of a hill to retake Outpost Frisco; and of Private First Class Ronald Leroy Coker on the narrow Vietnam jungle trail in the northwest sector of Quang Tri Province all serve as examples.

Men like Gunnery Sergeant Walsh who jumped on grenades consciously considered additional factors beyond their own survival before taking an action survival instincts demand. These men considered the presence of other men likely to be injured or killed by the detonation, overcame their own nervous system instinct for self-preservation, often called out to alert comrades, and quickly *decided* to cover the explosive device with their own bodies. Gunnery Sergeant Walsh accomplished this entire analytical sequence in the seconds between recognition of the grenade and its explosion. When the grenade landed in the trench, Gunnery Sergeant Walsh had time only to decide and then jump onto the grenade before it exploded.

His platoon's assault of the machine-gun emplacement allowed George Company to advance further towards Hill 362 and hold the ground they had won. The remnant of his platoon survived. Gunny Walsh, 22-years-old, died in the grenade's blast.

Gunnery Sergeant William Walsh was initially buried at the 5th Marine Division Cemetery on Iwo Jima. His remains were later brought back to the States and re-interred in Arlington National Cemetery on April 20, 1948. He is buried in Section 12, Gravesite 487.

Marines have continued to go into battle since Iwo Jima. Another generation of Marines is at war. They will continue to be brave in combat. It is certain that others will sacrifice their own lives that their companions can return home, and some will go above and beyond what is expected of them and earn Medals of Honor.

Marines continue to cradle grenades to preserve the lives of others. The most recent Marine to do so was in Iraq on April 22, 2004: Corporal Jason Lee Dunham from the small town of Scio, on the Genesee River in the Allegheny Mountains of western New York. Prior to that date, while in Iraq, Corporal Dunham thought about and prepared for what he would do if a grenade were ever tossed among his squad mates. His lieutenant suggested to him that any such attempt would likely prove fatal. Corporal Dunham was readying himself to do something that few would ever think about doing. When the time came, it was a deliberate action, not a reflexive or impulsive act.

CHAPTER 16
...But Not Forgotten

"...so many acts of courage and bravery that it's
almost impossible to remember them all."

Captain James G. Headley, USMC
Iwo Jima, Company L, 3rd Battalion, 25th Marines

Web logs got their start in December 1997, as the new millennium
was approaching. On a Sunday in January 2008, a new "blog" appeared
on the Internet. The lead story was about a local man who had died at
war sixty-two years earlier. The "blogger' had discovered the hometown
hero and wanted others at home and in the classrooms to remember
him. As it turned out, the community needed no reminders.

The lack of *easily* accessible information in public sources can be
deceiving. Relying on Internet searches for public records and phone
calls to the Chamber of Commerce do not necessarily yield an accurate
perspective of whether or not a community has honored its own Medal
of Honor Marine. Local newspaper archives and contacts with city and
high school librarians can prove to be invaluable.

This particular Marine had earned a posthumous Medal on Iwo Jima and had been counted among the thirty-four recipients forgotten at home. Indications were that his family had moved at some point from his birthplace, perhaps resulting in a lack of remembrance later. The Internet blog and a call to the librarian at the high school he had attended changed these conclusions.

The extended exploration into Joseph Rudolph Julian's life had results. The roster of the forgotten was going to be shortened by one.

Adelard Julian and his younger brother had been born and raised in the village of Fiskdale, in Sturbridge, central Massachusetts. A few miles from the Connecticut border and sixty miles southwest of Boston, Sturbridge is a small rural town nestled within forested, rolling hills, and sloping meadows. Carved out as receding glaciers scoured the landscape, the New England town sits on Westville Lake and is surrounded by ponds, other lakes, two state parks, and other small towns with old Victorian Main Streets. The Quinebaug River flows into Westville Lake. Water being so abundant, dams were built to manage farming and floods.

The towns in Worcester County, where Sturbridge is located, were named for bridges and groves with good reason. Covered bridges over the swift-flowing streams in the many valleys were a common sight. With sixty-six square miles of water, nearly five percent of its territory, the county is a fisherman's dream.

When the two brothers had their own families, they lived close to each other in Fiskdale. Their children were playmates, cousins who would remain lifelong friends. Patriotism and the New England work ethic were strong influences in the Julian family. Adelard worked most of his life in the Sturbridge Cloth Mill. Two of his children would enlist in the Marines when the United States entered WWII. Adelard's brother went off to the European front with the Army in WWI, was gassed and shelled, and came home with the lifelong psychological wounds common among the war's combat veterans. [1]

Adelard married Rosalda. The couple raised their son and two daughters through the era of World War I and the Great Depression.

[2] Joseph Rudolph Julian, or "Rudy" as he was called by family and friends, was born April 3, 1918. Rudy was two-years-old when his sister, Gloria, was born, four when Lorraine was born. He would be a well-loved big brother.

Rudy was an energetic and active boy, remembered as having been "into everything" by his mother. He had a warm, easy smile and pleasant nature, enjoyed play and sports, and was at home in the outdoors. Music was an enjoyment for him. He liked to sing, play guitar, and hum on his harmonica. Not shy in front of others, Rudy sang in a minstrel group and in the St. Anne's church choir. Christmas, with its many carols, would always be a memorable season for the family.

Rudy's relationship with his father was a close one. He and Adelard went off hunting and fishing together whenever they could. The woods behind Saint Anne's Shrine were good hunting grounds for squirrels and rabbits. Hunting trips north to track deer in Maine were cherished times for father and son. Rosalda kept boyhood photos of Rudy with abundant catches of fish or holding his deer rifle across his chest in an "inspection arms" position, a pose he would snap to later on Marine rifle drill fields.

Like all things to which he turned his attention, Rudy took his school studies seriously. Getting an education was his predominant interest. His Catholic faith was an integral part of his life, and he would be seen serving on the altar during Sunday Mass at Saint Anne's Church, a practice he continued later as a Marine in places that had neither marble altars or shrines.

Rudy might have grown up on an Americana post card, but the idyllic scene did not go unbroken. He was in elementary school in October 1929, when the stock market crashed. He listened as Adelard and Rosalda worried about financial matters. The family would never be destitute, however, because Adelard's job continued. Craftsmen, artisans, farmers, and construction laborers could still find work, and the growing American Optical Company still provided employments for those with the New England work ethic. There was also work to be had at the construction site of an historic, old village going up on the Quinebaug, a favorite stop for Massachusetts' tourists.

A quiet, rural town, Fiskdale, did not have a high school. After graduating from eighth grade at the Fiskdale Town Hall, Rudy traveled five miles down Old Sturbridge Road to attend Mary E. Wells High School in Southbridge. He was popular with the girls and dated throughout high school.

While Rudy attended high school, American newspapers carried the stories of events in Europe. Adolf Hitler became Chancellor of Germany in 1933 and then Führer in 1934. Hitler's politics and racism were evident. The red and black swastikas became a symbol of "Aryan superiority," the drive for racial purity, and the genocide of all peoples considered "non-humans." Another World War was not yet on the minds of the Julians or Americans, although it was just a few years away for Europeans.

When he graduated from high school around 1936, economic times were tough and good jobs were a blessing. Rudy went to work in Old Sturbridge Village for American Optical Company, the world leader in the manufacturing and sale of eyeglasses. Wanting to further his learning, and honing his manual skills, he began trade school there. Cabinet making became his specialty.

And besides the Great Depression, other storms and disturbances were just years away for Rudy and the Julians. Late on the afternoon of September 21, 1938, after three days and nights of downpours, rising rivers and streams, "the Great Hurricane" having destroyed one thousand miles of New England shoreline, rolled off the Atlantic Ocean and ravaged the Sturbridge area. Dams gave way, floods inundated towns and farms, streets and roads were made impassable, homes and businesses collapsed, and forests were felled. Afterwards Sturbridge went about rebuilding itself. A year later, a storm of a different kind began its move across the Atlantic Ocean, bringing with it more fury and devastation than any Category 5 storm could ever muster. At its center was Germany's Führer. Hitler and the Germans invaded Poland on September 1, 1939. England and France declared war on Germany and World War II was underway in Europe.

When the war broke out in Europe, Rudy, still employed at American Optical, was 21-years-old. He had a girlfriend he might have married, but the approach of war concerned him. The call up of American men for the draft was affecting cities and towns. Rudy had a sense that he would be called to serve his country and was hesitant to get married if he was only to leave a wife behind as he went to war.

Rudy wasted little time after Pearl Harbor was attacked in December 1941. Rather than wait to be drafted, two days after the attack he went to Springfield and enlisted in the Marines, the only military branch in which he wanted to serve. Older by a few years than many of the young men streaming to recruiting offices, he was leadership material from the start. He went to Parris Island in January 1942.

The average stature of Marines in WWII was a height of five-foot-nine-inches and a weight of 160 pounds. The majority of the Medal of Honor recipients were of average height and weight. Standing at six-foot-two and weighing 200 pounds, Rudy was one of the tall, athletically built Marines. His striking appearance, along with his maturity, leadership, and skills in getting men to perform in a military manner made his success in the Marines apparent early on in his training.

After his own basic training, he remained in Parris Island, assigned to duties as a Drill Instructor, where he rose in the ranks quickly. One photo shows him with his "Smokey the Bear" drill hat cocked to the side, eyes bright, and smile beaming. His heart was divided, intent on the preparation of men who were going to risk their lives for their country, but wanting to be among those with whom he had been trained. While proficient at training others, Platoon Sergeant Julian put in requests to join his cohort that had been sent overseas. He also visited Fiskdale every now and then. His parents, sisters and neighbors were all proud of him. His last visit was in September 1944. He seemed more serious than usual to his mother, seeming to have a sense of what was ahead for him.

Platoon Sergeant Julian had been assigned to the 1st Battalion, 27th Marines, 5th Marine Division. That December, he convinced his sister, "Julie," (Lorraine) to travel down from San Francisco to meet him for dinner in Los Angeles. Four years younger in age, she was also a Marine by then, working in the West Coast Public Relations Office.

Brother and sister met at a little restaurant, reminiscing about home, playing the piano, and singing together. Saying goodbye outside the restaurant, both trying to smile hopefully, would remain a lifelong memory for Julie. She was the last in the family to see Rudy. Soon after, he embarked to travel to the war in the Pacific and the island of Iwo Jima.

On the morning of February 19, 1945, Platoon Sergeant Julian landed on 500-yard-long Red Beach 2 and led a platoon of Marines up the first terraced incline of volcanic ash onto Iwo Jima. They fought their way for two and a half hours to reach Airfield No. 1, protecting the right flank of 5th Division, and veered north up the western side of the island on the first day.

In the days that followed, subsisting on K-rations and water, sometimes slogging through cold, drizzling rain, there was little opportunity for rest or sleep. Artillery and mortar explosions, enemy infiltrations and counter attacks, and the cries of comrades wounded and killed interrupted nights. Platoon Sergeant Julian slowly advanced with his men past Airfield No. 2, Hill 362-A, beyond the Nishi Ridge, past Kita village and Hill 362-B.

The Marines were pushing the enemy north beyond the airfields, but the intensity of the battle indicated that the end was not near. A damaged B-29 *Superfortress* bomber made the first emergency landing on the airfield secured by the Marines on March 4th. Although the relief of the fliers was worth celebrating, Marines had already died by the hundreds to ensure a safe landing site for aircrews. Encountering mazes of caves, pillboxes, minefields, and barrages of mortars and grenades, Platoon Sergeant Julian led his platoon for nineteen days into the northern most reaches of Iwo. Casualty numbers were high. Then the advance stalled as the Marine line faced Kitano Point and Hill 165.

The stories of the Marines on Iwo Jima make it clear that turning the outcome of an engagement with the enemy by initiating a one-man assault was a common action on the enemy-held island. Franklin Sigler, Doug Watson, Douglas Thomas Jacobson, and Andrew Jackson Lummus, Jr. all earned Medals of Honor for doing so. Platoon Sergeant

Julian's Medal Citation provides another example of this kind of heroic action.

On March 9, his company assaulted the Japanese fortified trench positions and encountered a withering barrage of mortars and machine-gun fire. Having moved only yards in the last day, his commander, Captain Julian, no relation to the Sturbridge family, was killed right in front of him. Having seen nineteen days of carnage, in a rage, Platoon Sergeant Julian positioned his men to provide him supporting fire, grabbed demolition charges and white phosphorus grenades and then attacked a pillbox on his own. He destroyed the emplacement, killing two crewmen, then followed five others into a trench and killed them. Returning for more explosives, he and another Marine charged ahead again and demolished two more cave emplacements. One more enemy pillbox remained pouring fire upon the stalled company.

Platoon Sergeant Julian returned again to his platoon, acquired a bazooka, and launched a one-man assault against the last enemy fortification. He destroyed the pillbox with four rockets. In the same moment that he launched the fourth rocket, he was killed by enemy gunfire from another position.

Platoon Sergeant Joseph Julian, 26-years-old, was cited for his significant contribution in advancing his company and forcing a breakthrough to Kitano Point. He was among the 5,931 Marines who died and the 17,372 who were injured in the bloodiest battle in the Corps' history. The family was notified by a telegram sent by the Defense Department.

As the Marines were securing Iwo, the Julian family would be rocked again by news from the Defense Department. Rudy's first cousin, 20-year-old Army Medic Corporal Rosaire M. Julian, first wounded in January 1944, at the Anzio, Italy landings, was killed March 26, 1945, when an enemy shell struck his boat as his unit crossed the Rhine River from France into Germany. He is counted among the WWII service personnel whose remains were not recovered for burial or return home. Rosaire's 17-year-old brother, Rolland Julian, was still in high school when the news reached home. Having learned of his cousin's bravery on Iwo Jima and now his brother's death on the Rhine, Rolland wanted to join the war effort. His parents would not sign the age waiver, having lost one son and a nephew close to them to the war. Yet, the memory of bravery has lasting effects. Rolland waited until his next birthday, and although the war had ended, he enlisted in the Marines in 1946.

Sergeant Rudy Julian's remains were first interred in the 5th Marine Division Cemetery on Iwo Jima. Following the war he was brought home and buried at Long Island National Cemetery, Farmingdale, New York, as his parents requested. Friends of Adelard and Rosalda tried to persuade them that Arlington was a fitting cemetery for their son. [3] The relationship they had enjoyed with Rudy had been close, and Virginia was too distant for the Julian family. The Long Island National Cemetery was 172 miles from Fiskdale and brought Rudy as close to home as he had been since enlisting in the Marines.

For years, Rudy's companions came by the Fiskdale apartment to visit his parents after the war. Rosalda kept a display of photos, medals, letters, and memorabilia in tribute to her son. Adelard died in 1957, and Rosalda moved to Southbridge in 1984. As families do when fathers, sons, brothers, uncles, and cousins go off to war and die in combat, the Julians remembered Rudy's bravery generation after generation. Gloria and Julie, his sisters, each had two children, twin nephews and two nieces who would hear often about Rudy, the uncle they never had a chance to meet. Gloria and Julie eventually made their homes in Florida and Texas. The bonds within the extended families remained close. Ralph Julian, a distant cousin, named one of his sons after Rudy. An inspiration to new generations, a distant second cousin, two generations removed, was also named Rudy Julian in remembrance of the family hero.

Rosalda Julian died in Southbridge in 2000, at the age of 94-years, a mother who thought of her son every day. Beyond his extended family, the question and concern of this research about the Medal recipients was whether the communities of Fiskdale and Sturbridge had remembered Rudy.

Worcester County stretches from the south to north borders of the state, encompassing 1,579 square miles. No fewer than 101 towns spread across the county. Rudy was acknowledged to be the only Southern Worcester County WWII veteran to receive the Medal of Honor. Although his record was added to the Find-A-Grave Web site on May 4, 2000, according to available public records, it appeared as if he might have been forgotten in Sturbridge. At least that is what it seemed. In reality, Rudy had been for years in the minds of many in his birthplace.

The Town of Sturbridge dedicated a stone monument topped with the Medal of Honor insignia in memory of Sgt. Rudy Julian in front of the Town Hall on Main Street on May 24, 1986. The Gold Star monument, with the image of the Iwo Jima flag raising was dedicated nearby in 1987. Platoon Sergeant Joseph "Rudy" Julian's name is inscribed on the monument along with three other local men who died in World War II. One of them is his first cousin, Corporal Rosaire Julian, who died on the Rhine River. The townspeople of Sturbridge did not want the memory of the Marine to be limited to a name on monuments, however. A Wall of Honor is dedicated to Rudy in the American Legion Champeau-Vilandre Post 109 Hall.

The 50th anniversary of the battle for Iwo Jima was celebrated across the United States in spring 1995. The tributes to those who fought on the island were special and heartfelt in Sturbridge. On Sunday, March 19, 1995, American Legion Post 109 and the Tantasqua High School, presented a benefit in Rudy's honor at the high school auditorium. Within the program, *The Great American Broadcast of 1945*, was an article providing details of Rudy's life, photos of him in uniform, a letter from one of his sisters, the Marine who had tried to enjoy a night out with him in Los Angeles before he left for Iwo Jima, a Tribute to a Veteran contributed by an 11th Grader, and business ads saluting their local hero. Post 109 also initiated the Joseph "Rudy" Julian Scholarship Trust Fund. The annual Memorial Scholarship is awarded to students at Tantasqua Regional High School, located in Fiskdale, for service to school and community.

For more than 100 years the Town of Sturbridge has held a Memorial Day parade and community wide celebration to honor its veterans. The tribute on May 28, 2007, included veterans, local organizations, American Legion Post 109, Sturbridge Historical Society Patriots, firefighters, Scout troops, Little League and Pop Warner participants, the Tantasqua Senior High School band and trumpeters, Burgess Elementary School students, and the Marine Corps Color Guard. The American Legion firing squad fired a salute at the North Cemetery.

At the Town Hall ceremonies, final tributes were made in front of the Gold Star Monument and the Honor Roll of Veterans of World War II and the Korean and Vietnam Wars. The Julians and other Gold Star families were paid a special recognition. [4]

Even local historians were unsure if hometown residents were familiar with Rudy's heroics. The *Thinking Out Loud in Sturbridge* blog was founded November 25, 2007. On Sunday, January 6, 2008, the lead story was about Joseph Julian. "The character, courage and strength shown by Joseph Julian reflect directly on the place where he was born, and raised, and onto the parents that raised him." The article asked that others at home and in the classroom remember his story.

In the next day's comments, Agent Thomas A. Chamberland, Director of Veteran's Services and American Legion Post 109 Commander, responded, wanting to clear some things up. He reported that Sturbridge had not forgotten Rudy Julian. The Gold Star monument on Main Street outside of Tom's office was dedicated in tribute to Rudy in 1987. He reminded the blog author of the 1995 Iwo Jima anniversary, the scholarship, and the Wall of Honor.

Year after year, particularly around the Memorial Day holiday, Rudy's heroism is remembered in a local *Sturbridge Villager* newspaper article. [5] Marine Medal of Honor recipient Joseph Rudolph Julian clearly will not be forgotten in Fiskdale or the Town of Sturbridge. Remembering a native son's bravery makes a difference.

CHAPTER 17
The World At War

There's trouble in the wind, my boys, there's trouble in the
wind, Oh it's "Please to walk in front, sir," when there's trouble
in the wind. [1]

Rudyard Kipling (1865 – 1936)

When the Second World War began for America in 1941, the Marines
were responsible for holding on to islands that the Japanese coveted in
the Pacific. Fewer than two years later, the Marines were tasked with
retaking a chain of Japanese-held islands starting in the Solomons east
of New Guinea and leading all the way up to mainland Japan. The
fighting was always fierce because the Japanese were entrenched and
bunkered in and did not intend to give up the islands to the Marines
landing on the beaches. The fighting was also typically done at close
quarters, using small arms, rifles, machine guns, flamethrowers, hand
grenades, bazookas, satchel charges, bayonets, and hand-to-hand combat. Casualties in large numbers were an expected occurrence wherever
Marines landed on beaches in World War II.

The hardships and traumas of the island battles included seeing
wounded comrades struggle in the throes of agony, or lie incapacitated

and exposed to further enemy fire, or overcome by pain and calling out for help or rescue. It was in the presence of such suffering, and sometimes because of it, that eighty-two Medals of Honor were awarded to Marines during WWII. The majority of these awards (76) were earned in clusters during well-known operations: Guadalcanal and Bougainville in the Solomon Islands, the low-lying, coral atoll of Tarawa in the Gilbert Islands, Namur of the Kwajalein Atoll, Guam, Tinian, and Saipan in the Marianas, Peleliu in the Palau group, Iwo Jima in the Izu Shoto Islands, and Okinawa Shima in the Ryukyu Islands. Six individual Marines earned this distinction in somewhat isolated engagements like Engebi Island, off the Eniwetok Atoll of the Marshall Islands and Makin Atoll in the Gilbert (now Tungaru) Islands.

All 82 Medal recipients went "above and beyond" what was asked of or required of them. Many did so by acting in defense of fellow combatants, even to the risk of one's self. Among these were twenty-eight Marines (34% WWII Marine Medal of Honor awards) who made decisions about grenades and the safety of comrades. The toll for those willing to sacrifice themselves on a grenade included two actions on Bougainville, three in the Marshall Islands Atolls of Roi, Namur, and Eniwetok, two on Saipan, two on Tinian, six on Peleliu, eight on Iwo Jima, and five on Okinawa. In fact, of the eleven Marines who distinguished themselves and earned Medals of Honor for their valor on Okinawa, the first five did so by hurling themselves upon grenades.

Wesley P. Phelps was one of the six on Peleliu Island who made a decision about an enemy grenade that landed in his foxhole.

Another young man from Kentucky

The northwestern part of Kentucky is a rolling region rich in bluegrass, farmland for tobacco and other crops, horse farms, and coal reserves. Neafus, too small to be located on maps or to have its own schools, is a town sitting at the intersection of Butler, Grayson, and Ohio Counties on Route 736.

When Athel Phelps was 22-years-old, he married 16-year-old Lida Jones on March 22, 1903. They owned a 70-acre farm near Rosine. The couple soon began having children, six altogether, and mostly boys. Their last child was Wesley P. Phelps, born in Neafus on June 12, 1923. Three months earlier, Luther Skaggs, Jr. had been born in Henderson, about sixty-five miles northwest.

Wesley was born three years after his sister, Ada Bell. They happened to celebrate their respective birthdays one day apart. In 2003, Ada Bell was the last of the children to die, having been twice married, given birth to four children, and lived to be 83-years-old.

Wesley went to the Ohio County schools and helped out on the family farm. He made a hobby of making and tinkering with one-tube radio sets in his free time. He walked about three miles east of the farm to attend Horse Branch High School. When Wes graduated in 1942, his father was nearing his mid-sixties. The last of the children on the farm and his parents' sole support, Wes was motivated to further his early hobby by building a career in the growing specialty of radio repairs.

Seeking to excel is evident among Medal of Honor recipients.

Although it might seem inconsequential, Wesley's interest in radio sets and electricity was one aspect of his bravery and demonstrated a trait that was characteristic of the Medal recipients. When he turned his attention to an interest of his, an impulse to achieve excellence was triggered.

Whatever their interests might be, the recipients wanted to be the best at it they could be. Family and friends remembered many of them as wanting "to be the best at whatever he did." Among those who were interested in academics, "A" grades, finishing at the top of the class, and listings on academic honor rolls was frequent. At least seven of the men earned college scholarships for academic or athletic performance in high school. Among those who worked prior to entering the Marines, many were remembered as the "hardest worker" or "best employee" on the job.

Of the recipients who were athletic, many were not satisfied to just be on a team. They also competed in sports that required individual and single effort, like boxing, wrestling, swimming, tennis, golf, and marksmanship. Sixteen of the recipients were described as a star or captain of an athletic team, winning state titles, winning a championship, being selected or nominated as an All-Conference, All-State, or All-American athlete, or being entered into a Hall of Fame for collegiate performance. Five participated in professional or semiprofessional sports before earning recognition in combat.

Once in the Marines, the recipients tended early to distinguish themselves in training, drills, military skills, and physical performance. Most earned advances and promotions expeditiously. They were drawn to specialties that challenged them. If assigned to mundane, simple, or inconsequential duties they sought reassignment. Staying overly long in unchallenging circumstances could elicit grumbling and forthright complaining.

Wes Phelps might have been only five-foot-one-inches tall, but he was smart and industrious. Not content to stay on the farm after graduating from high school, he went up the road to Owensboro on the Ohio River to study basic electricity. Four months later he went east into the heart of Kentucky. He studied radio repair at a Lexington trade school for three months. Not quite satisfied with his education and expertise, Wes continued on to the Johnson Pre-Frequency Modulation School to learn about field radio and aircraft radio receiver repair. Without realizing it, Wes had also prepared himself for a military specialty. Less than a year after finishing high school and before he could put his advanced technical education to civilian use, the Marines drafted him on April 9, 1943.

Private Phelps completed boot camp in San Diego and was assigned duties in the Marine's Signal Battalion to implement his expertise in radios. After a month of that, he was provided two more months of education in the special weapons course. When he was finished with his training in August, Private Phelps was an expert in radios and in the use of the Browning 30-caliber Heavy Machine Gun.

October came and Private Phelps embarked aboard ship, headed for battle. He joined the 3d Battalion, 7th Marines in December. A few days later, the day after Christmas 1943, he departed with Company M for the landing on Cape Gloucester, New Britain, a place far different than Kentucky bluegrass country and tobacco farms. It was called

"The Green Inferno" with good reason. Private Phelps waded through three feet of rough surf after leaving an LST and made his way to the beachhead on the inland flank near the enemy airfields and the Japanese fortress of Rabaul, well to the east. He was going to be on Cape Gloucester for the next four months.

Ahead of Private Phelps were enemy forces determined to fight to the death, a maze of trenches and bunkers, Hell's Point, Suicide Creek, Target Hill, a monsoon deluge that went on for days, biting winds, jungle rot and malaria, impassible vegetation, tall, cutting Kunai grass, insect-infested swamps, overgrown trails, muddy inclines, gorged streams and drenched jungles.

When the 1st Division left Cape Gloucester in April 1944, Private Phelps had been a Marine for one year, a third of which had been spent surviving in combat. He went with the Division for more amphibious landing practice in the Russell Islands and a promotion to private first class.

Private First Class Phelps was reassigned to Company K, 3d Battalion, 7th Marines as a light machine gunner. There would never be free time again for him to build one-tube radio sets. The bloody landing at Peleliu Island was five months away.

His last twenty days

The Japanese were skilled tacticians, anticipating where Americans would attempt to land forces on the islands. They prepared defensive fortifications, using the cover and concealment of jungle habitat to their best advantage. And when they established fields of fire with machine guns, rifles, and mortars, they ensured the impact would be scathing to any Marines who tried to advance onto the island toward them.

Like Guam, the Atolls, and the Solomons before, and as Iwo Jima and Okinawa would be later, coral-decked Peleliu Island was a place where Marines sacrificed their blood and lives in large numbers. The small, six-by-two mile island sits in the Palau archipelago abreast the Philippine Sea. Low-lying coral foundation and impregnable vegetation, hiding numerous lakes and lagoons, render most of the archipelago uninhabitable. Humans could be found on only eight of the

Terence W. Barrett PhD

200 Palau Islands. Over 10,000 well-equipped Japanese infantrymen waited for the Marines on Peleliu.

The Japanese had built an airfield on the flat southern side of the island and a phosphate refinery on Peleliu's northern tip. The Marines' 1st Division was given the mission to seize the airfield, cut the island in two, and then clear it of enemy forces both north and south. The Marines had been briefed that a gentle, rounded hill in the center of the island was the only terrain feature in the six miles separating the airfield and phosphate plant. By the time the Marines secured shadeless Peleliu, with its dozens of coral ridgelines, and the last enemy resistance ceased on the night of November 24-25, eight Marines had earned Medals of Honor in the first twenty days of battle. Six of these men hurled themselves onto grenades to protect comrades from injury and death.

On Friday morning, September 15, 1944, five battalions of Marines in amphibious tractors (LVTs) formed into lines stretching along a half-mile of sea and turned toward the beaches on the western side of Peleliu. Private First Class Phelps, standing shoulder to shoulder with other Marines, bounded toward the coral reef ringing Peleliu Island. As he peered over the gunwale of the LVT, he could barely see through the smoke, dirt, and water spouts along the beaches ahead, ample evidence of the explosive pounding by naval gunfire and aerial bombing prepping the landing site. To his right was the flat rise of the southern portion of Peleliu, the 3d Battalion, 7th Marines' objective on the right flank of the landing force.

To Private First Class Phelps' left was an unexpected and impressive sight. The rounded hill the Marines had been briefed about was actually a range of connected mountains rising from about 50 feet just to the north of where the airfield was located into one large mountain mass reaching to an elevation of 300 feet. That massif was named "Momoji" on Japanese tactical maps. The Americans named it the Umurbrogol Massif. The Marines who fought for three weeks in the encirclement and siege of Umurbrogol would refer to its limestone and coral ridges as *The Pocket*.

250

Private First Class Phelps focused his attention directly ahead. The LVT crossed the coral reef and raced across a 150-yard wide lagoon toward Orange Beach 2, just 4,000 yards south of Umurbrogol. He jumped from the amphibious tractor at 8:32 AM and battled his way ashore on the right flank. The Japanese poured fire into the Marines from their fortified positions, established in caves and caverns within the coral ridgelines. King Company fought inland, sustaining numerous casualties. The slow advance required the assault of one cave, dugout, and fortified shelter after another. The initial 100-yard advance onto the island took the first hour on shore. By dusk on D-Day, Marines held the left flank of the beachhead at *The Point*, the southern half of the airfield, and about one quarter of Peleliu's southern tip on the right flank.

Private First Class Phelps got what sleep he could, finding little protection in the rocky coral terrain. The Japanese used the protection of the dark, moonless night to leave their concealed positions and counterattack. The next morning King Company with the 7th Marines plunged further into the jungle scrub and tangles to the south. Daylight combat and nighttime counterattacks would be the rhythm of Private First Class Phelps' life for the next nineteen days.

The daytime temperatures on Peleliu reached from 105 to 115 degrees. The Marine assault forces emptied their canteens, hoping for refills. Supply officers tried to get halizone tablets to the front line so water taken from the island's stagnant pools could be purified. The Navy Corpsmen did what they could to ensure the Marines had salt tablets to compensate for heavy perspiration. Already slight of stature, Private First Class Phelps could not sustain effort if he lost much more body weight. Heat prostration casualties began to match the numbers of battle injuries in the battalions. The infrequent rains did not bring relief, but only turned the warm air muggy and the ground muddy.

By 3:30 PM, September 18, the third day after the landing, the 7th Marines had captured the lower third of Peleliu, having destroyed an elite enemy infantry battalion in fortified defensive positions. The 1st and 5th Marine Regiments had crossed the island, secured the airfield, and moved their lines forward to the southern rise of the Umurbrogol Pocket.

What had appeared in the aerial reconnaissance photos as a "gentle, rounded hill in the center of the island" was a piece of terrain about a mile long and four football fields wide. Far from "gentle," a better descriptive word would have been "treacherous." The Umurbrogol Massif was a jumble of steep peaks and sheer cliffs, sharp coral ridges, box canyons, narrow valleys, knobs, hollows, sinkholes, and heavy jungle cover scrub grass. The Japanese held the high ground upon the massif and used it to their advantage. Within the Pocket, the defenders had filled caves, tunnels, and underground installations with artillery, weapons caches, munitions, and food and medical supplies. One cave and tunnel complex sheltered more than 1000 enemy troops. Enemy fire from the high ground was always heavy and well directed. For the Marines assaulting from below, the coral terrain was rocky and provided little cover, but for the green jungle vegetation.

For as small and unimposing as the island might have seemed during the planning stages, when the invasion operation was over, commanders' reports of the battle included such place names as "the Point," "Bloody Nose," the "Coral Badlands," "Radar Hill," "Wildcat Bowl," "the China Wall," "Horseshoe Valley," "Death Valley," "the Five Sisters," "the Five Brothers," Hill 120 (actually a ridge), Garekoru, Ngardololok, Negesebus, Kongauru, "Hill Row," Amiangal Ridge, Kamilialul Ridge, Higashiyama, and The Pocket.

When the 7th Marines completed the "mopping up" in the southern sector of the island, the two battalions were ordered to turn north to engage in the encirclement of the Pocket. King Company and the 3d Battalion moved inside the West Road to attack coastal Umurbrogol from the south. Although the Pocket was not necessarily impregnable, the terrain, as much as the enemy defenses, hindered progress up the massif. The forward lines encountered intense defensive fire day after brutal day. Marine flame-throwing squads and mortar teams silenced individual caves, concrete pillboxes, and blockhouses as they were discovered.

Private First Class Phelps slugged his way along the left flank of Peleliu as King Company fought its way north on the West Road into the northern sector of the island. Providing a communication line around the Pocket, 3d Battalion skirted the northern edge of the massif and came back south along the East Road to secure Boyd, Pope's, and Walt Ridges on Umurbrogos' east side. [2] The encirclement of the Pocket was complete, but the battle for the massif was far from over.

Besides the advantage of higher ground, the Japanese had the cover of concealed emplacements and clear fields of fire. Artillery and mortar fire from enemy positions on Umurbrogos continued. From caves above the battalion and the King Company line, the enemy directed blazing fire upon the Marines and prevented further movement into the Pocket. The advance halted for days as the two forces resorted to hand grenade attacks in an effort to oust each other from the coral hillsides. The Marines would move ahead yards, seeking protective cover in the broken ground during daylong firefights and savage exchanges of hand grenades. At night the companies withdrew to better-protected dugouts and depressions in the coral ridges as the grenade exchanges continued. Marine casualties were mounting.

Now in the Third Operational Phase of the Peleliu campaign, the Marines had secured their key objectives and most of the island. The 7th Marines, having taken so many casualties, would finally be relieved on Thursday, October 5.

On October 3, four battalions of Marines attacked the eastern ridges. The next day, D-Day-plus 19, King Company advanced along Boyd Ridge toward Hill 120. Meeting fierce resistance, unable to hold the hill, the Marines, at times huddling together to fight off grenade barrages, withdrew and took up defensive positions. That night, Company K dug into a line across one slope of a coral ridge. The Japanese were within hand grenade range on the opposite slope, and the Marines could expect a night of aggressive counterattacks on their line. The men in forward positions, especially those in listening and observation posts, were the first defense against enemy infiltration.

Private First Class Phelps had been attacking enemy fortifications on the coral ridges of Umurbrogos for two weeks. He was in a forward defensive machine-gun position on the ridge crest on the night of October 4. Having been in this situation more than once, he and Private First Class Richard Shipley, his companion in the foxhole, had prepared themselves. The attack was ferocious when the aggressors came. The two Marines fought off the onslaught. In the fury of the exchange, a grenade landed in their foxhole.

Private First Class Phelps saw it first.

"Look out, Shipley!"

As he shouted the warning, he rolled on top of the grenade. The explosion shattered his body and killed him instantly, but his immediate reaction had saved the life of his companion. Private First Class Richard Shipley had hardly a scratch from the shrapnel.

Private First Class Wesley Phelps, 21-years-old, was among the 1,121 killed, 5,142 wounded, and 73 missing Marines of the 1st Division on Peleliu Island. He was initially buried in the United States Armed Forces Cemetery on Peleliu. He was later brought home and re-interred in Rosine Cemetery, Rosine, Kentucky. Both his parents are buried there, having outlived their son. His brother Estill, sister-in-law Gracie, and his sister Ada Bell Sikes also have gravestones nearby.

Rosine Cemetery is a small country site, where fewer than 300 locals are buried. Stepping into the cemetery, Wesley's gravesite is easy to find, not because the cemetery is small, but because a tall monument stands over his grave. Above his name, the Eagle, Globe, and Anchor symbol of the USMC is etched into the monument's upper portion. Above the Medal of Honor stars etched along the crest, stands a bronze eagle with outstretched wings.

Information about how Wesley is remembered today is limited. His biography on Wikipedia and other Web sites does not include his photograph. His official USMC photo can be viewed at the United States Marine Corps History Division, *Who's Who in Marine Corps History* Web site. Wesley's name is included on Kentucky's Medal of Honor Memorial erected in Louisville, Kentucky, on Monday, November 12, 2001, along with Luther Skaggs, Jr., Richard E. Bush, and fifty-three other Kentuckians. At that time, the Memorial was the only one "in Kentucky honoring the Commonwealth's Medal of Honor recipients, and the only state memorial of its kind in the U.S." [3]

Beyond the impressive monument in Rosine Cemetery, whether a tribute has been dedicated to Wesley in Neafus or Rosine or Horse Branch High School is unknown. His family does remember him. Wesley's great nephew, Justin, left a *Rest in Peace* note on the Find A Grave Web site on November 5, 2010. [4]

CHAPTER 18
The Last Island 1945

"I can see now why mothers cry. Their sons
go off to war like lambs to slaughter." [1]

Sandy Walmsley
U.S. Navy Hospital Corpsman Second Class
First Marine Division
Out of Da Nang, South Vietnam

The Marine's Pacific Island Campaign had reached the last island by April 1945, only ten days after Iwo Jima was declared secured. If the war were not brought to a close, the next beach landing would be 360 miles north on Mainland Japan, a most unwelcome prospect. Before the war ended in the Pacific, eighty-two desperate days of island combat remained for the Japanese as they faced another Marine assault.

More than 80,000 Marines participated in the battle for Okinawa. They landed in waves north of the Bishi River on Easter Sunday, April 1, 1945. They fought inland across the island, then north in the conquest of the upper island. Within eleven days, the Marines had surrounded the enemy stronghold on Mount Yae Take on upper Motobu Peninsula.

After a month of fighting, having taken Yae Take in uphill assaults from one lower ridge to the next higher one, the Marines redeployed south to press the defenders along the western coastal flank in the southern sectors. There the enemy was putting up a fitful defense at the Shuri defensive perimeter, trying to hold on to the little bit of island left to them. The Japanese were also planning offensive actions in the hope of repulsing the American advance.

Two Medal of Honor Marines on the list of the forgotten thirty-four were moving south from Yae Take toward Shuri. The details of Corporal John P. Fardy's life were sketchy at first and little could be discovered about his bravery. More than was initially known about Private Dale Hansen was eventually learned through further investigation. During the first five years of researching their backgrounds, when more had been uncovered about Private Hansen than about Corporal Fardy, this chapter reflected the difference in remembering a man's bravery or allowing his life to be forgotten. That difference no longer applies to their two stories.

A First Generation American

The surname Fardy, pronounced FAR-day, is derived from the Irish-Gaelic name, O'Fearadaigh. The original ancestors populated County Wexford, on the east coast of Ireland where the River Slaney empties into the Irish Sea. ² The Fardys were farmers and ranchers and men of the sea, sailing, working in harbors, and laboring on docks. When they began immigrating to America, a good number of the families settled along the western shores of Lake Michigan. Early arriving Fardys can be traced to Sheboygan, Milwaukee, Waukesha, and Kenosha, Wisconsin and down to Chicago, Illinois. Some Fardys rose to positions of prominence, appearing often in newspapers. For example, James Francis Fardy was born in Illinois in 1880, after his parents had immigrated from Ireland. James went to law school and started out as a defense attorney in Chicago in the early 1920s. When four men were arrested for the May 12, 1921 murders in a small town, James assisted their defense attorney, the renowned Clarence Darrow. James, a Democrat, was eventually elected to a Chief Justice position in Chicago's Superior Criminal Court.

John Peter Fardy was born in Chicago. Researching his background and lineage proved to be complicated by the fact that other Fardy families were in Chicago at the same time with similar first names. Beyond his immediate family, no evidence was discovered to indicate if John had any relatives, uncles or aunts or cousins, among all the Fardys in the area, or living in or around his neighborhood. Having come from Ireland before John was born, both his parents might have been the first from their own families to come to America.

Martin Joseph Fardy was born in County Wexford, Ireland, on January 26, 1887. [3] Mary Kilkerman was born two years later in the same small town. [4] Mary immigrated to America in 1914, at age 25. Martin followed a few years later, just as the United States was entering World War I, and found work on Chicago's south side. He was employed as a "fireman" at Armour & Company, Union Stock Yards, working around steam boilers in the power plant in the years when Chicago was still viewed as the top meat-manufacturing city in the world. Whether they had already been betrothed while living in Ireland, Martin and Mary married at some point, lived on South Lowe Avenue, and began their family. Their first child was Mary Therese, born February 2, 1918. [5]

At the time of the 1920 U.S. Census, Mary's younger sister, Catherine Kilkerman, age 26 and also born in Ireland, was living with them. Catherine was working as a telephone operator at that time. What became of her is unknown, as no other Kilkerman information could be found in the records. The closest Kilkerman families appear to have resided in Bakersville and Coshocton, Ohio.

When Mary was pregnant with their second child, the Fardys needed more living space. They moved to an apartment at 4458 Emerald Avenue, closer to Martin's work. Their second daughter, Anne, was born on May 4, 1921. John was born the following year on August 15, 1922. As the three children grew up they would hear a bit of the Irish brogue dialect when their parents disciplined them.

In the years before the Depression, when gangland battles added to the noise and notoriety of the windy city, life seemed to be prospering for the Fardys. Martin had worked his way up to a "fire inspector" position for the meat packer. In the summer of 1926, before Mary Therese started off to third grade, Mary took the children on a trip, crossing the Atlantic Ocean on a ship to Ireland. [6] Due to the economic collapse just years ahead, this is likely the only time the children were able to see the emerald green hills and their grandparents and extended family. According to the *Republic's* ship manifest, they departed from Cobh, on Ireland's southeast coast, leaving Cork Harbour on August 25, 1926 and arriving back in New York on September 4. It is possible that John celebrated his fourth birthday in County Wexford, the land of his ancestors. Whether he remembered his first ocean crossings aboard a ship seventeen years later when he sailed the Pacific with the Marines would be conjecture.

Martin Fardy moved his Irish Catholic family one more time, away from his work at the Armour & Company, Union Stock Yards, 41st Street and Racine Avenue. Mary found an attractive six-family brownstone apartment building she liked in a nice Irish neighborhood, close to church and schools. For the remainder of their school years, the three Fardy children lived at 8144 South Calumet Avenue, in the Saint Clotilde Parish, four miles west of Rainbow Beach Park on Lake Michigan. Mary stayed at home, helping her children to get through school.

Fardy family events appeared in local newspapers long before John earned a Medal of Honor on a Pacific island.

Mary Fardy, social and outgoing, believed in service and was active in church activities, especially when the three children were all in their teens. She was hostess at their home for a semi-monthly, Friday evening meeting that entertained twelve Lambda Sigma Tau sorority sisters on October 2, 1936. [7] The next month she was on a party committee for the Third Order of Saint Francis. [8] In early 1937, she was a committee co-chair on the St. Joseph auxiliary of the Mayslake Preparatory Seminary, planning a party to help raise funds for the college library. [9] The next year, Mary was a member of the Sophomore Mothers of the Mercy High School auxiliary and served on another party committee. [10] A few months before John and Anne graduated from high school, she conducted a Sunday evening benefit card and bunco party at Saint Paul Hall, at Clark and Polk Streets, to help fund a project to build a Catholic chapel in China. [11]

Martin took his Irish Catholic heritage seriously. He was a member of an Irish trade union, as were his coworkers and his friends, some of who were asbestos workers, insulating pipes and boilers around Chicago. In late summer 1937, when John was nearly 15-years-old, Martin attended a Friday through Monday retreat at the Hillsdale Saint Francis Retreat House with 300 members of Asbestos Worker Union Chicago Local 17. A photo of him kneeling in front of a Station of the Cross on the friary estate, rosary beads in his hands, was featured in *Life* Magazine. [12] Based on John's senior high school photograph taken two years later, it appears that father and son resembled each other. [13] Martin clearly valued work, service, and faith, and providing his children a good Catholic upbringing and education was important to him.

Beginning in fall 1932, John's eldest sister, Mary Therese, walked one block from home to the all-girls Mercy High School where the Sisters of Mercy Community were the teachers. She graduated with the Class of 1936 (Mercian Yearbook).

Anne, a popular and active girl, followed her sister to Mercy High School, starting in 1936. According to her senior yearbook, she was on the Hi Ray staff, enjoyed Dramatic Art, was a member of the Sewing and Library Clubs, and had been Medical Missions President, an organization whose members sewed vestments and altar linens for the foreign mission churches. [14] Anne had definitely become skilled at a sewing machine and enjoyed making her own clothes. One of her creations was described in the local newspaper: "Her gown was venetian-embroidered net over eggshell taffeta." [15] That gown earned her the featured role in the annual Mercy High School fashion show, the Style Promenade, her senior year. A classmate wrote about Anne: "So fresh and cool as a secluded pine woods...possesses quiet ability...breaks all records for making life agreeable...displays decided interest in Missions." As a patron of the high school, Mrs. Mary Fardy's photograph was also in the yearbook. Anne graduated with the Class of 1940 after she had just turned 19-years-old.

John, an "ordinary" and "a nice quiet kid," began attending the Saint Clotilde Grammar School, three blocks south of the apartment building, in September 1928. Based on his birth date, he would have been younger than most of his classmates. At the time, students registering for Catholic grade school had to have turned six-years-old by September 1. John had just made that cutoff date by sixteen days, and his mother did not want to wait another year to start him in school. His classmates could have had birthdates going back to September 2, 1921. At some point in their education, and for a reason now long forgotten, John and his older sister, Anne, ended up in the same grade.

John continued his Catholic education at the all-boys Leo High School on West 79th Street, a mile west of Calumet Avenue. His teachers were the Christian Brothers of Ireland. Like John, the majority of his fellow students probably had parents or grandparents whose manner of speech resounded with an Irish lilt. Unlike John, who was a light-haired, blue-eyed, young man, most of his classmates had dark or red hair.

In 1936, John stepped into a high school that was always renowned in Chicago for its academic and athletic prowess. [16] Leo High School also had a reputation for being somewhat "straight-laced and rigorous" regarding the discipline of its students. The Christian Brothers believed that "obedience to superiors in every way, shape and manner is essential for the conducting of any organization" and that obedience had to be learned early in life. Even though his days in the Leo halls were not going to be like the San Diego Recruit Depot for John, the expected code of conduct at the high school provided some preparation for what was ahead in his life. However often he thought of the school's motto, *Facta Non Verba,* his actions would one day emulate the phrase; Latin, meaning *Deeds not Words.*

Besides book learning and academic lessons, Leo promoted extracurricular activities for the students. The idea was to provide additional opportunities to improve a boy's mind and further develop his body. The publication of an impressive monthly school newspaper, *The Oriole,* was one example of an extracurricular that reflected the Leo experience. Besides current front-page news, points of interest and concern, Honor

Roll lists, editorials, and messages from the faculty, the newspaper included a sports page and routine columns for Class Notes, Seen and Heard, Around the Corridors, CISCA (Chicago Inter-Student Catholic Action), Science Club, Debate, Dramatics, the Mothers and Fathers Clubs, Band, Glee Club, Hobbies, and class officer elections.

The October 1936 issue would have been the first to go to print when John was a freshman. The last issue while he was enrolled at Leo was March 1940. A review of the 1938-40 issues found only three mentions of him in his last two years of high school. He was never listed among the Honor Roll students nor was he ever elected to be a class officer. John did not play on any athletic teams. He was not in the Glee Club, Dramatic Club, or any other club. His photograph was not on any page of *The Oriole*. His only extracurricular activity listed in the 1940 senior yearbook, *The Lion,* was Public Speaking. Looking at the activities of the 184 members of his class, most of whom had numerous extracurriculars under their names, John was among the thirty-five students who had participated in two or less activities during their years at Leo; ten with two, fifteen with one, and ten with no extra activities. [17]

J. Fardy is pictured in the Leo yearbooks four times. He stood at the end of a top row among classmates in his freshman and sophomore pictures. He was standing beside a boy by the name of J. Auman when the freshman photo was taken for the 1937 *Lion* yearbook. John was in the middle of the top row in his junior year picture. He appears to have been among the taller boys in his class and by his junior year appears to have been broad in the shoulders. [18]

John's name appeared in print in *The Oriole* three times while he was a student. The first time was in the December 1939 issue when he was midway through his senior year. Thomas Drury, a kid from the Saint Margaret parish and the senior class editor, counted John among his good friends. According to Tom in his *That's What I Want For Christmas* column, J. Fardy thought "maybe a new name would be nice." Apparently, some at Leo did not pronounce John's surname in its proper Gaelic. In the January 1940 issue, the second time his name was in print, John was listed on Page One as one of five soon-to-be-graduates from Saint Clotilde. His name also was partially mentioned on Page Two of the same issue. Thomas Drury tendered an apology to

John F. for his comment in the last issue. That was the extent of the attention garnered by John as a Leo *Lion.*

At the time, his was the largest graduating class in the school's history. Eighty classmates went on to college, nine with scholarships to prestigious universities. John was not an academic standout at Leo, carrying a C+ academic average in his four years at the high school. When he graduated with the 184-member Class of 1940, John was ranked 138, at the lower 25th percentile. [19]

The Class of '40 held their senior prom on Friday night, June 7, at the swanky Drake Hotel Grand Ballroom on Lake Shore Drive, featuring the Charlie Straight orchestra, a favorite among swing dancers. There is no one to remember if John had a date for the prom, liked to dance, or even if he had a girlfriend.

John graduated from Leo two months shy of his eighteenth birthday. On October 16, 1940, President Franklin D. Roosevelt signed into law the first peacetime selective service draft in U.S. history. All men between 21- to 31-years residing in the Unites States were to report to their local draft board to pick up a draft registration card. John was three years away from having to register for possible selection into military service.

Life went on for the Fardys in expected ways once John was out of high school. The unexpected was still eighteen months in the future. Remaining in Chicago and not entirely sure what he wanted to do with his life, John was willing to try things. In order to improve his job prospects, he decided to further his education. He went over to Fox Secretarial College on West 93rd Street for a year to learn typing, then up to the Illinois Institute of Technology (Armour) on East 33rd Street the next year to study mechanical engineering.

John's sisters, still living at home, continued their educations as well, attending Chicago Teachers College. Their photographs can be viewed in the archived yearbooks at the Chicago State University Library. They are both in the 1941 *Emblem* yearbook, Pages 36, 38, when they both still had much to smile about. Mary's engagement to Harold John Wilkening, a young man who lived in the apartments at 7945 Langley Avenue, nine blocks away from the Fardy apartment building, was announced in early September 1941. [20] No date had been set for

John to become a brother-in-law, but the attack on Pearl Harbor three months later and WWII changed the planned Fardy-Wilkening union.

Four months after the engagement had been announced Harold, six-foot-tall and 175 pounds, one month younger than Mary, enlisted in the Army Air Corps on January 15, 1942. His voluntary enlistment was for "the duration of the War, or other emergency, plus six months, subject to the discretion of the President or otherwise according to law." Harold was single when he enlisted and went to war. He did not return to Mary, but remained in the service afterwards and rose to the rank of first sergeant. He died in Tennessee on April 17, 2004, at age 86. [21]

Anne's photo appears on Pages 48, 89 of the 1942 *Emblem* yearbook, indicating that she participated in the Social Science Major and Geography Clubs. Mary is pictured again among the graduating seniors in the 1943 yearbook on Page 32. When she graduated, John was at the San Diego Marine Recruit Depot. Anne was in the June 1944 graduating class, pictured on Page 16 of that year's *Victory Emblem*. She had been in her sophomore year when the Japanese attacked Pearl Harbor. As written in her senior yearbook (pp 17-18), many changes followed for her when the war began. "There were adjustments to be made, more mental than physical...Life took on a deeper significance...there were much deeper undercurrents." When Anne graduated, her younger brother was on a South Pacific Island called Pavuvu, resting between amphibious landings.

According to the Cook County Marriage Index, Mary was single until after the war. On January 3, 1947, she married Joseph T. Martin, an Army veteran and later a Chicago policeman. [22] Anne also married a man devoted to service—John J. Thometz, a 1945 graduate of Loyola University, who had a long career as a family doctor. John, the son of a west side dentist, had been awarded a scholarship to the prestigious university in 1939, having ranked the highest "among the public school entrants in the examinations." [23] Mary and Anne's brother was not in Chicago to attend their weddings.

America's military had been dangerously undermanned as the country looked to its possible entrance into the war on behalf of its allies. A second draft registration was ordered on July 1, 1941, for all men who had reached 21-years since October 1940. John had a little more than two years to complete his mechanical engineering degree and find his career before becoming eligible to be drafted into the armed services.

Three more registrations were ordered in 1942 after the attack at Pearl Harbor. All men 20-21-years and 35-44-years of age were ordered to report to their draft boards on February 16, 1942. John was six months away from his twentieth birthday. On April 27, 1942, men between 45-64-years of age, but not liable for military service, were ordered to pick up their draft registration cards. Then on, June 30, 1942, the registration age was lowered to all men 18- to 20-years-old. When sixteen Class of 1942 Leo graduates, sophomores when John was a senior, later arrived for their September 1942 engineering classes at Armour, he was no longer enrolled at the Institute.

Martin Fardy, John's father, walked into the local Draft Board office in 1942 and registered. [24] That he was 55-years-old at the time was likely a factor in his not receiving a draft notice. John decided to leave school and took a position as a draftsman at the Cornell Forge Company on Chicago's west side, south of the Midway Airport. He had also registered for the draft and was now at the right age to expect his draft notice at any time.

The Marines made their assault on the beaches of Guadalcanal in the Solomon Islands in August 1942. For the next six months, the battles on the island would be the center of the war news. Before November the Marines had defeated the Japanese in three major battles, the Navy had engaged in five intense battles off the island, and Marine aviators were earning the title of *Ace* in dogfights over Guadalcanal. John certainly was aware of the struggle in the Pacific, and perhaps had more personal feelings about it. Young men who had attended Leo with him were Marines fighting along jungle trails.

The impact of the war on the community and families began slowly to find its way into the pages of Leo High School's newspaper. In the February 1942 issue, two months into the war, *The Oriole* reported that the Latin and English teacher had been "called to the colors to fight for our country." The paper also informed "the Leoites" that the Department of Defense had requested the nation's high schools to begin making model airplanes for its various war training needs. Not much more notice was given to the war until the start of the next school year and the October 1942 issue. That front page highlighted two alumni who were among the many Leo graduates who were by then doing their part in the Armed Services. One was from the Class of 1930 and the other more recent graduate was from the Class of 1941. Both had younger brothers in the high school.

Larry Spillan, Class of 1941, from Saint Leo Parish, was a year behind John at the high school. Wearing number 58 on his black and orange jersey, he had been an outstanding left end on Leo's undefeated 1940 Catholic Champs football team, making "beautiful tackles," pulling down quarterbacks, and blocking kicks. He had also been a four-year class officer and was considered to be "[a]mong the most distinguished graduates in the armed services." Private Spillan had participated in what would become the famous August 17, 1942 raid by the "Submarine Raiders at Makin Atoll," Carlson's 2d Marine Raider Battalion. *The Oriole* would receive more news about Larry in December—the news would come from the Navy Department.

The November issue informed the students that those who turned 18-years-old would have to register for the Draft and would have the opportunity to enlist in the service branch of their choice or wait to be drafted.

On December 18, 1942, a commemorative plaque was dedicated to the 466 Leo graduates in the war, three of whom had died. The plaque was hung on the wall of the auditorium vestibule.

The January 1943 *Oriole* reported in a twelve-line, front-page column that Laurence Patrick Spillan, Jr. and Joseph Auman, both Marines from Saint Leo Parish, had made the "Supreme Sacrifice." Both had been in the early battles on Makin Atoll and Guadalcanal Island and had died on Guadalcanal. Both had brothers still at Leo. The details of their deaths were unknown. A longer column reported that seven seniors from the Class of 1943 had already enlisted or been drafted.

The Raider Battalions had been formed in February 1942. The Marines who volunteered to join the "elite" Raiders and were accepted by the commanders had to be physically strong, able to make long, fast marches, and be endurance swimmers. Joe Auman had been a Marine for nineteen months when the Raiders were created. Larry Spillan had been out of Leo for only eight months and not long out of the San Diego Recruit Depot. It is probable that Joe and Larry had remained in contact after Joe enlisted, and that once Larry had enlisted, the two friends decided to volunteer together for the Raiders.

Private Spillan had been a member of the Leo High School Glee Club. It is easy to imagine him and Private Auman proudly singing the Marine Corps Hymn together after a tough day of training: "...First to fight for right and freedom..." Or, maybe, singing familiar refrains of the Leo Fight Song: "Then all their might against the foe is hurled. Tis' then the foe shall feel the Lion's might." Whatever the case might be, they both were going to put those words into action as the Marines took the fight to the Japanese in the Pacific. These were the kind of young men who had considered John Fardy a friend.

Private Spillan, 20-years-old for six weeks, had landed during a downpour at Aola Bay on the northeast coast of Guadalcanal with Company C, 2d Marine Raider Battalion on November 4, 1942. [25] He participated in what would be called "Carlson's Long Patrol," a northwest march behind enemy lines along a jungle trail, across seven rivers, headed toward Lunga Point and Henderson Field. The Marine column hiked nearly 150 miles in twenty-nine days.

By November 11, Armistice Day in the States, Private Spillan had marched twenty-five miles with his company. After cold morning chow of rice, raisins, and tea, the companies set out from Binu Village into chest-high Kunai grass, moving toward the jungle. The enemy forces, desperately fighting out of an encirclement, attacked the column at 10:00 AM, near the Metapona River and Asamana Village. Intense mortar, machine-gun, and rifle fire pinned Charlie Company down. Easy Company was dispatched to reinforce the embattled company. The fighting continued until after sunset. Twelve Marines died during the "Battle at Asamana." [26] Two of them had grown up together in Saint Leo Parish. Private Spillan was listed among the missing-in-action, and then was reported KIA, body never recovered. [27] His remains are believed to have been interred in a field in the Asamana area.

The Leo students, and probably John Fardy, would not know much more about Joseph Auman until the October 1943 *Oriole* was published.

Wanting to better inform the student body, Leo had asked the alumni in the services to remain in contact with the school. Letters and phone calls came in response and continued for the duration of the war. A new, front-page column was launched in the March 1943 *Oriole*: "News From Leo Men in the Armed Services." The students began reading updates on various alumni, many of whom they would have known from previous classes. No fewer than twenty-two of John Fardy's 1940 classmates were mentioned in the *Oriole* columns by the end of the war. A good number of them had been in the newspaper while they had been outstanding Leo students and athletes. The reports of alumni killed in action, wounded in action, missing in action, and held in prisoner of war camps increased beginning in the October *Oriole*.

Out of high school for three years, John Fardy was drafted into the Marines on May 8, 1943, as the last *Oriole* issue was being distributed to the 1943 graduating class. John said goodbye to his parents and sisters on South Calumet Avenue and left for the San Diego Marine Corps Recruit Depot. Neither Mary Therese nor Anne were married at the time John left home. Private Fardy spent the next five months in California and it is unknown if he ever took leave to return to Calumet Avenue in his Marine uniform.

After his initial recruit training, Private Fardy requested assignment to the Japanese Language School, before which he was promoted to private first class in July. After a month at language school, he was reassigned to the special weapons school at San Diego and trained to be an automatic rifleman. He left the United States in October 1943, to participate in the island campaigns with his comrades. At that time, the Leo student body was reading the first *Oriole* of their new school year.

As the Leo Class of 1944 and Edward Auman began their senior year, the October 1943 *Oriole* front page printed a service photograph of a smiling USMC Private Joseph M. Auman. The 21-year-old 1940 alumnus, among the first Leo war dead, had been killed by a bullet to his face on Guadalcanal, November 11, 1942, with Easy Company of Carlson's 2d Raider Battalion. [28] Joe Auman and Larry Spillan, friends since their grade school days, serving together in the Raiders, had died in the same battle at the Metapona River. For his extraordinary heroism, Private Auman had been awarded a posthumous Navy Cross, the second highest award for valor in all the military branches. Edward was proud of his big brother, but he also had some concern for his other brother. William Auman, Class of 1941, was a private first class in the Marines and was preparing to go into the Pacific islands with an anti-tank battalion.

By the time the November *Oriole* issue was published, fourteen of the previous year's Leo graduates were also serving in the Marines. The December 1943 issue reported on the back page that the War Department was honoring Private Joe Auman by naming a destroyer escort (DE-674) after him. When the December 1943 *Oriole* went to print, another of Leo's 1940 graduates was aboard a different troop transport ship in the Solomon Sea.

Private First Class Fardy served as an automatic rifleman with Company C, 1st Battalion, 1st Marines, 1st Marine Division and first stood up to the rigors of combat at Cape Gloucester on the northwestern tip of volcanic New Britain Island, a place the Marines would remember as *The Green Inferno*. The principle objective of *Operation Backhander* was to capture two enemy airstrips and then clear the island of enemy forces. Three hundred and ten Marines would give their lives in the fight to take 130 miles of the island, and another 1,083 would be wounded.

The city kid from Chicago who had been uncertain about a career came ashore on Yellow Beach 1 at 2:00 PM on the day after Christmas 1943, and stayed until April 25, 1944. Private First Class Fardy was in terrain unlike any he had encountered in Saint Clotilde parish. He advanced with Company C through swamps, monsoon deluges, swollen streams, shin-high mud, mangrove forests, jungles, high kunai grass, and insect hordes. The ever-drenched company skirted the ridges of Hell's Point, slowed more by the environmental conditions than by the banzai counterattacks. By day five, Private First Class Fardy was in the middle of the Marine front line sweeping across the airstrips all the way to the northern beaches. He and the 1st Marines spent another four months on New Britain.

Following the successful Cape Gloucester operation, Private First Class Fardy trained with the division for their next amphibious assault—Peleliu Island. The 1st Division waded through the surf and struck the beaches of Peleliu on September 15, 1944. Private First Class Fardy fought his way off White Beach 1 on the left flank of the assault under the enemy barrage from The Point and Bloody Nose Ridge on the Umurbrogal massif. By September 21, the 1st Marines had suffered 1,749 casualties in the capture of the Peleliu airfield and in the routing of the Japanese from caves in the coral ridges inland from the airfield. Weeks of intense fighting remained. Private First Class Fardy departed from Peleliu with the regiment in early October when the island had been secured. He was then a veteran of two bloody island campaigns.

More practice landings were ahead and mainland Japan began to loom in the consciousness of the Marines. Back home, the January 1945 *Oriole* issue reported that the 1945 *Lion* yearbook was to be dedicated to the alumni in the services and to the twenty-three Leo war dead. Before the school year was over, fifteen more former students would die in combat.

How many American high schools can claim that two classmates who had once stood beside each other would later be counted among the most valorous of Marines, one earning a Navy Cross and the other a Medal of Honor?

There is a good chance that Private First Class Fardy knew about Joe Auman's Navy Cross, not because he had read issues of the Leo *Oriole*, but because the heroism of the Marines on Guadalcanal had become legendary within the Corps during the war. Also, John had once stood shoulder to shoulder with Joe in the top row of freshman when their 1938 *Lion* yearbook photograph was taken. To have been in high school corridors with a Raider Battalion Marine and Navy Cross recipient would have been a source of pride. There is an equally good chance that the Marine from South Calumet Avenue never knew that the USS *Joseph M Auman* (APD-117) was commissioned April 25, 1945. On that date, John Fardy was surviving enemy artillery, mortar, and rifle fire barrages during assaults on a mountain fortress called Mount Yae Take on an island peninsula named Motobu.

Having demonstrated leadership in two bloody assault operations, Private First Class Fardy was promoted to corporal, December 21, 1944, and assigned duties as a squad leader. With little more than three months to train in his new position, he would be remembered later as a "stouthearted leader and indomitable fighter."

Company C went into action again. With nearly two years in the Corps, in his third amphibious assault, Corporal Fardy participated in the *Operation Iceberg* Easter Sunday, April 1, 1945, landing and sweep to the north tip of Okinawa, 360 miles from Japan. During the early days of the battle, as the regiments fought their way up Motobu Peninsula and captured Mount Yae Take, the 1st Marines were kept mainly in reserve, dealing with night patrols, ambushes, and sniper attacks. Then on April 27, they were ordered to turn south to relieve the Army units that had encountered bitter Japanese resistance in their sector of operation.

Corporal Fardy was headed into Okinawa's southern highlands, the concentric Japanese defenses around Shuri Castle, and what was later to be considered the most intense, nightmarish fighting on the island. He crossed over hillcrests, moved through cliffs and draws in the region of Awacha Pocket, and survived massive enemy counterattacks.

After weeks of combat, the Marines moving south to Shuri had taken on a weary, haggard appearance: days without shaving or bathing, uniforms muddied, torn, and often soiled by blood, their own and that of their companions. Many had that distant stare in their eyes, "the thousand yard stare," yet were determined to finish the fight.

Every day families in the States were receiving telegrams, sometimes followed by condolence letters from commanders.

On May 6, after five weeks battling on Okinawa, in continuous cold rain and mud, Charlie Company, moving closer to its final objective on the Asa Kawa River, engaged a well-defended, heavily fortified Japanese emplacement. Having received his mission orders from his platoon sergeant, Corporal Fardy led his squad along a drainage ditch when a force of concealed defenders opened fire upon them with rifles and other small arms. He quickly deployed his men into defensive positions along the drainage ditch, giving time to assess the situation. The enemy soldiers kept the squad pinned down with relentless fire. Because the ditch afforded the Marines some protection against small arms, the Japanese attacked with grenades.

When one of the explosive devices rolled into the ditch among his men at 11:30 AM, Corporal John Fardy, 22-year-old squad leader, jumped on it immediately, taking the full force of the detonation himself. He survived the blast with multiple fragmentation wounds to his abdomen and chest and was evacuated to a field hospital. He died the next day, May 7, having been a Marine one day short of two years, and was buried in Grave 417, Plot 1 of the 1st Marine Division Cemetery on Okinawa.

When the telegram arrived on South Calumet Avenue, Martin and Mary Fardy hung a Gold Star in their front living room window to let neighbors know that their son had sacrificed his life on behalf of freedom. For the first time in their lives as parents, their son was going to be on the front page of a newspaper. John's death was reported on Page One of local Chicago newspapers on Wednesday, June 27, 1945. One of seven "Southtowners" identified to have recently died in combat war zones, his was the first name of the seven listed. The location and details of his death were "undisclosed." Under his name in bold print, John's background, including that he had graduated from Leo High School, was described in ten lines of print. By war's end, he was listed among 253 Southtown men who had died in the Pacific. [29] No one in South Chicago knew the significance yet of the young man's sacrifice.

Corporal Fardy was the last Marine in the Second World War to hurl himself on a hostile grenade to protect companions from injury and death. More died in the combat on Okinawa, and six more Marines were awarded Medals of Honor. A week after his death, Corporal Fardy's young Charlie Company friend from Ada, a small, rural town of about 2,000 people in northwestern Minnesota, also earned a posthumous

Medal of Honor. Corporal Louis James Hauge, Jr., 20-years-old, assigned a machine-gun squad leader position, charged a heavily fortified hill and died in a "heroic one-man assault." The Marines dedicated a camp on Okinawa in Corporal Hauge's memory after the war and the Navy named a ship in his honor in 1984.

The Marines finished the fight for Okinawa in June. The War in the Pacific ended in August 1945, and the servicemen began returning home. The October 1945 *Oriole* reported on its back page that six alumni had been listed among the war dead in the summer months leading up to the war's end. Michael Kelly, Class of 1943, was killed May 20, when an enemy suicide plane struck the USS *Thatcher* off the beaches of Okinawa. In another column five graduates from the 1945 class were reported to have traveled to the South Carolina Parris Island Marine Recruit Depot. Eight others had also "answered Uncle Sam's call to arms" and were serving in other military branches.

Two photographs, side by side, of the two Auman brothers, Joe and William, in their Marine uniforms appeared on the front page of the November *Oriole* Issue. Edward, Class of 1944, had received a letter from his brother's commanding officer. Private First Class William Auman, having been overseas for one year, had been killed in action on Okinawa in May. Four Leo alumni had died in May during the battle for Okinawa. The news about only two of them had reached the high school.

America would soon be celebrating a New Year. Families were making the adjustments to having "their boys" back home. There were parades and "Welcome Home" parties. There were things to look into, like employment, the G.I. Bill for education, and veteran benefits for home mortgages. The Leo veterans of war began visiting their alma mater to the accolades of the younger students.

For families like the Fardys and Aumans, for whom sons and brothers would not be returning home from war, it was obviously different. As Christmas approached, there would be no joyous carols. Although the hopeful message in Bing Crosby's rendition of "I'll Be Home For Christmas" had been popular for three years, it had only a melancholy ring for families with a Gold Star in their windows. In their homes there would be the quiet of anguish.

By the close of 1945, three members of the 1940 Class had been reported to have been killed in action during the *Oriole's* three-year coverage of the war, two others were missing in action, and three had been reported to be prisoners of war. As had been true when he was a student at Leo, students reading *The Oriole* remained unaware of John Fardy's activities and heroism. The last time his name had been in the school newspaper was when the editor printed a friendly apology for having found amusement in the pronunciation of his last name.

Then the staff of the *Oriole* did something in the March 1946 issue that had never been done before. Corporal John Fardy's senior year photograph was printed on the front page. The newspaper reported that his death had been discovered in February. The few details were given in nine succinct lines. The one photograph of Corporal Fardy on Web sites today seems to be a color-enhanced portrait of a smiling young man who had not yet been in combat. The portrait is similar to the photograph printed in *The Oriole* with Marine Dress Blues superimposed upon it.

Beside John's photo was one of a smiling Lieutenant George Karl in aviator helmet and goggles. George had lived five blocks to the east of the Fardys and was two years behind John at Saint Clotilde Grammar School and at Leo. A Marine fighter pilot who had been providing close air support for the Marines assaulting Shuri Castle, he had likely at some point flown over Corporal Fardy leading Marine grunts in the ground fight. Lieutenant Karl was killed in a dogfight over Okinawa on May 16, 1945.

In his four years of high school, John had never been on the Leo Honor Roll, had not been elected to any office, and had not had time for extracurricular activities. Yet, in his two years in the Marines, this first generation American acquired the skills of an automatic rifleman, was twice promoted into leadership positions, and distinguished himself by earning the highest honor for valor his nation extends to its citizens.

Such Sons as These

Three weeks before Corporal Fardy smothered a grenade to protect the men under his leadership, historic changes occurred in

Washington, D.C. that would affect how his Medal would be presented. The Commander-In-Chief's responsibilities, including the award-ing of Medals of Honor, were transferred when President Franklin D. Roosevelt died and Harry S. Truman succeeded to the presidency on April 12, 1945. President Truman awarded no fewer than 219 of the total number of Medals of Honor earned in WWII and at least 123 of the posthumous awards. His signature was affixed to all but one of the Medal Citations for Marines on Iwo Jima and Okinawa. [30]

Before President Truman had any notice of Corporal Fardy's valor, he addressed the Joint Session of the Congress on May 21, 1945, announcing that he was going to present a Medal of Honor to Army Tech Sergeant Jake Lindsay. "This is one of the pleasant duties of the President of the United States," he remarked. President Truman under-stood the Medal to represent the kind of honor all strive for, but few achieve. He urged Congress to consider the magnitude of such bravery. "I hope that every man and woman in our Nation today will reverently thank God that we have produced such sons as these. With their high courage as an inspiration, we cannot fail in the task we have set for our-selves." [31]

After that day, over the next five years, President Truman sum-moned another eighty-five servicemen and their families to the White House to receive their Medals. He made a point of telling the recipients that he would rather have the Medal of Honor around his neck than to be president. One of his last presentations for the WWII recipients was to Justice M. Chambers on November 1, 1950.

A task President Truman did not find so pleasant was pre-senting posthumous awards. From the start of his presi-dency, he adhered to a "definite policy" of not presenting posthumous Medals of Honor to the next of kin at the White House. The Medals were instead carried by his representatives to the recipient's hometown or to a location of the family's choosing.

Consistent with President Truman's policy, Corporal Fardy's family was not summoned to receive his Medal of Honor at the White House. A year after the war ended, John's Medal was presented to Martin and Mary Fardy at ceremonies conducted by the Chicago Detachment of the

Marine Corps League on September 15, 1946. A photo of Lieutenant Colonel Peter A. McDonald, USMC, presenting the Medal to Martin and Mary appeared in the Saturday, September 28, 1946, *Chicago Daily Tribune.* The accompanying column, MEDAL OF HONOR IS AWARDED TO AN ABSENT HERO: Parents Get Son's Medal, reported that Corporal Fardy's parents had attended a quiet ceremony the night before in the Roosevelt room of the Morrison Hotel, a premier high rise on West Madison and Clark in the downtown Loop.

Corporal John Fardy's family and friends from Saint Clotilde Grammar School and Leo High School first learned the details of his valorous actions when they heard or read his Medal of Honor Citation. While they might have remembered the quiet, modest boy John had been throughout his school years, his Citation described the kind of man the 22-year-old Marine had grown to be.

As remembered by Marines who had fought with him on Cape Gloucester, Peleliu, and Okinawa, Corporal Fardy had certainly acted above and beyond what is asked of any service man or woman. More than that, he had been a strong and determined leader, refusing to be "bested" in a fight with an enemy, and had made prompt decisions in dire and terrible circumstances. Concerned for the men for whom he was responsible, he had willingly risked his own life to protect them from certain death. Corporal Fardy had rendered valiant service to the Corps and to the country. Having demonstrated the kind of unwavering spirit and unassailable character that inspires others, his bravery had brought the highest credit upon him.

Those present at the memorial ceremony were likely moved by the description of his valor, but what they likely did not realize was that, by itself, his Citation did not fully convey the distinction Corporal Fardy's actions had earned him. Some facts were likely unknown by those attending the ceremony. An estimated 80,000 Marines had faced the Japanese defenses during the eighty-two days of fighting on Okinawa. All who went ashore that Easter morning were brave. Before the island was secured, more than 3,400 Marines were killed in action during the battle, and nearly another 350 died of their wounds afterwards. Of all in the three Marine divisions in the fight, Corporal Fardy was one of only eleven Marines to have been awarded a Medal of Honor, ten of which were posthumous awards.

That he ranked 138 of 184 Leo Class of '40 graduates became a meaningless number on Okinawa. John Fardy's life and valor serve as reminders that academic performance alone is not predictive of later heroic bravery. And as far as the Marine Corps was concerned, Corporal Fardy had finished at the top of his class.

A month after the award ceremony, on October 28, American Community Builders developers held a press conference in the Palmer House Hotel in downtown Chicago. They announced their plan to build a new community just southwest of Chicago Heights to provide housing for veterans returning from the war. The self-governing suburb would be called The Village of Park Forest. More announcements followed nine months later.

In the December 1946 *Oriole*, John's photograph appeared on the front page for the second time in the school's history. The two-column headline proclaimed: *GRAD WINS CONGRESSIONAL MEDAL OF HONOR POSTHUMOUSLY*. A summary of his Citation described how he had thrown himself on a grenade, absorbing the blast of the explosion to protect his comrades. Archived copies of *The Oriole* after 1946 were not available for review, so whether or not John's name or photograph ever appeared in print at Leo High School again is unknown. However, the South Chicago community would read about him in the years ahead.

Column headlines on the front page of the Friday, July 30, 1948, *Chicago Heights Star* read "Park Forest Streets Will Honor Heroes: To Be Named for Winners Of Congressional Medals." Noting the importance of remembering "deeds of heroic bravery on World War battlefields," the community developers felt "that the contribution of these heroes is the truest example of the best traditions of the American way of life, and to perpetuate the memory of these deeds we believe that it is quite fitting to name the streets in Park Forest after Congressional Medal of Honor winners from the State of Illinois." John Fardy was listed with four other Marines among the recipients to have streets named in their honor. The dedication of Fardy Avenue was meant to ensure that John's name would "be perpetuated for posterity in the new city." [32] It appears that the developers at some point changed their plans about street names.

Park Forest, encompassing five square miles and 65 miles of streets, became a model middle class community, earning the All-America City award more than once. A drive around the suburb today finds streets named in honor of Marine Medal of Honor recipients Joseph J. McCarthy, Kenneth Bailey, John Leims, and Robert Dunlap. There is no Fardy Avenue to be found in Park Forest, on the city maps, or in the street indexes. [33]

A "Fardy Road issue" was addressed at a The Town of Mukwonago Board meeting in 2005. Mukwonago is in the southern portion of Waukesha County, Wisconsin. Given that the streets in town tend to be named for the city founders and prominent residents, and given the number of well-known Fardys in that region going back to the 1800s, that road probably had no connection to the Marine from Calumet Avenue in South Chicago. [34]

The Quiet of Bravery

Funeral ships like the USAT *Cardinal O'Connell* began transporting the thousands of "repatriated" war dead from the Pacific back to the United States in October 1947. John Peter Fardy was brought home from Okinawa to Chicago for reburial on American soil in early April 1949. The Chicago Detachment of the Marine Corps League ensured military honors were extended to him.

Nearly six years had passed since John had last walked down the street with his family to attend Sunday church services. The parishioners of Saint Clotilde, Saint Leo, Saint Margaret, and the other South Chicago Catholic parishes had entered the fifth week of Lent, known as Passiontide week. Church altars and vestibules were shrouded in black draperies as Palm Sunday approached. Easter Sunday was ten days away. It was a fitting time for Martin and Mary Fardy to have their son brought home.

That Thursday, April 7, 1949, the temperatures rose into the mid-50s, and the winds picked up, gusting between eighteen and twenty-one miles per hour. Light rain showers fell for a while early in the afternoon.

John Fardy's funeral procession made its way from South Chicago and traveled nine miles southwest of Calumet Avenue to 6001 West 111th Street in Aslip Village, Worth Township, Cook County. Just blocks away from Fox Secretarial College, where John had been enrolled nine years earlier, the procession turned into the Catholic Archdiocese of Chicago's Holy Sepulchre Cemetery. Beyond the front gate, the cars turned left at the first road, and slowly filed to the eastern end of Section 23. John Fardy was laid to rest in Grave 3, Lot 16, Block 3. [35]

Holy Sepulchre Cemetery lists John among its 21 famous burials, including U.S. Army Medal of Honor recipient, Anton L Krotiak, who was killed in combat the day after John died and is buried twenty rows away and six blocks over from him in Section 23. Private First Class Krotiak's flat stone marker bears the Medal of Honor inscription. Among the other notables in Holy Sepulchre are five U.S. Congressmen, Mayor Richard Daly, another mayor, a New York Jets football player, two American League baseball players, two entertainers, and two criminals. Only six of the famous people had been buried at the cemetery by 1949, when John's remains were returned home.

John is not alone, without family, at Holy Sepulchre Cemetery. His father and mother are buried beside him. Records indicate that Martin J. Fardy passed away February 3, 1957 at age 70. [36] Mary Therese (Fardy) Martin, living in Fontana, Wisconsin at the time, arranged for her father to be buried two lots east of John. Mary Fardy died on July 2, 1975, and was buried between her son and her husband.

Had the couple from Ireland ever had the chance to tell grandchildren stories about John and his heroism and death on Okinawa? Three generations have been born since Martin and Mary raised their children on South Calumet Avenue. As was discovered in the search for Ken Worley's background, tracking extended family can be a challenge. If nieces or nephews had ever learned about John and his Medal of Honor, they would not have had their uncle's surname, but rather would have had the last name of Martin or Thometz. A March 6, 2009, *Chicago Tribune* obituary answered some questions.

Mary T. Martin, 91-years-old, died March 5, 2009, in Tinley Park, Cook County, about seven miles south of her brother's grave in Holy Sepulchre Cemetery. [37] She had been a dedicated parishioner of St. Julie

Billiart, a large Roman Catholic Church, and was a supporter of its Youth Program. She was buried at Saint Mary's Cemetery, five miles west of St. Clotilde and South Calumet. [38] Mary Therese is with her husband, Joe, who was buried May 18, 1983, and two sons, one of who died four months before his grandmother, Mary Fardy, and the other who died one year after in 1976.

According to the *Tribune* obituary, Mary and Joe Martin had two daughters and six sons, John's nieces and nephews. [39] The Martins named their eldest son, John, after the Marine who had sacrificed his life on Okinawa just four years earlier. Like his uncle, John graduated from Leo High School, Class of 1967. [40] Mary and Joe had eighteen grandchildren and twelve great-grandchildren. This means that the four generations of Martin and Mary Fardy descendants who might have remembered John at Memorial Day celebrations numbered at least forty direct family members.

During the ongoing search, no records were found to indicate whether Anne (Fardy) and John Thometz also had children. From available archives, except for the March 2009, *Chicago Tribune* obituary, Anne was last mentioned in the 1945 newspaper article announcing her brother's death. As late as June 2011, she and John were living on Chicago's north side. It was learned that Anne and John did have five children, some of who now reside in Wisconsin, and "a lot" of grandchildren. [41] At the time of this printing, Anne was 90-years-old.

John was initially included on the list of the thirty-four forgotten Medal of Honor recipients because his history seemed as quiet as he is remembered to have been as a kid. Most of what was described above about his high school days was undiscovered for the greater part of the search for information about him. A short blog article on a Web site made a difference. [42]

Pat Hickey, the Director of Development at Leo High School and a regular columnist for the *Chicago Daily Observer*, is the son of a WWII Marine. He understands how quiet the nature of bravery can be. Pat's father served with Able Company, 1st Battalion, 3d Marines, 3d Marine Division during the battle for Guam in the Marianas, July 21 to August 10, 1944. The 1st Battalion's landing zone was on the left flank of the beach assault at Adelup Point. During the first night of the assault to secure the beachhead and capture the heights of Chonito Cliff and Bundschu Ridge, Private First Class Luther Skaggs, of the 2d Battalion, earned a Medal of Honor. In the first two days of the battle, 615 1st Battalion Marines were killed, wounded, or missing. By day three, Able Company had almost been obliterated from the battalion. As Pat Hickey grew up, his father never mentioned the fight on Chonito Cliff. [43]

Pat's September 27, 2010, article …*With Both Hands: Leo High School's Medal of Honor Hero—Cpl. John P. Fardy* provided otherwise unreported details of John's early life and reopened the search for the young Marine's background. [44] That Pat had earlier mentioned John in his 2005 book describing Leo High School alumni who had served honorably in WWII indicated that John was remembered in Chicago. "John Fardy '40 smothered a grenade with his body in order to save his comrades, on Okinawa." [45]

There was more. Every year on the Friday before Veterans Day, John is remembered during Leo's Veterans Observances. About 500 veterans attended the November 2010 tribute. Additionally, the original plaque dedicated to the Leo WWII Veterans in 1942 eventually included John. Leo replaced that plaque with a newer one at some point after 1990. What happened to the original plaque is not known. [46]

Leo High School has a student body numbering about 250 young men. Each of them, year after year, as was true of the Leo *Lions* going back into the late 1940s, has remembered John P. Fardy. That they do is as much a tribute to the faculty and graduates of Leo High School as it is to the Marine from South Calumet Avenue.

Holy Sepulchre's 320 acres have changed since Martin, Mary, Mary Therese, and Anne Fardy stood beside John's grave. In 1949, the cemetery had been open for only twenty-six years and fewer than 20,000 people were buried there. Since John's funeral, shrines to various Irish saints, a chapel, and a mausoleum have all been erected on the grounds, and since John's funeral, more than 70,000 Catholics have been interred there.

Today, looking from either end of Holy Sepulchre's Section 23, Block 3 is a long row of flat stones lying between rows of upright headstones and monuments. Without a cemetery map or directions from staff, John's grave would be difficult to find. On the map, Grave 3, Lot 16 is five rows in from the front access road. Looking for his grave or approaching it from the road, the location and view of John's lot are obscured by tall Flanagan and Mussatto upright monuments in front of his grave, and Brett and Marker monuments standing behind it.

The WWII-era, flat, granite, government marker at the foot of John's grave is now weathered and gray. A passerby would not know that he had earned a Medal of Honor; there is no inscription on his marker detailing his medals. As was true in his school years, now at rest, John's heroism is quiet and does not draw much attention to him.

Exactly sixty-two years after John's funeral procession took him to Holy Sepulchre Cemetery, Paul and Patty Becka went to the cemetery in April 2011, to pay their respects. Having traveled more than 525 miles to visit family in North Chicago, they went out of their way to stop in Aslip to find his resting place, a Marine they had not known.

The air was a bit cooler than it had been on that same day in 1949, and the sky was overcast, threatening a light drizzle throughout the day. The lawns were greening and the gusts of winds rustled the few crisp brown leaves scattered about the ground, remnants yet of the previous autumn. The evergreen trees provided some color to Section 23, but the branches of the maple trees remained barren of leaves.

Standing at his grave, the CPL 1 Marines 1 Marine Division inscription meant something to Patty Becka. She is the daughter of a Korean War-era USMC veteran. The absence of any MOH recognition on John's marker was also noteworthy to Paul and Patty. After visiting the grave, they went to the cemetery office and talked to the manager, Ray Pawlak, about the matter. Ray explained that a replacement stone might be possible and gave them the phone number for the VA Memorial Program Service, Status of Headstones and Markers division. At this printing, efforts are underway to either replace or upgrade John's military marker so that those walking by his grave will know that this quiet young man's exceptional valor earned him a Medal of Honor and a place in Marine Corps history.

"We will get this done." [47]

The impact of one man's valor across generations is evident in South Chicago. As Corporal Fardy had inspired his Charlie Company squad mates to charge a fortified Japanese emplacement on Okinawa, his bravery stirred the spirits of those who remembered him sixty-six years after he had earned a Medal of Honor.

Pat Hickey is an ardent supporter of all things Leo, even though he is not a graduate of that high school. In April 2011, he informed alumni that John Fardy's military marker at Holy Sepulchre Cemetery did not have the Medal of Honor insignia. The alumni understood the significance of the WWII commemorative plaque they had so often walked past or stood before in the Leo auditorium vestibule. The Alumni Association decided to do something about the apparent oversight at Holy Sepulchre. James Furlong, Class of 1965, Richard Furlong, Class of '59, James Farrell, '61, John Gardner, '75, Mike Holmes, '76, and Mark Lee, '85, wanted anyone walking by Corporal Fardy's grave to know of his gallantry, and they got busy.

A first priority was to find the Martin and Thometz families, descendants of John's two sisters. John Martin was discovered to be a Leo High School Class of 1967 graduate living in Tinley Park, and Mary Colette was located in a western Chicago suburb. Jim Furlong got right on the phone to both of them. John Martin, his uncle's namesake, was honored and humbled by the attention that Leo was extending to the uncle he had never known. He had been told long ago that his uncle had been an "ordinary" man. John Martin, now in his early sixties, did not think that his siblings or his Thometz cousins, or their children, had ever been much aware of their uncle's courage. John did express complete confidence that the family would fully support the Leo alumni in their efforts to recognize his uncle and was happy to be involved. [48]

Determined that a renewed tribute be extended to John Fardy, the alumni made proposals to Maurice Moore's Memorials, across the street from Holy Sepulchre Cemetery, Chicago's own 2d Battalion, 24th Marines, 4th Marine Division, the Illinois State Commander of the Military Order of the Purple Heart, the Congressional Medal of Honor

Foundation, Chicago's Marine Corps League, Tom Day, founder of Bugles Across America, local bagpipers, and the Leo High School football team. They invited Marine Medal of Honor recipients to be guest speakers. Major General James E. Livingston, USMC (Ret.), who had earned a Medal of Honor in Vietnam, alerted the Medal of Honor Foundation regarding the unfolding events in Chicago. The Leo alumni were planning for an unveiling of a redesigned monument near the day that would have been Corporal Fardy's 89th birthday—August 15, 2011. They had four months to achieve this undertaking and organize a military ceremony. In addition to John Martin and Mary Colette Dillon, the alumni hoped to send invitations to Anne Thometz and as many Martin and Thometz nephews and nieces as they could locate. Anne (Thometz) McGuire, Corporal Fardy's niece, hoped to attend the ceremony.

The efforts of the Leo Alumni Association are honorable and fitting—not just in paying tribute to Corporal John Fardy, but also in doing all they could to involve the Fardy descendants. Heroic valor within a family is an esteemed legacy, and the generations that follow deserve to recognize the significance of their inheritance.

John is among ten U.S. Marine Medal of Honor recipients from WWII the State of Illinois claims as its own. He is listed among all of Illinois' recipients at the State Military Museum in Springfield.

Saepe Expertus, Semper Fidelis, Fratres Aeterni

The translation of the extended USMC motto is "Often Tested, Always Faithful, Brothers Forever." The Brothers Forever part explains a lot about what happened on Okinawa and all the Pacific islands. John Fardy had only sisters as he grew up, then he went to an all-boys high school. It does not appear that he participated in any team sports. While he likely had friends among his school classmates, what John learned of brotherhood likely began at the San Diego Recruit Depot.

Marines naturally looked out for each other, sharing a family-like bond. That they experienced comrades as brothers helps to better understand why the Medal of Honor recipients were so readily willing to put themselves in harm's way, disregarding danger, to rescue their comrades and to act in defense of fellow combatants, even at their own risk. The sense of brotherhood, combined with the *esprit d'corps* attitude, was accentuated in combat situations and often fueled brave actions.

If this was the case with comrades in arms, imagine a Marine's reactions if his own biological brother was injured and dying.

Before he had finished his own training in South Carolina, Private Franklin Sigler had received news of his brother's death in the Pacific Campaign. The death of his brother, a Marine, no doubt had an impact on Private Sigler's actions eight months later when he stepped onto an enemy beach. Imagine the impact if he had been right beside his brother when he was killed in action on a beach far from home and family. Dale Hansen lived that reality, or so he thought.

A Brother's Death

Patriotism ran deep in the Hansen blood. Peter Hansen and Lillian Lena Marie Schulz married and lived on a farm northwest of Omaha in Cuming County, Nebraska. Peter served in the Army during WWI, and when he returned home, he and Lillian started their family. Their first son, Dale Merlin Hansen, was born December 13, 1922, in Wisner, a town of under 1,000 Nebraskans on the Elkhorn River, off Route 275.

The land around Wisner is flat and fertile and nourished by plenty of moisture. Farms and ranches flourished through the hard work of families dedicated to the land.

The second Hansen boy, Donald, was born a year after Dale, and then Forrest was born in 1929. Perhaps due to the economic turmoil of the Great Depression and the foreclosures on farms brought on by the Dust Bowl years in other states, Peter and Lillian had no more children for a while. Their fourth boy, Larry P., was born in 1939, when Dale was going into his senior year in high school. The eldest Hansen son had a special affinity for his "baby brother." The four Hansen boys were close to each other, and worked and played together. [49]

Dale worked on the farm while he went to the county schools and grew to be five-foot-nine, 140 pounds. His recreation consisted of playing on sandlot baseball and softball teams and riding horses. Graduating from the Wisner high school in 1940 when he was 17-years-old, Dale went to work on the family farm. John Fardy, four months older than Dale, graduated at the same time up in Chicago.

By 1944, wartime production in America had begun to pull the nation's economy into recovery. Allied forces were planning on pushing the German forces back across the Rhine River and the Marines were planning an invasion of Saipan and hopping islands all the way to Japan. Casualty rates were anticipated to be high and the need for replacement drafts was apparent.

Like John Fardy the year before, the Marines drafted Dale Hansen for service on May 11, 1944. He and Donald decided to go into the Corps together, enlisting after Dale's draft notice was delivered to the farm. The two brothers trained together in San Diego and Camp Pendleton, were assigned together, and sailed into the Pacific together in November. Dale, the Nebraska farmer, had been trained to be a Browning Automatic Rifleman. On the training range, he earned an Expert Automatic Rifleman's badge, demonstrative of a drive to be the best at whatever he did. Later, he would learn the skills of bazooka-use while at Pavuvu in the Russell Islands, where he and Donald saw some combat.

The Hansen brothers were assigned to Company E, 2d Battalion, 1st Marines and trained with the company for amphibious landings. Assigned together as a bazooka team, they went ashore behind the first assault waves on Okinawa's beaches, on D-Day, April 1, 1945. Once ashore, one explosion would forever change their lives.

During the initial phase of the island assault, Private Donald Hansen sat down on a land mine. Severely injured in the detonation, he was evacuated from the island and treated on a hospital ship. He survived his injuries, spent two years in a California hospital, and was medically discharged from the Marines.

Private Dale Hansen never learned of his younger brother's survival. He continued ahead with Easy Company for the next thirty-seven days, certainly taking the images of his brother with him, and scoured the northern section of the island with his company. In spite of the ongoing battles, Private Hansen remembered his youngest brother back in Wisner. He took time to mail home a coconut from Okinawa with Larry's name inscribed in the shell. He would not have many more opportunities to let his family in Wisner know he was thinking about them.

The 1st Marines were turned south. Private Hansen and Corporal Fardy, in two different battalions, were moving along the western coastline of Okinawa into the island's center where the Japanese had dug in, fortified, and concealed their positions. Once redeployed in the south, Easy Company battled the entrenched hostile units a yard at a time in Urasoe. They approached Hill 60, a two hundred-foot rise in the terrain, in early May. Private Hansen had been a Marine for almost a year.

Easy Company's attack on Hill 60 stalled. The hill defenders had machine-gun pillboxes and mortar positions supporting the troops in the trenches, and their fire was accurate and devastating. Private Hansen was going to demonstrate a characteristic common among heroically brave Marines: acting with one's own initiative when under duress.

The ability of recipients to react quickly to critical events unfolding around them was related to an innate confidence in themselves and their drive to get things done. When situations demanded reaction, they did not need to wait for orders, directions, or a call to duty. No matter their rank or position in the group, they began to take matters into their own hands. This characteristic is consistently noted in citations describing actions that went *above and beyond the call of duty*.

Because they also tended to be quick to act, men like Private Hansen at times appeared to react to events without thinking. They seemed able to discern the important elements of a situation and to act almost instinctively. This appears to reflect a pattern of behavior rooted in early experience. Having participated in play or sports that required spontaneous reactions, having practiced skills, and having repeated drills, they appear to have developed the habit of automatically acting rather than needing time to "think things through."

Able to recognize the importance of taking immediate action in critical situations, the recipients were undeterred by obvious risk or danger. Their Medal Citations attest to this characteristic, describing them as having acted "unhesitatingly," "instantly," "immediately," and "deliberately."

Private Hansen proved to be no exception to this rule. On the day Corporal Fardy died of his grenade wounds in a field hospital, the

Marine from Wisner, who was afterwards described as "cool and courageous in combat" during the battle for Hill 60, took his own initiative on May 7, 1945. Recognizing the most tactical positions on the enemy outpost, Private Hansen crawled into an open area with his rocket launcher, fired, and destroyed a pillbox. Exposed to enemy fire, his weapon was disabled before he could fire again.

Undeterred, Private Hansen grabbed a rifle and charged a ridge alone. Leaping across the crest, he engaged six Japanese soldiers who were firing into his platoon. Having killed four of them, his rifle jammed, giving the remaining two hostiles the chance to charge him. After disabling them both with his rifle butt, Private Hansen climbed back down the ridge and supplied himself with another weapon and grenades.

Remaining at the lead of Easy Company's assault on Hill 60, and showing "complete disregard of all personal danger," he charged the ridge again, attacking and destroying a mortar position. Eight hostiles died during his second one-man attack and Company E advanced, eventually overwhelming the Japanese outpost.

Four days later on May 11, Private Dale Hansen, 22-years-old, was killed by enemy sniper fire during the fight for Wana-Dakeshi Ridge. He died one year to the day after the Marines had drafted him.

Larry was five-years-old when the news of his brother's death reached home. Donald remained in the California hospital recuperating from his injuries. Private Hansen was buried in the 1st Marine Division Cemetery on Okinawa. His Medal of Honor was presented to Peter and Lillian Hansen at Memorial Day ceremonies in Wisner on May 30, 1946, nearly four months before John Fardy's parents received his Medal in Chicago. Dale's body was returned to Wisner in 1948.

Wisner City Cemetery is located on the southeast edge of town, beside St. Joseph Catholic Cemetery. Twenty-eight Hansens from various families lie in the cemetery. Peter died in 1972, at the age of 76-years. Lillian lived to be 85-years-old, dying in 1985. The parents, laid to rest beside Dale, lived to see most of the tributes extended to their son.

Dale's is an impressive gravesite. The gold Medal of Honor symbol is engraved in his white marble headstone, which resembles the stones at Arlington. A bronze plaque is affixed to the granite cover over his grave. Larry Hansen, living in nearby Norfolk, continues to tend to the family gravesite. He ensures that a small, blue Medal of Honor flag flies at the foot of his beloved brother's grave, that flowers are there at Memorial Day, and that a wreath is there at Christmas time.

Dale's brothers, Donald, Forrest, and Larry, all married and raised families. Eight nieces and one nephew would hear the proud stories about their Uncle Dale. Now, their children are also learning about the valor of the two Hansens on Okinawa over sixty years ago.

The Marines did not forget Private Hansen either. In 1956, when they transformed central island Kin Airfield on Okinawa into a base, they named it Camp Hansen as a memorial to the fallen private. Camp Hansen is the second-northernmost major Marine installation on the island, one of ten Marine camps comprising Marine Corps Base Camp Smedley D. Butler, named after another cherished Medal of Honor recipient. Camp Hansen is the Central Training Area for the Marines on Okinawa.

Driving through or visiting Wisner would give the impression that Dale's heroism has been forgotten. Except for his well-kept grave in Wisner Cemetery, there is no public monument or town hall memorial. Appearances can be deceiving. In fact, as is the case at Leo High School in Chicago, every student who attends Wisner-Pilger High School is likely familiar with the hometown Medal of Honor recipient.

More than twenty years had passed since the fight at Wana-Dakeshi Ridge, but Dale Hansen remained in the memory and traditions of the Marines, as well as in his hometown. The Marines commissioned a tribute and presented a memorial display to the city of Wisner in 1967. Since then, the oil painting of Private Hansen in uniform wearing the Medal of Honor, a brass plaque describing his heroism, and a copy of his Citation have been kept on display at Wisner-Pilger High School, *Home of the Gators.* The Private Hansen display is near the front entrance of the high school, in the hallway outside the school office, in view of the approximately 270 students from grades 7-12 on their way to the cafeteria. The community welcomes people to visit the display whenever the school is open. [50]

The Nebraska Hall of Fame was established in 1961 to officially recognize prominent Nebraskans. [51] The Hall of Fame honors people (1) who were born in Nebraska, (2) who gained prominence while living in Nebraska, or (3) who lived in Nebraska and whose residence in Nebraska was an important influence on their lives and contributed to their greatness. Busts of inductees sit in niches or on pedestals in a hall off the Nebraska State Capitol Building's Rotunda in Lincoln.

One of the notables was William Frederick "Buffalo Bill" Cody who, over time, lived in the state for an aggregate of about five years. "Buffalo Bill" received the Medal of Honor in 1872 for gallantry as a civilian scouting for the 5th Calvary at Fort McPherson, Nebraska. A congressional ruling in 1917 resulted in the revocation of his Medal shortly after his death, because he had been a civilian when he earned it. The Army returned his name to the Medal of Honor rolls in 1989.

Nebraska Legislative Bill #1212 passed August 25, 1969, declaring that all Nebraskans who received the Medal of Honor were to be inducted into the State's Hall of Fame. The names of each Nebraskan recipient were to be inscribed on an appropriate plaque. The Medal recipients were "selected" on November 3, 1973, and the plaque was dedicated May 5, 1974. Dale Hansen's family was at the capitol for the dedication.

Twenty Medals of Honor are accredited to Nebraska. Eight other recipients were born in Nebraska, but their awards were accredited to other states, because they had either moved or enlisted outside of Nebraska. Besides Dale's, plaques for five other Marines are displayed in the Hall: James Meredith, (aka: Patrick F. Ford, Jr., Spanish-American War), Harold William Bauer (World War II), Edward Gomez (Korean War), Ronald L. Coker and Miguel Keith (Vietnam).

The names of John Peter Fardy and Dale Merlin Hansen are no longer included in the list of forgotten Marine Medal recipients. Their heroism is a cherished memory in their hometowns.

CHAPTER 19
Self-Inflicted Death Before Dishonor

"You want courage—
I'll show you courage you can't understand." [1]

Bruce Springsteen
"Nothing Man"

Corporal John P. Fardy was never on an academic honor roll during his school years. Perhaps his teachers and classmates would not have expected him to at some point demonstrate valor under rigorous conditions. His Marine instructors at the Recruit Depot, however, likely had a sense of it as soon as he stepped onto the drill field.

A certain amount of pride is instilled in an individual who completes Marine recruit training. Rooted in the Corps' history, traditions, and values of *honor, courage,* and *commitment,* that pride begins to emerge as a recruit learns more about the service branch he has entered. By the time the recruits march in front of the Recruit Depot dignitaries' observation deck during graduation ceremonies, their pride is more than evident.

For most men and women who serve with an eagle, globe, and anchor emblem on their collars, the sense of pride for being in a Marine uniform will continue through their service and beyond. To have served with honor, especially on a battlefield, has an impact across a lifetime, even following discharge from the Corps. Sometimes the pride can be tarnished by life events, but it never completely fades, no matter how many years have passed since the Marine marched in formation for the last time. Should it happen, the loss of honor can be devastating and demoralizing for a Marine. What living with honor, courage, and commitment means to a Medal of Honor recipient, as well as all Marines, can be seen in something as simple as a tattoo.

His heroic actions culminated on the night of October 24, 1942, and into the next morning. Comrades would remember later that Sergeant John Basilone kept his machine gun firing through three days and nights of enemy assaults against a ridge on Guadalcanal. He went without sleep, rest of any sort, or relief. After the island and Henderson Field were secured, Sergeant Basilone was returned to the States to promote a war-bond campaign. Much was made of the tattoo on his left arm, *Death Before Dishonor*.

Having requested return to his unit, Gunnery Sergeant Basilone was with the 5th Marines on D-Day, February 19, 1945, for the landing on Iwo Jima at Red Beach 2. He refused to bunch up or hesitate in the black volcanic sands on the beach as the landing forces stalled under the withering Japanese fire. He encouraged and cajoled his unit forward and pushed them off the beach. Alone, he charged an enemy blockhouse and destroyed it and its occupants. As he pressed the assault with his platoon, an artillery shell exploded at his feet at 10:45 AM, killing him and four other Marines. Gunnery Sergeant John Basilone was 28-years-old.

On a different island, in an earlier battle, Private First Class Richard Beatty Anderson charged onto Roi Island at noon, February 1, 1944. Three hours later, the company had made its way to the center of Roi airfield, about two-thirds of the way across the island.

In the ongoing battle, Private First Class Anderson took cover in a fifteen-foot-deep crater with other Marines. He attempted to throw an armed grenade out of the crater over his shoulder, but the explosive rolled back towards him. Instead of vacating the hole or yelling at the others to do so, putting them at risk of enemy fire, Private First Class Anderson threw his body over the grenade. He cradled it in his groin, curled around it, and shielded the others from the explosion. The detonation was contained, but Private First Class Anderson was grievously wounded. Both of his hands were blown off, as were parts of his abdomen, chest, and face. He clung to life long enough for a corpsman to administer morphine and plasma and to be evacuated to the beach to be treated by surgeons. He was taken aboard the USS *Callaway* where he died of his wounds.

Private First Class Richard B. Anderson, 22-years-old, had died in his first day of combat. Those who treated him would remember the tattoo on his arm declaring *Death Before Dishonor*.

Death Before Dishonor. Another way to say this is *Life With Honor.*

There can be no question that the Medal of Honor recipients acted with honor, and that the respect and admiration and tributes extended to them afterwards had been rightfully earned.

Like all the recipients, John Lucian Smith had earned his Medal. A life lived with honor was important to him. Initially, when little information was readily available about his family and childhood, and whether he had been remembered and acknowledged in his hometown could not be determined, his name was added to the list of the forgotten. And a question emerged. Was there no tribute to him because of the manner in which he had died?

John was born December 26, 1914, in Lexington, Oklahoma, the day after Christmas and seven years after Oklahoma had entered statehood. His was a small hometown of fewer than 1000 souls, sitting on less than 1.5 square miles of Oklahoma land. Lexington is in the center of the state, off the main highway, thirty-five miles south of Oklahoma City. The Canadian River, the largest tributary of the Arkansas River, runs past the town on its western side. The North Canadian River flooded for three days when Johnny was eight-years-old, in October 1923, and the floodwaters caused extensive damage in downtown Oklahoma City.

As described earlier in the story of Ken Worley, experiencing early personal challenges is a background factor identified in the Medal recipients' childhoods that influenced both the development of a strong personal character and later heroically brave actions. This was true for John L. Smith, who learned early to face adversity while growing up in Lexington.

The possibility of flooding was just one of the challenges of growing up in Lexington, many of them related to weather. The region is like a tornado alley, experiencing above-average numbers of storms violent enough to erase towns from the map and lives from the census. Record-setting storms devastated the state when John was a boy. He was six-years-old when the third deadliest tornado in Oklahoma history, an F4, hit well northeast of his hometown on May 2, 1920, destroyed the tiny town of Peggs, and killed seventy-one "Sooners." Ten years later, on April 25, 1930, another F4 tornado struck down at Bethany west of Oklahoma City, killing twenty-three people, the ninth deadliest tornado in the state's history. [2]

As Johnnny neared his fifteenth birthday, the nation plunged into a deep economic depression. The following year began a decade of blizzards, freezing and baking temperatures, droughts, floods, tornadoes, hail storms and dirt storms, and static electricity disruptions from all the blowing particles.

As one unusually hot summer followed after another, the land dried out. Droughts ensued, the winds came, and the red Oklahoma soil mixed with the black dust of Kansas, and the gray dust from Colorado and New Mexico and filled the atmosphere with dark, fearful clouds. Families lost their farms and many Oklahomans migrated west looking for work in what became known as the Dust Bowl years.

The severe dust storms that could reduce visibility to just a few feet had names like *Black Bizzard* and *Black Roller*. Destructive enough to topple hundreds of homes, over 500,000 residents of the Great Plains states were left homeless. Alcohol intoxication, "mental breakdowns," and despair descended upon many of the small towns. So did resilience, strength, and humor.

The challenges John faced were not just about the Oklahoma weather. He also demonstrated an early pattern of putting himself into challenging situations in which brave actions were a likely eventuality. Saying that men like John found themselves in circumstances in which heroic actions were elicited, in part misses an important point. All the Medal recipients repetitively across their lifetimes deliberately placed themselves into challenging and risk-filled situations. They did not just happen to be present when circumstances demanded their actions. If life did not challenge them enough, they generated their own challenges. It is as if individuals with such personality characteristics design their own early endurance tests.

Of the 181 recipients researched from the three wars, at least twenty-six participated in sports requiring individual contests like boxing and wrestling. Seventeen went beyond academic and athletic challenges while in school by joining military organizations like ROTC and PLC. Wesley Lee Fox was early on intrigued by the mystique and challenge of the Marines, and Bruce Wayne Carter had wanted to be a Marine since early in his childhood. Ultimately, putting themselves into challenging situations was demonstrated by the forty-two who dropped out of school to join the Marines as well as by the additional thirty-three who enlisted right after graduating from either high school or college.

That this pattern of seeking challenges was a part of John's life became clearer when Volume 1, Number 1, of *The Barker* was published in July-September 2007. The Lexington High School Alumni Association staff planned to feature a section called *Big Dog* to acknowledge a notable alumnus in each issue of their official newsletter. Their first alumni profile was of John L. Smith and new information about his early family life came to light. [3]

Robert Owen Smith was a rural-mail carrier who delivered the mail by horse and buggy and sometimes by mule-drawn mail cart. [4,5] Civic-minded, he was also a school board member. Being of service and having a job to do were important to him. Robert married Pearl Gertrude Fennel and the couple had three sons. When Robert went to work in a postal uniform, including a cap, he sometimes put one or other of the boys on the cart. His eldest son, Robert Owen Jr., was born in 1905, when Owen was 34-years and Pearl 24-years-old. The second son, Haskell, followed the next year. The eight-year gap in age between Haskell and Johnny meant that the youngest Smith boy was on his own as he passed through the Lexington school system. [6]

When John was born, the family was living in a rented house called "Hawk's Place" on the edge of town. By the time of the 1930 U.S. Census, Robert had moved the family to a house he had bought closer to the center of town. [7]

John's two older brothers would remain in Norman and Oklahoma City, working and raising their families. Classmates later remembered the youngest Smith boy as popular and a good student at Lexington High School. He was also a natural athlete. He played football with the Bulldogs, though he had yet to reach his full size. His competitiveness and drive for excellence were evident when he played tennis or golf. He would be remembered later for playing eighteen holes with a zero handicap.

John also had a penchant for numbers, strategy, thinking quickly, and putting on a "poker face." His skill and enjoyment in card playing might have been noted as an extracurricular activity for him. "Smitty," as many across his lifetime liked to call him, graduated from Lexington High in 1932 and wasted little time in getting on with life. His travels had begun.

John went sixteen miles up Route 77 to Norman and joined 4879 other students at the University of Oklahoma (OU) in 1932. He intended to be a businessman. He chose accounting for his major, and would pass the state certified public accountants' examination. Participating in the Army Reserve Officer Training Corps (ROTC), his leadership skills became evident as he rose to the rank of ROTC Cadet Lieutenant. Intramural football, handball, and tennis provided outlets for his athleticism. [8] He likely continued playing cards with friends and classmates.

For two days, April 10-11, 1935, a dust storm reduced visibility to less than two blocks on the Norman OU campus and covered almost all of Oklahoma. As John's junior year neared its end and another week of classes was to begin, twenty of the worst Black Blizzards hit the Prairie States on April 14, 1935. The giant, thick dust storm filled the afternoon horizon over the panhandle and northwest region. The midday midnight darkness triggered visions of the world's end. Remembered by many as the worst day of the 1930s, "Black Sunday" inspired an Associated Press reporter to coin the term "dust bowl."

Besides accounting, John L. Smith was learning to be undaunted by black clouds, choking dust, poor visibility, and airborne particles flying in his face. Getting where he was going was to be determined by his character, not by "blackness" or the uncertainty of survival.

Despite 1936 being one of the harshest Dust Bowl years, significant things happened on the OU campus. The Museum of Art, originally located in Jacobson Hall, was founded, opening with over 2,500 items on display. Jessie Lone Clarkson Gilkey, the girls' glee club director, penned the "OU Chant," the loyalty song that continues to resonate at most major OU events. And John L. Smith graduated in May, with a degree in Business Administration.

John's OU alumni status is one reason he was included on the list of the thirty-four forgotten Medal recipients. Although the OU Army ROTC official history is proud to claim John as one of its own, the University does not appear to give the Marine much acclaim. This might be related to OU's view of what makes a person's life honorable. OU does count many of its former students as prominent local and national notables. According to the List of University of Oklahoma People, the notables include sixty-three athletes, twenty-two lawyers, judges, justices and politicians, eighteen entertainers and Hollywood actors like James Garner and Ed Harris, and twenty-two "others," including a shuttle astronaut, an Apollo 13 astronaut, and a Miss America. [9] Another Web site, Ranker.com, does list John L. Smith as 176th of 348 notable OU graduates. [10]

Being a notable OU graduate was not much on John's mind in 1936. Maybe there was not much work in accounting during the Depression years, or maybe that career was too "safe" for someone like John. After graduation, he was appointed a second lieutenant in the Army Field Artillery. His ease with numbers now turned to figuring ground coordinates, distances and ranges to targets, bracketing of targets, lethal radius of artillery rounds, and firing for effect. Second Lieutenant Smith had a yearning for more adventure and risk than he found in the Army. He resigned his commission in July, accepting a second lieutenant's commission in the Marine Corps. [11] Standing tall at six foot, with hazel eyes, Second Lieutenant Smith looked the part of a Marine officer.

Record heat hit Oklahoma in July and August 1936, producing the highest temperatures ever recorded officially in Oklahoma. Three northern towns reported 120 degrees Fahrenheit and Oklahoma City recorded its all-time high temperature, 113 degrees Fahrenheit, on August 11. Having acclimated to seething climates, Second Lieutenant Smith left this kind of heat behind him, better prepared for other kinds of extremes.

After attending the Marine Basic School at Marine Barracks, Navy Yard, Philadelphia, Pennsylvania, Second Lieutenant Smith fulfilled his two-year field artillery commitment in duty assignments at Quantico, Virginia, Washington, D.C., and Parris Island, South Carolina. By 1938 he had earned a promotion to first lieutenant and a transfer to be trained in a much-desired Military Occupational Specialty. First Lieutenant Smith was transferred to Pensacola Naval Air Station in July 1938, to begin flight training, transitioning from accounting to artillery to firing for effect to aviation, airspeed, and angles of attack. He graduated the following July, earning his aviator wings and the designation of Naval Aviator, and was initially assigned to a dive-bomber squadron. Americans wondered if they could stay out of the war that was realigning the borders between European countries.

Like the Black Sunday dust storm, the dark cloud of war loomed to the west. The Japanese had begun their incursion onto the Chinese mainland in July 1937. Chiang Kai-shek had completed the Burma Road late in 1938, linking southwest China to the Bay of Bengal to keep supplies coming into China. CAMCO had contracted with Generalissimo Chiang to provide air protection over the Burma Road. And, within two years of First Lieutenant Smith pinning on his aviator wings, American pilots, having hired on as air commandos were going to be on ships headed to Kunming, China.

By January 1941, civilian contractors had begun constructing a military base and airstrip on Wake, two thousand miles to the west of Pearl Harbor. Wake Island, Midway, and Hawaii formed a defensive triangle in the Pacific between Japan and the United States. The strategic importance of tiny Wake was that, of the islands in the defensive triangle, it was the closest U.S. possession to mainland Japan. It was primarily viewed as an advanced listening post in the defensive stance against Japan.

Like other Pacific islands, the three small islands comprising the 2.5 square miles of Wake are the remnants of the rim of an ancient, extinct underwater volcano. Twenty miles of coastline, white rock and sand, were fringed by a coral reef. Inland, the narrow flat island is covered with short green scrub, thick brush, and wiry vegetation. A single road with its two bridges connected the three uninhabited sections and Pan Am's civilian airfield.

Intelligence briefings kept secret information circulating among the Navy and Marine pilots. With thoughts of Wake Island and Midway kept to himself, First Lieutenant Smith returned to Lexington in April 1941. His mother, Pearl, had died on the 17th. Loaded down with grief, the approach of war, the likelihood of engaging experienced enemy pilots in aircraft reputed to be superior to the dive-bomber he flew, he returned to the east coast with much to ponder. First Lieutenant Smith would have to force darker aspects of his life into a corner of his mind in order to focus his concentration on flying.

In late spring 1941, John went to an Officer's Club party in Norfolk, Virginia. [12] Louise Maddox Outland, a Norfolk native, was there. Louise was a true Virginian. Her father was a Virginia House Delegate and her family was prominent in the community. Her sister, Jean, was married to Walter P. Chrysler, Jr., the son of the automobile designer and founder of the Chrysler Corporation. In 1933, Louise had begun her studies with the Class of 1937 at the College of William and Mary in Williamsburg, about forty-five miles and an hour's drive from home. When John met her at the Officer's Club, Louise, 24-years-old, was working on her master's degree at Old Dominion University. [13]

Both John and Louise were ambitious and driven to excel in life. She was engaging and well read and interesting in conversations. She easily made friends wherever she was—a nice complement to John's somewhat quiet and inward nature. They married at her parents' Norfolk home at 122 Hardy Avenue a few months after meeting at the Officer's Club party. As quick as their courtship was, three years passed before they could start their family.

In August 1941, 525 military men were garrisoned to Wake; 240 Marines provided security against what seemed a probable attack by Japanese forces. They began digging trenches, foxholes, and sandbagged gun emplacements, and positioning eighteen artillery pieces. By December, Wake had 3-inch antiaircraft batteries, 5-inch seacoast artillery batteries, .30 and .50 caliber machine-gun batteries, and six 60-inch searchlights posed seaward. There were not enough Marines yet on the islands to man all the positions. Shortly, Wake and its Marine defenders were going to earn the reputation as the *Alamo of the South Pacific.*

Days before the December 7 attack at Pearl Harbor, twelve Marine pilots attached to Fighting Squadron 211 ferried aging F4F *Wildcat* fighters onto Wake Island. The Japanese attack on Wake began the day following the surprise attacks on Hawaii and Midway. America had declared war upon the Imperial Empire, and the Marines waited for the attack that was certain to come. When it was unleashed just before noon on December 8, the attack came first from aerial bombardments.

Twenty-seven Japanese bombers flew out of dark rain clouds, mist, and fog over the island and scoured Wake with their bombs. Eight Marine fighters sat in a row on the flight line waiting to be fueled. In the attack, seven of them were destroyed, a couple with their pilots aboard. In the seven-minute raid, forty-five Marines and civilians were killed or wounded. Thirty-two of them were airmen. The enemy planes returned for three straight days of bombardment.

The Marines under siege on Wake held on for thirteen days. During those days, Captain Henry "Hammering Hank" Talmage Elrod earned the first Medal of Honor among the Marine WWII aviators. The Marines named their camp on Espiritu Santo and the main road to the Officer Candidate School at Quantico in his memory. On May 12, 1984, the Navy launched the USS *Elrod*, FFG-55, a guided missile frigate, with his name on the hull. The University of Georgia, where Henry had lettered on the 1932 *Bulldog* football team, at the same time Smitty was attending OU, made sure the Marine aviator was remembered. On November 9, 2002, an impressive red and black granite monument to Henry T. Elrod and twenty other *Bulldog* athletes who have died in wars was dedicated on the Georgia campus. At the top of the monument are engraved the words: Those Who Served in Honored Glory Rest Lest we Forget. [14]

Lest we Forget is the underlying purpose in all the memorials, monuments, and tributes to the Marine Medal of Honor recipients. *Lest we Forget* is the reason to ensure that any recipients remaining on the list of The Forgotten Thirty-Four are remembered in fitting ways.

After December 7, 1941, and before Captain Elrod earned his Medal of Honor on December 23, the USS *Saratoga* left San Diego and arrived near Hawaii on December 14. The USS *Tangier*, a sea plane tender, left from Pearl Harbor as both joined a task force sent to relieve the Marine garrison at Wake Island and reinforce the depleted Fighting Squadron 211. The dive-bomber squadron to which First Lieutenant Smith was assigned was enroute to Wake.

On December 17, 1941, Scout Bombing Squadron VMSB-231 in their aging two-man, Vought SB2U-3 *Vindicator* dive-bombers flew from Hawaii to Midway. Wake fell to the enemy on December 23 before the relief force could arrive, and the dive-bomber squadron was redirected to Midway, one of the islands the Japanese intended to claim as their own. The defense of the island and its airfield was vital.

In his first few months on Midway, First Lieutenant Smith quickly demonstrated his flying skills. Commanders saw the potential in his flying skills, although his officer performance evaluations had often posed questions about his "presence of mind." He was transferred from dive-bombers to the fighter squadron and promoted to the rank of captain. Captain Smith, 27-years-old, was called back to Pearl Harbor in April and ordered to organize a new fighter squadron, as preparations were underway to recapture Guadalcanal from the enemy.

In one month's time, he turned a group of fledgling student aviators into pilots as he prepared to take men into aerial combat. Captain Smith was an exacting taskmaster who expected discipline and excellence from his pilots and ground crew. He had gained a deep respect for Japanese pilots and their Zeros while flying against them on Midway, and understood what his squadron would face once in combat.

As Lieutenant Colonel Chambers would later do with a battalion of infantrymen, he trained the aviators thoroughly and relentlessly. Smitty would also be remembered as sometimes moody and demanding. Fellow aviators who served with him viewed him as tough and abrasive. He had the kind of determination that made it nearly impossible to steer him away from a course he determined to be set. Overcoming life challenges had given him a deep confidence in himself and fueled an evident ambition to be the best at whatever he did. [15] Enemy pilots were going to discover this in the Solomon Islands.

Marine Fighter Squadron 223 (VMF-223) was commissioned on May 1, 1942, at Marine Corps Air Station Ewa, Oahu, Hawaii. Captain Smith's Squadron was first called the "Rainbow" Squadron. A year later, after they had distinguished themselves in battles, and when Captain Smith had more of a say in what the squadron would be called, its nickname was changed to the "Bulldogs" in May 1943. VMF-223 remains so named today. Classmates and alumni from Lexington High School saw in this designation their motto "Once a Bulldog...always a Bulldog."

Keeping his focus on what was ahead for his squadron in the Solomons would have been at times challenging for Captain Smith. News from home and thoughts for Louise could be worrisome. An F4 tornado, the fifth deadliest in Oklahoma history, struck Pryor, northwest of Peggs, and killed fifty-two on April 27, 1942. Less than two months later, on June 12, 1942, thirty-five Sooners were killed when the seventh deadliest F4 tornado hit Oklahoma City. Captain Smith had to let the Sooners deal with the devastation in their state as they had always done. In just two months, he would be flying his own Grumman F4F *Wildcat* into formations of Japanese fighters; as devastating to them as the F4 storms so familiar to him in Oklahoma.

The Battle for Midway began when the Japanese fleet was observed approaching on June 3, 1942, intent on invading Midway and capturing the airfield. The next morning, Squadron Commander Major Henderson, with Captain Richard Eugene Fleming on his wing in a new SBD-2, led VMSB-241 in an attack against the Japanese aircraft carriers and battleships. Major Henderson was killed and Captain Fleming assumed command of the division as the squadron unsuccessfully attempted to sink the carrier *Hiryu*. By the time he was able to return to Midway, enemy fire had hit his *Dauntless* 171 times. He had two minor wounds. Captain Fleming returned to the air that afternoon in a *Vindicator*, in a flight that turned out to be uneventful. [16] On the morning of June 5, Captain Fleming led VMSB-241's second division back into the fight to take on the heavy cruisers *Mogami* and *Mikuma* that had collided in the night near Midway. Historical accounts vary as to what happened, but those who survived Midway have their version.

Early in the engagement, in a screaming dive on the cruiser *Mikuma* that would be remembered by survivors of both sides in the war as an unquestionable act of bravery, Captain Fleming released his bomb, scoring a hit on the ship. His plane was pierced by antiaircraft fire from the cruiser and burst into flames. Rather than pulling out of the dive, Captain Richard Fleming, 24-years-old, flew the *Vindicator* directly into the enemy cruiser. The SB2U-3 hit the after-turret of the ship, putting it out of action, and caused a fire on the starboard side of the ship. The fire triggered an explosion in the engine room that crippled the ship and left it a target for further VMSB-241 bomb runs. The *Mikuma* sank on the afternoon of June 6. [17]

Captain Richard Fleming was the second Marine aviator to earn a Medal of Honor in WWII. On June 16, 1943, the Navy launched the

Destroyer Escort-32 with his name on the hull. The South St. Paul Airport is named in his honor, as is Squadron Detachment #410 at the University of St. Thomas.

Following Wake and Midway, Marine pilots understood the risk of dying in the cockpit of an airplane.

Guadalcanal, ninety by twenty-five miles in size, is the largest island in the southern end of the Solomon Islands chain in the South Pacific. Seeming to rise out of the sea when seen from a distance, a mountain range runs along the length of the island, and divides it into northern and southern sides. At the center, the Haiacha ridgeline includes 7,713-foot Mount Popomaneseu and Mount Makarakomburu that reaches an elevation of 8,028 feet. A few narrow trails and foot-paths provided the only passage across the mountain range.

A rugged place, plush green, covered by extremely dense jungle growth, Guadalcanal's interior seemed impassible. The dense vegetation included groves of bananas, coconuts, and pineapples. Coconut palms and cocoa trees gave little shade to the coral beaches. Colonists had earlier come to Guadalcanal with the hopes of harvesting rubber and gold. The small hills on the north side of the island were covered by Kanai grass. Movement through the blades of tough grass sliced through clothing, cut into skin, and left bloody red welts.

Most of the island's flat land is on the northeast side. That is where the Japanese had scraped out the beginnings of an airfield on a plantation at Lunga Point, east of the Lunga and Matanikau Rivers. Savoy and Tulagi Islands were in sight across the sound. Barely inhabited by small numbers of natives, a few dirt roads provided passage across the flat areas. The high rainfall coming from the mountain range often produced a rain shadow over the dryer plains of North Guadalcanal, turning roads to shin-high muddy ruts during the rains, engulfing trucks up to their axles. Hiking turned to slogging.

On Sunday morning, August 2, 1942, with three hours notice and no time to send goodbyes, Captain Smith and his twenty VMF-223 pilots left Marine Corps Air Station Ewa, Oahu, Hawaii on the transport

William Ward Burroughs. Their nineteen Grumman F4F *Wildcat* fighter planes, along with twelve dive-bombers of VMSB-232 traveled aboard the small escort carrier USS *Long Island* (CVE 1). The impact of Wake and Midway and what was ahead in the fight to wrench an island from the grasp of the Japanese was as much on the minds of families back home as it was in the plans being briefed by the VMF-223 pilots. Louise traveled to Lexington to stay with Captain Smith's family for a short while.

The Marine's amphibious assault hit the Guadalcanal beaches on August 7. They captured the nearly completed enemy airstrip on August 8, and then fought to finish and hold the airfield. After two weeks at sea, in the morning of August 20, the two squadrons launched from the carrier 190 miles from Guadalcanal, code-named *Cactus*, and landed on unfinished Henderson Field in the late afternoon, two weeks after the Marines had first taken the airfield from the Japanese. The morale of the Marines dug in on the island improved immeasurably.

The first Marine fighter squadron to arrive in the Solomons, Captain Smith and the other pilots of the "Cactus Air Force" were going to prove themselves in combat operations against experienced enemy fighters over Guadalcanal. In the conquest of Chinese territory and Pacific islands, the Japanese pilots had earned the reputation of being skilled, intrepid warriors. That being true, reputation and reality are sometimes at odds with each other. Captain Smith would later acknowledge, "...they were just as scared of us as we were of them." [18]

That night, Marines on the ground fought the battle at Tenaru River sandbar a mile and a half from Henderson Field.

The next day around noon Captain Smith patrolled the air with three other *Wildcats*. Six enemy aircraft approached Guadalcanal. His mouth went dry, his heart was pounding, and his eyes squinted as he opened up with his six .50 caliber wing-mounted machine guns. The belly of the enemy plane split open and belched thick black smoke. Captain Smith had shot down his first Mitsubishi Type "O" Carrier Fighter, later called Zeros or "Zekes."

Four F4Fs were out of the fight after the first day of action. His own *Wildcat* was grounded for eight days for repairs. VMF-223 would be slowly depleted of aircraft and pilots as the squadron remained active on Guadalcanal into October. Six of the original Fighting 223 pilots would be seriously wounded and taken out of action.

Second Lieutenant Erlwood R. Bailey was the first of Captain Smith's pilots to die in the skies over Guadalcanal, on August 24. Replacement pilot Second Lieutenant Lawrence C. Taylor also died that day. Second Lieutenant Bailey had been married in Honolulu the day before the squadron left for the Solomons. What does a squadron commander write to console a one-day bride waiting for her young husband to return home from war? Second Lieutenant Roy A. Corry, who had flown at Midway, died August 26.

A hilltop, rickety, wooden *Pagoda* at Henderson Field served as headquarters for the Cactus Air Force throughout the first months of air operations on Guadalcanal. A tent served as their Ready Room for flight briefings and debriefings. Pilots share an enthusiasm for debriefing air missions and fighting tactics. Until comrades begin to die. Within a few days of landing on Guadalcanal, the chatter was dimmed. Trying to lock away the war into one of those corners of the mind, the crews sat around in front of their tents in their pajamas at night.

Some nights they listened to Japanese radio broadcasts playing songs from back home, trying to laugh off the propaganda "Tokyo Rose" spewed in her sultry voice, warning of their impending annihilation having been abandoned by the Navy. They listened to a few old phonograph records and bantered with each other. They recalled the women of Honolulu and the lives that waited for them back in the States.

The unthinking mention of a pilot killed in action brought silent pause. All in the squadron would bring home memories of standing around footlockers at the death of friends, as personal effects were packed away. The loss of a comrade was not the best thing to have on one's mind when retiring for the night, with battles blazing on nearby ridges and offshore Navy engagements seeming to present distant fireworks displays. A little sake or whiskey loosened tight nerves and permitted a few hours of sleep. [19, 20]

The air defense over Guadalcanal slipped into a routine. The aviators slept in mud-floored tents on grassy high ground above their nearby aircraft and sometimes ankle deep muddy parking ramps and taxiways. They bathed in the Lunga River, fighting off flies and wary of leeches and crocodiles.

The time between dawn and sunset was about eleven and a half hours. Patrolling the skies during the daylight hours, the squadron developed its own routine as the fight for the island continued. Captain Smith launched the early four-plane fighter patrol at 0545, expecting it to return by 0830. The second patrol left the airstrip at 1400, remaining airborne until 1830.

Enemy planes were not the only airborne danger to Captain Smith's pilots. Hordes of malaria-infested and dengue-infested mosquitoes patrolled Guadalcanal. After landing, the Marines on the island fought off malaria, dysentery, dry rot, and dengue fever as well as the attacks of the Japanese. The headaches, abdominal pains, vomiting, nosebleeds, and lethargy that came from a dengue infection meant an aviator would be grounded from flights for a day or two. An underground sick bay was established for the sick and wounded.

Nine-point-five degrees south of the equator, 600 miles east of New Guinea, the climate on tropical Guadalcanal could be severe, stifling hot and humid. During the months VMF-223 was flying missions, the weather was the island's most bearable, moderated by the southeast trade winds. The average daytime temperature was 83 degrees; nights were cooler, averaging about 73 degrees.

The quality of aircrew meals between missions deteriorated as the air campaign continued. The chicken, steak, and hot stores from supply ships quickly dwindled when the Navy pulled away from the island. Breakfast, lunch and dinner soon became canned meat. When that was gone, the air and ground crews subsisted on rations captured from the Japanese: canned snails, hardtack, rice, after the worms were picked out, and moldy oatmeal.

Although coconuts were plentiful, the aircrews quickly discovered that eating them could cause diarrhea: not a pleasant in-flight event.

Candy bars and cigarette cartons were sometimes delivered by torpedo plane from a nearby carrier, and carefully rationed into 160 portions. The conditions at Henderson Airfield eventually caused the ground crews to take on an emaciated look.

Known to be single-minded, dedicated to the mission, and having experienced the extremes of drought, heat, tornadoes, and dust storms in Oklahoma, Captain Smith remained resolute despite the extremes of life on Guadalcanal. By the time he had been on the island for only eight days, he had shot down four more enemy aircraft, becoming one of the first Marine Aces in the war.

On Sunday, August 30, 1942, his most remarkable day of flying, Captain Smith bested two enemy pilots in less than five minutes in an air battle over Iron Bottom Sound. In one head-on fight, both planes firing machine guns and neither giving way to the other, tearing past each other at 500 knots, a 20-mm shell ripped through his wind screen and past his face. Smitty blew the Zero out of the sky just before the two fighters might have collided, with less than fifteen feet separating them. He watched the Zero go into its fatal dive, the cockpit aflame, and the enemy pilot's hair "burning like a torch."

By the end of the day's engagement, Captain Smith had four confirmed kills in fifteen minutes, bringing his total to nine, making him the leading Marine Ace at the time. His aviators knocked fourteen of twenty-two Zeros out of the sky.

As well as the *Wildcats* were fighting, they were also being riddled by the Zeros' dual 20-mm cannons and two .30-caliber machine guns. By nightfall of August 30, fourteen VMF-223 *Wildcats* had been downed, destroyed, or rendered out of action. Ten planes remained in the "Rainbow" squadron, five of them operational aircraft.

Among the brave, competition is an aspect of friendship and affiliation.

VMF-224 arrived on Guadalcanal August 30, under the command of Captain Robert E. Galer. Bob had been an engineering major at the University of Washington, one year behind Greg Boyington. He and Greg had entered the Cadet program together from Seattle and remained long-time friends. The pilots of VMF-223 and VMF-224 began flying missions together that afternoon. Promoted, Major Galer would accumulate fourteen victories over the Solomons, earn a Medal of Honor, and eventually retire from the Marines as a brigadier general.

While the squadrons and their commanders might have competed for the highest number of air victories, the bonds formed in combat are strong. Major Galer, an Ace, was married between overseas tours. Lieutenant Colonel Smith was his best man. [21]

The annual rainfall on the island was nearly eighty inches with a slight decline in moisture between May and September. The mountain range caught the trade winds and generated the high rainfall in the interior. A rain shadow often dropped over Henderson. The number of Captain Smith's air victories continued to accumulate through September, in spite of the rainy days when VMF-223 saw little air-to-air combat.

"Down time" on the island was not necessarily restful. Battles raged on the airfield perimeters. And there were letters to write—to home and to families he had never known. These letters were the result of a grim fact: his pilots continued dying. Second Lieutenant Zenneth A. Pond died on September 10 and replacement pilot Second Lieutenant Richard A. Haring on September 13. The strain under which his men were operating showed on the squadron commander's face.

Henderson Field was under frequent bombardment from land, air and sea. Bomb and shell craters collected rainwater. The burning wreckage of *Wildcats* and scout-bombers sometimes lit up the runways after nighttime Japanese air attacks. The Japanese wanted Henderson Field back and the Marines prepared for an attack they knew was coming.

After shooting down his tenth enemy aircraft, Captain Smith wrote home to Louise on September 12, that he had "been bombed almost every day since I've been here... We are shelled or bombed nearly every night. Am getting so used to it that I wake up, smoke a cigaret[te] and go back to sleep again." [22]

A letter to Louise on October 5 reflects the mix of thoughts that challenged the squadron commander's evenings. "...One thing I do know is that I am going out of here alive and well. ...Have lost the best I started out with. ...would have rather it had been me instead of him. Hope I can see his family when I get back and tell them what a swell Marine he was. ...Really no justice in war, or he certainly would have gotten through. ...I am proud to get it [the Navy Cross], except that they think that it is good payment for seeing young pilots who are sharing my tent go down in flames day after day. I don't mind saying that I am sick of the whole mess." [23]

A high, grass-covered ridge of coral rock protected the airfield's south perimeter. About 1,000 yards from the runway, the ridge radiated a mile south away from the airfield. Marine Raiders were dug in along the ridge in defense of the squadron operations. On September 11, enemy bombers peppered the ridge. A Japanese naval bombardment of the ridge began at 10:00 PM. About a half-hour later, mortars and machine guns opened up from the jungle, and the enemy attacked the Marine line at the lagoon. An enemy brigade of over 3000 soldiers advanced towards the airfield.

The outnumbered Marine line, at times cut off from each other, at times breached, and pushed back towards Henderson, held the ridge during three nights of engagements. The final attack began at nightfall, just before 7:00 PM on September 13. Two hours later an intense mortar barrage pummeled the ridge and at 10:00 PM the enemy brigade surged forward. Thirty-four Raiders died during the three days of fighting on the ridge and 129 were wounded. Afterwards, Marines referred to the site as Edson's Ridge or Bloody Ridge. Colonel Merritt Austin Edson and Major Kenneth D. Bailey were both awarded a Medal of Honor for their leadership on the ridge.

In late September, a five-day battle ensued about 8,000 yards west of Henderson Field on the Matanikau River. Three U.S. Marine companies under the command of famed Lieutenant Colonel "Chesty" Puller were surrounded by Japanese forces, took heavy losses, and were evacuated under intense fire. There was good reason the aviators on Guadalcanal tended to wear pistols on their hips.

Again promoted, Major Smith took the remainder of VMF-223 to the air against a raid by Japanese bombers and fighters on October 2. Having shot down one Zero, two others slipped in behind him. Unable to maneuver out of their gun sights, the Zeros shot up Major Smith's *Wildcat*. With the floundering aircraft barely keeping flight, he forced the plane to make a landing in a clearing about six miles short of Henderson Field.

Major Smith hiked alone for two and a half hours through jungle and coconut grove, fording tangled jungle streams to the airstrip, alert for patrols of Japanese soldiers who roved crash sites for downed pilots. As he wrote in a letter three days later, he "...got back damn fast thru some pretty thick jungle." [24] Along the way he found the crash site of one of his young pilots downed earlier in a September 13 engagement. Second Lieutenant Noles "Scotty" McLennan had been just a few years out of Yale. His body was not recovered at the wreckage site.

The squadron commander led a patrol away from Henderson to search for Second Lieutenant Charles "Red" Kendrick's plane, downed during the day's air battle. When they found the plane tumbled over in a field, their companion, a year out of Harvard Law School, was in the cockpit, his finger still tight around the machine-gun trigger. They buried him beside the F4F-4, Tail Number 02110. [25, 26]

Second Lieutenant Willis S. Lees, III was also lost from the Fighting 223 that day. After lining up the two footlockers with the others, the pilots gathered quietly in front of their tents before trying to get some sleep. Only nine of the original twenty VMF-223 pilots were left. Eight planes were airworthy.

Admiral Chester Nimitz, Commander of the Pacific Fleet, sailed to Guadalcanal in early October on an inspection tour. In front of a small formation of war-weary Marines, the Admiral pinned a Navy Cross on Major Smith's chest.

The Ace flew into the air over Henderson Field for the last time on October 10, 1942. Before the *Wildcats* of VMF-223 returned to the airfield, they had shot nine more Japanese Zeros from the skies. The final tally for the squadron commander was nineteen air victories in fifty-four days. Under his able leadership, VMF-223 accounted for eighty-three enemy aircraft destroyed. At that time Major Smith's air victories placed him as the top Ace among Marines. By war's end, he would be listed as the sixth highest of the Marine Corps Aces.

As the squadron prepared to leave Guadalcanal, some of the Marine Raiders came by the Ready Tent to say goodbye. To show their appreciation for the air cover provided to them by the first squadron to join them in the fight, the Raiders presented Major Smith a cake iced with smooth, chocolate frosting and a tribute written in white confection. The exhausted and battle-worn remnant of VMF-223 departed from the island on October 12.

When they left Guadalcanal, Major John L. Smith, 27-years-old, and his remaining pilots carried the footlockers of their six lost companions aboard ship with them.

Early in the war, the nation needed to hear that the Japanese invaders, who were imagined to be fanatical and invincible, could be stopped and pushed back to their own island. It was an era before television, when citizens relied on radio broadcasts, movie matinee newsreels, magazines, newspapers, and personal appearances to acquaint themselves with celebrities and heroes. Then, weekly issues of *Life* Magazine, fifty-two a year, could be purchased every Monday at a newsstand for ten cents. For the most part in the years leading up to Pearl Harbor, movie stars, politicians, and athletes donned *Life's* cover. Periodically, a cover photo would be related to the war raging in Europe and America's preparation for possible entry into the conflict. In 1942, after the Pearl Harbor attack, twenty-seven *Life* cover stories brought some aspect of the war into America's homes. And in 1942, December 7, the first anniversary of the attack, fell on a Monday, when people would be looking at the latest *Life* issue.

Having arrived in San Francisco on October 17, 1942, like other of the nation's early war heroes, Major Smith was tasked to travel the country to promote and support the War Bond effort. He appeared on the Friday, November 13, 1942, KGLO-CBS radio "Kate Smith Hour." The broadcast took place before the University of North Carolina naval preflight cadets at Chapel Hill. The first Oklahoman to receive a Medal of Honor, he visited his Lexington hometown for a parade in his honor.

The accolades were nice in their way, but did not quell the realization that the war continued.

Major Smith was interviewed frequently about his aerial combat experiences. *Life* Magazine dispatched Richard Wilcox to go meet the Marine Ace in Norfolk, Virginia. The story of *Captain Smith and His Fighting 223*, sharing eight magazine pages with twenty-one advertisements, was featured in the December 7, 1942, *Life* issue. One photograph was of the nine pilots who returned home sitting and standing in front of the Ready Tent. Everyone passing a newsstand could see the photograph of VMF-223's squadron commander on the cover, gazing confidently into the South Pacific skies from the cockpit of his *Wildcat.* [27] It was a fitting story, symbolic in a way, for the nation that for a year had remembered Japanese planes sinking five battleships, obliterating lines of airplanes, and killing over 2400 Americans at Pearl Harbor. American aviators, led by men like Major John L. Smith, were in the Pacific punching back in a big way.

The Palace Drug Store in Lexington received 100 copies of *Life* instead of the usual two copies delivered there.

Eleven of the first twenty-five Medals of Honor earned by Marines in WWII were awarded to aviators. Seven of these went to pilots who flew out of Henderson Field on Guadalcanal and became Aces over the Solomon Islands between May 1942 and January 1944.

For his actions, Major Smith became the third Marine WWII aviator to be awarded a Medal of Honor. He met President Franklin D. Roosevelt on February 24, 1943, and was presented his Medal.

Promoted and assigned to training new pilots again, Lieutenant Colonel Smith spent two years in the States after Guadalcanal. He had been a Marine, focused on Corps' duties and commitments, longer than he had been a husband. So, he and Louise took what time they could to get reacquainted while he was back in the States. The December 7 *Life* Magazine story of John setting the American record for the most planes shot down by that time in the war ended with a photograph of the smiling couple on the couch in Louise's parents' home in Norfolk, where they had been married a year earlier.

The Smiths decided to begin their family. Caroline Maddox Smith was born August 17, 1944. The first of John and Louise's three children, she studied to become a doctor. Their two sons, John Lucian, Jr. and Owen Ballard were to be post-war babies, born May 4, 1946, and March 15, 1950, respectively. [28]

As much for his family, John's thoughts were for the Marines moving up the chain of South Pacific islands. Newspaper clippings during this time illustrate how often Major Smith thought, and spoke, about the pilots under his command. The same was true in his letters to Louise. This was common among Medal of Honor recipients who survived their wars. Richard Bush, who later in the war cradled a grenade on Okinawa and survived, perhaps said it as well as any of the recipients who returned home: *"I wasn't out there alone that day on Okinawa. I had Marines to my right, Marines to my left, Marines behind me and Marines overhead. I didn't earn this alone. It belongs to them, too."* [29]

Lieutenant Colonel Smith requested reassignment to the war zone. Marine Air Group (MAG)-32 flew the Douglas *SBD Dauntless* aircraft dive-bomber. The motto on its patch said *Parati Servire*, Latin meaning "Ready to Serve," and its mission was air-to-ground support. The MAG was positioned in Hawaii in mid-1944, preparing for its participation in the campaign to retake the Philippines. Lieutenant Colonel Smith joined them at Oahu. When MAG-32 landed at Emirau Island in November 1944, he was its Executive Officer. Between then and June 1945, Lieutenant Colonel Smith led his aviators in numerous combat engagements over various Philippine islands, from the Bismarck Archipelago all the way up to the Sulu Archipelago.

At the war's conclusion, Lieutenant Colonel Smith returned to the U.S. and remained in the Marines. Promoted to Colonel in 1951, he spent most of his service on the East Coast, in addition to tours away from home in Europe, a few years on the West Coast, and a tour in Korea when the war ended there in 1953. The 1951 movie, *Flying Leathernecks*, closely based on John's experiences, cast John Wayne as a WWII Marine squadron commander.

His children remembered Colonel Smith as a loving husband and a caring father. He coached them in baseball when they were young. He taught them to play poker and canasta, and to play competitively. The hometown folks, proud of their native son, put up a sign in front of his boyhood home. Colonel Smith took his family to Lexington in 1956 and again in 1966 to visit family and old friends. Photos of the family by the commemorative sign went into family albums. [30]

Colonel Smith retired from the Marines in 1960.

John's aviation and leadership experience were of value in the civilian aerospace industry community. Hired to work at Grumman Aircraft Engineering Corporation on Long Island, he worked briefly in the defense industry. He then accepted an executive position with North American Aviation (NAA), in southern California.

NAA had long focused on manufacturing aircraft. During the war years the company had built military fighters and bomber aircraft. The development of the X-15 was considered its greatest achievement in the mid-1950s. North American decided to turn its attention to the space program in 1960, just as Colonel Smith was retiring from the Marines. The firm designed the Apollo Moon-landing vehicle and the Saturn V launch vehicle. Later, it built the Shuttle Orbiters. In January 1967, when the launch pad fire killed three Apollo astronauts, the company's technical and managerial competence came under scrutiny and criticism.

North American hoped the B-1 bomber contract won in 1970 would improve its reputation and production efforts. By 1986, 40,000 people were working on the program. From the outset, the B-1 project triggered controversy. Costs escalated. The bomber's reliability and performance were criticized. Funding for the contract, as well as jobs, were threatened at times. [31] By that time John was no longer working at NAA.

Thirty years after he had taken command of VMF-223 and earned a Medal of Honor over Guadalcanal, John Smith was laid off from his North American Aviation position in 1972. It might be unimaginable, but sometimes for a brave man, an Ace, the loss of a job can pose the same threat and danger to the life as flying into a formation of enemy planes firing 20-mm machine-gun shells through his wind screen and past his face.

Like most of his generation, the generation journalist Tom Brokaw termed *The Greatest Generation*, John had returned from WWII, tucked his war experience into that corner of his mind, and turned his attention to being productive and raising a family. And like others, including fellow Medal of Honor recipients, he struggled to keep combat's impact at bay. Medal recipients had to find ways to manage the kind of "nervous system agitation" that is normal for those returning from combat. Even if it manifests as depression, having productive challenges provided outlet and meaning. Loss and failures in life could become intense experiences for such men because of their competitive natures. Other characteristics including no fear of death, pragmatic or fatalistic attitudes toward death, and the pattern of taking action as well as initiating attacks against the odds, could mix with depression.

John's children later accepted that their father had come home with and, as time passed, was increasingly affected by "battle fatigue," the condition that would be called post-traumatic stress syndrome after Vietnam. For some Medal of Honor recipients, like John, it appears that the belief that there was nothing more to accomplish, that their individual best had already been attained, or that only decline or despondency lay ahead, could trigger taking action even against depression. For these men, *Death before dishonor* is more than a tattoo, e-mail signature, or title to a 1987 action movie. [32]

On Tuesday, June 13, 1972, a ten-line AP wire appeared in newspapers across the nation. John Lucian Smith, 57-years-old, had died on Saturday, June 10, in Encino, California. Having lived a life with honor, he was overtaken by sadness and despondency and took his own life. He was buried in Section 3, Site 2503-H-2 at Arlington National Cemetery. [33]

The manner in which death comes does not diminish Life with Honor.

In addition to the Egyptians as far back as 2100 BCE and the Hebrew Bible's King Saul, the Roman legions, Japanese samurai, and Aztec warriors accepted death, even if self-inflicted, as preferable to a shameful defeat or loss.

Three suicides, including John's, are recorded among the Medal of Honor recipients, all veterans of WWII. All three had accomplished much after the war, had led exemplary and distinguished lives, earned pensions, and would have earned guaranteed government retirements, as well as probable acclaim within their communities. All three killed themselves on weekend nights, perhaps when memories of war crept out from the shadows of repressed memories.

For such warriors, if life seems to hold no more, or if some shameful experience seems to have evolved, or if they fear that they have been, or will be forgotten, death can seem preferable to a life without honor.

Merritt "Red Mike" Edson had earned his Medal of Honor on the ridge above Henderson Field at the same time Major Smith was shooting down enemy planes and becoming an Ace. "Red Mike" had for years been retired from the active Marines. He had kept busy serving in various positions: executive director of the NRA, President of the 1st Division Association, member of the VFW National Security Committee, President of the Marine Corps War Memorial Foundation charged with development of the Arlington Iwo Jima monument, member of the Defense Advisory Commission on Prisoners of War, Director of the National Savings & Trust Company, a position with the Boy Scouts of America National Committee, public speaker, and consultant to the CIA. His two sons were on their way to their own experiences in the Marines.

It would have appeared to those who knew him well that the only real disappointments in his later life had been not earning another general's star, not being elected a Senator from Vermont, inability to maintain a vigorous state of physical health, and not achieving financial prosperity. But obviously there was more, because on Saturday night, August 13, 1955, at age 58, Red Mike pulled his car into the family garage, closed the door, and let the engine run. His wife discovered him dead the next morning. Merritt Edson was buried in Arlington National Cemetery, Section 2, Site 4960-2. The USS *Edson*, DD-946, was launched January 4, 1958.

William G. Harrell was the youngest of the recipients to take his own life. Having lost both hands to a grenade on Iwo Jima, Bill returned home to Texas, married, had four children with his wife, Olive, and rose to the position of Chief of the Prosthetics Division in the Veterans Administration. He remained an expert marksman throughout his civilian life. At the age of 42-years, after a Saturday night party, in an event lacking explanation on August 9, 1964, he shot and killed a husband and wife in his home, then killed himself. [34] He was buried at Fort Sam Houston National Cemetery, San Antonio.

Sergeant William G. Harrell had attended Agricultural and Mechanical College of Texas (later Texas A&M University) for two years. Texas A&M University renamed a dormitory in his honor on March 1, 1969. One of seven Texas Aggie Medal of Honor recipients, every new Texas A&M cadet must learn his name. William Harrell is honored in the Sam Houston Sanders Corps of Cadets Center and the Texas A&M Memorial Student Center. The students at the University of Washington who objected to a memorial for their alumnus, Greg "Pappy" Boyington, might have learned something about honor from the Texas A&M cadets.

Questions remained to be answered about events following John L. Smith's death. How was he remembered in Lexington? Did the commemorative sign remain in front of his old home? Did his suicide tarnish the memory of the honorable life he had lived?

On November 24, 2006, during season one, the History Channel aired *Dogfights, Guadalcanal*, featuring the "courageous airborne actions" of Marine Captain John Smith. Then, *US Marines Battle of Guadalcanal*, a 1940s newsreel, circulated on the Internet March 3, 2008, and on his son's Web site, December 16, 2008. [35] Owen Smith continues to update johnluciansmith.blogspot.com with photographs, historical documents, and text about his father.

In July 2008, the University of Oklahoma housed a large, temporary exhibit dedicated to OU students who had served in World War II. The patriotic exhibit was located at Oklahoma Memorial Stadium and included a modest and dignified display honoring John L. Smith and two other OU Medal of Honor recipients. When the larger exhibit was dismantled, the Assistant Curator, John Lovett, decided to make the Medal of Honor display permanent. Moved to the Western History Collections museum inside Monnet Hall, it resides with a special collection of historical materials and archives documenting the American West. [36]

Celebrating the *USMC!* , a color photograph of Major Smith, back in the cockpit of his *Wildcat* on Guadalcanal, gazed again from the cover of the Spring 2010 *Centennial of Naval Aviation* magazine.

And in Lexington, Oklahoma?

Leaving Purcell, Oklahoma, on Route 77 and approaching from the west, a sign welcomes travelers to Lexington. Behind the sign at the intersection of West Broadway Street and East Washington Street is a small, triangular section of land called Veterans Park. Around May 19, 1995, atop a silver pole, a plaque with Major John Lucian Smith's picture and an acknowledgment of his being an "Ace of all Aces" was dedicated in the park's east entry as a tribute to him. Today, there is a white metal gate at that entrance on NW 4th Street. Under the flagpole is a small plaza with five standing, rectangular granite monuments, the central one six-feet-tall. The names of all the Lexington men and women who served in the Armed Forces are chiseled into the stones. John's plaque stands among them.

On the northern end of Lexington, where North Main Street ends at Route 77, within sight of Lexington High School four blocks directly east, is another small, triangular section of land, 89er Park. At the northeastern edge of the park, near a green pavilion, stands a granite monument dedicated to Colonel John Lucian Smith. The plaque on the monument's face includes a replica of the December 7, 1942, *Life Magazine* cover, and a proud declaration "Birthplace and Boyhood Home." [37] This monument might stand on the location of John's birthplace home, "Hawk's Place," which was torn down at some point. [38]

What became of the commemorative sign in front of John's boyhood home was not known at the time of this printing.

John L. Smith's service to his country and his life after retiring from the Marines reflected the Marine Corps' values of *honor, courage,* and *commitment*. His self-inflicted death did not diminish the honor and tribute due to him. It is clear that those in Lexington, Oklahoma, understand this truth, and that John is remembered in his birthplace.

Another name was removed from the list of The Forgotten Thirty-Four.

CHAPTER 20
Long Remembered, Gradually Forgotten?

"Thus did this man die, leaving not only to young
men, but also to the whole nation, the memory
of his death for an example of virtue and fortitude."

2 Maccabees 6:31

Korea

When America sent its military forces to Korea in 1950, the Communist (North) Koreans were the identified enemy. Diplomats and high-ranking military officials had been reassured that China would not enter the conflict. This was a justifiable concern to anyone who might have recalled Empress Dowager Tsu Hsi's imperial edict issued from the Forbidden City in Peking, China, prior to the Boxer Rebellion of 1900.

When foreign powers attempted to bring their unwanted influence into the region, the Empress subtly warned that hundreds of millions of Chinese would rise up, gather, and "prove their loyalty to their emperor and love of their country."

As the Marines had deployed to Korea, tens of thousands of China's armed and uniformed inhabitants were being massed in the southeastern province at the border with Korea. In the dark of night, undetected, they would slip in to the northern mountains of Korea and wait for their chance to spring upon American forces. They did in November 1950.

The Marines were in combat in Korea from 1950 to 1953. During those years 4,267 Marines gave their lives. Another 23,744 were wounded in action. Beginning with D-Day and the invasion at Inchon, until the conflict was arbitrated into an armistice on July 27, 1953, forty-two Marines distinguished themselves by performing above and beyond what was expected of them and were awarded Medals of Honor. Ten of these Marines were added to the roster of recipients unheralded in their hometowns.

In contrast to WWII, American involvement in Korea seemed brief and the general public tended to overlook the conflict. The American economy was booming, most of the veterans of WWII had settled in, and the average citizen was focused upon getting his or her fair share of the abundance. There seemed barely enough time to get the reporters to the divided nation: a couple of amphibious landings, some encirclements, a lot of battles for hills, a movie or two, and the engagement was over.

Tributes were paid with as much admiration as in the previous war to most of the Medal of Honor Marines who had died in Korea. Surviving Medal recipients were often grand marshals at hometown annual Veterans Day parades and highlighted at July 4th and Memorial Day ceremonies. Yet, while hometowns did take pride in the heroism of their native sons, it was not with the same fervor as those from WWII had experienced upon their return.

The Korean Conflict is commonly called The Forgotten War with good reason, especially by the veterans who returned home to very little acknowledgment or acclaim afterwards. Perhaps that helps make sense of the impression that ten hometowns had not acknowledged the recipients' contributions to freedom and to the honor they brought to their communities.

Even for a Marine Medal recipient who had been remembered at home after Korea, forgetting could be a slow, drawn out process.

William A. Kelso was born May 13, 1904. He was from Texas and might have had some Native American ancestry in his bloodline, as a granddaughter remembers him receiving checks from the Native American Heritage Foundation later in his life. His father, William M. Kelso, a Texas native, had been a Texas Ranger in the 1920s. There are hints that his grandfather had also been a Texas settler and Ranger in Kerr County and was wounded in a battle with a band of Comanches at Boneyard Waterhole, northwest of San Antonio, in 1856.

Virginia Farned was born September 22, 1914. She was originally from Mississippi. How she met William A. Kelso, when the two of them arrived in California, and where they married was information later unknown to their grandchildren. [1] The couple lived for a while in the small-town Madera area, northwest of Fresno. Their first daughter, Jeanne, was born there, followed by their only son, Jack, on January 23, 1934. William decided to move his family down Route 99 past Fresno to Caruthers, another small town of about 1,317 residents at that time. He and Virginia had four more daughters once settled there.

Moving about was characteristic of being a Kelso. Texan William's own siblings were spread out across three states. His brother, James, remained in Texas, while Robert had migrated to New Mexico. One sister, Dena Chisholm, lived nearby in Fresno, and another, Kelly Friedrich, lived in Texas. Although William's children would have no fewer than seven paternal cousins, there would not be many opportunities for the cousins to get together. Family ties were important to the Kelsos, however, and distance among family members did not diminish the bonds among them.

Jack William Kelso grew up in the central San Joaquin Valley of Southern California, between the Sierra Nevada and Coastal Mountain Ranges, west of the Sequoia National Forest. As Jack grew through his boyhood and adolescence, he worked on his father's farm.

Jack had family around him, a good number of them women who adored him: an older sister, Jeanne, and four younger sisters Nina (born in 1937), Billie (1938), Mary (1942), and Alice (1945). His maternal grandmother, Eula Farned, lived in Chowchilla, north on Highway 99. Being a big brother, looking out for little sisters, was a part of his life.

Besides hard work, important attributes among the Kelso men were also honor, integrity, and service. Jack's father had a cotton and grape ranch near Caruthers. Community minded, William was an officer in the Caruthers Lions Club and believed in helping others. His son would follow that example, work hard, and wait for his chance to be of service.

America entered the Second World War as Jack's eighth birthday was approaching and events would soon bring the war close to home. Japanese families lived and worked in Caruthers and in the rural areas of the San Joaquin Valley. On February 14, 1942, President Roosevelt signed Executive Order 9066 calling for the removal of United States residents of Japanese descent to Relocation and Internment Camps. The Manzanar Camp was opened in March, just ninety miles due east of Caruthers at the eastern base of the Sierra Nevada Mountains. Neighbors and schoolmates of the Kelsos vacated their homes and moved to the camp. More than three years passed before they were permitted to return to the San Joaquin Valley.

Jack's uncle, James W. Kelso, was 20-years-old when the war began and was inducted into service in 1943. He served as an Army Private First Class with the combat engineers in the Aleutians Islands. He was stationed at the Santa Barbara redistribution facility in the latter part of the war, five hours from the Kelso fields and vineyards. Some news of the war with the Japanese came first hand to Jack during visits from his uncle. What discussions about the Japanese and the Internment Camps the family might have had at the dinner table is unknown. What can be certain is that Jack developed a deep sense of patriotism and service.

Before any news of Allied victories reached America, Jack's Texas grandmother, Mary, died, and his grandfather, the former Texas Ranger, moved to Caruthers to ranch in 1942. Throughout Jack's childhood, before the rumors and news of war began, the nation's families could find evening entertainment listening to radio broadcasts of shows that would later be broadcast from television sets. The shout of "Hi-yo, Silver! Away!" could bring children scurrying to the radio set to hear the latest escapade of *The Lone Ranger*. By the time Grandpa William was living on Route 1, two *Lone Ranger* movies had also thrilled children in the theaters. Jack did not have to wait for a radio episode or go to a theater to enjoy stories of the Rangers. He could just sit on the front porch with Grandpa William and hear about the adventures of real Texas Rangers.

While *The Lone Ranger* might have provided some distraction from the war, the war was hitting home in the Fresno area. Private First Class Joe M. Nishimoto was born in Fresno on February 21, 1919. He had been interned in one of the Relocation Camps before he joined the United States Army. He died in combat in the Vosges Mountans near La Houssiere, France, at the age of 25-years on November 15, 1944. He received a French-American commemoration for heroic actions on November 7, the week before he was killed in action. Private First Class Nishimoto's body was brought back to California, and he was buried at Washington Colony Cemetery seven miles north of Caruthers, on South Elm Avenue, four miles from the Kelso property and just west of Highway 41. The original marker placed over his grave would be changed after 1998. Regional newspapers for the 1944-50 period that were available in archives make no mention of Joe. Whether the Kelsos were aware of him is unknown.

The Kelso children started their formal education at Monmouth Elementary School and then graduated into the Caruthers' schools. Jack was still in elementary school when WWII ended and neighbors returned from the Manzanar Internment Camp. As he started at Caruthers High School, the post-war economic boom was underway, and the Second World War was finding its way into the final chapters of American History textbooks assigned to high school students. As a "Blue Raider," Jack was active and involved. Athletic and competitive, he earned trophies in track, which were displayed in the school hallway. Jack had a natural talent for running.

And before Jack graduated, America entered another war on behalf of an ally. When Jack turned seventeen in January 1951, midway through his junior year, the Marines had been at war in Korea for less than a year. Jack might have been influenced by memories of his Uncle James' WWII Army service, or by stories of a great grandfather, a Texas Ranger wounded in the Boneyard Waterhole Battle nearly one hundred years earlier, or by Hollywood's version of WWII heroics. Whatever the influences might have been, high school, small-town Caruthers, and farming were not going to be enough to hold him in San Joaquin Valley. Jack wanted to join the Marine Corps.

His parents tried to persuade him to finish high school and wait until he was older to make this decision. Jack was determined. He told William and Virginia their choices; either give permission for him to go into the service or he would find another way to enlist. The Kelsos signed on the line permitting their son to go to war. [2]

Jack Kelso was on the move.

That May 15, 1951, Jack made the fifteen-mile trip up to the Fresno Post Office and recruiting station to enlist in the Marines. In July, he finished his recruit training in San Diego. From there, he went to Camp Pendleton until January 1952. During his first seven months as a Marine, Jack was close enough to Caruthers for family visits. His proud parents had attended his graduation ceremonies from the San Diego Recruit Depot and probably hoped that he would be assigned duties that would keep him at Camp Pendleton. The nation was adjusting to the fact that the boys had not returned home from Korea by Christmas, as General MacArthur had promised President Truman on October 15, 1951.

When Jack traveled to Hawaii and then on to Korea in April 1952, Virginia made sure that she wrote to him often. Like mothers across time who have watched their sons go to war, she believed that letting him know about everyday things at home could bring him some comfort.

Private Kelso [3] got news from home that the Caruthers District Fair, always a big event in Fresno County, had been scheduled for October

16, 17, and 18. William, Virginia, and his sisters waited anxiously for Jack's letters to home.

Private Kelso (MCSN: 1190839), 18-years-old, was assigned duties as a rifleman with Company I, 3d Battalion, 7th Marines in Korea. The older, more experienced men might have looked out for the young replacement, but he soon showed his own mettle in battle. His would be an example of many of the actions characteristically demonstrated by heroically brave men.

During one three-day battle in August when enemy forces were trying to dislodge the Marines from an outpost hill, "far forward of the main line of resistance," Private Kelso rushed from his position with Item Company through hostile artillery and mortar fire to re-supply another company with ammunition. On his return, he carried casualties down the hill with him to friendlier lines.

Private Kelso had experienced San Joaquin Valley August days when temperatures could rise into the mid-80s and 90s, with gentle evening westerly winds cooling the air, and little precipitation. The heat of August was stifling in Korea, and heat and fatigue casualties were plentiful in extended battles, just as frostbite casualties were in winter. Other Marines were assisting in the re-supply of the beleaguered unit on the hill. Most were relieved of the endeavor after several trips to prevent the inevitable heat collapse.

During the August battle, Private Kelso refused to be relieved. Maybe his endurance was honed in the work experience on his father's farm in the San Joaquin Valley summers, maybe it was boyhood hikes and climbs in the Sierra Nevada mountains, maybe training and competing in track, or maybe it was just the character of this young man. After running over twenty trips back and forth through the pounding barrage, Private Kelso finally collapsed from the re-supply effort and was evacuated. For that effort, he was awarded the Silver Star for gallantry in battle. A Department of Defense photograph shows Private Kelso, under combat helmet and in combat fatigues, smiling as a commander pinned the Silver Star above his heart.

It is uncertain if Jack was promoted to Private First Class after he earned his first award for valor. Most records continue to refer to him as Private Kelso, while others refer to him as Private First Class Kelso. His promotion to Private First Class might have been posthumous.

No matter the rank worn on his collar, the men in Company I respected a Marine who looked out for his companions. Private Kelso would give them even more to respect and admire six weeks later.

In late September, Private Kelso's parents received a package. Major General E. A. Pollock of the 1st Marine Division had signed a Citation, awarding their son a Silver Star Medal for "conspicuous gallantry and intrepidity in action against the enemy . . . from August 13th to 15th." The Citation and Silver Star arrived on the farm just a week before a telegram was delivered.

Despite the award for valor, the Kelsos worried about their son and brother. William and Virginia did what they could to keep life normal for their four youngest girls. By the time the Silver Star had arrived, their eldest daughter, Jeanne, had become Mrs. Baxter, but Nina and Billie, in their early adolescence, and Mary and Alice were still at home. Alice Kelso was only seven-years-old. [4] Reading letters from Jack and news about the approaching local Fair Days were ways to ease the mounting apprehensions in the Kelso home.

While news headlines followed the 1952 presidential campaign and wondered with General Dwight D. Eisenhower if his vice-presidential running mate, Senator Richard M. Nixon of California, had inappropriately received $18,235 in an expense fund beyond his salary and senatorial allowances, Caruthers Fair board members planned the judging for a horse show, for a livestock and poultry competition, and for the crowning of a queen. Ruth Elaine Andersen, the 1951 queen would be on hand, and Beverly Klepper was considered a strong contender for the title.

The Caruthers High School senior class worked out the details for their *From Caveman to Classroom* float. Although the float later won its division, the joy felt by seniors like Martha Nabors, Bobby Shiflett, Dewey Short, Cecil Lane, Gerald Sedo, Edna Fincher, Roberta Glass and Dale Trimble would not be what it might have been. These "Blue Raiders" had walked the high school hallways for a year or two with Jack Kelso. Some of the seniors had been looking out for Nina and Billie Kelso.

Private Kelso mailed letters home to Route 1, Box 167, Caruthers whenever he had a chance. Whether or not the Caruthers District Fair was on the young Marine's mind, his home and family were. In one letter, he wrote that he hoped to have enough "points for rotation" out of Korea in time to be home for Christmas with his parents and five sisters.

Having worried about their brother off in a war the nation seemed not to be paying much attention to, the letter provided the girls some comfort and reassurance.

Celebrating his eighteenth family Christmas was not to be for Jack.

Item Company, under the command of Captain Anthony J. Skotnichi, was in a vital position at Combat Outpost Warsaw, near Sokchon, on the night of October 2, 1952. It was not a quiet night. A numerically superior enemy force attacked with mortars, grenades, and rifle fire. Both Private Kelso's platoon commander and platoon sergeant were taken casualties.

Without leadership to direct their defense, the rancher's son attempted to reorganize his squad. He exposed himself to intense enemy fire as he maneuvered about the men. As the attack escalated, unable to repulse the enemy charge, Private Kelso and his fire team were forced back to positions in a fortified bunker. As the enemy directed fire against it, the bunker provided little better protection than the trenches. An enemy grenade landed in the emplacement, exposing the fire team to imminent danger. Private Kelso immediately grabbed the explosive, rushed out of the bunker, and threw it back towards the enemy. The grenade detonated as it left his hand. Seriously wounded and again under close enemy fire, he returned to the bunker with the four other Marines.

The five men were pinned down and in the perilous position of soon being overrun when Private Kelso directed their escape from the bunker. He moved into the open, exposing himself again to the intense hail of enemy fire and brought his fire to bear on the advancing force. His action gave the other Marines the opportunity to vacate the bunker and move to more secure ground. He did not join them.

Private Kelso, 18-years-old, was killed by hostile fire as he provided the covering fire that protected his fire team in their escape. His comrades in Item Company recovered his body after the enemy assault was repulsed. The Kelsos received a telegram informing them of their only son's death. The circumstances of how he had been killed were not provided. The family would learn of his heroism later.

Jack Kelso was buried on December 8, 1952, at Washington Colony Cemetery. The cemetery, established in 1888, is a peaceful place surrounded by quarters of almond tree groves, tree nut groves, fruit tree orchards, and grape vineyards. Jack was buried near Joe M. Nishimoto. His flat, bronze military marker, with the Medal of Honor inscription, is now weathered and faded. The rank engraved on his marker is PFC. The main office of the cemetery has maintained a display with Jack's photo, his Citation, and the ceremonially folded American flag.

The Kelsos moved to Route 6, Box 342, at Dinuba and Marks Avenue, north of Caruthers. They continued to receive letters from Marines who had served with Jack and who wanted his family to know how much his bravery had inspired them.

Captain Skotnichi, I Company commander, wrote Mrs. Kelso, noting her son's persistent great courage. He described Jack's death during the fierce and heavy attack, brought down by "bullets from an enemy submachine gun." The Item Company commander confirmed what Jack's family already knew; that he "was a fine lad and a good Marine" and that "[h]is cheerful personality brought him many friends." The captain also acknowledged that Jack's courage had "gained for him the respect of all who served with him."

Then General Lemuel C. Sheperd, the Commandant of the Marine Corps, wrote the Kelsos. His letter was a notification that their son had been recommended for and awarded a Medal of Honor. The Commandant did not specify what heroic action had earned Private Kelso this distinction. Local Fresno Marine officials speculated that the Medal might be further recognition of his August heroics for which he had already been awarded a Silver Star.

Accompanied by a photograph of a smiling Private Jack W. Kelso in his Marine Dress Blue uniform, a headline on the Tuesday, July

7, 1953, *Fresno Bee Republican* front page announced, "Congressional Medal Is Awarded Fresno Hero."

He is the fourth youngest Marine to have earned a Medal of Honor in all wars.

Newspapers reported that Vice President Richard Nixon would present a Medal of Honor to the family on Wednesday, September 9, 1953. [5] William and Virginia Kelso met Vice President Nixon at the tree-shaded parade ground, 8th and I Streets Marine Barracks, Washington, D.C. They also met the families of S.E. Skinner, W.E. Schuck, Jr., L.G. Watkins, and John D. Kelly, whose sons had also been awarded Medals for actions in Korea. Staff Sergeant William Schuck was a 3/7 Marine who had died in July 1952, and Staff Sergeant Lewis Watkins was another 3/7 Marine who had been killed five days after Jack. The Kelsos learned more of their son's "valiant fighting spirit, aggressive determination and self-sacrificing efforts on behalf of others" when Vice President Nixon read the Citation to the assembled families. The Silver Star mailed to them by the 1st Division commander and Jack's Medal of Honor were for two different actions in combat. When the vice president handed Mrs. Kelso the Medal, she dropped her black handbag to the floor. Vice President Nixon instantly recovered the bag, handed it to her, and gave a reassuring pat to her arm. Photos of Virginia Kelso in tears appeared in the next day's newspapers.

Afterwards, the 7th Marine Regiment named their parade grounds in Korea in Private Jack W. Kelso's honor.

Remembering the bravery of one individual can cross generations and impact those who come afterwards. Perhaps the roots of bravery are to be discovered in genetically transferred DNA, or in the stories learned in childhood, or in the parades of uniformed men and women passing through a town square.

Jack's five sisters all married and raised families. In all, he would have nine nephews and eight nieces who would learn of, and be proud of, his heroism. Both of Nina's sons entered the Marines. One of Mary's sons enlisted in the Marines, was deployed for *Desert Storm* and then served in *Operation Iraqi Freedom*. Alice's two daughters, Sherri and

Kathy Clifford, were particularly close to their grandparents, who they remember as having "just loved kids." The two girls were often in the care of William and Virginia, who took them on camping trips and told them stories about Jack. Later, when Grandma Kelso brought out her photo album and mementoes of their uncle, the elder of the two girls began her own scrapbook to share with her three children. As often happens among heroes and Medal of Honor recipients, Jack had become a family legend. [6]

In February 1953, the Fresno County Foundation for the Mentally Retarded was formed, and turned to establishing a school with classrooms, a cafeteria, cottages for living quarters, sheltered workshop, daycare center, and school grounds with recreational facilities for training hundreds of area mentally retarded children and young adults. Frank F. Pimentel, a Caruthers rancher and sweet potato culture developer, was among the group that founded the project. The school was to be named the Kelso Community Village, in memory of the late Marine. The Foundation presented Mr. and Mrs. Kelso an honorary membership on January 14, 1954, and the couple would work at the school as the years passed. [7]

In June 1954, Charles S. Colhouer, a real estate man, donated an eight-acre plot of land near 404 South Hughes and White Bridge Avenues for the school. Commuters taking off from or landing at the downtown Fresno-Chandler Executive Airport would have a good view of the Village, sitting a few city blocks northwest of the airfield.

The Kelso site was developed one building and one donation at a time. The Fresno Carpenters' Local, Friends of Retarded, Fresno Labor Council, architects and draftsman, engineers, home contractors, North American Aviation Employees Donate Once Club, and the Ladies Aid to Retarded Children dedicated themselves to the task. Donated materials, cash gifts, fund raisers, and volunteer labor, including more than fifty volunteer workers, began the first building, Colhouer Hall, in 1956.

Nearly five years after William and Virginia accepted their son's Medal of Honor from the Vice President, they stood among 300 others attending the ribbon cutting ceremony on February 24, 1958. The

Marines presented them a flag in honor of their son. Then a Marine Honor Guard stepped sharply to the flagpole and raised the flag over the new Kelso School. The Marines would remain involved as the years passed and the school grew. On Friday, September 25, 1958, the Department of the Pacific Marine Band performed at the Kelso Village to help promote the Foundation's fund raising drive.

The facility became known as Kelso Village School and eventually comprised 12,000 square feet in a cluster of five buildings. Around 1969, under the auspices of the Fresno Association for Retarded Citizens, the school was renamed the Kelso Activity Center. In August 1971, various contributors and volunteers constructed a $10,000 recreation playground. By 1972, when most of its students were over 21-years of age, Kelso also began considering the needs of neglected senior citizens. An adult day program, day training activity center, and a seniors' program were implemented to help meet the growing community needs.

At the entrance to Colhouer Hall, a 14x17 inch plaque in tribute to Jack Kelso's "valiant services to his country" during the Korean War had been fixed to the foyer wall. Anyone who entered the first building constructed on the eight-acre site, and took the time to read the plaque, would know that the Kelso facility had been dedicated in his name. Given that the Kelso Activity Center eventually provided services to 200 students and their families, it seemed that many in the Fresno area would remember Jack Kelso.

The Caruthers Marine who died at Combat Outpost Warsaw long remained in the memories of his comrades and the Fresno community, as well as his family. At an Armed Forces Day luncheon in Fresno, sponsored by the military affairs committee of the Fresno County and City Chamber of Commerce, Friday, May 17, 1963, Jack's parents donated his Medal to the Marine Corps. Brigadier General John F. Dobbin, USMC, accepted the Medal on behalf of the Quantico, Virginia Marine museum. [8] In February 1964, the 12th Marine Corps District presented a charter for the newly organized Fresno Chapter of the Marine Corps Reserve Officers Association, named the Jack W. Kelso Chapter.

The Lemoore Naval Air Station was commissioned in 1961, just twenty miles to the southwest of Caruthers. Navy and Marine aircraft began maneuvering near the Kelso family fields and vineyards where Jack once toiled. The Marines based at NAS Lemoore held their November 10, 1997, Marine Corps Birthday Ball in honor of Jack. His mother, then 83-years-old, along with a maternal aunt, Jack's sister, Nina, and his niece, Sherri, and her husband were guests of honor.

The National Museum of the Marine Corps (NMMC) in Quantico loaned the Kelso display to the Marine Corps Recruit Depot San Diego Command Museum, located at the front entrance of the Main Gate, Gate 4. The Kelso exhibit, opened spring 1998, in San Diego, was showcased in the 2nd floor Medals and Decorations Room beside the Chesty Puller display case. [9] Jack's nieces had a chance to visit the display while it was there. The NMMC recalled the loan several years ago. Once back in Quantico, the Kelso display was on the main exhibit floor at the NMMC.

The May 1998, Memorial Day ceremony celebrated at Washington Colony Cemetery was dedicated to Jack Kelso's memory.

Was he remembered in Caruthers?

Jack Kelso's Caruthers High School classmates graduated while he was fighting in the Korean hills. Some of the younger students who had known and looked up to him had started another school year when news of his death reached their town. For the next couple of years, they likely thought of him when they passed by his track trophies in the school hallway. As they graduated, they might have wondered what would become of those trophies when the new high school, then under construction, was opened. The school building Jack attended remained on the West Tahoe Avenue and Raider site until 1955. Three years after his death, the new high school was completed there. Year after year, 18-year-old students graduated from the high school on the edge of town.

Jack's memory went with them.

Nine years had passed since the last time Jack had walked in the Caruthers High School halls. His father had remained involved with the students and was then working as a janitor in the school. If the question had been raised at that time whether the "Blue Raiders" remembered the valor of the janitor's son, as it had once been described in a Citation signed by President Dwight D. Eisenhower, the graduating class of 1960 would have had a resounding answer. Before they left to pursue their lives, the student body, led by Mary Bennetts, presented a memorial gift to their school. On Tuesday, May 31, 1960, a 9x12 inch plaque honoring the memory of Jack Kelso was dedicated and fixed to the campus flagpole. Jack's father had built that flagpole. William and Virginia were present at the ceremony. [10]

When inquiries were made in 2009, current faculty and staff at the high school could not confirm if the plaque and Jack's track trophies remained at Caruthers High School. Jack's niece believed that the plaque was still on the flagpole.

Available records indicate that thirty-five Fresno area men died in WWII. Only one of them was a Medal of Honor recipient, and his name was not added to the record until 1998. When a 1996 study was conducted to investigate whether Asian Americans had been discriminated against in the awarding of medals for valor during WWII, Joe M. Nishimoto was one of twenty-two Asian Americans to have been determined deserving of America's highest medal for valor for his actions on November 7, 1944. President Bill Clinton awarded his posthumous Medal of Honor to Joe's family in 1998. Eight Fresno area men died in Korea. Jack Kelso is the only Medal of Honor recipient among them. His Medal is accredited to Caruthers, his home of record. Another local man earned a Medal and survived the war. Rodolfo Perez "Rudy" Hernandez, born April 14, 1931, the son of a farm worker, was raised in Fowler, a small town eight miles northeast of the Kelso ranch. He joined the Army in 1948, when he was 17-years-old. Two weeks after Jack Kelso had enlisted in the Marines, Corporal Hernandez earned a Medal of Honor on May 31, 1951, when he single-handedly stopped a Communist attack and continued to fight, although wounded and without ammunition, until he was felled by a grenade blast. "Rudy" now lives in Fayetteville, North Carolina. Later, sixty-seven area men would die in Vietnam. The other four Medals of Honor accredited to

Fresno are from that war and none of the four recipients were born in California. One of these is Kenneth Lee Worley.

While the White House was deciding about Joe M. Nishimoto, businessmen in Caruthers were making their own decisions about those who had served the country in war. The Caruthers community wanted to remember and honor all those who had ever resided in Caruthers who had served their country in any one of the six military branches. The Caruthers Chamber of Commerce, Caruthers District Fair Association, and Caruthers Lions Club all took an active part in the initiative. Stockman's Bank donated the land for the project on L Street, Beer Monuments contributed the brick trim, and the Fresno Legion of Valor Museum provided its assistance. The memorial was dedicated on April 27, 2002.

Driving from agricultural fields onto West Tahoe Avenue, the main street through town, the Caruthers Veterans Memorial comes into view on the right side of the road. [11] It is an impressive sight. An olive drab green, 1942 57-mm artillery canon stands sentinel in front of the flagpole. The American flag flies sixty feet above the plaza, the black and white POW*MIA flag beneath it. The Wall of Names, over ten feet tall and twenty-four feet long, includes seven panels on its face, each panel with three columns of names. More than 500 names are inscribed on the Wall.

From a distance at the curb, the American eagle symbol on the top panel is easily distinguished. Over the Eagle are the words "For God and Country"; under one wing is the name Jack W. Kelso and under the other, Joe M. Nishimoto. If he was ever forgotten at home, Jack Kelso has been remembered again in Caruthers.

The Kelso buildings are razed.

According to U.S. Census data, the population size of Fresno, like most cities, grew during the same years the Kelso Activity Center was increasing the services provided to developmentally disabled children and adults. In the 1990s, Fresno's population growth was nearly twenty-one percent. Since 2000, the growth was another sixteen percent and Fresno became the sixth largest city in California. During all the years of growth, Fresno Yosemite International Airport became the major air transportation center for the city and the San Joaquin Valley. Not so many commuters looked down at the Kelso Activity Center on takeoff and landing.

And, ground highway traffic management took precedence over preserving the memory of Private Jack William Kelso, USMC Medal of Honor recipient. Crossing into the new century, the city planned for the westward extension of Highway 180, claiming the land to Marks and Brawley Avenues. The eight acres on South Hughes Avenue north of Whites Bridge was in its path. The city bought the eight acres on which the Kelso Activity Center had been sitting for nearly fifty years. The project went to bid in October 2006.

The Kelso property sale money went to the purchase of a $1.2 million dollar, 15,000-square-foot building housing the Association of Retarded Citizens (ARC) Fresno Enrichment Center. Moved to the city's northwest, the new Enrichment Center sits at the junction of Marty and Selland Avenues. The contributions of Mr. and Mrs. William Kelso, the fundraising efforts of the Marines, and the sacrifice of Private Jack Kelso appear to have been forgotten in Fresno.

When contacted, some of the ARC-Fresno staff who had entered Colhouer Hall in the years just prior to the closing of the Kelso facility, remembered the wall plaque that had hung at the entrance to the building, but could not recall to whom or to what it was dedicated. The wall plaque seemed to have been lost when the Kelso buildings were razed.

ARC Fresno Executive Director Lori Ramirez knew better. She had retrieved the 14x17 inch plaque from a workman after the Kelso Activity Center had been dismantled. She kept it safely stored in a closet in her office, unsure what to do with one of the remaining mementos of the original Center. [12]

Today, it is difficult to find family connections to Jack Kelso. A dozen or so Kelsos currently live in Fresno, descendants of long-ago immigrants from Scotland and Ireland. Those contacted knew of no direct relationship to Jack, or his father William. Only one knew that a Kelso had been awarded a Medal of Honor. He had once worked at

NAS Lemoore and remembered a memorial display with Private Kelso's photograph, plaque, and Citation on a wall at the Marine Group's Headquarters Building. He had noticed the display because he shared the Marine's last name. [13] That information suggested that a call to NAS Lemoore might lead to the discovery of another tribute to Jack.

The Marine Aviation Training Support Group 23 is located at NAS Lemoore, providing administration, logistical, and training support to all Marines aboard the Air Station. Starting with a clerk answering the phone at the Group's Headquarters Administration Building, going up the chain of command to the Executive Officer, as well as the Group's historian, who took time from his busy morning to investigate a display case, the Marines did not know of any display with photograph and citation dedicated to the memory of Private Jack Kelso.

There is, however, a display in tribute to Joe Foss and Marian Carl, "Cactus Air Force" aviators of Guadalcanal, at Headquarters Building 730.

Further searches for Jack Kelso's extended family might have ended were it not for Internet blog sites and social networking sites like Facebook and Twitter. Pieces of history unknown to distant researchers emerged fifty-six years after the legacy began, because two nieces acknowledged their uncle on Web sites.

On December 15, 2008, two and a half years after the Kelso name was deleted from the ARC Fresno facility, Kathy "Kay" M. Clifford posted a story, entitled *My Uncle, My Hero*, on the Fresno area Community Correspondent Web site. [14] Her sister, Sherri Clifford Alcorn, posted a comment on another Web site. [15] Jack Kelso still had family in the communities surrounding Caruthers.

Sherri and "Kay," the daughters of Jack's youngest sister, Alice, knew much about their family history. Their grandparents and their mother had told them about the uncle they had not had a chance to meet and how he had lost his life in Korea and earned the Congressional Medal of Honor. They are obviously proud to talk about him and remember him as a hero, an uncle loved by the generations who have followed. In addition to Sherri's two sons, daughter and two grandchildren, and Kay's three daughters, there are fourteen other surviving nieces and nephews who are raising families of their own. Now their children have learned about a great-uncle and enjoy sharing the story of his valor with friends and classmates.

Besides Jack's early death in Korea, the Kelso generations have weathered many tragedies. William M. Kelso, the former Texas Ranger, outlived his grandson, dying at the age of 90-years, on the night before the eighth anniversary of Jack's death. He is buried near his grandson at Washington Colony Cemetery. [16] Jack's father was killed in a car accident in 1986 and was also buried near his son. William's accident seems to have been a harbinger of more family tragedies ahead. Alice, Jack's youngest sister, was killed in a car accident caused by a drunk driver in 1991. She was 46-years-old. One of Mary's sons, Jack's nephew, was also killed in a traffic accident. Virginia Kelso died in 1999 and is buried beside her husband. Dena Chisholm, Jack's aunt, and Jeanne Kelso Baxter, his older sister, are both buried near him. [17] The causes of their deaths are unknown.

Three of Jack's sister's Nina, Billie, and Mary, remained alive as of this printing, two living in Selma, California, and one living in Arizona. Nina and Billie are in their 80s, and Mary's 2012 birthday will put her into that decade as well.

A Marine's bravery, unfettered by time

It just so happened that Sherri was living just a few blocks from the relocated Fresno ARC facility in 2009. When she learned of her uncle's plaque stored in the director's closet, it stayed on her mind. Her decision would ensure that Fresno would remember Jack Kelso again.

In early April 2009, Sherri Alcorn called Lori Ramirez at the Fresno ARC to inquire about her uncle's plaque. She wondered if she could have it. Lori, pleased to have contact with a Kelso family member, at first thought to give the plaque to Sherri, but then thought she should present the idea at the next Board meeting.

The following Monday she did just that and a long discussion ensued. The Board wanted Jack to be remembered at the agency. The final decision was that Lori would erect a formal display of the plaque somewhere in the ARC facility. A replica of the memorial plaque would be made to provide to Sherri. Later the Board decided that the original plaque would be erected in the ARC facility park in September, 2009, so that it would be within the view of even those just passing by. [18]

Medal of Honor recipients belong as much to the community as they do to their families.

It is as a son said at a ceremony honoring his father. "Pappy belonged to the nation." [19]

American Legion Post 55 members from Easton, Boy Scouts, Cub Scouts, Future Farmers of America, a retired *Fresno Bee* reporter, and local church members began arriving at Washington Colony Cemetery on Saturday, May 29, 2010. They brought with them small American flags, ribbons, crosses, and flowers. As the groups spread out, they located the graves of nearly 900 veterans, ensuring that a memorial was placed at each one.

Jack Kelso's was among those graves.

An eight-year-old girl pulled her wagon, full of flags. This was her eighth Memorial Day weekend trip to Washington Colony Cemetery, and she understood the purpose of her endeavors. Drea Barberich, granddaughter of the event's organizer, Kathy Barberich, spoke with certainty.

"It supports what they did for us. They fought for us." [20]

When Jack Kelso died, the end of the conflict in Korea was only nine months in the future. He was the thirty-sixth Marine to earn a Medal of Honor in Korea. The first had been First Lieutenant Baldomero Lopez, Jr. who jumped on a grenade to protect the men under his command from harm at 5:33 PM on September 15, 1950, the first day of the invasion at Inchon. A photo taken from behind of First Lieutenant Lopez leading his platoon over the seawall moments before he gave his life can be found on the walls of many halls of fame and Marine recruiting offices. Six more Marines earned Medals after Jack Kelso, bringing the total to forty-two recipients. Staff Sergeant Ambrosio Guillen was the last Marine to distinguish himself by demonstrating heroic bravery in the Korean War, earning his Medal on July 25, 1953, during the battle for Boulder City, or Hill 111 on tactical maps. The armistice was signed on July 27, 1953, ending the Korean conflict two days after the platoon sergeant's actions had taken place. Today, a junior high school and a Veteran's Home in El Paso, Texas, bear the honor of his name.

Jack Kelso's name was removed from the list of the thirty-four forgotten Marine recipients. Of the nine other recipients from Korea who were included on the list, eight had died before him, and one died after him in March 1953. The accounts of these nine Marines are recalled in the next three chapters.

CHAPTER 21
The War That Was Forgotten

"The greatest use of life is to spend it for something that will outlast it."

William James

What is there to last longer than the recognition of another person's bravery?

At the close of World War II in 1945, Japan was forced to give up its 35-year rule of Korea. The mountainous peninsula was divided at the 38th Parallel, the south under the occupation of United States forces and the north under Soviet Union control. Kim Il Sung, head of the Korean Communist Party governed the nine million people in the north. In the south, the Republic of Korea, Syngman Rhee was first elected chairman, then president, of the republic to rule 21 million constituents.

This division did not sit well with Kim Il Sung. Tensions between the two "freed" populations escalated, but the engagements between North and South Korea along the 38th Parallel raised little concern in

American homes. In 1949, after four years of occupation, the United States withdrew most combat forces from South Korea, leaving behind a small Army advisory group in support of the Republic of Korea (ROK) Army.

With Soviet support, intent on Communist unification of the peninsula, the North Korean People's Army (NKPA) crossed the 38th Parallel on June 25, 1950, and drove south. Within weeks, the defenders were pushed back to the port of Pusan in the southeast.

About 4,700 Marines of the 1st Provisional Marine Brigade were dispatched from California in early July with orders to reinforce the beleaguered U.S. Eighth Army, the ROK Army, and other UN forces. The Marines landed on August 2, taking their positions on the Pusan Perimeter on August 4. The Pusan Perimeter encompassed about 50 miles from east to west and about 100 miles from north to south. Geographic features determined the rectangular Perimeter. Mountains formed the northern line from Waegwan to Yongdok. The Naktong River formed most of the western boundary. The communists intended to drive the defenders, with the ocean to their backs in the east and south, right off the peninsula.

Throughout August, the line held against the northern invaders. The U.S. and ROK Armies planned the breakout from the Pusan Perimeter in September. It was to coincide with amphibious assaults by the Marines on the west coast, just beneath the 38th Parallel. The tide was about to turn against the NKPA.

The first wave of Marines who would help turn the tide landed at Wolmi Island at 6:33 AM, September 15, 1950. The assault forces moved rapidly inland as the Marines took one objective after another, crossing the island. By 7:50 AM the Marines had secured the causeway leading to Inchon, on the mainland. The invasion of Inchon began at 5:33 PM. The Marines remained in combat on the Korean peninsula until the July 27, 1953 armistice.

During the ensuing three years, forty-two Marines distinguished themselves by performing above and beyond what was expected of them and were awarded Medals of Honor. Twenty-eight of these did not return alive from Korea. Fourteen survived their actions. Thirty-one have been remembered with significant tributes. At this writing, three survive.

Among the forty-two Marines who earned Medals of Honor in Korea, besides Jack Kelso, the other recipients who seemed to have had no memorials dedicated to them and to have been unheralded in their hometowns included Stanley Reuben Christianson, James Irsley Poynter, Lee Hugh Phillips, James Edmund Johnson, David Bernard Champagne, Whitt Lloyd Moreland, John Doren Kelly, Daniel Paul Matthews and Frederick William Mausert III. Further research removed Stanley Christianson and Frederick Mausert from The Forgotten Thirty-Four listing.

YEAR 1950

Stanley Reuben Christianson was born January 25, 1925. His was a family that liked to stay close to each other. His parents, Simon and Inga Christianson lived on a farm near Mindoro, Wisconsin, a small, unincorporated rural town in Farmington, about fifteen miles northeast of La Crosse. While his parents lived their lives in Wet Coulee, when his five sisters and three brothers married, they moved to their own places in other towns on Route 108, all within ten miles of their birthplace.

Stanley did not marry, nor move down the road. After attending Rhyme School, he farmed for a while at Wet Coulee. Tilling, planting, and harvesting might have been enough for him at a different time, but news of a war had been daily on the minds of Americans for nearly a year, and he wanted to do his part. Stanley enlisted in the Marines on October 2, 1942, when he was 17-years-old. After training, he joined the 2d Marine Division and traveled to the Pacific islands where he spent the next two and a half years. He fought across the coral beaches in four major amphibious assaults at Tarawa, Saipan, Tinian, and finally Okinawa. His actions in the Pacific earned Stanley a commendation for meritorious service.

Between the Wars

At the close of the war, Stanley was 19-years-old. He was honorably discharged in December 1945. War and combat had changed his outlook and returning to Wisconsin farming held no allure. Stanley reenlisted in March 1946 and served in a number of stations distant from Wisconsin, including a tour as a Drill Instructor at Parris Island, South Carolina. In August 1950, after nearly eight years of service, he sailed to Korea with the 1st Marines.

He was going to distinguish himself in battles again.

Unlike his service in WWII, however, his experience in Korea was brief, as it was for many. His combat service in Korea extended across fourteen days.

Private First Class Christianson was an automatic rifleman with Company E, 2d Battalion, 1st Marines. He landed with them on Blue Beach at Inchon on September 15 and fought with them along the main road to Seoul.

Three days after the landing he earned a Bronze Star Medal for valor on September 18. While his platoon was assaulting an enemy position, they received fire from well-concealed enemy soldiers attempting to flank the platoon and attack in their rear. Private First Class Christianson stood in an exposed position to draw fire at himself. Once locating the enemy, he returned fire on their positions and directed the exacting fire of other members of his unit. His actions resulted in the North Koreans abandoning their attack and withdrawing. Private First Class Christianson received a citation for materially aiding Easy Company in the continuation of its mission.

When the 5th Marines diverted north to Kempo Airfield, the 1st Marines continued east along the road to Yongdungpo and then across the Han River into western Seoul. In their approach to Seoul, they encountered intense daily resistance. By late September, Easy Company was engaged with North Korean units at Hill 132. [1] On September 28, the company deployed its platoons into defensive positions for the night. Private First Class Christianson was with another Marine at a forward listening post covering the approach to their platoon's flank.

The North Koreans began an attack in the early morning darkness. Detecting the enemy's approach, Private First Class Christianson sent his companion back to the platoon area to alert the command and, without orders, remained alone at the post forward of the company's line.

The enemy soldiers might have passed his post without discovering his position, but to give Easy Company more time, Private First Class Christianson opened fire upon the North Koreans with his automatic rifle, alerting them to his position. They attacked the listening post with automatic weapons, incendiary grenades, and rifle fire. Severely outnumbered, Private First Class Christianson took almost an entire enemy squad out of the fight as they swarmed about him. Before his position was overrun, he killed seven hostiles and wounded more.

Private First Class Christianson was killed at his post.

By that time, of the forty-four Marines in his platoon who landed at Inchon, only seventeen remained. Corporal Watters of Milwaukee, who served in the same platoon, recommended Private First Class Christianson for the Medal of Honor.

By remaining in the forward position instead of withdrawing to his platoon's line of defense, as might have been expected, Private First Class Stanley Christianson, 25-years-old, diverted the initial enemy attack long enough to give his platoon members time to occupy their fighting positions and ready themselves for what was meant to be a surprise assault on their flank. Forced to withdraw from the engagement on Hill 132, however, the North Koreans instead sustained forty-one fatalities, more than that wounded, and three prisoners captured.

When his photograph and the story of his death during the fighting in Korea appeared in Wisconsin newspapers, his parents were contacted by Mrs. Gordon Watters, informing them of the details of the battle and Medal of Honor recommendation. [2] Ten months later, Stanley's parents, three sisters, and a brother traveled together from Wisconsin to Washington D.C. for the posthumous presentation of his Medal of Honor, presented to Simon and Inga at the Pentagon by Secretary of the Navy Dan A. Kimball on Aug 30, 1951.

Private First Class Christianson remains La Crosse County's only recipient of the Congressional Medal of Honor.

Stanley Christianson was buried in a family section at Wet Coulee Cemetery, a small public cemetery cared for by the Town of Farmington. [3] He is one of only two service veterans buried there. His father was buried beside him in 1959, and his mother on the other side in January 1974. Inga is reported as the last person of eighty-one interred in the .794 acre cemetery. Wet Coulee is now inactive. [4]

Public records available during this study initially indicated that no tribute or memorial had been dedicated to Stanley in his hometown. Searching the Internet with the key words Stanley R. Christianson USMC yielded only what has already been described. Local Farmington newspapers were contacted in July 2008, fifty-eight years after his death, but did not respond. There was more to uncover.

A search of 1078 Marine Corps League Detachments across all the states for any named in tribute of Medal of Honor recipients, identified MCLD #347, chartered January 1, 1953. Named the Amundson/Christianson Detachment, the members meet in Onalaska, Wisconsin, north of La Crosse and eleven miles southwest of Mindoro. The Amundson name was unfamiliar, but the Christianson portion of the Detachment name, the location of MCLD #347, and the charter date all suggested a connection to Stanley Christianson.

On December 6, 1941, Private Leo DeVere Amundson, USMC, reported to the Marine Detachment aboard the USS *Arizona*. His Home of Record was La Crosse. His birthdate and birthplace are not provided on the historical USMC Web sites, nor is a photograph of him available. Leo was one of seventy-three Marines who died aboard the USS

Arizona on December 7, 1941. [5] Amundson family members are buried at Lewis Valley Lutheran Cemetery and Farmington Cemetery west of Mindoro. Private Leo Amundson is entombed in the USS *Arizona* Memorial at Pearl Harbor, Honolulu, Hawaii. Leo Amundson shares the honor of Marine Corps League Detachment #347 being named for him with another local Marine hero, Stanley Christianson. This shared honor was not the only tribute the Mindoro area extended to Stanley, however.

The last major battle of World War II began April 1, 1945 on the Island of Okinawa. Private First Class Christianson fought with the Marines until the island was secured on June 21. Three days later a ceremony took place in Veterans Memorial Park, off Highway 90, one mile west of West Salem, Wisconsin, and eight miles due south of Mindoro. On Sunday, June 24, the official procession turned off State Highway 16 at the park entrance, crossed over the Lagoon stone bridge, and stopped just past Shelter #1. At curbside a bronze plaque bolted to a standing, isosceles trapezoid-shaped rock was "Dedicated to all service men and women of La Crosse County." The well-tended plaque, facing towards the La Crosse River to the west, stands beside the base of the flagpole.

Private First Class Christianson was not named specifically, nor was his valor on Tarawa, Saipan, Tinian, and Okinawa cited. At the time of the dedication, the Marines were still in the Pacific preparing for the invasion of mainland Japan and would be there even after the August 15 announcement of Japan's surrender.

As a boy, when there was a chance to travel away from the family farm into nearby Western Wisconsin bluffs and valleys, Stanley would take it. He would have been familiar with, and maybe climbed, the weathered stone outcroppings of various vibrant colors there. The Badger State's native stones, created by epochs of wind, rain, and blizzard, have long been the source of building materials. The handcrafted cultured stone, with its rough and weathered appearance, adds a sense of endurance and character, whether used to build a fence, wall, fireplace, pillar, monument, or church edifice. [6] When Stanley looked out at the Wisconsin outcroppings, it is unlikely he ever imagined that the favored ledgestones would one day be fashioned into a monument to honor him.

On July 4, 1959, nearly nine years after Stanley gave his life on Hill 132 in Korea, another procession made its way into Veterans Memorial Park, and stopped at the flagpole for a dedication ceremony.

Behind the American Flag in the Memorial Park, fixed between two white ledgestone and mortar pillars, standing over five-feet-tall on a stone platform, is a white on bronze plaque dedicated to Stanley R. Christianson. Under his USMC photograph are inscribed details of his Medal of Honor actions and his Wet Coulee family background. [7]

A few paces behind the Stanley Christianson monument, over his right shoulder, a shiny olive drab, 46-ton M26 Pershing tank, with its 90-mm long-barrel gun and boat-hull-like underside, is parked on its own platform. The M26 tank was familiar to Private First Class Christianson. Marine M26 Tank Battalions went ashore as part of the first landing wave at Inchon and provided support for the ground troops fighting in the hills on the way up to Seoul.

The monument, shaded by trees, and its continued maintenance, demonstrate the pride La Crosse County continues to find in its only Medal of Honor recipient.

Closer to his family home, there is more proof that Stanley has not been forgotten.

Travel two-point-two miles east of Mindoro on County Road DE, turn south on County Road C for one mile, then right onto Amundson Road for a half-mile. Turn right at the intersection with Christianson Road, excavated by the Onalaska National Guard after Stanley's body was returned to the States in 1951. Just up the road on the right hand side, a chain link fence encircles Wet Coulee Cemetery.

The Trane Company of La Crosse donated a flagpole in 1978, and the La Crosse County Veterans Allied Council erected it over the Christianson family plot, Block 1, Lot 3, Site 7. [8] The Town of Farmington carefully maintains the small, hillside cemetery. The trees and lawn have a manicured appearance. Flowers and floral arrangements are often left at Stanley's gray, standing headstone with its bronze military marker.

Among other Marine Medal of Honor recipients from Korea honored at home, Stanley Christianson's name was removed from the Forgotten Thirty-Four roster.

STANLEY R. CHRISTIANSON
1925 — 1950

Pfc. Stanley R. Christianson was posthumously awarded the Congressional Medal of
Honor for his heroic action against enemy
forces at Hill 132 at Seoul, Korea, September 29,
1950. While he was manning a listening post
in the early morning hours the enemy made
an attack. Pfc. Christianson quickly sent
another Marine to alert the platoon. He
remained in his position with full knowledge
that he had slight chance of escape. He fired
relentlessly at hostile troops, attacking
furiously until he was fatally struck down.
His devotion to duty was responsible for
repulsion of the attack, accounting for seven
dead in the immediate vicinity and a total
of 41 enemy destroyed by the platoon. His
self-sacrificing action in the face of overwhelming odds sustain and enhance the finest
tradition of U. S. Naval Service. Pfc. Christianson was also awarded the Bronze Star Medal
for heroic action in Korea on September 16,
1950. He was one of nine children born to
Simon and Inga Christianson on a farm in
Wet Coulee near Mindoro, Wisconsin.

Erected 1959

CHAPTER 22
Heroic Lives, All Too Short

"Although no sculptured marble should rise to their memory,
nor engraved stone bear record of their deeds, yet will their
remembrance be as lasting as the land they honored." [1]

Daniel Webster (1782-1852)
American statesman

The youngest among them was a teenager. Five were in their early twenties, two just barely. The eldest among them was 33-years-old. They went to war and went above and beyond. Six were brought home: one to be buried in a National Cemetery, and four to be buried in hometown cemeteries. Two were not returned home.

The following accounts are short, based on available information about each of the seven Marines. They are written in the order in which the Medals were earned.

James Irsley Poynter

He was born in Saybrook, Illinois, a village of less than one square mile on the Sangamon River, and is variously claimed as a native of nearby Bloomington. Jim's parents, Eugene Lonzo and Molly Isabell, were from the county adjoining Daniel Boone National Forest in south central Kentucky. Jim was their ninth child. He had five older sisters and three brothers. One more sister was born many years after him, and lived less than a year. By the time Jim was born December 1, 1916, the family had already changed location to Illinois.

What opportunities might have drawn Eugene and Molly away from Kentucky is unknown. The Saybrook area experienced frequent annual tornadoes, and a fire in 1912 had left the center of the village in ruins. Seeking better circumstances did seem to have been somehow ingrained into the family, as evidenced in their marital experiences. Four of Jim's nine siblings married more than once. One of his older sisters married three times. Records indicate that Jim married twice and had six children.

No information was accessible for his school experience or of his life in Saybrook prior to WWII. Jim appears to have already been married to Dorothy Terry and to have had two sons, Albert Edwin and James Irsley, Jr., when war broke out in 1941. [2]

Pearl Harbor was attacked six days after Jim turned 25-years-old. He enlisted in the Marines two months later and survived five of the bloodiest campaigns in Marine Corps history: Guadalcanal, Southern Solomons, Saipan, Tinian, and Okinawa.

Jim came back to the States at the end of the war, returned to civilian life, and decided to settle in Downey, California. At some point his first marriage ended and Jim married Kathren G. Morrow. They had a son and three daughters born one year after each other between 1947 and 1950: Sharon Sue, Lois Jean, Patricia Lee, and Byron Eugene. [3] Although his eight grandchildren would hear about him, Jim would never have the opportunity to know them. The combat veteran decided to rejoin the Marine Reserves in Los Angeles in July 1950. By September's end Jim was in Korea.

Sergeant Poynter, by then 33-years-old, was combat experienced and mature. He was assigned duties as a squad leader in Company A, 1st

Battalion, 7th Marines. Taking his squad into action during the capture of Seoul, fighting from one barricade to the next, he demonstrated the same kind of aggressiveness against the enemy as he had during the island campaigns of WWII. He was recognized for his valor at Seoul between September 24 and October 4, 1950. For his able and "outstanding leadership" of his squad, he was awarded a Bronze Star with a Combat V device, indicating that he had demonstrated heroism in combat.

Following the taking of Seoul, the 1st Battalion, 7th Marines were quickly redeployed to North Korea's east coast, ready to move north to the Chosin Reservoir. To reach the reservoir, their column was going to march through places called the Sudong Gorge, Funchilin Pass, Hell Fire Valley, and the Toktong Pass on their tactical maps.

"Jump-off" came early in the morning, October 31. The Marines spent the day climbing a one-lane mountain road. That night, having passed the village of Majon-dong, the battalions were settled into a narrow valley between Hungnam and the Taeback Plateau, bordered on the west by a dry riverbed. The valley was encircled by hills, steep and high, some rising taller than 1,500 feet. Rocks were everywhere.

Sergeant Poynter briefed his squad that they were about thirty miles below the Chosin. A tiny village called Sudong-ni was to the north of the valley. He encouraged them to get as much sleep as possible. In the morning, they were to continue through the village, into the Funchilin Pass, and on to the reservoir. He also let them know that the imposing hill just ahead of them and between Able Company and Sudong-ni was designated as Hill 532.

The night was chilled and sleeping bags were hardly enough to keep the weary Marines warm. That did not matter, really, since they would have little time to sleep. What Sergeant Poynter, his squad, and Able Company commanders did not know was that the Marines were about to have their first engagement with an army division of the Chinese Communist Forces (CCF). And it was going to be a brutal fight.

The CCF came in the dark of night, a multitude blaring bugles and shouting, charging down the hills and up from the riverbed. Machine gun and rifle fire shattered the quiet of the valley. Parachute flares burst overhead, giving a glow to the valley, casting undulating shadows on the valley floor. The agonizing cries for "Corpsman!" soon began.

This is how the days and nights ahead would be as the Marines moved north and fought for every yard out of the Sudong Gorge.

November 4, 1950

In the fifth day of fighting in the valley, Able Company pushed the fortified enemy forces off Hill 532.

Sergeant Poynter knew what to expect. He established his squad in hasty defensive positions, in line with the rest of the platoon. The enemy, reorganized and combined with other units, charged the hill in a violent counterattack. The advancing force greatly outnumbered the Marines.

Sergeant Poynter was wounded in the assault and his squad sustained devastating casualties. He maintained command of his remaining men, directing their fire. The enemy reached the crest of the hill, pierced the Marine's defensive line, and surrounded the squad's position. His squad was at risk of being overrun as the encirclement tightened. Sergeant Poynter engaged the enemy soldiers with his bayonet. The hand-to-hand combat was desperate and frenzied, and he killed at least three of the Chinese soldiers.

Maintaining his tactical sense of the situation despite the close-in fighting, Sergeant Poynter saw three enemy machine-gun teams preparing to set up within twenty-five yards of his position. Understanding the ruinous power about to be unleashed upon his men, he reacted decisively. Sergeant Poynter gathered hand grenades from wounded Marines near him and charged alone into the open. He attacked the first, then the second machine-gun emplacement with grenades, destroying the emplacements and killing the crews. As he reached the third machine gun, he was wounded again by enemy fire.

Before he died, Sergeant Poynter put the third emplacement out of action with a grenade.

His one-man attack caused disorganization among the advancing soldiers and inspired the remnant of his own squad to regain the initiative and force the enemy back down Hill 532. Doing so, the entire platoon was able to maneuver itself into a more advantageous position within Able Company's line of defense. When the battle was over and the 7th Marines marched north out of Sudong, more than 1500 Chinese infantrymen were lying dead on the ground and the CCF 124th Division was out of the fight for the rest of the war.

Sergeant James Irsley Poynter was buried with full military honors in Fort Rosecrans National Cemetery, San Diego, California, Section O, Grave 729. Reports that he had been awarded a Medal of Honor on February 1, 1952, appeared in a UP newspaper article, also indicating that the Medal was to be presented to Mrs. Kathren Poynter. [4] She and their two-year-old son, Byron Eugene, were presented the Medal at the Pentagon by Secretary of the Navy Dan Kimball on September 4, 1952. The Marines remember Sergeant Poynter from time to time. Fifty-three years after his death on Hill 532, Gunnery Sergeant Keith A. Milks, a Marine historian and author, wrote Sergeant Poynter's story in "The Lore of the Corps: Marine veteran reenlisted and gave his life in Korea." [5]

Lee Hugh Phillips

Medal of Honor recipients often faced early challenges in life. These challenges resulted either from life situations in which the boys had no direct part or from deliberate choices they made. In other words, if they were not challenged by early life experiences, they found ways to challenge themselves.

Developing the character inclined to heroic bravery involved routinely putting themselves into situations in which they would be challenged and tested and in which they had an opportunity to excel. Their response to most challenges was to face them directly or to find a way to triumph. Some of their responses would have been immediate and spontaneous, perhaps impulsive. Others were thought out, planned, and rehearsed in their minds. Lee Hugh Phillips' life provides examples of this trait.

Lee was born on February 3, 1930. He might have seemed like a questionable leader type around his hometown of Stockbridge, on the southeast side of Atlanta, Georgia. He went to school in Ellenwood, seven miles from home. He left school when he was 15-years-old and went to work in Atlanta, first as a picture frame painter, then as a department store clerk. At some point, Lee's mother remarried and moved to Hapeville, on the edge of the Atlanta International airport.

Bosses liked his work and each would have continued his employment had he wanted to stay. Instead, Lee enlisted in the Marines weeks before his eighteenth birthday, giving Ben Hill, on the southwest side of Atlanta, as his home of record. When he said goodbye to his parents and two sisters, Mary and Martha, to leave for Korea in September 1950, he had served fourteen months of his enlistment, had been promoted twice, and had reached the age of 20-years.

Corporal Phillips was a squad leader with Company E, 2d Battalion, 7th Marines and participated in offensive operations at Seoul in late September. Afterwards, when the Marines bypassed the 38th Parallel, he made the landing in the east on Kalma Peninsula at Wonsan and moved his way up the central sector of Korea towards the Chosin Reservoir.

The North Korean People's Army (NKPA) had prepared fortified defenses along the main routes of advance. They held the high ground on strategic hills and armed themselves in trenches and dugouts. They also knew they were reinforced by divisions of Chinese Communist Forces. The NKPA soldiers did not leave their hills without a determined fight.

On one such hill early in the drive north, the 7th Marines encountered frenzied resistance outside of Sudong-ni. The North Koreans repelled five assaults against their position and held Hill 698. Corporal Phillips explained the objective to his squad on November 4. They fixed their bayonets onto their carbines, preparing to ascend a hill occupied by an entrenched force of much larger numbers. Corporal Phillips took the lead position and led the charge up the steep slope. There was no element of surprise and the enemy was waiting.

The Koreans immediately responded to the charge by unleashing a storm of mortar rounds, machine-gun fire, and rifle fire. The squad was quickly taking casualties and pinned down by the blockade of explosions. The onslaught did not cause Corporal Phillips to stop for long, though. From his point position, he rallied the squad and moved them up the slope under bombardment. Only five of his men remained when he reached the crest of the hill. An enemy squad immediately attacked the Marines, intent on pushing them off the hill.

Medal of Honor recipients contend with adversity rather than withdraw from or submit to it.

On the crest of Hill 698, Corporal Phillips charged into the enemy squad with grenades and rifle fire, encouraging his men to follow him. They did, overwhelming the squad sent against them, and infiltrating further into the enemy emplacement. One fortified position remained, manned by four North Koreans, holding on to an almost unreachable, rocky precipice.

Corporal Phillips quickly gave directions to the three men remaining in his squad and led the charge. Under the covering fire of his men, he climbed the outcrop and, holding his position with one hand, lobbed grenades into the fortification with his other. When he climbed into the destroyed fortification, he had only two squad members left. The remaining three Marines quickly organized themselves in the stronghold. A squad-size enemy force just as quickly counterattacked. Directing their fields of fire against five-to-one odds, Corporal Phillips and his two men repulsed the counterattack. That portion of the road out of Sudong and on to the Chosin was now open. This was the same day Sergeant Poynter died.

November 27, 1950

His decimated squad was manned with replacements. Corporal Phillips led them north with Easy Company, making it to the southeast corner of the Chosin Reservoir. He continued with them to Yudam-ni, pushing the North Koreans to the Yalu River. On November 27, at 8:00 AM, after three months of fighting in Korea, the 7th Marines began the planned push west to join the right flank of the U.S.

Eighth Army. In the effort to take the high ground on the steep Southwest Ridge of Yudam-ni, Corporal Lee Phillips was killed in the advance. His comrades buried him at the Chosin Reservoir during the battle, and his body was not recovered.

His name is engraved on the *Wall of The Missing* at the National Memorial of the Pacific in Honolulu, Hawaii.

If arranged in the order of dates of heroic action, Lee Phillips would be the eighth Marine to earn the Medal of Honor in Korea. However, based on the date of the award's authorization, official records list him as the fortieth Marine recipient in Korea. The Medal he had earned three weeks before he was killed at Yudam-ni was announced on January 19, 1954, three years after his death. [6]

His Medal was received by his mother, Mrs. Izora B. Cantrell of Hapeville, Georgia, at a ceremony at the Pentagon on March 29, 1954, presented by Secretary of the Navy Robert B. Anderson.

Although his body was not brought home to Georgia from the Chosin Reservoir, it is possible today to leave a commemorative flower or wreath in his honor. The twenty-three-acre Marietta National Cemetery is in downtown Marietta, Georgia, on the northwest edge of Atlanta. The cemetery, now closed to new internments, was placed on the National Registry of Historic Places in 1998. More than 10,300 Union officers and soldiers who died in the Civil War are buried there. [7] At one edge of the cemetery, at Grave 8 in the shaded Memorial Area B, stands a white marble headstone. It is in the front row, easily viewed by visitors making their way along the stone walkway. Engraved on the headstone is "In Memory Of Lee H. Phillips." The Medal of Honor insignia is below his name. Two headstones to the left, a standing, ground level plaque explains: "The markers in this Memorial Area honor veterans whose remains have not been recovered or identified..." [8]

Lee Phillips' headstone is one of only two in the Marietta National Cemetery dedicated to a Medal of Honor recipient. The other recipient was a private in the New York Infantry who died in the Civil War at Peach Tree Creek on July 20, 1864.

A search for Lee among rosters of Georgia's famous people did not yield much. Poets, actors, comedians, athletes, writers, singers, musicians, conductors, journalists, Pulitzer Prize winners, diplomats, a painter and sculptor, a serial killer, an old west hero who fought at Tombstone's OK Corral, the U.S. Girl Scouts founder, a jurist, a supreme court associate justice, a civil rights leader, the first appointed woman U.S. senator, a secretary of state, and a U.S. President are listed as notable. [9] The timeline of his life was included in *Our Georgia History*. [10]

To date, Lee Phillips, Medal of Honor recipient, is not counted among Famous Georgians.

James Edmund Johnson

He was a New Year's baby, born in 1926, and lived at 816 North Garfield in Pocatello, Idaho.

Throughout Jim Johnson's life, crowds were drawn to him. He played on his high school junior varsity basketball team for two years, while WWII played out in Europe and the Pacific. His father had fought with the 11th Marines in WWI, and Jim felt the call to arms himself before he finished high school. On November 10, 1943, when the Marine Corps turned 168-years-old, and when Jim was 17-years-old, he enlisted in the Marines.

Immediately after his infantry training in California, he traveled further into the Pacific, joining the Marine Regiments serving in the island campaigns. After experiencing combat on Peleliu and Okinawa, he returned to San Diego for a brief tour and was discharged from the service in February 1946.

Jim went home to Pocatello, took a job as a machinist in the Naval Ordinance plant and went to college in Bellingham, Washington. He also found that he could not settle into postwar civilian life. Instead, he reenlisted in the Marines in January 1948, fewer than two weeks after he had turned 22-years-old. That June, Second Lieutenant Johnson reported to the Officer's Basic School in Quantico, Virginia and joined the Fifth Basic Class, USMC.

Like Jim, many of his fellow classmates had come from the enlisted infantry ranks, promoted within the Meritorious Staff Non-Commissioned Officers program. Second Lieutenant Johnson would have to apply himself to keep his officer rank. Meritorious commissions did not guarantee success at the Officer's Basic School. Neither did a college degree. As was true across the many years of Basic School classes, 25% of the Fifth Basic Class did not make it to graduation.

Second Lieutenant Johnson was a standout among his classmates in various ways, some professional, some not. He was remembered as good-natured, without "a mean bone in his body," and as a man of good cheer even in stressful circumstances. The photograph of him on Web sites today, would seem to confirm one characteristic attributed to him by staff and students alike at the Basic School. He seemed always to have a quirky little grin, leaving classmates to wonder what was on his mind. Often it was a mischievous prank of some sort he was planning for one of them. The targets of his pranks found it impossible to be long annoyed with Second Lieutenant Johnson, and no one stayed mad at him for long. When ranked by classmates on various personality and professional characteristics, he was predictably found at the top of popularity ratings.

Highly adaptive coping mechanisms

What people today call *defense mechanisms* are mental tactics by which a person protects one's self from distressing realities. The mechanisms are so habitual and automatic that they sometimes reside outside the awareness of the person who employs them. To early analyst Sigmund Freud that meant defense mechanisms were in the unconscious. In a sense, defense mechanisms are internal cognitive reactions to stress. Today, such reactions are more commonly referred to as *coping devices*.

Like all people, Medal of Honor recipients developed personal skills, or tactics, to manage stressful and challenging experiences. Their coping skills take a variety of forms. Some result in higher functioning despite stressful events. These allow a person to adapt productively to stress and to make the most of their circumstances. For these individuals, encounters with stress promote their personal development and elevate their performance.

Defense mechanisms do not necessarily result in welcome outcomes. Some actually lead to poor interpersonal functioning, resulting in distortions and manipulations of reality, irrational reactions, acting out behaviors, and, in the extreme, psychotic breaks from reality. People who employ such mechanisms in stressful circumstances tend to "come apart," or decompensate as stress increases. They do not function well in many areas of life.

Men like Second Lieutenant Johnson tend to react to stress in adaptive ways, thereby maximizing their efforts to master life events. They establish affiliation with others rather than secluding or isolating themselves. They are prosocial rather than antisocial. They channel anger and aggression into athletic endeavors. They assert themselves rather than cowering or passively withdrawing when challenged. They seem to evince an innate optimism in themselves, in life, and in outcomes. And, many of them have the tendency to recall adverse events with humor.

Where Second Lieutenant Johnson truly excelled at The Basic School was in map reading, the use of infantry weapons, and leadership skills during field exercises. When training in the role of Fire Team, Squad, or Platoon Leader, he ran about shouting encouragement, the grin on his face indicative of how much he enjoyed the challenge of taking a ridge from a hidden aggressor squad.

If there was an obstacle to Jim keeping his officer's commission, it went beyond playing pranks on classmates. From month to month he ended up with a larger bill at the Officer's Club bar than his salary could cover. He took some well-intended scoldings from classmates about the bar tabs, promised to reform, and then spent a good amount of time the next month back at the Club. His drinking and his mounting debt seemed problematic to his commanders. About a month before the Fifth Basic Class graduation, Second Lieutenant Johnson was deprived of his commission and was returned to the enlisted ranks. [11]

While assigned duties in Quantico, Sergeant Johnson met Mary Jeanne Wright from Salisbury, Maryland. They were married on October 15, 1949. He was then an accounting instructor for a year in Washington, D.C., having joined the Marine Corps Reserves after his commission was revoked. He was recalled to active duty with the Reserves during the summer of 1950. In August, he was home for the birth of his daughter, Stephanie, and then departed for Korea five days later.

The Chosin Reservoir

Sergeant Johnson was assigned to the 11th Marines, the unit in which his father had served two wars previously, and then to a provisional rifle platoon in Company J, 3d Battalion, 7th Marines. He was given the duties of squad leader. After Inchon and Seoul, Sergeant Johnson, along with the rest of the First Marine Division, made his second amphibious assault, landing at Wonsan on the east coast of the Korean peninsula, October 26, 1950.

The mission moving the Marines was to drive 125 miles north to Changjin Lake, and then push northwest across the Taebaek Mountains with four Marine rifle battalions and three artillery battalions to close the gap with the U.S. Eighth Army's right flank. They pushed their way fifty-five miles to Hamhung. From that point, they fought day and night, from one hill and village to the next, north along 70 miles of single-lane, dirt and gravel road with its steep climbs and drops to Changjin Lake, also known as the Chosin Reservoir.

The place names would become as familiar to Marines as *Iwo Jima*.

Sergeant Johnson led his squad north, climbed the difficult eight-mile Funchilin Pass up 2,500 feet to Koto-ri, passed through Hell Fire Valley, continued north to the high plateau where the village of Hagaru-ri once sat on the southeast corner of the reservoir, and then fought northwest another thirty-five miles through the Toktong Pass, Chinhung-ni, and to the staging area at Yudam-ni. Sergeant Johnson would pass through Hagaru-ri only once.

Major General Oliver P. Smith, commanding the Division, had ordered the construction of an airfield, supply dump, and ammunition dump in the flattened area of Hagaru-ri, to ensure adequate support for the Marines at Chinhung-ni, Koto-ri, Hagaru-ri, and Yudam-ni, who would be in mutual support of each other across the thirty-five miles of narrow, winding, climbing, tortuous road.

Sergeant Johnson, having spent nearly six years of his life serving as a Marine, was among the nearly 7,000 Marines of the 5th and 7th Marine Regiments who reached Yudam-ni, west of the Chosin Reservoir. When his former Basic School classmates encountered him there, they had no trouble recognizing him. Despite the nighttime temperatures of minus thirty-five degrees, he greeted them with the same good cheer he had shown them at Quantico, and always the devilish grin.

Enemy forces attacked nightly to probe Marine positions and defenses. To complicate matters, a Siberian cold front blanketed the region on November 14. The frozen ground did not give easily for Marines to prepare foxholes and defensive trenches.

On November 26, three days after Americans celebrated Thanksgiving Day, a holiday that had been declared just nine years earlier by President Roosevelt, the Marines prepared to move west from Yudam-ni, sending companies out on patrol to probe the enemy defenses and gather information about the ridges ahead in the Taebaeck Mountains, the spine down the center of the Korean peninsula. The terrain was rugged, snow covered, and thickly wooded.

It was also thick with enemy forces.

The Chinese Communists had been secretly massing forces across the Yalu River into Korea for over a month. Four Chinese armies with ten divisions and an estimated 120,000 soldiers waited to sweep down the east and west sides of the Chosin reservoir. Their orders from China's Chairman Mao Zedong were to annihilate all the Marines between Yudam-ni and Chinhung-ni and to wipe clean the Marine command post from Hagaru.

By morning of November 27, the Marines, with the Chosin at their back, were prepared to "jump off" into the Taebaeck Mountains and link with the Army. They were about to learn that the enemy armies planned to tighten a circle around them. The Chinese divisions had been divided to make nearly simultaneous attacks at Yudam-ni, the Toktong Pass, Hagaru-ri, and Koto-ri and to block the road out of the Chosin. At each of their objectives, they came in human wave assaults. More than 20,000 Chinese regulars attacked at Hagaru, threatening to overrun the Marine command post.

By the third day of battle at the Chosin, on Wednesday, November 29, it was clear that the Marines were not going to push through the Taebaek Mountains. Orders were passed to Major General Smith to withdraw from the Chosin and return his Marines to Tongjoson Bay for evacuation from North Korea.

While the Marines fought their way out of the Chinese encirclement, news broadcasts back in the States reported the "Retreat." Americans waited to learn about the loss of the Marine Division. When asked by a journalist how the retreat was expected to progress, Major General Oliver P. Smith had his own comment about the ongoing events. Two weeks later, his answer was quoted at the start of a national magazine article. Enjoyed by Marines ever since, the retort continues to be repeated in various forums today.

"Retreat, hell! We're not retreating, we're just advancing in a different direction." [12]

Any doubts in Major General Smith's assertion would be answered by the fact that ten Marines who fought at the Chosin Reservoir were awarded Medals of Honor.

Since the landing at Wonsan, Sergeant Johnson had remained at the lead of his squad through thirty-eight days of intense fighting. The convoy was readied to move in an orderly withdrawal back down the road to Hagaru-ri. The Marine regiments would be there by the afternoon of December 3. Sergeant Johnson was no longer among his men.

The "Breakout"

The "advance in a different direction" began on December 1. As the convoy of Marines started south from Yudam-ni, to Hagaru, the 3rd

Battalion, 7th Marines was tasked to cover the rear of the column in the vicinity of Yudam-ni. To do that, they had to strike first, capturing Hill 1542 and Hill 1419 in order to place themselves between the Chinese and the convoy on the road.

The Chinese held the peaks against the Marine assaults, but the companies dug in on the eastern slopes, preventing the enemy from attacking the road. The convoy passed south by afternoon and the 3/7 followed. That night and into the morning of December 2, 1950, the Marine rearguard fought to secure the Toktong Pass. As Jig Company maneuvered, Sergeant Johnson's platoon was out in the open and exposed to enemy fire. From entrenched and concealed positions, a large enemy force advanced. Because they were wearing the uniforms of friendly forces, procured from American casualties and prisoners, the Marines hesitated.

As the Chinese closed the distance, the enemy attacked the platoon.

The platoon commander was absent at the start of the assault, so Sergeant Johnson assumed leadership. He moved about the platoon, organizing the men into a hasty defense and directed their fire effectively to fend off the attack. Despite the intense enemy fire and barrage of explosions, he shouted encouragement to the platoon as the firefight continued. As they fought, orders came down for Sergeant Johnson to move the platoon from its open location in the engagement, a challenging maneuver while under fire. He moved among his men, passing along the order.

Sergeant Johnson did not withdraw, although greatly outnumbered and wounded. To provide protective cover as the platoon displaced, he took an exposed position, firing into the advancing enemy force with his weapon. Alone, he slowed the enemy assault enough to give time to the entire platoon to reposition with the larger Marine force.

When last seen, Sergeant Johnson was engaging the hostile force in close hand grenade exchanges and hand-to-hand combat. He was directly credited with the successful displacement of his platoon. Among his Basic School companions, it came as no surprise that he would die so fellow Marines could live. It was an action typical of him. Sergeant Johnson was never seen alive again.

The Marine "advance in a different direction" to Hagaru was completed on December 4. The breakout continued from there two days later. The Marines reached the outskirts of Hungnam on December 13. One hundred ninety-three U.S. Navy ships were waiting in the port. As the evacuation of UN troops and 98,000 Korean civilian refugees got underway, the Marines set up a defensive perimeter around Hungnam to prevent the pursuing communist forces from entering the port city. While skirmishes with the enemy continued for eleven more days, the engagements were hardly like the brutal battles along the road to and from the Chosin. The last of the Marines were evacuated from Hungnam by 2:36 PM on Christmas Eve, December 24, 1950.

All the Marines in Jig Company, 3d Battalion, 7th Marines knew that Sergeant James Johnson did not board a ship and leave North Korea from Hungnam. He had been declared "missing in action" on December 2, the same day he was last seen covering the withdrawal of his platoon in the Toktong Pass. In reports, he was counted among the 4,385 Marine battle casualties from the Chosin Reservoir Campaign. [13] Other reports and recommendations regarding his heroic actions and his being "fully aware that his voluntary action meant certain death or capture" began working their way up the chain of command.

On Tuesday, December 4, 1951, General Clifton B. Cates, 19th Commandant of the Marine Corps notified Mary Jeanne Johnson in Washington, D.C. that the Marine Corps was conferring the Medal of Honor upon her husband for his actions near Yudam-ni. General Cates told Mary Jeanne that his office was going to hold the Medal "with the hope that he would be available for the award sometime in the near future." [14]

After the Korean War ended, Sergeant Johnson was declared "presumed dead, killed in action" on November 2, 1953. His Medal of Honor was presented to his wife and three and a half-year-old daughter on March 29, 1954, at the same Pentagon ceremony for Lee Phillips and William Mathews. [15] Mary Jeanne's aunt, Mrs. Joseph Dean, accompanied her to the Pentagon to hold on to Stephanie's hand. It is unclear if either Jim's mother, Mrs. Juanita Hart, left her home in San Diego, or his sister, Mrs. Edwin L. Hanke, left hers in Pocatello, to attend the presentation in Washington. After the ceremony, Idaho Republican

Senator Henry Dworshak took Mary Jeanne and Stephanie to visit the vice president's office. A photo of the White House visit appeared in the Pocatello newspaper. [16]

A headstone "In Memory Of Sergeant James E. Johnson" was erected in the Memorial Section H, Lot 451, at Arlington National Cemetery, Virginia.

From out of Texas they came.

Going back to the American Indian Campaigns of 1863-90, eighty-two Medal of Honor recipients have hailed from the State of Texas. Sixteen of these were Marines in World War II, the Korean War, and the Vietnam War.

From World War II, the Marines included Staff Sergeant William James Bordelon, San Antonio, Sergeant William George Harrell, Rio Grande City, First Lieutenant William Deane Hawkins, El Paso, First Lieutenant Jack Lummus, Ennis, and Private First Class Charles Howard Roan, Claude. Those from the Korean War included Staff Sergeant Ambrosio Guillen, El Paso, First Lieutenant Frank Nicias Mitchell, Indian Gap, Private First Class Whitt Lloyd Moreland, Waco, and Second Lieutenant George Herman O'Brien, Jr., Fort Worth. From the Vietnam War were Lance Corporal Richard Allen Anderson, Houston, Private First Class Oscar Palmer Austin, Nacogdoches, Lance Corporal Thomas Elbert Creek, Amarillo, Sergeant Alfredo (Freddy) Gonzalez, Edinburg, Second Lieutenant Terrence Collinson Graves, Corpus Christi, Lance Corporal Miguel Keith, San Antonio, and Private First Class Alfred Mac Wilson, Abilene.

Of the sixteen Marines, only George Herman O'Brien, Jr. and William George Harrell returned home after their battles and wars.

In tribute to the sixteen, no fewer than six ships, one room, three halls, one barracks, two schools, a high school rifle team, one infantry officers' course, one Veteran's Administration Medical Center, one veteran's home, one Dining Hall, one Enlisted Club, one University dormitory, one Marine Association Chapter, one American Legion Post, two boulevards, and one athletic award have been dedicated in their names.

The Commemorative Air Force National Headquarters is located in Midland, Texas. Within is O'Brien Hall, named in honor of George H. O'Brien, Jr., a native of Midland. Second Lieutenant O'Brien earned his award in 1952 at the battle for The Hook, in Korea. He came home to Texas, led an exemplary life, and died March 11, 2005. George was laid to rest in the Texas State Cemetery in Austin, Texas. An eight-foot bronze statue of him as he would have appeared on The Hook was dedicated on Memorial Day, May 26, 2008, in the hall named for him.

The Texas Medal of Honor Memorial, honoring all the Medal of Honor recipients from Texas, is located in O'Brien Hall. The eighty-two names are listed around the base of the George O'Brien statue. As a further tribute to honor the sixteen Marines, the Texas Marine Medal of Honor Monument was dedicated in a ceremony on Memorial Day weekend, May 25, 2007. Whitt Lloyd Moreland's name can be found on both memorials.

Whitt Lloyd Moreland

The Private First Class celebrated his twenty-first birthday in Korea with his comrades of Company C, 1st Battalion, 5th Marines. There was no doubt in their minds where he had come from. The proud "twang" was clear—he was a Texan. Most called him Moreland; those closest to him called him Whitt. His full name would have been familiar only to those on both sides of his family.

Whitt Lloyd Moreland was born in Waco, in McLennan County, on March 7, 1930, and raised in Austin, in Travis County. It might be that both his parents, Lloyd and Patsy, were originally from Arkansas. Whitt's first name was derived from his mother's side of the family, the Whittingtons. His middle name was obviously also his father's first name.

The pioneering Whittingtons came to Arkansas in 1834, settling in Mount Ida, a small town in the mountains of Ouachita National Forest in western Arkansas. The available records do not indicate when Lloyd and Patsy came to Waco to have a family. Whitt's sister, Elizabeth Ann, was born when he was 12-years-old. His brother, Lloyd W. Jr., was born in 1948 while the family still lived in Austin. Lloyd Jr. would have very few memories of his big brother.

Whitt played football for two years at Junction High School, from where he graduated in 1948. He enlisted in the Marines the following September and served a year's enlistment. Whatever his future plans might have been, he went into the Marine Reserves in September 1949. Because Marines were dying at war, and units needed replacements, Whitt was activated for service at the end of November 1950. He was transferred to Korea early in 1951 and would be in combat zones for fewer than five months.

Private First Class Moreland was an intelligence scout for Company C when he celebrated his last birthday. Charlie Company was engaged in operations against the enemy at Kwangch'i-Dong. On May 29, 1951, the company was facing an enemy force maintaining advantageous positions on a hill. When a rifle platoon was assigned the mission to overrun the enemy defenses, Private First Class Moreland volunteered to participate in the assault.

"Here I am, send me!" [17]

Medal recipients like Private First Class Moreland volunteered to go into harm's way, demonstrating a readiness to encounter injury and pain, as well as threats to life and limb. It is that spiritual something that permeates the willingness to put one's self in danger on behalf of others.

As the Charlie Company platoon charged the emplacement, Private First Class Moreland provided effective covering fire, significantly assisting in the taking and securing of the position. Observing another fortified bunker about 400 meters further along the ridgeline of the hill, he led a party of Marines through the enemy's fields of fire to reach it. As they closed on the bunker, the enemy countered with a barrage of hand grenades.

Private First Class Moreland kicked the projectiles off the ridge, neutralizing their explosions. As he kicked at the last of the grenades, he lost his balance, slipped, and fell to the ground. Without time to regain his feet, he shouted a warning to his companions and rolled on top of the grenade. Dying in the explosion, Private First Class Whitt Moreland, 21-years-old, spared his fellow Marines injury.

On Monday, August 4, 1952, fourteen months after Whitt died protecting comrades from a grenade detonation, Lloyd and Patsy Moreland, along with Whitt's 9-year-old sister, Elizabeth Ann, drove to the State Capitol Building in Austin. In an "impressive capitol ceremony," in front of a "great throng" of spectators, USMC officers from the Austin area presented Whitt's parents his Medal of Honor, handing it to Patsy on a silver pillow. The Marines also unveiled a large portrait of the young Marine and presented it to the Moreland family on behalf of the people of Austin. Whitt's parents "sadly and proudly" accepted the tributes. [18] What eventually became of that portrait could not be determined in this research, but it likely remained in the Moreland family, perhaps passed down to a niece or nephew.

When Whitt's body was returned to the United States, he was buried in Whittington Cemetery in Mount Ida, Arkansas. The small, rock-fenced cemetery, established for descendants of the original Whittingtons, sits on top of a wooded knoll. Lloyd and Patsy Moreland were also both buried among the Whittingtons more than thirty years after Whitt returned home.

His name was included on Texas monuments with other Medal of Honor recipients. Fifty-four years after he had died, some looking at the memorials might have wondered who Whitt Moreland had been. One Texan remembered him well. Whitt was mentioned in a Memorial Day weekend release from House Representative Charles "Doc" Anderson's Capitol Office on Tuesday, May 24, 2005. [19] In *Gone, But Not Forgotten—Looking Back At Mclennan County Military Heroes*, Representative Anderson described walking by a display of all the Texas Medal recipients every day at the State Capitol Building in Austin. The display included three Medal of Honor recipients from McLennan County. Representative Anderson remembered Whitt among the

"heroes of our area who distinguished themselves with honor and bravery in combat. The release notes that "[f]inding out more about these
individuals only deepens the respect." Representative Anderson then
told Whitt's story in a short paragraph.

Representative Anderson had good reason to remember Whitt
Moreland. He was also born in Waco and was almost six-years-old when
Private First Class Moreland sacrificed himself to protect his companions.

Whitt Moreland was the seventh Marine Medal recipient to save
companions from a grenade's explosion in Korea. Nine more would
do so before the war ended. On May 28, 1952, a 19-year-old corporal
would be the eleventh.

David Bernard Champagne

Dave was born in Waterville, in central Maine, on November 13,
1932. The town sits in a valley cut by the Kennebec River. His family moved south from the Pine Tree State to Wakefield, in the south
central region of Rhode Island, where bodies of water are plentiful.
Narragansett Bay, Point Judith Pond, Silver Lake, Worden's Pond, and
various other small ponds surround the small town. The University of
Rhode Island is a few miles up the road.

Dave went to the Wakefield public schools. His uncle worked at
the local theater and got Dave a part time job showing movies while he
was in high school. Dave's older brother, Carl, was already in the Air
Force when he finished high school. Carl later remembered Dave as a
"good, all-around kid."

The war that had been expected to end by Christmas, 1950, had
continued after the breakout from the Chosin Reservoir. *The Frozen
Chosin Few*, as the veterans from the fight would be called, were not
home yet.

Dave traveled up to Boston, Massachusetts, on March 7, 1951,
and enlisted in the Marines. Private Champagne went through recruit
training at Parris Island, was promoted to private first class, and was
transferred west to Camp Pendleton for intensive combat training.

With two sons now in the military, and a war going on in Korea, Dave's family in Wakefield understood the purpose for a Marine receiving combat training. His transfer to California put him too close to Korea for those in Rhode Island. Worried as they were, the Champagnes were encouraged in July when the United Nations leaders and the Communist leaders began their "Peace Talks." They hoped there would be a resolution to the conflict before any more troops were sent to the embattled nation.

Private First Class Champagne let his folks know that he had received his orders to go to Korea. Like Private First Class Moreland, Dave was going to celebrate a birthday after arriving in Korea. And it would also be his last birthday.

Talk of Peace Did Not End the Dying

Private First Class Champagne was assigned to 1st Platoon, Company A, 1st Battalion, 7th Marines, and went immediately into combat. Having participated in three successive campaigns, he was promoted to corporal and raised to a fire team leader position.

In addition to stalemates and see-sawing fights for hills, South Korea's President Sygman Rhee declaring martial law in Pusan on May 27, 1952, was another indication that peace negotiations were not bringing an end to the battles. The next day, Able Company was tasked to assault the fortified enemy position on Hill 104 and Tumae-ri Ridge.

In the dark of night, May 28, Corporal Champagne reviewed the mission with his men. Then he maneuvered the fire team through a barrage of enemy fire. Under his direction, charging with bayonets up the steep slope, the fire team overpowered enemy trenches and strongly defended bunkers. When the platoon reached the crest of the hill, he positioned his team in a trench in a defensive line with mutually supporting fields of fire, ensuring they were prepared for the inevitable counterattack. He had done this all before.

Single-minded

As children, many Medal recipients were remembered as having had a "strong will," being strong-minded, being determined, or as being "stubborn." Once set on a course of action, they were difficult to redirect or deter. They would not be easily talked out of their plans. When they had an objective in mind, some might have said they were overly "preoccupied."

Parents and teachers often view this trait as frustrating. Partners in relationships might accuse a single-minded individual of "caring" only about their own point of interest. Bosses, commanders, and peers tend to view single-mindedness as strength and resource when goals are set and actions are required.

Men with this sort of "preoccupation" do not give up on attaining goals they have set for themselves.

The artillery and mortar shells came first on Hill 104, and then came the human wave of enemy soldiers. Corporal Champagne, intent on holding the crest of the hill, was seriously wounded in the leg by a bullet round that spun him to the ground. He refused evacuation to the Marine lines three football-fields-length to the rear. He stayed in order to help stave off the enemy effort to retake the commanding hill emplacements.

Determination propelled the hostile force to charge more fiercely. The rate of machine-gun, automatic weapons, and rifle fire intensified, as did the exchange of hand grenades. The noise was deafening.

A grenade landed in the trench among his team members, and Corporal Champagne reacted immediately. The Chinese were closing on the trench. He stooped, grabbed the grenade, and threw it down toward the charging enemy force. The device exploded as Corporal Champagne released it, blowing off his hand, showering him with shrapnel, and blasting him out of the trench. He was now exposed to the enemy charge. As he struggled to get himself back into the trench, and before he could be pulled back in, he was wounded again by a mortar detonation.

Private First Class William A. Powers was a fire team member on Hill 104, and also from Rhode Island. Surrounded by charging Chinese soldiers, he turned over his team leader and held him briefly. [20] Corporal David Champagne, 19-years-old, died in the trench on the crest of Hill 104. His platoon commander, Second Lieutenant Carl F. Ullrich, would never forget David's courage and considered himself lucky to have led such "truly wonderful men." [21]

David was brought home and buried in Saint Francis Cemetery, in Waterville, Maine, his birthplace. His 15-year-old brother, Reginald, received his Medal of Honor in July 1953, during ceremonies held at Wakefield's Old Mountain Baseball Field. The award was accredited to Rhode Island because Dave reported Wakefield as his hometown.

No available record attests to whether any Wakefield school has a commemorative plaque in his memory. But, David Champagne had not been entirely forgotten in Rhode Island. When the First Session of the 105th Congress convened in January 1997, forty-five years had passed since David Champagne's act of heroism. Had he survived the war in Korea, he would have been 64-years-old.

In June, Rhode Island House Representative Robert A. Weygand and Senator Jack Reed introduced bills to designate the United States Postal Service facility located at 551 Kingstown Road in South Kingstown (Wakefield) as the "David B. Champagne Post Office Building." According to the record of that session (111 Stat. 1455), on the Marine Corps' 222nd Birthday, the House of Representatives passed 2013/Public Law 105-70 on November 10, 1997. [22] 1998 Library of Congress records note the naming of the building on Kingstown Road as the "David B. Champagne Post Office Building." In the January 1998, Rhode Island General Assembly, the State House extended congratulations for the dedication of the David B. Champagne Post Office to be held on May 29, 1998. [23] On October 21, 1998, S.973 Bill, regarding the Wakefield Post Office was referred to the House Committee on Government Reform and Oversight. William A. Powers, Dave's Marine companion who had held him as he died on Hill 104, was reported to have been in Wakefield during a ceremony to name the Wakefield Postal facility in honor of his former fire team leader. [24]

How well David is truly remembered today in Wakefield is difficult to determine. Telephone calls to various postal employees in Wakefield consistently provided the same information. The employees reported that their building, as well as any other government building in their community, was not named in the young Marine's honor. Could it be that twelve years after the dedication of the David B. Champagne Post Office, that postal employees are unaware of the tribute and of the name of the building in which they work? Or was there a point in time in which Public Law 105-70 was obstructed or reversed?

A testimony to the enduring nature of bravery, even when it appears to have been forgotten, is the fact that David B. Champagne's heroics are remembered in print from time to time. In its February 16, 2004, issue, the monthly magazine of the Marines, *The Leatherneck,* remembered him in "The Lore of the Corps: Team leader showed courage on Hill 104." [25] Then, in June 2010, Carl F. Ullrich, his 1st Platoon commander in Korea, wrote a tribute to David in the Norfolk, Virginia newspaper. David is also listed among Maine's "Hometown Heroes" because he was born there, even though he moved to and enlisted in the Marines from another state. [26]

John "Jack" Doren Kelly

Jack was born July 8, 1928, in Youngstown, Ohio. Although he was more than four years older than Dave Champagne, he and the Marine from Rhode Island shared many similarities. Both had moved to a neighboring state before starting grade school, both were high school graduates, and both had decided to enlist in the Marines in 1952. Both had experienced training at Parris Island and Camp Pendleton, were transferred to Korea, served with the same battalion, and fought in the same locations. Although Jack was in Korea for a shorter time than Dave, he died on the same day and on the same embattled hill.

After moving from Youngstown to Homestead, Pennsylvania, small mill-town life on the Monongahela River southeast of Pittsburgh suited Jack's family and they stayed. At some point in his life, his mother, Emma Kelly, was widowed and he was without a father. Jack continued his education at Arizona State College after graduating from high school in 1947. He attended there for four years, but not long enough to graduate with a degree. When the hostilities broke out in Korea, he found it hard to concentrate on his studies. Home on summer break, Jack went to Pittsburgh and enlisted in the Marines in August 1951.

By early 1952, Private First Class Kelly was a radio operator with Company C, 1st Battalion, 7th Marines in Korea. His duties were to keep the company commander in contact with Battalion headquarters and with support units and to call in friendly artillery fire upon the Chinese positions. He was responsible for keeping the radio equipment in sound working order, which sometimes meant taking cover in ditches and shell holes because the antennas on his radio made him a good target for enemy forces intending to disrupt command communications among the Marines. Private First Class Kelly's responsibilities were important because on May 28, 1952, a platoon from Charlie Company was to provide the covering fire for the lead assault platoon going up Hill 104. Corporal Champagne, in Company A, was in the vanguard of the attack.

The covering platoon was soon under assault by an enemy force that outnumbered them and had them pinned down. Mortar rounds and grenades were exploding all about them and the enemy soldiers kept an intense volume of machine gun and small-arms fire on the Marines.

Wanting to be in the forefront of the action

Private First Class Kelly might have remained with his radio equipment, within a "relatively safe" perimeter of Marine riflemen. Earlier the previous year, he could have stayed at Arizona State College, also. Doing so was not in his nature. Instead, Private First Class Kelly volunteered to leave his radio equipment with another man and to engage in an assault on critical enemy positions. He initiated a one-man attack by charging into the enemy fire and silencing an enemy emplacement, killing two of the hostiles. Private First Class Kelly advanced further, bravely charging toward a fortified machine-gun bunker, and was seriously wounded. Unstoppable, he was able to close on the bunker in spite of his wounds. He destroyed it with grenades, killing three more enemy soldiers.

Private First Class Kelly, wounded and blooded, continued forward away from the Marine line, driving himself toward another bunker. Reaching it, he inserted his carbine into the bunker's opening and fired into its occupants.

Private First Class Kelly, 23-years-old, was shot again as he fired into the bunker and fell mortally wounded. His courageous charge rallied the men of his platoon to surge against the hostile force, overwhelming them. The platoon took its objective, held it for a time, and then relinquished it to the human wave of Chinese soldiers. So went the hill battles in Korea.

Private First Class John D. Kelly's "great personal valor" and "extraordinary heroism in the face of almost certain death" were cited in the posthumous award of his Medal of Honor, signed by President Eisenhower. His mother, 64-year-old Emma Kelly, was notified of the award on July 3, 1953. She was asked to pick a date and place for the presentation of the Medal at her convenience. [27] Sad of expression, Mrs. Kelly's photograph holding a picture of her son in his Dress Blue Marine uniform appeared in AP news articles. She decided to go to Washington to accept the award. [28] Mrs. Kelly and Jack's older brother, Eugene, traveled to 8th and I Streets Marine Barracks, Washington, D.C. at the expense of the USMC. [29] They met Vice President Richard Nixon there on Wednesday, September 9, 1953. Mrs. Kelly also met William and Virginia Kelso and the families of S.E. Skinner, W.E. Schuck, Jr., and L.G. Watkins. [30]

Jack is buried at Jefferson Memorial Park in Pleasant Hills, Section 20, Site 319, Allegheny County, Pennsylvania.

Besides the characteristics of volunteering for a challenging task potentially dangerous to himself, initiating a one-man assault, and demonstrating leadership that inspired others to take action despite the imminent danger, Jack Kelly demonstrated another trait common among Medal of Honor recipients. Men like Jack Kelly are more comfortable being in the lead than being left behind. If Jack's grade school and high school classmates had ever read his Citation, they likely would have recognized this attribute to have been present in his childhood. If on a camping trip in the Allegheny Mountains as a boy, Jack would have been the first out of the station wagon, looking for a good spot to set up the tent. On a hike through the woods, he would have been most comfortable in the "pathfinder" position.

When they were boys, the recipients would have been so intent on being in the action, that when ill, injured, or in pain, they would have been more concerned about what they were missing out on rather than taking time to deal with the illness or injury. They were likely to shortcut recuperation and healing, going against doctors' recommendations, and probably ranted against inactivity. The recipients would have been unlikely to feign illness or injury for attention or to get out of responsibilities.

In combat, they ignored injuries and wounds, insisted on remaining at their posts, refused first aid or to be evacuated, or returned to duties against medical orders.

The characteristic of wanting to be in the forefront of the action was quite evident when the recipients participated on athletic teams and made them likely candidates for captain positions. "Sitting it out" on the bench was intensely frustrating for them. As Marines in combat situations, the recipients seemed to want to be where the fighting was the fiercest, at the point of the action, attack, or battle.

The enlisted men among recipients, like Jack Kelly, could be expected to do whatever they could to be at the head of a patrol. For example, Private First Class Bruce Carter, a grenadier with Hotel Company, 2d Battalion, 3d Marines, 3d Marine Division, felt most comfortable at the point position. He earned a posthumous Medal of Honor jumping on a grenade to protect fire team companions on a hill near Cam Lo, Quang Tri Province, Vietnam.

The officers among the recipients readily moved forward into the fight, rather than finding protected positions from which to shout orders. Baldomero Lopez charged out of the landing craft, up a ladder, and over a seawall at the head of his men at Inchon. "Red Mike"

Merritt established his headquarters positions as close to the front lines as possible and left the command post to be among his men in the fight rather than giving commands over a radio.

Daniel Paul Matthews

Brothers have a bond with each other. Whether they are together in a family or in the Corps. That bond must be much the stronger if the brothers are twins.

Dan came into the world on New Year's Eve, 1931 with a twin brother, David. They spent their youth in Van Nuys, California, playing and going to school together. Dan played on the football and track teams in high school and felt a strong impulse to go his own way. He left high school when he was 16-years-old and went to work as a concrete-mixer operator. Three years later, February 1951, with the war in Korea going into its second year, he enlisted in the Marines. Dave enlisted in the Navy.

Two years after that, Dave would escort his twin brother's body home from Korea to Van Nuys.

The Outpost War

Following the battles of the second Korean winter, the 1st Marine Division was repositioned to the western side of the Main Line of Resistance (MLR). On March 24, 1952, the Division assumed responsibility for approximately thirty-five miles of frontline. The Marines were south of Panmunjom and were responsible for the defense of the Pyongyang Seoul corridor. This was a treacherous region of ridges and streams.

The Marines began employing their own tactics. With small units, they established observation outposts on barren, rocky hills, ridges, and high ground several thousand yards in front of the MLR. Companies were established in defensive positions on the hills to monitor enemy movements and to call in artillery barrages. The outposts, critical in maintaining the MLR from enemy incursions, were isolated and dangerous places.

Engagements at the outposts were on a smaller scale than previous battles and successful defense of key positions depended upon the leadership of small unit commanders. While the fights involved smaller numbers of combatants, the extended thunder of battle and the streams of casualties making their way down the hills made the MLR seem miles away when an outpost was under siege.

At night, Marine patrols were sent out from the outposts to harass enemy positions.

To the north of the line of outposts sat jagged granite peaks. The Chinese considered the elevations to be high enough to command sections of "no man's land." They moved battalion and regiment-sized infantry forces into entrenchments along the heights of the peaks to bring withering machine-gun fire, grenades, mortar shells and small-arms fire down upon any unit attempting an assault on their positions.

They did not just sit and wait for the Marines to come.

Aware of the Marine outposts on the edge of "no man's land," the Chinese closed on the outposts by digging trenches, building bunkers, and establishing fields of fire for mortars and artillery. They set up ambushes, probed the outposts for weak spots, and directed nighttime attacks against them. They attacked in battalion-sized engagements; nearly 1300 Communist soldiers assaulting the outpost hills in a series of overwhelming waves of infantrymen, often outnumbering the Marines twenty-to-one.

There was little rest or sleep for the Marines manning the string of forward positions. The Outpost War was underway and some of the most vicious, often hand-to-hand, seesaw fighting during the Korean War occurred at places like Bunker Hill, the Hook, Reno, Vegas, Carson, Seattle, Detroit, Warsaw, Berlin, East Berlin, Ronson, and Elko.

After his training at the San Diego Recruit Depot and assignment to Camp Pendleton, Dan Matthews worked his way up in the ranks and earned one leadership position after another. Promoted to corporal in March 1952, his promotion to sergeant came four months later. Sergeant Matthews was a skilled infantryman, dedicated to those under his command.

Having been stationed in California for two years, his orders to Korea came in January 1953. Sergeant Matthews joined Company F, 2d Battalion, 7th Marines in February as a squad leader. Even though the cease-fire talks at Panmunjom remained suspended when he arrived, a winter lull during January-February had quieted things a bit for the Marines along the MLR. All the same, Sergeant Matthews was quickly thrown into combat.

On March 26, 1953, the Chinese forces initiated a major offensive against the hilltop outposts on the right side of the Marine's thirty-five-mile line. Fox Company was in place on high ground called Vegas Hill. By March 28, enemy units had been able to entrench and fortify themselves on Vegas. The enemy had already repulsed six assaults against their position as the Marines tried to overrun them.

Sergeant Matthews led his squad up the slope in the seventh attempt to take the fortification. They advanced only far enough to come within the range of a concealed machine-gun position at the crest of the outpost, which sprayed them with deadly fire and pinned them down. One of the Marines was seriously wounded and incapacitated. A corpsman braved the enemy fire to reach the man, but then, both now exposed to the machine-gun fire, was unable to move the Marine to a safe location.

Sergeant Matthews, under fire himself, quickly appraised the situation. He maneuvered himself to the rocks at the base of the machine-gun fortification, jumped onto the rocks, and charged alone into the emplacement firing his carbine. Although caught by surprise, the machine-gun team was able to turn the weapon upon him, severely wounding him as he approached.

Sergeant Matthews killed two of the machine gunners and chased off the third, occupying the machine-gun nest alone. With the machine gun silenced, his squad members were able to assist the corpsman and remove their wounded comrade from the fields of fire. The remaining squad members advanced up to Sergeant Matthews' position. By the time they reached him, he had died from the wounds inflicted by machine-gun shells. Sergeant Matthews was one of the 1,000 Marine casualties sustained in the defense of Vegas, Reno, and Carson hills.

When his comrades brought his body down from Vegas Hill, the ceasefire and truce in Korea were only four months away. Two months later in May, his body was transported home by ship, accompanied by his 21-year-old twin, David. Dan was buried in Glen Haven Cemetery, San Fernando, California. A flat, bronze, military marker with the Medal of Honor Star lies upon his grave.

Not much more could be discovered about Daniel Paul Matthews. The Medal of Honor award was announced on January 19, 1954. [31] His parents, Mr. and Mrs. William C. Matthews, met the parents of Corporal Lee Phillips and the wife and young daughter of Sergeant James Johnson at the March 29, 1954 ceremony at the Pentagon.

Jack Kelso and Stanley Christianson's names were removed from the roster of the Thirty-Four Forgotten recipients because extended research verified that they had received fitting tributes in their hometowns. The seven Marines whose stories made up this chapter had also been counted among the ten who had earned Medals of Honor in Korean battles and then had been forgotten. All seven recipients remain on the roster. David Champagne's name might be removed if further inquiries in Rhode Island can verify that the Post Office in Wakefield conspicuously bears his name or that a plaque has been affixed to the lobby wall, letting all those entering the building read about his heroic bravery.

One more forgotten recipient from Korea remains. He had earned his Medal of Honor four months after Whitt Moreland and eight months before David Champagne and Jack Kelly. Based on what was initially discovered about him, his short biography would have been included in this chapter. However, in the end his story required its own chapter. Further investigation and contacts with his family disclosed much more about him. The stories of the forgotten Medal recipients from Korea end with his in the next chapter.

CHAPTER 23
Move About and Be Forgotten

"...numbered among the dead.
Contemplate the mangled bodies of your
countrymen, and then say,
What should be the reward of such sacrifices?" [1]

Samuel Adams (1722-1803)
American Founding Father

Checking the rolls of Medal of Honor recipients accredited to Pennsylvania, one finds Frederick William Mausert, III, USMC, accredited to Dresher, Pennsylvania. Yet, there is little to discover of this Marine in Dresher. How is it that the Keystone State lists Frederick as one of its own hometown heroes?

Which state gets to claim a Medal of Honor recipient a native son can be a tricky business. It is based on the background information the recipient provided upon entering the service. Birthplace and current address, family information, education, medical history, employment history, religious preference, criminal record, and emergency point-of-contact all go on enlistment forms. Officially, the Home of Record becomes the town where the serviceman was living at the time of entry into the service or where he went to enlist. Which proud state claims a recipient as its own comes down to the Birthplace and Home of Record on the enlistment forms. While the Birthplace can claim the recipient when a Medal of Honor is awarded, the Home of Record is customarily where the Medal will be officially Accredited.

Gathering accurate historical information about military enlistees like Frederick Mausert poses challenges. Available public records are not always reliable and tracking backwards from the records can lead one away from the truth. Information having been directly provided by a young recruit can be suspect. Enlistees have sometimes shaded the truth in order to improve their chances to enter the Corps.

Birth dates and birthplaces provided by the enlistee, school records, health records, and delinquent records can prove to be other than what the recruiters put into the files. Getting to the origins of a recipient's life can proceed along dark, back and blind alleys.

Frederick Mausert's background is an example of giving misleading information to a recruiting office. Kenneth Lee Worley's and Gregory "Pappy" Boyington's histories are also examples. So is Private First Class Jack Lucas', who convinced his mother to give him permission to join the Marines, then forged her signature on an enlistment waiver saying he was seventeen, so he could enlist at the age of 14-years. The youngest Marine to ever be awarded the Medal of Honor, he cradled two grenades under his body on Iwo Jima.

The backgrounds in which some Medal of Honor recipients had been raised can lead a researcher to wonder if being forgotten results from claiming no single community as one's own, or from coming from a broken home and being bounced from place to place.

Though rates of migration and mobility have varied within the United States across time, families and individuals accept the stresses inherent in "moving on" as a normal aspect of life. According to population researchers Patricia K. Hall and Steven Ruggles, [2] interstate migration was at the highest in America in the decades prior to the Civil War and then began a steady decline afterwards.

The forty-two Marine recipients from Korea were all born in the era when the mobility rate among white Americans remained a steady 23% of the population. At least seventeen of these men, including Frederick Mausert, made significant moves in their childhood, amounting to forty percent of the group, a difference of seventeen percent in contrast to the general population and much higher than would have been expected.

For the entire group of Medal of Honor recipients across three wars, the largest percentage did not make significant geographical relocations in childhood. Sixty-eight percent grew up and went to school in the towns of their birth. The moves they might have made were within easy distance of their early community. A good number of these men likely went to elementary, junior high, and high schools with children they had known for a good portion of their lives. For these men, the opportunity for stability and a connection to community was present.

The total number of recipients who moved in childhood was 32%, again, higher than would have been expected in the general population. The larger-than-expected numbers of men who moved is an intriguing finding. The reactions and adjustments a child must make to a move to an unfamiliar place are in part reflections of the child's age, experience, and character. Among those who will be heroically brave later, a move can present an early, perhaps frightening, challenge to be overcome.

While geographical relocation can be said to have affected a significant percentage of the recipients in some manner, moving in childhood alone cannot be said to be a determining factor in the development of heroic bravery. Nor can it be accepted as a justification for not remembering a recipient in his birthplace or hometown. In each war, far more Medal of Honor recipients were remembered than forgotten in spite of having moved from their birthplace. Of the recipients across all three wars who had moved, 80% were paid a significant tribute.

Among the thirty-four Marines who appeared to have had no honor extended to them beyond their Medals, either in their hometowns or otherwise, twelve had moved in childhood. Those who moved account for 35% of the forgotten men, a percentage similar to the overall number across the three wars. Again, while moving from their hometown occurred at a higher percentage among these men than evident in the general population, the increase does not seem to account for their being forgotten in their home communities.

Frederick William Mausert, III was not from Dresher, Pennsylvania, the place to which his Medal of Honor was Accredited in 1952. He lived near there for only a short time. What he was doing in Dresher would be hard to discover. As were other aspects of his life.

Upon his enlistment, Frederick provided the USMC some auto-biographical information, for example reporting that he was born on May 2, 1930. That would have made him just 18-years-old when he was filling out his entry papers. Frederick was a year off, since his birth certificate was issued in Mary McClellan Hospital, Cambridge, New York, on May 2, 1931.

Cambridge, at an elevation of 496 feet and due east of Saratoga Springs, sits in a valley between the Hudson River of upper New York and the Green Mountains of Vermont. The intersection of New York, Vermont, and Massachusetts is about twenty miles down the road. In 1931, the town was less than one square mile in area, rural, and a reflection of the Irish, English, German, and Italian farmers who had immigrated there in the previous generations. Farming always remained the mainstay of the economy. However, there were other ways to earn a living and support a family.

Frederick III was born into a family that did not settle long in one place. His mother, Gwendolyn Sharp, had moved with her family to Cambridge around 1924, having been born further north in either Salem or Granville on November 10, 1910. Fred "Fritz" Mausert, II had moved up to Cambridge from North Adams, Massachusetts.

"Fritz" was the second son of Henry L. and Sadie Buxton Mausert, German and English descendants. His older brother, Clayton, was seven years senior. Another brother, Ryerson, was seven years younger. Rancor erupted between the two younger brothers during the late Depression years, and they had little to do with each in their adulthood. For their children, the cousins, Grandpa Henry would be the common, if tenuous, thread in their extended family life. [3]

Grandpa Mausert was a man others admired. He was hard working. Although life and the times could be tough, he did not smoke, drink alcohol, or swear to take the edge off. Seen as a "straight arrow," he was someone for grandsons to admire. Henry L. owned the White Swan Hotel in Greenwich, opened in July 1926, eight miles northwest of Cambridge on Route 372. The hotel sat on a corner at the top of a hill, with a bend in the Batten Kill River behind it, and facing the downtown Greenwich square. The White Swan also housed a movie theater.

"Fritz" Mausert II and Gwen met in Cambridge and married there. Young when married, "Fritz" had health problems, was seldom well, suffered from a bad back, and had difficulty walking upright, but he wanted to be a businessman. He had a chance to do that when he and Gwen moved into the White Swan Hotel to run the movie theater. They were residing there with other Mauserts when their first son was born. Gwen was 20-years-old at the time. Although both parents were working at the theater, the hotel dining room, bar, and dance floor, as well as the hill and village square provided ample places for their son to play as he passed through his toddler and early childhood years.

Without knowing more than his enlistment application data and Frederick III's Medal Citation, one might conclude that his familiar name, derived from his formal name Frederick, might have been Fred. His great uncle, Frederick I, and his father were both called "Fritz." Gwen had followed the Mausert family tradition of naming a son after the father, but she chose to call her son "Rickie," the name by which extended family, neighbors, babysitters, and friends knew him.

What family members called each other mattered. Gwen was young when she became a mother. Although she and Rickie would always share a close relationship, she preferred that he not call her "Mom" or "Mother." A beautiful woman who never looked her true age, Gwen enjoyed the attention of others. Not wanting to be seen as maternal, she insisted that Rickie call her either by her name, Gwen, or "doll." [4]

With a theater in the family, Hollywood movies played a part in Rickie's life. He was born in the era when silent movies came to an end, and the "talkies" spread across the globe. Livened chatter on porch stoops, on street corners, across town squares about *The Public Enemy* (1931), *It Happened One Night* (1934), *Mutiny on the Bounty* (1935), *Dangerous* (1935), *Boys Town* (1938), and *Gone with the Wind* (1939) could distract people from their financial woes.

The White Swan theater introduced locals to gangsters like James Cagney, scary monsters like Boris Karloff as Frankenstein, stormy lovers like Clark Gable and Joan Crawford, Detective Charlie Chan, Johnny Weissmuller, the Olympic swimming champion swinging from jungle vines as Tarzan, the slapstick comedy of the Three Stooges, and curly-haired child stars like Shirley Temple. At the matinees, cartoon characters like Popeye and Betty Boop and Walt Disney's Donald Duck could entertain children.

The screen image that most likely left a lasting impression on Rickie was one of a then-B-actor who had his first major movie role the year before Rickie was born. In 1930 Greenwich folks watched a western, *The Big Trail*, and the major motion picture debut of John Wayne.

There were strains on the extended Mausert family that would eventually divide Fritz and Gwen and would add challenges to Rickie's early life. For Grandpa Henry, running a small town hotel in the Depression era was not lucrative business. Winters in small, upstate towns further decreased business. Rather than operate at a loss, many owners closed their doors during the snowy seasons and wintered in Florida. For those relying on the hotel, bar, and theater business, winter slow downs or closings could increase financial woes.

There was also that other social factor—thirteen years of Prohibition. When the sale of alcohol for public consumption was outlawed in 1920, various businesses beyond bars and taverns were affected. The saloons in hotels had been a source of good income.

Henry L. kept the White Swan afloat as best he could. Prohibition was officially repealed in the United States on December 5, 1933, with the ratification of the Twenty-First Amendment. Hotel owners decided whether to maintain an alcohol-free establishment or to unlock the doors to dusty saloons.

Opening a bar would not be enough to save the White Swan. As the Depression continued into the early 1930s, movie theater owners also felt its economic effects. Hollywood productions suffered and theater attendance dropped. And questions were being raised within the Mausert family about how Fritz II was conducting business and keeping the books at the theater.

Like the hotel and theater, Fritz and Gwen had fallen on hard times, but tried to make their marriage work. A second son, John, was born to the Mauserts on January 19, 1937, named after his maternal grandfather, John ("Jack") Sharp. Now an older brother, Rickie watched as his parents' marriage crumbled. The couple separated soon after John was born and eventually divorced on July 16, 1940.

The acrimony between Gwen and Fritz must have been intense. The boys spent little time afterwards with their father or his family. The younger Jack had no relationship with, nor memories of, his biological father. In a legal action on August 1, 1956, around the time he died, Frederick W. Mausert II was removed as parent and natural guardian of the boys. More than fifty years passed before John met paternal cousins he did not know and learned about the extended family on his father's side he had never been encouraged to contact.

During the break up of their parents' marriage, the two brothers were moved to the Town of Jackson in the Annaquasicoke community, three miles north of Cambridge Village. In 1937, around the same time the White Swan went into bankruptcy, and when Rick was six-years-old, the boys began living with their maternal grandparents, Jack and Lucy Sharp. Grandfather Sharp held the Cambridge Waterworks Superintendent position. The family lived in the superintendent's bungalow at the springs.

Rick's progress through school is murky history. School attendance records for that era in Annaquasicoke have been lost, and he gave the Marines information on his enlistment forms that seems unlikely. There was a one-room schoolhouse called "Sunrise" a mile down the road from the waterworks. A former Annaquasicoke babysitter, Viola

Gulley, thought that Rick probably began school there. He was not an exemplary student.

Grandpa Sharp died while Rickie was attending grade school. No longer the Waterworks Superintendent's wife, Grandma Sharp moved the boys to Washington Street in Cambridge Village. Then they moved a block down the street, across East Main Street, to Grove Street. From there, Rickie had only a short, three-block walk along Main to get to the Cambridge Union School. More than fifty years later, Mrs. Kathleen Squires recalled attending the Cambridge Union School with the Mausert boys and babysitting for them. A photo now hanging in a local bank shows young Rickie on the steps of the Cambridge Union School with his 6th grade class. [5]

Once he was living in Cambridge, Rick might have been influenced by the tribute the community had paid to a local Marine. Earl Wesley Maxson was born to be a captain. He was elected captain of one of the early Cambridge High School football teams in 1904. An inspired athlete, he also wanted to be a Marine. He wanted it so much that he enlisted midway through the team's championship season. He had found his career, and worked his way up the ranks. In a WWI battle in Europe, Captain Earl Maxson initiated a charge across No Man's Land. He died in the action, but his memory came home to Cambridge. The local American Legion Post 634 was named in his honor. [6]

Fewer than twenty years later, young Rick Mausert was living on Washington Street in Cambridge Village. It was a small town, and he likely knew the story of Captain Maxson's patriotism.

Rickie was 10-years-old when America entered WWII. As was true for so many, his life was going to again change dramatically. Five months after the attack at Pearl Harbor, Gwen Sharp Mausert married Mr. Wentworth Barnes, on May 20, 1942.

Harkening back to the White Swan theater days, movie matinees with their war newsreels became a part of Saturday afternoons in Cambridge. War movies soon were projected onto theater screens and into the minds of adolescent boys like Rickie. *The Fighting Seabees* (1944)

Back to Bataan (1945) *Sands of Iwo Jima* (1949) and *Flying Leathernecks* (1951) all featured John Wayne. What seems to be true is that the swaggering kind of heroism portrayed by John Wayne on the screen was going to have an effect on Rickie.

Although it had no known immediate impact on him, both of his Mausert uncles, having been serving in Company K of the Massachusetts Army National Guard, were called to service at the War's outbreak and became career Army officers. Clayton had served in WWI, was gassed in Germany, and suffered the loss of his sense of smell and taste. After his discharge from active service, he worked as a Prudential insurance salesman. He was already a captain and company commander when Ryerson Sr. joined the Army Guard unit. They both eventually retired as full colonels.

Rick apparently told companions later that his father had joined the Marines and was killed in the Pacific Islands campaigns during the war. Perhaps that was a way to explain his father's absence from his life. Maybe it was the way he wanted to think of his father, as strong and heroic. Not much is known about Fritz II's life after the White Swan closed, but it can be certain he was not eligible for the military because of his poor health. He actually died either in Prescott or Phoenix, Arizona, around 1956, a sympathetic figure to those who remember him.

Around 1944 when Rick was 13-years-old and too young to be on his own, Grandma Sharp died. The next four years of his life are obscure to those who have researched his background. Rick was never a Cambridge Central High School *Indian*, where he would have first enrolled in 1945. Greenwich Senior High School is on Gray Avenue, just a few blocks north of where Rick would have played as a boy at the White Swan Hotel. Available records indicate that he was never a student there. Information Rick later provided to his Marine recruiters seems to include a bit of his own fabrication.

Based on information given them by Rick, Marine records indicate that the Mausert family relocated to Brooklyn and that Rick went to elementary school there. Family memories include no ties to Brooklyn. Rick seems to have wanted the Marines not to be able to learn where he had been most of his youth before walking into the recruiting station.

Once Grandma Sharp died, Rick did not have much extended time living together with his brother in the same place. Gwen and Wentworth Barnes moved to various places looking for employment opportunities. At the end of WWII until about 1949, they worked in New York City. After their grandmother's death, Rickie and John were often left in the care of others, sometimes with family, other times with non-related families, and predominantly not together. John was shuttled back and forth between New York and Pennsylvania. Extended family believes Rick left New York after his grandmother's death. A cousin told a local Cambridge historian that he moved to Massachusetts to live with his father's family.

When the hotel business had gone bankrupt in Greenwich, Grandpa Henry moved to a chicken farm for which his son, Clayton, held title in Woodford, Vermont, 25 road miles southeast of Cambridge. Four to five thousand chickens pecked away in the large field behind the barn. Rickie showed up unannounced from time to time at Grandpa Henry's chicken farm. He had hitchhiked or taken a bus from wherever he happened to have been, his cousins never certain where that was. He traveled by himself, stayed a few days, and left.

Despite their five-year age difference, Rickie and his cousin, Rye, enjoyed each other's company. They were country boys, often hunting or hiking into the woods.

Rickie liked to sit behind the barn, enjoying slow drags on a cigarette. He also liked to shoot his .22 caliber pump action Remington rifle. Rickie was a marksman, remembered as having a "dead eye" aim, quick reactions, and being a "cracker jack shot."

One spring when he was about 14- or 15-years-old, he shot a chicken in the head at eighty yards, just as he said he would. Another time, when Rye was rummaging around at the bottom of a deep, dump hole on the edge of the farm, he pulled up a rotten rug, and a big, black milk snake coiled and reared menacingly. Rickie killed the snake with a single shot from above and behind his cousin.

Around 1947, Gwen and Wentworth lived for a time in Riverdale, on the northwest edge of the Bronx borough in New York City.

Kingsbridge and Marble Hill are adjacent neighborhoods. The family was reunited under the same roof in this middle-class neighborhood. Because Rick was now well into his teen years and uninterested in family time, he and his brother still did not see much of each other.

Rick did not acknowledge his time in the Bronx later when he enlisted. For his own reasons, he would have the Marines believe that he had moved from Brooklyn to south central Massachusetts, where he lived a few years in Monson, a small rural town among forests and rolling hills in Hampden County. Rick did possibly spend some time in Monson. His father had remarried, and his second wife was from the Springfield area. To the east, Monson is nearby. Fiskdale/Sturbridge, Iwo Jima Medal of Honor recipient "Rudy" Julian's hometown, is just fifteen miles to the east.

Rick claimed to have participated in basketball, baseball, and track while attending the Monson high school. There is a photo of him as a teenager, baseball and glove in hand, wearing a baseball cap and a dark letter sweater with a big H (and what might be a C) on its front. No official school records validate his attending Monson Junior or Senior High School. However, the H on his sweater might tell a story.

Balancing independence, affiliation, and competitiveness

Rickie shared a variety of the personal qualities identified among other Marine Medal of Honor recipients, the sort of characteristics that predispose an individual to brave acts when in dire circumstances.

He is remembered as having been independent, a trait consistently reported of the recipients. Starting early in their lives, others came to depend upon them, to look to them to take action, to expect them to initiate effort, and to get things accomplished. The recipients themselves seldom looked to others to do these very things, seldom waited to see who else might stand up to face the challenge.

Such independence does not mean the recipients had a desire to stand alone or apart from others. Among brave men, it is quite the contrary. Independent in initiative and action, yes, but at the same time welcoming affiliation with others. Affiliation can mean the condition of connection, allegiance, or association. In a sense, it was a belonging these men sought.

The Medal recipients demonstrated both the desire to have associations with others and an ease of being in the midst of others. They preferred the company of boys and men like themselves. Few, if any, would have been remembered as being "a loner." From this preference to associate with others is affiliation derived, and joining teams and participating in groups is a demonstration of affiliation.

At least sixty-one recipients were members of athletic teams in high school or college. Sixteen joined clubs or other extracurricular activities other than athletics while in school. Four participated in the Boy Scouts of America. Of the thirty-seven who graduated from college, twelve were members of national Greek fraternities. Seventeen participated in the Reserve Officer Training Corps (ROTC), the Marine's Platoon Leader Course (PLC), or the National Guard while in high school or college.

The tendency towards affiliation provides a balance to competitiveness in their lives. While such men might not want to be *bested* by others, they also tend to look out for those with whom they affiliate. They do not want family friends, companions, or comrades to be bested by others either.

Acting independently and being competitive can create problems in early life and affiliations can break down. The three characteristics require the kind of balance teenagers often find elusive.

In addition to being independent, Rickie had the kind of personality that made affiliation natural, perhaps even easy, for him. He was engaging in such a way that others were drawn to him. No matter where he went, girls found him charming. Although some would later recall him to have been rambunctious, others saw him as a "free spirit," nice and fun to be around. Sometimes there was a bit of a swagger in his gait. Time and maturity would temper that.

There is little doubt that Rickie was also competitive. He was the type of boy who would want to set up a target, get his rifle, and challenge someone to a bullseye contest. When he put on a baseball glove for a sandlot pickup game, it would be as much for a chance to win, as it would be for the fun of it. According to his cousin, Rickie was not always a "good sport" about losing.

When Rickie seemed to be too independent and without enough discipline, Gwen thought a private school might settle her teenage son down. Maybe students at the school wore sweaters with a big H on the front, like the one he had on in that photograph. A hint exists that Rick was sent to Hotchkiss School, a boarding school in Lakeville, Connecticut, about 75 miles south of Cambridge, on Wononpakook Lake.

The Hotchkiss School encouraged personal integrity and liked to develop students who would be responsible citizens committed to service to others. The *Bearcats* school colors are dark blue and white. Peter Rawson, the Hotchkiss School archivist, searched through various school records back to 1944-48 and could find no trace of Rick having been a student at Hotchkiss. [7]

Rick's cousin thinks that Holyoke Catholic High School might be the school to which Gwen sent Rickie. Perhaps he had once been an Irish Warrior (a Gael), proud to wear the Green & Gold sweater. At the time he was a teenager, the school was located in Granby, Massachusetts, about fifteen miles northwest of Monson. The current Principal at Holyoke Catholic, Sister Cornelia Roy, SSJ, researched the archived school records. There was no sign of Rick in the records. [8]

Whatever the school, Rickie's propensity for leading others began to emerge. His cousin remembered him to have gotten into trouble for having once run away from the school to go to a ballgame, taking a few classmates with him. And whatever the private school might have been, he was not a student there for long. Whether he actually graduated from high school, and from where, are facts hard to pin down. Just like it was hard to pin Rickie down in one place.

Before turning 17-years-old, Rick had moved again to the Dresher-Glenside, Pennsylvania area, just northwest of Philadelphia. There were family connections in Dresher, and John, their mother, and stepfather lived there awhile. The Barnes family eventually lived in Baltimore,

Maryland. John was adopted by Wentworth on July 25, 1957, and took the Barnes surname as his own.

One challenge in discovering the details of Rick's background can be linked to his use of the Mausert or Barnes names. There were times that Rick also took Barnes as his last name, though the name change was never legalized. As had been the case in the search for Kenneth Worley, school records might have had Rickie Mausert enrolled under a different name. The girls he dated in high school might know more about his school history than the Marine recruiters. [9]

It does not seem that Rick had yet been finished with high school when he lived in Dresher. Although a high school and seminary were nearby, his academic education was over. Rick got a job at a hardware store in Glenside. He did not work there long. Ever making his own way, Rick broke with a family tradition.

Rather than join the Army of his uncles, Rick chose instead to enlist in the peacetime Marine Corps on June 21, 1948, a month after his seventeenth birthday, and perhaps at the end of a school year. The last time his cousin saw him, Rick was in his Dress Blue uniform, standing at about five-foot-ten-inches tall, and weighing in at a trim medium build of about 180 pounds. Rye idolized his cousin all the more.

When Rick left for recruit training at Parris Island, he had lived in and moved from at least six towns. Greenwich, Jackson, Cambridge, and Riverdale, New York, Monson, Massachusetts, and Dresher, Pennsylvania were places where he had gone to school, played, walked the streets, had girl friends, and worked. His family knew that he had enlisted in the Marines. The questions later would be how many friends, baby sitters, teachers, classmates, neighbors, and bosses remembered him, or had a thought like "What ever became of Rickie Mausert?" Had he been forgotten in Cambridge because he had moved about so much that people just lost track of him? When the Philadelphia newspapers reported that his Medal of Honor award was being accredited to Dresher, how many people beyond his Glenside Hardware boss would say that they had known him when he lived in Dresher?

Standing at The Punchbowl

The discipline and camaraderie Rick experienced in the Marines might have been what his mother had hoped to provide him by sending him to a private school. In the Corps, he was able to find a balance for his independence, need for affiliation, and competitive drive. In three years time, Rick trained and earned promotions. By the time he was a sergeant, he was serving as a radio technician with the Marine Air Wing at MCAS Cherry Point, North Carolina. It was a good MOS, but not enough for Sergeant Mausert. What he wanted harkened back to shooting a black snake at a dump pit with his .22 caliber pump action Remington rifle, mixed in with the USMC doctrine that, regardless of MOS, "Every Marine is, first and foremost, a rifleman."

On June 29, 1950, President Harry Truman ordered American infantry forces into South Korea. The Marines were in the fight early, holding on to the Pusan perimeter. Sergeant Mausert volunteered for a change of MOS to infantryman and was transferred to Camp Lejeune for additional training.

Marine regiments landed at Inchon on September 21, 1950, fought their way to Seoul, made another amphibious landing at Wonsan in late October, and fought to and from the Chosin Reservoir in November and December. While undergoing infantry training, Sergeant Mausert talked often with his mother about the eventuality of his going into combat.

The Marines drove to take the eastern tip of the Hwachon Reservoir above the 38th Parallel in April 1951, when 500,000 Chinese embarked upon a spring offensive. By June, the Marines had taken the ridgeline of an ancient collapsed volcano in the Central Korean Mountains twenty miles northeast of Hwachon. The tactical position overlooked a deep, almost perfectly circular valley of four to five miles in diameter. West of the Soyong River and surrounded by mountain ridges reaching from 1,000 to 2,000 feet high, the valley was nicknamed *The Punchbowl*.

U.N. forces settled into a defensive line as truce negotiations got underway. Firefights between the adversaries were sporadic. While families back home in the States hoped for an end to the hostilities, the Marines were not fooled by the lull. Anticipating that the communists were only maneuvering to regroup their forces, the Marines prepared for battle.

Sergeant Mausert remained at Camp Lejeune, concerned that the war would end before he could get himself to Korea. His mother worried, likely remembering the significance of Gold Stars in the front windows of homes not too may years earlier during WWII. The bond between Rick and Gwen had always been close, and while he wanted to go to war, he did not want his mother to worry after him.

Gwen sent a "beautiful" cake to Sergeant Mausert for his 20th birthday that May. Her son had been keeping some news from her. In a letter he wrote on May 31, 1951, scrawled across four-pages of USMC Camp Lejeune letterhead paper, he acknowledged being uncertain of writing. [10] He was to report to Treasure Island, California in eight days, for transfer to the First Marine Division fighting in Korea. Combat was what he had trained to do and wanted to do. Expressing love for his country, Sergeant Mausert was happy to be finally able to put his long, endless training into action and go fight with "the best of outfits."

Having left adolescence behind at Camp Lejeune, Rick had matured beyond adolescent attitudes while a Marine. Like so many on the way to war, he keenly felt the love and affection toward family, his mother and Jack. He asked that his mother and brother not worry about him, believing he would return home "a man with a level head," and "all the better" for his experience.

The Marine sergeant expressed regret for mistakes made earlier in his life and the hurts he had caused his mother. Being respected by others had become meaningful to Rick. He had also come to value personal character above other things. He had learned that braggarts and liars are not respected by other men. He wanted Jack to grow into an honest and successful man. Rick recommended that his mother keep his younger brother from "the booze" and from following him into the military service.

Wanting the connection to family, Sergeant Mausert asked his mother to write how things were back home, wondering if Wentworth had a job. He expressed appreciation for the cake his mother had sent him, having shared it with his comrades who sent along their thanks.

In closing, the son expressed his love again for his mother and told her not to worry about him. Then he went off to war. A telegram arrived for Gwen Mausert Barnes in Baltimore four months later.

In July 1951, the 7th Marines regiment was put into Reserve in the long Inge Valley, fifteen miles from the *Punchbowl* and the Main Line of Resistance (MLR). Setting up a tent camp, they ate their C-rations warmed up, trained for the battle they were sure was ahead, and slept securely at night.

After his arrival in Korea, Sergeant Mausert was assigned duties as a squad leader in the 2d Platoon of assault Company B, 1st Battalion, 7th Marines, 1st Division. Those who served with him remembered him as having been diligent and detailed in training his men, sincere and dedicated. Proficient with firearms, he sometimes liked to carry a BAR, the Browning Automatic Rifle, although it was not a sergeant's weapon. Such Marines were viewed as "Gung Ho." [11]

On August 22, the communists broke off truce negotiations.

And the Marines were ordered to seize the rest of the *Punchbowl*. The 7th Marines were trucked out of Inge and moved into place. The North Koreans and Chinese had had more than enough time to position artillery, mortars, and machine guns to rain down a barrage into the *Punchbowl*, and they seemed to have held the advantage. The days were chilled and gray, the rains were heavy, and the roads were poor that September. Temperatures were dropping as winter approached.

Three battalion commanders passed the orders down the Marine ranks.

On the night of September 8, 1951, 5-foot-7-inch, Second Lieutenant Eddie LeBaron, 2d Platoon Commander, advised his squad leaders of their situation, mission, objective, and enemy ahead. [12] They were to take "Objective B," Hill 673, on Kanmubong Ridge from the North Koreans.

From their position on Yoke ridge, Baker Company faced the seasonal rains, muddy roads, and strongly fortified, well-entrenched enemy forces in the Songnap-yong vicinity. The enemy troops were dug into bunkers near the crest of the bleak, 2,208-foot hill. The log entrenchments were protected under many feet of dirt and rocks.

Interconnecting trenches between the forward slope and the rear of the hill allowed for replacements and re-supply.

Sergeant Rickie Mausert was soon to enter history.

The Marines called Hill 673 "Old Baldy" for good reason. For more than a week their artillery, mortars, and Corsairs when the visibility allowed it, had pounded the hill, turning trees into stumps. The gray clay of the slopes had been turned into ankle-deep powder.

Sergeant Mausert took the orders from Second Lieutenant LeBaron to take Hill 673 back to his men, offering them encouragement and trying to quell their apprehensions. Before dawn the next day when the order to "Saddle up!" came at 0300, they would be on the right flank of the assault.

Marines knew from experience that North Korean soldiers were hard-fighting and would not yield unless overrun. Even then, they would counterattack. The squad would charge against the strongly-entrenched enemy, crawl up the towering hill if they had to, but they would advance. Sergeant Mausert reminded them that they were Marines, and that the North Koreans had learned to fear them.

The Marine offensive would not achieve its objectives until September 16.

When the orders came, Sergeant Mausert's squad left the "safety" of their foxholes, fixed their bayonets, waded across a stream, and maneuvered toward Hill 673. The waiting enemy aimed down on them.

Despite the fierce fighting, mine fields, and concealed tunnels, the Marine battalions advanced into the Punchbowl. They met strong opposition and made little progress up the objective. The enemy defenses halted the 1st Battalion on the face of the hill. The craters, depressions, and urgently dug holes on the hill provided little protection. As the days and nights of the assault passed, the numbers of casualties were high. On September 11-12 alone, twenty-two Marines were killed and another 245 were wounded.

Ordered to advance against the formidable enemy stronghold on September 12, Baker Company was pinned down on Old Baldy, unable to move up the slope. The artillery and mortar rounds and the crossing fire of machine guns ripped into Sergeant Mausert's squad. Wounded

Marines fell in exposed positions, while others were forced by the barrage to remain in whatever protected spots they could find.

Sergeant Mausert was known to write motivational quotes on slips of paper and repeat them to his men. Perhaps he was familiar with some of William Blake's writings and remembered:

"O for a voice like thunder, and a tongue

To drown the throat of war!–When the senses

Are shaken, and the soul is driven to madness,

Who can stand? When the souls of the oppressed

Fight in the troubled air that rages, who can stand?" [13]

Of his own initiative, Sergeant Mausert stood and charged into a minefield under heavy enemy fire and returned two wounded men to the Marines' line. During his rescue of comrades, he sustained his own serious head wound. Insisting on staying in the lead of his squad, he refused to be evacuated for medical attention.

Then, second platoon was ordered to attack the hill fortifications. From the valley behind them, Marine tanks pounded the bunkers ahead of them with 90-mm rounds.

Sergeant Mausert voluntarily took the lead position in a bayonet charge against a machine-gun bunker. He was struck in the helmet by a bullet and knocked to the ground, stunned. He quickly stood again and continued forward ahead of his squad, throwing a grenade and obliterating the enemy emplacement that had knocked him into the clay.

His squad took more casualties as he led them up Old Baldy against one bunker after another. The enemy increased their defensive fires as the squad neared their objective on the knife-crested ridge. Sergeant Mausert "regrouped" the remnants of his squad.

Despite the deafening noise, pounding explosions, and withering enemy machine-gun rounds biting into the ground and filling the air all around him, he again stood exposed, carbine firing, and moved alone toward the gun emplacement. By drawing fire to himself, he allowed his men to reposition themselves to continue their advance. Sergeant Mausert was seriously wounded again, and when the corpsman reached him, he again refused aid or evacuation.

He moved his squad against the enemy's topmost bastion positions, both forces firing fiercely against each other. Undaunted by the machine-gun fire, he rushed into it throwing grenades and destroying another enemy position. Comrades would later remember Sergeant Mausert singing the Marine Corps Hymn as he plunged at the final machine-gun bunker. [14]

Sergeant Mausert demonstrated leadership, initiative-taking, unquestionable concern for wounded companions, determined resolve to follow the orders he had been given, and the drive to take his objective although seriously wounded and under intense duress. He was cited for leading and inspiring his men to overwhelm and secure a nearly impregnable enemy-held ridge.

Sergeant Mausert was killed in the final flurry of grenades and machine-gun fire as he rushed the last enemy emplacement. The remainder of his squad took the crest and secured Hill 673.

Ernest Hemingway's World War I novel *A Farewell to Arms* was published in 1929. In it, two characters have an often-quoted discussion about the experiences of a coward and a brave man. It cannot be known if Rick Mausert read Hemingway, but he believed in inspirational words. After his death, a card was found among his personal belongings. [15] Printed on it was the quote that became familiar to the nation in his childhood: "A Coward Dies a Hundred Deaths, A Hero Only Once."

According to Jim Hughes of Dearborn, Michigan, a fire team leader in the 1st Platoon, the Marines dedicated a bridge over the Soyang River to honor Sergeant Mausert in late October—early November 1951.

From wayward to heroic

His heroic death might inspire others if they learned of his actions. His actions might also cause one to pause and wonder. Besides bravery, what might propel a young man to charge into an enemy machine-gun emplacement? What might another person have done in Rick Mausert's situation on that hill?

Sergeant Mausert had once been a kid who moved restlessly from place to place, who seemed wayward, and who was perhaps capricious in terms of having a fixed destination for himself. He had learned early to be independent, and he moved about on his own. That he did so, gives just a hint of his bravery. Then, something in his character moved him to enlist in the Marines. Once he put on his uniform, the Corps began to further shape the character that had not yet been fully realized within him.

Sergeant Mausert, like all Marine recruits, would have learned about Sergeant Major Daniel J. Daly in history and traditions class and in "bull sessions" with drill instructors at Parris Island. Dan Daly's devotion to the Corps and his fearless attitude toward combat have grown to be exemplary, perhaps the epitome of Marine tradition and expectations. His attitudes and actions resound down through the generations of Marines.

Dan Daly was twenty-five when he enlisted in the Marines. He earned his first Medal of Honor when he was twenty-six and his second when he was 41-years-old. In both events, he defied death and fought to overcome overwhelming odds. In the 1900 Boxer Rebellion in China, defending a position alone, he inflicted nearly two hundred casualties on attacking rebels. During the Haitian insurrection in 1915, he was among a detachment of thirty-five Marines ambushed from three sides by 400 insurgents. He earned his second Medal for fighting them off all night and leading the men out of the encirclement to the safety of a nearby fort in the morning.

Renowned for being one of only two Marines to earn two Medals of Honor in separate events, Sergeant Daly is also remembered by all Marines for one action in particular. At the outbreak of WWI, First Gunnery Sergeant Daly was assigned duties in France at the head of a machine-gun company. He was involved in a series of combat actions in 1918, including the Toulon Sector campaign, Aisne Operations, the historic Belleau Wood battle in June, the St. Mihiel Offensive, and the Champagne Offensive at Blanc Mont.

While his company was positioned near Belleau Wood on June 4, Gunnery Sergeant Daly might have had recollections of the bombardment he had been under in those desperate times in Peking, except that the ferocity of the enemy fusillade was greater in France.

The town of Luce le Bocage sat at the outskirts of Belleau Wood. The Germans had a large force in the sector and intended to hold there. The Marines were ordered to take the Woods. As they advanced, they encountered heavy artillery fire and determined German resistance. The hostile fire turned the advance into a blood bath for the Marines.

Sergeant Daly's company walked head on into machine guns and stalled. Pinned down by a greater number of Germans with greater firepower, unable to maneuver to advance, flank, or withdraw, the Marines faced gradual annihilation under the persistent and withering machine-gun fire.

Gunnery Sergeant Daly, having earned two Medals of Honor previously in perilous situations and then 43-years-old, would have no part in being pinned down. He ordered his men to charge the machine-gun emplacement, jumped to the lead, and shouted out above the sounds of battle.

"Come on, you sons of bitches! Do you want to live forever?"

His men followed him in the frontal assault, overtook the machine-gun position, and continued their attack forward until American forces had taken the entire town of Luce le Bocage. Belleau Wood would belong to the Marines.

Gunnery Sergeant Dan Daly survived Belleau Wood and went on to distinguish himself. On June 5, he extinguished an ammunition dump fire at Luce le Bocage. On June 7, while under an intense enemy barrage of artillery, he moved from one machine-gun position to another over a wide length of the front, encouraging his men to maintain their fighting spirits. On June 10, he assaulted a machine-gun emplacement alone with his automatic .45 pistol and hand grenades and silenced it. On the same day, while the village of Bouresches was under German assault, he removed wounded Marines to protected positions while under heavy fire. He was himself wounded in action on June 21 and then twice more on October 18, refusing to be evacuated from his company.

After a career spanning thirty years of honorable and legendary service and extraordinary actions, he lived to retire from the Marines. He returned to his boyhood home and worked as a bank security guard for seventeen years on Wall Street in New York City. He was 63-years-old when he died in 1937. Dan Daily probably does not know that his legend lives on. According to Marine lore, he would be one of the honored few on guard at the gates of Heaven, too focused upon his current duty assignment to be concerned about whether or not people on earth think about him.

And Gunnery Sergeant Daly's exhortation has resonated in the instructions of drill sergeants and in the minds of recruits ever since Belleau Wood.

"Do you want to live forever?"

Although brave deeds can have similar appearance, the essence of bravery is clearly not the same for all individuals. Psychological impulses in desperate circumstances vary from one person to the next. Courage takes different forms among those who find themselves in life-threatening situations and the inner forces that propel them into action vary.

For example, historian Jon T. Hoffman provides a distinction among men recognized as brave in combat situations: some resolutely override their nervous systems in order to act bravely; others get so caught up in the adrenaline flows triggered by events that they disregard all dangers; and then others lacking any noticeable fear of death, or perhaps seeking death, seem to relish putting themselves into situations in which death is a very real possibility. [16]

The conclusion that Rickie's background predisposed him to having suicidal impulses or a death wish might be reasonably proposed. Careful consideration would seem to suggest otherwise. For one thing, suicide requires that the person consciously intends to die and deliberately acts in some fashion to bring his/her own life to an end. Nothing in the records hints at Sergeant Mausert's intention to die in Korea on Hill 673. To the contrary, his letter to his mother suggests he intended to return home from Korea.

To be *willing* to die is not the same as wishing to die.

When Sergeant Mausert stood up and charged into machine-gun fire, Gunnery Sergeant Dan Daly would have understood this action as not suicidal, but duty. Marines tend to take their own heroism for granted.

Marines who served with Sergeant Mausert in Korea would have found it difficult to understand how he could be forgotten in his hometown. He had demonstrated a variety of character traits that had inspired not just the men under his leadership, but also Marines who heard about his charge up Hill 673. If any doubts exist about that, Corporal Leonard R. "Shifty" Shifflette would lay them to rest. Corporal Shifflette went into the *Punchbowl* that day with assault Company A ("Stable Able"), 1st Battalion, 7th Marines. He retired from the Marine Corps in 1970 and began writing poetry in 1997. One of his 1998 poems is a reminder of men like Sergeant Mausert. [17]

The heroically brave actions in combat that inspire others can be attributed to a combination of character traits possessed by Sergeant Mausert. Two of these characteristics would have been evident to the Marines around him, including his commanders, who wrote recommendations for the awarding of a Medal of Honor: a sense of duty and no apparent fear of death.

A sense of duty

The concepts of duty and loyalty are closely associated. A duty is something akin to a task to which a person is assigned or of which s/he takes charge. Duty implies a sense of obligation or commitment. Accepting a duty means you cannot walk away from it. Commitment ties you to it. Loyalty has a feeling of being free, not constrained by command. True fidelity, allegiance, or faithfulness cannot be demanded; these must be given. Heroically brave individuals feel loyalty to those to whom they are affiliated.

The idea of duty goes beyond loyalty. Sense of duty is a prosocial attitude affecting various aspects of social interactions. Duty is part of what leads people to keep agreements and contracts. It is what leads people to do their part on teams and in organizations. It is in part why projects are completed by deadlines. Sense of duty is sometimes what keeps a marriage intact; it is often what leads a spouse to remain faithful.

The sense of duty seems to first emerge in late childhood and throughout adolescence. Developing over time, this characteristic tends to become stronger and more deeply ingrained as a person matures. In part taught by example, by lecture, and by conditioning, it is also part nature of the individual.

Sense of duty first appears in small matters as a child learns to complete tasks or chores before turning to play. The completed task begins to take on an importance it did not initially have and begins to evolve into what is commonly referred to today as "staying the course." In time, completion and fulfilling one's obligation becomes as important as the task itself. Fulfilling one's duty is an accomplishment in and of itself, separate from the outcome of the task.

Some children seem to relish the tasks to which they are assigned. On the other end of the spectrum, there are individuals who throughout life will have no sense of duty, except to themselves. Responsible people take their duties seriously. This does not mean they necessarily like the task, it means they feel an obligation to complete it. The person will put the task or obligation ahead of his own interests. Responsible people also at times feel compelled to take upon themselves duties that belong to others. Some will become the "poster children" for the maxim, *If you want something done, give it to a busy person.*

Sergeant Mausert had been given mission orders. He had a duty to take the crest of Hill 673 and to do so by leading his men there. Like the other Medal recipients, he accepted his duty and went beyond it.

The attitude of duty eventually translates into broader contexts, like self-sacrifice. The Medal recipients seemed to have learned a moral principle; when they saw someone in need, they had to step forward. Some definitely grew up in churches that taught that Heaven was attained through giving up of one's selfish interests. A good number of the recipients enlisted in the Marines because they understood that their families were in financial difficulty and felt obligated to find a steady income in order to help out. Others felt a patriotic duty to do so. Somehow they had learned that life in America had benefited them and that they were obligated to reciprocate when the nation needed them to do so.

No apparent fear of death

Fear of death is strictly a mental experience, based on the recognition of one's mortality. Fear of death is more about apprehension and anticipation of a possibility, than it is about a present danger. In this regard fear of death is more closely associated to anxiety than it is genuine fear. Humans definitely can be afraid of death without being in a situation in which life is threatened in any realistic manner.

Those who study death and grief have determined that beliefs and understandings about death vary with age. Children do not understand the realities and permanence of death in the same way adults do. Although teenagers can have what seems like a morbid fascination with death, appearing even to have death wishes, they typically view death as distant and themselves as somehow invulnerable. Adolescents contemplating suicide seem also to believe that they will remain somehow present to witness their memorials or that they will enjoy the notoriety and attention their own death will bring them. Adolescence seems to bring some mental aspect of immunity from death.

An individual can be afraid of an imminent danger and experience the fear emotion without any thoughts of death. Fear is an agitation of the nervous system, generated by an immediate presence of a danger and a mental recognition of the threat.

Marines going to war understand that they will be in circumstances in which death is a possibility. If they consider it at all, they also know they are not going to live forever. Realistically, any Marine who charges across a battlefield into enemy gunfire is defying death. Yet, the Medal recipients will see it differently.

The recipients' nervous systems registered natural fear. Their heroically brave actions are a reflection of what they chose to do in the face of real danger. That they experienced fear is natural; that they had no concern for imminent death is likely.

Before leaving Camp Lejeune, Sergeant Mausert expressed the belief that he would return home after the war. Some of the recipients believed they were not going to be coming home, others never gave a thought to their fates, eager to be involved in the challenge, risk, and excitement of a good fight.

Perhaps those who were still in the latter stage of adolescence might have retained a sense of invulnerability or immortality. The older recipients, especially those who had already experienced combat, knew better. The range of ages among the recipients indicates that no apparent fear of death is an attitude, or cognitive structure, which is not reserved only for the young.

Merrit A. Edson, described as "fatalistic and nonchalant about the prospect of death," [18] time and time again demonstrated "absolute disregard for his own safety." [19] He did not hesitate to stand in the open without his helmet on his head while directing his men in action while under fire. Long before he had earned a Medal of Honor, he had accepted the belief that death comes when it is ordained to arrive for each individual.

Some adults deal with the reality of inevitable death by believing that one's death is predetermined. Some force, God, fate, or other has set when and how it will happen, and there is nothing a person can do about it. A person can neither avoid nor cause his or her own death until the moment occurs in which it is meant to happen.

Many men in combat fully believe that they will survive in battle only if they have been marked to do so. Whether or not an enemy sniper will kill you when you stand up in an open field of fire is not determined by the sniper's skill and aim, but by whether or not that particular sniper holds the bullet that already *has your name inscribed on it*.

Among all the recipients, fear of death seems not to have been a preoccupation of any kind. Their assigned responsibilities and objectives outweighed all consideration that one might die. As described in their stories, many of the recipients had survived previous wars and battles. Sixty-three men survived their heroic actions. Six of these died in later battles. It is possible that men with little innate fear of death who then survive armed engagements, experience even less concern for their own mortality.

Some who survive battles do experience a sense of invulnerability. Having been surrounded by death, they grow more confident, certain, and, perhaps, bold. Others who survive early battles begin to think that their time is coming, and there is nothing to do about it but go on and face it. In either case, the recipients refused to be bested, by the enemy and even by death.

By the time he was on duty in Peking, Dan Daly had reached the level of adult thinking in which death is accepted as a permanent end to life on this plane. He had lived through the fury of horrendous battles and survived all his wars. By the time he took a job as a security guard what might there have been left in life for him to fear?

Local newspapers inform the communities.

News of Sergeant "Rickie" Mausert's death in Korea began appearing in newspapers in November 1951. North Adams is forty miles south of Cambridge and across the state line into Massachusetts. Rick's father had been raised there, his grandfather still lived there, and Rick had shown up unexpectedly there at times during his adolescent wanderings. *The North Adams Transcript* carried the news about Rick's death and his Medal of Honor between November 1, 1951 and September 5, 1952, in at least six articles. The emphasis in each was that Rick was a local man's grandson. Rick was identified as a Greenwich native. That he had also lived in Cambridge was seldom mentioned. [20]

How little the local New York area knew or remembered about Rick Mausert was reflected in a Monday morning newspaper column about his death three weeks after he was killed on Hill 673. The misinformation in *The Troy Record* eighteen-lines included that Rick was a private in rank, not a sergeant, that he was Frederick Jr., rather than Frederick III, that he was killed on October 12, having been slightly wounded two days earlier, that he had graduated from Greenwich High School in 1949 and enlisted in the Marines shortly afterward, when he had in fact enlisted in June 1948, and that he had been in Korea for nearly a year. [21] *The Troy Record* also reported later that Rick had once lived in Troy and that Gwen was currently a resident there. Troy, New York, is only twenty-five miles south of Cambridge. Gwen was living in Baltimore at the time of Rick's death.

The confusion about his hometown and birthplace was apparent in the newspaper reports. Adding information that he had provided in his enlistment papers, the towns that could claim some connection to the Medal of Honor recipient then included Greenwich, Jackson, Cambridge, Troy, Riverdale, the Bronx, and Brooklyn, New York,

North Adams and Monson, Massachusetts, Baltimore, Maryland, and Dresher, Pennsylvania. Perhaps Rick was eventually forgotten in the towns once newspaper stories about him no longer showed up in print because he had moved so often in childhood that no town was really sure he could be claimed as a native son.

Rye Mausert was informed in a phone call from his father in Korea that his cousin had been killed in action. He does not remember there being any local media attention to Rickie's death at the time.

Sergeant "Rickie" Mausert, 20-years-old, was brought home and buried in Arlington National Cemetery, Section 12, Site 5559, on January 3, 1952. Lieutenant Colonel Ryerson N. Mausert represented the family at the military funeral services.

The awarding of his Medal of Honor was announced on July 1, 1952. The North Adams, Massachusetts, newspaper reported the award with a bold headline the next day. Rick's grandfather, Henry L. Mausert, was still living at 103 Main Avenue at the time. The basis for the Medal would not be disclosed until the presentation of the award, but AP outlets were assuming it was related to his death during "the bloodiest fighting of the Korean war" on the slopes of Heartbreak ridge. The article also mentioned that Rick's uncles, Clayton and Ryerson, were Army lieutenant colonels. Ryerson, then a Pentagon advisor, had received a Silver Star earlier as a battalion commander in Korea. [22]

Gwen Mausert Barnes and Rick's brother, John, accepted the Medal from Secretary of the Navy Dan Kimball in a ceremony at the Pentagon on September 4, 1952. Kathern Poytner was at the same ceremony. [23]

As the Marines had advanced upon Hill 673, elements of the U.S. Eighth Army, 2d Division had also advanced toward *Bloody Ridge* and the three hills known collectively as "Heartbreak Ridge." The Hills 851, 931 and 894 were in the vicinity of the Punchbowl's western edge and Taeu-san.

One of the Army Airborne Rifle Regiments was under the command of Colonel Ryerson Mausert, Rick's uncle. The regiment repositioned into the hills secured by the Marines. Colonel Mausert would not find out until the reading of his nephew's Citation at the Pentagon ceremony, that he had stood on Hill 673 the day after his nephew had earned the Medal of Honor there.

The public record provided no indication that a ship, building, monument, or memorial had ever been dedicated in Frederick W. Mausert's honor. Forty years after he died on that desolate hill in Korea, a hometown historian considered the fact that Rick had never received the recognition he deserved.

Was he forgotten because he had died in his act of heroism and news did not reach Cambridge? Was it because he had come from a broken home? Had been bounced from place to place in his childhood and lived in no single community long enough to claim it as his own? No matter the reasons, Memorial Day, 1991, would change all that.

Dave Thornton is a retired Cambridge high school theater arts and English teacher. Long serving as the town historian and archivist, he wrote a weekly newspaper column about the local history. His page appeared in *The Eagle* for over ten years, encompassing more than a million words of Washington County history. His research would bring the memory of Rick Mausert home to Cambridge.

More than thirty years had passed since Rick had given his life on Hill 673, when Dave began a systematic study of *Washington County Post* back issues. Within the weekly's microfilm archive, he discovered the story of Marine Sergeant Frederick W. Mausert, III being awarded the Medal of Honor in Korea for sacrificing his life after repeated acts of heroism. The story and obituary had also been circulated in Pennsylvania newspapers, identifying the young man as a former resident of Dresher.

Dave began researching the background of Rickie Mausert, tracking down family, friends, and babysitters, interviewing those he could, and writing. He had located Rickie's mother, retired in Florida, and interviewed her in 1990, as well as his uncle, Ryerson Mausert, Sr. [24]

Dave also initiated community-wide efforts to establish an archive and to raise permanent honor rolls to all veterans from the Cambridge area who had served honorably from the Revolutionary War through Vietnam. From his research and The Honor Rolls project, Dave published a series of booklets to revitalize the community's pride in its veterans. Rick's story appeared in the Korea book.

Although Dave was doing what he could to raise funds for the project, he knew the effort to honor veterans would require community involvement. He approached the Old Cambridge American Legion Captain Maxson Post 634 members with Sergeant Mausert's story, but none of the veterans remembered him. As in other American communities with hometown Medal of Honor recipients, there can be resistance to paying tribute to a Marine no one remembers.

Dave's diligence in reminding the town of the heroism of its sons, and the importance of keeping their stories vibrant for future generations was augmented when another Marine came to town to visit. Joseph A. Lenard, from Webster, Massachusetts, graduated from high school in 1950, joined the USMC, and fought with them in Korea. He was a veteran of the battle at, and breakout from, the frozen Chosin Reservoir, when ten divisions of Chinese were given orders to annihilate a Marine regiment in November 1950.

Joe came home, finished a degree from Worcester Polytechnic Institute, and worked for IBM in Poughkeepsie and Fishkill, NY. He made it a mission in his life to visit the homes of First Marine Division Medal of Honor recipients when he had spare time. Forty-two Marines had received the Medal in Korea: twenty-eight of them had not come home. Joe had fought beside seven of the recipients at the *Frozen Chosin*.

Having retired from IBM, Joe stopped at the Cambridge Legion Post one night and asked the bartender if he knew that a Medal of Honor recipient had been raised in Cambridge. The bartender was unfamiliar with Rick's valor and Medal of Honor, but knew of Dave Thornton's initiatives. The bartender called him, Dave went to the Post to meet Joe, and a new collaboration began. As a result, Joe would gain the support of the First Marine Division Association and Dave would reinvigorate the local veterans. Their resolve sparked community interest.

Dave, Joe, and the Legion Post planned with representatives of The First Marine Division Association. They assembled Memorial Park on Memorial Drive, on the south side of West Main Street in 1990, close to the site once occupied by the old Cambridge Union School.

Today, under the shade of trees, bordered by manicured lawns and well-tended gardens, on the faces of a semicircle of large granite stones, bronze plaques provide the long, alphabetical rosters of local veterans who served in each of the wars and the men and women "who paid the supreme sacrifice." On the largest of the stones, the Honor Roll rosters include names from WWI and WWII, 179 names from Korea and 224 from Vietnam. Rick's name is inscribed at the top of the Korean War Era plaque, with two others Killed In Action.

On Wednesday, January 9, 1991, the Associated Press released Dave's article, Cambridge Honors Forgotten Hero of Forgotten War, telling Rickie's story and announcing that a memorial was going to be dedicated to him during the May 25 Memorial Day ceremonies. Honoring Rick was to be the highlight of the annual Memorial Day parade and service.

Rickie's mother traveled to Cambridge for the dedication. A 20x32 inch bronze plaque, detailing Rick's Medal of Honor Citation, provided by The First Marine Division Association, was to be mounted on a large, natural Ice Age fieldstone, directly behind the flagpole. The First Marine Division Association was also contributing a smaller plaque to go inside a public building in Old Cambridge.

In his Saturday May 25, 1991, article, Dave updated the community on the Memorial Dedication Ceremony. The monument to Rick was unveiled, the stone having been worked into a smooth face by the American Legion veterans. Visitors taking the sidewalk to the Honor Roll rosters first approach Rick's monument, standing tall and alone in its own garden, in front of the other monuments. The sidewalk around Rick's stone is in the shape of a pentagon, a reminder of the five-pointed bronze Medal of Honor.

The Memorial Day dedication in Cambridge was an opportunity for Barnes and Mausert cousins to catch up on forty years of life. Cousin Rye hosted a "family reunion" at his home after the dedication. Thirty-two family members were captured in photographs. John's long-time wish to have more family than just his parents had become a reality. Like John, his daughter, Carrie Barnes Osak, and her husband met extended family members for the first time.

When the Osaks began their own family a few years after the reunion, having first a daughter, then three years later twins, a boy and girl, Rick remained in their thoughts. As they grew up, the Osak children. Shannon, Ryan and Rachel took great interest in the story about their mother's uncle. The entire family visited Rick's grave in Arlington National Cemetery in spring, 2008. Ryan was very impressed.

Shannon, 15-years-old, did a research project and presentation about her great uncle, a story in which her teacher and class were fascinated. The Osaks keep Rick's picture on display at home, happy when people ask about it, and sensing a proud kinship when others are "fascinated by the history of this very brave man."

Bravery inspires one generation after another.

The Cambridge branch of the Glens Falls National Bank & Trust on Main Street has a permanent tribute to Rickie in its lobby. Dave Thornton formed a committee of local Marine veterans to plan, establish and manage the display. Gwen Sharp Mausert Barnes had been impressed with the way Cambridge had honored her son. She believed his Medal of Honor belonged in his birthplace. Gwen died October 10, 1994, knowing that her son had been remembered.

By then living in Southington, Connecticut, John brought his brother's Medal and presented it to the town at a later Memorial Day celebration. Having not had time or opportunity to know his older brother well, the Medal did not provide John a sense of pride. Instead, it was a reminder that he had lost a brother in war, a brother who had adopted a John Wayne view of heroism, a brother he would never see again.

In addition to Rick's Medal of Honor and the First Marine Division Association plaque, the bank display has photos of Rick across his all-too-short lifetime.

Frederick "Rickie" William Mausert III was no longer forgotten in his hometown.

CHAPTER 24
Remembering or Forgetting is Sometimes a Family Matter

"The hero is one who kindles a great light in the world, who sets up blazing torches in the dark streets of life for men to see by."

Felix Adler (1851-1933)
American educator

That is true, as long as the world and men are permitted to see the hero.

During a telephone conversation, a mid-ranking Alliance police officer acknowledged having never heard of Ron Coker. It was fall 2009, and Ron had been dead for forty years. The officer had been born well after Vietnam, so events of that war and its local impact were understandably beyond immediate awareness. Then again, a Memorial Day celebration at the Court House and the naming of an airport road to the Medal of Honor Marine had taken place four months earlier. The police officer likely represented a larger segment of the town and county.

The community tribute to Ron had been long overdue.

Ronald Leroy Coker was born on August 9, 1947, in Alliance, Nebraska, a rural town of around 8,129 souls. The Box Butte County seat, seventy-four percent of the county population resided in Alliance. In the far western panhandle region of the state, agriculture and ranching predominated.

Ron's grandparents had moved to the Sand Hills to help lay out the county lines, formed in 1886. The Cokers were surveyors; the Heaths were assessors. The families laid the foundations of their homes miles north of town with about nine miles between their respective homesteads. The Heaths eventually cleared an acre for a family cemetery.

Cecil Leroy Coker, born May 29, 1898, and sometimes called "Roy," was an Army veteran of WWII. He married 25-year-old Nellie Fern Heath on January 18, 1943, and had four children, each birth separated by about fifteen months. Janet was their first child, born January 27, 1945, before the war ended. Three sons followed: Charles, March 23, 1946, Ron, and last was Ray, on September 6, 1948. [1]

Ron grew up in sand hills terrain, in easy travel distance of a National Forest, state parks, recreational areas, and Chimney Rock, one of the most famous landmarks on the Oregon Trail. He lived on Long Lake Route during his childhood and adolescence, about eleven miles northeast of Alliance. The closest town of any size was Scottsbluff about fifty miles to the southwest, with about 15,000 inhabitants.

Life on the farm in the early days was without amenities. The Cokers had no phone or electricity. Kerosene lamps provided the indoor lighting. Television, of course, was years in the distance. News traveled slowly. This was evidenced in Ron's own life; when Ron was about five-years-old, his parents drove off for town one day and did not return. Three days passed with Janet taking charge of the family. Not until an uncle came to the farm did the children learn that their parents had been hospitalized after a car accident. Whatever life brought their way, the only choice the Cokers accepted was to deal with it and move on.

Ron attended both District 78 Rural Elementary School and Alliance High School. The grade school, Grades 1-8, had one teacher, Lloyd Goldstedt, who began teaching there in fall, 1947. Teaching eight grades might have seemed much, but was made easier by the fact that only ten students attended. [2]

A country kid, Ron liked having something to do with his hands. He enjoyed baking and was sometimes caught with flour on his face, hands, and clothes. When Mr. Goldstedt suggested that someone bring in a sheep skin for a school project, Ron complied, bringing a skin in a sack that Friday. Not realizing that Ron had taken the initiative to skin a dead lamb, and that the sheep skin was raw, Mr. Goldstedt directed his young charge to hang the sack in the hall, where it remained over the weekend. By Monday the stench had permeated the school; windows and doors were left open for days afterwards.

In one school photo, Janet, Charlie, Ron, and Ray are to Lloyd's left, four Bauer children to his right, and two Trenkle boys sit in front of him. Dick Bauer, a grade ahead of Ron, remembered that he and Ron were so bashful through school that by the time they graduated from the high school, they had seldom talked to each other and knew little of each other.

The descriptions of Ron by those who had known him are consistent; he was a "down-to-earth" young man. If there was a theme song to his life in Nebraska, it might have been:

"Let me ride through the wide open country that I love,
Don't fence me in.
Let me be by myself in the evenin' breeze,
And listen to the murmur of the cottonwood trees,
Send me off forever but I ask you please,
Don't fence me in." [3]

Once an Alliance High *Bulldog*, Class of '65, Ron wore his black cowboy hat wherever he went. Popular in school, his friends called him "Cisco," borrowed from the TV series they had watched as children in the early 1950s, *The Cisco Kid*. [4] Ron participated with friends in the Future Farmers of America (F.F.A.). He appeared in a Senior Annual photo, wearing the distinctive jacket with its emblem above the heart, working over a buffing wheel.

While attending Alliance High, Ron drove his pickup truck over to his uncle's to help out on the farm, passing Fairview Cemetery, final resting place of his maternal ancestors.

On the first day of junior year, Ron asked Karen Ball if he could sit down beside her in homeroom. The tall, lean young man, 6'3" and 180 pounds, introduced himself and they began visiting. Karen shared a quality with Ron to which he could relate. She tended to be bashful. Getting to know each other sometimes entailed passing notes back and forth, sometimes sauntering together in the hallways as he walked her to a class.

Ron experienced a disappointment later that year. Having waited, by the time he asked Karen to the Junior Prom, she already had a date. She offered to instead go to the Senior Prom with him, an agreement he was happy to accept. Looking ahead, Ron signed Karen's '64 Annual. "Well next year will be our last year at A.H.S. Let's make the best of it."

The Senior Prom theme was *Underwater Paradise*, with blue and white crepe stretched above the gym floor to imitate waves above the dancers, fish and sea horses dangling about. Initially hesitant about his dancing skills, Ron's confidence emerged once he and Karen stepped onto the gym floor. He watched her movements and quickly learned the steps, wanting then to remain under the waves for nearly all the dances. Shy perhaps, Ron had a good sense of humor. His grin and smile were ever-present, his laughter infectious. At the prom dinner, the steaks were so tasty that he debated and bantered with another friend whether the beef had come from Herefords or Nebraska Black Angus.

Ron graduated from Alliance High School in 1965 with about 134 classmates. That summer, he traveled down to Denver, Colorado, to attend a diesel mechanic school. Ron took the initiative to do this, an aspiration of his, believing the training would allow him to be of more assistance on the family farm. [5] There for six months, he learned to operate a yellow Caterpillar D-4 tracked bulldozer, "The Crawler." Ron had always taken to machinery, fixing equipment and implements around the farm and working on his cars. Riding his Harley Davidson motorcycle with friends held a special place in his heart.

Ron's life plans changed before he graduated from the Denver Auto Mechanic School. Nellie Coker, his mother, died on October 6, 1966, at the age of 49-years and was buried in the family cemetery. Ron was home for his mother's funeral and did not return to Denver afterwards.

Cecil moved into Alliance, residing at 908 Mississippi Street, several blocks east of Central Park. He lived there for a couple of years, then sold his property and moved to Rapid City, South Dakota. Ron's father lived five years longer than Nellie, dying June 9, 1972, at the age of 74-years.

Ron remained in Alliance working, having three different employers in the next two years. For the last fourteen months of his civilian life, Ron worked as an assistant well driller for Meder Smith, Inc., driving a water truck and helping to drill, install, remove, or repair irrigation and stock wells and their pumps.

Ron does not appear to necessarily have had aspirations to be a Marine. He was 20-years-old when he received a notice from his Selective Service Board, January 4, 1968, to report for induction. Whatever might have been his attitude about the Marines and the war, Ron is one of only two of the fifty-seven USMC Vietnam Medal of Honor recipients to have been drafted into service while busy doing other things. His thoughts about this would be expressed in letters home within the year.

Ron decided to go to the Denver recruiting office and enlisted in the Corps, April 16, 1968. After his father, he designated his friend, Richard L. Taylor, as next to be notified in emergencies. He added Jack Taylor and Paul Snyder as character references.

The *Tet* Offensive in Vietnam, which had been much in the news, was winding down. The siege at Khe Sanh had ended the week before when the NVA troops withdrew from the area. Public antiwar sentiments were spreading. President Lyndon B. Johnson, watching his approval ratings slipping significantly in public opinion polls, had weeks earlier announced a halt in U.S. bombings over North Vietnam in order to get Hanoi to participate in peace talks with the United States in Paris. He also had announced his unexpected decision to not seek re-election.

Private Coker reported to the San Diego Recruit Depot. In Aptitude and Assignment Tests, he scored highest in automotive information, electronics information, arithmetic reasoning, and mechanical aptitude. His General Classification Test (GCT), a general learning ability test to assist placement into training schools, indicated he was in the upper third of enlistees tested. He was Drill Instructor material. On the rifle range with an M-14, his final qualification score earned Ron a Marksman Badge. After graduating from the Recruit Depot, he went through infantry training in Camp Pendleton. Ron was promoted to private first class. He had his orders to Vietnam.

In a chance meeting at the Alliance Jerry Lynn Drive-In, Ron ran into Karen while he was home on leave that fall. She was married by then and her husband was serving on a ship off the Vietnam coast. As the two caught up on events in their lives, Ron confided in his friend. He had a feeling he could not evade: a fear he was not going to be returning to Alliance from Vietnam.

The family gathered with Ron in the Alliance City Park Shelter House to say goodbye to their Marine before he departed for the war. He took his niece, Robyn Nicodemus, for her first ride on a Harley, a memory she cherishes to this day, and left for Vietnam on September 23, her fourth birthday. No one today remembers what happened to Ron's Harley after he was buried at home.

During his presidential campaign, Richard M. Nixon had promised to end the war in Vietnam and win the peace. Once in office, President Nixon agreed to the bombing halt of North Vietnam cities that had gone into effect on November 1, 1968. The North Vietnamese made a reciprocal pledge to cease their attacks on major South Vietnamese cities. As Americans hoped for peace in Southeast Asia, the infiltration of enemy troops and weapons down the Ho Chi Minh trail into South Vietnam increased.

As the four parties at the Peace Talks argued about seating arrangements around the conference table, Private First Class Coker, a rifleman, arrived in the Republic of Vietnam on November 6, 1968. He was assigned duties with Company M, 3d Battalion, 3d Marines, 3d

Marine Division in Con Thien, Quang Tri Province, in the northwest of the country. Known as *America's Battalion*, these Marines had been in Vietnam since May 12, 1965, and had fought battles at Khe Sanh, the Rockpile, Cam Lo, Gio Linh, and Con Thien.

An easy-going young man, Private First Class Coker made friends among his Second Platoon, Third Squad mates. He seemed always ready to help others and never to be angry about anything. Photographs show him among companions, taller than most, always smiling. He adjusted to the life in bunkers at Con Thien during monsoon season. The platoon pulled escort duties, went out on patrols to locate the enemy, provided road sweeps to make sure supply convoys could get to their destinations, and set up in ambush sites.

Lance Corporal Ronald Edgar Playford was Private First Class Coker's team leader. From Yelm, Washington, a small town just south of the Fort Lewis Reserve and the Puget Sound, he had been in Vietnam since the previous March and was knowledgeable about life in "the bush." He mentored Private First Class Coker on how to survive as a point man.

Late in 1968, a primary NVA staging area was identified well south of the 3d Battalion area, southwest of An Hoa in Quang Nam Province. Intelligence units referred to the location as Base Area 112, near the Arizona Territory. Along a major infiltration route between Da Nang and Tam Ky, BA 112 warehoused enemy supplies, logistical facilities, and training supports.

To get to the rugged mountains in which the enemy staging area was located, the Marines had to conduct clearing operations from the Liberty Bridge, across the rice paddies, south to An Hoa. CH-46 helicopters carried the first companies of Task Force Yankee in on the morning of December 7. *Operation Taylor Common* was underway.

Two days later *America's Battalion* was sent to the Arizona Territory to augment the three other rifle battalions of TF Yankee. Within a week, Private First Class Coker dug in on FSB Mace, near the western edge of BA 112, about twelve kilometers southwest of An Hoa and southwest of FSB Lance on Hill 575. Once established on the ground, experiencing mortar barrages and ground assaults, the companies began fanning out from the fire support base into inhospitable terrain to clear out caves, tunnels, and bunkers. Private First Class Coker crossed swollen streams and muddy rice paddies and climbed slippery inclines through choking vegetation. The Marines fought off "trench (immersion) foot," booby traps, relentless NVA snipers, and well-entrenched enemy forces.

For the first time, Private First Class Coker saw Marine M-48 tanks with Christmas trees on the turrets and lights decorating the 90-mm guns. And just before Christmas, some family back at home learned of the 30,000th American KIA.

Private First Class Coker's willingness to go "above and beyond" what was demanded of him was demonstrated in January 1969, while he was in the Arizona Territory and after he had been in-country for three months. He submitted an application for voluntary assignment to the Marine Corps Combined Action Program (CAP), acknowledging his willingness to extend his overseas tour if necessary.

Begun in 1965, the CAP provided a squad of Marines and one Navy Corpsman for six months in isolated villages, the "Villes," from Chu Lai to the DMZ. Occupying and controlling areas uncovered by the forward movement of the U.S. and ARVN forces, CAP Marines were typically surrounded by jungle, endangered by Viet Cong booby-traps, and in the midst of potentially hostile Vietnamese civilians. [6]

The CAP's primary mission was local defense. Coordinating with Popular Force (PF) members, the Marines gained knowledge of the local area, people, customs, government, and Viet Cong activities. They trained the PF, increasing their combat effectiveness. Living among the people, the CAP Marines also attempted to isolate Vietnamese civilians in the selected villages from the battles and help them survive the war. Records indicate that thousands of Vietnamese benefited from the CAP program until its end in 1971.

Having been nominated for the CAP, Private First Class Coker filled out a questionnaire. He believed the ARVN were good men, but admitted having no feelings for the PF soldier because he did not know anything about them. The three things he liked most about his assignment in Vietnam were: "the chance to see another country, also helping people get a start in the right ways, it also gave me a chance to decide what to do in life." His assignments around An Hoa were noted to be those he liked most since his enlistment.

Private First Class Coker wanted to volunteer for the CAP "so that I can help the people get educated in life and keep them from becoming Communists." He believed he could help the people improve their lives. He also wanted to have a more permanent placement, have additional responsibilities, and earn higher promotion. On January 30, 1969, Mike Company commander, Captain B.J. Williamson, helped Private First Class Coker, signed his request and forwarded it on, recommending approval.

For two months under fire by small arms, 50-caliber machine guns, and rifle grenades, the Marines cleared large arms caches as they found them in the Arizona Territory. A complex could store dozens of 122-mm rockets, dozens of smaller rockets, and thousands of mortar rounds. By mid-February, BA 112 appeared neutralized, while enemy activity along the DMZ had increased. Hanoi launched a wave of attacks against cities throughout South Vietnam.

Most of the task force was ordered to return to An Hoa by February 16. Having participated in all three phases of *Operation Taylor Common*, the 3d Battalion returned to Dong Ha Combat Base, Grid Coordinates YD 245599. Private First Class Coker had earned a reputation for caring about his Marine comrades in this Operation.

By the time *Operation Taylor Common* ended on March 8, 1969, 183 Marines had died in BA 112 and 1,487 were wounded. *Menu,* the secret bombing campaign against Cambodia, would begin soon.

Fire Support Base Alpine, (Lang Hoan Tap), Hill 807, at Grid Coordinates XD 761531, was about as far west from Dong Ha as Marines might be choppered. The Laotian Border was just six miles west. Khe Sanh was to the east. The enemy infiltration route from the north across the DMZ was nearby. The 1st Battalion, 4th Marines held the FSB with a battery of both 105 and 155 Howitzers. Fire Support Base Argonne, at Grid XD 756532 on Hill 1154, was up a valley, a mountain or two to the north and west, almost on the Laotian border and the DMZ. Assignments at FSB Argonne definitely put Marines "in the bush."

At 8:00 AM, March 21, Private First Class Coker marched to the helicopters with Mike Company, flew from Dong Ha parallel to Route 9, past the Rockpile and Khe Sanh, and assumed responsibility for security of Fire Support Base Alpine from Company C.

The enemy had accurate maps of both Marine positions and their 82-mm mortar and sniper fire kept the two Fire Support Bases hunkered down day and night. There would be little quiet for the rest of Private First Class Coker's days, during *Operation Purple Martin*.

At 8:20 AM, the enemy launched an 82-mm mortar attack from the north. The Alpha Command Group bunker, directing operations at FSB Argonne, was hit, instantly killing two Battalion commanding officers and wounding many other Command Group personnel. The Marine security details kept up their own mortar fire against the suspected enemy positions. The exchange continued without respite all day and into the night.

Mike Company was set up in bunkers on the sides of Alpine, away from the batteries on the flat top of the hill. They could hear the sounds of the enemy mortar rounds popping out of their tubes and soaring inbound. Squads walked the perimeter, went on patrols in a radius of three to four kilometers, established ambushes, set up in forward observation posts, manned listening posts, and ran for the shelter of their bunkers when mortars "popped off." They bathed in and filled their canteens from rain-filled bomb craters or in the river that ran down the middle of the valley. They slept when they could.

A flare ship came on station over the hills at 10:00 PM that first night to provide continuous illumination over the fire support bases. The flares lit up the night skies until 6:30 AM in order to hamper an enemy counter attack. After midnight, the Battalion called in an aerial support ship, AC-130H/U Spectre/Spooky, to blanket the area with deadly fire where the enemy mortar teams were suspected to be. A ground explosion indicated that at least one enemy position was hit. At 6:30 AM, March 22, the flare ship was relieved.

The NVA went into action right away. Forty-five 82-mm mortar rounds hit the Bravo Command Group at FSB Alpine, wounding five Marines and damaging two artillery pieces. The Battalion fired back with 60-mm mortars and artillery into the grid position from which the attack had come. An Aerial Observer controlled two fixed-wing missions over the hills.

That night, Mike Company Commander Captain B.J. Williamson gave the mission statement to the Second Platoon Commander, First Lieutenant Richard Hoffman, who passed it to Staff Sergeant Clifford Goodau, who gave the orders to Lance Corporal Playford, Corporal Gifford T. "Tiny" Foley and the other team leaders. The fifteen Marines of Third Squad were to "Saddle up" in the morning, go into the hills as a Killer Team, and destroy the Mortar Pit. [7]

As on earlier days, 82-mm mortar rounds pounded into the flat tops on Sunday morning, March 23. Marine patrols fanned out from the bases and swept the surrounding bunker complexes. Third Squad moved off FSB Alpine moving east across the valley then north. By nightfall, they had reached the base of their objective at Grid XD 746547. They were about fifteen miles northwest of Khe Sanh.

Meeting the enemy at the Mortar Pit

In the dark, silently, they moved up the northern side of the hill and set up an ambush site behind the suspected enemy position. To be sure they were on the correct hill, they called for an artillery strike on the Mortar Pit. Two friendly rounds exploded on top of them. Those rounds proved to be the extent of the night's action. There was no enemy contact, as Third Squad remained at 100% alert throughout the night. That meant no one slept.

Sounds of war came with the dawn on March 24. From somewhere nearby came a burst of automatic weapons fire that struck FSB Alpine. The base answered with 81-mm mortars.

With Private First Class Coker out on point, Third Squad started down the south side of the hill, advancing quietly. About one hundred yards down from their ambush site, they found the Mortar Pit, which seemed abandoned. The mortar tube and twenty 82-mm rounds were unmanned. The team collected the ordnance and continued down the slope of the hill.

Descending another one hundred yards, Private First Class Coker ran headlong into three NVA mortarmen making their way up the hill from the creek below. The point man immediately opened fire with his M-16, but the weapon jammed. The crack of AKs returning fire was brief. The M-60 gun team opened up on the enemy, and the NVA turned and ran for the creek. Staff Sergeant Goodau directed the squad to get off the trail and cut through the heavy bush straight down the steep ravine to the Creek. Near the bottom, closing in on the enemy, the lead fire team came to a *Big Rock*. A narrow trail, wide enough for only one Marine to pass, cut between the hill and the side of the Big Rock. The creek was in sight. What was not in sight was the enemy three-man cave beneath the rock.

Lance Corporal Playford ran down into the cut first with Private First Class Coker right behind him. Three Marines jumped up on the Rock hoping to catch the NVA in the sights of their M-60 before they reached the Creek. The crack of AK-47s just below them echoed up the hill.

The NVA had waited in their concealed position until Lance Corporal Playford was directly in front of them and opened fire on the team leader. He was down, fully exposed in the open draw, but not alone. Without thought, Private First Class Coker demonstrated a trait common among the Medal of Honor recipients.

Concern for others

When he had filled out the CAP questionnaire, Private First Class Coker expressed his intention to assist the Vietnamese people, believing he could help them improve their lives. Friends and family who had known him as a boy and as an adolescent would not have been surprised about what he was about to do.

Most Medal recipients are remembered to have demonstrated efforts to respond on behalf of others, as well as looking out for themselves while growing up. As brothers, they helped younger siblings with chores and homework, included them in play, and tried to help them learn activities. They also looked out for siblings, protecting them in various ways. While they might have picked on siblings in normal family rivalries, they would not allow others to do so. They often argued cases with their parents on behalf of younger brothers and sisters.

When friends were in trouble, the Medal recipients helped out in any way they could. They encouraged friends to try things, and to "hang in there" when things got difficult. As boys, the recipients were willing to come to the assistance of strangers, as well, for example stopping to help people stranded on roadsides, holding doors for those carrying packages, picking up items dropped by others, chasing down a letter blown out of someone's hand by a gust of wind.

By the time Ron was in combat, as was true of all the Medal recipients, coming to the aid of a fellow Marine was not just an impulse, it was a habit.

Despite the intensity of the hostile fire, Private First Class Coker shouted excitedly to Lance Corporal Playford, assuring him that he would get him out of the enemy guns' line of fire. Advancing towards the wounded squad member, Private First Class Coker was wounded himself by small-arms fire. Wounded in the chest and throat, he crawled within close enough range to toss a hand grenade into the cave, diminishing the hostile firepower a degree. Reaching his companion, Private First Class Coker grabbed him, trying to pull him back from the draw. The squad, unable to either get to the draw or provide covering fire, shouted encouragement to him as the NVA fired steadily at them.

NVA soldiers typically carried a pouch of Chi Com stick grenades. This explosive was a smaller and lighter version of the German WW II "Potato Masher" grenade. The Chi Com usually had a bamboo handle with a wooden or cork-like screw cap. Its friction-type fuse was activated when the cap was pulled off. The Viet Cong liked to attach a wire to the cap and run the wire across a trail, hoping an American would trip across the booby trap and detonate the Chi Com.

From the protection of their cave under the Rock, the NVA began tossing Chi Coms. One landed almost on top of Lance Corporal Playford. From atop the Rock, J. D. Murphy screamed a warning.

"CHI COM!"

Private First Class Coker instantly grabbed the explosive in his hands and rolled away from his comrade. The stick grenade exploded before he could discard it, severing both his hands. Bleeding profusely, Private First Class Coker reoriented himself and crawled resolutely back to Lance Corporal Playford. With the stubs of his wrists in the team leader's cartridge belt, he again began dragging him toward safety. The squad threw helmets and flak jackets into the open draw, hoping to give the two some protective cover. Grenades continued to detonate near the two seriously wounded Marines, one piercing Private First Class Coker's chest and cutting open his face. Determined to pull his comrade to safety, he continued to crawl across the open area, eventually withdrawing far enough for others to rush forward to the wounded Marines and pull them to cover.

The squad had seen enough. They generated enough sustained firepower at the enemy position to allow the M-60 team to skirt to the left of the Rock and lay about 100 rounds into the cave. The team made sure; the three NVA in the cave were dead.

Having persevered in spite of absorbing piercing wounds to his chest, arms, legs, face, head and neck, fracturing of both legs, and amputation of both hands, Private First Class Coker's wounds were too many and too severe for Doc Roberto Valencia Jr.'s first aid efforts to save his life. The young man from Nebraska had given in full measure.

Neither Private First Class Coker nor Lance Corporal Playford survived the patrol to the Mortar Pit. The Third Squad strained to get their two fallen companions back to Fire Base Alpine, traveling along the rock-strewn creek bed. They carried with them two captured AK-47 rifles, six Chi Com grenades, the twenty 82-mm mortar rounds, and three NVA helmets. Once at the base of Alpine, they would face the ascent to the flat top.

HM3 Cliff "Doc Hoppy" Hopkins was the senior Corpsman on Alpine. Informed of the inbound casualties, he set up LZ Alpine in the valley and arranged for a medivac chopper to pick up the casualties at the base of the hill. They were waiting when the Killer Team came out of the mountains.

Staff Sergeant Goodau understood that recommendations for a Medal of Honor required eyewitness accounts. He told his squad to write down everything they had seen at the *Big Rock* and submit it to him. He intended to recommend Private First Class Coker for the Medal of Honor. The seven descriptive statements were making their way up the Chain of Command by April 21.

Private First Class Ronald L. Coker's body was returned to Alliance on April 4 for burial at the family's Fairview Cemetery as his father wished, next to his mother, beside the expansive prairie, and with military honors. He had reached the age of 21-years.

Forever honoring his memory

Cecil Coker was still residing on Mississippi Street in Alliance.

Four Star General Leonard F. Chapman, Jr., Commandant of the Marine Corps, wrote to Cecil on April 8, extending his sympathies. "However, I am sure you will be comforted in some measure by the knowledge that your son served his country faithfully and that his friends share your grief."

Dated as received April 14, another letter arrived for Cecil from Company M Commander Captain M. B. Riley. "In the time Ronald was with the Company he made many good friends. He was well known and liked by all of us. Your loss is a son, ours a dedicated and faithful fellow Marine. Be assured we share your sorrow."

A letter from President Nixon followed. "The only consolation I can offer is that the nation he died to serve shares your grief and will forever honor his memory." [8]

On September 15, 1969, Admiral John J. Hyland, Commander in Chief, Pacific Fleet, signed the Seventh Endorsement to Captain Riley's April 21 letter recommending Private First Class Coker for a posthumous Medal of Honor award. The recommendation was forwarded on to the Joint Chiefs of Staff Chairman and then to the Secretary of the Navy.

For Private First Class Coker's actions in defense of fellow Marines against enemy forces, Vice President Spiro T. Agnew presented the Medal of Honor to his father, Cecil, at a White House ceremony in the East Room. Ron's sister and brothers also attended. The Cokers were not alone, either. The East Room was crowded that Monday, April 20, 1970. The parents of thirteen other Marines were present to accept awards on behalf of their sons.

Despite the president's promise that the nation would "forever honor his memory," not much public notice was given to Ron's life and heroism. Information about him in the public venue is minimal. The rural elementary school he attended was closed many years ago. There was neither a memorial to him at the school before it closed, nor is there one at the Alliance High School.

The two Coker brothers had strong feelings associated with recognition of their brother's heroism. In post-WWII America, not many families had to deal with the death of three beloved family members in less than six years. That sort of grief can be disruptive and enduring. Naturally, one loss following another brings with it a good share of anger. Their mother died late in 1966, Ron died two and a half years later, and then their father.

Three years after Ron's death, his father was living in Rapid City, South Dakota. He had remarried a Rapid City woman by the name of Flora Napier Allen and the couple was living in her home. Cecil was having health problems and seeing doctors at the V.A. hospital in Hot Springs, south of the city. [9]

On the night of June 9-10, 1972, one of the deadliest floods in U.S. history hit the city. In a period of hours 238 people lost their lives, and five were missing. Among the dead were three National Guardsmen, three firefighters, seven airmen from Ellsworth Air Force Base, one police reserve officer and other rescuers. 3,057 Rapid City residents were injured, including 118 who were hospitalized. Insurance records listed 770 permanent homes and 565 mobile homes destroyed. An additional 2,035 permanent homes and 785 mobile homes were damaged. Thirty-six businesses were destroyed and 236 more damaged. Over 5,000 vehicles were destroyed. [10]

Cecil and Flora Coker died in the Rapid City Flood, their house ripped from its footings with them inside and swept along in the surging water.

Lost with Cecil were all of Ron's medals, including the Medal of Honor. The Marines would have replaced each of the lost medals, but the family did not submit any requests to replace the tributes to their brother's valor. [11]

Cecil was brought home to Alliance and buried in Fairview Cemetery beside his wife and son.

Ron Coker's name is included with six other recipients from Vietnam on the Medal of Honor plaque housed in the Nebraska Hall of Fame at the State Capitol. The dedication ceremony was May 5, 1974. The name of Miquel Keith, a Marine from Omaha, was also inscribed on the plaque. According to Ron's sister, Janet, the Coker family did not know anything about the ceremony at the State Capital. [12]

The Coker family continued to grow and in time five nephews and five nieces learned of their uncle's bravery. Janet had three sons and a daughter, Joel, Robyn, Michael, and Gerald. Joel died and is buried beside Ron in the family cemetery. Charlie had five children, two sons and three girls. [13] His oldest son, Donald L. Coker was also a Marine. Charlie died December 6, 1997, and is buried near his brother and nephew in the family plot in Fairview Cemetery. Ray Coker, Ron's younger brother, had one daughter.

Ron's gravesite at Fairview Cemetery was a source of conflict for many years. His family preferred for him to be close to other family and that his grave be simple. Any suggestion that Ron be re-interred in a Veteran's Memorial Park is vehemently resisted. At one point, the community surrounded his gravesite with a base of white stones and an ornamental white picket fence, a tribute to his having earned a Medal of Honor. The fence made Ron's grave stand out among all the other burial sites in the cemetery.

Had Cecil Coker remained alive, he would have been unhappy about that fence. Ron's older brother knew that and agreed. Ron had always been a "free spirit," not one who was comfortable with posts, pickets, and rails. The expanse of land and open space were most important to him. Charles Coker, every part a cowboy, could hear a song's familiar refrain: "And I can't look at hobbles and I can't stand fences. Don't fence me in. No. Poppa, don't you fence me in." [14] Charles went out to the cemetery and kicked down the fence. Its remnants are now the front gate to the cemetery.

Around Memorial Day, 1990, J. D. Murphy received a call from the V.A., asking if he had served with Ron in Vietnam. They told J.D. that Ron's grave had been vandalized, resulting in the discovery that he was a Medal of Honor recipient. A ceremony was planned for him in Alliance. It was the first the former squad mate knew of the Medal's awarding. J.D. had Ron in mind often over the years, as did other Marines who had fought at FSB Alpine. In 2002, Rick Bartholomew, a 3d Platoon, Mike Company, 3/3 Marine from upstate New York, included a short rendition of Ron's actions at The Rock in his book, *Dig In.* [15]

In the nearly twenty years between the time when Charles removed the fence from around his brother's grave and Memorial Day, 2009, a number of seemingly unrelated events worked toward establishing a lasting tribute to Ron in his hometown. The first significant event actually went back to the December 1941, attack on Pearl Harbor. Months after the attack, the U.S. Army had purchased 31,489 acres of open landscape one mile south of Alliance. Five thousand construction workers came to town to erect 775 buildings and by July 1942, four 9,000-foot runways had been laid down.

The Alliance Army Air Field was ready to train C-47, C-53 transport, and CG-4 glider aircrews. By autumn of the next year 12,500 military personnel were based at the field. When the war ended with the Japanese surrender, the airbase was declared a surplus asset. Buildings were sold and a portion of the field was opened as the Alliance Municipal Airport. Nebraska Historical Marker 416 was placed on Airport Road near the site of the World War airbase. [16]

Then in 1995, local Alliance leaders had an idea for a veterans' cemetery that they suggested to the City Council. The High Plains Veterans Cemetery Task Force took on the project and worked on it for thirteen years. In 1997, the city donated land that had been part of the 1940's Air Base.

During the 2006 legislative session, legislation necessary to create the State Veteran's Cemetery System was passed. In September 2008, the Department of Veterans Affairs announced a $2.9 million grant to establish the Nebraska State Veterans Cemetery in Alliance. The 21-acre cemetery to serve western Nebraska veterans and their eligible dependents was to be developed in phases. The groundbreaking ceremony for the cemetery was held Friday, October 10, 2008.

Another event occurred within the city limits. The Knight Museum is maintained by the City of Alliance. Situated on the west side of Central Park, between Sweetwater and Niobrara Avenues and E 10th and E 12th Streets, the Shelter House is nearby. A separate Foundation established the Sallows Military Museum to celebrate the town's military history. The Military Museum features artifacts from the WWII Alliance Airbase and Box Butte County history involving all the military services from World War I, World War II, the Korean War, Vietnam and the Gulf War, honoring the hometown men and women who have served their country. [17]

Before the museum was opened in 2004, the Foundation Committee considered naming the museum in honor of Ronald Coker. His family would not approve. The Cokers wanted Ron remembered as a brother and uncle. [18] Apprehensive that his memory would be sensationalized, or that he would be the focus of adulation out of character with who he had been, his family resisted any public recognition of his heroism. The Museum does display information about the Marine Medal of Honor recipient, but any efforts to pay specific tribute to him were protested by his siblings. Tensions among Ron's family, the community, and the museum continued to hamper efforts to pay a fitting tribute to him.

Ron's heroism was not forgotten, and the issue of public recognition would be resolved.

Memorial Day and Veterans Day celebrations tended to rekindle the memory of Ron Coker in the Alliance region. In the words of Felix Adler at the start of this chapter, Ron was a young man who set up "blazing torches in the dark streets of life for men to see by." And his brand of heroic bravery continued to inspire others who learned of him, as demonstrated in a Nebraska Panhandle hospital on November 10, 2007, a day when Veterans Day and the Marine Corps birthday coincided.

One man helped put up a display to honor hospital employees, men and women, who were veterans. A memorial to U.S. Marine Corps Private First Class Ronald L. Coker was part of the display, including his Medal of Honor Citation.

In the employee's words, "I cannot describe the sense of awe and feeling of respect that came over me as I read his citation while working on the display...that same sense of awe and respect is held by myself and countless others for the display of professionalism, duty and devotion exhibited by our armed service personnel these past four years...'Inspiring Initiative.' 'Selfless Devotion to duty.' 'Indomitable courage.'...Some fine men and women." [19]

The next Veterans Day, 2008, a radio station acknowledged Ron. KNEB, AM 960/FM 94.1, an affiliate of the Rural Radio Network, is located in Scottsbluff, Nebraska. The station wanted to pay tribute to the sacrifices men and women from the region had made in the Armed Forces. The station established a special Weblog to honor the Veterans, inviting listeners to write and pay tribute to Veterans. Ron's Citation and Marine photograph were added to the Veterans Day blog.

The relationship between Private First Class Coker's family and the community regarding memorials to him was getting worked out as the 40th anniversary of his March 24 sacrifice in Vietnam approached. The Alliance American Legion Post 7, the city and county commissioners, and local businesses organized and coordinated with the family for a special tribute to their native son.

County Commissioner Casper "Cap" Brixius, Gunnery Sergeant Chanin Nuntavong, USMC Recruiting Station, Denver, Chief Master Sergeant Robert M. Quinn of Buckley Air Force Base, Colorado, Senior

Master Sergeant Curtis Watkins, USAF (Ret.), and the 140 Mission Support Flight, Colorado National Guard exchanged e-mails and phone calls regarding plans for a display.

The Alliance Museum had its "annual feed" on March 17, 2009, to raise money for its Military Museum. Leading up to that event Ron's sister, Janet, Karen (Ball) Greenly, and his sister-in-law put together a large display about Ron, including their scrapbook and Karen's photographs from Vietnam. The display was by the front door of the museum so all would pass by it on their way to the feed.

Museum organizers informed Karen that they were really busy on other projects at the time, and could not do much about Ron. They would find a time during the meal to "mention" that it had been forty years since Ron's death, and "might put a little something" in the newspaper about the display.

The next month, April, Janet Coker Artz and Robyn Nicodemus, her daughter, mailed out a flier announcing the Ronald Coker's Memorial Day Celebration, May 25, 2009, to honor Ron. [20] The colorful invitation displayed a photograph of Ron in his Dress Blues, a Purple Heart Medal backed by the American flag, an image of the Medal of Honor, and a description of the day.

The family was going to provide food and drinks, music, entertainment, and a short program to honor the community's Vietnam veterans. The students of the two Alliance grade schools, the middle school, and the high school were invited to enter a contest with a poster or an essay, expressing what it meant to them to have a hero like Ron Coker from their community.

A long table was to be set up for people to display their scrapbooks, and hopefully to stand around and tell the stories of men who had left home and family more than forty years before to fight in a war that for a long while seemed to have galvanized the nation into its own battling factions.

The Wednesday, May 20, 2009, *Alliance Times-Herald* provided details of the Ron Coker Memorial Day Presentation. Photographs of the Memorial Day observance filled a quarter of the Tuesday, May 26, *Times-Herald* front page. "A great light was going to be kindled" in Alliance.

The Patriot Guard Riders (PGR) put out an alert to its members on May 20, following the announcements about the Ron Coker Presentation. The motorcycle group is dedicated to *Standing for Those Who Stood for Us*. Just after 10:00 AM, Monday, May 25, the sound of thirty-five motorcycles echoed at the corner of East 5th Street and Box Butte Avenue in Alliance. The Patriot Guard Riders were arriving at the Box Butte County Courthouse under the guidance of Ride Captain Rodger Clark. The fifty-two PGR members formed into the Flag line at 10:45 AM. [21]

The community ceremony in front of the Courthouse began at 11:00 AM. The cool, Nebraska wind kept the many flags fully extended and waving. One of those flags immediately to the right of the speakers was the bright red flag of the 3rd Marine Battalion, held firm throughout the half-hour ceremony at the waist of Ron's 32-year-old nephew and former Marine, Donald L. Coker. Legion Executive Board member Dick Foland introduced the speakers and directed the events. A Color Guard presented and posted the Colors. The National Anthem was sung. [22]

Following the Invocation by Pastor Jim Rowe of the First Baptist Church, himself a veteran, Lieutenant Colonel Richard Hoffman, USMC (Ret), remembered his time with Ron in Vietnam. Ron's platoon commander described him as a tall, good-looking young man, quiet, who was well liked and had a keen sense of humor. When Ron said something, it was remembered as meaningful. The Medal of Honor recipient had been proud to be a Marine. His sense of duty had been strong.

Major Ted Hempel, USMC (Ret), 2004 Sallows Military Museum President, read Ron's Citation. Mary Crawford acknowledged the veterans and Ron's family and comrades on behalf of Representative Adrian M. Smith (R), Nebraska Congressional District Number 3. After the presentation of wreaths, a squad fired a rifle gun salute of three volleys. A bugler sounded Taps.

The official dedication of a road in Ron's name by the county commissioners followed the Benediction, and Robyn Nicodemus, representing her uncle's family, expressed her thanks to all who had worked toward honoring Ron and who had gathered for the Memorial.

"You did not desert me, my brothers in arms." [23]

The seven members of Ron's unit who had traveled to Alliance for the celebration were recognized. They had come from California, Texas, Arkansas, Colorado, and Wisconsin to honor their companion. [24]

Of the fifteen Marines who went on patrol to the Mortar Pit and fought at the *Big Rock*, Ron was among three who did not return from Vietnam. Five died in the years between 1984 and 2004. Seven patrol members survived as of May 2009. All have remembered their Nebraska comrade.

The Patriot Guard Riders led the procession from the County Courthouse. The motorcade, including vehicles with Ron's family and the men who served with him in the 3d Battalion, went south to East 3rd Street, and then three miles east on Highway 2 toward the Alliance Municipal Airport. At County Road 57, they turned south again, past quarters of irrigated corn crop circles until west of Skyview Golf Course.

From the highway to the Nebraska State Veterans Cemetery, they had traveled the one-mile section of county road that is now Ronald Coker Lane. The PGR then escorted the vehicles back to Central Park for a reception to celebrate the "memories of a HERO," a "beloved brother, uncle, friend, and comrade." Piles of white t-shirts with Ron's photograph on the front, a Marine Corps emblem on the back commemorating the 40th Anniversary Celebration on the back, were available to all.

Robyn had arranged for special entertainment for the celebration. Monica Harvey sang in tribute to Ron and the veterans. Monica is with the Veterans Music Ministry and travels with the Moving Wall, in great measure volunteering her time and talent to bring healing to those who have served in wars. [25]

Lieutenant Colonel Hoffman and County Commissioner Casper "Cap" Brixius, a former Marine, extended a tribute to Janet Coker Artz and Ray Coker at the Shelter House, the very place the family had gathered in 1968 before Ron left for Vietnam. They presented a glass-covered "shadow box," a wood-framed military display case with red background, carefully crafted by Senior Master Sergeant Curtis Watkins, to the Coker family.

Within the case is a new Dress Blue Uniform Jacket with white belt and gold buckle, donated by Gunnery Sergeant Nuntavong. Chief Master Sergeant Quinn of Buckley AFB had replaced the medals and ribbons lost in the Rapid City flood. Ron's medals are pinned across the chest and his gold, Private First Class stripe on red flash is sewn to the left sleeve. A replacement Medal of Honor had not yet been provided by the Department of Defense. When available, the Medal will be displayed around the collar of the Dress Blue jacket. A framed picture of the Medal of Honor is included in the lower portion of the case.

A United States flag that had flown over the capitol building in Washington, D.C., and the Nebraska State Capitol Building in Lincoln, is folded into the upper left corner of the box, five white stars on the blue field showing. Displayed beside the uniform jacket are a bronze plaque of Ron's Citation and his photo, his ribbons and badges, and USMC and 3d Battalion, 3d Marines emblems. The Colorado ANG 140 Mission Support Flight had provided a new set of dog tags.

His sister, brother, nieces and nephews, in-laws, and high school friends continue to hold Ron's memory dear. Ronald Osborn and other classmates whose photos can be found in the '65 *AHS Bulldog* annual wanted to be sure that visitors to the Alliance Sallows Military Museum recognize their admiration for Ron Coker. They decided to contribute a display case to the museum in tribute to their friend. The three-foot-wide by three-foot-deep by six-foot-high case is made of solid oak construction with inlaid details of grained purple heart wood. The engraving and scrolling on the outside of the case includes Ron's name and an acknowledgment, *From AHS Class of 65*. A photograph of Ron, a display Medal of Honor, his Citation, ribbons and miniature medals including a Purple Heart, National Defense Service Medal, Vietnam Service Medal with one bronze star, and Vietnam Campaign Medal, a photograph of his platoon, other photographs, and USMC memorabilia are displayed inside the partitioned case. The *Bulldog* Class of 1965 hoped to have the case standing in place by Memorial Day, 2011. [26]

Among the others who remember Ron Coker each year when the anniversary of his death arrives are the Marines of Third Squad, Second

Platoon, Mike Company, 3d Battalion, 3d Marines who were with him when he died protecting a companion from a grenade.

And after Memorial Day, 2009, all who travel Ronald Coker Lane to the Nebraska State Veterans Cemetery, the Skyview Golf Course, or the Municipal Airport will know that the City of Alliance and Box Butte County remember and honor him.

Ronald Coker's name no longer belongs on the list of forgotten Medal of Honor Marines.

CHAPTER 25
Vietnam: A Nation Turns Away.
And slowly turns around.

"These boys out here have a pride in the Marine Corps
and will fight to the end no matter what the cost."

Second Lieutenant Richard C. Kennard [1]
Forward observer, Peleliu, World War II

Even if the cost is being scorned, mocked, and then forgotten at home.

Nine biographies comprise this chapter. Each is short because little information could be compiled about these Medal recipients. The irony in this is that their heroic actions took place in the most recent of the three wars studied.

While they appeared to be forgotten at the start of the *Semper Fidelis* study, this changed for several of these nine recipients as the years unfolded. A post office building has been dedicated to one of them. For another, a Public Broadcasting Station documentary was recently produced. For a third, a state governor ensured a plaque was dedicated at the elementary school the Medal recipient attended. More recently, another has had a section of a state highway dedicated in his name. These tributes serve as further examples that heroic bravery inspires others to take action, even after forty years have passed.

Heroism goes to Vietnam

Army Major Dale R. Buis and Master Sergeant Chester M. Ovnand were the first American military men killed in combat in Vietnam when the guerrillas struck an American compound twenty miles northeast of Saigon on July 8, 1959. [2]

Fewer than two years later when President John F. Kennedy took office in January 1961, there were 900 American servicemen on duty in South Vietnam. Seven hundred forty-six were Army advisers assigned to the Military Assistance Advisory Group. Five aircrewmen had died the previous year. Most Americans were unaware of the conflicts brooding in Indochina, and the Marines had not yet arrived in force in Vietnam.

By mid-1961, President Kennedy began authorizing troop increases and at the end of his first year in office, the official number of military personnel in Vietnam had grown to 3,200. An estimated thirteen servicemen had either been killed or wounded that year. The conflict in the divided country was escalating, but the first public demand that American troops be withdrawn was a year and a half in the future.

The first 450 Marines landed in Vietnam with fifteen combat helicopters in April 1962. The Marine air unit was based near Soc Trang, one hundred miles southwest of Saigon. In under four-months' time they flew fifty combat troop lifts and 130 landings in Landing Zones (LZs) against the Viet Cong. These Marines were relieved in August by a second helicopter squadron that moved its base to Da Nang. Fifty-three American servicemen were killed in 1962, another fifty-six wounded. Among the dead were five Marines. [3]

President Kennedy needed an assessment of the combat situation in 1963. The president was receiving contradictory reports about how the ground war between the North and South forces was evolving, and he was in a quandary, both over sending further aid to the South Vietnam government and whether or not to increase American military involvement in the conflict. In September, he sent Marine General Victor Krulak and a senior Foreign Service officer to Vietnam on a fact-finding mission. General Krulak focused on the Army of the Republic of Vietnam (ARVN) successes against the Viet Cong insurgents in the rural and village regions, while Joseph Mendenhall concentrated on civil unrest in the urban areas, particularly in Saigon and Da Nang. President Kennedy's deliberations were made no more certain by the divergent reports provided to him by the two advisors upon their return. Characteristic of the president, he quipped, "You two did visit the same country, didn't you?"

When President Kennedy was assassinated on November 22, there were an estimated 16,500 U.S. servicemen in South Vietnam. American financial aid to Vietnam reached over five hundred million dollars. By December, the possibility that President Lyndon Johnson was ready to send 100,000 troops into the war was clear. In 1963, 118 American servicemen had been killed in combat and another 413 had been wounded. Ten of the KIAs were Marines.

In spring 1964, the first Marine ground unit was detached to Vietnam to collect signals intelligence. By year's end another five Marines had died in South Vietnam. The first combat infantry Marines in Vietnam began arriving in force in Da Nang in early 1965. American college students also began marching that year. About 12,000 students demonstrated in front of the White House on April 17, protesting the war–508 Marines died in Vietnam in 1965. Four Marines earned Medals of Honor, the first two posthumously: First Lieutenant Frank Stanley Reasoner, Lance Corporal Joe Calvin Paul, Corporal Robert Emmett O'Malley, and First Lieutenant Harvey Curtiss Barnum, Jr.

The Marines remained in country until mid-1971. Following the departure of the main combat forces, a contingent of Marines remained behind to provide security and evacuation forces in support of U.S. personnel. The names of 13,091 Marines are inscribed on the black Memorial Wall in Washington, D.C., all killed-in-action between 1962 and 1975. The last two Marines to die on Vietnam soil, Corporal Charles McMahon, Jr. and Lance Corporal Darwin Lee Judge, were killed during the American Embassy evacuations in a rocket attack at Tan Son Nhut Airport, four miles north of central Saigon, on April 29, 1975. Their names are engraved on Panel 01W, Line 124 of the Memorial Wall. Another 51,392 Marines suffered battle wounds and came home from Vietnam with Purple Hearts. [4]

An estimated eighty-five Marines are also counted among the 1,835 American servicemen who remain missing-in-action from Vietnam: either lost in battle or captured, taken prisoner, and not seen again. [5] An additional 155 Marines are listed as killed-in-action, body not recovered. [6] The Joint POW/MIA Accounting Command (JPAC), with its mission to give a full accounting for all America's military personnel who did not come home from wars, continues to find and identify missing servicemen in Southeast Asia. Most recently, remains of U.S. Air Force pilot, Major Thomas Beyer, missing in Quang Tri Province since July 1968, were brought home to Fargo, North Dakota, on December 15, 2010, for burial. [7] "Until they are home," JPAC's motto, gives hope to some of the families of the 240 unaccounted for Marines.

In whatever battles Marines find themselves, there will be among them some who are willing to cradle a grenade to save their companions. This was as true in Vietnam as it was on Bougainville, Iwo Jima, Peleliu, Okinawa, Chosin, and Panmunjon. Of the fifty-seven Marines awarded Medals of Honor during their ten years of fighting in Vietnam, twenty-three (40%) hurled themselves on top of grenades. All but one of these twenty-three were awarded the honor posthumously.

The first Marine in Vietnam to hurl himself on a grenade to protect others was a staff sergeant, born in the early Great Depression years and well before the start of WWII.

YEAR 1966

Peter Spencer Connor

Harold E. and Katherine Connor, of South Orange, New Jersey, had five children, three boys and two girls. Peter Spencer Connor was born to them on September 4, 1932. Two years after he had graduated from high school in 1950, Pete enlisted and served with the 5th Marines in

Korea for the last year of that war. He completed his first enlistment in assignments at Camp Lejeune and returned to civilian life in New Jersey in February 1955.

Having remained a member of the Ready Reserve, Pete reenlisted in the Marines six years later in 1961, serving in a variety of duty stations in the next four years on the east and west coast and overseas. Pete was promoted from Sergeant to staff sergeant on May 1, 1965. That August, he arrived in Vietnam as a platoon sergeant in Third Platoon, Company F, 2d Battalion, 3d Marines, 3d Marine Division (Reinforced).

The Sarge was an *old grunt* in his unit in Vietnam, his second war. By then he was also one of the *married grunts*. He and Eleanor had a daughter, Cecilia, born in 1959, two years before his reenlistment. The Staff Sergeant would be the fifth Marine to earn a Medal of Honor in Vietnam. Every year at the Our Lady of Sorrows High School in South Orange, New Jersey a student is given an award for good sportsmanship in his name.

On February 25, 1966, Staff Sergeant Connor's company was on a search and destroy mission in Quang Ngai Province, seeking out tunnels, caves, spider holes, and the Viet Cong. Viet Cong insurgents had engineered extensive tunnel complexes, linked to caves natural to the region. Foxtrot Company had been encountering periodic small-arms fire as they advanced.

While leading his platoon, Staff Sergeant Connor recognized the small opening of a camouflaged enemy emplacement ahead of him, a spider hole, an entry and exit point to underground tunnels and bunkers. Booby traps were frequent near these holes and within them. The common way of dealing with such enemy positions was to make them inhospitable to the inhabitants by throwing explosives into them. The less preferred method was to crawl into the hole, seek out the hostiles, and engage them with rifles, handguns, or hand-to-hand fighting.

Staff Sergeant Connor took the initiative upon himself and prepared to charge the spider hole, a distance of about fifteen meters in front of him. He pulled the safety pin from a hand grenade in preparation of being able to quickly drop it down the hole. The safety mechanism of the grenade malfunctioned and its fuse immediately activated, giving Staff Sergeant Connor only seconds to discard the device before it exploded. He quickly assessed the situation, accepting the responsibility for the device and its activation.

Taking responsibility is characteristic of Medal of Honor recipients.

The basic meaning of responsibility is that a person who is responsible is *able to respond*. This *ability to respond* can be evident in having the ability to act without the guidance or direction of others, in being the cause or source of an action or event, in being personally accountable for outcomes, in being capable of making rational and moral decisions, in providing the care of others or property, and in being trustworthy, dependable, or reliable.

A person's ability to respond develops with time, maturity, and experience. Therefore, responsibilities increase in number, frequency, and magnitude as a person grows towards and into adulthood. Those who will prove to be responsible adults will have demonstrated some ability to respond in childhood and adolescence.

As boys and young men, the Medal recipients could be given responsibilities that they took seriously. Many were given leadership positions in clubs and organizations. Employers trusted them. Some were in the position to watch out for and guide young children. John Leims was the sports editor of his high school newspaper and an assistant scout master in the Boy Scouts of America. Jimmie Dyess was the assistant director of a boys' summer camp.

At least eighteen of the recipients grew up on farms and had daily chores to accomplish before going to school. Many of the recipients were working while in high school; they were store clerks, newspaper carriers, stock boys, life guards, apprentices to skilled laborers, truck drivers, and assistants in their father's trades. Fifty-six of them had been working at jobs, some of them for many years, before enlisting in the service to go to war. Among them were fire fighters, policemen, draftsmen, welders, businessmen, engineers, electricians, mechanics, machine and equipment operators, factory and foundry workers, and lawyers.

There is a touch of dedication evident in their acceptance of responsibility, as well. Many recipients were helping out their parents and families financially, and some were providing sustenance for their own families.

Being accountable for one's actions

Accountability is related to responsibility, but the two are not exactly the same. Accountability might be better viewed as the ultimate responsibility, and often the harder to accept. Accountability means to be able to give an accurate account of one's actions and, thereby, take responsibility for them.

While a team shares responsibility for the outcome of a game, each player is solely accountable for his/her own performance. Accountability cannot be shared. A completed pass play in football is a shared responsibility among quarterback, blockers, and receiver. When a receiver *blames* the quarterback for his dropping a pass, he denies accountability. Blaming others for one's performance or actions is an avoidance of accountability and a denial of responsibility for the outcome of one's actions. Because Medal of Honor recipients so often took their own initiatives, they seldom blamed others for events. Responsibility and accountability are resounding features of their actions.

Staff Sergeant Connor's actions demonstrated these characteristics, as did the actions of Medal recipients in previous wars.

Sergeant Herbert Joseph Thomas, Jr., 25-years-old, was the first Marine in WWII to sacrifice his life by diving onto a grenade for the sake of comrades, November 1, 1943. As he was lobbing grenades toward an enemy machine-gun crew at Cape Torokina, Bougainville, jungle vines deflected one grenade. The explosive bounced back into the Marines gathered for the assault. Sergeant Thomas immediately threw himself onto the grenade, fully absorbing the explosion and protecting his men from injury.

Private Joseph William Ozbourn, 24-years-old, was among the assault forces that landed on Tinian. On July 30, 1944, advancing in the middle of a five-man, line-abreast fire team, against enemy soldiers resisting in pillboxes and dugouts on the right flank, the Browning automatic rifleman pulled the pin from a grenade in preparation to throw it into the opening of a dugout. Before he could do so, an explosion at the entrance wounded all five men and temporarily stunned them. Unable now to either toss the grenade into the dugout or to throw it beyond the proximity of the other four wounded Marines, Private Ozbourn clutched the grenade to his body and fell on it. Although the explosion took his life, his four companions were spared from the blast.

As described earlier in Chapter 19, Private First Class Richard Beatty Anderson, 22-years-old, died in his first day of combat, February 1, 1944, three hours after charging onto Roi Island in the Marshall Islands. During the intensity of the battle, he pulled a live grenade from a canister. Although it should not have been armed as it came out of the container, it was. Somehow the safety pin had been dislodged from the grenade. Shared responsibility.

He attempted to throw the armed grenade out of the crater over his shoulder, but the explosive rolled back towards him. Instead of vacating the hole or yelling at the others to do so, putting them at risk of enemy fire, Private First Class Anderson threw his body over the grenade, shielding the others from the explosion. Accountability.

First Lieutenant Baldomero Lopez, Jr., 25-years-old, was the first Marine in Korea to earn a Medal of Honor. He climbed over the seawall at Inchon, Korea, at the lead of his platoon on September 15, 1950. When he sighted an enemy pillbox spraying the beach with fire, keeping the Marines pinned down, he did not order a squad to charge at it. Instead, he moved into the open, exposing himself to fire, and skirted alongside a bunker, preparing to assault the enemy position with a grenade. As he pulled the pin from a grenade and readied to throw it with his right arm, he was struck in the right shoulder and chest by automatic weapons fire.

Seriously wounded, First Lieutenant Lopez fell backward and dropped the charged grenade to the ground. Gathering his senses, he crawled forward to the explosive device only to discover that his injuries prevented him from grasping and throwing it. Rather than endanger the lives of his men, he swept the grenade beneath his body with his injured arm and curled himself around it.

Marines who followed Staff Sergeant Connor to war would also earn Medals for this kind of responsibility and accountability. Nearly three years after Staff Sergeant Connor stepped on to Vietnam soil, Lance Corporal Roy Mitchell Wheat, 20-years-old, and two other Marines were providing a security detail for a construction crane and its crew along Liberty Road, near the Dien Ban District, Quang Nam Province. Lance Corporal Wheat went reconnoitering to ensure there were no Viet Cong to their rear.

Making his way back to the others, he inadvertently stepped on an antipersonnel mine and halted within ten feet of the team's position. The hissing sound of the burning, timed fuse was evident. Lance Corporal Wheat and the other two Marines near where he stood recognized the sound of a *Bouncing Betty* device. The concealed mine was the type to bound several feet into the air, detonate in a tremendous explosion, and disperse shrapnel all around in a lethal ball.

All three Marines were immediately in jeopardy. Lance Corporal Wheat had been the one who unintentionally triggered the bouncing mine. He shouted a warning to his companions and dived onto the mine, smothering it with his body. The antipersonnel mine did not bound into the air as designed, but it did detonate. Lance Corporal Wheat took the full impact of the explosion himself, only weeks after he had turned 20-years-old. Lance Corporal Roy Wheat died so that two other Marines could continue in the performance of the duties for which they had been trained. Accountability.

While these five Marines were sharing responsibility with other Marines for the outcome of an engagement, while they were definitely protecting others, they were also accepting accountability. Full acknowledgment for their brave actions belongs to them, solely.

The same can be said of Staff Sergeant Connor.

Fifteen meters separated Staff Sergeant Connor from the enemy spider hole he had intended to close with the armed grenade he held in his hand. And only seconds separated him from safety and the device's explosion.

There was not time for Staff Sergeant Connor to reach the spider hole. Jungle growth prevented him from throwing the grenade any distance from his position. The men of his platoon were in positions all around him, and he could not throw the explosive in any direction without it detonating in the proximity of some of them. He decided to hold the grenade to his own body rather than to let its explosion endanger others.

Staff Sergeant Connor survived the detonation. Severely wounded, he was evacuated from Quang Nag Province and died eleven days later aboard the USS *Repose*. Thirty-three-years of age when he pulled the pin from that grenade, Staff Sergeant Peter Connor is the oldest of the Marines awarded the Medal of Honor for absorbing the blast of a grenade to protect companions in combat.

Peter Connor is buried in Fort Rosecrans National Cemetery, San Diego, California, Section A-e Grave 1005, 2420 miles from his hometown in Orange, New Jersey.

The veterans from the Korean War might not have been shown the gratitude they deserved when they returned home, but they were not blamed or disrespected for having gone to war. The servicemen who went to Vietnam returned to encounter both blame and derision for having answered the call to arms, and most of the criticism they faced came from their own generation.

By the time Peter Connor's body was brought home, the questions about, and protests against, American involvement in Vietnam were growing. A few young men were burning their draft cards, the "beatniks" were writing antiwar stanzas in coffee houses, and some college students were burning the Flag during demonstrations. And politicians were blurring the lines of responsibility for the war.

At a ceremony in the White House Rose Garden on May 2, 1967, President Johnson presented a Medal of Honor to Staff Sergeant Connor's widow, Eleanor. The president took this occasion to make some unfortunate remarks, as reported by the journalists present, blaming dissenters for the Marine's death in Vietnam. President Johnson's comments sparked more controversy regarding his conduct of the war. [8] The politicians and protesters alike, safe at home to debate their views, ignored their shared responsibilities to the men and women deployed to Vietnam. From the presentation to Eleanor M. Connor in the Rose Garden forward, honoring heroic bravery was not going to be open to the public. President Johnson would not permit media at White House award ceremonies. Very gradually, hometowns were less welcoming of their native sons and daughters as they returned from the war. Perhaps it was inevitable that in some places Medal of Honor recipients would not be remembered with a tribute to their bravery.

YEAR 1967
Douglas Eugene Dickey

Mr. and Mrs. Harold E. Dickey, of RD 1, Rossburg, Ohio, looked ahead as the second Christmas following the end of World War II approached. Americans had turned their attention to economic recovery and prosperity in the aftermath of the war. Christmas shoppers could again turn their attention to store front windows and worry less about rationing. Hometown newspapers carried more news about local events and less about the Allied military occupation forces remaining in divided Germany, or the U.S. Nuremberg Military Tribunals that had begun on December 6, 1946, to determine the fates of Nazi war criminals.

Mr. and Mrs. Dickey were watching events closer to home on the western edge of Ohio, waiting for a gift to arrive, wondering if they were going to have to take a drive thirteen miles south of home. They did. Doug was born on Christmas Eve, 1946, at Wayne Hospital in Greenville, the seat of Darke County. He grew up in Rossburg, with three brothers and a sister.

Rossburg is a rural village covering about one-tenth of a square mile. It is surrounded on all sides by squares of agricultural fields. When Doug was born, the population of less than two hundred people was predominantly of German descent. Farming was the mainstay of the economy. Most residents who did not farm had to travel an average of twenty-two miles to go to work.

When Doug was eight-years-old in 1954, a local bandleader purchased some property two miles north of Rossburg and built a clay oval racetrack. Called Eldora Speedway, within a few years the track became a showcase for sprint auto races. [9] It is possible that Doug's father at times took him and his brothers up to the speedway for some entertainment.

Since Rossburg was too small to have its own schools, Doug likely went to grammar school and high school in Ansonia, five miles down County Road 118, or in Mississinawa Valley to the west. He graduated from grammar school in 1961 and from high school in 1965.

What Doug did during the six months following his high school graduation is unknown. However, he made a decision to leave Rossburg. On December 13, 1965, two weeks before his nineteenth birthday, he went down to Cincinnati and enlisted in the Marines. He was following a family tradition. One of Doug's older brothers was a Marine corporal and an uncle was a Marine sergeant. [10]

By October 1966, he had been promoted to private first class and been transferred to Vietnam. He joined Company B, 1st Battalion, 4th Marines, 3d Marine Division then involved in *Operation Prairie*, a search and destroy mission in the Ngan Valley, just south of the DMZ and about fifty-five miles northwest of Hue.

Before a year passed, Private First Class Dickey would be involved in a series of operations against the Viet Cong in Quang Tri Province. By the time he turned 20-years-old, he was an experienced combat Marine who had been twice wounded in action. In November, he was moved over to Charlie Company, 1st Battalion. The company engaged the Viet Cong just south of the DMZ in *Operation Deckhouse*. Then in early 1967, Private First Class Dickey traveled into a wide, flat valley near Duc Pho during *Operation Desota* to see if the Marines could provoke the Viet Cong into a fight.

Following that operation, three months after his twentieth birthday, and probably a month before his next promotion, Private First Class Dickey went out with the 2d Platoon, Company C, on March 26, 1967. The NVA had positioned company-sized units in the Gia Linh District of Quang Tri Province with orders to fight. Charlie Company went out looking for them during *Operation Beacon Hill 1*. This was Private First Class Dickey's fourth major combat operation. Second platoon passed through dense jungle. According to the 1/4

Operations Log, at around 11:30 AM Charlie Company began receiving sniper fire, which intensified into a brief firefight at 12:45 PM. [11] Private First Class Dickey and the Marines were closing in on their objective.

A battle broke out with the NVA and Viet Cong at 4:00 PM when Company C was hit with 82-mm mortars, heavy automatic weapons, and small-arms fire. The foliage was deep, the enemy was in well-concealed positions and trenches, and the engagement occurred at close range. By the time it ended at 7:30 PM, Charlie Company had lost eight Marines and a Medevac helicopter had been downed.

During the battle, Second Platoon's radio operator was incapacitated by injuries. The corpsman aided the immobilized man as best he could, but the radioman was out of the fight. Private First Class Dickey understood that Marines depend upon radio communications to maintain command, control, and support during a fight. He had also been in three other operations and knew that radiomen and their equipment were primary targets for enemy fighters. Private First Class Dickey volunteered himself to take over the radioman's equipment and duties, making himself a target-of-opportunity to the Viet Cong.

As Private First Class Dickey came forward to take over the radio, an enemy grenade landed among the group.

"Grenade!"

The warning, familiar to Marines in the jungles, mountains, hamlets, and rice paddies of Vietnam, echoed over the sounds of gunfire. Private First Class Dickey instantly jumped on the grenade, protecting the injured Marine, the corpsman, and the nearby platoon members from the explosion, fully absorbed by his own body. "He must have realized it was too late for us to take cover," recalled corpsman, HM3 Gregory R. Long. "He gave me one short glance and lunged forward, deliberately covering the grenade with his body." [12]

Lance Corporal William L. Dorsey witnessed the explosion from a distance, believing that the grenade must have killed several of his comrades. Then he heard someone say, "Oh God! He jumped on it to save our lives." Five survived the blast because Private First Class Dickey had been willing to volunteer and sacrifice himself to protect others. His was the only life claimed by that grenade. [13]

On Monday, April 3, 1967, the Defense Department identified Private First Class Dickey as one of nine Ohioans killed in Vietnam in the previous weeks. [14] Doug's remains were brought home and buried in Brock Cemetery, a small, rural cemetery four miles east of Rossburg, at the intersection of Brock-Cosmos Road and Route 127.

Private First Class Douglas Dickey was the third Marine in Vietnam awarded the Medal of Honor for the *conspicuous gallantry* demonstrated by sacrificing his life rather than protecting himself from a grenade. On Tuesday, April 16, 1968, his Medal was presented to his parents by Secretary of the Navy Paul Ignatius and USMC Commandant General Leonard Chapman at the Marine Corps Barracks in Washington D.C. Some newspapers carried a front-page photograph of Mr. and Mrs. Dickey accepting their son's award. [15] The same photograph appeared within the pages of other newspapers. [16] A photograph of a smiling Private First Class Dickey in his Marine Corps olive drab cotton sateen utility uniform and cap, probably taken before he graduated from the San Diego Recruit Depot, accompanied short columns in some newspapers reporting the awarding of his Medal. [17] Other newspapers briefly mentioned the award without any photograph. [18]

By the time Doug's remains were brought home to Rossburg, newspapers were printing headline stories about war protests, the questioning of American presence in Southeast Asia, drug busts, and crime. The week after Mr. and Mrs. Dickey traveled to Washington, one reader expressed his dismay that genuine acts of patriotism and heroism were given little print. In a letter to Robert W. Lee, Editor of the *El Paso Herald-Post*, Army Lieutenant Colonel Raymond E. Messier wrote that one-inch of space, a column-filler, hidden and tucked away at the bottom of page two, was inadequate mention of Private First Class Douglas Dickey's posthumous award. Recognizing that Medals of Honor are not freely awarded, earned by great sacrifice, he believed that America's youth were entitled to know more about such valor. [19]
Forgetting bravery has a cost.

There are some numbers that give credence to the idea that a monument to Doug in Rossburg is warranted. The Ohio Historical

Society has a Web site with a *Beyond the Call of Duty* page. The purpose of the page is stated as: "Commemorating Ohio's heroes, who for their undaunted courage in the service of the United States of America received the nation's highest military award, the Congressional Medal of Honor." [20] All 319 Medal of Honor recipients connected to Ohio are listed on the site. Two hundred fifty-one recipients are accredited to the Buckeye State, 144 of whom were born in the state and another 107 who had either moved to or enlisted from Ohio. Only seventeen of the Ohio recipients are U.S. Marines. Ohio claims another sixty-eight recipients who were born in Ohio, but had their Medals accredited to other states.

Pinpointing birthplaces and homes of record of the 251 Ohio recipients on a map gives another indication of why Rossburg has good reason to take pride in remembering there own Medal recipient. Doug is one of only two recipients from Darke County. The other recipient is Isaac James, from Mississinawa Township, just to the northwest of Rossburg. Isaac was born in neighboring Montgomery County, but was residing in Mississinawa when he entered the service. He was a private in the Northern Army during the Civil War and earned his Medal in Petersburg, Virginia, April 1865, near the end of the war. More than 100 years passed before Darke County could claim another Medal recipient.

Douglas Dickey has the distinction of being the only Medal of Honor recipient born and raised in Rossburg, Ohio.

Considering that, today, Ohio is home to nearly 11, 500,000 people, [21] the chances of a small town being able to claim one of the state's 251 Medal recipients as a native son are unimaginably small. Based on the number of people living in Ohio, the 251 recipients accredited to the state would account for .00002183 of the population. Rossburg is just large enough to show up on road maps and have its own postal zip code. The 2000 U.S. Census for the rural village notes that 224 people, sixty-two families, reside in eighty-nine houses there. Whether any of Doug Dickey's four siblings or nieces and nephews remains in Darke County could not be determined.

For such a small town, traffic on Broadway, the main north-south thoroughfare through Rossburg, can be heavy. Several times each year, nearly 20,000 NASCAR fans make their way to the Eldora Speedway to enjoy the spectacle of short track auto races. In 2004, the State of Ohio honored the builder of the speedway by dedicating Highway 118 in his name, from Ansonia through Rossburg and up to St. Henry. Broadway and Highway 118 are the same road in Rossburg. Whether any of the thousands of NASCAR fans driving quickly through Rossburg know that the village is the hometown of a Medal of Honor recipient who was killed in action in Vietnam is doubtful. That sort of recognition would depend on a prominent monument or memorial to Private First Class Douglas Dickey somewhere along Broadway.

Lawrence David Peters

For Larry Peters, September was a momentous month. It was the month in which he was born, in which he enlisted in the Marine Corps, in which he completed his recruit training at Parris Island, in which he received his last promotion, and in which he died in action against an enemy.

Larry was born in Johnson City, New York, on September 16, 1946. The city, home to about 14,000 people mostly of Irish, English, and German descent, sits along the Susquehanna River in the central portion of the state in the foothills between the Allegheny and Appalachian Mountain Ranges. He graduated from grade school and junior high in Johnson City.

At the beginning of his junior year at nearby Binghamton North High School, Larry enlisted in the Marines two days after his seventeenth birthday. He graduated the next year in 1964, said goodbye to his mother and his sister, Shirley, completed his initial and advanced infantry training, and returned to Binghamton for a year, serving in the Reserves. He entered the Regular Marine Corps in January 1966. Then a corporal, Larry requested assignment to Vietnam in early 1966 and arrived there in May, joining Company D, 1st Battalion, 3d Marines, 3d Marine Division. He averaged a promotion in seven-month intervals, reaching the rank of sergeant on September 1, 1966.

Sergeant Peters demonstrated such leadership ability that his superiors often assigned him positions of greater responsibility. Prior to his promotion to sergeant, he served as a fire team leader, squad leader, and then as the noncommissioned officer in charge of the Combined Action Company. After his last promotion, he served as the company gunnery sergeant, a temporary additional duty, then served with the Military Police Company for three months.

In July 1967, his next assignment was as a squad leader with Company M, 3d Battalion, 5th Marines, 1st Marine Division. On September 4 of that year, Sergeant Peters led his squad in an advancing offensive against enemy forces in Quang Tin Province during *Operation Swift*. As the Marines of Second Platoon approached, enemy mortars, machine guns, and small-arms fire opened up on them from a trench. Mike Company reacted to provide tactical support to the platoon under fire.

Sergeant Peters maintained the leadership of his squad, maneuvering them into position to attack the enemy force firing from high ground. Subjected to intense fire all around him, he stood his ground in an open area in order to direct his squad's firepower against crucial enemy positions on the knoll. He took a round in his leg, temporarily immobilizing him. But, rallying himself quickly, Sergeant Peters moved the attack forward, shouting orders to his squad, until the men were pinned down by the ferocious salvos expended by the defenders. His concentration fully upon his mission, disregarding the enemy fire and the danger it represented, Sergeant Peters exposed himself further to reposition his men and direct their fire upon the enemy. A mortar round exploded near him, wounding him in the face and neck.

Wounded this second time, Sergeant Peters remained fully aware of the progress of the battle. He witnessed enemy personnel on his flank moving discretely to get into a position to attack the platoon. He immediately stood erect and began firing bursts into their camouflaged positions. The enemy reacted by firing back at him, thereby revealing their own positions and bringing fire upon themselves from the adjacent platoon they were attempting to infiltrate. The knoll remained his squad's objective. Sergeant Peters encouraged and directed his men in the continued assault, seeking to force the advantage over the enemy positions. At this pivotal point in the engagement, he sustained a third and fourth wounding.

His serious wounds did not sap him of the leadership that had been noted all along in his Marine career. He continued to direct his men until he lost consciousness and fell. In full sight of the enemy and his men, his life ended. The death of their sergeant in action galvanized the squad's fighting spirit, though. Refusing to be pinned down any longer, they established fire superiority over the enemy position, regained their momentum, and pushed the assault forward.

Marines like Corporal Raymond B. Harton remembered Sergeant Peters as one of the bravest men they had ever seen and acknowledged him for saving their lives on that September day in 1967. [22]

Sergeant Peters fell in battle less than two weeks short of his twenty-first birthday. He is buried in Chenango Valley Cemetery in Binghamton. His original flat granite marker is now faded from forty-three years of weathering. A more recent bronze marker, on a standing granite base, has been added, highlighted by the Medal of Honor star.

Two and a half years passed before Vice President Spiro T. Agnew presented Sergeant Peters' Medal to Mrs. Mildred Peters, of Binghamton, New York, at a White House ceremony in the East Room. Mrs. Peters stood among the parents of thirteen other Marines awarded the Medal on Monday, April 20, 1970. The media was not permitted access to the ceremony and the Vice President's remarks were not released to the public.

The family members who met at the White House that Tuesday in April represented a cross section of American life from east to west coast. Among those Mrs. Peters was introduced to in the East Room were: Mr. and Mrs. Fred Prom, Pittsburgh, Pennsylvania, Mrs. Rebecca Johnson, Charleston, South Carolina, Mr. and Mrs. Robert Jenkins Sr., Interlachen, Florida, Mr. and Mrs. Howard Williams, St. Clair, Michigan, Mr. and Mrs. Walter Burke, Monticello, Illinois, Mr. Cecil Coker, Alliance, Nebraska, Mr. and Mrs. Ross Creek, Amarillo, Texas, Mr. Fred Wilson, Odessa, Texas, Ken Worley's foster parents, Mr. and Mrs. Donald Feyerherm, Mr. and Mrs. Frank Austin, Phoenix, Arizona,

Mr. and Mrs. Samuel Phipps, of Reseda, California, and Mrs. Alice Maxam, formerly of Glendale, California.

Six of their sons are included in this book.

William Thomas Perkins, Jr.

Bill was born in Rochester, New York, on August 10, 1947, and started elementary school there. His brother, Robert, was born five years later. When Bill was eight-years-old, William T. Sr. and Marilane Perkins moved the family to north of Los Angeles, California. All around their new home were mountains and forests, parks and reserves: scenic and rough places like Angeles National Forest, the San Gabriel Mountain Range and Switzer Falls, Topanga State Park, Malibu State Park, Point Mugu State Park. Outdoor recreation like camping, hiking along canyon trails, wading into rocky creeks, skiing, fishing, and wilderness excursions were all common local pastimes.

The San Andreas Fault was within miles of home. The first California earthquake of significant magnitude occurred in that region in 1769. During the years between 1955 and 1965, the fault was relatively quiet and earthquake disasters were not a part of the family's experience. Perhaps only symbolic of Bill's later actions, living along the San Andreas Fault can require a disregard of potential dangers and disasters.

Bill was in proximity of Hollywood and had an interest in acting. He was given child parts in West Coast productions of Broadway plays, on stage with various screen actors, like Vincent Price. His attention expanded into the technical aspects of theater and motion picture photography. [23] His developing skills likely would have grown into a career.

Outgoing and engaging, Bill maintained a large group of friends at James Monroe High School in Sepulveda, home of the *Vikings*. He was avid about swimming, competing on the *Vikings* swim team and earning a certification in SCUBA diving. [24]

Within a year of the *Valhalla* Yearbook heralding the graduating class of 1965, after briefly attending Pierce College in Woodland

Hills, and apprenticing at the Valley Music Theater, Bill enlisted in the Marines with his friend, Jim Prudy, on April 26,1966.

Combat Photographer

Maybe it was living in the beauty surrounding him in California or some other early influence, but Bill had developed a knack for cameras. So much so, that the Marines assigned him as a Headquarters photographer right out of his recruit and infantry training schools. In less than a year past his enlistment date, he was promoted to private first class and lance corporal. The Marines then sent him to the U.S. Army's Motion Picture Photography School in New Jersey. His promotion to corporal was a certainty.

Lance Corporal Perkins had found his specialty. He was a combat photographer. He went to Vietnam as such in July 1967, eventually to be assigned to Company C, 1st Battalion, 1st Marines, 1st Marine Division in Quang Tri Province. That August he turned 20-years-old and was promoted to corporal.

"Every Marine is, first and foremost, a rifleman. All other conditions are secondary."

General Al M. Gray, USMC, Commandant of the Marine Corps 1987-91, said it. He knew what he was talking about. He had enlisted in the Marines at the start of the Korean War and, as a major, had commanded battalions in Vietnam. He was in Da Nang commanding the 1st Radio Battalion when *Operation Medina* began. One of the Marines participating in *Operation Medina* proved to be an example of first being a rifleman.

The Hai Hang Forest, full of color and natural beauty, spread from the Central Highlands of South Vietnam westward into Laos. The landscape consisted of steep hills and bug-infested, steaming jungle valleys. In October 1967, search and destroy missions were being planned for the forest southwest of Quang Tri. October might have meant cool autumn weather in other parts of the world, but in the Hai Hang, the temperatures could climb above 100 degrees Fahrenheit by midday.

The air temperature never determines the missions Marines undertake; it is all about the enemy situation. Despite the conditions in the Hai Hang Forest, the search and destroy operation got underway. *Operation Medina* kicked off at 4:30 AM on October 11.

Corporal Perkins went into the field on October 12, carrying his camera equipment with Charlie Company. He was not on a photo assignment a *National Geographic* photographer might celebrate, but rather embarking upon a major reconnaissance mission deep into the Hai Hang Forest. While he was filming in the area of a helicopter landing zone (LZ) near the Command Post, a force almost triple in size of Charlie Company attacked at the point of the LZ. Headquarters came under intense fire.

Corporal Perkins was a skilled, competent photographer, but he was first and foremost a Marine rifleman. As the fierce enemy assault escalated, he huddled in the proximity of First Lieutenant Jack Arden Ruffer, Lance Corporal Dennis Antal, and Lance Corporal Fred Boxhill. Corporal Perkins observed an enemy grenade fall in the midst of his three fellow Marines. Without hesitation, he instinctively abandoned his camera, shouting a dreaded warning to them.

"Incoming grenade!"

Corporal Perkins dived onto the grenade just before it exploded.

Ten Marines of Charlie Company died during *Operation Medina* and another sixty-four were wounded. The three men who were fortunate enough to have been under the watchful eye of a combat photographer survived the battle.

Corporal William Perkins was buried in San Fernando Mission Catholic Cemetery, Mission Hills, California, Los Angeles County, in sight of the wilderness surroundings of the San Gabriel Mountain Range. His exceptional courage and selfless devotion to his comrades earned him the distinction of being the only combat photographer to ever receive the Medal of Honor. President Nixon presented the posthumous award to his parents at the White House on Friday,

June 10, 1969. By that time, a new policy was being implemented–
White House posthumous award ceremonies were conducted in
private.

Before Memorial Day 1972, nearly five years after their son had
died in the Hai Hang Forest, William Sr. and Marilane Perkins were
in North Carolina in front of the 2d Marine Division's Headquarters,
Camp Lejeune's Building 2. They were there to dedicate the Perkins
Memorial Photographic Laboratory in honor of their son. A Memorial
Plaque was placed on the laboratory building in tribute to "A combat
photographer who gave his life for his fellow Marines." [25]

More than forty years have passed since Bill Perkins dived on a
grenade to save the lives of others. If it were known in greater detail,
Bill's background information would likely be as inspiring to others
as his heroic bravery. [26] There can be no doubt that he made friends in
his short life who would not forget him. His friend Craig Ingraham
produced a documentary, *Above and Beyond: The Story of Cpl. William T.
Perkins, Jr. USMC*, in 2006.

Marines visiting Perkins Memorial Photographic Laboratory
Building have a chance to learn about their heroic combat photgra-
pher. There is no indication in public venues that students attending
Sepulveda's James Monroe High School, actors who play on the stages
on which he performed, or residents of his hometown remember Bill
Perkins today. Nor does he seem to be remembered in Rochester, New
York, his birthplace.

YEAR 1969
Alfred Mac Wilson

Odessa, Texas, an oil-field town, lies in the arid southern portion
of the Cap Rock Escarpment, about 260 miles south of Amarillo. The
rippled region around Odessa lies between areas of juniper-covered hills
in the east and the rugged Texas high plains to the west. A meteor
long ago impacted Texas and left a huge scar of a crater about twelve
miles southwest of Odessa. Forty miles west is the southeastern corner

of New Mexico. The land in the Escarpment seems expansive between restaurant stops. A map might locate five towns in all of Ector County.

"Mac" Wilson's story did not begin on the Escarpment, though. He was two-years-old when Fred V. and Edna O'Neal Wilson moved from Olney, Illinois to Texas in 1950. His older sister, Marilyn Sue, was five. The family put down roots in Odessa, west on HW20 from Midland. They lived at 221 Neal, on the north side of town one block west of the Odessa airfield.

The family stayed in place and "Mac" had little memory of Illinois, Olney, or anything else but Texas. He and his older sister now belonged whole-heartedly to The Lone Star State. He enjoyed most being "country," but did not take well to being called Alfred. The name was a little too "fancy." He made friends easily in the neighborhood, playing soldiers with them, digging foxholes and dashing about in vacant lots around Neal.

Mac attended Burleson Elementary, Crockett Junior High, and Odessa Senior High School. He played on the OHS "Bronchos" football and track teams, proud to wear the high school's red and white. He was a friendly person, respected even among his older, upper classmen. Those who knew him recognized his unselfish nature. He joined clubs and had numerous hobbies, most of them having to do either with outdoor activities or athletics. Having enjoyed the comradeship of teammates throughout his school years, when Mac graduated from high school in 1967, he took the "short" 140-mile drive up Interstate 20 to Abilene to join the Marines with three of his high school friends. He was 19-years-old.

Private First Class Wilson arrived in Vietnam in July 1968, just weeks before Lance Corporal Kenneth Worley hurled himself upon a grenade. Once involved in combat operations in Vietnam, the notable differences in background and childhood experiences between these two young men seem to be insignificant. At their core, they had become Marine riflemen.

Private First Class Wilson was assigned rifleman duties in Quang Tri Province, first in Company D, 1st Battalion, 27th Marines, 1st MARDIV, then with Company M, 3d Battalion, 9th Marines, 3d

MARDIV. The NVA was massing forces in sanctuaries within the twenty-two-mile A Shau Valley near the Laotian border and the 9th Marines were going to be tasked to deny them their safe haven.

Phase I of *Operation Dewey Canyon* began in late January 1969. By its conclusion, the 9th Marines would make incursions into Laos in order to interrupt the enemy's two-way traffic across the border. In early March 1969, as Phase III of the operation was coming to a close, Mike Company went out on a reconnaissance-in-force mission near Fire Support Base Cunningham, near the northern edge of the A Shau Valley. Mike Company would be well-supported. FSB Cunningham was under the command of a Marine who had three years earlier earned a Medal of Honor in December 1965, Captain Harvey Curtiss Barnum, Jr.

Private First Class Wilson was a First Platoon squad leader, under the command of First Lieutenant Dwight Krinze of New Hampshire. As the company returned from the mission on March 3, the last official day of *Dewey Canyon*, a well-concealed enemy force attacked First Platoon. Grenades and automatic weapon fire pinned down the center squad.

Private First Class Wilson deployed his squad in the rear of the column to engage the hostiles with a base of fire, allowing the lead squad to flank the enemy position. As the fight continued, his machine gunner and assistant machine gunner were among the disabled casualties. The column was seriously disadvantaged with the machine gun silenced. Leading another Marine, Private First Class Wilson charged across the fire-swept distance to the machine-gunners' position. As they recovered the weapon, an enemy hand grenade landed between the two men, tossed from behind a tree.

Private First Class Wilson, the squad leader, shouted a warning to his fellow Marine and unhesitatingly jumped on top of the grenade. Witnessing his actions and the sacrifice of his life inspired First Platoon to successfully drive the counterattack into the enemy force and defeat them.

Private First Class "Mac" Wilson, the Texan, was 21-years-old when he gave his life for a Marine comrade. He was among the 130 young Marines who died during the *Dewey Canyon* mission, considered by Marine historians to be the most successful regimental campaign of the Vietnam War. Another 932 men left the A Shau wounded. [27]

"Mac" Wilson was brought home to the town he loved, escorted from Vietnam by Sergeant Jerry Pruitt, USMC, a childhood friend also of Odessa. He was buried at Sunset Memorial Gardens Cemetery, Plot Prayer Section, Lot 54, Grave 4, on the southeast edge of town. Two months later, his grieving friends from Odessa High School's Class of 1967 would return to Sunset Memorial Gardens to attend funeral services for another fellow graduate. On May 11, 1969, two weeks before his 20th birthday, USMC Private First Class Robert Nelson Newman was killed in action in Quang Nam Province.

Mac's mother, bereft and struggling, would learn only a little about her son's heroism and would not be alive to receive news from the president or read newspaper headlines about Mac a year later. Edna Wilson, 52-years-old, died of a heart attack on June 6, 1969, three months after Mac's death. She was buried right beside him in Sunset Memorial Gardens.

On Saturday, April 18, 1970, newspaper headlines across America announced the safe return from space of the three Apollo 13 astronauts. A beaming President Nixon personally welcomed them home in Honolulu after their four days of peril in a damaged spacecraft. [28] That same Saturday, the White House announced news more pertinent to Odessa, Texas. Mac Wilson had been awarded the Medal of Honor, to be presented to his father on Monday. Mac's photo and news column shared the front page headlines in Odessa beside the Apollo 13 story.

On April 20, 1970, Vice President Spiro T. Agnew presented the Medal of Honor to Fred Wilson and Mac's sister, Marilyn Sue Whitehead, at the White House. Among the others present for the ceremony, accepting honors on behalf of sons, were Donald and Rose Feyerherm, Cecil Coker, Mildred Peters, and Mr. and Mrs. Samuel Phipps.

Fred Wilson had many years ahead to take pride in his son's heroism, but he would not learn of the many tributes paid in honor of Mac. Fred died in 1996. [29]

More years passed. As for so many recipients' family members, his life and death seemed like "it was just yesterday" to Sue Wilson Whitehead, living in San Angelo, about 120 miles east of Odessa. Mac had two nephews and three nieces he never knew: Lloyd, Vickie, Debbie, Angie, and Robert. Their seventeen children would all know about their great-uncle who died in a war far from Texas.

Besides the generations that followed Fred and Edna, Mac's memory continued to touch others; among them were his 1967 classmates. Odessa High School keeps a roll of notable "Bronchos" alumni, including Grammy Award-winning country artists, the Gatlin Brothers, a representative to the Texas Legislature, Miss West Texas 1970 and Miss America USO Show who toured South Vietnam during the war with Bob Hope, a former University head football coach, and an actress and actor. The Class of 1967 ensured that Mac was remembered as a cherished Notable Alumni.

When nearly forty years had passed since his heroic death, it might have seemed that the tributes to Mac Wilson were only the memories held by his family and high school friends and his name on the Texas Medal of Honor Memorial in Midland and the Texas Marine Medal of Honor Memorial in the Woodlands. Except that the Texans of Odessa did remember his legacy, his noble and heroic character, and the tribute he had brought to their community. Despite the passage of time, they wanted "a fitting and meaningful tribute to a proud Marine who served selflessly on behalf of his town and nation." Early in 2008, local surveys began to surface showing strong favor for a draft of a bill to be entered in Congress.

In a tearful presentation on July 8, 2008, to the House of Representatives in the 110th Congress, 11th District of Texas Republican Representative K. Michael Conaway proposed H.R. 6437, legislation to name the Post Office in Odessa in Corporal Mac Wilson's honor. On October 7, 2008, Public Law 110-349 was approved.

Thursday morning, February 5, 2009, was crisp and breezy as a couple hundred people gathered at the downtown Odessa's main Post Office building, located at 200 North Texas Avenue, for a ceremony beginning at 10:00 AM. Sue Wilson, U.S. Rep. Mike Conaway, and Mayor Larry Melton were all present. Among the invited guests were Dwight Krinze, Mac's former platoon commander and Kevin P. Keilty, a fellow squad leader who had traveled from North Carolina. The Odessa High ROTC presented the American flag and the school's choir sang Lee Greenwood's by now anthem-like "God Bless The U.S.A." Under the ceremony shelter a shiny 2.5-foot x 2-foot dedication plate was unveiled, declaring the Law. [30]

The Corporal Alfred "Mac" Wilson Post Office Building was officially dedicated.

Lester William Weber

Lester made adjustments to changes in his life. He was born west of Chicago, in Aurora, Illinois, on July 30, 1948. When his parents divorced, he and his two brothers moved with their mother closer to the Windy City. Les went to St. Isaac Jogues Grade School in the town of Hinsdale. He graduated from there when he was thirteen and went on to Hinsdale High School on South Grant Street. In 1965, the high school became Hinsdale Central.

Les was outgoing and made friends easily all through his school years. He was also athletic and competitive. Starting in grade school, he played Little League baseball, wearing the *Pirates* uniform. One of his closest friends was Pat Quinn. The two were in the same Cub Scout pack and went to school together, Pat one grade behind Les. Although they played for different Little League teams, rivalry did not sever the bond between them. Lester's friendship and their mutual competitiveness remained a lifelong memory for Pat Quinn.

Seldom Inactive

As young boys, the Medal recipients, like Lester Weber, were often described as inquisitive and "always getting into things" or wanting to "try out new things." Some bounced from one activity to another when their interest waned in what they had been doing. The activities that truly captured their attention and in which they enjoyed being involved at times seemed to have distracted them from "the more important things" like homework or chores.

Beyond his high school studies, whatever activities or distractions that might have captured Les' attention while he was enrolled at Hinsdale Central, one thing can be certain. Vietnam was on the nightly news, and the war was on Les' mind. When some of his friends and classmates were starting their first term in college in September 1966, Les went the thirteen miles to Chicago and enlisted. And as those same friends were finishing up their college freshman year, he completed his special weapons training, received his first promotion, and was ordered to Vietnam in July 1967. Evaluations noted that Private First Class Weber had excelled in training. Companions remembered him as always trying to be the best at all things required of the "grunts." Once in Vietnam, Private First Class Weber demonstrated leadership in his assignment as ammunition carrier and was put into a squad leader position. In less than four months in Quang Nam Province, he was promoted a second time.

When Private First Class Weber received his promotion, his childhood friend, Pat Quinn, was in his first semester at Georgetown University.

The records do not indicate how Lance Corporal Weber spent whatever free time he had around Da Nang during his first thirteen-month tour of duty. There were other sights besides jungle-covered mountains and cratered hilltops. Despite the dangers, Marines sometimes did take scenic tours out of Da Nang on their off time. Famous sites included the 15th Century trading post, Hoi An Ancient Town, sitting on the Thu Bon River thirty miles south of Da Nang. The My Son Sanctuary, 69 kilometers southwest of Da Nang and 40 kilometers west from Hoi An, is a large religious complex of brick temples and stone towers built during the Champa dynasty in a green-covered mountain valley in the Duy Xuyen District.

The records do indicate that Lance Corporal Weber served out his first tour of duty and requested that his time in Vietnam be extended for six months. Five months into his extension he was transferred to Company M, 3d Battalion, 7th Marines and assigned duties as a Second Platoon machine-gun squad leader. On February 23, 1969, near the end of his tour, a squad of Marines on patrol around the hamlet of Bo Ban, in Hieu Duc District, southwest of Da Nang came under assault by an entrenched battalion-size force of Communist guerrillas. Bo Ban was the hamlet where Lance Corporal Ken Worley had earned a Medal of Honor six months earlier. Second Platoon was quickly dispatched to help extract the squad.

As the rescue force moved through a rice paddy of high grass, the platoon also came under intense fire. Lance Corporal Weber reacted immediately, charging into the tall grass in the direction of the enemy fire and assaulted a squad of concealed enemy soldiers. He killed one and forced eleven others to withdraw under his fire. Then he overcame a second insurgent in hand-to-hand fighting.

As the battle continued around him, Lance Corporal Weber spotted two hostiles protected by a dike and firing upon his squad mates. He again raced across a fire-swept area and dived into the enemy position, wrestling their weapons from them and killing them both. His one-man assault diverted the enemy fire from his comrades to himself as he yelled directives and encouragement to them. He spotted another enemy soldier in front of him and again dashed into the open, firing at the hostile.

Fully exposed to enemy fire, Lance Corporal Lester Weber, 20-years-old, was fatally wounded. He was the third of five Marines from 3d Battalion, 7th Marines to earn a Medal of Honor in Vietnam in less than a three-year period of time. The first had been Lance Corporal Roy Wheat, of Kilo Company, and the second, one year later, was Lance Corporal Ken Worley, Lima Company. Two more followed Lance Corporal Weber. Lance Corporal Jose F. Jimenez, Kilo Company, was killed in action in August 1969. Lance Corporal James Howe, India Company, earned a posthumous award in May 1970.

The available newspaper archives did not provide many facts about the awarding of Les Weber's Medal of Honor. His remains were brought home and interred in Clarendon Hills Cemetery in Darien, Illinois. A bronze and granite marker sits on his gravesite. His Medal was received by family from President Nixon in a private ceremony in the East Room at the White House on Tuesday, February 16, 1971. From that date on, it would appear that little attention was given to his heroic bravery.

Some hints that Les Weber had not been forgotten in the Chicago area slowly began to emerge during the search for him. First was the discovery that the Lester Weber Memorial Northern Illinois Leathernecks Motorcycle Club is named in his honor. Then, when the Moving Memorial Wall was scheduled to be in Naperville in late June 1999, *Daily Herald* staff writer Stacy St. Clair reminded residents of Chicago's west suburbs of Lester's self-sacrifice in the tall grass of a Vietnam rice paddy. [31]

At least one person needed no reminders of Lester. Patrick Joseph Quinn III, his childhood friend, had never forgotten him. In 2002, Pat was campaigning on the Democratic ticket for election to lieutenant governor. That summer, he took his younger, 17-year-old, son to visit the Vietnam Memorial Wall in Washington. They found the name on Panel 31W, Row 029 and talked about Lester Weber. When back in Illinois, the Quinns began researching Lester's heroics, coming to better understand the significance of a Medal of Honor. The politician decided that the Marine from Hinsdale deserved a tribute and intended to do something about it once the election was over.

Pat Quinn was sworn in as the 45th Lieutenant Governor of Illinois January 13, 2003. The day of his inauguration he called a state senator for some help. Although the lieutenant governor was a Democrat and the senator was a Republican, they had something in common. They had both grown up in Hinsdale. Senator Kirk Dillard was only 13-years-old when Lester charged into enemy gunfire near Bo Ban Hamlet.

On Sunday, May 25, 2003, Lieutenant Governor Quinn, Senator Dillard, and John Krepp, Lester's cousin, were at St. Isaac Jogues

Elementary School to help unveil and dedicate a memorial stone plaque in Lester's honor. The plaque was set in the ground under the flagpole at the front door of the school, a reminder to all of a young man's determination to make a difference in the lives of companions. [32]

Pat Quinn assumed the seat of 41st Governor of Illinois on January 29, 2009. Perhaps another tribute to his friend, Lester Weber, is ahead.

Jimmy Wayne Phipps

Santa Monica, California, neighbors thought of the Phipps family as friendly and close to one another. Jimmy was born on November 1, 1950, the second oldest of three boys. Jimmy was one of those outgoing, kind-hearted young men and liked to help his little sister, Cordy, with her homework. [33]

Keeping his attention focused on studying academic lessons posed a challenge while he was attending Venice High School. The war in Vietnam had been in news broadcasts for years, and Jimmy was in a hurry to do something momentous with his life. When he turned 17-years-old, he dropped out of Venice High School and talked his parents into signing permission for him to go to Culver City to enlist in the Marines. It was early January 1968. The *Tet* Offensive was just weeks away in Vietnam.

Private Phipps completed his basic training, individual combat training, and basic infantry training schools in the average time. Then he went to more schools for air technical training and combat engineering. He had by that time had more continuous schooling than he would have had had he remained in high school. This was practical learning, however, that he took to and that he would soon be able to put to use.

His first promotion came a month before his 18th birthday. Private First Class Phipps was progressing up through the ranks as would be expected of a capable Marine. The month following his birthday, he was transferred to the Republic of Vietnam in December 1968.

Private First Class Phipps joined the Marines of Bravo Company, 1st Engineer Battalion, 1st Marine Division, based near Da Nang.

He was a combat engineer and quickly established himself as a Marine who liked to help others out when they needed it. He was the kind of enlisted man who often shared laughs with his commanding officers. He seemed always to have a "shy grin" on his face, as if he was up to something. [34]

At the time he arrived in Vietnam, Marines in the Da Nang area were busy conducting ambushes and small unit actions, seeking out enemy infiltrations in places like Happy Valley, Arizona Territory, Dodge City and the Que Son Mountains. Reports of large enemy build-ups around Da Nang were arriving at the Division Headquarters. Patrols were going out on sweeps, finding weapons caches, encountering mines and entrenched enemy forces, and bringing back their own wounded. Rocket and 82-mm mortar attacks and scattered ground attacks increased on the hills occupied by the Marine Regiments.

Operation Taylor Common had just kicked off.

The 5th Marines were stationed at An Hoa Combat Base in Quang Nam Province, south west of Da Nang. Their area of responsibility was the An Hoa Basin.

The overgrown trails through the valleys provided a major enemy infiltration route just to the west of An Hoa. The NVA and Viet Cong units had gained local support in isolated villages and hamlets and had been warehousing supplies and digging out logistical facilities. Situation maps designated the location as Base Area 112. The maps did not show the thick brush, hedgerows, and elephant grass that sheltered the villages. Company patrols increased in the An Hoa basin. The mission was "search and clear."

Attached to Company C, 1st Battalion, 5th Marines from February into April 1969, Private First Class Phipps went into the field with the rifle company, serving as its combat engineer. He was at An Hoa when the base was attacked on Sunday afternoon, February 23.

Rockets and mortar rounds pounded the base for hours. Sapper teams infiltrated the base defensive perimeter. The ammunition and fuel storage areas served as major targets for the enemy, detonating massive explosions and fires in the dumps. When the attack was finally repulsed, 15,000 artillery rounds and 40,000 gallons of fuel had been destroyed. Afterwards Private First Class Phipps went into "the bush" on patrols in search of the NVA, destroying enemy fighting holes and bunkers around outlying villages.

Private First Class Phipps was wounded in action twice during this first stint with Charlie Company.

Following the attack at An Hoa, in March 1969, President Nixon ordered the secret bombing in Cambodia to begin. It was kept secret, in part, because of the mounting protests against the war. While Private First Class Phipps was patrolling jungle trails, 300 "radical" students at Harvard University seized the administration building on April 9, throwing out eight deans and locking themselves in to protest the university's ROTC program and the war. The next morning local police were called in to forcibly remove the demonstrators from the building. More students voted to strike against university policies and boycotted classes.

Private First Class Phipps had left high school to join the Marines and go to war. What he thought of the social and political upheavals going on "back in the world" cannot be known. What is evident is that he continued to volunteer beyond what was asked or expected of him. He returned to Bravo Company in April 1969.

Even in a theater of war, life within an Engineer Company could seem mundane and garrison-like for a young Marine who wanted to do something momentous. Being attached to a rifle company and going on patrols, locating and destroying enemy ordnance and hidden explosive devices with C-4 plastic explosives was more to the liking of Private First Class Phipps.

American communities were busy finishing up plans for May 30, Memorial Day celebrations. At the same time, other plans were underway. The young people of America who had graduated from high school and gone on to college in the four or five years before Private First Class Phipps left Venice High School had been significantly affected by the war. Referred to as the *Baby Boomer Generation*, a large and growing number were opposed to the country's involvements in Southeast Asia. Their brand of music reflected their antiwar sentiments.

Organizers of the Woodstock Music and Art Fair were hard at work. They had leased a pasture near Bethel, Sullivan County, New York. They needed to get facilities arranged for the Aquarian Festival Grounds, and headline performers under contract to provide the music for the concerts planned from Friday evening, August 15, to Monday morning, August 18.

"In-country" while all this was going on, Private First Class Phipps volunteered in mid-May to return to the field a second time with Charlie Company, 1st Battalion, 5th Marines. The company was operating patrols in the "Arizona Territory," an area of flooded rice paddies near An Hoa hamlet. Two NVA regiments were known to be operating in the vicinity.

Third Platoon went out on patrol the morning of Tuesday, May 27, 1969, under the command of First Lieutenant Michael R. McCarty. The patrol discovered an unexploded 175-mm high explosive artillery round next to a village hut. Without a combat engineer along and out of C-4 satchel charges, the platoon commander noted the location on his grid map and reported the artillery round when back within the company's perimeter. [34, 35]

Having flown across the Song Thu Bon River in a re-supply helicopter, Private First Class Phipps went out on afternoon patrol with First Platoon to find and either disarm or destroy the round. By the time he found the dud 175-mm round, he had used up his demolitions. He determined that the round was probably attached to another explosive device and would act like a booby trap to friendly troops. Working in a two-man team, Private First Class Phipps and the other Marine did just as they had been trained to do.

Private First Class Phipps waited for the platoon members to respond to his warnings to move to protected positions. He carefully began to fix a hand grenade in place to destroy the round and the fused secondary explosive device he had discovered attached to it. Before he could finish his work, the enemy fuse ignited. Private First Class Phipps understood the situation. The explosive device would detonate itself and the 175-mm round before he could move out of range. The explosion was also likely to reach his team assistant and his platoon commander, Second Lieutenant Neil Meier.

Private First Class Phipps cradled his hand grenade to his chest and dived onto the artillery round and secondary device. His quick, decisive action meant that his body took the full force of the multiple explosions and that the two Marines standing within less than ten feet of the detonation survived. When Private First Class Jimmy Phipps sacrificed his life for his comrades he was seven months past his 18th birthday. He is the third youngest Marine to have earned a Medal of Honor.

The Nation would have a chance to be introduced to Private First Class Jimmy Phipps a month after he was killed, if people looked closely enough.

Americans paid forty cents for a copy of *Life* Magazine in 1969, when the toll of American dead exceeded 36,000. Early in June, the Pentagon released the names of all 242 Americans killed in hostile action in Vietnam during the week from Wednesday, May 28th, through Tuesday, June 3.

Life Magazine's June 27th cover story was "The Faces of the American Dead in Vietnam War, One Week's Toll." [36] The twelve-page story consisted of the 242 names, photos (25 were not available, seven of whom were Marines), age, rank, and hometown of the war fatalities. Each page held twenty photos, a "gallery of young American eyes." For some, the last available photo was a high school yearbook picture. The majority of the casualties, 191 KIA, served in the Army. Two were Navy Corpsmen and one a Gunner's Mate Third Class. [37]

Forty-eight of the men were Marines, forty-six enlisted men and two officers. All but one 36-year-old staff sergeant were between the ages of 18- and 23-years. Two were privates, twenty-two were privates first class, thirteen lance corporals, eight corporals, one a 20-year old second lieutenant, and one a 23-year-old first lieutenant.

Although he died the day before the count of the 242 began, a photograph of Private First Class Phipps in his Marine Corps Recruit Depot San Diego helmet and utilities appeared at the crease of Page 25, second row from the bottom. He was one of the six 18-year-old Marines pictured. Two other privates first class who died that week had enlisted from cities not too far from Jimmy; one was from Garden Grove and another from Ojai.

The article did not intend to speak for the dead. "We cannot tell with any precision what they thought of the political currents which drew them across the world. From the letters of some, it is possible to tell they felt strongly that they should be in Vietnam, that they had great sympathy for the Vietnamese people and were appalled at their enormous suffering. Some had voluntarily extended their tours of combat duty; some were desperate to come home. Their families provided most of these photographs, and many expressed their own feelings that their sons and husbands died in a necessary cause."

The magazine article emotionally affected the nation. Since details of the actions in which the men were killed were not provided, readers would have no inkling that a Medal of Honor recipient was among the 242. In fact, on the same day Jimmy earned his Medal, U. S. Army Sergeant Charles Clinton Fleek, 21-years-old of Petersburg, Kentucky, serving with Company C, 1st Battalion, 27th Infantry, 25th Infantry Division, earned a Medal for smothering a grenade with his body to protect companions around him in Binh Duong Province, north of Saigon. His picture appeared on Page 21.

Before the June 27 magazines arrived at news stands, the body of Jimmy W. Phipps had been returned to California and buried in Woodlawn Cemetery, Santa Monica. Like all *Life* readers, his parents, brothers, and sister would not have known a Medal recommendation was working its way up the chain-of-command to the president. His award was not made public until ten months later.

Jimmy's parents were among the other twelve Marine families provided Medals of Honor during the private ceremonies conducted by Vice-President Spiro Agnew, April 20, 1970, in the East Room of the White House. [38]

Today, his flat, bronze military marker reminds visitors that he had earned a Medal of Honor, Purple Heart, and GS, (Gallantry Cross) in Vietnam.

His extended family remains proud of the sacrifice he made. [39]

Today's Web sites give evidence to the impact of bravery and the importance of remembering. In the past few years, blog messages have appeared around Memorial Day remembering the family, friends, and comrades who were pictured in that June 27, 1969, *Life* Magazine.

The Marines take pride in the fact that Jimmy Phipps was one of their own. They named the Enlisted Barracks, Building 2002, at Marine Corps Base, Quantico, Phipps Hall in his honor. [40]

On the west coast, where Jimmy spent his childhood, Building 62500, the Combat Engineers Building at Marine Corps Base, Camp Pendleton, California, is about fifty miles south of Santa Monica and Venice High School. The building is located in the 1st Marine Division area in the northwest region of the base, through the HWI-5 Cristianitos Road Gate, to San Mateo Road, past the 5th Marines swimming pool, to 2nd Street, before reaching B Street. Encircled by lush trees, a half-block-long, Building 62500 runs parallel to the street. On June 28, 1990, twenty years after Mr. and Mrs. Samuel W. Phipps accepted his Medal at the White House, General Alfred M. Gray, Jr., Commandant of the Marine Corps, approved the naming of the Combat Engineers Building in honor of Private First Class Jimmy W. Phipps. [41] A call to the Marines working in Building 62500, and an inquiry about the building, will give proof that combat engineers remember their Medal of Honor recipient.

Outside of the Marine tributes and his grave at Woodlawn Cemetery, available information does not tell how Jimmy Phipps is remembered and honored in the places he journeyed during the first seventeen years of his life.

Ralph Ellis Dias, 1969 draws near to its end.

As the following biography and the one in the next chapter suggest, there must be something about spending a childhood in the western Allegheny Mountain foothills and treading elevations over 1,350 feet that makes young men robust and resilient.

Ralph Dias was born July 15, 1950, in Indiana, Pennsylvania, a small town forty-four miles northeast of Pittsburgh. The Two Lick Reservoir is just east of Indiana and the river runs through the town. The Yellow River State Park is five miles east, Crooked Creek State

Park to the west. The region is a place inviting to a little bit of rugged, out doors activity.

Ralph was the seventh of eight Dias children. His brothers were Wilbur or "Wib," James, and Bill, and his four sisters were Wanda, Nancy, Leona, and Jean. Wilbur, born in 1936, was a U.S. Marine for as long as Ralph could remember. His older brother had served in the Korean War and would later also be a Gulf War Desert Storm veteran. [42] Ralph had relatives in Leetonia, Ohio, and spent portions of his childhood there.

Ralph had an attitude about going to high school similar to other Medal recipients. Two years at Elderton Joint High School in Shelocta was enough education for him. Rather than complete a third year, he decided in the fall of 1967 that, since he was recently 17-years-old, he was old enough to be a Marine. He went over to Pittsburgh in October, enlisted, went to Parris Island, received some special infantry training in Camp Pendleton, and stayed on base with the 28th Marines for a year.

With a year and a half of time in the Marines, well-trained and gaining in experience and rank, Private First Class Dias was ordered to Vietnam in April 1969. He had already earned a reputation of always being ready to do what was needed. That sense of him was similar to how he was remembered by his siblings. Forty years after Ralph left for Vietnam his sister, Nancy, would recall how he "always put everyone else first."

The rugged Que Son Mountains southwest of Da Nang in the Quang Nam Province, ringing the basin plains that ran down to the South China Sea, were not like the rolling Allegheny Mountains. The gnarled mountain slopes were covered in triple-canopied jungle and the densely forested peaks could reach to summits nearly 1,500 meters above sea level. Sheer, one hundred foot cliffs dropped along the mountainsides. Where there was no jungle, the brush, scrub, and elephant grasses were just as efficient in concealing tunnels and caves. Often shrouded in fog and mist, the dusty roads and trails into and through the Que Son Mountains were quickly turned to mud in torrential downpours. Unlike the Alleghenies, the area was a hot, combat zone, and not amenable for recreational hiking or camping.

Private First Class Dias arrived on Hill 55 and was assigned to Company D, 1st Battalion, 7th Marines as a rifleman. In seven-months time he earned a number of medals and commendations.

American families, like the Dias' back in Ohio and Pennsylvania, were buoyed by the Presidential Order to reduce U.S. troop strength in Vietnam. Between July 4 and November 7, 1969, the 3d Marine Division was redeployed from Vietnam, the first full division to depart. Maybe sons and daughters would be home soon.

In his November 3, 1969, Monday night Address to the Nation, President Nixon informed the public that he had begun secret negotiations with Hanoi to bring an end to the war in Vietnam. He expressed his willingness to withdraw all American forces from South Vietnam. The secret talks did not slow the enemy intentions. They planned to establish what they called "strategic springboards" from which they could launch counter-offensives to push American forces out of Vietnam. Enemy maps had circles and arrows at places like Ban Son and Hill 952. Nine days after the president surprised the nation, news of the war would strike more to the hearts of Dias family members in the Village of Leetonia, Ohio, and Indiana, Pennsylvania.

On Wednesday, November 12, 1969, a Marine platoon was pinned down in action with the enemy on Hill 952. In dire circumstances, a 1st Battalion, 7th Marine reaction force was sent in to assist them. When the call came for Third Platoon, Delta Company, under the command of Second Lieutenant Paul Gibbs, Private First Class Dias was eating a can of crackers and jelly, talking with a friend, Rod Sharp. "Always ready to do what was needed," Private First Class Dias immediately ran across the stream toward the sounds of gunfire. [43, 44] Running *toward* the sound of gunshots is an action common among warriors.

The hostile fire was fierce and the reaction force was quickly pinned down themselves. The Marines could not advance nor withdraw without coming into the sights of enemy weapons. Casualties in the stalled units increased. Private First Class Dias took stock of the situation and took action. He noted that the most aggressive enemy fire was coming from a machine-gun bunker across an open area from the Marines' positions. He charged into the open, firing as he went, in an effort to silence the machine gun and bring relief to the pinned down force. Enemy snipers took advantage of his unprotected assault and shot and seriously wounded him.

Undeterred, Private First Class Dias pulled himself across open ground to the temporary shelter of a rock, which protected him from the enemy's line of fire. Rather than remaining in "relative safety," he re-gathered his determination and charged ahead toward the machine-gun emplacement. He was wounded a second time and collapsed to the ground. Now severely disabled, unable to walk, he crawled another fifteen meters toward the bunker and found a rock to shield himself. Enemy fire continued to be intense, keeping all the Marines in check: except for Private First Class Dias.

Carrying on his duty in spite of grievous, debilitating, and life-threatening wounds

As demonstrated so commonly among Medal of Honor Marines, despite his severe wounds, Private First Class Dias exposed himself to throw grenades at the bunker. After several unsuccessful attempts, he realized that his position did not allow an accurate toss. He moved further into the open area to a more advantageous position. While positioning himself, he was wounded for a third time by a nearby sniper. Rallying again, he rose up and threw a grenade, at the same time taking an enemy round that ended his life. Four wounds to stop him, but not thwart him. Private First Class Dias' last grenade achieved his objective, the destruction of the machine-gun emplacement.

Ralph E. Dias, 19-years-old, was returned to the United States and buried one hundred miles west of his Pennsylvania birthplace, in Oakdale Cemetery. Owned by the Village of Leetonia, Columbiana County, Ohio, a small town like the one he had grown up in, the gated cemetery spreads across 24 acres on County Road 416.

As had happened for fifty-one Marines before him in Vietnam, Private First Class Dias' Delta Company commander gathered reports from the Third Platoon members who had witnessed his actions, and forwarded the recommendation for a Medal of Honor to senior military officers. An investigation for justification of the award would be conducted, and final authorization by the President of the United States would lead to an announcement from the White House or the Department of Defense. The Dias family would have no true idea of the extent of Ralph's bravery until the posthumous presentation of the Medal.

1970 passed, then 1971. 1972 came and went, and so did 1973. Obviously, the awarding of his Medal had not been expedited. A variety of factors impeded the process, but did not entirely stop it. Into early 1970, Marine commanders were being directed to turn over their tactical areas of responsibility to U.S. Army command and to South Vietnamese forces. The 7th Marines departed Vietnam on October 1, 1970, less than a year after Private First Class Dias gave his life on Hill 952. The last Marine tactical unit left Vietnam on March 14, 1973.

The political situation in Washington was, perhaps, not conducive for recognizing heroism in Vietnam. Beyond their families, Americans seemed not much in the mood for welcoming home servicemen or honoring those who arrived in flag-draped coffins. President Nixon became embroiled in the Watergate break-in scandal and would resign his office in August 1974. Most American military combat forces were out of Vietnam by then.

Nine months before the fall of Saigon to Hanoi and the evacuation of the U.S. Embassy, Ralph's mother and the Dias family traveled to Washington D.C. They met with Vice President Gerald R. Ford on July 17, 1974, at the Blair House to be presented Ralph's Medal of Honor. Ralph's mother later contributed his Medal to be displayed at the Ohio Military Museum in Massillon.

One of Ralph's nieces, Tracy Dias, was just two-years-old when her grandmother went to Washington to receive her uncle's Medal. When Tracy was 18-years-old, in 1990, she began looking for information about Ralph, trying to find out everything she could about him, and discovered that her family did not want to discuss what had happened. She had a daughter the following year, then a son in 1995. She proudly named her son Ellis, her uncle's middle name. Tracy wanted her children to know all about her hero, her Uncle Ralph, but no matter where she searched over a ten-year period of time, she "kept hitting dead ends." Worried that her uncle's memory was going to be forgotten, Tracy wrote about him often. [45]

If a 28-year-old niece could find little to nothing about her uncle by 2000, it seemed reasonable to conclude that Ralph had been forgotten in the communities where he had lived prior to enlisting in the Marines. Several more years would pass before this impression changed.

Oakdale Cemetery is proud that Ralph Dias, a Congressional Medal of Honor recipient, is interred there, making special note of this on their Web site. There is no doubt that someone remembers and cares about Ralph. His grave is just inside the front gate, near the flagpole that flies a United States Flag once flown at Arlington National Cemetery. Above his flat, bronze military marker, on a brick foundation, stands a shining black monument. His name is engraved under the Medal insignia, and under that is *Greater love hath no man than to give his life for his country.* [46] His Medal inscription is written in full on the reverse side of the monument. Knee-high American flags are posted on either side of his monument, usually circled by flowers. Visitors still leave remembrances to him at the base of his monument. A ceremony is held at his graveside annually on Memorial Day.

Indiana County, Pennsylvania, where Ralph was born and went to school was also proud to claim the young Marine as a native son. By 1991, the Vietnam Veterans of America chapter in Indiana County had been named the Ralph Dias Chapter 286. The *Indiana Gazette*, the local newspaper delivered up the road to Shelocta, periodically remembered him in articles in the 1990s and 2000s. [47] Then, on Memorial Day, 2001, a plaque was dedicated to Ralph on a monument outside the American Legion Post 493 on Mullen Avenue in Homer City, Indiana County. [48]

Along with these remembrances, Ralph's was among the names in an alphabetical listing of 255 Pittsburgh dead in a 1997 *Post-Gazette* Special Report: *Reflections of Vietnam: 25 Years later. Remembering the Fallen: Soldiers from Western Pennsylvania killed in the Vietnam War.* [49] His story was featured in a later April 25, 2000 article: *Profiles in courage: The area's other Medal of Honor winners. Vietnam, 25 years later.* [50]

A tribute long overdue

Jason Wilson, a native of Martins Ferry, across the Ohio River from Wheeling, West Virginia, was fifteen-months-old when Ralph Dias was brought home and buried in Ohio. Ralph had been dead for nearly thirteen years when Craig Brown was born. Craig lived in Salem, Ohio, west of Leetonia. One thing Jason and Craig had in common was that their hometowns were in Northeast Ohio, the 30th State Senate District.

The eight miles between Salem and Leetonia were just a few minutes drive on Route 344. Those became miles familiar to Craig. He was a distant cousin to the Dias family and the stories of Ralph's bravery in Vietnam, and who he had been as a son and a brother, were stories told to him by his grandmother and cousins.

Being of service to others had become a tradition in the Dias and Brown families. Craig Brown began serving as Columbiana County Recorder, January 1, 2005. During his first four-year term, he also began working out an idea and coordinating efforts with the Leetonia VFW Post 5532 and an Ohio State Senator.

The VFW Post Commander, Paul Kramer, expressed a view common among those who remember a Medal of Honor recipient whose bravery has faded from the wider community's memory; "I think it is long overdue."

Jason Wilson assumed the office of 30th State Senate District Senator on January 2, 2007. He and Craig Brown got right down to important business.

Six months after taking office, Senator Wilson stepped forward at the Senate Chamber, Columbus, Ohio, on Wednesday, June 13, 2007, after the 1:30 PM reconvening. He introduced Senate Bill Number 181 to enact section 5533.371 of the Revised Code to rename a portion of State Route 344. [51] The bill was passed by the Ohio State Legislature late in 2008, and signed into law by the governor early in January 2009. The bill designated the portion of State Route 344 commencing at the western boundary of Leetonia and extending eastward through the Village to State Route 11 to be renamed in honor of Ralph Dias.

On Memorial Day weekend, May 24, 2009, family and friends and politicians gathered in Oakdale Cemetery for the annual tribute to Ralph Dias. From there, they proceeded to a dedication ceremony down to the road so often traveled by Craig Brown and the Dias extended family. The road signs into and out of Leetonia now alert travelers that they are on the "Pfc. Ralph Dias Memorial Highway." [52]

YEAR 1970
James Donnie Howe

In the northwestern tip of South Carolina, in a Blue Ridge Mountain county that shares a border with North Carolina, are small towns like Six Mile, Cateechee, and Liberty. Greenville is about a twenty-minute drive east on Highway 123.

Greenville is where Robert Allen Owens was born, September 13, 1920. When Robert was a boy, his family had moved twenty miles up the road to Spartanburg, a city about one-third smaller than Greenville and the place he considered his home. Sergeant Owens, USMC, went ashore on the northwest corner of Cape Torokina with Company A, 1st Battalion, 3d Marines, the 3d Marine Division on November 1, 1943. Disregarding all danger to himself, he charged the front of a 75-mm gun emplacement that had been blowing landing craft out of the water. Silencing the big gun and its crew, Sergeant Robert Owens, 23-years-old, died within less than an hour of his first day in combat.

Robert Sidney Kennemore had also been born in Greenville, on June 21, 1920, three months older than Robert Owens. For a while, he attended high school in nearby Simpsonville. When he was fifteen, Robert Kennemore moved to Chicago to find work. He enlisted in the Marines in 1940 and two years later went to war at the Battle for Guadalcanal. Staff Sergeant Kennemore remained in the Marines after the war. He embarked for Korea with the 2d Battalion, 7th Marines in September 1950.

In late November 1950, the Marines were engaged in the brutal campaign against the Communist Koreans and Chinese at Chosin Reservoir. They were fortunate to have seasoned combat veterans like Staff Sergeant Kennemore among their young Marines.

Commanding a Marine platoon from a machine-gun position under siege, directing the fire of his squad into the charging hostile force, Staff Sergeant Kennemore spotted an enemy grenade land among his machine gunners. He immediately stomped the explosive device into the snow and mud and kept his foot pressed down upon it. The blast dismembered his legs and propelled his body into the air. His action cost him both his legs, but not his life.

Easy Company rallied and eventually repulsed the enemy, holding on through the night attack. Staff Sergeant Kennemore was found in the morning light, his legs just frozen stumps partly encased in blood-soaked snow. The freezing nighttime temperatures at Yudam-ni likely saved him from bleeding to death. His comrades successfully evacuated him from the Chosin, down 78 miles of hard-fought road.

The oldest of the Marines in Korea to muffle a grenade's explosion was eventually returned to California for a year's care and convalescence at the Oakland Naval Hospital. He left the hospital and the Marines in October 1951, and traveled to the White House in November 1952, to receive the Medal of Honor from President Harry S. Truman. Robert Kennemore died on April 26, 1989, and was buried in the San Francisco National Cemetery, San Francisco, California.

Maybe there is something in the Blue Ridge Mountain air.

Seneca is a town of about 6,000 people in a Blue Ridge Mountain county sharing a border with Georgia. Longnose, Big Stakey, and Musterground Mountains are within sight. The area has a small-farm culture, and forest and wilderness areas like Devils Fork State Park, Sumter National Forest, Ocanee State Park, Table Rock State Park, and

Lake Keowee are almost within easy hiking distance from town. For a while, Lewis George Watkins called Seneca his home, spending only part of his childhood there.

The Watkins family one day moved to Greenville, a short thirty-minute drive up Route 123 from Seneca. Lewis graduated from high school in Greenville. He worked within the local police department for a year, then enlisted in the Marines in September 1950, when he was 25-years-old, on the same day the Marines assaulted the beaches at Inchon, Korea.

On the night of October 6, 1952, the enemy overran Outpost Frisco and established themselves in defensive positions in trenches along the crest of the hill. USMC Staff Sergeant Watkins' platoon was tasked to counterattack and retake the hill. In the darkness of the following morning, he led his unit in the assault against grenades and rifle fire. Wounded himself in the charge up the hill, his men pinned down by intense fire, he took an automatic rifle from a wounded Marine and directed its fire against an enemy machine-gun emplacement. His supportive fire allowed the advance to continue as he directed his unit forward.

When he and several of the platoon members reached the crest, they worked their way along the trench. An enemy hand grenade landed in their midst, and Staff Sergeant Watkins reacted immediately. He pushed the others out of the way, put himself between them and the grenade, picked it up from the trench bottom, and poised to throw it out of their proximity. The grenade detonated while he held it, killing him instantly.

At the age of 27-years, Staff Sergeant Lewis Watkins was the second oldest Marine to have sacrificed his life to a grenade to save comrades in Korea. He was buried at National Memorial Cemetery of the Pacific in Honolulu.

One ship, one U.S. Post Office, and two Marine Corps League Detachments have been dedicated to the honor of these three Marines from the northwest corner of South Carolina.

Jimmie Howe was born in Six Mile on December 17, 1948. The town of around 500 residents, fifteen miles to the northeast of Seneca and eight miles southwest of Pickens, the county seat, was one of the smallest in the county. At the time Jimmie was born, Six Mile was a one-street town without a stoplight, stretching out to about one-square mile. The main occupation of its residents was cotton and corn farming. One of the favored childhood recreations was a swim in the Six Mile Creek. Jimmie's school years were spent in Six Mile and in Cateechee Mill Village and Liberty.

There is no information available to determine if he knew anything about the heroism of the three Marine Medal recipients, his fellow Blue Ridge Carolinians, or how he might have been influenced by their legacies. Robert Owens had been dead for five years when Jimmie was born. Jimmie was almost four-years-old when Lewis Watkins earned a Medal of Honor and died and when Robert Kennemore met President Truman at the White House to receive his.

Closer to home, however, as small as the town was, Jimmie might have known some of Furman L. Smith's family, or at least heard about him. Furman was also born in Six Mile. He was a 19-year-old private in the U.S. Army during WWII and died in Italy on May 31, 1944. The Smiths would have been proud of Furman, even had he not earned a posthumous Medal of Honor for refusing to leave wounded comrades behind and standing off an attack of eighty German soldiers. [53]

Furman's grand military funeral in Six Mile was just four months before Jimmie was born. Most of the town turned out for it and over one hundred cars lined the route of the procession on its way to the Pleasant Hill Baptist Church graveyard. The eight pallbearers were all in uniform. The procession included a 15-man military band and a column of marching soldiers. Not long after his funeral, the dirt road where Furman had grown up, leading out of the west side of Six Mile, was graded and paved and designated the Furman L. Smith Memorial Highway. As Jimmie Howe was growing up, stories about Furman Smith would have been common lore in Six Mile. [54]

Jimmie graduated from Cateechee Elementary School in 1960. After one year at Liberty Junior High School, he set out to make his way in the world in June 1961, and ended up working for a painting contractor five miles east down the road in Easley. Although education abounds in that region of South Carolina, and locals could apply to nearby Clemson University, South Wesleyan University, Anderson College, or North Greenville College, Jimmy did not appear to be much interested in academia. He did, however, have a yearning to go further than Pickens County.

Seven years after he left junior high, and one month from his twentieth birthday, perhaps because his options seemed limited, Jimmy Howe enlisted in the Marines on October 31, 1968. When he said goodbye to his parents and four sisters in Liberty to go to Parris Island in the southeast corner of the state, the distance might not have seemed *too* great that they would not be seeing him again. But there was the war in Vietnam.

Three months after he had enlisted, Private Howe left South Carolina for Camp Lejeune, North Carolina, still not so far away from home. After three more months there he was promoted to private first class and transferred to Vietnam in June 1969.

Private First Class Howe would not return to the Blue Ridge Mountains. Instead, he would make a decision to save companions south of Marble Mountain, east of Da Nang.

Assigned to duties as a rifleman with the 1st Marine Division, Private First Class Howe took to combat situations and was promoted again six months into his tour in Vietnam. He was also assigned the duties of radio operator with Company I, 3d Battalion, 7th Marines in operations against insurgents in Quang Nam Province. This was the same company in which Jack Kelso and Lewis Watkins had served and for which they had sacrificed their lives in October battles in Korea. And as "Jack" Doren Kelly learned in Korea, and Marines in Vietnam understood, radio antennas presented an opportune target for enemy snipers.

Lance Corporal Howe, called "Mouse" by his friends, was proficient with radio equipment and liked to entertain the men in his platoon by bringing them the sounds of country music while in bivouac areas.

On May 6, 1970, India Company was in defensive positions just 800 meters from the South China Sea, near the village of Viem Dong, south of Marble Mountain. The enemy launched an attack in the dark of the early morning. Lance Corporal Howe and two other riflemen were in a position behind a thicket of bamboo in an area of sandy beach.

Under attack by grenades, the three Marines moved across sand dunes to give themselves a better position to bring suppressive fire against the enemy. As the assault continued, a grenade landed among the three comrades. With no hesitation, Lance Corporal Howe yelled a warning to the others and dived upon the grenade, sacrificing his own life to protect them from the explosion.

When he died near the bamboo thickets, Lance Corporal James Donnie Howe was 21-years-old. Seventeen months had passed since he had left his home in Liberty, South Carolina to train to be a Marine. His tour of duty in Vietnam would have ended two months later. His battalion was withdrawn from the country five months later in October. He was the last Marine until Iraq to be awarded the Medal of Honor for smothering a grenade to save comrades.

Lance Corporal James "Mouse" Howe's remains were returned to South Carolina. He is buried in Liberty Memorial Gardens Cemetery at Alta Vista and Summit Drives. [55] Among 689 others buried in the city cemetery, Jimmie is the only "famous internment" listed on the cemetery rolls. But, for a long time it was a small number of people who would think to go to Liberty, South Carolina, and pay him their respects.

Time passed.

The town of Pickens, South Carolina, is the county seat. According to census data, the population was 3,012 in 2000. [56] There are a lot of Marines living in and around Pickens. They fought in Vietnam and other wars and came home. Sometimes, one or another of them stood on East Main Street, between Pendleton and Court Streets, out in front of the Pickens County Courthouse in Legacy Square. For many, standing there would bring a sense of solemnity. Between the flagpole at the sidewalk and the stairs up to the courthouse is the Pickens County Veterans Memorial Marker. A standing granite monument, it was dedicated "In honor of All Men Who Paid the Supreme Sacrifice For Freedom in

War." Lying in front of the monument are two flat markers. The citizens of Picket County placed the left marker, now weather worn, in 1959. The marker is dedicated to three soldiers from Six Mile, Liberty, and Pickens who received posthumous Medals of Honor in WWII and Korea. The soldier listed at the top is Private Furman L. Smith. The right flat marker, unfaded, was added after Vietnam. It is dedicated to Marine Lance Corporal James Donnie Howe, from Six Mile, South Carolina. [57]

The Marines got together from time to time and talked about things. They understood the valor required of one of their own to earn a Medal of Honor. They remembered and talked about the young Marine who did not come home to live out his life and whose flat bronze grave marker over at Liberty Memorial Gardens Cemetery bore the Medal of Honor insignia. Thirty years after Jimmy Howe shouted a warning to his comrades and threw himself upon a grenade, the Marines from Pickens County began planning and organizing.

Their objectives were accomplished on August 7, 2003, when the Marine Corps League chartered the James Howe/Luke Cissons Detachment #1145. Nearly eighty MCL officers and members from all over South Carolina went to Pickens to attend the Charter Ceremony. A Congressional Medal of Honor and Citation were presented to members of Jimmie's family, having been repaired by the new Detachment after fire and water had damaged the original awards. The new officers were installed. The Detachment Charter was presented to the Detachment's first commandant. Photographs give evidence that Raider, the Detachment's bulldog mascot, was in attendance and parade-ready, wearing his red, white and blue scarf.

The members of MCL James Howe/Luke Cissons Detachment are proud to meet together the first Monday evening of each month.

Nine months later, the memory of James D. Howe came to the floor during the 115th Session of the South Carolina General Assembly. On May 19, 2004, the General Assembly acknowledged that most Medal of Honor recipients are "ordinary Americans from ordinary backgrounds who, under extraordinary circumstances and at great risk to their own lives, performed an incredible act or a series of acts of conspicuous valor that clearly sets them apart from their comrades." Sponsored by 123 Representatives, the Assembly chose to publicly recognize and honor the memory of James D. Howe and passed Joint Resolution 5294, commending the brave and courageous native South Carolinian for his extraordinary actions. A copy of the resolution was to be forwarded to Jim's family. [58]

During the 115th Session, the members of the General Assembly also passed Joint Resolution 5297, commending the extraordinary heroism and valor of Lewis G. Watkins. On May 14, 2007, the United States House of Representatives considered a bill introduced as HR 1335. That Bill became Public Law No: 110-59, designating the United States Postal Service facility located at 508 East Main Street in Seneca, South Carolina, as the "S/Sgt. Lewis G. Watkins Post Office Building." [59]

South Carolina cherishes it heroes. It was considerate of the General Assembly to write a commendation recognizing James Howe's bravery. One of South Carolina's mottoes is Dum Spiro Spero, meaning "While I Breathe I Hope." The hope regarding Jimmie Howe is that his memory will not fade like flat markers on the ground tend to do.

There are state and county roads around Six Mile that are designated only with numbers. And, the Six Mile Post Office at 598 North Main Street, a small structure with fifteen parking spaces across the road from Six Mile Elementary Daniel Area School, does not appear to have its own name. Perhaps one day the General Assembly of the Palmetto State will remember again Jim Howe's extraordinary heroism and valor and dedicate a highway or building in his honor.

That is the hope.

CHAPTER 26
Remembering Steel Town and the Trees of Lebanon

"I have grown tall as a cedar on Lebanon."

Ecclesiasticus 24:13 [1]

For a particular tree to appear as a simile in a sacred text, it must be special. The Lebanon cedar was known throughout the ancient Mediterranean cultures. A coniferous evergreen, the tree grew abundantly in the mountains above 3,300 feet. Tall and strong, with trunks over eight feet in diameter and heights reaching beyond 130 feet, its timber was preferred for shipbuilding and its resin and bark were believed to possess medicinal and spiritual properties. The cedar's enduring strength and imposing image ensured its status "as a legacy to all future generations."

William David Morgan was going to be remembered as a tall and strong young man. His bravery has by now left an image across three generations. Little was known about him initially. Discovering his background, and the influences that took him from his home in

Pennsylvania into a far-away, restricted, enemy stronghold, occurred across years of searching.

Mount Lebanon, Pennsylvania, covering just less than six square miles of land, is an affluent suburb fifteen minutes south of downtown Pittsburgh. Called Lebo by locals, the town was named for two Cedar of Lebanon trees planted on the Bower Hill Road property of one of the first southern Allegheny County settlers. Gently rolling, tree-lined residential streets make it a lovely place to live.

Fifty percent of Lebo's residents were of German and Irish ancestry, proud and solid. St. Patrick's Day was as much a celebrated holiday as Labor Day and Memorial Day. Neighbors tended to be close and friendly with each other and kept their neighborhoods in good order. Family life was a priority, and ensuring children had a good education was part of that. The greatest portion of the residents had a high school or higher education (more than 95%) and greater than half had a college degree or higher (more than 60%). The unemployment rate in town was low historically; always well below the state and national levels.

Lebo neighborhoods drew their lines by which of the seven elementary schools the kids attended. For example, residents living on the north end of Mount Lebanon, where Bower Hill intersects with Washington Road, would say they lived in the Lincoln area. That meant the kids went to Lincoln Elementary. The middle class Lincoln neighborhood had a mix of nationalities, with sections of large and small residences. Many were called "Pittsburgh style" homes: three-story, brick houses with little space between them. The neighborhood butted up against the Beverly Road business district, a place where kids and teenagers could cluster around shops, a bakery, and restaurants. Down in the central area of town, near the Galleria Mall, was the Markham area, meaning the children attended Markham Elementary. That might also mean a family was sending their children to the *rich kids school*. In all the seven neighborhoods, there were no "bad" schools. Solid.

Billy Morgan grew up in Mt. Lebanon. Before he finished high school, his life was twice affected by the death of a parent. The effects of the first death would not have been very obvious, as it occurred years before he was born. The impact of the second death was profound.

Billy's father was John Morgan. He had been born in Wales around 1885 and immigrated to America in childhood before the turn of the century. John married and had a daughter, Betty, who was born around 1915. John's wife died of cancer, and for a long time Betty had no mother. A widower, John believed in work and that is what he did, ensuring he provided for his daughter. Billy's mother was born Helen Reining in 1912. Helen believed in work and service herself. She finished nursing school during the Depression and began supporting herself as a single woman while still living at home. [2]

When John Morgan met Helen, his daughter, Betty, was nearly finished with school. John and Helen both wanted a family, with children in the home, and decided to marry. Their wedding took place around 1940, when John was fifty-five and Helen was twenty-eight. Both continued to work until their family had grown to include Betty and two boys.

Solid

Solid is a good word to describe the life John and Helen Morgan wanted for their children. They would have two sons who would grow to have enduring strength and who, in their own ways, would ensure bravery would be a legacy passed along to future generations—like the cedars after which Mt. Lebanon was named. Jay was their firstborn son, November 28, 1942. Nearly five years passed before his brother, Billy, was born on September 17, 1947. Betty, the boys' half-sister, was not home much while Jay and Billy grew up. In fact, she married just after WWII ended, moved on with her life, and had very little relationship with her two half-brothers. Billy would hardly know her at all.

John Morgan worked in insurance and financial planning at K. Richard & Co. downtown near the Village Square area. He was earning enough income that Helen stopped her nursing career to be at home for their boys. John talked frequently about his sons to his coworker, Jim Christ, who would later recall how proud the Morgans were of Billy.

The family resided in the Lincoln area of Mt. Lebanon, west of Washington Road. One of the Morgan's close neighbors on Edward Avenue was Frank Sgro, who would later feel proud to have had the opportunity to watch the brothers grow up.

Billy followed Jay in many things, looking up to his big brother. Both were athletic, so play revolved around sports. There were two small parks within walking distance of home, Meadowcroft and Church Place Parks, where the boys could meet friends and play ball. Just a few blocks further from home, across Washington Road, was Mt. Lebanon Cemetery. The gates never closed there, and young and old walked and rode bicycles along the curving, tree-lined roads. Sixty-five acres of sprawling park, kids liked to play in the cemetery, families had picnics, and teens sometimes found it a good place to "make out." [3] From time to time, Billy might have taken bicycle rides with friends there. Many years later, it would be where his friends went to visit and pay their respects to him.

John and Helen encouraged success in school and work for the two boys. School came first. Getting to Lincoln Elementary was easy for Jay and Billy, a walk of five or six blocks to the west end of tree-lined Edward Avenue, across two avenues, over a fence, and into the Meadowcroft ball diamonds and playgrounds behind the school. The school is on the corner of Ralston Place, kitty corner to the Beverly Road business district. Although there were shops and businesses nearby, part-time jobs were not plentiful for older children and teenagers in the 1950s. So, for work, the boys mowed lawns in the summer and shoveled snow from the neighbors' walks in winter for spending money. Physical work.

While Billy continued passing through the elementary grades, Jay went to Mellon Middle School on Castle Shannon Boulevard, a block south of the cemetery and the metro tracks. For the first time in his life, Billy was not following his brother to school. Later, when he graduated from Lincoln, Billy went in the other direction, attending Jefferson Junior High, down Bower Hill Road to Moffett Street, about a mile walk, and a half hour from home. Since the family did not have a car, walking was a means of staying physically fit, especially if he got a late start from home and had to run to avoid tardy slips and detentions.

Up to this point in their lives, the challenges that Jay and Billy had faced were primarily related to academic achievements, athletic performance, and earning spending money. There were more personal challenges and important life decisions ahead. Events in their lives and the personal character they each possessed were determinants in those decisions.

John Morgan died in 1961 at the age of 76-years, when Billy was 14-years-old. Jay had graduated from Mt. Lebanon High School the previous year and was in his first year at Gettysburg College, where he continued to play football. Billy and his mother now lived alone. Helen returned to nursing work in Pittsburgh to ensure there was enough for her sons to continue their educations. Four years later, Helen sold the home on Edward Avenue and moved in with her mother and sister, Bill's grandmother and aunt. The change in family residence occurred shortly after Jay graduated from Officer's Basic School at Quantico. [4]

Death of a parent

At least nineteen of the Medal of Honor recipients experienced the death of a parent while they were growing up. Fifteen of these were WWII recipients; afterwards the number of those who experienced a parent's death declined. Most of the deaths recorded were of fathers. Of the working class, these fathers often died in accidents: for example two were firemen, one a police officer, one a miner, and one a farmer. When George Phillips was three-years-old, both his father and mother were killed in a car accident. From extrapolated estimates, an additional seven men possibly experienced the death of a parent, bringing the total to twenty-six. All told, about 14% of the recipients grew up in a home in which a parent had died.

Death of a parent is a disruptive event in a child's life, affecting children and adolescents in ways different than it does adults. While making necessary adjustments, the surviving parent reasonably becomes less available. The child's sense of stability, safety, and predictability are undermined. Relationships, educational pursuits, and recreational activities are altered. Parental death can stall, retard, or accelerate a child's personal development.

Jackie Lucas was 10-years-old when his father died in 1938. He recalled being "rambunctious" and "shattered," full of resentment and anger a good amount of the time afterwards. For a year, he was "a mean kid," so much so, his mother sent him to a military school in hopes of providing him more discipline. He channeled his anger into competitive sports and excelled.

When the Japanese bombed Pearl Harbor, Jack was 13-years-old. He took the attack personally and was enraged. He enlisted the following August, his sole purpose to kill Japanese. When he was assigned duties that kept him out of the fight, he again became a discipline problem for the Corps and spent time in the brig. [5]

Hank Elrod, who died on Wake Island and was the first Marine aviator to earn the Medal of Honor in WWII, was already 22-years-old and a student at Yale University when his father died in 1927. College educations were hard enough for farming families to provide with the economy in decline, and Hank decided to do his part in providing sustenance for his bereft family. He gave up his university goals, went home to Georgia, and enlisted in the Marines.

Death within the family was more common during the childhood years of the WWII recipients than it was for those in the Vietnam generation. Census data by decades shows that in the early 1900s, between 30 and 40 percent of all children lost a parent or sibling to death before they left their adolescence. The mortality rates of parents gradually declined as the century progressed. In the 1990 Census approximately five to six percent of children had experienced the death of a parent before reaching the age of 18-years.

The recipients as a group did not experience the death of a parent at a rate significantly different than the general population. Death of a parent, per se, did not likely determine their later heroic actions. More likely it is the challenges grief brings and the efforts to face and overcome them that are the precipitants to bravery.

Bill Morgan was in his last year of junior high when his father died. As adolescents are able to do, he kept his grief private and carried on in school. Bill played scholastic football and track at Jefferson, competing against neighborhood rivals at Mellon Middle School. Some of those rivals would become his classmates, teammates and friends a year later at Mt. Lebanon High School, which was less than a mile down Washington Road from Mt. Lebanon Cemetery.

Bill made friends easily. Among those who would carry fond memories of him across their lifetimes, telling stories of him to their own children, were John Dragonas, Joe Robinson and his wife, Sue, Paul Kmec, Ken Wentzel, and Peggy and Al Williams.

Social as he was, Bill was also competitive. Joe Robinson would stretch into the chocks on the track and race against him in the 100-meter dash. Bill was the better sprinter, and Joe could never beat him. The two teamed up and melded their talents on the high school football team. Bill was tall and played end. A capable receiver, he would sprint across the scrimmage line, find an opening in the defense's backfield, and be there to catch Joe's pass, even if the ball did not always arrive where Bill was. He could dash at opponents, never cowered by knowing that others intended to knock or tackle him to the ground.

The impression Bill made on others is evident in the words of *Blue Devils* who walked the same high school hallways as he did. Susan Fleming Morgans, for example, was in the 1965 Graduating Class, a year ahead of Bill. She became the Editor in Chief of the monthly *Mt. Lebanon Magazine.* She married one of Jay Morgan's best friends from high school. [6] She writes about Bill Morgan occasionally. In one article, she described him for readers who might not have known him personally: [7]

"In 1966, Bill Morgan was a typical Mt. Lebanon High School senior, if there was such a thing. Well-liked but not the most popular guy in the school, good looking but not a knockout, a good player but not the star of the football team, a good son and brother, a loyal friend, an all-around nice guy." The article was topped by a photograph of Bill at the railing of Navy heavy cruiser USS *Newport News,* tall and trim in his shipboard Marine Regulation C-Class uniform, private first class stripe on his sleeve and his Rifle Marksman Badge on his chest. [8]

There had been strong influences in his life to lead Bill to want to put on that uniform. Patriotism and military service were important in the Morgan family.

Bill was finishing his freshman year at Mt. Lebo High in the spring of 1964 when the first Marine ground unit was sent to South Vietnam. His older brother, Jay, was finishing up his studies at Gettysburg College and was making some decisions. In the first quarter of Bill's sophomore year, Jay went into the Marines, in October 1964. He was not the first Marine in the family, since an older cousin was already in the service and would retire as a Marine Lieutenant Colonel. By the time Jay completed Officer Candidate School in Quantico and pinned second lieutenant bars on his collars, news of service-related deaths had been arriving in American homes for three years; twenty Marines had died in Vietnam. The first combat infantry Marines in Vietnam were arriving in force in Da Nang mid-way through Bill's junior year, in early 1965. As Americans watched nightly news reports of the escalating conflict, another 508 Marines died in Vietnam that year. And the war came home to Edwards Avenue. Jay Morgan served a tour in Vietnam at Hawk Missile Batteries at Da Nang and Chu Lai. Helen Morgan read her first son's letters from the war zone to Bill.

Although there were seven universities and colleges within ten miles of his home, Billy decided to get away for college. He traveled to Hiram Scott College, Scottsbluff, Nebraska in the summer of 1966, right after having graduated from Mt. Lebanon High. Ron Coker had left Alliance for Denver the previous summer. Bill had not been a stand-out student, and in order to play football at Hiram Scott, he had to do some preseason school work.

His friend John Dragonas was with him. John, of Greek ancestry, was known as "Drag." They went to Hiram Scott together to play football. Their mutual friend and teammate, Joe Robinson, went on to Ohio Northern University. He became an attorney.

Jay passed through Scottsbluff while on leave from the Marines to pay his little brother a visit. Bill was finding college studies a bit much, so while Drag stayed on at Hiram, Bill withdrew after a few months in Nebraska and returned to Mt. Lebo in the fall. He took a job selling pots and pans in a local department store. Not seeing this as an occupation that could take him into the future, Bill made a decision. [9] Again, he followed his brother, and would not spend much time or many holidays with friends and family in Lebo again.

In November, Billy Morgan decided to enlist in the Marines, reporting to Parris Island in January 1967. Private Morgan met a lot of young men in the Third Recruit Training Battalion, where Spirit and Discipline were proud words. The Battalion was comprised of five companies, typically each with six platoons. Sixty to eighty recruits would have been in his platoon, about 420 in the company, all wanting to be Marines. As had been true in Mt. Lebo, MCRD Parris Island was a place where Private Morgan would have forged lifelong friendships.

At the completion of recruit, individual combat, and Sea School training in six months time, Private Morgan was promoted to private first class. His promotion to lance corporal came eight months later. By then, he was out to sea. His frequent letters home to his mother were a comfort for her. Having two sons, her only children, in the Marines during the war had to have been a source of apprehension.

For nine months, Private First Class Morgan served first with the Marine Detachment afloat. He and thirty-four other enlisted Marines and two officers provided internal ship security aboard USS *Newport News* (CA-148). Among other duties, the Detachment provided the Guard of the Day, supervising the main deck and conducting magazine security patrols.

The heavy cruiser, looking like a scaled-down WWII battleship, departed Norfolk, Virginia, on Tuesday, September 5, for an eight-month deployment. [10] The young Marine made a five-day journey through the Caribbean, which ended at the Panama Canal on Sunday morning, September 10. The crew and their security forces enjoyed one evening's liberty before launching again the next day.

Six days into the Pacific, Private First Class Morgan turned 20-years-old.

On September 21, *Newport News* cruised into Pearl Harbor, Hawaii, and docked near the USS *Arizona* Memorial. Private First Class Morgan had opportunities during the next four days to tour Pearl Harbor and enjoy liberty in Honolulu and on sunny Waikiki Beach in sight of Diamond Head.

The ship was underway again on September 25, stopped briefly on the island of Guam on October 2, then docked at Subic Bay, Central Luzon, in the Philippines on October 5. This two-day stay was the last before sailing to Vietnam. Days of liberty for Private First Class Morgan would be infrequent in the months ahead.

Being aboard a Navy cruiser in wartime, with its nine eight-inch, twelve five-inch, and twelve three-inch guns, is not just a "sea cruise" with stops in port for liberty. Nor is it quiet. Thundering noise like he had never heard in the Allegheny heights was going to punctuate six months of Bill Morgan's life.

On Monday morning, October 9, Private First Class Morgan looked out at the South Vietnam coastline from Da Nang's outer harbor. Attached to the US Seventh Fleet's Task Group (TG), the *Newport News* became the flagship for the fleet Commander, ComCruDesFlot 3. The commander gave his ship a new call sign, "Thunder," and quickly got down to the business of *Operation Sea Dragon*.

The ship's mission was to provide interdiction fire north of the Demilitarized Zone, to destroy military supply routes, bridges, trails, camps, artillery fortifications, bunkers and radar sites, and to destroy shoreline traffic, meaning gunboats and waterborne logistics craft like supply barges. Also, because the Marines on shore, with "feet dry," were calling in missions for naval gunfire support, the cruiser would aim its guns over American allied troops in the South in places like Quang Tri, Dong Ha, Gio Linh, Cam Lo, and Con Tien.

The *Newport News* opened up with her eight-inch guns on shore targets at 11:00 PM that night, and kept firing them for the next twenty days. The concussion along the deck and bulkheads, the persistent pounding, and the echoes of distant explosions became the rhythms of Private First Class Morgan's days as the flagship sailed along the north coastline from the Demilitarized Zone (DMZ) into the Gulf of Tonkin during its first service "on the gunline."

A respite from the war zone began October 29. Dropping anchor in Hong Kong harbor on Monday, October 30, the ship and its crew were provided five days of rest and relaxation: relaxation not being a sure thing. The Marines were briefed on precautionary protocols before disembarking from the ship for liberty, especially since Hong Kong was in the midst of its 1967 riots. Armed militia of the People's Republic of China (PRC) had agitated Hong Kong's pro-communist leftists to participate in large-scale demonstrations against British colonial rule. Waves of bombings and gunfights erupted. British troops and the Sha Tau Kok (the Hong Kong Police) clashed with Chinese demonstrators on the border of China and Hong Kong as *the Newport News* anchored.

Newport News left Hong Kong the morning of November 4 and returned to Vietnam's coastline to provide naval gunfire support between November 5 and 12. The ship then departed the Gulf of Tonkin for Yokosuka, Japan, to take care of needed repairs. Docking on November 13, the crew spent six days in the port, given several evenings' liberty ashore before departing on the 19th. The cruiser rejoined the Task Group.

Private First Class Morgan was "on the gunline" a second time, this time for 38 days, again experiencing the sound of incoming enemy rounds. During its participation in 1967-68 *Operation Sea Dragon*, *Newport News* was under fire of enemy coastal defense batteries on seventeen separate occasions and was frequently strafed with shrapnel. Prior to Christmas, 1967, Private First Class Morgan would have some news for the folks in Mt. Lebo.

Tuesday, December 19, 1967.

Newport News and another ship were seven miles off the coast of North Vietnam. Twenty to twenty-eight separate enemy shore batteries simultaneously opened fire on the ships. "Thunder" was going to earn a new nickname that she would carry throughout the war. While exchanging fire and silencing most of the enemy positions, the ship's

Captain maneuvered the heavy cruiser so adeptly that over 300 enemy rounds bracketed *Newport News* without scoring any direct hits. This engagement led American forward observers to nickname the ship "The Gray Ghost from the East Coast."

NBC-TV's war correspondent, Howard Tuckner, was aboard *Newport News* during this engagement. His broadcast was aired during the Huntley/Brinkley Report on NBC-TV Evening News. Chief D. Goad was a member of the crew. Ruby and Mike Goad (age seven-years at the time) audiotaped the three-minute segment, now maintained on the ship's Web site (along with a short movie of the attack). The sounds familiar to Private First Class Morgan, eight-inch guns and ship's buzzers, punctuated the broadcast. [11]

Private First Class Morgan celebrated his first Christmas away from home, afloat in the Gulf of Tonkin, North Vietnam. He saw the New Year in at Sasebo, Japan, during an eight-day rest and relaxation stay from December 27 to the morning of January 4, 1968. *Newport News* was back in the Gulf of Tonkin on January 10, 1968.

Private First Class Morgan had been in the Marines for a year and the Vietnamese New Year holiday and the North's *Tet* Offensive were twenty days away.

Until January 22, the flagship's guns were seldom silent. *Newport News* answered calls several times daily for strike missions against key targets inland and to stop the southerly flow of waterborne logistic craft. She then moved south to the DMZ. Except for a brief hop to Subic Bay in February for a minor overhaul, there was no more respite from the war for Private First Class Morgan. Between January 23 and April 18, the cruiser provided naval gunfire in support of 1st Marine Regiment, 3d Marine Division operations on the beach in I Corps, staying in sight of the coastline.

Private First Class Morgan's promotion to lance corporal came in March. The guns continued. *Newport News* fired on targets around the clock for periods sometimes lasting several successive weeks.

As those in Mt. Lebo who had celebrated St. Patrick's Day the previous night were waking up for work on Monday morning, Lance

Corporal Morgan tried to catch some sleep as *Newport News* fired 1777 rounds on enemy targets in a ten-hour barrage that started on the night of March 17 and continued well into the morning of March 18.

Safe departure from a war zone

When "Thunder" turned away from Vietnam on April 19, Lance Corporal Morgan had spent more than fifty days patrolling North Vietnam's coastline. He had listened to 59,241 rounds of high-explosive ammunition pound from the naval guns as *Newport News* conducted 841 missions against the enemy. During this deployment, he had celebrated with the crew the sinking of seventeen waterborne logistics craft, damage to fourteen others, destruction of several enemy bunker and radar sites, and destruction or damage to bridges, barges, trucks and roads.

Now, leaving the war zone for another brief stay in Subic Bay, while the Viet Cong and the North Vietnamese Army continued the Tet Offensive, Lance Corporal Morgan had time for some thinking. His Southeast Asia deployment had lasted six months, while the Marines on the ground remained in-country for thirteen months. He was single and married men, some with children, were going into combat and not going home, ever. He had served in the protected environs of a steel ship, whereas his fellow Marines were living in log and sandbag bunkers, trudging through rice paddies and along jungle trails, and climbing up and down steep mountain slopes.

While the Marines were under siege on the hilltops at Khe Sanh for 77 days from January 21 until April 8, 1968, less than two weeks earlier, *Newport News* was able to make a quick sail to Subic Bay and back. Unlike the experiences of Marines below the DMZ at the Rock Pile, Cam Lo, and Con Tien, Lance Corporal Morgan had never been concerned that the ship might be overrun by a battalion of enemy soldiers. And some of the friends he had made in Parris Island had likely been killed in action.

A characteristic common among Medal of Honor recipients was simmering within Lance Corporal Morgan: wanting to be in the action and at the forefront of the action. For a young man like him, observing naval missions "on the gunline" off the coast of Vietnam might have been too much like watching the action play out in front of him from the sidelines during the first half of an important *Blue Devils* football game. Lance Corporal Morgan would soon tell an old Mt. Lebo neighbor what he concluded about all this.

Newport News departed Subic Bay on April 21, 1968, and made its way back to the Atlantic, again passing through the Panama Canal. Families and friends were waiting to welcome home the sailors and Marines when the Navy cruiser arrived in Norfolk and docked at Pier 5 on May 13. Bill's family was on the dock waiting, happy and relieved that he was safely home. Their mood was to be tempered by the news of a decision he had made before *Newport News* had come into port.

CHAPTER 27
Sparing a Family Man From Combat

"Men have for ages done what afterwards was called heroic—
they call it foolish if they live to speak about it—to
protect their fellow man and to come to his aid." [1]

Sandy Walmsley

Lance Corporal Morgan enjoyed some leave in Mt. Lebanon after his
first tour of duty, visiting family, friends, and neighbors. Frank Sgro
remembered talking to him about his service. The maturing young
Marine, trained to be an infantry rifleman, did not think he had done
his part yet, nor believe he had done enough. [2] He had already "reupped"
for another tour, ensuring he would serve on the ground in Vietnam.
His friend, Al Williams, recalled Bill saying that, because he was single, he wanted to spare a family man from combat. [3]

Willing to risk

People sometimes view men who seek out personal challenges as *risk
takers*, some to the point of being called *reckless*. Men with the capacity

to act heroically brave are capable of taking risks without undue apprehension. The Medal recipients were not prone to anxiety reactions, nervousness, or worry. They had learned from early experiences that their endeavors resulted in achievement.

Overcoming early challenges seems to have resulted in an unquestioned confidence for most of the Medal recipients. They tended to believe that positive outcomes followed their efforts and did not anticipate dire or dreadful outcomes to their actions. Bill likely gave no serious or lingering thought to the possibility that he might die in combat.

In the months before *Newport News* returned to Norfolk, President Lyndon B. Johnson had decided to lower the numbers of replacement combat troops being sent to Vietnam in response to the enemy's early 1968 country-wide offensive. The president's announcements did not change Lance Corporal Morgan's mind. He was transferred to Vietnam in July 1968, serving as a rifleman, fire team leader, and squad leader with Company H, 2d Battalion, 9th Marines.

There are small coincidences in all lives. Lance Corporal Morgan had gone to a high school nicknamed the *Blue Devils*, had joined a service branch in which the warriors were sometimes called *Devil-Dogs*, [4] and then been assigned to a regiment with a patch proclaiming its nickname, "Hell In A Helmet." As interesting as coincidences might be, Lance Corporal Morgan immediately had more pressing things to consider.

The intense fighting of the Tet Offensive continued until September 23, 1968. Having survived the seige, the Marines had abandoned Khe Sanh in July, near the time Lance Corporal Morgan arrived. Assigned to Vandegrift Combat Base (VCB) on Route 9 in northwest Quang Tri Province, just east of Khe Sanh, Lance Corporal Morgan was now a member of what their commanding general referred to as the *Mountain Regiment.*

Life at VCB was nothing like what Lance Corporal Morgan had known on tree-lined Edward Avenue, or shipboard on the *Newport News.* The outer perimeter of the base was circled by rolls of three-coil, barbed concertina wire, not to be jumped over like the fence behind Mt. Lebo Lincoln Elementary. When he walked a guard post along that perimeter, especially during the night watches, Lance Corporal Morgan would have been alert for enemy forces intent on breaching the Marine defenses.

Trench walls were constructed of sand bags, logs, and dirt-filled ammo boxes. Sleeping quarters consisted of plywood bunk beds in sand-bagged bunkers carved into the sides of the hill. Amenities included rubber inflatable mattresses and vinyl poncho liners. Essential belongings were stored in his olive drab, waterproof ("willy peter") bag. Rain gear was going to be a necessity. [5]

Cleared of most vegetation, the red dirt of VCB, whether slurping mud that gulped boots and vehicle tires or dry dust blown by winds and helicopter blades, was a constant coating for equipment, clothes, and skin. The red became a life-long memory for those who served on that hill and returned home. Dirty clothes were a constant, although sometimes they might be cleaned in the stream at the base of the mountain or by standing out in the rain.

When Lance Corporal Morgan arrived at Vandegrift the air temperatures were climbing. Temperatures got into the 120s in August. Due to the seasonal heat, when not wearing camouflaged jungle utilities, "cammies," and flak jackets, the "off-duty" ensemble tended towards shorts and t-shirts, or just shorts, and jungle boots. Bugs were ever-present, especially in August, and scorpions frequently shared the bunks with the Marines. The rats skulking among garbage cans knew no particular season.

Meals most often came out of C-ration boxes. Getting to the chow hall to eat off paper plates with plastic spoons was not always an option. Anyway, for many a rifleman the C-rations were preferred over the one-course meals served up by the cooks. With the heat, physical exertion, and skimpy meals, weight loss was a given.

Noise at VCB was persistent. Of course there was the sound of grenades, rockets, and mortars, artillery, and small-arms and machine-gun fire. The hum of generators keeping electricity available in the more crucial bunkers was obscured by the engine sounds of 6x6, deuce and a half (two-and-one-half-ton) cargo trucks and jeeps, and CH-46 Sea Knight and AH-1 Cobra helicopters.

The possibility of explosions when walking in the proximity of 55-gallon drums of diesel fuel had to be repressed in one's mind. Marine fuel and ammunition dumps were favored targets of Viet Cong and North Vietnamese Regular Army attacks. On a Sunday afternoon the previous September 3, 1967, at Dong Ha, the enemy launched a 140-mm rocket attack that blew up a fuel dump holding 40,000 gallons of aviation gas and an ammunition dump containing 20,000 tons of C-4 plastic explosives, artillery shells, and various types of ammunition.

"Off-time" at Vandegrift could be spent cleaning weapons and filling sand bags. Power napping, tossing a ball, running for passes, playing cards or pranks on one another, listening to music, and talking about home were suitable recreations.

Bill's promotion to corporal came on September 1, 1968, after two months in Vietnam. The rains also came in September. He celebrated his twenty-first birthday among Hotel Company, 2/9 comrades in sand-bagged bunkers and, before the year was out, proved himself in combat in two major operations. With six months experience as a corporal, he would lead a squad into one of the last offensive operations conducted by the Marines in Vietnam, the two-month-long *Operation Dewey Canyon*. [6]

The Chaine Annamitique mountains run from North Vietnam south along the Laotian and Cambodian borders. Within the mountains, jungle trails, dirt roads, and tunnel systems comprised an enemy supply route, the Ho Chi Minh Trail. The NVA had established artillery bases in Laos in support of the Trail.

Six miles to the east, running north-south along the western edge of Vietnam, in places only a few miles from the Laotian border, the deep A Shau Valley was a twenty-two-mile piece of terrain formed by the Rao Loa River. The valley floor was flat and covered in head-high elephant grass. Heavily forested mountains abruptly rising to over five thousand feet shielded the valley on either side, and triple-canopied jungle tended to make movements within the region impervious to aerial observation. Thick bamboo stands provided the enemy abundant places to hide.

Fifty miles south and east of Vandegrift Combat Base, the A Shau served as a stronghold and staging area for the North Vietnamese forces moving along the Ho Chi Minh trail. Stockpiling weapons, munitions, and supplies within, the enemy considered the A Shau a relatively secure base and safe haven for their forces. Over 5,000 men were estimated to be garrisoned there throughout 1968. One site was called Base Area 611.

Intelligence reports reached 3d Marine Division Headquarters at Da Nang and command at Vandegrift in early January 1969. The enemy, capitalizing on the monsoon season and ongoing Paris peace talks, was gathering in great numbers in the A Shau Valley. The task of denying the enemy access of the valley was given to Colonel Robert H. Barrow's 9th Marines. Planning began to "saddle up" three battalions. *Operation Dewey Canyon* was underway and Corporal William Morgan was going to do more than his part on the western border of South Vietnam in a war far from home.

As they had in the Pacific Island campaigns of WWII and in the mountain ranges of Korea, the Marines planned meticulously. *Operation Dewey Canyon* was divided into three phases. First was the movement and positioning of air assets for air-to-ground support, which began January 22. Second was the movement of the three *Mountain Regiment* battalions out of Vandegrift Combat Base to the northern edge of A Shau. The third and final phase was the sweep of the A Shau Valley and return of the battalions to VCB.

Although Corporal Morgan had grown up in the foothills of the Allegheny Mountains, no Pennsylvania valley was like the treacherous environment he was entering. Wade Berliner could understand this. He had also graduated from Mt. Lebanon High School, was with the 9th Marines at the start of *Dewey Canyon*, but rotated out during the operation. He learned later of his fellow *Blue Devil's* actions in the A Shau. [7]

The 9th Marines moved from the "security" of Vandegrift on January 31 and crossed the Song Thach Han and the Da Krong River. Ahead were dense jungle, monsoon rains, fog and mud, and slippery mountain inclines. But most dangerous were concealed enemy forces. The NVA had its own intelligence methods and was waiting. They also had the heavy artillery in protected positions on high ground inside

Laos to bring fire down on anyone bold enough to interfere with their supply route. They did not intend to abandon the A Shau.

The deep jungle in which the Marines maneuvered could obliterate visibility at times, meaning that platoon and squad members could be out of sight of each other. The enemy ambushed and attacked from concealed positions with machine guns and small-arms fire. Enemy mortar rounds and rocket-propelled grenades slowed, but did not stop, the advancing *Dewey Canyon* force.

Lance Corporal Thomas P. Noonan, Jr., Company G, 2nd Battalion, earned a posthumous Medal of Honor on February 5, rushing to the aid of four Marines wounded in an ambush.

Of the columns moving south, the companies of the 2d Battalion were west of the Da Krong River and closest to the Laos border.

The Marines dug in fire bases on hill tops along the way to provide artillery support for Phase III and to keep their supply and return route open. The terrain and distance from VCB would require that Henderson, Tun Tavern, Shiloh, LZ Dallas, Razor, Cunningham, and Erskin be re-supplied by helicopter. Having reached the Phase III Line, the three battalions began the advance into the enemy's stronghold, Base Area 611, on Tuesday, February 11. On February 13, Lance Corporal Thomas Elbert Creek earned a posthumous Medal during the ambush of a convoy re-supplying VCB.

By February 20, Corporal Morgan and Hotel Company had fought their way through enemy resistance, heavy monsoon rains and nearly continuous fog to their area of operation on the Laotian border. In ten days of fighting, the Marines had advanced, countering enemy ambushes and night assaults, and watched the NVA retreat into their havens across the "neutral" Laotian border. From a forested mountain ridge overlooking Laos, Hotel Company could see enemy convoys, trucks by the hundreds, traversing Route 922 about a half mile away.

If the Marines were to prevent enemy access into the A Shau and deny them their sanctuary, incursions into Laos seemed provident. Captain David F. Winecoff, Hotel Company Commanding Officer, called in a fire mission on the heavy truck traffic observed on the night of the 20th. Captain Winecoff was concerned for his Marines. [8] They were not in the best of condition, without rest and worn by the daily movement and combat. But Hotel Company was also "all up for" getting down from the ridge, crossing the border, and setting up ambushes on the road.

Dawn came on February 21, as did a message from Colonel Barrow. Hotel Company was to disregard the border and ambush the trucks moving along Route 922. Captain Winecoff briefed his platoon commanders at 6:30 PM. Waiting for dark, they moved out towards the road. By 1:00 AM, the company had covered the 900 meters into Laos and established an ambush site. Within minutes of getting into position enemy trucks could be heard in the distance, moving down the road the NVA believed to be their own.

Waiting quietly and patiently, letting a little traffic pass through the ambush site, steely nerves must have been raw. The dimmed headlights appeared at 2:30 AM. As three trucks came into the kill zone, the column of eight trucks stopped.

Captain Winecoff set off the claymores and the Marines opened fire on the three vehicles with small arms and automatic weapons. The forward observer called in artillery on either side of the company's position. Within minutes Captain Winecoff called for cease firing.

After ensuring that everything was destroyed, Hotel Company moved out to its rally point 600 meters away. Three trucks destroyed, eight NVA soldiers killed, and no Marine casualties by enemy fire was reported to 2d Battalion command. Hotel waited for daylight, re-supply, and rest.

In the following days the three platoons would conduct patrols inside the Laotian border. Corporal Morgan did what he could to keep his squad of Marines loose. Having a "huge sense of humor," he made light of the perilous circumstances Hotel was in.

First Lieutenant Wesley Lee Fox, 37-years-old, had led Company A, 1st Battalion from Vandegrift on January 31. By February 22, Alpha Company's roster carried 153 men. On that day First Lieutenant maneuvered his platoons from a ridge overlooking Laos, down to a stream where enemy forces had been observed. From concealed positions, the NVA attacked with machine guns, small arms, and mortars.

Under fire, his radioman and fire support observers killed, his officers either killed or wounded, twice wounded himself by shrapnel and bleeding heavily, First Lieutenant Fox directed his company's actions and coordinated fire, air, and artillery support. The sounds of battle reached Hotel Company patrolling forward of Alpha.

The enemy force repeatedly charged and the Marines of Alpha Company repulsed them each time with grenades and deadly automatic weapons fire. First Lieutenant Fox continued to fight and direct his men. Unable to dislodge him and the platoons, the NVA withdrew from the engagement, leaving 105 of their dead soldiers in the jungle. When the echoes of the fight subsided in the jungle, First Lieutenant Fox reorganized Alpha's survivors into a defensive perimeter, refusing medical aid from the corpsmen. The company had secured its position near the creek by late afternoon. Eleven of their own were dead, and another fifty-eight were medevaced with disabling wounds.

In the days that followed the fight by the stream on the Laotian border, down to sixty-six Marines, Alpha continued to fight off enemy attacks, ambushes, mortar assaults, and inhospitable weather. Casualties continued to be taken. When Alpha Company walked out of the A Shau Valley, three quarters of the men had sustained casualties, including their commander.

Alpha Company was finally airlifted out on March 18. First Lieutenant Fox, the only officer remaining to lead Alpha Company through its travail in A Shau, earned a Medal of Honor.

The Marines counted on their artillery support and during *Dewey Canyon* it came in spades. Captain Harvey Curtiss Barnum, Jr. was in Vietnam for a second tour in 1968-69, serving as commanding officer of Echo Battery, 2d Battalion, 12th Marines. His battery had built a series of fire support bases beneath the DMZ and participated in a lot of combat. Echo Battery, established at Camp Cunningham overlooking the A Shau Valley, provided the fire support for the 9th Marines who went into the valley.

Captain Barnum was more closely associated to Corporal Morgan than anyone could have known during the advance into the A Shau. He had earned a Medal of Honor during his first tour in Vietnam as a

25-year-old first lieutenant during *Operation Harvest Moon* in December 1965. Then the Marines were moving along Route 586, four miles west of Highway 1, about six miles south of Hoi An, and eight miles inland from the South China Sea. The heavily populated terrain was rugged: jungle-covered hills, rich farmland, and extensive rice paddies. During the monsoon season, the flooded fields and muddy hillsides were all the more treacherous for Marines on patrols.

At the small village of Ky Phu, Viet Cong forces ambushed the Marine column in a fight that continued for four hours. For his valor at Ky Phu, First Lieutenant Barnum was awarded a Medal of Honor on February 27, 1967. At the time of the battle, he had been attached to Company H, 2nd Battalion, 9th Marines as a forward observer.

Corporal Morgan was now in Laos with the same company.

Following the first successful ambush in Laos, further ground interdiction of Route 922 had been approved by higher command. The mission order was for Hotel Company, now followed by Echo and Fox Companies, to go down Route 922 and drive back eastward to the Vietnam border, forcing the enemy into the waiting 1st and 3d Battalions.

Near exhaustion from days of patrolling, Hotel began the march at 5:00 PM, February 24, cutting itself off from re-supply of such essentials as 60-mm mortar ammunition, C-rations, and beer. Corporal Bill Morgan was going to distinguish himself with acts of valor his comrades would always remember.

After marching six hours into the darkness, expecting enemy movement, Hotel Company set up a hasty ambush on the road. Six NVA soldiers walked into the kill zone at 11:00 PM. Only two escaped the night firefight. The Marines stayed in place and waited for daybreak. They were about fourteen miles west of A Luoi Village and Hamburger Hill and three quarters of a mile into Laos. [9] Tensions were high now that the NVA knew they were interfering with traffic on Route 922.

In the morning, Hotel Company, flanked by Echo and Fox Companies, began to move eastward, back toward the border. They encountered a fortified NVA force manning a gun emplacement.

Eight enemy soldiers were killed in the engagement. Two Marines died and another seven were wounded, Hotel's first casualties in Laos.

Captain Winecoff took stock of the situation. The company had now accounted for three trucks destroyed, sixteen NVA soldiers killed, one 122-mm field gun and two 40-mm antiaircraft guns captured during their Laos incursion. His orders were to push whatever enemy might be between the company and the border into the A Shau. Captain Winecoff sent out a patrol to determine what was ahead. Corporal Morgan moved out with them.

The patrol was ambushed at a bunker complex heavily fortified by a NVA force, estimated to be fifteen enemy soldiers dug in and primed for a fight. The advance of Corporal Morgan's squad was immediately halted by intense fire of rocket-propelled grenades and automatic weapons. The squad experienced several casualties, and could not advance or withdraw. Two of the wounded were in exposed positions and attempts to reach them by fellow Marines proved unsuccessful.

Quickly assessing the situation across an open road, as he had so often done on the football field, Corporal Morgan identified the hostile bunker putting the most fire against the pinned down squad. Rather than sending a Marine in his charge into a killing zone, the squad leader told Tom Ward, 18-years-old, to provide covering fire and took the initiative himself to rush through tangled jungle underbrush, reaching the clearing in the road. Corporal Morgan shouted encouragement to the wounded Marines and charged across the road at the bunker through machine-gun fire and exploding grenades.

In plain sight of the bunker, the NVA soldiers were forced to turn their weapons away from the downed Marines onto Corporal Morgan. They poured devastating rounds in his direction as he assaulted their position alone. He got to within about twenty feet of one bunker before being shot in the head. [10]

For those moments, Corporal Morgan's lone assault was sufficient to divert the enemy fire away from his squad mates. Relieved briefly of the heavy volume of fire, the squad was able to evacuate the wounded members from the field of fire. The remnant of the squad, including PFC Robinson Santiago, Tom Ward, and Allen H. Brooks, reorganized and regained the advantage, advancing against the bunker and over-running the enemy position. Once reinforced, the patrol silenced the enemy positions, capturing a second 122-mm gun and killing two NVA soldiers.

In selflessly charging the bunker, Corporal Bill Morgan sustained fatal wounds. He was 21-years-old. Two other Marines died in the February 25 ambush and five were wounded. Private First Class Santiago was killed later in the day.

Their deaths were officially recorded as having occurred in Quang Tri Province, South Vietnam. Corporal Morgan's Medal citation, vague about the location, notes that he was killed in action southeast of Vandegrift Combat Base. No mention is made of the A Shau Valley or Laos.

That piece of history would not generally be known for more than twenty years; except by those who had been there.

Hotel, Echo and Fox Companies continued the advance east for another six days, bringing their dead and wounded with them. By March 1, they were nearly a half-mile from the South Vietnamese border. When the three companies were lifted from the jungle in helicopters, March 3, and returned to VCB, on paper Marine operations ended in Laos.

End of action reports recorded the results of the 2d Battalion's Laos incursion: 48 NVA soldiers killed, enemy supply trucks destroyed, 122-mm field guns, 40-mm antiaircraft guns, ammunition, and twenty tons of foodstuffs and supplies captured. Friendly casualties: eight killed and 33 wounded.

After the Laos incursion

On the last day of the *Dewey Canyon* offensive, March 3, Private First Class Alfred Mac Wilson, earned a posthumous Medal of Honor, when he shouted a warning and unhesitatingly jumped on top of a grenade to protect a fellow Marine near FSB Cunningham.

During the slow withdrawal of the 9th Regiment's battalions from the valley, on March 5 Private First Class Robert Henry Jenkins Jr. was manning a machine gun with a 12-man recon team in defensive positions at the Argonne Fire Support Base south of the DMZ. A platoon-size enemy unit launched an attack against their positions, assaulting with mortars, automatic weapons, and hand grenades.

When the attack commenced at Argonne, Private First Class Jenkins and another machine gunner, Private First Class Fred Ostrom, immediately took cover in a two-man fighting hole, quickly delivering devastating fire into the oncoming North Vietnamese soldiers. During the fight, a grenade wounded Private First Class Ostrom, blowing off part of his right hand and arm. The two friends continued in the defense of Argonne until a hand grenade landed in their fighting hole.

Private First Class Robert Jenkins, 20-years-old, earned a posthumous Medal when he pushed the other Marine to the ground and jumped on top of him. By his action, he "absorbed the full impact of the detonation" and shielded his comrade from certain death. Private First Class Jenkins' injuries were serious, but he held on to life for a while longer before he "succumbed to his wounds."

At its conclusion, *Operation Dewey Canyon* was considered an overall success. 1,617 NVA were reported killed, 500 tons of arms, munitions, supplies, and stocks of rice were either captured or destroyed, and the A Shau was denied as an enemy staging area for as long as the *Mountain Regiment* remained in the valley. Marine casualties included 130 killed in action and 932 wounded. Six Marines would be awarded Medals of Honor.

Dewey Canyon is considered one of the most successful operations in the 9th Marines' history in Vietnam. [11]

More important than score keeping to Corporal Morgan's squad and platoon companions and to Captain Winecoff was the bravery they had witnessed. The recommendation for Corporal Morgan's Medal of Honor award began moving up the chain of command.

As the investigation of events would prove, there was no doubt that Corporal Morgan had acted in a manner characteristic of Marines awarded a Medal of Honor. He had done more than was asked or required of him, had charged into an enemy of unequal odds, had taken on his own initiative a challenging task potentially dangerous to himself, and had demonstrated leadership which inspired others to take action despite imminent danger. Most evidently, Corporal Morgan had put himself in harm's way, disregarding danger, to rescue other Marines.

Saturday, March 1, 1969.

A Marine lieutenant from the Pittsburgh Recruiting Office knocked on Helen Morgan's front door. She knew immediately when she saw the young man in uniform standing there why he had knocked. The news of Bill's death devastated the family. His body, having been carried out of Laos by his squad, including Tom Ward who had known him for only five weeks, was brought home.

A memorial donation of two dozen roses arrived at the funeral home from Pittsburgh. The florist referenced a letter he had received from a former employee. Bill Rice was a Hotel Company Marine, a squad leader in Bill's platoon. Touched by the loss of his friend, he had written the florist, told him the "sad news," and asked him to send the flowers on behalf of the platoon. They had pooled their funds to pay for the flowers.

Bill Morgan was buried in Mount Lebanon Cemetery, in his aunt's family plot, up on the ridge near the soldiers' graves. His grave in Section 8 is marked with a simple, flat bronze plaque encased in granite stone common to veterans' memorial parks across the country.

Jay Morgan, sensing some responsibility for his little brother's choices to enlist in the Marines and go to Vietnam, resigned his officer's commission three months later in June. A big brother's sense of duty to look out for a younger brother brings a grief difficult to resolve. The family and Mt. Lebanon were unaware that an investigation was underway to determine if Bill's selfless sacrifice and valor justified the awarding of a Medal of Honor.

Helen received a phone call from the White House in late summer, 1970, informing her that President Nixon had signed a Medal of

Honor award for her son. She was asked to keep this information secret and to not involve the media. Jay received a similar call, by then having returned to civilian life and living in Centerville, Maryland.

That August, Helen, her mother and sister, Jay and his half-sister, Betty, and Bill's Marine cousin, Lieutenant Colonel Samuel E. Englehart, went to Washington and were guests of the Marines in a hotel the night before the ceremony. On August 6, 1970, only Bill's mother, brother, and sister were permitted into the East Room, although his cousin was able to convince one of the Marine escorts to trade places with him so he could also attend the presentation. [12]

When a Medal of Honor is "presented to the family," the award has been made posthumously. Although being brought to the White House to receive the award can be exciting, and the family members are certainly proud to be there, the ceremony is also sad and somber. When the Morgans entered the East Room, they found it crowded with the grieving families of other servicemen killed in Vietnam.

On that day, Medals were presented to the families of: Lance Corporal Jose Francisco Jimenez, USMC, William Atkinson Jones, III, Colonel, USAF, Gary Lee Miller, First Lieutenant, U.S. Army, John Earl Warren, Jr., First Lieutenant, U.S. Army, William David Port, Sergeant, U.S. Army, Robert David Law, Specialist 4th Class, U.S. Army, and Thomas Joseph McMahon, Specialist 4th Class, U.S. Army.

Helen Morgan returned to Mt. Lebanon with her son's Medal. Most of the Marines were out of Vietnam within ten months of her trip to Washington. America's political and social turmoil continued, and President Nixon's Watergate scandal took center stage for the media. The Paris Peace Agreement was brokered in 1973 to bring an end to the conflict between North and South Vietnam, and all sides disregarded the Agreement before another year had passed. Four and a half years after Helen had been in the East Room, the U.S. Embassy in Saigon was evacuated on April 29-30, 1975, and the Vietnam War ended for America. Once back home, the Vietnam veterans began their slow, arduous healing.

And for nearly twenty years after he died charging a fortified enemy bunker, it seemed that Bill Morgan's memory had been left in Laos, west of the A Shau Valley.

CHAPTER 28
An Act of Bravery is Like
a Seed of a Lebanon Cedar

"So go rest high on that mountain,
Son your work on earth is done."

Vince Gill [1]

Community attitudes regarding the war in Vietnam and those who
fought in it were riddled with tension. President Nixon's wish that a
family keep secret the posthumous presentation of a Medal of Honor
reflects his growing and pervasive suspiciousness of anything public.
There was just so much going on behind closed doors that he feared the
leaking of news he preferred to keep from the media.

The nation's tension was reflected in Mt. Lebo's hesitation to extend
a tribute to their native hero. But for his family and friends, the only
acknowledgment of his Medal of Honor might have remained the
insignia on his grave marker. In the early stages of this study, indications in available public records were that no other memorial had been
dedicated to Bill Morgan. This account of his life would have ended

here and been barren of many of the family details already described. A niece who loved and admired the uncle she had never met changed that.

John Dragonas could not forget the sacrifice his friend had made. At a Class of 1966 reunion the discussions of Bill Morgan's bravery increased. Bill's best friend would not let the matter rest. "Drag" is remembered by former teammates to have been "the driving force in getting several beautiful memorials dedicated in our community and in the school" and to have "put in hundreds of hours in his efforts to memorialize not only Bill, but all of the other deceased veterans from our community." [2]

"Drag" contacted more friends, neighbors like Frank Sgro, other Vietnam veterans, and the Marine Corps League.

Mt. Lebanon Park is the city's main park, adjacent to and below the *Blue Devils* football stadium and high school. It has baseball diamonds, basketball courts, tennis courts, picnic pavilions, a playground, and swimming pool. A recreation center with a regulation size ice rink and recreation building opened there in 1977.

The road into the park was renamed Morgan Drive in 1987, in honor of the native son.

At the entrance to the park, off Cedar Boulevard, is a carefully-tended roundabout, an often-photographed sight. The roundabout's center is circled by a brick curb and walkway. Green cedar and fuchsia ground cover provide color, as do the short shrubs and plants. At the very center is a lamppost, circled by bricks, approached by sidewalks from three directions, spaced 120 degrees apart. Each of the three sections in the roundabout has a tree within its center.

The section of the circle first passed when entering the park is what captures a photographer's attention. Under an evergreen tree is a standing, gray granite monument, flanked by shin-high American flags on both sides. Two bronze plaques fill the street-side face of the monument. The top plaque identifies Morgan Drive as dedicated to Bill for being awarded the Medal of Honor, briefly citing his "conspicuous gallantry." The lower plaque, with insignias of five military services, is a tribute to Vietnam veterans and a memorial to honor all American Veterans. The names of the eleven men from Mt. Lebanon who gave their lives in Vietnam are listed in three columns under the insignias: six officers and five enlisted men, one other Marine besides Bill, four Army, three Air Force, and two Navy servicemen. [3]

Near the walk a bronze over blue-colored street sign heralds the main road throughout the park as Morgan Drive. The blue portion holds the five star Medal of Honor insignia. The ground around the monument is decorated by silver lambs ear.

Also dedicated Memorial Day, 1987, the roundabout is an impressive tribute to a young man whom others were proud to call son, brother, uncle, cousin, friend, teammate, schoolmate, fellow alumni, and neighbor.

Proud of her son, the Memorial Day parades and tributes were still painful reminders of an unbearable loss for Helen. When Morgan Drive and the monument were dedicated, she had already outlived her youngest son by eighteen years.

They fell in battle by acting bravely; by remembering and honoring their bravery, they rise again.

The memory of Bill Morgan went beyond Mt. Lebanon, Pittsburgh and Western Pennsylvania. Rick Barney, Class of 1983, left Mt. Lebo for the Marines. After recruit training he was stationed for a time at the Philadelphia Navy Yard, at the confluence of the Schuylkill and Delaware Rivers. The Yard held a lot of history for Marines. Their first pilots, the likes of Gregory "Pappy" Boyington and John L. Smith, received flight training there and the first Officers Basic School was also located there. And, as meaningful to Marines, the Navy Yard was the final resting place for some local USMC English Bulldog mascots—the "Teufel-hundens."

Building 100 Barracks, at the corner of South 13th Street and Constitution Avenue, held memories for Rick Barney. On one wall in the wing in which he stayed were a photograph of Bill and a copy of his Medal of Honor citation. Several years before the Memorial Day, 1987, dedication to Bill, the tribute on the wall gave Rick a sense of pride that Bill had graduated from his high school and had served in the same branch of service as he did. [4]

There is no point in going to the Navy Yard today to look for Bill Morgan's photograph. The Philadelphia Navy Yard was closed on September 30, 1995. Building 100 now stands as part of a renovated, 1,220-acre Business Center. No information is available regarding what became of the display honoring Bill on that wall.

Solid were the relationships Bill had had with friends and neighbors, classmates, and the Mt. Lebanon community. In no way had he been forgotten. And still is not.

His friend John Dragonas, Jim Christ, his father's coworker and a Korean War veteran, got together with T.J. McGarvey, a Vietnam veteran of Upper St. Clair, the Marine Corps League, and the city commissioners to propose that a tribute to Bill be installed at the high school. T.J. McGarvey was the author of a poem, "Welcome Home," and was instrumental in establishing the Pittsburgh Vietnam War Monument along the north bank of the Allegheny River, dedicated on Veterans Day, 1987.

By the early 1990s, public wounds about American involvement in wars away from home were mending. *Operation Desert Shield* and *Operation Desert Storm* transfixed the nation when General H. Norman Schwarzkopf, Jr. successfully led American forces into a confrontation with Saddam Hussein in the deserts of Kuwait.

On Saturday, June 15, 1991, the Mt. Lebanon community turned out at the *Blue Devils* football stadium behind the high school on Cochran Road to welcome home the troops from *Operation Desert Storm*. Helen Morgan and family were there. Harvey Curtiss Barnum, Jr., retired from the Marine Corps for three years and at the time serving as the Principal Director, Drug Enforcement Policy, Office of the Secretary of Defense, spoke at the ceremony. A state senator, state representative, and U.S. Representative also spoke about the dedication and valor of Mt. Lebanon's young citizens.

Former and current *Blue Devils* filled the stands, some of them Vietnam veterans. Marine Corporal Rick Barney, just home from *Desert*

Storm attended the ceremony, proud to be from a town that would raise and remember a Marine like Bill. [5]

The 122-member USMC Battle Color Detachment, the Marine Drum and Bugle Corps, and the Marine Silent Drill Team stepped onto the astro turf field at 7:00 PM. [6] A portrait of Corporal Morgan, a smiling image in Dress Blue uniform, wearing the Medal of Honor around his collar, medals above his heart, ribbons on his right chest, was unveiled during the ceremony. The Vietnam Veterans of Pittsburgh commissioned the portrait with the decorations for valor that Corporal Morgan had never had a chance to wear in life.

The impact of a tribute to heroic bravery

One who attended the ceremony at the *Blue Devils* stadium wrote to the *Pittsburgh Post-Gazette* afterwards expressing "special thanks to all the people and the Marines who organized the dedication...They were all so awesome, I can't put into words how I felt watching those wonderful Marines perform, with shivers up and down my spine, and misty eyes." [7]

Today, the glass-covered, wood-framed, commemorative display case, with a deep blue background, is kept on what might be called a Wall of Honor in the high school auditorium lobby, one of the main entrances to the school. Bill's painting, a photograph of his Medal on a white background, and his citation are enclosed. His name is inscribed on the Washington D.C. Vietnam Veterans Memorial Wall, Panel 31W, Line 054. A rubbing taken from The Wall on April 15, 1993, was added under his portrait.

To the right in an adjoining case, are three individually-framed photographs of the Morgan Drive monument and two plaques. The ceremonial American flag stands in a tall display case to the right. Another display case to the left holds photographs and brief biographies of Mt. Lebanon High School alumni who are currently, or were recently, serving in the Armed Forces. An adjacent case on the far left of Bill's display is dedicated to the annual winners of Great Alumni awards. [8]

Students moving between classes during the school day pass the Memorial display. And because the *Blue Devil* auditorium is used for assorted school and community night functions, Lebo community members frequently view the display. Every year the ninth-grade social studies students stand in front of the Memorial as part of their social studies curriculum.

The *Pittsburgh Post-Gazette* published a Special Report in 1997. *Reflections of Vietnam: 25 Years Later. Remembering the Fallen: Soldiers from Western Pennsylvania killed in the Vietnam War* was an alphabetical listing of names compiled from the military records used to create the Washington, D.C. Vietnam Memorial Wall. William Morgan and Ralph Dias were listed among 255 Pittsburgh dead. [9] The stories of the two Marines were featured in a later April 25, 2000, article: *Profiles in courage: The area's other Medal of Honor winners. Vietnam, 25 years later.* [10]

As the 35th anniversary of his death approached, Bill Morgan was on the minds of many. Tom Ward had become a pharmacist in Saratoga, New York, and Bill was ever a part of his life. Tom planned to visit Mt. Lebanon to pay tribute to his former squad leader and made a strong suggestion to the city commissioners. When Commissioner Dale Colby, a Vietnam veteran, learned that Tom was traveling from Clifton, N.Y., he made a proposal that met with approval.

The City Commission designated February 25, 2004, as "Corporal William D. Morgan Day" in Mt. Lebanon. Several Vietnam veterans attended the Commission meeting, and T.J. McGarvey made a statement in support of the proclamation to honor Bill. That day, Tom and his wife, Joanne, visited Bill's gravesite at Mt. Lebanon Cemetery, the Park and high school memorials, and met some of Bill's friends. [11]

Gravitate towards and relate with other men of brave disposition

Something should be said about Bill's brother, Jay, his cousin the retired Marine, his friend, "Drag," his other teammates, Joe Robinson and Paul Kmec, his squadmate Tom Ward, Bill Rice who made sure roses were sent to his funeral services, and all the others who were drawn into relationships with Bill in his short life. His character is also a reflection upon them.

People across the age span tend to spend time with others of like interests and attitudes. It is a way to experience a sense of kinship beyond family. The tendency is apparent in early childhood when a toddler chooses which toys to play with or which playmate to move toward. The same tendency can be observed in the selection of adolescent peer relationships, athletic teammates, college companions, work associates, and retirement hobbyists.

It might seem obvious that a man who demonstrates heroic bravery would, by circumstance alone, be in the presence of other brave men. This is like saying that athletes tend to associate with other athletes. But what early influences and personal qualities initially trigger a young person's desire to act athletically? What impels a teenager to join the Marines and be among other Marines? The answers to such questions are found in childhood. Who Bill considered his friends and role models suggests much about his character, as well as it does about the character of those with whom he chose to affiliate.

The actions of the recipients in combat demonstrate personal and prosocial tendencies formed in childhood. These men stood out in memorable ways among the childhood peers with whom they shared common interests. As young adults, they chose to be among others who were also brave. And among their brave peers, they would distinguish themselves and stand out.

Heroic bravery is, after all, a higher degree of bravery.

Bill Morgan, like other Medal of Honor recipients, did not "come out of nowhere." He had left behind impressions on others emanating from his own patterns of behavior. Friends, neighbors, teachers, ministers, priests, and coaches remembered him.

And, like other recipients, he sought affiliation with others in childhood and put himself into situations in which his courage and endurance would be challenged. He was among others who were also willing to be challenged. Bill associated with boys and men who were competitive, striving, and who took risks.

The Marines with him at MCRD Parris Island, those who served with him aboard USS *Newport News,* and those who patrolled with him in the A Shau Valley all shared many of his characteristics. Perhaps, the quote of an anonymous Canadian citizen long circulated at the Pentagon, on Marine Corps bases, and on the Internet among Marines speaks to this perspective: "Marines are about the most peculiar breed of human beings, I have ever witnessed. They treat their service as if it were some kind of cult, plastering their emblem on almost everything they own...their high spirits and sense of brotherhood set them apart and, generally speaking, the United States Marines I've come in contact with are the most professional soldiers and the finest men I have ever had the pleasure to meet."

The connections to Bill and the impact of his heroic bravery are extensive.

Heroism's impact within a family is evident in Bill's. Jay Morgan married and had children. Bill has two nieces and a nephew who never had the opportunity to know him, except through stories. One niece posted a tribute to her uncle on his memorial Web site. [12] Jessica Morgan's message was the first indication during this research that Bill had a brother and surviving extended family. Bill's second cousin, who was nine-years-old when the Marine left for Vietnam, had a son in 1997 and named him William David Morgan Englehart. The family calls him Billy. [13]

John and Helen Morgan are both buried in Mount Lebanon Cemetery, close to their son.

Rick Barney, *Blue Devils* Class of '83, is now a police officer in Baltimore County, Maryland. He gets home to Mt. Lebo about five times a year. During a visit in early May 2009, he ran into Mr. Wentzel, his old gym teacher. As is always true for students, Rick had not known much about his teacher's background and earlier life. Rick mentioned the research about Bill and the forgotten thirty-four. Mr. Wentzel stopped him in mid-conversation and told him some surprising things. Rick's former gym teacher had walked the high school hallways with a Medal of Honor recipient. [14]

Ken Wentzel was a classmate of Bill's and had graduated with him from Mt. Lebo in 1966. The two had been close friends and played on the football team together. Mr. Wentzel had many memories of Bill. He told Rick about friends getting together when Bill was home in 1968 between his tours in Vietnam. Today, Ken Wentzel remains a close friend of John G. Dragonas, who is now living in Boca Raton, Florida. [15]

The impact of bravery upon future generations and the importance of paying tribute to Medal of Honor Marines are further exemplified in another comment posted on Bill Morgan's memorial Web site. Thirty-eight years after Bill died protecting companions in Laos, two generations later, May 14, 2007, a student at Mount Lebanon High School acknowledged his actions. [16]

Alex Anderson, then 14-years-old and a 9th Grader, had a class assignment to complete a Power Point. He chose to focus upon "a hometown hero," remembering that portrait inside the school's main entrance. He began searching out information. When Alex came upon the blog site, he decided to contribute his own thoughts. He wrote that whenever he passed the memorial display in the hallway and "gazed" upon Bill's picture, he thought "of all the people who went to Mount Lebanon who risked their lives in battle," about "what Corporal Morgan did for his country to save the lives of those two Marines," and that "there are no words that [he] could write that would express [his] feelings towards his great efforts."

Because the community cared enough about a native son to dedicate a display to place in the hallway, Alex Anderson was certain that Bill Morgan's "memory will always live on in the lives of all the students who walk the halls of Mount Lebanon High School." [17]

Heroic bravery inspires. It is to be remembered.

CHAPTER 29
The Pride of Their Communities
as well as Their Nation

"The world will little note nor long remember what we say
here, but it can never forget what they did here."

President Abraham Lincoln
Address at Gettysburg, November 19, 1863

Bill Morgan's was the last of the names removed from the list of the
thirty-four forgotten warriors. Sixteen of those studied in this work
have had suitable memorials dedicated to them, either prior to or during the progress of the *Semper Fidelis* research. Eighteen Marines remain
who seem now to be forgotten. If this is a factual rendering, the question remains, how will they be honored in their hometowns?

All the Marines listed below possessed personal characteristics and
qualities associated to their heroically brave actions. Although little has
been discovered about their early lives, because they acted with heroic
bravery in combat, it is inferred they demonstrated characteristics and
behaviors early in life and across their lifetimes that were true of all of
the 181 Marine Medal of Honor recipients initially studied.

Second World War
Luther Skaggs, Jr., Henderson, Kentucky
Richard Earl Bush, Bowling Green, Kentucky
Wilson Douglas Watson, Earle, Arkansas
Franklin E. Sigler, Montclair, New Jersey
William G. Walsh, Roxbury, Massachusetts
Wesley Phelps, Neufus, Kentucky
Korean War
James Irsley Poynter, Bloomington, Illinois
Lee Hugh Phillips, Ben Hill, Georgia
James Edmund Johnson, Pocatello, Idaho
David Bernard Champagne, Waterville, Maine
Whitt Lloyd Moreland, Waco, Texas
John Doren Kelly, Youngstown, Ohio
Daniel Paul Matthews, Van Nuys, California
Vietnam War
Peter Spencer Connor, Orange, New Jersey
Douglas Eugene Dickey, Greenville, Ohio
Lawrence David Peters, Johnson City, New York
William Thomas Perkins, Jr., Rochester, New York
Jimmy Phipps, Santa Monica, California

Heroically brave actions in combat can be attributed to some combination of personal characteristics that started in childhood. While all of the traits described in previous chapters might have been true of a few of the recipients, a variety of the characteristics and behavioral tendencies, if not all, would have been true of all of the men. Some things can be known about the now eighteen forgotten recipients with certainty. Like all the Marine Medal of Honor recipients, these men experienced early personal challenges. They learned to contend with adversity rather than withdraw from or submit to it and, as a result, developed strong personal character. They were willing to do what was asked or required of them and more. They stood up against formidable odds and took on challenging tasks, even if the action was dangerous to them. They sustained deliberateness of purpose despite extended duress, carried on in spite of serious and life-threatening wounds, and thereby inspired others to take action despite imminent danger.

Fall seven times; stand up eight. [1]

There are two additional personal characteristics necessary to heroic bravery. These were evident among the Marines on the Island of Samar, as well as at Iwo Jima and Khe Sanh. The Marines in Fallujah have demonstrated them. Every Medal of Honor recipient, whether honored at home or not, possessed these in full measure: resilience to adversity and a moral, religious, or spiritual center.

Resilience to adversity

Clarissa Pinkola Estes, psychologist and author, wrote, "Refuse to fall down. If you cannot refuse to fall down, refuse to stay down...." [2] Vivid illustrations of her words can be found in the Medal of Honor Citations of every Marine mentioned in this book. One such example is Private First Class Ralph E. Dias who definitely refused to stay down when he charged an enemy machine-gun bunker, was wounded four times, knocked to the ground, crawled forward with all the strength he could gather, and rallied one last time to rise up, throw a grenade, and destroy the bunker.

Reading any of the Medal Citations might draw forth the thought, "I could never have done *that.*" When bravery involves going above and beyond one's duty, sustained deliberateness of purpose despite duress, and carrying on in spite of wounds, the question can reasonably be asked, "From where does such strength and determination come?" What did it take for the recipients to refuse to fall down and to refuse to stay down? Only 19-years-old when he died in battle, Ralph Dias had already learned before he went to Parris Island and Vietnam to not give up and to get up when knocked down by life events.

Bravery begins in childhood and is evident in the common belief that "children are resilient." This typically means that children can deal with difficult experience and recover or *bounce back* from it. However, there is more to resilience than recovering and bouncing back.

Physicists, or engineers, and psychologists have different views of resilience and Ralph Dias' actions. A physicist might describe resilience as a property of matter that allows it to return to its original shape or condition after force or stress has been applied to it. The material object is able to bend or contort or compress while under stress, but then returns to its original state once the stress has been relieved.

Psychology also views resilience as related to stress. While a person can manage a certain amount of stress without being changed, the experience of some stresses results in the person being unable to return to the original condition prior to the stress. Stressful experience alters a person. In fact, some theories of individual development state that stress is a necessary ingredient in personal growth. Childhood reality is such that stresses are a normal and necessary aspect of a child's healthy development. In life, there is no avoiding stress. The key for any child is that the stress encountered be equal to the child's age, stage, or current mental, emotional, and physical capacities. In other words, how a child reacts to stress is, in part, determined by the character that has developed within the child by the point in life when the stress occurs. [3]

Psychologically, resilience is more than managing encounters with stressful or harsh experience. Resilience is the ability to develop in spite of it, to adapt positively to it, and to grow from it. Resilience is identified as part trait or attribute of person (resiliency), part attitude (or thought), and part ability: a blending of strength, endurance, and adaptability. Resilience develops over time, likely associated to the encounters with realistic and reasonable stresses, and what might be called *diligent striving*. A person learns to manage. And once a child has learned to manage, he or she will tend to remain resilient across a lifetime. [4]

Diligent striving is an applicable term for understanding the Medal of Honor recipients and their bravery. To strive is another way to say endeavor toward or to seek. All humans strive, and what any person seeks is a demonstration of their character. As described in their backgrounds, among the experiences the Medal recipients endeavored toward were challenges, affiliation, risk, improvement in performance and life situations, and accomplishment. The *diligent* part of the term *diligent striving* is most relevant to understanding the actions of the recipients. Diligent means persevering and constant in effort. As demonstrated by the Medal recipients, an aspect of bravery is to continue endeavoring toward the objective no matter the odds, obstacles, or setbacks. Like the recipients, those who are diligent seldom give up.

The reality of resilience is that all children do not possess it and that the children who do, do not possess it in equal degrees. [5] Like all other human competencies, resilience might be barely noticeable for one child, or it might be obviously present in great degree. One child gives up and the other prospers. Children with little resilience can appear to be overcome or overwhelmed by their experiences and are unable to "bounce back." Children lacking resiliency might demonstrate failure to thrive, might fall apart under stress, or might just give up on life because they cannot long bear its difficulties. Children like the Medal recipients have extraordinary levels of resiliency, and rather than waiting for life to unfold, seem habitually to seek challenges that test their own limits. What seems insurmountable to one child looks merely like a challenge to another.

The Medal of Honor recipients provide examples of resilient responses, starting in their childhood, continuing into their combat experiences, and for those who survived the war, in the aftermath of their battle service. As boys, the recipients demonstrated the characteristics and competencies common among resilient children: they possessed a good share of optimism, energy, enthusiasm, and curiosity about the world around them. They were active, had a strong tendency toward humor and laughter, had talents in some areas, established close relationships with supportive and loving caregivers, and had supports in the wider community. Their mothers would likely have described these boys in their preschool years as affectionate, cuddly, good-natured, easy-tempered, and a delight to handle.

As resilient children demonstrate once in school, the Medal recipients developed a positive social orientation to others. They were comfortable in interpersonal relationships. Other children gravitated toward them, and their peers evidently accepted them. Teachers likely viewed them as active, sociable, easy to get along with, independent, and self-confident.

The recipients tended to have a positive self-concept, were good communicators, and were achievement-oriented in life pursuits. Employers described them as hard working and dependable. As adolescents and young adults they typically developed and sustained strong relationships with competent adults, especially mentors and coaches.

A summary of factors associated to the healthy development of resilience described by Clinical Psychologist H. Katherine O'Neill closely fits the characteristics of the Marine Medal of Honor recipients. Individuals who demonstrate resilience in the face of stress and trauma tend to maintain close and positive relationships with important others; accept help and support; participate in groups; give help to others; are able to think realistically and keep things in perspective; set and work towards attainable goals; develop habits of effective problem-solving; have a positive view of themselves; maintain a hopeful and optimistic outlook; take care of their own basic physical, emotional; and psychological needs; and have a spiritual connection. [6]

Without having studied psychology, President Theodore Roosevelt also had a fitting description of these men one hundred years ago:

"The credit belongs to the man who is actually in the arena; whose face is marred by the dust and sweat and blood; who strives valiantly; who errs and comes short again and again...who at the best, knows in the end the triumph of high achievement, and who, at worst, if he fails, at least fails while daring greatly...." [7]

Should the question be asked, could the bravery of men like these truly be forgotten, there is an answer. One thing to learn from the lives of Ken Worley and the other recipients who were honored in their hometowns long after they had earned their Medals is this: the memory of one person's heroic bravery has its own resiliency. What seems forgotten will bounce back and be remembered—even if forty years have passed.

Religion, morality, and a spiritual center

Semper Fidelis means "always faithful." *Esprit de corps* means that a common spirit of enthusiasm, pride, and honor exists within a group. Marines accept that there is something powerful beyond themselves in which to believe, and they intend to remain faithful to it—always. For some Marines, that might simply mean that they have put their faith in the Marine Corps and their fellow Marines. In addition to *esprit de corps*, the lives of the Medal of Honor recipients suggest an association between religious and spiritual beliefs and acting heroically brave. Some sort of faith-based or moral structure, or the belief in some power beyond one's self, is likely an important aspect of heroic bravery.

Having morals and religious beliefs are two distinct things.

Moral attitudes begin to develop in childhood, before religious beliefs do. The basic principle in morality is: Do the right thing. Built on that foundation, other moral lessons are taught to children, like: Be good. Be kind to others. Help others. Share what is yours with others. Be thankful for what is given to you. Respect your elders. Tell the truth.

The prosocial attitudes demonstrated by all Medal recipients are rooted in moral attitudes learned early in life.

All religious beliefs derive from the sense that there is some great power determining existence. There is a life beyond the world we see. There is something more beyond a person's awareness. Each life has value and meaning. There will likely be an accounting after death.

Heroic bravery is part moral, part prosocial, part spiritual, and, perhaps, part religious. It is most certainly a demonstration of faith. Bravery is also nondenominational, that is, not determined by particular religious beliefs. Among the Marine Medal recipients were Protestants of various denominations and Catholics. Religion, church attendance, familiarity with the Christian Bible, and prayer life seems to have been common among them.

While many of these young men might not have viewed themselves as religious, devout, or "God fearing," none of them could be identified as atheists prior to their entry in the Marines. Others of them were obviously serious about religion. Several had been altar boys.

"Red Mike" Edson's family thought he would likely go to the seminary because of his interest in church-related activities. His decision to join the Marines was unexpected.

John Leims attended a Preparatory Seminary before graduating from high school.

Mitchell Paige described his mother's advice when he walked away from home to enlist for service in WWII: "Trust in the Lord, son, and He will guide you always." Then, on the morning after the events on Guadalcanal that resulted in his receiving the Medal of Honor, the Bible fell out of his pack to the very passage to which his mother had alluded. [8]

Joe Foss carried a Bible in the pocket of his flight suit.

Ross Franklin Gray, who earned his Medal on Iwo Jima, was considered such a devout Protestant that his comrades called him "The Deacon."

Joseph "Rudy" Julian served at Mass during the fight for Iwo Jima.

After 30 years of service in the Marines, retiring at the rank of colonel when he was 58-years-old, then working in social services, Carl Leonard Sitter, veteran of Hagaru-ri and the Chosin Reservoir breakout, entered the Union Theological Seminary in Richmond, Virginia, at the age of 75-years to earn a Masters of Divinity. He wanted to be a Presbyterian minister. [9]

Family and fellow Marines remembered Roy Mitchell Wheat, who died in Quang Nam Province, Vietnam, as an avid churchgoer.

The lesson to be learned from this is: teach a child moral behavior, introduce a child to religious beliefs, help a child develop a spiritual center and view of life and the potential for later heroic behavior is enhanced.

"Tell a man he is brave, and you help him to become so." [10]

As described at the start of this book, only from *spirit* can come inspiration. Without question the Medal of Honor recipients possessed admirable *spirit*. Vigorous spirit is a quality that can be breathed into those who witness and read about their heroic bravery. To tell the story of their bravery is to give inspiration.

Lance Corporal Kenneth Lee Worley, USMC, 20-years-old, died August 12, 1968, in an early morning ambush in Bo Ban Hamlet, southwest of Da Nang, Quang Nam Province, Republic of Vietnam. The memory of his bravery lay quietly on a flat military grave marker for thirty-four years. MOH. PH.

Then between 2000 and 2003 in three communities distant from each other, he and his heroic bravery were remembered: in Westminster, California, by a military historian who wanted to give a home to an "orphaned" Marine; in Farmington, New Mexico, his hometown, by a local military historian who wanted to bring honor to a native son; and in Fargo, North Dakota, by a psychologist wanting to better understand the roots of heroic bravery.

Ken Worley's legacy is now left to his countrymen to inherit and pass along from one generation to the next.

Of the eighteen Marines in the list above, as Major General James E. Livingston, USMC (Ret.) wrote in his Foreword:
"We must remember them."

NOTES

CHAPTER 1

1. British Prime Minister, author, 1804-1881. His speech in the House of Commons, February 1, 1849.
2. Long Beach, CA, *Press-Telegram* Newspaper Obituary, August 23, 1968.
3. Some of this information was not initially available in the records. Donel L. Swisher, Ken's foster sister, provided information more later in correspondence, May 12, 2008.
4. Mother of Eight Seeks Job as President. San Mateo *The Times*, Tuesday, February 16, 1971. This AP story was also front-page news for The Modesto Bee.
5. Unselfish Marine wins Medal of Honor. Sante Fe *The New Mexican*, May 19, 1970. Pg A2.
6. Vietnam Weekly Casualties Statistical Summary, No. 759-68 (C-159).
7. Unselfish Marine wins Medal of Honor. *The Santa Fe New Mexican*, May 19, 1970, Pg A2.
8. Unless otherwise cited, Donel L. Swisher provided information regarding the Feyerherms in correspondence.
9. Mother of Eight Seeks Job as President. San Mateo *The Times*, Tuesday February 16, 1971.
10. This is the former Fresno Selective Service System Induction Center from which Ken enlisted and which relocated 200 miles north to Sacramento in June 1996. Retrieved from mepcom.army.mil/meps/sacramento/index.html.
11. Ceremonies at White House, MEDAL OF HONOR CITES GALLANTRY IN VIETNAM. *The Tribune-Review*, (1910-80) Edmonds, Washington, front-page, Wednesday, April 22, 1970. Also, in the *Everett Herald*, April 22, 1970.
12. Medal of Honor to 15 Killed in Vietnam. *Cedar Rapids Gazette*, April 20, 1970, Pg 23.
13. As viewed at Google Earth, Edmonds Washington, 98020.

14. SSgt Don Franklin Worley volunteered for a sensitive assignment for which even his wife had to sign a secrecy agreement. Taking temporary leave from the Air Force, he accepted a civilian position with Lockheed Aircraft. He was to run Lima Site 85. The clandestine radar site was situated at the top of mile-high Phou Pha Thi Mountain in the Annam Highlands, near the village of Sam Neua, Houaphan Province, Laos. The place was "neutral," internationally prohibited for American military personnel at the time. Despite the sheer cliffs on the mountain's three sides, Communist forces overran the site on March 11, 1968. Although some of the Americans were rescued by helicopter, SSgt Worley was among the eleven who were either killed or captured at Lima Site 85. His remains were never located. He is listed among Vietnam's POW/MIAs. Dr. Kara Rachel Worley, Resident Physician, University of New Mexico, Don Worley's niece, brought this event to light. Correspondence July 6, 2008.

CHAPTER 2

1. The accounts described in this text have been extracted from this larger study, completed in 2006.
2. From the USMC Historical and Museum Division, Historical Documents Section.
3. Marion F. Sturkey. *Warrior Culture of the U.S. Marines*. Plum Branch, South Carolina: Heritage Press International, 2001.
4. From the Congressional Medal of Honor Society, cmohs.org.
5. Retrieved from cmohs.org, May 14, 2009.
6. Washington, D.C.: Government Printing Office, 1973.
7. *For The Fallen*, a seven-verse poem dedicated to the war dead and often quoted at Memorial Day celebrations. Appeared in *The Times*, September 21, 1914.
8. Lauren Edson Lewan, February 28, 2000. Retrieved from Dan Marsh's usmcraiders.com/guestbook5.htm.
9. Retrieved from sherrysmith-fbb.com/news, August 20, 2008. Sherry Smith, an IFBB Professional Female Bodybuilder, is a niece of John Lucian Smith.

10. Sharon Corby's message, June 28, 1999. Retrieved from mishalov. com/Phipps.html.
11. Sherri Clifford. *You Are Our Hero. We Love You.* Retrieved from homeofheroes.com/myhero, February 15, 2009.
12. Jessica Morgan, niece, message left on October 23, 2004. Retrieved from virtualwall.org/dm/MorganWD01a.htm.
13. Retrieved from texasmarinemedalofhonor.com.
14. Mike Prager. In proud landing, it's Pappy Boyington Field. *The Spokesman-Review*, September 23, 2007.
15. Secretary of State Matthew Dunlap. *The Congressional Medal of Honor Project.* Retrieved from maine.gov/sos/kids/cmoh/.
16. Michael T. Gams. Enclosing Dunham's Story in History. *Marine Corps News*, July 15, 2009. Corporal Jason L. Dunham, a squad leader for Company K, 3d Battalion, 7th Marines, earned a posthumous Medal of Honor in Al Anbar Province, Iraq, April 14, 2004. The DDG-109, USS *Jason Dunham* will be the 56th ship. Built by Bath Iron Works in Bath, Maine, the ship was christened August 1, 2009 and commissioned in 2010. On March 14, 2006, President George W. Bush authorized that U.S. Post Office building in Scio, New York be named after Corporal Dunham.
17. Republican Vice-presidential nomination acceptance speech, July 27, 1920.
18. Jim Proser and Jerry Cutter. *"I'm Staying with My Boys..." The Heroic Life of Sgt. John Basilone, USMC.* Also, James Brady. *Hero of the Pacific: The Life of Marine Legend John Basilone.*
19. This is the former Fresno Selective Service System Induction Center from which Ken enlisted and which relocated 200 miles north to Sacramento in June 1996. Retrieved from mepcom.army.mil/meps/ sacramento/index.html.

CHAPTER 3

1. Cover Them Over, *Farm Legends*, 1875, Pg 87. Also, Jeannette Leonard Gilder, George Parsons Lathrop. *Representative Poems of Living Poets*, (Cassell, 1886), University of Michigan, Digitized September 1, 2006.

2. Correspondence dated Sunday, January 4, 2009.

3. Correspondence with David Noyes, October 24, 2009.

4. A eulogy delivered by a British Army officer at a Royal Cumbrians soldier's memorial, 1885: from the movie, *The Four Feathers*, Paramount Pictures, 2002.

5. Correspondence, February 21, 2009.

6. *Medal of Honor Lance Cpl. Kenneth Lee Worley*. Posted at marzone. com/7thMarines/message_board/, May 26 2003.

7. Byron Weber. Posted at marzone.com/7thMarines/message_board/, August 23, 2004.

8. *Orange County Register*, May 23, 2004. Copy provided by Victor Vilionis, September 3, 2009.

9. Correspondence, September 4, 2009. Dennis is now Reader Engagement Editor at the newspaper.

10. Ray and Susan Jackson. *America's Youngest Warriors, Volume II*. Tempe, AZ: Veterans of Underage Military Service, 2002, pp 364-66.

11. Information noting Bruce Salisbury was provided in correspondences with him beginning July 13, 2008 and continuing to this printing.

12. As recalled by Ann Phelps, correspondence, August 26, 2009.

13. Richard Melzer. Sunstone Press: Santa Fe, NM.

14. Retired First Sergeant Jack Closson, USMC, put the author in contact with Ken Worley's foster family. His foster sister, Donel Swisher, who was 13-years-old and in the eighth grade at the time Kenny entered the family's life, provided much additional personal background about him.

15. *Bedford Gazette*, Friday March 29, 1907.

16. Michelle Seeber. *Clovis News Journal*.

17. Jeanne Williams. *Temple Daily Telegram*, April 28, 2008.

18. Initial information regarding Ken's biological family was provided by Sharon Houston. Telephone interviews: August 12, August 16, and August 18, 2008. Also, a series of correspondences between August 27, 2008 and January 7, 2009.

19. LEGAL NOTICE Nm.7149—Apr. 30, May 1. *3. The Hayward Daily Review*, April 30, 1963, Pg 6.

20. *Farmington Daily Times*, Sunday, July 13, 2008.
21. See Bernard C. Nalty. *The Right To Fight: African–American Marines in World War II*. History and Museums Division, Headquarters, U.S. Marine Corps, Washington, D.C., 1995. Confirmed in correspondence, Joan Earnshaw, June 22, 2009. Following an inquiry by Brigadier General Thomas V. Draude, USMC (Ret.), Robert Aquilina of the History Division also provided documents confirming Brigadier General Joseph W. Earnshaw's (USMC, Deceased) command of the 52d Defense Battalion. Brigadier General Draude, describing his own experiences in Vietnam in a phone conversation on April 21, 2011, also referenced a meeting Marine General Victor Krulak and Foreign Service officer Joseph Mendenhall had with President Kennedy, described at the start of Chapter 25.

CHAPTER 4

1. Dates were initially derived from freepages.genealogy.rootsweb. ancestry.com/~mckaughan/combined/names14.htm, and then were cross-checked at other sites.
2. Retrieved from boards.ancestry.com/surnames.horlacher/28/mb.ashx.
3. As recorded in Wise County, *Texas Marriage Book 1*, Pg 123.
4. From Hale County, Texas, Cemetery Records. Retrieved from unger.myplainview.com/cemetery/cemetery.php
5. From *History Of Arizona; Biographical Volume III*. Phoenix: Record Publishing Co., 1930, Pg 329. Retrieved from rootsweb.ancestry. com/cgi-bin/igm.cgi?op=GET&db=1777&id=I3874
6. Ibid.
7. *My Family Tree*. Retrieved from bryanbrazil.com/family/person/1/i_ I63387/william-oliver-tuttle.
8. Lois Monson, enthusiastic and determined ancestry researcher in Fargo, ND provided the references to the 1920 U.S. Census, the Texas Registry records, and the Oregon Death Index in May 2010. Joan Earnshaw later confirmed these findings from her own search.
9. Retrieved from rootsweb.ancestry.com/cgi-bin/igm.cgi?op=GET& db=1777&id=I0213, Known Descendants of William Sibley of England, compiled by Bernie Schwinty.

10. Retrieved from bryanbrazil.com/family/person/1/i_I63387/william-oliver-tuttle.
11. Lois Monson. In correspondence May 10, 2010.
12. Joan Earnshaw. In correspondence, August 11, 2009.
13. Had served as Assistant Pastor at Park Presbyterian Church of Los Angeles in 1922. *Herald and Presbyter, Volume 93*. Harvard University: Monfort & Company, 1922.
14. Joan Earnshaw provided *Record of Marriages, No 6926*, on August 19, 2009.
15. Correct spelling is Winkelman.
16. Bruce Salisbury, correspondence, August 20, 2009.
17. Sharon Houston, phone conversations, August 16, August 20, 2009.
18. Bruce Salisbury in correspondence, April 19, 2009. Announcement and wedding photo in Hayward *The Daily Review*, Sunday, November 11, 1962, Section II, Pg 3. The Hayward connection seemed to prove unlikely after a photo comparison between the bride and an earlier photo of Betty Sue Peace. Also the Hayward Betty Worley had three other brothers: Lester, Norman, and Robert.
19. Also *Oakland Tribune*, Southern Alaraeda County Section Thursday, Aug. 17,1961, Pg 4-A.
20. *The Hayward Teen Review*, Pg 12. Also, December 6, 1958, Pg 13.
21. *The Hayward Teen Review*, May 2, 1959, Pg 12.
22. Joan Earnshaw. In correspondence, June 24, 2009.
23. Joan Earnshaw. In correspondence, June 25, 2009.
24. Ann (Salisbury) Phelps provided this and the following in correspondences June 27, 2009, August 26, 2009, August 27, 2009, and November 3, 2009.
25. Edward Eggleston. *The Hoosier Schoolmaster:A Story of Backwoods Life in Indiana*. New York: Grosset & Dunlap. Written in 1871, last published in 1913.
26. Ann (Salisbury) Phelps largely provided the description of childhood Farmington.
27. Eg: *Albuquerque Tribune* March 3, 1952, May 1, 1952, September 29, 1952, October 31, 1952, and *The Farmington Times*, September 2, 1952.

28. Ann Phelps reported that this old building is now a part of the Senior Citizen Complex on La Plata Street. A designated walkway across Wall Avenue now connects the complex and former school.

29. Bruce Salisbury, a Farmington classmate of Glen Rickelton's, provided this in correspondence, Saturday, July 18, 2009. See also *The Aztec Local News, The Talon,* Vol. 17 No. 8, April 16-30, 2009, Pg. 11. Bruce provided the correct location of the drug store in correspondence, Sunday, July 17, 2011.

30. Sharon Houston also provided information about the Allen Street neighborhood.

31. Sharon Houston, phone conversations, August 16, August 20, 2009.

32. Information disclosed later during this research, reported that Ken had accidentally shot himself in his foot with a rifle. Provided by Michael Doyle, World just learning mystery of Vietnam-era Marine hero, *McClatchy Newspapers*, posted on Friday, October 30, 2009.

33. Her junior photograph appears in the Spartan's 1967 *Olympian* Yearbook. The school is located at 1200 West Rumble Road, abutting the Davis Community Park.

34. Quonieta (Feyerherm) Murphy provided additional background information to augment her sister, Nell's, recollections in a telephone conversation, July 29, 2008.

35. Bruce Salisbury provided photograph on the next page of Kenneth Worley's monument at All Veterans Plaza, Farmington, New Mexico.

CHAPTER 5

1. *The Coldest War: A Memoir if Korea,* New York: Thomas Dunne Books, 1990, Pg 9.

2. Rey Mejia. *His Name Was Worley.* Written around 1992. Rey was with Ken in Platoon 396, was transferred with him to Vietnam in 1967, and then was transferred to the 5th Marines in mid-December 1967. He saw extensive combat during the 1968 Tet Offensive, was in the A Shau Valley, and then in Operation Hue City. Rey was wounded twice in Hue and hospitalized. Correspondences June 8, 2009. The following MCRD account is based on Rey's descriptions, provided through Donel Swisher and Bruce Salisbury.

3. David Noyes. Correspondence and phone conversations in January and February 2009.
4. Comments left at The Virtual Wall by former Marines having served with Ken, Rey Mejia Friday, July 2, 1999; William Blancett Wednesday, August 16, 2000.
5. Quonieta (Feyerherm) Murphy. Correspondence on January 31, 2011.
6. Jack Shulimson, Leonard A. Blasiol, Charles R. Smith, David A. Dawson. *US Marines in Vietnam: 1968 The Defining Year.* History and Museums Division, Headquarters, U.S. Marine Corps, Washington, D.C., 1997, Pg 157.
7. Larry Muhlenforth, as quoted by Jim Radcliffe. Unsung Vietnam hero gets belated monument. *Orange County Register*, May 28, 2004.
8. Vietnam: The Hidden Charm. Da Nang City. Retrieved from OPENTOUR JSC, SINHCAFE, Viet Nam, October 24, 2007.
9. Daniel D. Poland. Correspondence, January 4, 2009.
10. Charles G. Black. As quoted in *Orange County Register*, May 23, 2004, Pg 4.
11. *Orange County Register*, May 23, 2004, pp 3-4.

CHAPTER 6

1. Lines from the Decoration Day poem *Cover Them Over. Poems.* Chicago: Lakeside Publishing, 1871, Pg 111.
2. Jim Radcliffe. Unsung Vietnam hero gets belated monument. *Orange County Register*, May 28, 2004. Copy provided by Victor Vilionis, September 3, 2009.
3. Theresa Walker. *The Orange County Register*, May 31, 2005.
4. Web site at lcplworleyym.com/
5. From *The Veterans' Voice* <vetsvoice@blackfoot.net>, August 04, 2009.
6. The Vietnam War Memorial was initiated by Westminster City Councilman Frank G. Fry in 1997 and completed in 2003.
7. Minutes of a regular Westminster City Council/Redevelopment Agency meeting, June 11, 2008. Retrieved from ci.westminster.ca.us.
8. Eric and Pati Walz provided photographs of the ceremony and their impressions of the event.

9. From daily-times.com/news/ci_9865036.
10. Opening line from article, City, veterans should resolve memorial issue. *Farmington Daily Times*, January 7, 2009.
11. From daily-times.com/ci_11390497 and daily-times.com/ci_11360032.
12. Staff Writer. Memorial finally planned for Medal of Honor troops. *The Daily Times*, April 29, 2009.
13. Retrieved from riverreachfoundation.com/main.htm.
14. Steve Lynn, reporter for *Farmington Daily Times*, provided description in correspondence, April 24, 2009.
15. Steve Lynn. Memorial is Farmington's first to Medal of Honor winner. *Farmington Daily Times*, April 27, 2009.
16. Memorial finally planned for Medal of Honor troops. *Daily Times*, April 29, 2009.
17. Steve Lynn. City to break ground on Medal of Honor memorial. *Daily Times*, May 21, 2009. Also Alysa Landry. Ground breaking solemn Medal of Honor Memorial. *Daily Times*, May 24, 2009.
18. Bruce Salisbury. In correspondence, Saturday, May 23, 2009.
19. *Kenneth Lee Worley Bronze Memorial Challenge*, message circulated 13 April 2009.
20. This is a 501 (3) (c) Public Charity.
21. Zimmerman, Dwight Jon and Gresham, John D. *Uncommon Valor: The Medal of Honor and the Six Warriors Who Earned It in Afghanistan and Iraq*. New York: St. Martin's Press, 2010.
22. Correspondence, August 8, 2009.
23. Bruce Salisbury. In correspondence, August 12, 2009.
24. Michael Doyle. Posted at mcclatchydc.com/staff/michael_doyle/story/77692.html. Reference provided on October 24, 2009 7:08 AM.
25. Correspondence, October 28, 2009.
26. Steve Lynn. Farmington Medal of Honor Memorial to be unveiled Saturday.
27. Bruce Salisbury. In correspondence, November 3, 2009.
28. This account adapted from Elizabeth Piazza, Mayor: Memorial 'is a legacy that will go on', *The Daily Times*, November 8, 2009.
29. Correspondence, July 30, 2010.

CHAPTER 7

1. Retrieved from *Arlington National Cemetery* Web site, May 14, 2000.
2. *Essays*, First Series, 1841, Heroism.
3. U.S. Army Space Missile Command. *The Eagle*, Vol 5, No. 2. March 1999, Pg 6.
4. Mary Jean Porter. Risked His Life to Save Other Marines. Pueblo, Colorado, *The Pueblo Chieftain*, June 29, 1995.
5. USMC Assistant Commandant, in Foreword, Jon T. Hoffman. *Once a Legend*, 2000, p xii.
6. Pen name for Samuel Langhorne Clemens, (1835 –1910). Quote in Pudd'nhead Wilson's Calendar, 1894.
7. *Arlington National Cemetery* Web site, May 14, 2000.
8. Major John Smith interview, USMC, Bureau of Aeronautics, 10 November 1942.
9. In November 2006, his victories over Guadalcanal were first featured in the History Channel's Dogfights series.
10. *The Beta Theta Pi* magazine Vol CXXIX, No. 4. Miami University, Spring 2002, Pg 24.
11. Jon T. Hoffman. *Once A Legend*, Pg 270.
12. Isaiah 6:8, the *New American Standard Bible*. Lieutenant General John R. Allen, USMC, quoted this verse in his August 15, 2009 eulogy for Captain Matthew Freeman, USMC, killed in action in Afghanistan, August 7, 2009.

CHAPTER 8

1. Lyrics from his song, *God Bless the USA*, Music Corp. of America, 1984.
2. Comment posted on Farmington, New Mexico's *The Daily Times* discussion forum, January 5, 2009.
3. The manuscript was first displayed at the Library of Congress, February 1942.

4. Greg believed he shared one quarter of his blood with the Hunkpapa Sioux natives on his mother's side. Sources vary regarding Greg's Sioux ancestry, some reporting that he was half-Sioux or quarter-Sioux. A few sources report that he was part Apache. Family members later would insist that Grace had no Native ancestors on either side of her family and that she had concocted the legend herself, perhaps in part to explain Greg's facial structure or to conceal his true paternity.

5. Baron, R. A. & Byrne, D. Social psychology: Understanding human interaction (6th ed.) Boston: Allyn & Bacon, 1991.

6. John Bolcer, University Archivist Special Collections, University of Washington Libraries, in correspondence, April 14, 2010, clarified some information regarding the spelling of Greg's last name and provided a link to the *Tyee* yearbooks at content.lib.washington.edu/cdm-ayp/search.php. Greg appears in Volumes 32, 33, 34, and 35.

7. Gamble, Bruce. *Black Sheep One: The Life of Gregory "Pappy" Boyington*. Novato, CA: Presidio Press, 2000, Pg 48.

8. References provided different dates for events in Greg's personal life. Dates cited in this text are those that best follow his memoirs or documented records.

9. From the list of WWII USMC Aces. Retrieved from acepilots.com/usmc_aces_list.html.

10. The number of aircraft shot down by Gregory Boyington is recorded variously. As a Marine pilot, he had 22 "kills." The record of 28 includes his six "kills" as a *Flying Tiger*.

11. *Life* Magazine, October 1, 1945.

12. Raymond "Hap" Halloran. Camp details were derived from his eulogy for Gregory "Pappy" Boyington written and delivered at Arlington National Cemetery, January 15, 1988.

13 Missing Ace Reported OK. *Oakland Tribune*, Wednesday, August 29, 1945, Pg C3.

CHAPTER 9

1. *Life* Magazine, January 26, 1959, Pg 70.

2. Lucy Malcolmson 'Stunned' at News of War Hero's Marriage To Frances Baker. Los Angeles, *UP, The Schenectady Gazette*, Thursday, January 10, 1946.
3. California: Born to Fight. *Time Magazine*, Monday, September 2, 1946.
4. *Baa Baa Black Sheep*. New York: Bantam Books, 1977, (First Edition, Putnam Publishing, 1958), Pg 339.
5. Los Angeles (AP), "Pappy" Boyington Seeking Divorce. Racine *Journal-Times*, Tuesday, March 31, 1964, Pg 4B.
6. Boyington's Daughter Gets Child. Long Beach, California *Press-Telegram*, Friday, May 4, 1960, Pg A-4.
7. Bruce Gamble, 2000, Pp 421-23.
8. Posted: April 8, 2002 1:38AM GMT, Message Boards, ancestry. myfamily.com
9. *"Black Sheep" Leader Takes Fourth Bride, The Yuma Daily Sun* Wednesday August 6, 1975.
10. Bruce Gamble, 2000, Pg 13.

CHAPTER 10

1. From *Ten Things Every American Student Should Know About Our Army in World War II,* May 2009, Vol 14 No 15. From a talk at the Foreign Policy Research Institute Wachman Center's History Institute for Teachers, held May 2-3, 2009. Captain Henry T. Waskow, U.S. Army, September 24, 1918-December 14, 1943, was killed in action, above San Pietro, Italy.
2. Retrieved from globalsecurity.org/military/agency/usmc/vma-214. htm.
3. Retrieved from collectair.com/ORIGINAL_ARTWORK.html.
4. Tom Griffin. Gregory Boyington—Our 'Black Sheep' Hero. *UW alumni magazine, Columns, A look Back at UW History,* December 1998.
5. washington.edu/alumni/columns/dec98/back_pages1298.html.
6. Some sources name seven Medal of Honor recipients associated to UW.
7. Retrieved from senate.asuw.org/secretary/min...02-07-2006.pdf.
8. Retrieved from uwfoundation.org/giving_opps/uw_wide_opps/ medalofhonor.asp.

9. University of Washington *The Daily*, Letters to the Editor, December 5, 2007.
10. University of Washington News Release, August 31, 2009: University of Washington to dedicate Medal of Honor monument.
11. *Pappy Boyington Field – A Campaign to Honor a Hero.*

CHAPTER 11

1. *Profiles in Courage.* New York: Harper & Brothers,1956.
2. For example, Department of the Navy, Naval Historical Center, history.navy.mil.
3. Karen D. Smith. *Supreme Sacrifice.* Retrieved from medalofhonor. com.
4. AP story, Kingsport, Tennessee, *Kingsport Times*, October 26, 1945.
5. Medal Winner at Iwo Jima is AWOL And Held in Jail. *The Moberley Monitor-Index*, February 14, 1963.
6. Arkansas World War II Hero Faces Army Desertion Charge. Fayetteville, *Northwest Arkansas Times,* February 15, 1963.
7. Medal of Honor Winner is Found: AWOL Since Fall. Edwardsville, Illinois *The Edwardsville Intelligencer*, February 16, 1963.
8. Medal of Honor Winner Transferred to Walter Reed. Lawton, Oklahoma, *Lawton Constitiution,* February 24, 1963.
9. May, 2005 issue.

CHAPTER 12

1. From the poem, *Monuments and Memories (For Those Who Never Came Home)*, on a bronze plaque at the entrance to The 'Striking Sixth' Memorial, Quantico National Cemetery in Prince William County, Virginia.
2. Mary Jean Porter. Risked His Life to Save Other Marines, Pueblo, Colorado, *The Pueblo Chieftain*, June 29, 1995.
3. William Honan. Ex-Marine Honored for Bravery in Korea. *New York Times*, April 8, 2000.
4. James E. Livingston, et al, Pp 134-35.
5. Iwo Jima Re-enactment Held in Texas. *Northwest Cable News,* Sunday, Feb 20, 2005

6. New York: Random House, 1998.
7. Peter Harriman and David Kranz. S.D. Loses Legend, American Hero. *The Argus Leader*, January 2, 2003.

CHAPTER 13

1. Clint Van Winkle. *Soft Spots: A Marine's Memoir of Combat and Post-Traumatic Stress Disorder.* New York: St. Martin's Press, 2009, Pg 68.
1a. See en.wikipedia.org/wiki/Henderson,_Kentucky, as of December 26, 2008.
2. Officer Calls Skagg's Conduct Greatest Inspiration Possible. *Ames Daily Tribune*, Thursday, February 22, 1945, Pg 5.
3. Rick Bell. *The Great Flood of 1937: Rising Waters, Soaring Spirits.* Louisville, Kentucky: Butler Books, 2007.
4. AP Survey Shows Congressional Medal Winners in Pacific Live Quietly. *Billings Gazette,* Sunday, August 14, 1949.
5. Courage. Long Beach, California, *Independent Press-Telegram*, July 1, 1962.
6. Retrieved from cmohs.org/society-history.php.
7. Highest Military Medal Century Old. *Fergus Falls Daily Journal*, Thursday, July 12, 1962.
8. Retrieved from mcleague.org.
9. Purple Heart Association of United States Formed. *Evening Sentinel,* September 22, 1932.
10. *Two Score and Thirteen, Volume 2 of Third Marine Division Association History, 1949-2002.* Third Marine Division Association, Inc, Turner Publishing Company, 2002.
11. At kentuckymarines.org/index.cfm/lutherskagg.html.
12. en.wikipedia.org/wiki/Glasgow,_Kentucky. Reviewed December 26, 2008.
13. Richard Goldstein. Richard E. Bush, Who Served on Okinawa, Dies at 79.
14. Retrieved from boards.ancestry.com/localities.northam.usa.states. kentucky.counties.barren/4054/mb.ashx

15. Jerry V. Stahl graciously provided this information in a telephone call, April 10, 2010.
16. Retrieved from leasingnews.org/archives/April%202008/04-16-08.htm.
17. en.wikipedia.org/wiki/Glasgow,_Kentucky. Reviewed April 6, 2009.

CHAPTER 14

1. Arthur N. Hill. Battalion on Iwo. *Marine Corps Gazette*. November 1945, Pg 27.
2. * indicates Posthumous Awards.
3. Benjamin Chambers, nephew to Justice Marion Chambers, first provided early family history. Phone conversation, Monday, May 4, 2009.
4. Stephen Hunter and John Bainbridge Jr. *American Gunfight: The Plot to Kill Harry Truman – and the Shoot-out that Stopped It*. New York: Simon & Schuster, 2005, Pg 102.
5. Benjamin Chambers first provided this reference. Phone conversation, May 4, 2009.
6. Rasmiliya Sporny. MU 'greats' elected to Hall of Fame. *The Parthenon*, July 3, 2003. Retrieved from marshallparthenon.com.
7. Jennifer J. Day. In correspondences April 19, 2009 to May 7, 2009.
8. Lieutenant Colonel Justice Marion "Mike" Chambers Jr. USMC (ret), took time to review, correct, and clarify factual material in the account of his father's life. In correspondences between November 15, 2009 and February 14, 2010.
9. The Tulagi account is adapted from Jon T. Hoffman, *Once A Legend*.
10. Arthur N. Hill. Battalion on Iwo. *Marine Corps Gazette*, November 1945, Pg 27.
11. Now a historic site, noted as Old Japanese Prison on tourist maps. See Loomis, Vincent and Ethell, Jeffrey. *Amelia Earhart: The Final Story*. New York: Random House, 1985.
12. Joseph H. Alexander. *CLOSING IN: Marines in the Seizure of Iwo Jima*. 1994.
13. Ibid.

14. Benjamin Chambers. Provided in phone conversation, Monday, May 4, 2009.

15. For example: Arthur N. Hill. Battalion on Iwo. *Marine Corps Gazette*, November 1945, Pg 27, and War on Japan's Doorstep. *Leatherneck Magazine*, November 1964, Pg 32.

16. Chalmers M. Roberts and Alfred E. Lewis. Assassin Slain, Another Shot at Truman's Door; Puerto Rican Terrorists Kill Guard, Wound 2; President Glimpses Battle's End from Window. *The Washington Post,* November 2, 1950. See also Stephen Hunter and John Bainbridge Jr. *American Gunfight: The Plot to Kill Harry Truman –and the Shoot-out that Stopped It.* New York: Simon & Schuster, 2005, pp 101-103.

17. Twins Steal Show As Father Get Nation's Highest Honor. *Mansfield News Journal*, November 2, 1950.

18. Stephen Hunter and John Bainbridge Jr., Pg 103.

19. Mike Chambers. In correspondence, February 14, 2010.

20. Charles R. Chambers. Retrieved from arlingtoncemetery.net/jmchambe.htm, June 4, 2005.

21. Benjamin Chambers provided copies, May 6, 2009.

22. August 3, 1982 Interment Ceremonies brochure provided by Ben Chambers.

23. Mike Chambers. In ccorrespondence, February 13, 2010.

24. West Virginians Awarded the Medal of Honor. *West Virginia History*, Volume XVII, Number 2, January 1956.

25. W.Va. Has 63 War Heroes Not 62: One Medal Winner's Name Was Overlooked. *Raleigh Register*, Beckley, West Virginia, Thursday, November 7, 1963, Pg 6.

26. Retrieved from files.usgwarchives.net/wv/statewide/military/medhonplaza.txt.

27. wvculture.org/HiStory/wvvets.html.

28. Retrieved from rootsweb.ancestry.com/~wvcccfhr/fame/wall.htm and cityofhuntingtonfoundation.com/pages/wall.htm: 2008 Induction Ceremony.

29. *Huntington Quarterly* Magazine Issue 35, 1999. Dagmar reference first provided by Benjamin Chambers, phone conversation, May 4, 2009.

30. James E. Casto, Associate Director for Public Information, Huntington, provided reference in correspondence, April 20, 2009.

31. Tim R. Massey. Wayne to honor late Col. Chambers. *The Herald-Dispatch*, January 9, 2002. Copy provided by Benjamin Chambers. May 6, 2009.

32. Retrieved from rockefeller.senate.gov/press/record_speech. cfm?id=292596&&.

33. Retrieved from legis.state.wv.us/Bulletin_Board/2004/rs/ House/H_DAILY_JOURNAL/February%2019.htm.

34. Special thanks to Jack Lengyel, Head Coach, Marshall University Thundering Herd football team, 1971-74 and Samuel Stanley, current Director of Athletic Development, Big Green, Marshall University for taking time to research this.

CHAPTER 15

1. U.S. Senator James Webb, author, from his speech at the Confederate Memorial, June 3, 1990.

2. Patricia K. Hall and Steven Ruggles. *Restless in the midst of their prosperity*. Department of History and Minnesota Population Center, University of Minnesota, June 2004.

3. William's cause of death is variously reported. The Arlington National Cemetery Web site reports he was killed in action. Other sources report that he was killed in a traffic accident either while on leave in New Zealand or on New Georgia Island in the Central Solomons.

4. Douglas Larsen. Marine Hero Braved Heavy Fire. *The Coshocton Tribune*, January 29, 1946.

5. AP Survey Shows Congressional Medal Winners in Pacific Live Quietly. *Billings Gazette,* Sunday August 14, 1949.

6. Top heroes honored. Long Beach, California, *Press-Telegram Monday,* October 31, 1977.

7. Mike Gardner. *The Humanity of Veterans Day*, posted November 11, 2008. Describing aspects of Sigler family life, also reported that Elsie Sigler "casually told a story about how she had sold the rights to Frank's story for $1.00 when Paramount Studios was making the *Sands of Iwo Jima*." Retrieved from blueweeds.typepad.com/blue_ weeds/family/.

8. Arlington National Cemetery Web site, September 18, 2004
9. Marines are not the only ones who have protected comrades from grenades. According to the Center for Mililtary History Online Web site, reviewed on June 4, 2008, of the 3,468 Medal of Honor recipients, no fewer than 142 men across services have earned the award by cradling a grenade.

CHAPTER 16

1. Mrs. Mel Blake, Southbridge Elementary Librarian, provided contact information for Rudy's extended family in correspondence, November 24, 2008. Rudy's first cousin, Rolland J. Julian, and his distant cousin Ralph Julian, who both continue to live in Sturbridge, provided some family history.
2. Steve Gilbert, historian, author, and contributor to *The Colonial Chronicle, A Newsletter of 18th & Early 19th Century North American Living History*. Information regarding Joseph Julian's life prior to his Marine service was derived from his article *Julian's valor has not been forgotten*. Agent Thomas A. Chamberland, Director of Veteran's Services in the Town of Sturbridge, contributed the article and other memorabilia.
3. Information regarding Rudy's family is derived from *The Great American Broadcast of 1945* Program, March 19, 1995.
4. Town marks Memorial Day; Ceremonies on tap in Sturbridge. Worcester *Telegram & Gazette*, Sunday, May 27, 2007.
5. Gus Steeves, staff writer. Iwo Jima vet, others honored by Historical Society. *Sturbridge Villager*, Friday, June 4, 2010, Pg 3.

CHAPTER 17

1. *Tommy*, in Complete Verse, Anchor Books: New York, 1988, Pg 396.
2. Pope's Ridge on Hill 100 was so-named following Captain Everett Parker Pope's actions there on September 19-20, 1944.
3. Retrieved from kymoh.com/about_kymoh.html.
4. Retrieved from findagrave.com.

CHAPTER 18

1. Micahel Takiff. *Brave men, gentle heroes: American fathers and sons in World War II and Vietnam.* New York, NY: Perennial, 2004, Pg 501.
2. From surnamedb.com/Surname/Fardy.
3. Lois Monson, ancestry researcher in Fargo, ND, provided many details of the Fardy background in February 2011. She referenced the 1920 U.S. Census, 1930 U.S. Census, Cook County, Illinois Marriage Indexes, WW II Draft Registration documents, the U.S. World War II Army Enlistment Records, and Ship Manifest records. Correspondences February 15-16, 2011. Birthdates for Martin and Mary do not always match up from one record to another, but various details like employment, residence addresses, and children's birthdates do match.
4. Mary's maiden name could not be confirmed. That she was a Kilkerman is derived from a single source, the mention of Martin's "sister-in-law" in the 1920 US Census data. Mary's date of birth might be in 1889 or November 6, 1895.
5. During the research into John Fardy's background, he was first believed to have been an only child until a 1945 newspaper article reporting his death was discovered. His two sisters were listed with his parents as his survivors. War Death Toll Up; 7 Yanks Die In Battle Zones. *Southtown Economist*, Wednesday, June 27, 1945, Pg 1.
6. Ship's Manifest record provided by Lois Monson. Mary is listed as 37-years of age. The three children's ages and birthdates in the manifest are consistent with other records.
7. Mary Fardy Is Hostess to 12 Sorority Girls. *Southtown Economist*, Sunday, October 4, 1936, Pg 12.
8. Gadabout's Notebook. *Southtown Economist*, Sunday, November 15, 1936, Pg 39.
9. Gadabout's Notebook. *Southeast Economist*, Thursday, January 7, 1937, Pg 8. Also, St. Joseph Auxiliary Gives a Benefit Party. *Southeast Economist*, Thursday, January 14, 1937, Pg 9.
10. Mercy High Auxiliary to Sponsor Party Wednesday. *Southtown Economist*, Sunday, March 20, 1938, Pg 8CW 12S.

11. Mrs. Martin Fardy to Be Hostess at Bunco Party. *Southtown Economist*, Wednesday, March 27, 1940, Pg 12.

12. Pious Workers Go on a Retreat: "60 Golden Hours" at Hillsdale Friary. *Life* Magazine, August 2, 1937, Pg 72. Correspondence on February 12, 2011, with Asbestos Worker Union Chicago Local 17 was unable to confirm that this Martin Fardy was a member of Local 17 or John's father.

13. Pat Hickey, Leo High School, provided links to John's 1940 senior photo, Senior Activities yearbook page, and the 1939-46 issues of *The Oriole* school paper in correspondences, February 15, 2011. John's photo was viewed on The Leo High School Alumni Association Web site at: leohsalumniassoc.com/images1940/ seniors_1940/pages/Seniors%20Du-%20Ha_jpg.htm.

14. From the 1940 Mercy High School yearbook. Material provided by Lois Monson.

15. Style Promenade Is Held At Mercy, *Southtown Economist*, Wednesday, May 22, 1940, Pg 27.

16. All material regarding Leo High School, its students, and the school newspaper was adapted from the 1939-46 issues of *The Oriole* found at The Leo High School Alumni Association Web site at: leohsalumniassoc.com/oriole1940/index.htm. Link provided by Pat Hickey.

17. From The Leo High School Alumni Association Web site at: leohsalumniassoc.com/images1940/seniors_1940/pages/Senior%20 Activities%20Dr-Gr_jpg.htm. Link provided by Pat Hickey.

18. From leohsalumniassoc.com.

19. Information retrieved from hickeysite.blogspot.com Monday, September 27, 2010, article, ...*With Both Hands: Leo High School's Medal of Honor Hero—Cpl. John P. Fardy*.

20. Mr. and Mrs. Martin J. Fardy, 8144 Calumet Ave., announce the engagement of their daughter, Mary Therese, *Southeast Economist*, Thursday, September 11, 1941, Pg 2.

21. From U.S. World War II Army Enlistment Records, 1938-46 and Social Security Death Index provided by Lois Monson.

22. Marriage license:{130B6447-EFC3-4EF7-B4C7-F98805075824}, File Number: 1949214. Cook County, Illinois Marriage Index, 1930-60, provided by Lois Monson.

23. Wins Award, *The Garfieldian*, May 18, 1939, Pg 11.
24. WW II Draft Registration, Serial No U-368, 8144 Calumet Avenue, Chicago, Telephone: Radcliffe 5771, provided by Lois Monson.
25. Confirmed in correspondence from Beth L. Crumley, CIV, Historian, USMC History Division, Historical Reference Branch, March 17, 2011. Beth provided both a Company C Muster Roll of Officers and Enlisted Men, as well as a copy of Evans F. Carlson's Operation Report of the period 4 November to 4 December 1942, dated December 20, 1942. Considerate and consistently helpful, Beth Crumley also forwarded April and May 1945 Muster Rolls for the 1st Battalion, 1st Marines on Okinawa; in correspondences, July to August 1, 2011.
26. Sergeant William Douglas Lansford, an Easy Company machine-gunner, 2d Raider Battalion. The Battle At Asamana: "We Caught Them With Their Pants Down." *Leatherneck* Magazine, November 2007, Pg 60.
27. Laurence Patrick Spillan, Jr. (339755), USMCR, Pvt, born September 15,1922, Date of Loss November 11, 1942. From dtic. mil/dpmo/wwii/reports/mar_m_s.htm and Chicago, Cook County Illinois Birth Certificate, provided by Lois Monson.
28. Different issues of *The Oriole* reported Joseph M. Auman as both a 1940 and 1941 class member. He was not pictured with classmates in what would have been his junior (1939) and senior yearbooks (1940) nor included in senior activities in the 1940 yearbook. It is likely that Joe left Leo High School after his sophomore year. He enlisted in the Marines on August 27, 1940, more than a year before America entered the war. His younger brother, William (Bill) was in the 1941 class and entered the service in June 1943.
29. 864 Southtown Men Killed; 253 Die In Pacific. *Southtown Economist—Victory Extra*, August 14, 1945, Pg 3.
30. To date, 464 Medal Citations have been awarded for actions during WWII, 266 of which are posthumous awards. These include awards that were made by presidents following later investigations of rediscovered lost documents, recommendations for upgrading, and allegations of racism. President Jimmy Carter awarded two Medals, including one to Guadalcanal veteran, Corporal Anthony

Casamento, USMC. President Bill Clinton awarded twenty-two Medals to Japanese Americans and seven to African Americans. He also presented the Medal to Major General James L. Day, USMC, who had earned the award as a corporal on Okinawa's Sugar Loaf Hill a week after Corporal Fardy had died on the island.

31. Retrieved from the President Harry S. Truman Library, truman-library.org/calendar and presidency.ucsb.edu. See in particular, March 13, 1946, Entry 12, Time 10:00 AM.

32. Park Forest Streets Will Honor Heroes—To Be Named for Winners Of Congressional Medals—Bravery Recalled, *Chicago Heights Star*, Friday, July 30, 1948, Page One. Also, Home Project's Street to be Named for John Fardy. *Southeast Economist*, Thursday, August 19, 1948, Pg 7.

33. Information derived from villageofparkforest.com.

34. docstoc.com/docs/34895209/MUKWONAGO-TOWN-BOARD-JANUARY-112_-2005.

35. Ray Pawlak, Holy Sepulchre Cemetery office manager, courteously provided the location and directions to John's gravesite, as well as a cemetery map showing the grave's location, on February 23, 2011.

36. Lois Monson provided Cook County Clerk's office, File 8172. Ray Pawlak provided confirmation and further information about Mary Therese Martin in phone conversations April 14-15, 2011. Holy Sepulchre files give Martin Fardy's age as 68-years. Depending on the records referenced, Mary Fardy was either 88 or 80-years-old when she died.

37. From Ancestry.com research, provided by Lois Monson.

38. Ray Pawlak provided details in phone conversations April 14-15, 2011.

39. Mary Collette (Tom) Dillon, John (Joan) Martin, Joseph (Maureen), Richard (Hannah), Ellen (the late Dave) Reppert, Michael, William "Billy" (deceased 3/10/75), and Gerard "Pudgy Joseph Martin (deceased 6/14/76).

40. James Furlong, Leo High School Class of 1965, Vietnam Veteran, U.S. Army, Distinguished Service Cross and Purple Heart recipient. Information provided in correspondence, May 5, 2011.

41. Ibid. Also, John J. Thometz, MD (retired), phone conversation, May 22, 2011.

42. Initially the accounts of the lives of John Fardy and Dale Hansen were meant to be a contrast between one hometown forgetting and another remembering a Medal of Honor recipient. John's biography was limited to three pages of text, based on his Citation, the usual Web site references, and a few archived Chicago newspaper articles. During the fourth rewrite of this book, Kim Crowley, editing, suggested adding some details to smooth out the transition from one paragraph to the next in John's short story. That led to the discovery of hickeysite.blogspot.com and Pat Hickey's recommendation to take a look at the archived issues of *The Oriole*.

43. Pat Hickey. In correspondence, February 19, 2011.

44. hickeysite.blogspot.com.

45. Pat Hickey. *Every Heart and Hand: A Leo High School Story*. Bloomington, Indiana: Author House, 2005, Pg 60.

46. Information provided by Pat Hickey in correspondence, February 19, 2011.

47. Richard Furlong, former president of the Leo High School Alumni Association, in correspondence, May 2, 2011.

48. James Furlong, in correspondence, May 5, 2011.

49. Lorraine Hansen of Norfolk, NE, Larry's wife, provided information regarding the relationships among the four Hansen brothers. Phone conversation, January 3, 2009.

50. Jason Minnick of Kuzelka-Minnick Funeral Home researched records and provided information regarding Dale Hansen's gravesite and Memorial display in phone conversations, January 2009.

51. R. Eli Paul, compiler. *Nebraska Hall of Fame*. Nebraska State Historical Society, 1997.

CHAPTER 19

1. "Nothing Man" lyrics and performance by Bruce Springsteen, 2002, in his twelfth studio album, *The Rising*.

2. Retrieved from srh.noaa.gov/oun/centennial/wxtimeline.php.

3. Retrieved from lexokalumni.org.

4. Smitty & Friends. *Time* Magazine, Monday, November 2, 1942. Retrieved from: time.com/time/magazine/article/0,9171,773829,00. html.

5. The author is grateful to Owen Smith for providing family details in correspondences, November 2008 to January 2009.

6. Owen Smith. Retrieved from johnluciansmith.blogspot.com.

7. Ibid.

8. Maj. John Smith Is Jinx to Japs. Kingston, New York, *The Kingston Daily Freeman*, November 10, 1942.

9. According to en.wikipedia.org/wiki/University_of_Oklahoma_ people, last reviewed February 21, 2011.

10. On www.ranker.com/list/notable-university-of-oklahoma-alumni-and-students.

11. Two Reserve Officers Join Marine Corps. *San Antonio Express*, July 15, 1936.

12. Owen Smith. In correspondence, January 5, 2009.

13. Portions derived from Louise Maddox Outland Smith's obituary, Norfolk, Cox Funeral Home, April 21, 2007. Retrieved from dmvobits.com/posts.cfm?st=54&obit=24144.

14. Dan Magill "Magill: Remembering former Bulldogs who gave their lives." Retrieved from onlineathens.com/stories/052509/foo_443545745.shtml.

15. Barrett Tillman. *Wildcat Aces of World War 2,* Oxford, United Kingdom, Osprey Publishing, 1995.

16. Hill Goodspeed. Always Faithful. *Naval Aviation News*, May-June, 2003.

17. Jon Guttman. A Marine at Midway. Interview of Sumner H. Whitten, *World War II Magazine*, July 2002.

18. Bureau of Aeronautics, Interview of Major John Smith, USMC, November 10, 1942.

19. *The Barker* Volume 1, Number 1. Retrieved from lexokalumni. org. John's son, Owen Smith, contributed much material for this article.

20. Mainland. *The Galveston Daily News*, December 13, 1942.

21. The Japs Better Look Out. Zanesville, Ohio, *The Times Recorder*, November 6, 1944.

22. Owen Smith. Retrieved from johnluciansmith.blogspot.com, December 11, 2008

23. Retrieved from johnluciansmith.blogspot.com, June 8, 2009.

24. Letter to Louise, October 5, 1942. Retrieved from johnluciansmith. blogspot.com, June 8, 2009.

25. Peter B. Mersky. *Time of The Aces: Marine Pilots in the Solomons, 1942-1944*. Washington, D.C.: Marine Corps Historical Center, 1993.

26. Retrieved from aviationarchaeology.com/src/USN/LLOct42.htm.

27. Richard Wilcox, pp 120-130.

28. Owen Smith. In correspondence, January 5, 2009.

29. As told to *Chicago Tribune* reporter during a 1990 Medal of Honor gathering. Reported by Richard Golstein, Richard E. Bush, Who Served on Okinawa, Dies at 79, *New York Times*, June 13, 2004.

30. Owen Smith. In correspondence, January 5, 2009 and lexokalumni. org.

31. Retrieved from centennialofflight.gov/essay/Aerospace/North-American/Aero37.htm.

32. As worn by John Basilone and Richard B. Anderson, and signed by Mike Clausen.

33. Portions derived from Arlington National Cemetery Web site, August 21, 2003.

34. *San Antonio Express*, August 11, 1964.

35. Viewed at uk.youtube.com/watch?v=9FXP16oykv8&feature=related.

36. James S. Tyree. Medal exhibit puts heroes on display. *NewsOK*, July 13, 2008.

37. The dispatcher and an officer at the Lexington Police Department first mentioned the monument at 89er Park. Pastor Virgil "Buck" Jordan of Grace Chapel, 118 W. Broadway, was considerate with his time on Easter Saturday, April 11, 2009, drove to both parks during a phone conversation, confirmed the location of the monuments, and provided descriptions of them.

38. Retrieved from Owen Smith's johnluciansmith.blogspot.com. This monument and others dedicated to Medal of Honor recipients can be viewed at waymarking.com/waymarks (/WMACZR_Col_John_L_Smith_Lexington_Oklahoma).

CHAPTER 20

1. Personal data provided by Sherri Clifford Alcorn, granddaughter in a telephone conversation, March 26, 2009.
2. Information provided by Sherri Alcorn, Jack's niece, telephone conversation on March 24, 2009.
3. Sources differ regarding whether or not Jack Kelso was promoted once he was in Korea.
4. Caruthers Hero Is Killed In Action In Korean War. *Fresno Bee Republican*, Tuesday, October 21, 1952, Pg 18.
5. Marine Hero Awards Set. Lubbock, Texas, *Evening Journal*, September 9, 1953.
6. Sherri Clifford Alcorn provided information regarding events in Jack's family after his death, telephone conversation, March 26, 2009.
7. Information regarding the Kelso Village School, if not otherwise cited, was derived from *The Fresno Bee* articles dated November 18, 1954, December 9, 1956, February 9, 1958, February 24, 1958, September 25, 1958, December 22, 1958, November 5, 1959, March 29, 1960, February 17, 1963.
8. Marines Get Caruthers War Hero's Medal! *The Fresno Bee*, Saturday, May 18, 1963, Pg 2-A.
9. Stephen E. Duke, Deputy AC/S, G3, MCRD/WRR, San Diego and Barbara McCurtis, Director of the San Diego Command Museum, researched this piece of history on this study's behalf. Barbara McCurtis also provided a photograph of the MCRD Kelso display.
10. Plaque Will Honor Caruthers Marine Hero. *Fresno Bee Republican*, Sunday, May 20, 1960, Pg 3B.
11. Located at 2202 West Tahoe Avenue.
12. Phone conversation, January 26, 2009.
13. Jacob Kelso of Laton, California provided this information in a phone conversation, January 31, 2009. Jacob is not related to Jack William Kelso.
14. Found at communitycorrespondent.com, December 15, 2008.
15. homeofheroes.com/myhero. Retrieved February 15, 2009.
16. ExTexas Ranger, Grandfather Of War Hero, Dies. *Fresno Bee Republican*, October 4, 1960, Pg 2.

17. Information provided by Sherri Clifford Alcorn, telephone conversation, March 26, 2009.
18. Lori Ramirez. In correspondence, April 13, 2009.
19. Mike Prager. In proud landing, it's Pappy Boyington Field. *The Spokesman-Review*, September 23, 2007.
20. Brad Branan. Crosses, ribbons, flowers honor Valley vets. *The Fresno Bee*, Saturday May 29, 2010.

CHAPTER 21

1. Some sources report this as Hill 97.
2. Marine from Mindoro Killed in Hill Battle, Parents Learn. *The La Crosse Tribune*, October 18, 1950.
3. co.la-crosse.wi.us/townoffarmington/docs/cemeteries.htm updated May 30, 2008.
4. Retrieved from La Crosse Public Library Archives at lplcat.lacrosse. lib.wi.us/genealogy/cemeteryhistories.
5. Richard D. Camp. *Battleship Arizona's Marines at War*. Osceola, Wisconsin: Zenith Press, 2006, pp 70, 121.
6. For example, Weather Edge Ledgestone
7. Mary Kaufmann, La Crosse County Facilities Department, in a most considerate manner, provided current photographs of the Memorial and a Park map in correspondence, July 24, 2009. One of her photos appears at the end of this chapter.
8. Retrieved from La Crosse Public Library Archives at lplcat.lacrosse. lib.wi.us/genealogy/cemeteryhistories.

CHAPTER 22

1. *The Speeches of Daniel Webster and His Masterpieces*. Benjamin Franklin Tefft, Philadelphia: Porter & Coates, 1854, Pg 221.
2. Retrieved from freepages.genealogy.rootsweb.ancestry.com/~kykinfolk/ web/lewisgree/pafg59.htm#10793.
3. Posthumous Medal of Honor Awarded. Redlands, California, *Redlands Daily Facts*, February 01, 1952, reported that he and Kathren had a son and three daughters together.

4. *Independent Long Beach*, California, February 2, 1952.

5. *Marine Corps Times*. Republished in Leatherneck.com, December 29, 2003.

6. Dead Marine Heros Get Highest Honor. *Panama City News*, Florida, January 20, 1954.

7. Retrieved from cem.va.gov/cems/nchp/Marietta.asp.

8. Retrieved from freepages.genealogy.rootsweb.ancestry.com/~gnut/mnc.html.

9. For example, List of people from Atlanta, a list of famous people who lived in the area in and near Atlanta, Georgia, including both natives and residents. Retrieved from en.wikipedia.org/wiki/List_of_people_from_Atlanta.

10. *Corporal Lee Hugh Phillips*. From ourgeorgiahistory.com, Golden Ink, Woodstock, Georgia. Retrieved on December 1, 2006.

11. Fifth Basic Class material derived from R. E. Sullivan, Colonel, USMC (Ret.), January 12, 2000. Retrieved from *The Korean War* at rt66.com/~korteng/SmallArms/jim.htm.

12. War: Retreat of the 20,000. *Time* Magazine, Monday, December 18, 1950.

13. In addition, the Marines suffered an additional 7,338 non-combat, cold-weather casualties.

14. Marine Corps Confers MH Upon Lost Sergeant With Hope He's Alive. *Stars and Stripes*, Wednesday, December 5, 1951, Pg 4.

15. Honor Marines Posthumously. Hagerstown, Maryland, *The Daily Mail*, March 31, 1954.

16. Pocatello *Idaho State Journal*, Wednesday, April 7, 1954, Pg 5.

17. Book of Isaiah, 6:8.

18. Parents Accept Medal of Honor. *San Antonio Express*, Tuesday, August 5, 1952, Pg 12.

19. Retrieved from house.state.tx.us/news/release.php?id=1298.

20. Keith A. Milks. The Lore of the Corps, Team leader showed courage on Hill 104, February 16, 2004. Retrieved from leatherneck.com/forums/archive/index.php/t-12557.html.

21. '...i was stabbed by a bayonet.' Norfolk, Virginia, *The Ledger-Star*, June 25, 2010.

22. From: Final Listing For The 1st Session, 105th Congress, Pub. L. 105-1 through Pub. L. 105-153, December 22, 1997. Retrieved from archives.gov/federal-register/laws/past/105-first-session.txt.

23. 98—H9159. Retrieved from rilin.state.ri.us/billtext98/huose-text98/h9159.htm.

24. By Keith A. Milks. *The Lore of the Corps*, February 16, 2004.

25. Ibid.

26. As per homeofheroes.com/moh/states/me.html, retrieved on November 7, 2007.

27. Medal of Honor to Penna. Marine. *Lock Haven Express*, Monday, July 7, 1953, Pg 5.

28. Her Son Won Medal of Honor. *Charleston Daily Mail*, July 8, 1953, Pg 34.

29. Medal of Honor for Pennsylvania Hero. *The Chester Times*, September 10, 1953, Pg 45.

30. 5 Dead Marines Awarded Medals. *Billings Gazette*, September 10, 1953, Pg 1.

31. Two Young Marines Receive Congressional Medal of Honor. Kalispell, Montana, *Daily Inter Lake*, Wednesday, January 20, 1954, Pg 6.

CHAPTER 23

1. His speech delivered at the Philadelphia State House, August 1, 1776.

2. *Restless in the midst of their prosperity*. Department of History and Minnesota Population Center, University of Minnesota, June 2004.

3. Ryerson Mausert, Jr., provided information regarding the Mausert side of the family in enjoyable telephone conversations, 12-06-08 and 02-15-09.

4. Patricia and John Barnes provided information in correspondences, in particular material involving Rickie's younger brother.

5. Retrieved courtesy of Ken Gottry, kgottryjoy.gottry.com/CambHistory_WebSite/Frederick_W_Mausert_III.htm.

6. Dave Thornton. Tales of Old Cambridge. *The Eagle*, Vol. 27 No. 47 November 22, 2007.
7. Phone conversation on February 13, 2009 and correspondence.
8. Correspondence, March 9, 2009.
9. Posted by thedrifter, *Marine bond endures all*, December 20, 2007. Retrieved from leatherneck.com/forums/showthread.php?t=58603
10. John and Patricia Barnes provided a copy of this letter, February 6, 2009.
11. A term borrowed from the Chinese by Major Carlson when he was forming the 2d Marine Raider Battalion. Gung Ho means "To work together in harmony," and he used it as an enthusiastic expression to inspire his battalion. *Gung Ho!* was used as the title of the 1943 movie about the raid on Makin Island.
12. Believed to be Eddie LeBaron, NFL quarterback; Washington Redskins, (1952-1953, 1955-1959), and Dallas Cowboys (1960-63).
13. William Blake (1757-1827). In David V. Erdman, Harold Bloom, William Golding, *Prologue to King Edward the Fourth*, *The Complete Poetry & Prose of William Blake*. New York: Random House, Inc, 1997.
14. Letter from Jim Hughes to Joseph A. Lenard, April 29, 1991, retrieved courtesy of Ken Gottry, kgottryjoy.gottry.com/CambHistory_WebSite/Frederick_W_Mausert_III.htm.
15. Ibid.
16. *Once a Legend*, pp 208-209.
17. On a Hill in Korea. Retrieved from koreanwar—educator.org/topics/poets/p.shifflette.htm.
18. Jon T. Hoffman. *Once a Legend*, Pg 36.
19. Ibid, Pg. 208.
20. Local Man's Grandson Killed in Korea. *The North Adams, Massachusetts, Transcript*, November 2, 1951, Pg 3.
21. Native of Greenwich Loses Life in Korea. *The Troy Record*, November 3, 1951, Pg 9.
22. Congressional Medal Awarded Sgt. Mausert. *The North Adams, Massachusetts, Transcript*, July 1, 1952, Pg 3.

23. Marine's Mother to Receive Medal. *Gettysburg Times*, September 1, 1952, Pg 8, and Kin Get Medals of Honor of 3 Dead Marines. *The Winona Republican—Herald*, September 5, 1952, Pg 11.
24. Dave Thornton. In series of correspondences, November 28-29, 2008.

CHAPTER 24

1. Janet (Coker) Artz, Ron's sister, provided family information in correspondences April 24 and April 27, 2009, and in conversation at Fairview Cemetery, September 18, 2009.
2. Materials and photographs were provided by Karen (Ball) Greenly, October 9, 2009.
3. Lyrics by Robert Fletcher and Cole Porter, music by Cole Porter, 1934.
4. Phone conversation with Karen (Ball) Greenly, October 10, 2008.
5. Janet (Coker) Artz. In correspondence April 24, 2009.
6. Information retrieved from capmarine.com/.
7. Adapted from accounts of Jimmy D. Murphy and Gerald M. Blink. Retrieved from mikecompany33.com/MikeHistory.html.
8. Robyn Nicodemus, Ron's niece, provided letters and records, October 15, 2009.
9. Janet (Coker) Artz. In correspondence, April 24, 2009.
10. Retrieved from rapidcitylibrary.org/lib_info/1972Flood/index.asp.
11. Becci Thomas, curator of the Sallows Military Museum. In correspondence, Wednesday, July 16, 2008.
12. Janet (Coker) Artz. In correspondence, May 1, 2009.
13. Donald, Lyle, Ronda, Charlet, and Cristy Coker.
14. Lyrics by Robert Fletcher and Cole Porter, music by Cole Porter, 1934.
15. BookSurge Publishing, Amazon.com, Inc.subsidiary, 2002, Pg 116 and 117.
16. Retrieved from waymarking.com/waymarks/WM4HR8.
17. Dixie Nelson of the Alliance Chamber of Commerce first provided information about Ron Coker's display at the Sallows Military Museum. In correspondence, July 15, 2008.

18. Becci Thomas correspondence, July 16, 2008.
19. Comment to Greyhawk's *The Mudville Gazette* November 09, 2007, article from Chatter (and Numbers that Matter) Or: "How the War was Won (Part one)." Posted by bman November 10, 2007, 03:20 PM. Retrieved from mudvillegazette.com/archives/009692.html.
20. Received from Janet Artz, on April 30, 2009.
21. Retrieved from patriotguard.org/ALLForums/tabid/61/forumid/186/postid/1158223/view/topic/Default.aspx+Nebraska+State+Veterans+Cemetery+at+Alliance.
22. Memorial Day services county courthouse. Viewed at alliancetimes.com/Video.htm and youtube.com.
23. Dire Straits. *Brothers In Arms*. London: AIR Studios, May 13, 1985.
24. In correspondence, October 9, 2009, Karen Greenly reported that the Marines from the squad did not want their names mentioned in published material.
25. Provided by Robyn, in correspondence, October 11, 2009. See veteransmusicministry.com.
26. Karen (Ball) Greenly provided the description of the memorial case in correspondence, March 29, 2011.

CHAPTER 25

1. *Combat Letters Home*. Bryn Mawr, PA: Dorrance, 1985.
2. John S. Bowman. *The Vietnam War*, 1985.
3. According to Defense Intelligence Agency Reference Notes, Incident number: 62100606.KIA, LCpl Miguel A. Valentine, Jr. passenger, Cpl. Thomas E. Anderson, crewchief, Sgt. Richard E. Hamilton, gunner, Sgt. Jerald W. Pendell, passenger, and 1stLt Michael J. Tunney, co-pilot, were killed in an HMM-163 Sikorsky UH-34D helicopter crash out of Da Nang on October 6, 1962. Passengers also included HM2 Gerald Norton, Navy Corpsman and Lt Gerald Griffin, Navy Flight Surgeon. The flight was providing SAR protection for an ARVN troop lift, encountered mechanical failure, and crashed into a jungle-covered hillside, fifteen miles southeast of Tam Ky. The sole survivor, the pilot, suffered serious injuries.

4. USMC History and Museum Division. See also James E. Livingston, et al, Pg 145.

5. U.S. Department of Defense, Washington Headquarters Service News Release April 25, 2005 and correspondences with Robert Aquilina, CIV, USMC History Division, Reference Branch.

6. The MIA numbers cited here are estimates derived from a variety of sources regarding Americans unaccounted for in Southeast Asia. Numbers vary slightly among sources.

7. Amy Wiesner Willson. Services Planned for Vietnam War Pilot's Return, Funeral, *Army.Mil*, front page, December 14, 2010.

8. Walter Lippmann. *Salina Journal*, May 7, 1967, Pg 4.

9. Retrieved from en.wikipedia.org/wiki/Eldora_Speedway.

10. Marine's Parents Receive Son's Medal. *Sandusky Register*, April 17, 1968, Pg 10.

11. Retrieved from a 03-03-01 Note on virtualwall.org/, provided by a fellow Marine, gtcardi53@aol.com.

12. Marine Who Gave Life For Buddies Honored By Nation. *Mexia Texas Daily News*, April 16, 1968, Pg 1.

13. *Charleston Daily Mail*, April 16, 1968, Pg 1.

14. 9 Ohioans on death list from Viet. Elyria, Ohio, *Chronicle Telegram*, April 4, 1967, Pg 4.

15. Receive Son's Honor. *Joplin Globe*, Missouri, April 17, 1968.

16. Receive Son's Honor. *Northwest Arkansas Times*, April 17, 1968, Pg 6.

17. Parents Get Hero Son's Honor Medal. *San Antonio Express*, Texas, April 17, 1968, Pg 11.

18. Covers Grenade, Dies; Honor Rossburg Youth. Newark, Ohio, *Advocate*, April 16, 1968, Pg 13.

19. *El Paso Herald-Post*, Section B, Page 2 Monday, April 22, 1968.

20. Retrieved from ohsweb.ohiohistory.org/exhibits/moh.

21. Retrieved from development.ohio.gov/research/files/p0006.pdf.

22. Purple Heart Recipients directory, homepages.rootsweb.ancestry. com/~sebring/pstory.htm#petersl.

23. *The Van Nuys News*, May 24, 1972, Pg 3-A.

24. Retrieved from aboveandbeyondfilm.com/perkins/.

25. *The Van Nuys News*, May 24, 1972, Pg 3-A.

26. Little is known about the family of William Perkins. His younger brother, Robert Brian Perkins, an artist, died of cancer in 1978 at the age of twenty-five and is buried with him at San Fernando Mission Cemetery.

27. Wesley Lee Fox. *Marine Rifleman: Fifty-three Years in the Corps.* Washington, D.C., Brassey's Inc, 2002.

28. Odessa Marine Due Nation's Highest Honor. *The Odessa American,* Sunday, April 19, 1970, Pg 1.

29. Several sources noted his death to be in 1979, though this seems to be an error.

30. Veronica Sandate. 'Pure country' honored: Fallen soldier remembered with renaming ceremony. *Odessa American,* February 5, 2009. Retrieved from oaoa.com/news/wilson_25974___article.html/ mac_odessa.html.

31. Sunday, June 20, 1999, Pg 7.

32. Stacy St. Clair. Marine killed in Vietnam is honored: Memorial placed at Hinsdale school for winner of Medal of Honor. *Daily Herald,* May 26, 2003, Pg D-6.

33. Cordy Phipps Henry. Memorial left May 31, 2001, at virtualwall. org/dp/PhippsJW01a.htm.

34. Michael R. McCarty. *Lest We Forget.* May 23, 2008. Retrieved from aroundthescuttlebutt.blogspot.com/2008_05_01_archive.html.

35. Retrieved from mishalov.com/Phipps.html, message received on April 12, 1999.

36. *Life* Magazine, Volume 66, No. 25, June 27, 1969, pp 20-31.

37. Some sources note that more servicemen than the 242 died in hostile actions during that week. For example, the Army's 1st Battalion (Mechanized), 50th Infantry Association, reports that photos of Jerome Collins and Steven Grubb were not in the article. Retrieved from ichiban1.org/html/news.htm. Also U. S. Army Medal of Honor recipient First Lieutenant Robert Leslie Poxon, 22-years-old of Detroit Michigan, killed in action in Tay Ninh Province while serving with Troop B, 1st Squadron, 9th Cavalry, 1st Cavalry Division, June 2, 1969, was not mentioned in the article.

38. *The Van Nuys Valley News,* Tuesday, April 21, 1970.

39. Sharon Corby, cousin. Message received at mishalov.com/MedalofHonor, June 28, 1999.

40. As noted by Michael R. McCarty in *Lest We Forget*, May 23, 2008, aoundthescuttlebutt.blogspot.com/2008_05_01_archive.html.

41. Retrieved from patriotfiles.com, *Yearly Chronologies of the United States Marine Corps - 1990*.

42. Wilbur R. "Wib" Dias obituary. *Daytona Beach News-Journal*, May 9, 2010.

43. From *Vietnam Veterans Memorial Fund, Virtual Wall*, September 25, 1999.

44. Paul Gibbs. Message left at Medal of Honor, mishalov.com/Dias.html, May 6, 2003.

45. Tracy Dias LaFleme. Message left at Medal of Honor, mishalov.com/Dias.html, October 4, 2000.

46. Derived from "Greater love hath no man than this, that a man lay down his life for his friends." John 15:13.

47. For example, a short *What Once Was* paragraph, recalled Ralph's death, The *Indiana Gazette*, Tuesday, September 19, 2000, Pg 21, M-3.

48. Two medal recipients to be honored, *Indiana Gazette*, May 26, 2001, Pg 3.

49. Retrieved from post-gazette.com/newslinks/wallnames3.asp.

50. Retrieved from post-gazette.com/regionstate/20000425medalside8.asp.

51. Retrieved from legislature.state.oh.us/JournalText127/SJ-06-13-07.pdf.

52. Deanne Johnson, staff writer. A day for Dias: Leetonia soldier honored with highway designation. Lisbon, Ohio, *Morning Journal News*, May 24, 2009.

53. Retrieved from history.army.mil/moh.html, Medal of Honor Recipients, World War II (M-S).

54. Charles Daniel Taylor. *Twenty Miles to Rome: The Story of South Carolina's First Medal of Honor Winner in World War II*. A Clemson University Graduate School History Thesis, August 2009.

Retrieved from etd.lib.clemson.edu/documents/1285611727/ Taylor_clemson_0050M_10328.pdf.

55. On the west side if Liberty, at end of West Front Street, the cemetery appears as either Gantt Cemetery or Westview Cemetery on old maps.

56. United States Census Bureau Population Estimates.

57. Brian Scott submitted this page with photos, on September 25, 2008. The monument can be viewed at HMdb.org/marker. asp?marker=11770.

58. scstatehouse.net/sess115_2003-2004/bills/5297.htm.

59. Congressional Record (May 14, 2007) and govtrack.us/congress/ record.xpd?id=110-h20070514-17.

CHAPTER 26

1. *The Jerusalem Bible*, Doubleday, Garden City, New York, 1968.

2. Jay Morgan. Provided much of the family background in phone conversations April 8 and April 11, 2009 and in correspondence April 20, 2009.

3. M. A. Jackson. At the Cemetery. *Mt. Lebanon Magazine*, October 2003, Pg 38. Retrieved from mtlebanon.org/DocumentView. asp?DID=1824.

4. Jay Morgan. In correspondence April 20, 2009.

5. William Standring. The Story of Jack Lucas. *Marine Corps Magazine*, Summer 1996.

6. Jay Morgan. In phone conversation, April 8, 2009.

7. For example, mt. lebanon, about this issue, pg 1. Retrieved from mtlebanon.org/DocumentView.asp?DID=1820.

8. In Focus: HONORING A HERO. *Mt. Lebanon Magazine*, April 2004, Pg 64.

9. Jay Morgan provided this segment, in phone conversation, April 8, 2009.

10. Departs for WestPac. Retrieved from: uss-newport-news.com/hist/ firstDeploy.htm.

11. Thunder goes to War. Retrieved from home.att.net/~dgoad/photos3.html.

CHAPTER 27

1. Micahel Takiff, p 514.
2. In Focus: HONORING A HERO, Mt. Lebanon Magazine, April 2004, Pg 65.
3. Survivor salutes a Vietnam hero. Vince Guerrieri, Pittsburgh *Tribune-Review*, Wednesday, February 25, 2004.
4. The name "Teufel-hunden" was given to the Marines by their German adversaries in the WWI Battle of Belleau Wood and was afterwards traditionally accepted by Marines as an affectionate nickname for themselves. It was appropriate that the Corps had a dog as its mascot, later named for the most decorated of Marines, Chesty Puller.
5. Description of VCB adapted from *Pop a Yellow Smoke and Other Memories: A Marine's Poignant and Humorous Stories of Time in VietNam.* W. Charles Truitt, Ozark, AL: ACW Press, 2005.
6. The account of this operation was adapted from two primary sources: Wesley Fox and C. Douglas Sterner, *Operation Dewey Canyon*, homeofheroes,com/wesleyfox/, retrieved November 19, 2005 and Wesley Lee Fox, *Marine Rifleman: Forty-three Years in the Corps.* Washington, D.C., Brassey's Inc, 2002.
7. Retrieved from virtualwall.org/dm/MorganWD01a.htm. Comment posted June 8, 2005.
8. Reported in U.S. Marines in Vietnam High Mobility and Standown, 1969.
9. A Luoi is an ethnic Ta Oi village on Highway 548. HW 548 started in Laos, ran the length of the A Shau, and was a major branch of the Ho Chi Minh Trail. Just west of the village, Ap Ba Mountain in the A Shau Valley was Hill 937 (3,074 feet in elevation) on American tactical maps. A ten day battle occurred there May 10-20, 1969. The media referred to it as Hamburger Hill.
10. Survivor salutes a Vietnam hero. Vince Guerrieri, Pittsburgh *Tribune-Review*, Wednesday, February 25, 2004.
11. C. Douglas Sterner, Operation Dewey Canyon, Home of Heroes Website, 2005.
12. Provided by Jay Morgan in phone conversation April 11, 2009.

CHAPTER 28

1. Go Rest High On That Mountain, *When Love Finds You*. Nashville: MCA, June 7, 1994.
2. Ken Wentzel, Class of 1966, in correspondence, Sunday, May 31, 2009.
3. The author is grateful for the extra effort extended by Michelle Kramer, Interim Librarian, Mt. Lebanon High School, who provided photographs of the monument, April 18, 2009. See one of her photographs at the end of this chapter.
4. Correspondences, March 31, 2009 through April 2009.
5. Correspondence, March 31, 2009.
6. Earl Kohnfelder, Mt. Lebanon Welcome, *Pittsburgh Post-Gazette*, June 10, 1991, Page A2. Retrieved at docs.newsbank.com/s/ InfoWeb/aggdocs/NewsBank/0EADE859A869C895/0F3651C 2407CC74B. Reference provided by Michelle Kramer, Interim Librarian, Mt. Lebanon High School, April 18, 2009.
7. Rene Rabold Dormont, A Glowing Tribute, Pittsburgh Post-Gazette, June 27, 1991, Page S3. Retrieved at docs.newsbank. com/s/InfoWeb/aggdocs/NewsBank/0EADE89364AD1431/0F36 51C2407CC74B. Reference provided by Michelle Kramer, April 18, 2009.
8. Information, description and photographs kindly provided by Michelle Kramer, Interim Librarian, Mt. Lebanon High School, in correspondence, April 18, 2009.
9. Retrieved from post-gazette.com/newslinks/wallnames3.asp.
10. Retrieved from post-gazette.com/regionstate/20000425medalside8. asp.
11. In Focus: HONORING A HERO, *Mt. Lebanon Magazine*, April, 2004, Pg 65.
12. Jessica Morgan, niece. Retrieved from virtualwall.org/dm/ MorganWD01a.htm, message posted on October 23, 2004.
13. David Englehart, cousin. Retrieved from virtualwall.org/dm/ MorganWD01a.htm, message posted on November 12, 2007.
14. Correspondence, May 4, 2009.

15. Kenneth Wentzel. In correspondence, May 31, 2009.
16. virtualwall.org/dm/MorganWD01a.htm.
17. Carol Delfino. In correspondences, April 17-20, 2009. Phone conversation with Alex, April 21, 2009.

CHAPTER 29

1. Japanese Proverb.
2. *The Faithful Gardener,* HarperSanFrancisco, 1995, Pg 76.
3. The impact of trauma on child development requires special consideration in regard to resilience. Psychology has been carefully studying this at least as far back as the early 1960s. For example, physician C. Henry Kempe and colleagues identified the existence of a *battered-child syndrome* as a valid clinical condition in 1962. See their Journal of the American Medical Association article. Research findings generally suggest that the majority of children who encounter trauma, given time and a supportive response from caregivers, do in fact gradually return to "being themselves." It does appear that the majority of children have some degree of resilience.
4. Luthar, S. S., Cicchetti, D., & Becker, B. (2000). The construct of resilience: A critical evaluation and guidelines for future work. *Child Development, 71,* pp 543-562.
5. Anne Masten, Professor of Child Psychology, University of Minnesota, 1994, *Resilience in individual development: Successful adaptation despite risk and adversity. In M. C. Wang & E. W. Gordon (Eds.), Educational resilience in inner-city America. Hillsdale, NJ: Erlbaum.*
6. Professional conference, *After the tragedy: Resilience and posttraumatic growth.* Fargo, ND, March 21, 2003. H. Katherine O'Neill, PhD specializes in the study of trauma and disaster and the treatment of its effects.
7. Speech at the Sorbonne, Paris, France, April 23, 1910.
8. Reflections From An American Hero, *The Messenger*, Eldred WWII Museum, Eldred, PA, December 1999.
9. William Honan, Ex-Marine Honored for Bravery in Korea, *New York Times*, April 8, 2000.
10. Thomas Carlyle (1795-1881), *Past and Present*, 1843.

REFERENCES

Alexander, Joseph H. *Closing In: Marines in the Seizure of Iwo Jima.* Washington, D.C.: Marine Corps History and Museums Division, 1994.

Alexander, Joseph H. *The Final Campaign: Marines in the Victory on Okinawa.* Washington, D.C.: Marine Corps Historical Center, 1996.

Alexander, Joseph H. *The Battle History of the U.S. Marines: A Fellowship of Valor.* New York: HarperCollins Publishers, 1997.

Alexander, Joseph H. *Storm Landings: Epic Amphibious Battles in the Central Pacific.* Annapolis, MD: Naval Institute Press, 1997.

Alexander, Joseph H. *Edson's Raiders: The 1st Marine Raider Battalion in World War II.* Annapolis, MD: Naval Institute Press, 2001.

Ballinger, Lee. *The Outpost War: U.S. Marines in Korea, Vol I, 1952.* Dulles, Virginia: Brasey's, 2000.

Ballinger, Lee. *The Final Crucible: U. S. Marines in Korea, Vol II, 1953.* Washington, D.C.: Brasey's, Inc., 2001.

Bartley, Whitman S. *Iwo Jima, Amphibious Epic.* Nashville: Battery Press, 1997. Reprint of Historical Section, Headquarters USMC 1954 edition.

Bowman, John S: Ed. *The Vietnam War: An Almanac.* New York: World Almanac Publications, 1985.

Bradley, James. *Flags of Our Fathers.* New York: Bantam, 2000.

Brady, James. *Hero of the Pacific: The Life of Marine Legend John Basilone.* Hoboken, New Jersey: John Wiley & Sons Inc., 2010.

Cerasini, Marc. *Heroes: U.S. Marine Corps Medal of Honor Winners.* New York, Berkley Publishing, 2002.

Chapin, John C. *Breaching the Marianas: The Battle for Saipan.* Washington, D.C.: Marine Corps Historical Center, 1994.

Chenoweth, H. Avery. *Semper Fi: The Definitive Illustrated History of the U.S. Marines.* New York: Sterling Publishing Company, 2005.

Clark, George B. *His Road to Glory: The Life and Times of "Hiking Hiram" Bearss, Hoosier Marine.* Pike, New Hamshire: The Brass Hat, 2000.

Clark, George B: Ed. *United States Marine Corps Medal of Honor Recipients: A Comprehensive Registry.* Jefferson, NC: McFarland & Company, 2005.

Coram, Robert. *Brute: The Life of Victor Krulak, U.S. Marine.* New York: Little, Brown & Company, 2010.

Davis, Burke. *Marine! The Life of Chesty Puller.* New York: Little, Brown & Company, 1962.

Dekever, Andrew J. *Here Rests In Honored Glory: Life Stories Of Our Country's Medal Of Honor Recipients.* Bennington VT: Merriam Press, 2008.

Foss, Joe. *A Proud American: The Autobiography of Joe Foss.* New York: Pocket Books, 1992.

Fox, Wesley Lee. *Marine Rifleman: Forty-three Years in the Corps.* Washington, D.C., Brassey's Inc, 2002.

Gamble, Bruce. *The Black Sheep.* Novato, CA: Presidio Press, 1998.

Gamble, Bruce. *Black Sheep One: The Life of Gregory "Pappy" Boyington.* Novato, CA: Presidio Press, 2000.

Gayle, Gordon D. *Bloody Beaches: The Marines at Pelelui*. Washington, D.C.: Marine Corps Historical Center, 1996.

Hoffman, Carl W. *Saipan: The Beginning of the End*. Washington, D.C.: Historical Section, Headquarters USMC, 1950.

Hoffman, Jon T. *From Makin to Bougainville: Marine Raiders in the Pacific War*. Washington, D.C.: Marine Corps Historical and Museum Division, 1995.

Hoffman, Jon T. *Once a Legend: "Red Mike" Edson of the Marine Raiders*. Novato, CA: Presidio Press, 2000.

Hoffman, Jon T. *Chesty: The Story of Lieutenant General Lewis B. Puller*. Random House, 2001.

Hough, Frank O., Ludwig, Verle E., & Shaw, Henry Jr. *History of the U.S. Marine Corps in WWII Vol I-Pearl Harbor to Guadacanal*. PCN 19000262400. Historical Branch, G-3 Division, Headquarters, U. S. Marine Corps, 1968.

Hough, Frank O., Ludwig, Verle E., & Shaw, Henry I. Jr. *Pearl Harbor to Gaudalcanal: History of the Marine Corps Operations in World War II, Volume 1*. Nashville: Battery Press, 1993. Reprint of 1958 edition.

Krulack, Victor H. *First to Fight: An Inside View of the U.S. Marine Corps*. Annapolis, MD: Naval Institute Press, 1984.

Lanning, Michael Lee & Stubbe, Ray William. *Inside Force Recon: Recon Marines in Vietnam*. New York: Ballantine Books, 1989.

Livingston, James E., Heaton, Colin D., & Lewis, Ann-Marie. *Noble Warrior: The Life of Maj. Gen. James E. Livingston, USMC (Ret.), Medal of Honor*. Minneapolis, MN: Zenith Press, 2010.

Lucas, Jack H. & Drum, D.K. *Indestructible: The Unforgettable Story of a Marine Hero at the Battle of Iwo Jima.* Cambridge, MA: Da Capo Press, 2006.

Lundstrom, John B. *The First Team And the Guadalcanal Campaign.* Annapolis, MD: Naval Institute Press, 1994.

Mersky, Peter B. *U.S. Marine Corps Aviation, 1912-Present.* Baltimore: Nautical & Aviation Publishing Company of America, 1986.

Mersky, Peter B. *Time of The Aces: Marine Pilots in the Solomons, 1942-1944.* Washington, D.C.: Marine Corps Historical Center, 1993.

Miller, Thomas G. *Cactus Air Force.* New York: Harper and Row, 1969.

Mueller, Joseph N. *Guadalcanal 1942: The Marines Strike Back.* Oxford: Osprey Publishing, 1992.

Myers, William L. *Honor the Warriors: The United States Marines in Vietnam:* Lafayette, LA: Redoubt Press, 2000.

Nalty, Bernard C. *Cape Gloucester: The Green Inferno.* Washington, D.C.: Marine Corps Historical and Museum Division, 1994.

Norman, Michael. *These Good Men: Friendships Forged from War.* New York: Crown Books, 1989.

Paige, Mitchell. *A Marine Named Mitch.* New York: Vantage Press,1975.

Phillips, Michael M. *The Gift of Valor: A War Story.* New York: Broadway Books, 2005.

Pisor, Robert. *The End of the Line: The Siege of Khe Sanh.* New York: W. W. Norton & Company, Inc., 1982.

Proser, Jim. *"I'm Staying with My Boys..." The Heroic Life of Sgt. John Basilone, USMC.* Lightbearer Hilton Head Island, SC: Communications Co., 2004.

O'Brien, Cyril J. *Liberation: Marines in the Recapture of Guam.* Washington, D.C.: Marine Corps Historical Center, 1994.

Ricks, Thomas E. *Making the Corps.* New York: Scribner, 1997.

Robbins, James S. *This Time We Win: Revisiting the Tet Offensive.* New York: Encounter Books, 2010.

Ross, Bill D. *Iwo Jima: Legacy of Valor.* New York: The Viking Press, 1976.

Russ, Martin. *Breakout: The Chosin Reservoir Campaign, Korea 1950.* New York: Penguin Books, 1999.

Sherrod, Robert. *Tarawa: The Story of a Battle.* Fredericksburg, Texas: Admiral Nimitz Foundation, 1973.

Stanton, Shelby L. *Vietnam Order of Battle.* Mechanicsburg, PA: Stackpole Books, 2003.

Takiff, Micahel. *Brave men, gentle heroes: American fathers and sons in World War II and Vietnam.* New York, NY: Perennial, 2004.

Truitt, W. Charles. *Pop a Yellow Smoke and Other Memories: A Marine's Poignant and Humorous Stories of Time in VietNam.* Ozark, AL: ACW Press, 2005.

Walton, Frank E. *Once They Were Eagles: The Men of the Black Sheep Squadron.* The University Press of Kentucky: Lexington, KY, 1986.

Warren, James A. *American Spartans: The U.S. Marines: A Combat History from Iwo Jima to Iraq.* New York: Free Press, Simon & Schuster, Inc., 2005.

Weise, William. *Memories of Dai Do* (DVD). Marine Corps Association, 2004.

Wukovitz, John. *Pacific Alamo: The Battle for Wake Island.* New York: New American Library, 2003.

Williams-Burden, Bruce. *Luminous Base: Corpsmen and Helicopters, Courage and Sacrifice.* Luminous Book, 2010.

ABOUT THE AUTHOR

TERENCE W. BARRETT graduated from the College of Wooster, Ohio. After seven years in the U.S. Marine Corps, he earned advanced degrees from the University of Southern California, North Dakota State University, and the University of North Dakota. A licensed psychologist, he practices in Fargo, ND, travels across the states to present seminars, and teaches at North Dakota State University.

13481995R10349

Made in the USA
Lexington, KY
03 February 2012